Contents at a Glance

I Visual Basic Fundamentals

1 Building Your First Application 13
2 What's New with Visual Basic 6 31
3 Working in the Visual Basic 6 Programming Environment 49
4 Using the Intrinsic Controls 67
5 Working with Projects in Visual Basic 6 79
6 Working with Properties, Methods, and Events 89

II Programming with Visual Basic

7 Using Data Types, Constants, and Variables 109
8 Statements in a Program 131
9 Working with Conditional Statements 145
10 Working with Loops 159
11 Working with Arrays 181
12 Working with Strings and Typecasting 211

III Elements of Visual Basic 6

13 Creating Menus in Your Programs 247
14 Enhancing Your Programs with Forms and Dialog Boxes 267
15 Handling Keyboard and Mouse Input in Your Programs 291
16 Working with Time and Timers 317
17 Adding Graphics to Your Programs 333
18 Writing Reusable Code with Subs and Functions 347
19 Saving and Retrieving Your Data with Visual Basic 365
20 Deploying Your Visual Basic Applications 385

IV Advanced Programming with Visual Basic 6

21 Debugging Your Applications 401
22 Creating Controls On-the-Fly Using Control Arrays 421
23 Programming Beyond Visual Basic Using the Windows API 437
24 Adding Help to Your Programs 457
25 Using VBA to Connect Your VB Programs with Microsoft Office 475
26 Making Object-Oriented Programs with Visual Basic 509
27 Creating Your Own ActiveX Controls with Visual Basic 529
28 Creating VB Programs for the Internet 543
29 Making Programming Easier with Visual Basic Add-Ins 579

V Database Programming with Visual Basic 6

30 Database Basics and the Data Control 605
31 Making Reports in Visual Basic 6 621
32 Enhancing Your Programs Using the Advanced Data Controls 631

Appendix A 647
Appendix B 701
Glossary 781
Index 799

Bob Reselman

Wayne Pruchniak

Richard A. Peasley

Eric A. Smith

que

A Division of Macmillan Computer Publishing, USA
201 W. 103rd Street
Indianapolis, Indiana 46290

Using Visual Basic® 6

Copyright© 1998 by Que

International Standard Book Number: 0-7897-1633-x

Library of Congress Catalog Card Number: 98-84137

Printed in the United States of America

First Printing: September 1998

00 99 98   4 3 2 1

Trademarks

Warning and Disclaimer

Executive Editor
Bryan Gambrel

Acquistions Editor
Angela C. Kozlowski

Development Editor
Susan Shaw Dunn

Managing Editor
Jodi Jensen

Project Editor
Maureen McDaniel

Copy Editors
Kate Talbot
Rhonda Tinch-Mize

Indexer
Bruce Clingaman

Technical Editor
Dallas G. Releford

Software Development Specialist
Andrea Duvall

Production
Marcia Deboy
Jennifer Earhart
Cynthia Fields
Susan Geiselman

Contents

Introduction   1

Why This Book?   2

How to Use This Book   2

How This Book Is Organized   3

Conventions Used in This Book   7

I   Visual Basic Fundamentals

1   Building Your First Application   13

Writing Your First Application   14

Starting Visual Basic   14

Building the Calendar Feature   15

Adding a Clock Feature   18

Configuring the Timer Control   20

Using the Label Control to
Display the Time   21

Adding a Message   22

Improving Your First Application   26

2   What's New with Visual Basic 6   31

Getting a Quick Overview of VB6   32

Getting More Power from
Enhanced Controls   32
   The *Validate* Event and the
   CausesValidation Property   33
   Adding Excitement with the New
   Graphical Enhancements   34

Working with the New Controls   36
   Selecting Dates with the MonthView and
   DateTimePicker Controls   37

Making Movable Toolbars with the
CoolBar   37
Using Graphics with an ImageCombo   38
The FlatScrollBar Control   39

Working with the New Language
Features   39
   File System Objects   39
   New String Functions   41
   True Dynamic Control Creation   42

Learning About VB and the Internet   43

Finding Out About the New
Data Capabilities   44

New Object Programming Additions   46

**3   Working in the Visual Basic 6 Programming
Environment   49**

Understanding the Parts of the IDE   50

Adding and Removing Toolbars
in the Visual Basic IDE   51
   Using the Debug Toolbar   52
   Using the Edit Toolbar   52
   Using the Form Editor Toolbar   55
   Using the Standard Toolbar   55

Adding Controls with the ToolBox   57

Navigating Through the Form Window and
Code Window   60

Managing Applications with the
Project Explorer   61

Controlling Settings with the
Properties Window   62

Setting Form Position with the

Form Layout Window   63

Viewing the IDE   64

4   **Using the Intrinsic Controls   67**

What Are Forms and Controls?   68

What Are Intrinsic Controls?   68

Adding and Removing Controls   70

The Importance of Naming Controls   72

How to Size and Position a Control   74

Modifying a Form's Size   75

Working with Containers   75

Extending Visual Basic
by Adding Controls   76

5   **Working with Projects in
Visual Basic 6   79**

What Is a Visual Basic Project?   80

Using the Project Explorer   80

Creating a New Project   82

Changing a Project's Properties   83

Saving and Naming a Project   84

Opening an Existing Project   85

Adding Files to a Project   85

Removing Files from a Project   86

Using Project Groups   87

6   **Working with Properties, Methods,
and Events   89**

What Are Properties, Methods,
and Events?   90

The Relationship Between Properties, Methods,
and Events   93

The Importance of Event-Driven
Programming   94

Using Properties, Methods, and Events in a
Sample Program   96
    Creating the Interface   96
    Programming the *Form_Load*() Event
    Procedure   97
    Programming the *Click*() Event   100
    Adding Event Notification   102

II   **Programming with Visual Basic**

7   **Using Data Types, Constants, and Variables   109**

Storing Information in Variables   110
    Declaring Variables   111
    Naming Variables   112
    Choosing the Correct Variable Type   115

Making Explicit Declarations   117

Using Type Suffixes with Variables   120

Using Strings   121
    Using Variable-Length and Fixed-Length
    Strings   122

Determining Where a Variable
Can Be Used   123
    Making Variables Available Globally   124
    Keeping a Variable Local   125

Using Static Variables   126

Using Constants   126
    Using Constants Supplied by Visual Basic   127
    Creating Your Own Constants   128

Using the Assignment Statement   128

Revisiting the Addition Program   129

8 Making Statements in a Program   131

Using the Assignment Statement   132

Using Variable Default Values   133

Using Math Operators   134
   Using Addition and Subtraction Operators   134
   Using the Multiplication Operator   136
   Using the Division Operator   139
   Using Exponents   140

Setting the Order of Precedence in Statements   141

Concatenating Strings   142

9 Working with Conditional Statements   145

Making Decisions in Your Program   146

Writing *If...Then* Statements   146
   Writing a Single-Line If Statement   146
   Executing Multiple Commands in the Conditional Statement   149
   Using *If...Then...Else* Statements   150
   Working with Multiple If Statements   151
   Using Nested If Statements   153

Using the *Select Case* Statement   153
   Using Relational Operators in *Select Case* Blocks   157

10 Working with Loops   159

Putting Loops to Work   160

Using *For...Next* Loops   160
   Terminating the *For...Next* Loop Early   164

Using *Do...Loop* Statements   166
   Using *Do...While* Loops   166
   Using *Do...Until* Statements   170

Breaking an Infinite Loop   171

Nesting Loops   172
   Working with Multiple Loops   172
   Using Nested Loops to Eliminate Loops   174
   Loading Data with Nested Loops   176

11 Working with Arrays   181

What Is an Array?   182

Declaring Arrays   183
   Declaring an Array like Declaring a Single Variable   184
   Declaring an Array with the *To* Keyword   185

Changing the Number of Elements in an Array   185

Multidimensional Arrays   188

Using Loops to Traverse an Array   191

Adding Items to ListBoxes and ComboBoxes   193

Selecting Items from a List   196

Removing Items from a List   198

Clearing a List   199

Understanding ComboBox Styles   199

Using Arrays, ComboBoxes, and ListBoxes in a Sample Program   201

Examining ScoreKeeper's Event Procedures   202

12 Working with Strings and Typecasting 211

Manipulating Strings   212
Reversing the Order of Characters in Strings   212
Replacing Characters Within Strings   214
Concatenating Strings   217
Determining a String's Length with *Len()*   219
Truncating Strings with *Left()* and *Right()*   220
Using *Mid()* to Return Characters from Inside a String   222
Using *InStr()* to Search for Characters Within a String   224

Using Strings and Arrays of Strings   226
Splitting a String into an Array of Strings with *Split()*   227
Creating a Sublist from an Array of Strings with *Filter()*   230
Combining an Array of Strings with *Join()*   231

Changing a String's Case with *UCase()* and *LCase()*   233

Using String-Parsing Functions   235

Controlling Data Types with Typecasting   240
Changing Data Types with the Conversion Functions   241

Validating Data with *IsNumeric()*   242

III The Elements of Visual Basic 6

13 Creating Menus in Your Programs 247

Understanding the Windows Standard Menus   248

Using Visual Basic's Application Wizard   249

Using Visual Basic's Menu Editor   253
Setting Menu Properties   255
Adding Access Keys to Menu Items   256
Adding Shortcut Keys to Menu Items   258
Creating Pop-Up Menus   259

Creating Complex Menus   260
Adding Separator Lines to Menus   261
Using the *Checked* Property   262
Cutting, Copying, and Pasting with the *Clipboard* Object   263
Selecting Text in a TextBox   265

14 Enhancing Your Programs with Forms and Dialog Boxes 267

Creating Message Boxes with the *MsgBox()* Function and the *MsgBox* Statement   268
Adding Icons to Message Boxes   270
Retrieving a Value from the *MsgBox()* Function   271

Using Predefined Forms   275

Getting User Input from the CommonDialog Control   276
Retrieving File Information with the File Dialog   278
Selecting Font Information with the Font Dialog   281
Selecting Colors with the Color Dialog   283
Setting Printer Options with the Print Dialog   284

Making a Simple MDI Application   285
The *Appearance* Property   289
The *AutoShowChildren* Property   289

15 Handling Keyboard and Mouse Input in Your Programs 291

Understanding Device Input   292

Working with the *KeyPress* Event   293
Working with the *KeyUp* and *KeyDown* Events   297

Using the *KeyPreview* Property   302

Understanding Mouse Input   303
   Using the *Click* Event   303
   Working with *MouseDown* and *MouseUp*
   Events   306
   Working with the *MouseMove* Event   311
   Recognizing VB's Limitations with Mouse
   Input   313

16 **Working with Time and Timers   317**

Understanding Serial Time   318

Understanding the Timer Control   318

Using the *Time*, *Date*, and
Now Functions   320

Use a Timer to Build a Clock Program   321

Using the *Format()* Function   324

Calculating Date Differences   326

Using Static Variables with a Timer   329

17 **Adding Graphics to Your Programs   333**

Adding Graphics to a Form   334

Changing a Picture at Runtime   336

Making a Custom Button   336

Adding Graphics to Forms
with *LoadPicture()*   339

Making a Form Icon   340

Loading Files with a File List Box   342

Creating Special Graphic Effects   345

18 **Writing Reusable Code with
Subs and Functions   347**

Using Procedures in Visual Basic   348

Making and Calling a Simple Sub   348

Making Subs by Using Add Procedure   349

Making a Simple Function   351

Passing Arguments into
Subs and Functions   352
   Using Named Arguments   355

Exiting Subs and Functions   355

Understanding Scope   358

Documenting Subs and Functions   359

Determining Your Entry Point
with *Sub Main()*   361

✓ 19 **Saving and Retrieving Your Data with Visual
Basic   365**

Understanding Persistence   366

Working with Files to Store and Retrieve
Data   366

Saving Data with the *Open* Statement   367

Retrieving Data with Input Statements   371

Manipulating Graphics with *LoadPicture()* and
SavePicture()   373

Saving and Retrieving Data with the Visual
Basic Registry Functions   375
   Retrieving Values with *GetSetting()*   376
   Saving Values to the Registry with
   the *SaveSetting* Statement   377

Retrieving an Array of Settings
with *GetAllSettings()*   378
Deleting a Key Section with the
DeleteString Statement   378

Using File System Objects   379

**20 Deploying Your Visual Basic
Applications   385**

Working with Version Information   386

Compiling Your Project   389

Using the Package and Deployment
Wizard   391

IV Advanced Programming with
Visual Basic 6

21 Debugging Your Applications   401

Catching Undeclared Variables
with *Option Explicit*   402

Checking Code Segments
with Breakpoints   404
Monitoring Variable Values with
Watches   405
Monitoring Additional Variables with
Add Watch   406
Examining Code Line by Line with
Step Into and Step Over   408
Stopping at Selected Lines with Run to
Cursor   410

Using Advanced Debugging Tools   410

Using Find and Replace   413

Designing Applications for
Debugging   415

Creating an Error Handler   417

**22 Creating Controls On-the-Fly Using
Control Arrays   421**

What Is a Control Array?   422
Creating a Control Array at Design Time   422
Extending Control Arrays at Runtime   424

Working with a Common Event Handler   426

Grouping Objects with the
Frame Control   428

Using the Scroll Bar Controls   429

Using *For...Next* Loops with
Control Arrays   432

**23 Programming Beyond Visual Basic Using the
Windows API   437**

Understanding the Windows API   438

Working with the API Viewer   440

Monitoring Mouse Movement
with *GetCursorPos*   445

Keeping a Window Always on Top
by Using *SetWindowPos*   447

Dragging a Window by Using *SendMessage*   452

Enhancing a List Box with *SendMessage*   454

Providing Help for Your Programs   458

Using the Help Workshop   458

24 Adding Help to Your Programs   457

Making a Help File   462

Adding Help Files to Your Application   468

Making Context-Sensitive Help   469

25 Using VBA to Connect Your VB Programs with Microsoft Office   475

Working with VBA   476

Using VBA with Microsoft Office   477
Using the Record Macro Tool   478
Using the Object Browser   480
Making a Simple VB/Microsoft Office Application   482

Making a Spelling Checker with VB and Word   486

Making a Word Search Program   491

Working with Visual Basic, Access, and Excel   498

26 Making Object-Oriented Programs with Visual Basic   509

Understanding User-Defined Types   510

Making Objects from Classes   512
Creating a Class in Visual Basic   513
Adding Properties to a Class   515
Creating an Object from a Class   520

Making an ActiveX DLL   521

Working with Components   527

27 Creating Your Own ActiveX Controls with Visual Basic   529

Creating an ActiveX Control   530
Understanding the *UserControl* Object   533
Adding a *UserControl* to a Form   534

Adding Functionality to an ActiveX Control   535
Compiling Custom ActiveX Controls   538
Deploying Custom ActiveX Controls   540

28 Creating VB Programs for the Internet   543

Working on the Internet   544

Making a Simple Program with VBScript   546

Using VBScript with Internet Explorer   548
Working with HTML Elements   551
More on Scripts   557
Incorporating VBScript with HTML   558
Handling Events with VBScript   564

Understanding a DHTML Application   565
Programming a Simple DHTML Application   568
Rapid Development with DHTML Applications   570
Using DHTML with ActiveX Components   574
Compiling a DHTML Application   577

29 Making Programming Easier with Visual Basic Add-Ins   579

Working with Add-Ins   580
Attaching Add-Ins to the Add-Ins Menu   580
Attaching Add-Ins to the Add-Ins Toolbar   581

Using Add-Ins   582
Using the VB6 Application Wizard   582
Using the VB6 Data Form Wizard   588

Creating a Custom Add-In   593
How the Add-In Works   595
Understanding the Visual Basic 6 IDE Object Model   596

V Database Programming with Visual Basic 6

30 **Database Basics and the Data Control** 605

Understanding Databases 606
Understanding Database Terminology 607

Working with the Intrinsic Data Control 609
Connecting the Intrinsic Data Control to a Database 611

Creating Database-Bound Forms with the Data Form Wizard 614

31 **Making Reports in Visual Basic 6** 621

What's New with Reporting? 622

Building a Simple Report 623

32 **Enhancing Your Programs Using the Advanced Data Controls** 631

What Are Advanced Data Controls? 632

Adding and Configuring the ADO Data Control 632

Using the DataGrid Control 636
Selecting Grid Columns 637
Cleaning Up the Form 639
Configuring Other DataGrid Properties 640

Using the DataList Control 641
Configuring DataList Control Properties 642

Using the DataCombo Control 643

Working with the Data Form Wizard 644

Appendix A 647

Appendix B 701

Glossary 781

Index 799

About the Authors

Bob Reselman is a principal consultant with the Des Moines office of Cap Gemini, a worldwide consulting organization that helps businesses achieve transformation through technology. Bob enjoys hearing from other developers. He can be reached at reselbob@pionet.net.

Wayne Pruchniak has been a Human Factors Engineer with Gateway since 1995. He spends much of his time designing software and trying to make computers a bit less frustrating. After that, he can be found either listening to music, tuning his home theater, or modifying his car. He currently resides in Sioux City, Iowa, and can be reached at pruchnw@pionet.net.

Richard A. Peasley is also a principal consultant at Cap Gemini, practicing in the Information Technology Solutions Architecture group. His interests include learning new technology, trying to read technical reference materials, and teaching. When Richard isn't working, he's involved with his family and church in Elk Point, South Dakota. He can be reached at peaslric@pionet.net.

Eric A. Smith is a senior consultant with Information Strategies, a Washington, D.C.-based Microsoft Solution Provider. He specializes in Visual Basic development, but is also experienced in Web and database programming. He is a frequent contributor to Visual Basic Programmer's Journal and speaks at industry conferences. He is also the creator of Ask the VB Pro, a Web site that provides how-to information on Visual Basic (http://www.inquiry.com/thevbpro). Eric can be reached at eric@northcomp.com.

Dedication

I dedicate this book to my sister, Nancy, and the miracle of e-mail.

–Bob Reselman

I dedicate this book to my parents. Without you, I wouldn't be what I am today, and I never forget.

–Wayne Pruchniak

To my wife and best friend, Sonja Swanson, and our two daughters, Sara and Annie, for their support on the long weekends and late nights writing this book. They are my life.

–Richard A. Peasley

For Jodi.

–Eric A. Smith

Acknowledgements

I very much want acknowledge the patience, support and understanding of Angela Kozlowski, acquisitions editor extraordinaire. Without her continuing guidance and help, this would have been an impossible project to do. Also I want to acknowledge the continued perseverance of my wife, Dorothy Lifka, and my daughters, Alexandra and Genevieve, for allowing yet another book into their lives.

—Bob Reselman

I'd like to thank Bob Reselman for giving me the opportunity to help write this book. Also, thanks to Angela Kozlowski and Susan Dunn for their patience and advice. And thanks to everyone at Gateway for giving me the opportunity to work on many different things.

–Wayne Pruchniak

On the shoulders of giants and in the company of friends, the depth of our vision and strength extends. Bob, it is a privilege to work with you professionally and to know you as a friend. I would like to thank you for inviting me to the party, Wayne for joining the party, Angela Kozlowski for hosting the party and helping me work through a travesty of personal technical problems, and finally the editors and production staff for making the pieces whole. Without the great team at Que, books like these would not be possible. A commercial book is truly a collaborative work of art.

–Richard A. Peasley

Tell Us What You Think!

As the reader of this book, *you* are our most important critic and commentator. We value your opinion and want to know what we're doing right, what we could do better, what areas you'd like to see us publish in, and any other words of wisdom you're willing to pass our way.

As the Executive Editor for the Client/Server and Database team at Macmillan Computer Publishing, I welcome your comments. You can fax, e-mail, or write me directly to let me know what you did or didn't like about this book—as well as what we can do to make our books stronger.

Please note that I cannot help you with technical problems related to the topic of this book, and that due to the high volume of mail I receive, I might not be able to reply to every message.

When you write, please be sure to include this book's title and author as well as your name and phone or fax number. I will carefully review your comments and share them with the author and editors who worked on the book.

Fax: 317-817-7070

E-mail: cs_db@mcp.com

Mail: Executive Editor
         Client/Server and Database Team
         Macmillan Computer Publishing
         201 West 103rd Street
         Indianapolis, IN 46290 USA

INTRODUCTION

THIS BOOK IS NOT ONLY FOR beginning programmers who want to learn Visual Basic but also experienced programmers who are familiar with other programming languages and seek a working knowledge of Visual Basic. Every page of *Using Visual Basic 6* provides you with useful facts and techniques. The aim is to teach you how to program by showing you programs—sometimes step by step and sometimes with a conceptual, from-the-ground-up point of view.

The author of this book assumes that you have a working knowledge of Windows, that you've done word processing or used a spreadsheet, and that you know your way around the Windows interface. It's also assumed that you have a copy of Visual Basic 6, access to a computer, and time to review the topics and work with the examples in each chapter. Very, very rarely can someone read a book on computer programming and instantly "get it" without taking the time for some hands-on experience.

Learning a programming language is a challenging experience. The author and technical reviewers of this book are professional programmers who have made every effort to convey the fun and challenge of VB programming while addressing your need for relevant, easy-to-understand material. If Visual Basic programming is something that you want to do, either professionally or as a side activity, and you need a book that instructs in a clear, concise, real-world manner, this is for you.

Why This Book?

Have you ever purchased a *Using* book from Que? For many years, the *Using* books have proven invaluable to readers as both learning guides and references. The *Using* series is an industry leader and has become practically an industry standard. We encourage and receive feedback from readers all the time, using their suggestions whenever possible.

This book isn't a compiled authority on all the features of Visual Basic. It's a streamlined, conversational approach to productive, efficient programming in Visual Basic. Features of this book include

- *Relevant information written just for you.* We have carefully scrutinized which features and tasks to include in this book and have chosen those that apply to your everyday use of Visual Basic. Why invest in material that teaches you how to perform tasks you might never need to perform?

- *Reference or tutorial.* You can learn to quickly perform a task by using the step-by-step instructions, or you can investigate the why and wherefore of a task in the discussions preceding each task.

- *Wise investment.* We don't waste your valuable bookshelf space with redundant or irrelevant material, nor do we assume that you know it all or need to know it all. Here is what you need, when you need it, and how you need it—with an appropriate price tag.

- *Easy-to-find procedures.* Every numbered step-by-step procedure in the book has a short title explaining exactly what it does. This saves you time by making it easier to find the exact steps necessary for accomplishing a task.

How to Use This Book

You can use this book in various ways:

- *If you are a beginning programmer,* the best way to go about using this book is to read each chapter in sequence. Some chapters build on knowledge shared in previous chapters. If you skip around, you might be confused because you missed a concept or technique introduced in other areas of the book.

- *If you are an experienced programmer,* skipping around might be the better way to go. If you have mastered some of the conceptual items—such as variables, arrays, loops, and conditional statements—reading chapters at random would make the best use of your time. The book is designed so that each chapter can more or less stand on its own.

Each page of the book contains the main text and margin notes. These margin notes are helpful when you're looking for brief snippets of information. The book is also full of figures, code listings, and tables that you will find useful now and in months to come as you refer to this book in your day-to-day programming activity.

More than 20 working programs are associated with this book. You can download these from the book's Web site at http://www.mcp.com/info. When you locate the URL, you'll be asked to enter the book's ISBN: Enter 078971633x and then click the **Search** button to go to the **Book Info** page. You'll find references and listings that relate to the code throughout the book. Feel free to use the code in your own programming activities.

How This Book Is Organized

The book is organized into five parts. The first three parts give you a fundamental knowledge of the Visual Basic programming language and the Visual Basic programming environment; the last two parts cover advanced Visual Basic topics such as object-oriented programming, ActiveX control creation, Internet programming, data access, and databases.

Part I: Visual Basic Fundamentals

The chapters in this section introduce you to the basics of Visual Basic programming and working within the Visual Basic programming environment.

- Chapter 1, "Building Your First Application," helps you build a desktop calendar application from the ground up. Through hands-on learning, you develop an understanding of what Visual Basic is and how it works.

- Chapter 2, "What's New with Visual Basic 6," introduces you to the new features of Visual Basic 6 and the enhancements to previous versions.

- Chapter 3, "Working in the Visual Basic 6 Programming Environment," shows you how to work in the Visual Basic integrated development environment. The IDE enables you to make powerful programs quickly by taking the tedium out of Windows programming.

- Chapter 4, "Using the Intrinsic Controls," explains how to use the small, reusable programs that make VB so special.

- Chapter 5, "Working with Projects in Visual Basic 6," teaches you how to create different projects with different file types, describing how a Visual Basic project is organized and how to use the different file formats.

- Chapter 6, "Working with Properties, Methods, and Events," is about manipulating ActiveX controls by adjusting their various properties, using their methods, and responding to their events.

Part II: Programming with Visual Basic

The chapters in this section cover subjects that are fundamental to Visual Basic and also conceptually applicable to other programming languages.

- Chapter 7, "Using Data Types, Constants, and Variables," shows you how to control data and manipulate different types of information, known and unknown.

- Chapter 8, "Making Statements in a Program," teaches you how to make programming instructions in Visual Basic. Also, you learn how to do arithmetic calculations.

- In Chapter 9, "Working with Conditional Statements," you learn how to program to make decisions by using `If...Then` and `Select Case` statements.

- Chapter 10, "Working with Loops," shows you how to make statements in a repetitive, controlled manner.

- Chapter 11, "Working with Arrays," presents the concepts and techniques that you need to know in order to work with groups of variables.

- Chapter 12, "Working with Strings and Typecasting," describes how to examine, combine, and shorten strings. You also learn how to turn strings into numbers, and vice-versa.

Part III: The Elements of Visual Basic 6

The chapters in this section develop concepts and techniques that you learned in Part 1, while giving you a better understanding of Visual Basic as it relates to Windows programming.

- Chapter 13, "Creating Menus in Your Programs," shows you how to design menus, use the Menu Editor, and program menu items.

- Chapter 14, "Enhancing Your Programs with Forms and Dialog Boxes," tells you about the different types of forms, how to create multiple-document interface programs, and how to use the CommonDialog ActiveX controls.

- Chapter 15, "Handling Keyboard and Mouse Input in Your Programs," shows you how to make your programs work with a mouse. Also, you learn how to work with data coming from a keyboard.

- Chapter 16, "Working with Time and Timers," explains how to work the Timer ActiveX control to write programs that function in real time. Also, you learn how to use static variables.

- Chapter 17, "Adding Graphics to Your Programs," teaches you how to use the PictureBox and Image controls, as well as the various graphics functions internal to VB.

- In Chapter 18, "Writing Reusable Code with Subs and Functions," you learn to make user-defined subroutines and functions. Writing your own subs and functions paves the way for advanced object-oriented programming.

- Chapter 19, "Saving and Retrieving Your Data with Visual Basic," shows you how to read and write data to a file. Also, you learn how to use the `FileSystemObject`, which is new to Visual Basic 6.

- Chapter 20, "Deploying Your Visual Basic Applications," covers the concepts and techniques that you need to know in order to distribute your program to others.

Part IV: Advanced Programming with Visual Basic 6

This section introduces you to the advanced topics in Visual Basic programming and relates the language to ActiveX and Internet programming.

- In Chapter 21, "Debugging Your Applications," you learn how to write error-free code and make your applications more robust.

- Chapter 22, "Creating Controls On-the-Fly Using Control Arrays," shows you how to work with control arrays to write code once and yet have it apply to many controls.

- Chapter 23, "Programming Beyond Visual Basic Using the Windows API," teaches you how to work directly with the Windows application programming interface. You can use the Windows API to do things that standard Visual Basic won't let you do.

- Chapter 24, "Adding Help to Your Programs," shows you how to use the Windows Help Compiler to write interactive, context-sensitive help files.

- Chapter 25, "Using VBA to Connect Your VB Programs with Microsoft Office," teaches you how to use Visual Basic for Applications to interact with Microsoft Word and Microsoft Excel.

- Chapter 26, "Making Object-Oriented Programs with Visual Basic," introduces you to the fundamentals of object-oriented programming and describes how to create true OOP programs in VB.

- Chapter 27, "Creating Your Own ActiveX Controls with Visual Basic," shows you how to make ActiveX controls in VB that you can distribute to other programmers.

- Chapter 28, "Creating VB Programs for the Internet," explains how to create interactive Web pages with VB. This chapter covers the fundamentals of HTML, VBScript, and Dynamic HTML.

- Chapter 29, "Making Programming Easier with Visual Basic Add-Ins," teaches you how to enhance the Visual Basic programming environment. *Add-ins* are programs that you write in VB to use as programming helper applications. In this chapter, you learn to create an add-in that adds code headers to your user-defined subroutines and functions.

Part V: Database Programming with Visual Basic 6

This section shows you how to program Visual Basic to handle data access and databases.

- Chapter 30, "Database Basics and the Data Control," describes how to construct databases and use the data control to access and manipulate data.

- Chapter 31, "Making Reports in Visual Basic 6," demonstrates how to use Visual Basic's new data-reporting features.

- Chapter 32, "Enhancing Your Programs Using the Advanced Data Controls," shows you how to use the new ADO data control. This chapter also explains data designers, data providers, data consumers, and SQL.

Conventions Used in This Book

The following items are some of the features that make this book easier for you to explore:

- *Cross-references.* We've looked for all the tasks and topics related to a topic at hand and referenced them for you. If you need to look for coverage that leads up to what you're working on, or you want to build on the new skill you just mastered, these references direct you to the appropriate sections in the book:

SEE ALSO

> *See how to create an add-in that adds code headers to user-defined subroutines and functions on page 593*

- *Glossary terms.* For all terms that appear in the glossary, you'll find the first appearance of that term *italicized* in the text.

- *Boldfacing.* You can easily find the onscreen menu and dialog commands by looking for boldfaced text, as in the following example: From the **File** menu, choose **Save**.

- *Sidenotes.* Information related to the task at hand or inside information from the authors is offset in SideNotes—to avoid interrupting the flow of the text and to make it easy for you to spot valuable information. Each SideNote has a short title to help you quickly identify the information you'll find there.

Visual Basic's syntax for commands, scripts, and SQL statements also incorporates special elements. Look at the following syntax example:

```
For CounterVar = StartNum To EndNum [Step StepNum]
    statements
Next [CounterVar]
```

- Terms that are *italicized* are placeholders. When you use one of these terms in real life, you replace the italicized word with an appropriate value. For example, *StartNum* in the preceding code would be replaced with an actual number from which the loop starts.

- Brackets ([ ]) in command syntax indicate optional clauses. The brackets around [Step *StepNum*] in the preceding code indicate that you aren't required to provide the Step keyword or what size step the increment/decrement should be. When you use the command, don't include the brackets.

- A ¦ character indicates that you choose between one item or the other, not both. Again, don't use this character in the actual command.

- An ellipsis (...) in listings indicates a clause that can repeat or skipped code that's not pertinent to the discussion. Don't use the ellipsis in the actual code.

Most code listings include line numbers to make discussion about the code easier to reference. Don't include the numbers with any real-life Visual Basic code.

Note About the Microsoft Visual Basic 6 Working Model

The CD-ROM accompanying this book includes the Microsoft Visual Basic 6 Working Model. We have included it at no charge to you so that you can better evaluate the Visual Basic programming environment.

This version will allow you to do everything you can do with the Learning Edition of Visual Basic with the following exceptions:

- It cannot create executable files (.exe). Therefore, you need to run all your programs from within the Visual Basic environment.
- The Working Model does not include online Help.

Visual Basic Fundamentals

1   **Building Your First Application 13**

2   **What's New with Visual Basic 6 31**

3   **Working in the Visual Basic 6 Programming Environment 49**

4   **Using the Intrinsic Controls 67**

5   **Working with Projects in Visual Basic 6 79**

6   **Working with Properties, Methods, and Events 89**

Building Your First Application

Write a real application with Visual Basic 6

Learn about ActiveX controls

Use the Timer control

Manipulate data

Declare variables

Writing Your First Application

Who is the end user?

An end user is the person for whom the program was made–the person who uses the program.

The best way to learn programming is to do programming. Therefore, let's create a program. Your first program will be a Visual Basic Calendar, which allows the end user to

- View a calendar of the present month
- Browse months
- View a clock that presents the current time
- Read a secret message

If you think that this is too much functionality to implement for a beginner's program, don't worry; it's not. Visual Basic does most of the work for you. Unlike other languages, such as C++, where you have to program every little thing, Visual Basic brings a high degree of automatic programming to your fingertips. Thus, you can do a lot with not a lot of code.

However, don't misinterpret "not a lot of code" to mean "not a lot of power." Visual Basic is a very powerful language. You can write Visual Basic code that does "every little thing" if you want or need it to. You also can exploit the labor-saving nature of VB to implement a program quickly. The choice is yours. Visual Basic is versatile enough to be useful to a broad range of programmers—from beginner to seasoned professional.

Starting Visual Basic

The first thing you need to do is open a Visual Basic program. From the **Windows Start** menu, choose **Programs**, **Microsoft Visual Studio 6.0**, and then **Microsoft Visual Basic 6.0**.

When you start VB, you're taken to the Visual Basic *Integrated Development Environment (IDE)*. This is your programming workbench, the place where you create your programs (see Figure 1.1). Notice that the IDE presents what looks like an empty window containing some dots and a title bar with the word Form1. This window is a *form*, the primary building block of a Visual Basic application. An application can have many forms or one form; the application we're developing for this example has one form.

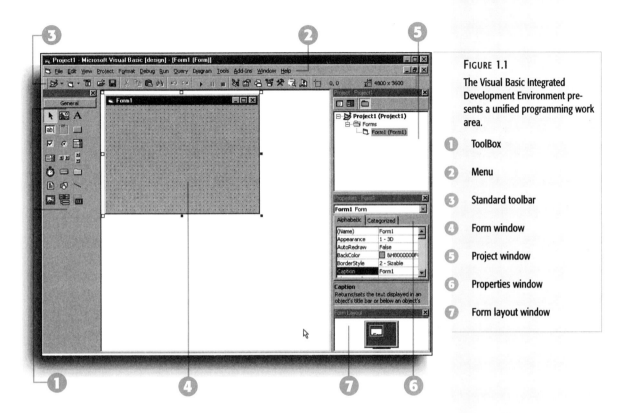

FIGURE 1.1

The Visual Basic Integrated Development Environment presents a unified programming work area.

1 ToolBox

2 Menu

3 Standard toolbar

4 Form window

5 Project window

6 Properties window

7 Form layout window

Building the Calendar Feature

Now let's build the features of your application. First, you need a calendar. You could build one from scratch, or you could add the calendar program that comes within VB to your application. Let's use the one that comes with VB (if you don't have a few years to learn VB at the expert level, it makes the most sense).

If you don't want to create the Visual Basic Calendar program from scratch, you can retrieve the finished code from the Web site dedicated to this book (http://www.mcp.com/info). You'll be asked to enter an ISBN; you need to enter 078971633x, and then click the **Search** button to go to the Book Info page for *Using Visual Basic 6*. After you download the code, double-click the file Project1.vbp for the Chapter 1 code. If you've installed Visual Basic on your system, double-clicking invokes the sample project within VB.

ActiveX controls

Another name for the little programs that come with Visual Basic is *ActiveX controls*. The calendar program that you add to your application is an ActiveX control.

Get the calendar program into the Visual Basic IDE

1. From the **Project** menu, choose **Components** (see Figure 1.2).

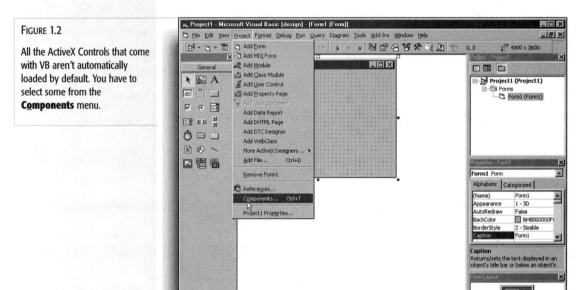

FIGURE 1.2

All the ActiveX Controls that come with VB aren't automatically loaded by default. You have to select some from the **Components** menu.

2. In the **Components** dialog, select **Windows Common Controls 2-6.0** and click **OK** (see Figure 1.3).

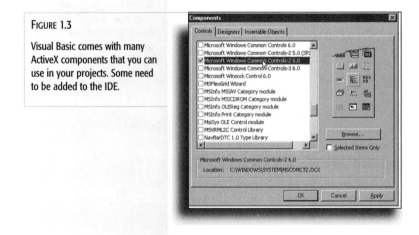

FIGURE 1.3

Visual Basic comes with many ActiveX components that you can use in your projects. Some need to be added to the IDE.

These steps added the calendar control to the Visual Basic ToolBox. The formal name for the control that you've inserted into your first application is the MonthView ActiveX control. We'll use this terminology from here on.

Now you need to add the control to the form.

Add the MonthView control to your form

1. Select the MonthView control icon from the Visual Basic ToolBox (see Figure 1.4).

2. Double-click the MonthView control icon to add the control to the main form (see Figure 1.5).

What is ActiveX?

ActiveX is a brand name from Microsoft that lets you create little programs, formally known as components and *controls*, that you can add to larger programs. These larger programs that you can add ActiveX components and controls to can be *stand-alone programs* or programs that run on the Internet. You can use Visual Basic to make your own ActiveX components and controls.

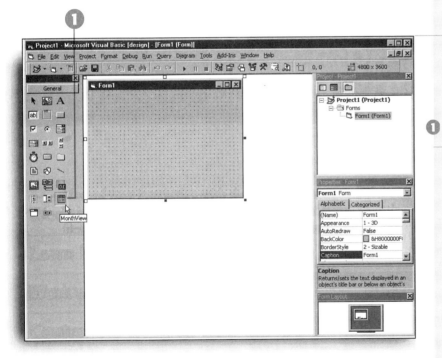

FIGURE 1.4

When you add an ActiveX Control from the Components dialog, it appears in the Visual Basic ToolBox.

① The MonthView control

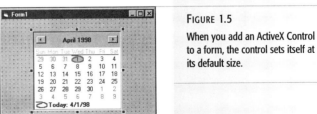

FIGURE 1.5

When you add an ActiveX Control to a form, the control sets itself at its default size.

You've just created your first program. Press **F5** or choose **Start** from the **Run** menu to run it [▶]. Click the End button [■] or choose **End** from the **Run** menu to terminate the program.

Adding a Clock Feature

The next feature to implement into your practice program is the capability to display the time. You'll use the Timer ActiveX control, which is *intrinsic*, meaning that it's standard to Visual Basic (built right into the core code). You never have to add it to the ToolBox; the Timer is always there (see Figure 1.6) Look at Table 1.1 to see the ToolBox icons and their associated ActiveX control.

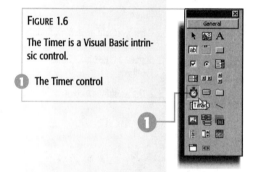

FIGURE 1.6

The Timer is a Visual Basic intrinsic control.

① The Timer control

TABLE 1.1   The Visual Basic Controls

Icon	ActiveX Control
▶	Not a control; enables the mouse pointer
A	Label
abl	TextBox
▭	CommandButton
⏱	Timer
🖼	PictureBox
xy	Frame

Icon	ActiveX Control
	CheckBox
	OptionButton
	ComboBox
	ListBox
	Vertical scrollbar
	Horizontal scrollbar
	DriveListBox
	DirListBox
	FileListBox
	Shape
	Line
	Data
	OLE
	Animation
	UpDown
	MonthView
	DateTimePicker
	FlatScrollBar

The latest additions to your IDE

Animation, UpDown, MonthView, DateTimePicker, and FlatScrollBar are all Windows common controls. When you selected Windows Common Controls 2-6.0 in the earlier steps, you put all these controls into your ToolBox.

Add the timer to your application

1. Make sure that the Pointer icon ▶ in the ToolBox is selected.

2. Put the mouse pointer on the MonthView control on the form, press your left mouse button down, and drag the control over to the right (see Figure 1.7).

3. Double-click the Timer control 🕑 in the ToolBox to add it to the form (see Figure 1.8).

FIGURE 1.7

You can move an ActiveX control around a form at design time by dragging it.

FIGURE 1.8

Controls appear in the middle of a form when you add them by using the double-click technique.

What's a windowless control?

If the Timer appears over the MonthView ActiveX control, don't fret; the Timer is a windowless control. A windowless control appears during design time but is invisible when you run your code. Don't mistake controls that can be made invisible at runtime as windowless controls; they aren't. You never see a windowless control at runtime.

Configuring the Timer Control

Although you've added the Timer to the form, it won't really do anything until you configure it to report time the way you want it to.

Configure the Timer to report the time

1. Select the Timer control on the form. (Make sure that the Pointer ▶ is selected in the ToolBox.)

2. In the Properties window, select the **Interval** property and enter the number **500** (see Figure 1.9).

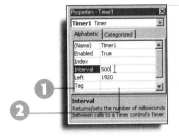

FIGURE 1.9

The Properties window is where you configure the settings for a selected ActiveX control.

1 Properties

2 Property values

Setting the value of the Timer's Interval property to 500 is operationally the same as configuring the Timer to do something every half a second. Now you have to program what you want the Timer to do every half second: to report the current time. You need a place in which to display the time. For this, use a Label control.

Measuring a second with the Timer

You set the increment of time measured by the Timer by using the Interval property. The Timer measures time in intervals of 1/1000 of a second. Therefore, to measure time in half-second intervals, set the value of the Interval property to 500.

Using the Label Control to Display the Time

Add a Label control to the form

1. Select the Label control icon [A] in the ToolBox.

2. Rather than double-click, draw a box on Form1 by dragging the mouse (see Figure 1.10).

FIGURE 1.10

You also can add a control to a form by selecting the control in the ToolBox and dragging to size.

3. In the Properties window, scroll to the BorderStyle property. Click the property and then select **1-Fixed Single** from the drop-down list (see Figure 1.11).

FIGURE 1.11

Some properties, such as the Label control's BorderStyle property, have values that you can set from drop-down menus.

Code the instructions that display the time in the Label control

1. Double-click the Timer control on the form. The Code window appears.

2. Add the following line of code to the Timer1_Timer() event procedure in the blank space between the line Private Sub Timer1_Timer() and End Sub (see Figure 1.12):
   Label1.Caption = Time

3. Run the code by pressing F5 (see Figure 1.13).

Adding a Message

For this program, a message appears when you click the CommandButton on the form. To implement this feature, first you must add a CommandButton to the form.

Add a CommandButton

1. Select the CommandButton control ▣ in the ToolBox.

2. Add a CommandButton to the form by dragging your mouse cursor across the form (see Figure 1.14).

What's an event procedure?

An *event procedure* is a piece of code that you write to execute a programming event. For example, when a user clicks a CommandButton, a Click() event is generated. Visual Basic provides a CommandButton_Click() event procedure that you can program to react to the CommandButton click. The same is true with the Timer. When a Timer's interval is reached, a Timer() event is fired. You can think of the code that you write in the Timer() event as "do this when the Timer's interval has been reached." Some controls have many events; some have only a few. It depends on the control. You can learn more about event procedures in Chapter 6, "Working with Properties, Methods, and Events."

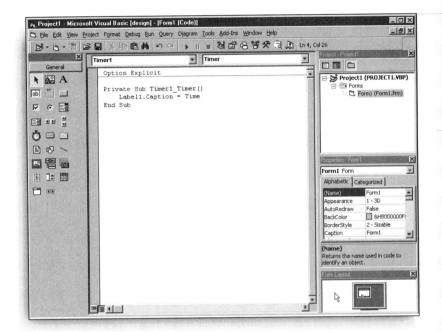

FIGURE 1.12

The Timer event procedure is fired every time its `Interval` is reached. If you set the value of the `Interval` property to 500, the Timer event is fired every half second.

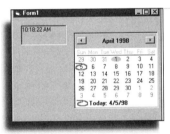

FIGURE 1.13

The Timer assigns the present time to the `Caption` property of the Label control in its `Timer()` event procedure.

FIGURE 1.14

Add a control by dragging if you want to custom-size it at a specific location.

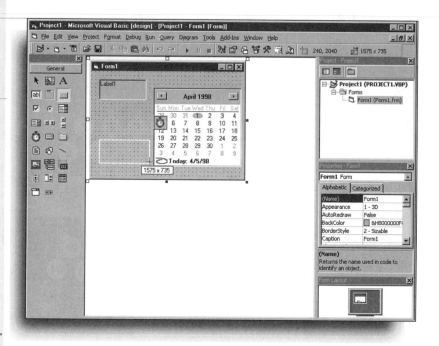

A control's *Name* property

All controls have a unique name. By default, VB assigns the value of the **Name** property to be the control's type name plus a number. For example, the default value of the CommandButton's **Name** property is **Command1**. If the value **Command1** is already in use, VB names the new CommandButton **Command2** (and so on). You can change the default value of a control's **Name** property only at design time. Also, the **Name** property of the control isn't something that end users see when the program is running.

Using listing code

If you don't want to type code from the book into your programs, you can use the code in the file referenced in the heading of the listing. You can get this code from the book's Web site (http://www.mcp.com/info). To access this code, open the file in a text editor such as Notepad. Then **Copy** and **Paste** the code from the text editor into VB.

3. Use the drag technique in Step 2 to add a TextBox above the CommandButton.

4. Double-click the CommandButton to expose the Click() event procedure.

5. Add the code in Listing 1.1 to the Command1_Click() event procedure (see Figure 1.15).

LISTING 1.1   **01LIST01.TXT—The Code that displays a secret message in the TextBox**

```
01  Dim strMsg As String
02  strMsg = WeekdayName(Weekday(Date), _
                False, vbUseSystemDayOfWeek)
03  strMsg = strMsg & " is the first day of the rest"
04  strMsg = strMsg & " of your life!"
05  Text1.Text = strMsg
```

6. In the Properties window, set the **Caption** property for the Command1 CommandButton to Click for a Secret (see Figure 1.16).

FIGURE 1.15

Notice that the code for the Command1_Click() event procedure doesn't have line numbers, which are used in this book for reference purposes. You shouldn't use them in code.

FIGURE 1.16

When you change the value of the CommandButton's Caption property, you change the text that the CommandButton displays within itself.

7. Save the code by selecting **Save Project** from the **File** menu.

8. Run the code by pressing the F5 key (see Figure 1.17).

The code in Listing 1.1 shows you how to work with variables. You can think of a *variable* as a storage container for unknown information that's to be provided at a later time or at another place in code. Line 1 of Listing 1.1 shows you how to *declare* a variable by using the Dim keyword as shown in Line 1. Line 1 creates the variable strMsg.

When you create a variable, it doesn't contain any data. To give the variable some value, you must assign some data to it. Lines 2 through 4 of Listing 1.1 assign value to the strMsg variable by

Saving projects

When you save a project, you should create a directory to hold all the parts of the project—project file (.prj) and forms (.frm and .frx). FRX files contain information about embedded graphics in a form.

continually adding new data to existing data. Finally in Line 5, the information stored in the variable strMsg is assigned to be the value for the Text property of the Text1 TextBox.

FIGURE 1.17

Click the CommandButton to fire the Click() event procedure that displays the secret message in the TextBox.

For more information on variables, what they are, and how to use them, see Chapter 7, "Using Data Types, Constants, and Variables."

Improving Your First Application

As you review the work that you've done so far, notice that some things need improvement. Figure 1.18 shows these shortcomings.

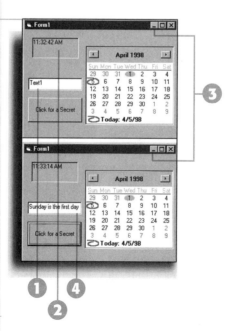

FIGURE 1.18

The upper form is the state of your program before the user clicks the CommandButton. The lower form is after the user clicks the CommandButton.

1 Default value of TextBox's Text property is confusing.

2 Clock is hard to read because the type isn't boldface.

3 Form can be resized, but controls can't be repositioned to accommodate resizing.

4 When the program is run, you can't view the secret message in its entirety.

Make the clock more readable

1. Press Shift+F7 to view the Object window.

2. Select the Label control in the main form.

3. In the Property window, scroll down to the Font property.

4. Click the **...** button to the right of the Font property (see Figure 1.19).

5. Select the **Bold Font Style** from the Font dialog (see Figure 1.20).

FIGURE 1.19

Clicking an **...** button opens a Property dialog.

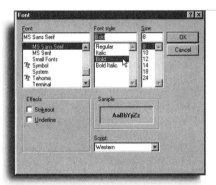

FIGURE 1.20

The Font dialog appears when you need to change the Font property of any control.

Improve the TextBox

1. Select the TextBox.

2. Scroll down the Properties window to the **MultiLine** property. Set it to **True** as shown in Figure 1.21.

3. Keep scrolling down the TextBox properties to the **ScrollBars** property. Set it to **2-Vertical** (see Figure 1.22).

FIGURE 1.21

Set the MultiLine property to True to make the text in the TextBox wrap.

FIGURE 1.22

If you set ScrollBars to 2-Vertical, up/down scrollbars appear. 3-Horizontal show sideways scrollbars, and 4-Both show scroll bars both ways.

4. Scroll to the **Text** property and delete the text Text1 from the drop-down list (highlight it and press Delete).

5. Increase the vertical size of the TextBox a small amount to accommodate the capability to display multiple lines of text.

Restrict resizing and assign a title to the form

1. Click the form. Be careful not to click any ActiveX control on the form; otherwise, you'll get the properties for the control rather than the form in the Properties window.

2. Select the **BorderStyle** property and set it to **3-Fixed Dialog** (see Figure 1.23).

FIGURE 1.23

Setting the BorderStyle property to 3-Fixed Dialog makes it so that the form can't be resized. Also, only the **Close** (×) button is shown in the title bar.

3. In the Properties window, set the form's **Caption** property to **First App**.

4. Save your work by choosing **Sa<u>v</u>e Project** from the **<u>F</u>ile** menu. Then run the code by pressing F5 (see Figure 1.24).

FIGURE 1.24
Your first application lets you view months and the present time, as well as display a secret message that users can view by scrolling through a TextBox.

Congratulations! You've made a very powerful program in Visual Basic by using the tools and building blocks that the language provides. Granted, a lot is going on behind the scenes that we might have covered in more detail, but you'll get more in-depth coverage in the following chapters.

For more information about the intrinsic controls that come with VB, read Chapter 4, "Using the Intrinsic Controls." To learn how to get around the VB IDE, read Chapter 3, "Working in the Visual Basic 6 Programming Environment." To get a clear understanding of properties, methods, and events, and how they relate to Visual Basic programming, read Chapter 6, "Working with Properties, Methods, and Events." Finally to get an in-depth view of the Timer control, read Chapter 16, "Working with Time and Timers."

What's New with Visual Basic 6

Learn about the CoolBar, DateTimePicker, ImageComboBox, and new data controls

Find out the new features of the Visual Basic language

Learn about IIS and DHTML applications

Learn about ActiveX Data Objects (ADO), the new data controls, data environments, and data reports

Getting a Quick Overview of VB6

If you're new to Visual Basic, the title of this chapter might be a little confusing. Clearly if you are a novice to the language, everything about VB is new. Even so, you shouldn't avoid this chapter. There's something in it for you, particularly in the sections focusing on the new ActiveX controls. For those of you who have done some work in other versions of Visual Basic, you'll find this chapter very relevant.

Saying that Visual Basic 6 has some interesting new features is nothing short of an understatement. Visual Basic 6 has so many amazing new features that overstatement is next to impossible because so much is new in so many areas. New controls allow your applications to incorporate the look, feel, and function of Office 97 applications and Internet Explorer. No more do you have to have at least one instance of a control on your form to create controls on-the-fly. With VB6, you add controls to your project dynamically with only code, and you can make custom ActiveX controls leaner and meaner than ever. You can even write server-side applications that use Dynamic HTML embedded with Internet Information Server DLLs.

This chapter gives some new features a bit more attention than others. Some new improvements involve working with larger-scale data access programs that might involve hundreds—if not thousands—of users on a corporate network or on the Internet. These types of Visual Basic applications, known as enterprise applications, are usually written with the Enterprise Edition of VB. These new enterprise features are referenced here but fall outside the scope of this book.

Getting More Power from Enhanced Controls

Before we look at the completely new additions to VB6, let's look at some enhancements to the features from the previous version.

> *For more information about how to add ActiveX controls to your project, see page 76*

What's Omitted

Keep in mind that some new features in VB6 have been omitted from this discussion. These features require more than an introductory knowledge to fully understand them. Many of these features that weren't discussed, however, are covered in later chapters, whereas others are described in the documentation that comes with the product.

Working with the Windows common controls

Most controls discussed in this chapter are *not* intrinsic (standard) ActiveX controls. Therefore, they must be added to your project from the Components dialog (choose **Components** from the **Project** menu). When you open the **Components** dialog, select **Microsoft Windows Common Controls**, **Microsoft Windows Common Controls-2**, and **Microsoft Windows Common Controls-3** from the list.

The *Validate* Event and the *CausesValidation* Property

The first enhancement that affects just about all intrinsic ActiveX controls is the addition of the `Validate` event and the `CausesValidation` property. Before VB6, if you had to check to see if a word was typed properly in a TextBox, you most likely would program the TextBox's `LostFocus` event handler to see if, indeed, the user entered correct data. If they hadn't, you could invoke the control's `SetFocus` method in which validation was occurring to keep the user from proceeding. Sometimes the logic of this programming could cause your users problems. If they never entered the right data, they would be locked into that one control—they couldn't even click a Help button. The new `Validate` event procedure and the `CausesValidation` property address this issue.

Listing 2.1 shows how to use the `Validate` event procedure to check a TextBox's data. The code relates to the illustration in Figure 2.1. If users don't type the word `Cherries` in the first TextBox, they can't proceed to the second TextBox. However, because the value `CausesValidation` property of the CommandButton is set to False, users can click it to help determine the right word to enter.

LISTING 2.1   02LIST01.TXT—Allowing Some Controls Event Handling Activity During Data Validation

```
01   Private Sub Text1_Validate(Cancel As Boolean)
02       'Make it so that if the user does not
03       'enter the word, "Cherries" in the TextBox
04       'the cursor will be returned this TextBox
05       If Text1.Text <> "Cherries" Then
06           MsgBox "You cannot go on!"
07           Cancel = True
08       End If
09   End Sub
10   Private Sub Command1_Click()
11       Dim strMsg As String
12       Dim strQuote As String
```

continues...

Using the CausesValidation property

Notice the **Cancel** *parameter* on Line 1. Visual Basic provides this parameter within the control's **Validate** event procedure. If you set the value of **Cancel** to **True** (Line 7), the program's focus won't be allowed to leave the control except to go to other controls that have their **CausesValidation** property set to **False**.

Listing 2. 1   Continued

```
13      strQuote = """"
14      'Make an instructional message
15      strMsg = "You must type the word," & strQuote
16      strMsg = strMsg & "Cherries" & strQuote & " "
17      strMsg = strMsg & "in the first TextBox."
18      MsgBox strMsg, vbInformation, "Instructions"
19      'The reason that you can click on this
20      'CommandButton even though the Cancel parameter
21      'of the Validate event handler is set to True
22      'is because the value of CauseValidation
23      'property of this CommandButton is set to false.
24   End Sub
```

Commenting code

The apostrophe (') before a line of code denotes a commented line. That line of code isn't run by Visual Basic.

FIGURE 2.1

The Validate event procedure allows you to check for correct data while still allowing you to access other controls during the validation process.

Adding Excitement with the New Graphical Enhancements

Visual Basic, as always, allows you to use graphics to make your programs come alive, and Microsoft has enhanced the graphical capabilities of many controls. First, the ImageList control now supports .gif files. This enhancement is substantial because just about every control that uses graphics has an ImageList control associated with it.

The ListView and TabStrip controls have been enhanced to allow you to use pictures and icons for decoration and description. Figure 2.2 shows you the new ListView control, to which you can add a background picture in the *client area*. The background picture can be centered, tiled, or placed at any corner. You can add check boxes to ListItems child objects within the control by setting the ListView's CheckBoxes property to True. Also, you can make the scrollbars of the ListView appear in the new flat style by setting the FlatScrollBars property to True. (If you want to see some of the ListView control enhancements demonstrated within a programming context, download the file VB6Ch2.zip and look at the project prjListView.vbp.)

Getting files From the Web site

The files referenced in this book can be downloaded from the Web site dedicated to this book. The source code can be found at http://www.mcp.com/info. When you get the URL, enter 078971633x, and then click the **Search** button to go to the Book Info page.

FIGURE 2.2

You now can have a background graphic in the ListView control client area.

Figure 2.3 shows you the new TabStrip control, which now allows you to place graphics in each tab. The control also has a new property, HotTracking, that you can assign at design time. If you set the value of HotTracking to True, the tab highlights when you pass the mouse pointer over it. As mentioned earlier, as with all the new controls, the TabStrip control has a Validate event procedure. (The example code for this control is in project prjTabStrip.vbp, in the VB98Ch2.zip file on the book's Web site.)

FIGURE 2.3

The TabStrip control has been enhanced to allow for icons on each tab.

The Slider control has a new property, Text. When you set a string to the value of the Text property, that string appears within a ToolTip window. The position of the ToolTip window is

determined by the Slider control's new `TextPosition` property
(see Figure 2.4). To see this code in action, review the project
prjSlider.vbp from the book's Web site.

FIGURE 2.4

The Slider control now has a
`Text` property that shows you a
ToolTip window.

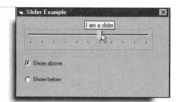

Many enhancements have been made to the ToolBar control.
You can now add drop-down menus to the toolbar by using a
ButtonMenu. The `Style` property supports a transparent setting
(`tbrTransparent`) that allows you to have the buttons on your
toolbar appear and behave like the buttons on the Internet
Explorer toolbar. Figure 2.5 shows the effect of the new transparent setting and a collection of buttons with each button having its own ButtonMenu. If you want to find out how to set up
your toolbar as shown in the figure, download the project
prjToolBar.vbp from the book's Web site. Open the project,
select the form, and then right-click the ToolBar control to view
the property page for the control. You then can review the various settings for the control.

FIGURE 2.5

The ToolBar control is enhanced
to provide ButtonsMenus and
hotspots. The control's property
page allows you to configure a
ToolBar at a very detailed level.

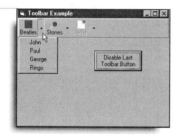

Working with the New Controls

Visual Basic 6 ships with many new ActiveX controls. Some of
these controls apply to stand-alone desktop programs; others
pertain to enterprise-wide data access development projects. In
the following sections, you'll see the new controls that relate to
your desktop development efforts.

Selecting Dates with the MonthView and DateTimePicker Controls

VB6 has two controls that provide you with a new way to view and select dates: MonthView and DateTimePicker. What's interesting about these controls is that they let you view and select dates within the context of a calendar. The MonthView control presents a full calendar that you can traverse from day to day or month to month. The DateTimePicker control is similar to the MonthView except that its calendar drops down when the user clicks the control's down arrow. Figure 2.6 shows you the MonthView and DateTimePicker controls.

Using all the new controls

All the controls discussed in this section are displayed and used within a single project, WhatsNew.vbp. You can download this code from http://www.mcp.com/info, as explained earlier.

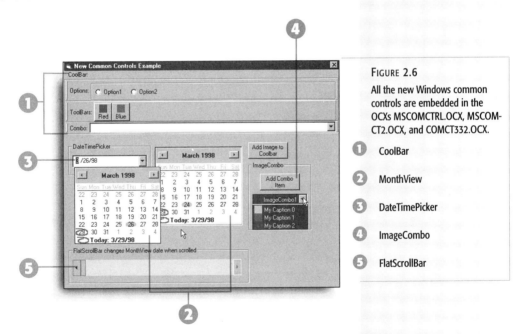

FIGURE 2.6

All the new Windows common controls are embedded in the OCXs MSCOMCTRL.OCX, MSCOM-CT2.OCX, and COMCT332.OCX.

① CoolBar

② MonthView

③ DateTimePicker

④ ImageCombo

⑤ FlatScrollBar

Making Movable Toolbars with the CoolBar

The new CoolBar control is similar to the *Coolbars* you've been using in Office 97 and Internet Explorer. A CoolBar is a toolbar that you can move on a form, and the CoolBar control is a *container* for other ActiveX controls. Thus, you can offer your users more flexibility and utility by embedding other controls within

CoolBar bands

A *band* is a bar within a CoolBar. A CoolBar can have many bands that can be moved about in the CoolBar client area.

Working with ImageLists

An *ImageList* is a "windowless" control that you use to store different types of graphics: bitmaps, gifs, icons, and so on. You associate an ImageList with a control by assigning the ImageList in question to a control's `ImageList` property. For example, to assign an ImageList named `ImageList1` to an ImageCombo, the code is `ImageList1.ImageList = ImageList1`.

the CoolBar. Figure 2.6 shows a CoolBar with three *Band* objects. The first Band contains two OptionButtons, the second contains a ToolBar control with three buttons, and the third band contains a ComboBox control. At *runtime* you can move the Bands around the Coolbar's client area any way you want.

Using Graphics with an ImageCombo

The ImageCombo control, new with Visual Basic 6, allows you to embed graphics within a ComboBox. To accomplish this, Visual Basic introduces a new *object*, the ComboItem, which encapsulates all layout and data properties that are needed to work with an ImageCombo. A ComboItem has a `Text` property for string display of a line within the ImageCombo and an `Image` property that can define the graphic to show on a line within the ImageCombo. As with most of the new graphical ActiveX controls, the ImageCombo has an ImageList from which it references images and pictures.

Use the code in Listing 2.2 to add a ComboItem that has a graphic to an ImageCombo. This code is from the `cmdAddCbo_Click()` event procedure of the **CommandButton** `cmdAddCbo`, which is part of the code from the project WhatsNew.vbp. You can download the code from the Web side dedicated to this book.

LISTING 2.2   02LIST02.TXT–Creating ComboItems and Adding Them to an ImageCombo

```
01    Static i%              'A counting integer
02    Static imgi%           'A index for a graphic
03                           'within an ImageList
04    Dim ci As ComboItem    'Object variable for a
05                           'ComboItem
06
07    'Get a reference to ComboItem object using
08    'a ComboItems Add method.
09    Set ci = ImageCombo1.ComboItems.Add
10    'Assign some data a line of text
11    'ci.Text = "My Caption " & CStr(i%)
12    'Add a graphic by referencing an index in the
```

```
13    'associated ImageList
14    ci.Image = imgi% + 1
15    'Make sure that you haven't exceeded the number
16    'of images in the ImageList
17    If imgi% = ImageList1.ListImages.Count - 1 Then
18        imgi% = 0
19    Else
20        imgi% = imgi% + 1
21    End If
22    'Increment the string counter
23    i% = i% + 1
```

Figure 2.6 shows you the result of clicking the cmdAddCbo button. Notice that the ImageCombo contains a graphic and a string.

The FlatScrollBar Control

Visual Basic 6 provides a new variation of the familiar scrollbar control: the FlatScrollBar. The FlatScrollBar is fundamentally the same as the ScrollBar, except that the FlatScrollBar has three Appearance styles: a standard style, a three-dimensional (beveled) style, and a two-dimensional style that becomes beveled when the mouse pointer hovers over it (refer to Figure 2.6).

Working with the New Language Features

In addition to enhanced and new ActiveX controls, VB6 also provides new features within the Visual Basic language itself. Again, if you have no previous experience with Visual Basic, the following sections might seem a bit baffling. You still might want to read through it anyway, however; these new features will make your programming efforts easier regardless of degree of prior experience.

File System Objects

In older versions of Visual Basic, if you wanted to get file system information or perform file system tasks, such as writing to a file

---

Code for the ComboItem

If you're beginning programmer, the code shown in Listing 2.2 is probably a little beyond your needs right now. This code is provided to show those with some VB background how to work with the newer features of the ComboItem object.

Internet Information Server

Internet Information Server (IIS) is a complex program, the function of which is to deliver information and files over the Internet. An Internet server is a physical computer, and IIS is software that runs on an Internet server. As you read in this book, you'll learn that you can use Visual Basic to write programs that are extensions of IIS, called IIS Applications. An application that runs on an Internet server is called a *server-side application*.

Microsoft Scripting RunTime component

If you plan to program with the FileSystemObject, make sure that you include a reference in your project to the Microsoft Scripting RunTime ActiveX component. You include a reference to the MS Scripting RunTime through the References dialog (choose **References** from the **Project** menu). Then select the **Microsoft Scripting RunTime** in the **References** list.

or changing a directory, you had a number of techniques available, most of which were quite laborious. In Visual Basic 6, all these chores have been contained with a new object, FileSystemObject, which is part of the Visual Basic Scripting Library. Thus, when you learn to use this object within VB6, you can easily transfer your knowledge to scripting within Internet Explorer or Internet Information Server to do system-level programming.

The FileSystemObject is quite complex. It's made of a number of objects and methods that encapsulate the file system functions, which you use to work with drives and files on a local machine or over the network. Table 2.1 describes the new FileSystemObject objects.

TABLE 2.1   FileSystemObject Objects

Object	Description
Drive	Provides properties and methods for describing and working with local and network drives
File	Provides properties and methods for working with files
Folder	Provides properties and methods for working with folders
FileSystemObject	Provides properties and methods for defining and working with collections of drives, folders, and files
TextStream	Provides properties and methods that allow you work with text files

If you want an introduction to the FileSystemObject, the project prjFileSystem.vbp is a small program that shows you how to use the various FileSystemObject features to find out how many drives are on your computer (see Figure 2.7). Also, when you select a found drive, the program reports back the amount of unused disk space on a drive. You can find the project prjFileSystem.vbp on the Web site dedicated to this book.

FIGURE 2.7

The project prjFileSystem gives you an introduction about how to use the FileSystemObject.

New String Functions

Visual Basic 6 provides a number of new functions for working with strings (see Table 2.2).

TABLE 2.2   **The New String Functions**

Function Name (Return Type)	Description
Filter (string array)	Allows you to filter a string for various substrings
FormatCurrency (string)	Allows you to format a string to currency
FormatDateTime (string)	Allows you to format a string to a time or date
FormatPercent (string)	Allows you to format a string as a percent
InStrRev (string)	Returns the position of one string within another string; unlike InStr, InStrRev starts at the end of the string being searched
Join (string)	Takes a string array and combines its elements into one string
MonthName (string)	Returns the name of a month when you have the number of the month (for example, 1 returns January)
Replace (string)	Replaces substrings within a string
Round (string)	Returns a rounded number as specified
Split (string array)	Splits a string into an array of strings
StrReverse (string)	Reverses the order of a string—for example, "cat" becomes "tac"
WeekdayByName (string)	Returns the day of the week

As you can see in Table 2.2, some new string functions return string arrays. The capability of a function to return an array is also a new feature in VB6.

Each new function listed in Table 2.2 could warrant a section of a chapter dedicated solely to it. Clearly, such description is beyond the scope of this chapter, but if you need more details for how to use a specific string function, read the documentation that comes with your edition of VB6 or Chapter 12, "Working with Strings and Typecasting."

True Dynamic Control Creation

On-the-fly versus runtime

The phrase *on-the-fly* is used when you are creating something while a program is running. Another term for the state when a program is running is *runtime*.

For those of you familiar with VB, you might know that in prior versions of VB you created controls on-the-fly by using *control arrays*. One drawback to creating controls with a control array was that at least one control had to be present on a form for you to create others *dynamically*. This is no longer true in VB6; you can create a control at runtime purely from code by using the Add method of the Controls collection.

Listing 2.3 shows you the code that you must use to create a CommandButton purely from code, without having to drag a CommandButton from the ToolBox first.

LISTING 2.3   02LIST03.TXT–The New *Add* Method for the Controls Collection

```
01   Option Explicit
02   'WithEvents is a way tell the program to
03   'respect all the events that are associated
04   'a CommandButton such as the click event.
05   Private WithEvents cmdMyButton As CommandButton
06
07   Private Sub Form_Load()
08       Set cmdButton = Controls.Add("VB.CommandButton", _
                                      "Button")
09       With cmdButton
10         .Visible = True
11         .Width = 3000
12         .Caption = "A real surprise"
12       .Top = 1000
14       .Left = 1000
15     End With
16   End Sub
17
18   Sub cmdButton _Click()
19       cmdButton.Caption = "At last, real OOP!"
20   End Sub
```

If you want to see this code in action, go to the project prjDynCtrl.vbp on the Web site dedicated to this book.

Learning About VB and the Internet

Visual Basic has been positioned very nicely for Internet development. You can use *VBScript* to write applications that run on your desktop computer with Internet Explorer. Also, you can use VBScript on the server side to work with Internet Explorer. Visual Basic 6 has sharpened the focus on Internet development; it extends your ability to write *server-side* applications for Microsoft's Internet Information Server by introducing a project type named IIS Applications. Also, Visual Basic extends and simplifies DHTML (Dynamic Hypertext Markup Language, the language used by all Web browsers) by introducing a project type named DHTML Applications. For more about programming with VB, VBScript, and DHTML, read Chapter 28, "Creating VB Programs for the Internet."

An IIS application is a Visual Basic program that resides server side as an extension of Internet Application Server. An IIS application is called by a *client* computer via the Internet. Although the Visual Basic IIS Application sends data back to the calling client through HTML, the actual calculation on the server-side computer is done by using compiled Visual Basic code. This enhancement is significant; before this, IIS Applications were written in C++ or, if you wanted to program IIS, you had to do it with VBScript under Active Server Pages (ASP).

A DHTML application is a project that presents a Visual Basic *Designer*, a tool that automates the writing of VB code. The DHTML Application Designer allows you to write DHTML code within the Visual Basic *IDE*. You can find the actual DHTML on the IIS Web server in the form of an *ActiveX DLL*. This is significant because DHTML is somewhat different than VB code. Thus, you're leveraging the inner workings of IIS and VB to actually translate VB into DHTML at runtime.

One problem with programming for the Internet is that the programming dynamic is stateless by nature. Interaction is analogous to a telephone call. Every time you contact a server on the

Working with DHTML

Dynamic Hypertext Markup Language is an extension of HTML (Hypertext Markup Language), the language of the Internet. All Web browsers, regardless of manufacturer, use HMTL to decode information passed through the Internet that's presented to end users. DHTML takes HTML one step further by permitting a greater degree of programmability to take place. Thus, with *DHTML* you can send code via the Internet that allows end users to move things around the computer monitor with a mouse, to hide things, or even to delete items.

VB's integrated development environment

IDE stands for integrated development environment. The Visual Basic IDE is your programming workbench, where you write and debug code as well as manage your applications. You'll learn more about the Visual Basic IDE in Chapter 3, "Working in the Visual Basic 6 Programming Environment."

Internet, it's as though you're making a telephone call to a stranger who has no prior knowledge of the information passed in any previous call. Therefore, working with a body of data that must be transmitted from session to session is difficult. Visual Basic uses a new feature within Internet Explorer, the Global Property Bag, to allow you to share information from session to session.

Microsoft has extended the Setup Wizard into a set of new tools to make publishing your application to and deploying it from a Web server easier. These tools—the Web Publishing Wizard and the Package and Deployment Wizard—come as part of your purchase when you buy your edition of Visual Basic 6. You'll take a close look at the Web Publishing Wizard and the Package and Deployment Wizard in Chapter 20, "Deploying Your Visual Basic Applications."

Finding Out About the New Data Capabilities

Visual Basic 6 supports ActiveX Data Objects (ADO). In prior versions of VB, data access was handled under the umbrella of Data Access Objects (DAO) and Remote Data Objects (RDO). ADO has combined and superseded these technologies. ADO is easier to use and has a broader scope of implementation. You can use ADO to connect to a database on a local desktop or to a remote database server. Also, ADO allows you to access more types of data—e-mail, for example.

The current ADO technology is contained within the new ADO Data control. The ADO Data control might look the same as the familiar Data control of prior versions, but when you look at the Property Page of the control (see Figure 2.8), you see a significant difference. The ADO control allows you to connect to a desktop database file or an ODBC server on a network, or you can create a new connection to another database.

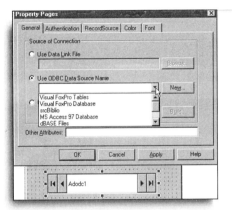

FIGURE 2.8

The ADO data control combines the functionality of DAO and RDO, as well as allows you to access non-traditional data types such as e-mail or files within the file system.

In addition to ADO, Visual Basic 6 also comes with a new set of tools and technologies that make data access easier. The Data Environment Designer allows you to view and manipulate data in various databases. Because data environments are objects in their own right, you can use them as you would a Data control. You can even *bind* other controls, such as a TextBox or Label, to a Data control.

Some new data controls allow you take advantage of the enhancements built into the ADO Data control. The DataGrid allows you to view your data in a row and column format. The DataList and DataCombo are similar to the DBList and DBCombo in earlier editions of VB; you can use them to get a pick list of data from an ADO control in a ListBox or ComboBox configuration. You also can use the more advanced FlexGrid and hierarchical FlexGrid controls to get a clear, visual view of complex data. Visual Basic also provides a new Data Setup Wizard to make deploying your larger-scale database applications easier.

Visual Basic 6 enhances its reporting capabilities with the Data Report Designer (see Figure 2.9), which lets you create, preview, and print reports in Visual Basic as you would in Access. (If you've worked in Access 97, you'll find the Data Report Designer familiar.) You set report controls from the new Data Reports Toolbox (VB also has some new IDE features) onto the Data Report form. Then you invoke the Data Report's

PrintReport() method. Granted, as you go along, you'll find things to be more complex. You can get more details on Data Environments and Data Reports in the chapters in Part V of this book, "Database Programming with Visual Basic 6."

FIGURE 2.9

The Data Report Designer brings the ease of Access 97 reporting to Visual Basic.

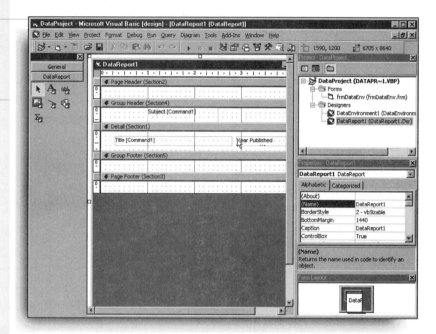

New Object Programming Additions

Visual Basic 6 has made creating classes and ActiveX controls a much broader activity. You can now save your custom-made class's data from session to session in a *Property Bag*. You can also create two new types of data-aware custom classes, Data Sources and Data Consumers. These types of data classes behave very much as the ADO Data objects, except they allow you to have more flexibility to suit your custom needs.

With regard to custom ActiveX controls, you now can make lightweight ActiveX controls in VB6. These types of controls are "windowless" and thus require fewer system resources than full-fledged ActiveX controls. To determine if an ActiveX control is indeed windowless, Visual Basic provides a new property, HasDC.

Probably the most helpful additions to Visual Basic 6 are all the new wizards that come bundled with it. Table 2.3 briefly describes each new wizard and add-in.

TABLE 2.3   Visual Basic 6 Wizards and Add-Ins

Wizard/Add-In	Description
All Editions	
Package and Deployment Wizard	Helps you prepare and deploy your application for desktop or network use.
Application Wizard	Helps you set up a framework for your application. It automatically adds menus, toolbars, resource files, intrinsic ActiveX controls, and data controls.
Wizard Manager	Helps you organize the various wizards that you can access within your IDE.
Professional and Enterprise Editions	
Data Object Wizard	Helps you create data objects bound to data controls and custom ActiveX controls.
Class Builder Utility	Helps you visually build custom classes.
ToolBar Wizard	Helps you visually create custom toolbars for your forms.
Data Form Wizard	Helps you create forms with controls that reference data in a database.
Add-In Designer	Helps you create custom VB add-ins.
Property Page Wizard	Helps you create property dialogs for the ActiveX controls you make in VB.
T-SQL Debugger	Helps you debug code that you write for Microsoft's SQL Server Database.
API Viewer	Helps you work with declares (functions), constants, and types from the Windows API.
ActiveX Control Interface Wizard	Helps you make ActiveX controls.

Using add-ins

An *add-in* is a Visual Basic tool that VB programmers make for other VB programmers. An add-in is written in VB and can run only within the Visual Basic IDE. The Application Wizard is an add-in, as is the Data Forms Wizard.

Working in the Visual Basic 6 Programming Environment

Work in the Visual Basic integrated environment

Learn how to work with toolbars

Work with multiple projects

Control the way you view the IDE

Understanding the Parts of the IDE

Defining IDE

IDE is an acronym for Integrated Development Environment. The IDE is the workbench on which you make your programs in Visual Basic.

The Visual Basic IDE is a collection of menus, toolbars, and windows that make up your programming workbench (see Figure 3.1). Each part of the IDE has features that affect different aspects of your programming activity. The menu bar lets you direct the overall activity and management of your programming. The toolbar enables you to access much of the menu bar's functionality through various toolbar buttons. Forms—the basic building blocks of Visual Basic programs—are presented in a Form window. You use the ToolBox to add controls to the forms of your project. The Project Explorer displays the projects on which you're working, as well as the different parts of each of those projects. You browse and set a control, form, and module's properties within the Properties window. Finally, you position and view a form or forms onscreen within the Form Layout window.

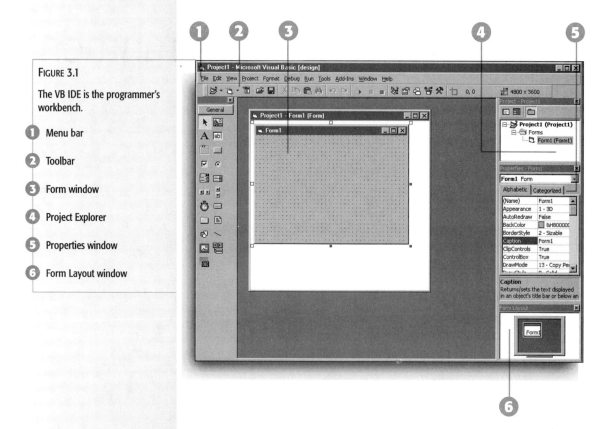

FIGURE 3.1

The VB IDE is the programmer's workbench.

1. Menu bar

2. Toolbar

3. Form window

4. Project Explorer

5. Properties window

6. Form Layout window

Adding and Removing Toolbars in the Visual Basic IDE

Toolbars are collections of small iconic buttons that reside in a bar underneath the menu bar. These buttons offer access to the most commonly used functions that you have in the Visual Basic menu structure. Toolbars are useful because rather than have to negotiate menus and submenus to do what you want, you click a specific button in the toolbar to call a specific functionality in the Visual Basic IDE.

Toolbars usually reside under the menu and can be grouped into a single bar. Also, you can drag a toolbar onto the IDE's Code and Form windows to have it "float" for more convenient access.

Add or remove a toolbar to or from the IDE

1. Right-click anywhere on the menu bar, or choose **Toolbars** from the **View** menu. The toolbar pop-up menu appears (see Figure 3.2).

ToolTips

ToolTips are little windows that appear when you hold the mouse pointer over a control or toolbar button for a few seconds. Inside these windows is some text that tells you what the control or toolbar button is about.

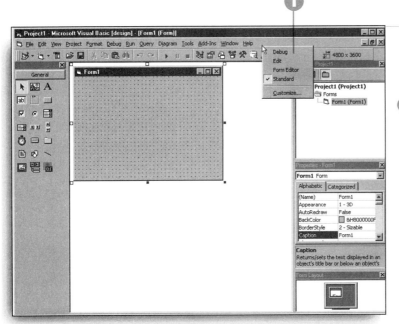

FIGURE 3.2

You select a predefined toolbar type by right-clicking the VB toolbar.

❶ Toolbar pop-up menu

2. Select the type of standard toolbar that you want from the pop-up menu. If a check is to the left of a toolbar type, that toolbar is already visible.

Using the Debug Toolbar

You use the Debug toolbar (see Figure 3.3) to test your program and resolve errors that might occur. When you debug a program, you do things such as run the code a line at a time, examine the values of variables, and stop the code at certain critical points or under certain conditions. For an in-depth discussion of debugging, see Chapter 21, "Debugging Your Applications."

Using the Edit Toolbar

You use the Edit toolbar (see Figure 3.4) when you're working with code in a Code window. The features of the Edit toolbar are similar to those of the **Edit** menu. You can **Cut** and **Paste** text. You can manipulate the layout of your code and do text selection, searches, and replacement. Also, you can use automatic coding features such as Quick Info.

An interesting VB IDE feature that the Edit toolbar uses is the Complete Word feature (also trademarked by Microsoft as Intelli-sense). This feature automatically completes a keyword for you. For example, if you were to type Ms into a code window and then invoke the Complete Word feature, Visual Basic would complete the word as MsgBox, an intrinsic Visual Basic function that displays a Windows message box. The Complete Word feature is very useful for avoiding syntax errors due to misspelling. For more information about the specifics of debugging, see Chapter 21.

FIGURE 3.3

The Debug toolbar enables you to access the debugging functions of the Visual Basic IDE.

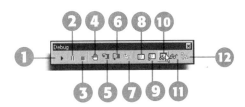

1. Puts program in Run mode

2. Temporarily stops program so you can inspect variable values and program flow

3. Stops program and resets IDE to Design mode

4. Sets a point in code to put program into Break mode

5. In Break mode, moves through code one line at a time

6. In Break mode, moves through code a procedure at a time

7. In a Step Into situation, moves out of procedure so you can move through large bodies of code quickly

8. Displays the Local window, which contains the Watch and Call Stack windows and lets you see the state of various code variables

9. Displays the Immediate window so you can enter small snippets of code to test

10. Displays the Watch window so you can view variable values

11. Displays the Quick Watch window so you can view the value of a single variable or expression

12. Displays the Call Stack window so you can see all functions and subs in force

FIGURE 3.4

You can access the extended **Edit** menu and some **Debug** menu functions from the Edit toolbar.

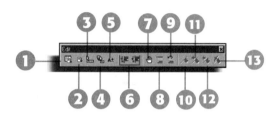

1 Displays an auto-complete pop-up window that displays all the available properties and methods

2 Displays a list of constants available for a given object

3 Displays the Quick Watch pop-up menu so you can view a variable definition

4 Displays the Parameter pop-up menu that lets you complete procedure statements

5 Invokes the automatic Complete Word feature so you can type a few letters of a word and have VB complete it

6 Moves code lines a tab stop so you can organize code layout quickly

7 Sets and releases a breakpoint on a line of code; useful when you want to run code to a certain point and then stop to inspect it

8 Creates a comment block by automatically adding an apostrophe to the beginning of a line of code

9 Removes a comment apostrophe

10 Sets a bookmark in code

11 Moves the cursor forward to the next bookmark that you've set in your code

12 Moves the cursor backward to the preceding bookmark that you set in code

13 Releases all bookmarks that you've set in the Code window

Using the Form Editor Toolbar

You use the Form Editor toolbar (see Figure 3.5) to size, move, and align controls on a form. The Form Editor toolbar has the same set of features as the **Fo̲rmat** menu.

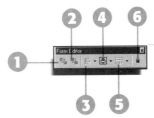

Notice the small downward-facing arrowheads to the right of the Align, Center, and Make toolbar buttons. These arrowheads indicate that a drop-down menu will appear when you select that toolbar button.

Working with forms and controls requires that sometimes you have to work with the ZOrder property of a control. ZOrder determines which control has the "right" to supersede the position of another control. Sometimes you might want one control to appear over another—an OptionButton over a PictureBox, for instance. You can accomplish this by dragging the OptionButton over the PictureBox. Alternatively, in code, you can set the value of the OptionButton's ZOrder property to 0. Then, no matter where you place the control at design time, the OptionButton will always be on top. When you place one control over another on a form, you're affecting each control's ZOrder property. The Z order determines the "top most-ness" of a control. Controls with a ZOrder value of 0 are always on top; however, if two controls each have a ZOrder value of 0, they nullify each other.

Using the Standard Toolbar

The standard toolbar (see Figure 3.6) is the central toolbar in the Visual Basic IDE. The standard toolbar offers many features found in the **Fi̲le**, **P̲roject**, **D̲ebug**, and **R̲un** menus.

FIGURE 3.6

The standard toolbar gives you fast access to often-used functionality and information.

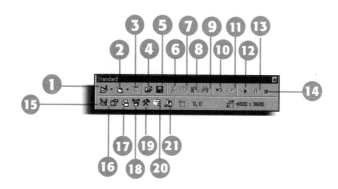

1   Add Project

2   Add Form, Module, and so on

3   Menu Editor

4   Open Project

5   Save Project Group

6   Cut

7   Copy

8   Paste

9   Find

10   Undo

11   Redo

12   Start

13   Break

14   End

15   Show Project Explorer

16   Show Properties Window

17   Show Form Layout Window

18   Show Object Browser

19   Show ToolBox

20   Selected Control x, y Position (in twips)

21   Selected Control Width × Length (in twips)

Adding Controls with the ToolBox

Controls are the building blocks with which you assemble your Visual Basic program. The ToolBox is a palette of controls, and you build your user interface by selecting controls from the ToolBox and placing them on your forms (see Figure 3.7).

Some controls are built into Visual Basic and can't be removed from the ToolBox; these controls reside within Visual Basic itself. These controls are known as *intrinsic controls*. Others live outside Visual Basic and reside in files that end with the extension .ocx. These controls can be added and removed from the ToolBox.

A full discussion of the ToolBox, intrinsic controls, and ActiveX controls takes place in Chapter 4, "Using the Intrinsic Controls."

SEE ALSO

➤ *No matter what ToolBox control you want, adding it to your form takes only a few steps, as shown with the command buttons in your first application, page 15*

FIGURE 3.7

This ToolBox shows both intrinsic controls and the extra ActiveX controls that ship with Visual Basic 6.

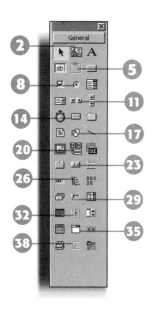

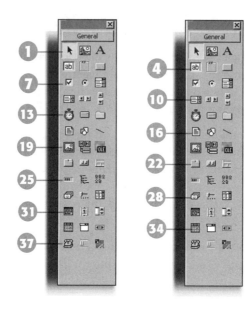

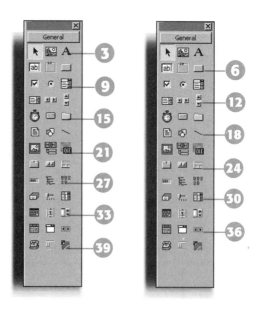

1 Pointer: Selects controls

2 PictureBox: Shows graphics

3 Label: Displays text

4 TextBox: Displays text and enables users to input text

5 Frame: Groups other controls

6 CommandButton: A "clickable" button

7 CheckBox: A group of CheckBoxes enables users to choose more than one item

8 OptionButton: A group of OptionButtons enables users to choose only one thing

9 ComboBox: Displays a drop-down list combination ListBox and TextBox

10 ListBox: Displays a list of text strings

11 Horizontal Scroll: Scrollbar for sideways scrolling

12 Vertical Scroll: Scrollbar for vertical scrolling

13 Timer: Enables things to happen at certain time intervals

14 Drive ListBox: Used for moving from hard disk to hard disk

15 Folder/Directory: Used for moving between folders (directories) on a hard disk

16 File ListBox: Used for selecting files in a folder (directory)

17 Shape: Used for making and displaying shapes

18 Line: Used for displaying lines

19 Image: Displays graphics more efficiently than the PictureBox

20 Data Control: Used for working with databases

21 OLE Container Control: Used for working with other insertable objects

22 TabStrip: An ActiveX control that you use for creating tabbed dialogs

23 ToolBar: An ActiveX control that lets you make collections of small CommandButtons on a single bar

24 StatusBar: An ActiveX control that enables you to display data at the bottom of a window

25 Progress Bar: An ActiveX control that enables you to communicate the "time to complete" status of a given process

26 TreeView: An ActiveX control that presents an Explorer-like hierarchical display of data

27 ListView: An ActiveX control that displays data similarly to the My Computer window in Windows—by large icon, small icon, or detail

28 ListImage: An ActiveX control that holds various graphics that you can reference (the graphics can be bitmaps, icons, or pictures in .gif or .jpg format)

29 Slider: An ActiveX control that enables you to set a value by moving a slider bar

30 ImageCombo: An ActiveX control that lets you list data in a CombBox fashion, but also with an associate graphical image

31 CommonDialog: Used to present the Windows 98 common dialog for working with files, printers, fonts, and colors

32 Animation: Lets you use pictures to create animation effects

33 UpDown: An ActiveX control that you can use to increment and decrement values in an associated control

34 MonthView: An ActiveX control that displays a calendar

35 MonthDate Picker: An ActiveX control that displays a drop-down calendar from which you can select dates

36 FlatScrollBar: An ActiveX control that presents scrollbars that have an enhanced graphical style

37 Comm: An ActiveX control that allow you to work with modems and other forms of serial communications

38 CoolBar: An ActiveX control that provides toolbars that can be moved and docked

39 RichText: An ActiveX control that lets you read and write text formatted as you would find in a word processor such as Word

Navigating Through the Form Window and Code Window

Just as controls are the building blocks that you use to assemble your Visual Basic program, a Visual Basic form is the foundation on which you build with those blocks. Forms reside in the Form Designer window (see Figure 3.8). You work in the Form Designer window to add controls to your form.

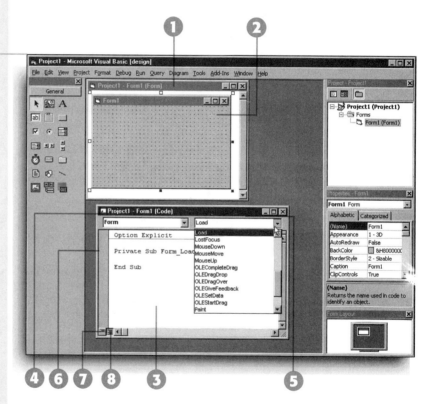

FIGURE 3.8

The Form Designer window is where you create forms for your Visual Basic programs.

1 Form Designer window

2 Form: Double-click form to view Code window

3 Code window: Write the code behind the controls and forms

4 Object drop-down list: Select the control to program

5 Procedure/Events drop-down list: Select the event procedure to which you want to add code

6 Margin Indicator bar: Set breakpoints automatically within the margin indicator

7 Procedure View icon: Click this button to view your code one procedure at a time

8 Full Module View icon: Click the button to view your code as a continuous text file with a line between the location in text when the sub or function begins/ends

For each Form Designer window, you can also open a Code window. Code windows are where you work with the Visual Basic code that you write "behind" your form (refer to Figure 3.8). You open a code window by double-clicking a form or a control on the form. You also can open a code window by choosing **Code** from the **View** menu. For how to access Code windows, review the process described for the application that you made in Chapter 1, "Building Your First Application."

Managing Applications with the Project Explorer

The Project Explorer in Visual Basic 6 helps you manage and navigate multiple projects. Visual Basic enables you to organize multiple projects into groups called *project groups*. You can save the collection of projects in your Visual Basic session into a project group file. Project Group files end with the extension .vbg.

The Project Explorer is a hierarchical tree-branch structure. Projects are at the top of the tree, and the project parts (forms, modules, and so on) descend from the tree. If you want to work on a particular part, you double-click the part to display it. If you want to see the part in a particular view—say, a form in a Code window—you select the form by clicking it once. Then click the View Code icon at the top of the Project Explorer window (see Figure 3.9).

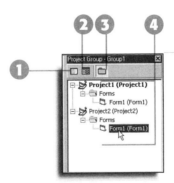

FIGURE 3.9

You can work with multiple projects in the Project Explorer window.

1. View Code icon: Shows the Code window of the item selected in the list window

2. View Object icon: Shows the Designer for the selected item, where appropriate

3. Toggle Folders: Shows project components in grouped folders or as an ungrouped list

4. List window: Displays a hierarchical tree of projects and project components within the IDE

As you become a more adept programmer and the scope and size of your programs grow to include multiple projects, you'll find the Project Explorer to be an extremely useful tool for doing large-scale programming. For example, if want to add a form to your project, you can do so by using the Project Explorer.

Add a form from the Project Explorer

1. Position the pointer on the white area of the Project window (**not** over a form or any other item on the tree view).

2. Right-click to display the Project Explorer context menu.

3. Choose **<u>A</u>dd** and then **<u>F</u>orm** (see Figure 3.10).

FIGURE 3.10

You can add or remove projects, forms, and modules to or from the Project Explorer by using its context menu.

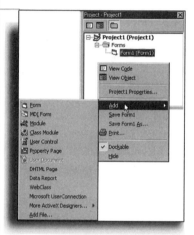

Controlling Settings with the Properties Window

Properties and values

The programming jargon for a property's setting is a property's *value*.

In the Properties window, you read, configure, and control the initial settings of the *ActiveX controls* in your program. As you become more familiar with Visual Basic programming, a good portion of your time will be spent learning, setting, and manipulating control properties. Because controls are the building blocks of Visual Basic programs, the Properties window is an essential tool to master. Figure 3.11 shows the structure of the Properties window.

SEE ALSO

➤ *To see how to use the Property windows to change property values within a form, see page 26*

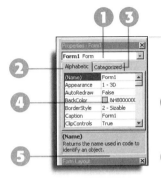

FIGURE 3.11

You set the attributes of a control with the Properties window.

1. Object box: Enables you to select the ActiveX control properties you want to list

2. Alphabetic tab: Displays properties alphabetically

3. Categorized tab: Displays properties by types or groups

4. Property list: Lists the property on the left and the property's value on the right

5. Description pane: Gives a brief description of the property

Setting Form Position with the Form Layout Window

The Form Layout window enables you to set the *runtime* position of one or more forms onscreen.

You position a form by moving its representation on the "computer screen" in the Form Layout window with your mouse. As you move the pointer over the small form in the Form Layout window, the pointer changes into a four-directional, arrow-headed cross. To position the screen, hold down your mouse button and drag the form to where you want it to be on the computer screen (see Figure 3.12).

FIGURE 3.12

The Form Layout window lets you position one or more forms as they appear onscreen.

The Form Layout window is a little tricky to use. Remember, the placement of a form in the Form Designer window doesn't affect the screen position of your program's form at runtime. If the IDE is in MDI display mode, you set the runtime startup position of a form in the Form Layout window. When the IDE is in SDI display move, there's no display of a Form Layout window. Thus, the position of the form onscreen is the startup position of the form at runtime.

MDI versus SDI

MDI stands for *multiple document interface*; SDI stands for *single document interface*. A multiple document graphical user interface is one that allows you to view multiple windows within a larger window—various Word document windows within the Word application window, for example. A single document interface is one where all windows appear independently of one another without the unification of a single *parent* window.

Viewing the IDE

You can view the Visual Basic IDE in two ways: with the multiple document interface (MDI) or the single document interface (SDI). MDI view shows all the distinct windows of the Visual Basic IDE as member windows within one large IDE window (refer to Figure 3.1).

In the SDI view (shown in Figure 3.13), distinct windows of the Visual Basic IDE exist independently of each other. There's no master window to contain and provide a unified feel to the IDE. Some people who've worked with previous versions of Visual Basic find working with the IDE in an SDI view a little bit easier in that it's similar to the earlier versions' environment; others find the unified layout of the MDI environment more appealing. There's no better or worse way; it's all a matter of work style.

FIGURE 3.13

The SDI view is the way the VB IDE looked before version 5.

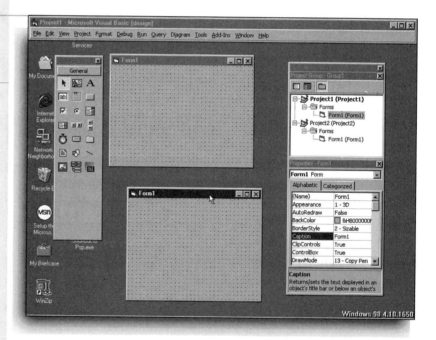

Change from MDI view to SDI view

1. Choose **Options** from the **Tools** menu. The Options dialog box appears (see Figure 3.14).

2. On the Advanced page, select the **SDI Development Environment** check box; then click **OK**. The Visual Basic IDE will reconfigure to the SDI view the next time you start a Visual Basic programming session.

3. Click **OK**; then terminate and restart Visual Basic.

FIGURE 3.14

You custom configure the IDE from within the Options dialog box.

Using the Intrinsic Controls

Add controls to a form

Size and position controls

Resize a form

Add controls to the Toolbox

What Are Forms and Controls?

Are there programs you can't see?

Although most programs you write will start with a form, not all programs use forms. These programs don't have any way for a person to use them directly; instead, other programs use them. Don't worry about this yet. Right now, just remember that people will be using your program and will use the controls you put on a form.

In Visual Basic, *forms* are the foundations you generally use to build programs. A form is where you put all the things that people interact with as they use your program. Those things you put on the form are *controls*, which enable the people who use your program to do things, such as enter text and click buttons.

Think of it this way: If you build a house, you start with a foundation—think of this as the form. On top of the foundation, you add all the things that allow you use the house: a floor, walls, and doors. These things are the controls.

What Are Intrinsic Controls?

Distributing intrinsic controls

When you distribute a program that includes intrinsic controls only, you don't need to include OCX files. All the intrinsic controls are contained within the Visual Basic runtime files, so they'll be available to your program as long as the runtime files are present on the system.

For the most part, you'll use a relatively small set of controls when you program in Visual Basic. However, these controls are very powerful. With them, you can add buttons, check boxes, labels, and text boxes to your programs. You can use them to see files on your hard drive right from your program. You can even read a database! These basic controls are *intrinsic controls*, and they're available in every edition of Visual Basic 6.

The intrinsic controls are available whenever you use Visual Basic. During design time, you can access them from the Toolbox (see Figure 4.1). Table 4.1 lists the intrinsic controls.

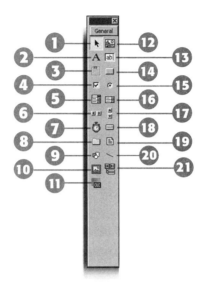

FIGURE 4.1

By using only the intrinsic controls, you can create powerful programs. To select a control, just click it.

1 Pointer

2 Label

3 Frame

4 CheckBox

5 ComboBox

6 HScrollBar (horizontal scrollbar)

7 Timer

8 DirListBox (folder or directory)

9 Shape

10 Image

11 OLE Container control

12 PictureBox

13 TextBox

14 CommandButton

15 OptionButton

16 ListBox

17 VScrollBar (vertical scrollbar)

18 DriveListBox

19 FileListBox

20 Line

21 Data

TABLE 4.1   **The Visual Basic 6 Intrinsic Controls**

Control	Description
Label	Displays text on a form
Frame	Serves as a *container* for other controls
CheckBox	Enables users to select or deselect an option
ComboBox	Allows users to select from a list of items or add a new value
HscrollBar	Allows users to scroll horizontally through a list of data in another control
Timer	Lets your program perform actions in real time, without user interaction
DirListBox	Enables users to select a directory or folder
Shape	Displays a shape on a form
Image	Displays graphics (images) on a form but can't be a container
OLE Container	Enables you to add the functionality of another Control program to your program
PictureBox	Displays graphics (images) on a form and can serve as a container
TextBox	Can be used to display text but also enables users to enter or edit new or existing text
CommandButton	Enables users to initiate actions
OptionButton	Lets users select one choice from a group; must be used in groups of two or more
ListBox	Enables users to select from a list of items
VscrollBar	Enables users to scroll vertically through a list of data in another control
DriveListBox	Lets users select a disk drive
FileListBox	Lets users select a file
Line	Displays a line on a form
Data	Lets your program connect to a database

Adding and Removing Controls

You can add controls to a form in two ways: by double-clicking and by drawing. You learned about double-clicking in Chapter 1,

"Building Your Application;" whenever you double-click an icon on the toolbar, the associated control appears on your form. When you do this, though, you can't control where the control goes: You're at the mercy of Visual Basic. When you draw a control on your form, you can put it wherever you want it.

Draw a control on a form

1. Click the control's Toolbox icon.

2. Move the mouse pointer over your form. Notice that your pointer is now shaped as a crosshair instead of an arrow. Click (and hold) the mouse button where you want the control to go.

3. Drag the mouse down slightly and to the left. As you move the mouse, notice that a box starts to appear (see Figure 4.2).

4. When the box is the proper size, let go of the mouse button. The control you selected now appears on the form.

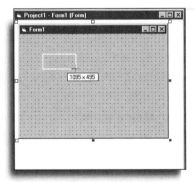

FIGURE 4.2

When drawing controls, use the box to approximate the size of your control.

Remove a control from a form

1. Select the control you want to delete by clicking it. The control you select will appear with a box at each corner and side (see Figure 4.3).

2. Press the Delete key.

You can also remove a control by right-clicking it. From the context menu that appears, select **Delete**.

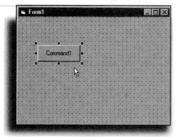

The Importance of Naming Controls

A control's name is one of its most important attributes because you literally refer to a control by its name whenever you want it to do something. Names are so important that every time you put a control on your form, Visual Basic automatically gives a name to it. If you add a CommandButton, Visual Basic names it Command1; if you add a TextBox, it's automatically named Text1.

However, naming controls like this can be confusing. For example, if you add six CommandButtons to your form, Visual Basic will name them Command1, Command2, Command3, and so on. If you need 100 buttons, Visual Basic will name the last one Command100. How are you supposed to remember what Command67 does? The trick is, rather than let Visual Basic name your controls automatically, you should do it yourself.

Name a control

1. After you add a control to a form, make sure that it's selected (it has a box at each corner and side when it's selected).

2. In the Properties window, click the control's name in the right column (see Figure 4.4).

3. Delete the current name and add the name you want.

A better name for a control is one that tells not only what type of control it is, but also what it does within your program. Can you see the value here? If you consistently give your controls descriptive names, you'll always know what they do. Naturally, there is a convention you can use to help you with this.

FIGURE 4.4
FIGURE 4.4
You can change a control's name in the Properties window.

This convention is quite simple. It consists of a short (usually three-letter) abbreviation that identifies the type of control (see Table 4.2), followed by a longer, friendly name that describes what the control does within your program. The abbreviation is lowercase, and the friendly name follows it immediately, without any spaces.

Friendly names

When naming a control, the first letter of the friendly name is generally uppercase. This makes it easier to read the control's name, because you can easily differentiate between the friendly name and the control's abbreviation.

TABLE 4.2   Common Prefixes for Naming Visual Basic Intrinsic Controls

Control	Prefix	Control	Prefix
Label	lbl	PictureBox	pic
Frame	fra	TextBox	txt
CheckBox	chk	CommandButton	cmd
ComboBox	cbo	OptionButton	opt
HscrollBar	hsb	ListBox	lst
Timer	tmr	VscrollBar	vsb
DirListBox	dir	DriveListBox	drv
Shape	shp	FileListBox	fil
Image	img	Line	lin
OLE Container Control	ole	Data	dat

For example, a CommandButton (which has the abbreviation cmd) used to close a program might be named cmdClose. If you use a TextBox (which has the abbreviation txt) for users to input their name, you might call it txtName. This convention becomes especially powerful when you use the same type of control multiple times. Say that you use two text boxes to capture a user's name. If you let Visual Basic name the controls, they will be

Text1 and Text2. If you take over and name them yourself, you can name them txtFirstName and txtLastName.

As you write Visual Basic programs, it's very important to name controls properly and consistently. As a programmer, though, you probably already know this.

How to Size and Position a Control

When you're drawing controls on a form, you don't have to be exact. It's very easy to make them bigger or smaller, and to put them in a different spot on the form.

Size controls with the mouse

1. In the Toolbox, select the Pointer tool (if it isn't already selected).

2. On your form, select the control you want to resize.

3. Grab a sizing handle with the mouse by moving the pointer over it and then holding down the left mouse button. You know when you're over the sizing handle because the mouse pointer turns into a double-sided arrow.

4. While holding down the mouse button, notice that a box appears (see Figure 4.5). The box shows you what the size of the control will be. When it's the right size, release the mouse button.

FIGURE 4.5

You can resize a control by dragging a sizing handle.

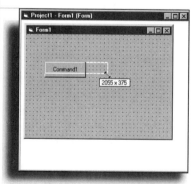

Changing the position of a control is also easy. Just click it to select it, and drag it to its new position.

SEE ALSO

➤ *To size and position a control through code by using the control's properties and methods, see page 96*

Modifying a Form's Size

Every new form you start using in Visual Basic will be the same size. However, this size probably won't be right for your program, so you'll have to resize it to better fit the controls you're using. You resize a form just as you resize a control: Grab one of its sizing handles with the mouse and drag it to the proper size (see Figure 4.6).

SEE ALSO

➤ *To resize a form through code by using the form's properties and methods, see page 96*

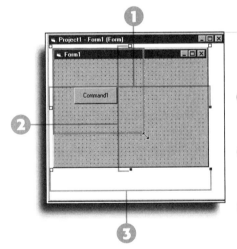

FIGURE 4.6

Resize your forms to better fit the controls you're using.

① Use the side sizing handles to make a control wider or narrower.

② Use the top and bottom sizing handles to make a control shorter or taller.

③ Use a corner sizing handle to change height and width simultaneously.

Working with Containers

A *container* is a control that can hold other controls within it, such as a Frame or a PictureBox—or a form. Controls inside a container are *child controls*. Child controls exist completely within their containers. This means that they can't be moved outside their containers (see Figure 4.7) and that when a container is deleted, so are any child controls within it.

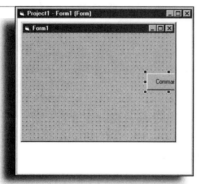

You can add a control to a container by using the drawing method. To do so, you must select the container on your form before you click the control in the Toolbox. Then draw the control inside the container.

The concept of container controls becomes especially important when you move and resize controls through code. For now, just remember that some controls can contain other controls and that any controls you put on a form are contained within the form.

Extending Visual Basic by Adding Controls

Although the intrinsic controls are powerful, they won't suit all your programming needs. Luckily, Visual Basic ships with many other ActiveX controls for you to use in your programs—they just aren't shown in the Toolbox by default. You have to add them.

Add controls to the Toolbox

1. From the **Project** menu, select **Components**.

2. In the Components dialog, make sure that the **Selected Items Only** check box is *deselected* on the Controls page. You then see a list of all ActiveX controls available on your computer.

3. From the list, select the control you want to add by checking its check box (see Figure 4.8).

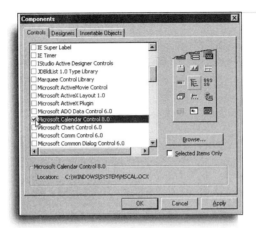

FIGURE 4.8

You can add ActiveX controls to the Toolbox by checking boxes in the Components list.

4. Click **OK**. The control you selected will now appear in the Toolbox, and you can use it just as you use the intrinsic controls (see Figure 4.9).

FIGURE 4.9

After adding the Calendar control, you can access it from the Toolbox.

SEE ALSO
➤ *For more information about using intrinsic controls, see page 14*

Working with Projects in Visual Basic 6

Creating a project

Changing a project's properties

Adding and removing files from a project

Using project groups

What Is a Visual Basic Project?

A project isn't the same as an application

A project is the thing you use to create an application, such as a "traditional" program, a dynamic link library, or an ActiveX control. Think of creating a Visual Basic program like baking a cake: you mix ingredients together, bake them, and pull a cake out of the oven. Similarly, you put forms, modules, and controls together, compile them, and get a Visual Basic application.

In Visual Basic, a *project* is the group of all the files that make up your program. These might include forms, *modules* (blocks of code not attached to a form), graphics, and ActiveX controls. Other types of files may also be part of a project, but don't worry about that now.

The first thing to keep in mind about a project is that as you create your program, each form, module, graphic, and ActiveX control is saved as an individual file (see Table 5.1).

TABLE 5.1   Common file types in a Visual Basic 6 project

File Type	Description
FRM	Form
BAS	Module
FRX	Automatically generated file for every graphic in your project
OCX	ActiveX control
CLS	Class module
VBP	Visual Basic project

Detailed information about all your program's files is stored in the *project file*. The project file lists all the files your program uses, as well as details such as the project name and how the IDE should be configured while you work on this particular project. Project files have the extension VBP.

Using the Project Explorer

You can keep track of all the files in your project with the *Project Explorer*, a window found on the right side of the Visual Basic IDE (see Figure 5.1). The Project Explorer provides a method to organize your project's files and allows you to access them individually in form or code view.

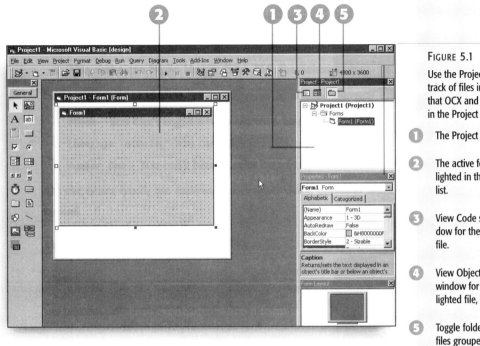

FIGURE 5.1

Use the Project Explorer to keep track of files in your project. Note that OCX and FRX files aren't listed in the Project Explorer.

1 The Project Explorer

2 The active form is the one high-lighted in the Project Explorer file list.

3 View Code shows the Code window for the currently highlighted file.

4 View Object shows the Form window for the currently high-lighted file, if available.

5 Toggle folders show your project files grouped in folders or in an alphabetical list.

Most of your interaction with the Project Explorer will be with its context menu. When you right-click one of your project's files, you'll see a menu similar to that shown in Figure 5.2.

FIGURE 5.2

Most of the interaction with your project will be through the Project Explorer's context menu.

The context menu allows you to

- View the file in a form window or code window
- View the properties of the file
- Add a form or module to the project
- Save the current file
- Delete the file from the project
- Print the file
- Make the Project Explorer float or dock it to the IDE
- Hide the Project Explorer

Creating a New Project

Every time you run Visual Basic, you'll see the New Project dialog (see Figure 5.3). From this window, you can simply select the type of project you want to create and click **Open**.

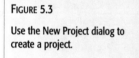

FIGURE 5.3

Use the New Project dialog to create a project.

It's also possible to start a new project while Visual Basic is already running.

Starting a new project

1. From the **File** menu, choose **New Project**. (You may be prompted to save the current project. If you need to save it but aren't sure how, see the later section "Saving and Naming a Project.")

2. In the New Project dialog, select the type of project you want to create and click **OK**.

Changing a Project's Properties

Many pieces of information are required to describe a project, including the project name, the version number, and the title that will appear in the title bar of the finished application. Many others can be accessed via the Project Properties dialog (see Figures 5.4 and 5.5).

FIGURE 5.4

You set your project's type, name, and help file on the General page. You can also add a project description.

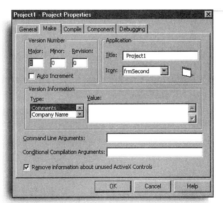

FIGURE 5.5

On the Make page, you can set your project's version number and version-specific information, as well as the project title and icon.

Access the Project Properties dialog

1. In the Project Explorer, right-click the project file (the first file listed).

2. From the context menu, select *ProjectName* **Properties**. The Project Properties dialog appears. (Or, from the **Project** menu, choose *ProjectName* **Properties**.)

Saving and Naming a Project

When you save your project, you actually save each individual part of your project (every form, module, graphic, and so forth) as an individual file, and then save the project file itself. When you save your project for the first time, Visual Basic automatically suggests a name for each file. This filename will be the same as the name of the form (or module, graphic, and so on), with an appropriate extension for the type of file you're saving (refer to Table 5.1). Thus, a module named modStart would be named modStart.bas because modules have the extension .bas.

Save a project

1. From the **File** menu, choose **Save Project**.

2. If this is the first time you've saved this project, or if you've added a form or module since the last time you've saved it, the Save File As dialog appears for each unsaved file (see Figure 5.6).

FIGURE 5.6

Visual Basic automatically suggests the filename frmFirst.frm for a form named frmFirst.

Changing filenames

You don't have to use the filename VB suggests, but you should be careful to use a name that allows you to remember what the file does. If you've already named your files with friendly names, following the VB convention will help you avoid confusion when your project contains large numbers of files. You also should always use the filename extension that Visual Basic suggests, to ensure that all your files can easily be found when you open a file from within Visual Basic.

3. Enter a name for the file and click the **Save** button.

4. The last file to save is the project file. If you've assigned a name to your project with the Project Properties dialog (refer to the section "Changing a Project's Properties"), VB automatically suggests *Project_name*.vbp as the file name. If you haven't assigned a project name, VB suggests a default name, such as Project1.vbp. When this happens, you should change the default name to something more friendly, such as SaveTest.vbp.

Opening an Existing Project

Opening files when you start Visual Basic

If you've worked on the file recently, open the **File** menu. At the bottom of this menu is a list of the files you have most recently worked on. Select the appropriate file to open it. If the desired project doesn't appear in this list, you'll have to look for it.

When you first start Visual Basic, the New Project dialog usually appears. You can save yourself some time by selecting a recent or existing project directly from this dialog. If you don't want this dialog to appear each time you start Visual Basic, deselect the check box at the bottom of this window.

Opening an existing project

1. From the **File** menu, choose **Open Project**. The Open Project dialog appears (see Figure 5.7).

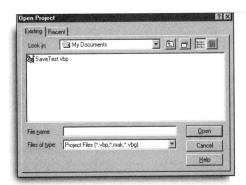

FIGURE 5.7

Open existing or recent projects with the Open Project dialog.

2. On the **Existing** page, switch to the folder in which you've saved your project. (If you've recently worked on the project, select your project from the list on the **Recent** page.)

3. Select the project and click **Open**.

Adding Files to a Project

Often, your programs will require more than one form or module. For example, if you want to have an About dialog in your program, it will require that you add a form.

You can add new files to your project in two ways: by selecting the file type (such as form or module) that you want to add from the **Project** menu, or by adding files from the Project Explorer.

Adding new files from the Project Explorer

1. Right-click inside the Project Explorer.

2. From the context menu choose **Add**, and then select the type of file you want to add.

Whichever method you use, you may be prompted with a dialog that allows you to pick a specific type of form or module to add (see Figure 5.8). Visual Basic provides templates for commonly used files, such as an About dialog, to save you the time and effort of creating it yourself.

FIGURE 5.8

Visual Basic contains many templates for creating commonly used forms.

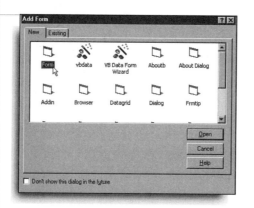

You can also add existing files to your project, which comes in handy if you want to use a form or module that you previously created for a different project. Adding an existing file is very similar to adding a new file, except that you choose **Add File** from the **Project** menu or from the Project Explorer's context menu (see Figure 5.9).

Removing Files from a Project

If there's a file in your project that you don't want (for example, a form you added accidentally or a module that contains a form you no longer need), you can remove it from the project list.

Removing a file from a project

1. In the Project Explorer, right-click the file you want to remove.

2. From the context menu, select **Remove** *filename*.

Why should you remove or delete a file?

If you don't remove an unnecessary file from your project, it will be included in your program after you compile it. Also, when you remove a file from a project, you don't actually delete the file from your hard drive. To delete the file completely, use Windows Explorer.

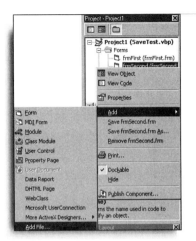

FIGURE 5.9
Add existing files to your project by selecting **Add File**.

You also can highlight the file in the Project Explorer and choose **Remove** *filename* from the **Project** menu.

Using Project Groups

Visual Basic 6 allows you to work with more than one project at a time. As you might imagine, working with multiple forms and modules that are used in different projects can get pretty confusing. To keep track of everything, you can use the Project Explorer and a *project group*, which is a collection of projects (see Figure 5.10). Project Groups can be saved as a file, just like a form, module, or project. They have the extension .vbg.

Add a project to a project group

1. Choose **Add Project** from the **File** menu.

2. In the **Add Project** dialog, highlight the type of new project you want to add from the **New** tab, or select an existing or recent project from the appropriate page of this dialog.

3. Click **OK**. Visual Basic automatically creates a project group and adds the new project to it, which you can see in the Project Explorer.

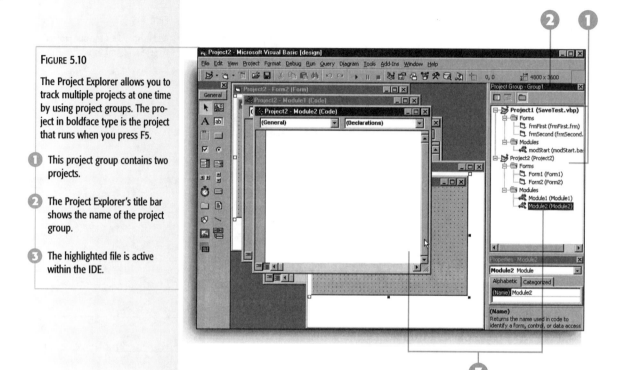

FIGURE 5.10

The Project Explorer allows you to track multiple projects at one time by using project groups. The project in boldface type is the project that runs when you press F5.

1. This project group contains two projects.

2. The Project Explorer's title bar shows the name of the project group.

3. The highlighted file is active within the IDE.

Project groups don't really become important until you start creating ActiveX controls, which require you to have multiple projects open at the same time. So don't worry about project groups right now. Just keep in mind that it's possible to have more than one project open at the same time.

Working with Properties, Methods, and Events

Modify objects by using properties

Manipulate objects by using methods

Write event procedures

What Are Properties, Methods, and Events?

Using containers

Remember that a container is an object–such as a form or the Frame or PictureBox controls–that can contain other controls.

Put simply, *properties* describe objects. *Methods* cause an object to do something. *Events* are what happens when an object does something.

Every object, such as a form or control, has a set of properties that describe it. Although this set isn't identical for all objects, some properties—such as those listed in Table 6.1—are common to most controls. You can see every property for a given control by looking at the Properties window in the IDE.

TABLE 6.1   Common Properties of Visual Basic Controls

Property	Description
Left	The position of the left side of a control with respect to its container
Top	The position of the top of a control with respect to its container
Height	A control's height
Width	A control's width
Name	The string value used to refer to a control
Enabled	The Boolean (True/False) value that determines whether users can manipulate the control
Visible	The Boolean (True/False) value that determines whether users can see the control

Another important property to consider is BorderStyle, which determines the *window elements* (title bar, Maximize and Minimize buttons, and so forth) a form will have. Table 6.2 summarizes the six BorderStyle settings; Figure 6.1 shows the same form, displayed with each setting.

TABLE 6.2   The Six Settings of the *BorderStyle* Property

Setting	Description
0-None	No borders, no title bar, not movable. Use this as a backdrop for a splash screen.

Setting	Description
1-Fixed Single	Not sizable by dragging borders but can have Maximize and Minimize buttons. Use this for any fixed-size window for which you want a button to appear in the taskbar.
2-Sizable (default)	Sizable by dragging borders and by using Maximize and Minimize buttons. Use this for typical programs.
3-Fixed Dialog	Not sizable and no Maximize/Minimize buttons. Use this for simple forms such as a password dialog.
4-Fixed ToolWindow	Similar to 3-Fixed Dialog except that the title bar is shorter and the title bar font and Close button are correspondingly smaller. Use this for floating toolbars.
5-Sizable ToolWindow	Similar to a 4-Fixed ToolWindow except that it's sizable by dragging the border. Use this for windows such as the Visual Basic Properties window.

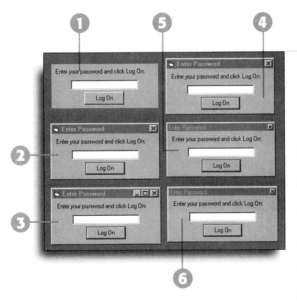

FIGURE 6.1

The BorderStyle property of a form can be set to one of six different styles. Notice that some styles can look exactly the same as other styles.

1 0-None

2 1-Fixed Single

3 2-Sizable

4 3-Fixed Dialog

5 4-Fixed ToolWindow

6 5-Sizable ToolWindow

Methods are blocks of code designed into a control that tell the control how to do things, such as move to another location on a form. Just as with properties, not all controls have the same methods, although some common methods do exist, as shown in Table 6.3.

TABLE 6.3   **Common Methods of Visual Basic Controls**

Method	Use
Move	Changes an object's position in response to a code request
Drag	Handles the execution of a drag-and-drop operation by the user
SetFocus	Gives focus to the object specified in the method call
ZOrder	Determines the order in which multiple objects appear onscreen

Events are what happen in and around your program. For example, when a user clicks a button, many events occur: The mouse button is pressed, the CommandButton in your program is clicked, and then the mouse button is released. These three things correspond to the MouseDown event, the Click event, and the MouseUp event. During this process, the GotFocus event for the CommandButton and the LostFocus event for whichever object previously held the focus also occur.

Again, not all controls have the same events, but some events are shared by many controls (see Table 6.4). These events occur as a result of some specific user action, such as moving the mouse, pressing a key on the keyboard, or clicking a text box. These types of events are *user-initiated events* and are what you will write code for most often.

Using GotFocus and LostFocus

The GotFocus and LostFocus events relate to most other events because they occur whenever a new control becomes active to receive user input. This makes GotFocus and LostFocus useful for *data validation*, the process of making sure that data is in the proper format for your program. Be careful, though! Improperly coding these two events can cause your program to begin an endless loop, which will cause your program to stop responding.

TABLE 6.4   **Common Events of Visual Basic Controls**

Event	Occurrence
Change	The user modifies text in a combo box or text box.
Click	The user clicks the primary mouse button on an object.
DblClick	The user double-clicks the primary mouse button on an object.
DragDrop	The user drags an object to another location.
DragOver	The user drags an object over another control.
GotFocus	An object receives focus.
KeyDown	The user presses a keyboard key while an object has focus.
KeyPress	The user presses and releases a keyboard key while an object has focus.
KeyUp	The user releases a keyboard key while an object has focus.

Event	Occurrence
LostFocus	An object loses focus.
MouseDown	The user presses any mouse button while the mouse pointer is over an object.
MouseMove	The user moves the mouse pointer over an object.
MouseUp	The user releases any mouse button while the mouse pointer is over an object.

The Relationship Between Properties, Methods, and Events

Although properties, methods, and events do different things, it's important to realize that they're often interrelated. For example, if you move a control with the Move method (most likely in response to an event), one or more of the control's position properties (Top, Height, Left, and Width) will change as a result. Because the control's size has changed, the Resize event occurs.

This interdependence means that you can sometimes accomplish the same task multiple ways in your code by manipulating object properties or methods. Consider the following code, which shows two ways to move a CommandButton:

```
'***********************************************
'Move the commandbutton by setting the properties
'***********************************************
cmdMove.Left = 100
cmdMove.Top = 100
'***********************************************
'Move the commandbutton by using the Move method
'***********************************************
txtMove.Move 100, 100
```

As another example, you can make a form appear and disappear from the screen by using its Visible property or its Show and Hide methods, as follows:

```
'***********************************************
' Make the form visible by setting the property
'***********************************************
frmMyForm.Visible=True
```

Right and bottom properties

It's important to remember that right and bottom properties don't exist in Visual Basic. Later, you'll see how to position an object by using the Top, Height, Left, and Width properties.

```
'*****************************************
' Hide the form by setting the property
'*****************************************
frmMyForm.Visible=False


'*************************************************
' Make the form visible by using the Show method
'*************************************************
frmMyForm.Show


'*************************************
' Hide the form by using the Hide method
'*************************************
frmMyForm.Hide
```

The Importance of Event-Driven Programming

When you create a program in Visual Basic, you'll generally be doing *event-driven programming*. Event-driven programming means that most of the code you write will be run as users do things within your program or even when certain things happen in Windows—when events occur. Of course, programming this way means that you have to know when events occur and have to write code that will make your program do something in response to the event.

Fortunately, Windows and Visual Basic do most of the work for you. Whenever an event takes place, Windows sends out a message to your program. Your program reads this message, and then runs the code you've attached to the event. If you don't specify code for an event, your program will simply ignore the event.

Generally, this code is known as a *procedure*, defined as any block of code that can be called from within your application. This code might be used to move objects around on a form, calculate a value from a formula, or write data to a database. No matter the purpose, a procedure always uses this format:

```
[Public¦Private] [Static] Sub¦Function¦Property _
    function_name (arguments) [As Type]
{...Your procedure code...}
End Sub¦Function¦Property
```

An *event procedure* is the place in your project where you put the code that will run when an event occurs. To write an event procedure, you must access the Code window for your object by doing one of the following:

- Double-clicking the object
- Selecting the object with the mouse and pressing **F7**
- Selecting the object and choosing **Code** from the **View** menu
- Selecting the object's form in the Project Explorer, clicking the **View Code** button, and choosing the object from the Code window

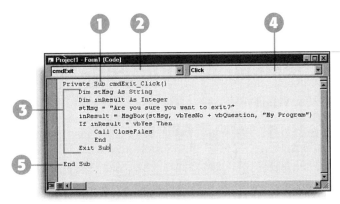

FIGURE 6.2

The code you write in an event procedure will run whenever the event occurs.

1. Beginning line of code block
2. Object selection drop-down list
3. Program code for the event procedure
4. Procedure selection drop-down list
5. Ending line of code block

Visual Basic automatically generates an event procedure when you select an event in the Code Window. In Figure 6.2, notice that you name event procedures by joining the object's name and the event name with an underscore character (`cmdExit_Click()`). When the event procedure in this example is run, it will display a dialog when the user clicks the CommandButton named `cmdExit`.

Using Properties, Methods, and Events in a Sample Program

Now is a good time to bring together everything you've learned about properties, methods, and events in an application named MoveIt (see Figure 6.3).

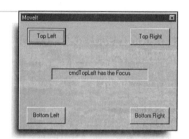

MoveIt consists of the form `frmMove`, which contains four CommandButtons placed in its corners. When you run MoveIt, clicking one of these buttons will move the form to the corresponding corner of the screen. In the center of the form is a label that will provide *event notification*—in other words, it will report information such as mouse movement and which button has the focus.

Create MoveIt (general steps)

1. Create the graphical user interface (GUI).
2. Program the `Form_Load()` event procedure.
3. Program the `Click()` event procedures.
4. Add the event notification.

Creating the Interface

Create MoveIt's GUI

1. Create a new project by choosing **New Project** from the **File** menu. Select **Standard EXE** from the New Project dialog.

2. In the Properties window, change the name of the project's form to frmMove. (You can call it something else if you want, but make sure that you're consistent.)

3. Add four CommandButtons to frmMove's corners and add a label in the center. You don't have to position the buttons and label exactly because you'll later put them in the proper locations by using code.

4. In the Properties window, name the label and the four buttons according to Figure 6.4.

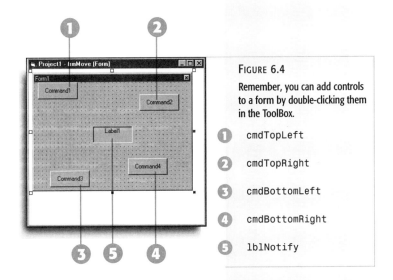

FIGURE 6.4

Remember, you can add controls to a form by double-clicking them in the ToolBox.

① cmdTopLeft

② cmdTopRight

③ cmdBottomLeft

④ cmdBottomRight

⑤ lblNotify

5. Now set the **BorderStyle** property of the form to **1-Fixed Single**. This ensures that the form can't be resized while the program is running. Also, set the label's **Alignment** property to **2-Center** and its **BorderStyle** property to **1-Fixed Single** to give the label a finished appearance.

6. Save the form and the project, using friendly names such as frmMove.frm for the form and MoveIt.vbp for the project.

Programming the *Form_Load()* Event Procedure

You can use the Form_Load() event procedure to prepare the form before showing it onscreen when your program is run. You will use this procedure to

Form_Load() event procedure naming

Whereas the event procedures for controls are named by joining the names of the object and the event with an underscore character, forms are different. No matter what you name your form, Visual Basic will always use the generic name Form instead of the name you choose. For example, even though the form in this example is frmMove, the name of the Load event procedure is Form_Load().

- Set the Caption property of the CommandButtons
- Set the initial text of the label
- Set the form's title bar text
- Set the position of the four CommandButtons, the label, and the form onscreen

Open the Code window for the Form_Load() event procedure by double-clicking anywhere on the form except the buttons, label, or title bar. Then, enter the code in Listing 6.1, being careful to change the names if you named your control differently.

LISTING 6.1   The *Form_Load()* Event Procedure Code for MoveIt

Commenting the code

You don't have to type in the comments (lines that start with the apostrophe (')) because these lines are for your information only. Be sure to read them, though.

```
01    'Set the Caption property of the CommandButtons
02        cmdTopLeft.Caption = "Top Left"
03        cmdTopRight.Caption = "Top Right"
04        cmdBottomLeft.Caption = "Bottom Left"
05        cmdBottomRight.Caption = "Bottom Right"
06
07        'Clear the initial text of the label
08        lblNotify.Caption = ""
09
10        'Set the form's title bar text
11        frmMove.Caption = "MoveIt"
12
13        'The rest of the code centers the form on the
14        'screen, sets the position of the four
15        'CommandButtons, and sets the size and
16        'position of the label.
17
18        'Center the form on the screen. This works by
19        'setting the Left side of the form to the center
20        'of the screen, less half the width of the form.
21        'Also, the Top of the form is set to the center
22        'of the screen, less half the height of the form.
23        frmMove.Left = (Screen.Width - frmMove.Width) / 2
24        frmMove.Top = (Screen.Height - frmMove.Height) / 2
```

```
25
26      'Set the Left edge of the buttons. The 200 setting
27      'for the left buttons sets a space between the edge
28      'of the form and the buttons. The right buttons are
29      'set by subtracting the width of the button from
30      'the width of the form, and subtracting 300 to
31      'set a space between the button and the form edge.
32      cmdTopLeft.Left = 200
33      cmdBottomLeft.Left = 200
34      cmdTopRight.Left = _
           frmMove.Width - cmdTopRight.Width - 300
35      cmdBottomRight.Left = _
           frmMove.Width - cmdBottomRight.Width - 300
36
37      'Set the Top edge of the buttons. This is done
38      'similar to setting the Left edge.
39      cmdTopLeft.Top = 200
40      cmdBottomLeft.Top = _
           frmMove.Height - cmdBottomLeft.Height - 500
41      cmdTopRight.Top = 200
42      cmdBottomRight.Top = _
           frmMove.Height - cmdBottomRight.Height - 500
43
44      'Set the size of the label
45      lblNotify.Height = 360
46      lblNotify.Width = 3000
47
48      'Center the label within the form. This is done
49      'similar to centering the form.
50      lblNotify.Left = _
           (frmMove.Width - lblNotify.Width) / 2
51      lblNotify.Top = _
           (frmMove.Height - lblNotify.Height) / 2 - 200
```

Figure 6.5 shows what the IDE will look like when you enter this code into the Code window. Setting these starting values is called *initialization*.

FIGURE 6.5

You write event procedures by
adding code to the code window
within the IDE.

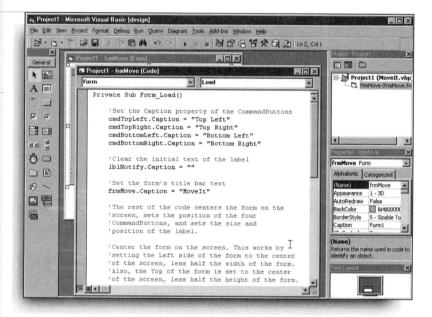

FIGURE 6.5

You write event procedures by
adding code to the code window
within the IDE.

Programming the *Click()* Event

We'll use the Click() event procedure to move the form around
the screen. To do so, double-click a CommandButton to view
the Code window. Then, enter that part of the code from
Listing 6.2 that applies to that CommandButton. Note that you
don't have to enter the first and last line, because Visual Basic
already creates that part of the event procedure. (Again, you
don't have to type the comments.) For example, you only have to
add lines 8 and 12 to the cmdBottomLeft_Click() event procedure.

The Screen object

As you add the code for the
Form_Load event procedure,
notice a reference to an object
called Screen. The Screen
object refers to your monitor screen.
For a detailed description of the
Screen properties, read the
online documentation that comes
with Visual Basic.

LISTING 6.2   The *Click()* Event Procedures for the CommandButtons

```
01   Private Sub cmdBottomLeft_Click()

02

03       'Set the value of the form's TOP property
04       'to the bottom of the screen but bring
05       'it up the height of the screen so that the
06       'bottom of the form is on the bottom of
07       'the screen
08       frmMove.Top = Screen.Height - frmMove.Height

09
```

```
10    'Set the value of the form's LEFT property
11    'to the far left of the screen.
12    frmMove.Left = 0
13
14  End Sub
15
16  Private Sub cmdBottomRight_Click()
17
18    'Set the value for the form's TOP property to
19    'the bottom of the screen, but bring the TOP
20    'up the HEIGHT of the form so that the bottom
21    'of the form is on the bottom of the screen.
22    frmMove.Top = Screen.Height - frmMove.Height
23
24    'Set the value of the form's LEFT property to
25    'the right of the screen but bring it across
26    'the screen the width of the form so that the
27    'right side of the form is on the right
28    'side of the screen
29    frmMove.Left = Screen.Width - frmMove.Width
30
31  End Sub
32
33 Private Sub cmdTopLeft_Click()
34
35    'Set the value of the form's TOP property
36    'to the top of the screen.
37    frmMove.Top = 0
38
39    'Set the value of the form's LEFT property
40    'to the left of the screen.
41    frmMove.Left = 0
42
43  End Sub
44
45  Private Sub cmdTopRight_Click()
46
47    'Set the value of the form's TOP property
48    'to the top of the screen.
49    frmMove.Top = 0
50
51    'Set the value of the form's LEFT property to
```

continues…

LISTING 6.2   Continued

```
52      'the right of the screen but bring it back across
53      'the screen the width of the form, so that the
54      'right side of the form is on the right
55      'side of the screen
56      frmMove.Left = Screen.Width - frmMove.Width
57
58  End Sub
```

Moving the form to the top or left of the screen is easy—set the Top or Left property of the form to zero. This always corresponds to the top or left of your monitor, respectively.

Lining up the form on the right side or bottom of the screen is a little harder because right and bottom properties don't exist. To place a form on the right side of the screen, you must set the Left property of the form to the Width property of the Screen object, minus the Width of the form (because the Width of the screen would be the right property of the screen, if the right property existed).

A similar technique is used to determine the bottom of the screen. If you were to set the form's Top property equal to the screen's Height property, you wouldn't see the form because it would be just below the bottom of the screen. To set the bottom of the form to the bottom of the screen, you subtract the value of the form's Height property from the value of the screen's Height property. This raises the form so that you can see it (see Figure 6.6).

Adding Event Notification

To finish MoveIt, let's add some code that will tell when certain events occur for the form and the CommandButtons. When users press or release the mouse button over the form, the text in lblNotify will change to reflect the state of the button. Also, when users use the Tab key or the mouse button to move from one CommandButton to another (which changes the focus from one button to the next), the text in lblNotify will change. Doing this requires you to write code in three different event procedures: the MouseUp and MouseDown event procedures for the form and the GotFocus event procedure for each CommandButton.

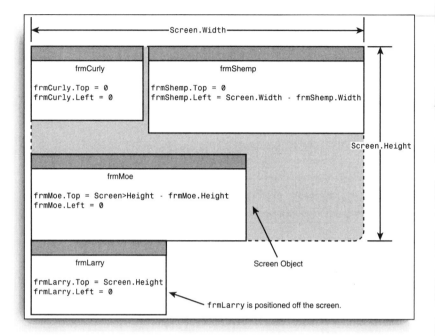

Enter the code from Listing 6.3 into the MouseUp and MouseDown event procedures for frmMain. (Remember that you don't have to enter the first and last lines.) To do this, open the Code window for the MouseDown event procedure by double-clicking the form and selecting **MouseDown** from the event procedures drop-down list (see Figure 6.7).

LISTING 6.3   Code for Reporting When Users Click and Release the Mouse Button

```
01   Private Sub Form_MouseDown(Button As Integer, _
                Shift As Integer, X As Single, Y As Single)
02
03       lblNotify.Caption = "MouseDown Event"
04
05   End Sub
06
07   Private Sub Form_MouseUp(Button As Integer, _
                Shift As Integer, X As Single, Y As Single)
08
09       lblNotify.Caption = "MouseUp Event"
10
11   End Sub
```

FIGURE 6.7

You can select an event procedure from the object's Code window.

When the program runs, if your mouse is over the form (not the CommandButtons or the label) and you click the mouse button, the text MouseDown Event appears in lblNotify. When you release your mouse button, the text MouseUp Event appears.

Last, add the code that will report which CommandButton has the focus. Enter the code from Listing 6.4 into the GotFocus event procedures for each CommandButton. Do this by double-clicking one of the CommandButtons and selecting the **GotFocus** event procedure (notice that Visual Basic selects the Click event by default). Repeat this procedure for each CommandButton.

LISTING 6.4   Code for Reporting Which CommandButton Has the Focus

```
01    Private Sub cmdBottomLeft_GotFocus()
02
03        lblNotify.Caption = "cmdBottomLeft has the Focus"
04
05    End Sub
06
07    Private Sub cmdBottomRight_GotFocus()
08
09        lblNotify.Caption = "cmdBottomRight has the Focus"
10
11    End Sub
```

```
12
13   Private Sub cmdTopLeft_GotFocus()
14
15       lblNotify.Caption = "cmdTopLeft has the Focus"
16
17   End Sub
18
19   Private Sub cmdTopRight_GotFocus()
20
21       lblNotify.Caption = "cmdTopRight has the Focus"
22
23   End Sub
```

That's it! Now you can run the program—just press the F5 key (see Figure 6.8).

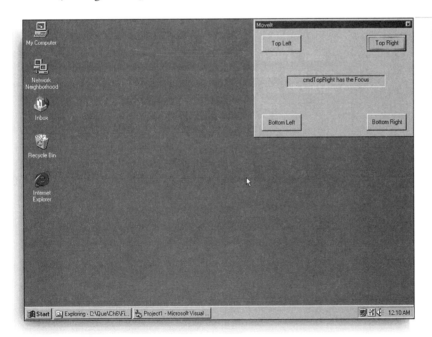

FIGURE 6.8

When you click a CommandButton, it automatically receives the focus. In Movelt, the focus is reported in `lblNotify`.

Programming with Visual Basic

7   **Using Data Types, Constants, and Variables 109**

8   **Making Statements in a Program 131**

9   **Working with Conditional Statements 145**

10   **Working with Loops 159**

11   **Working with Arrays 181**

12   **Working with Strings and Typecasting 211**

Using Data Types, Constants, and Variables

Declare variables

Work with data types

Represent data by using constants

Use scope to control data

Use naming conventions for clearer programming

Storing Information in Variables

Figure 7.1 shows a simple addition program, AddNum.EXE, from the project Addnum.prj from the file vb6cp07.zip on the Web site dedicated to this book. The program enables users to enter two numbers. When they click the + button, the program processes the total, which is then displayed in a third text box.

FIGURE 7.1

AddNum is a simple addition program that shows you how to use variables.

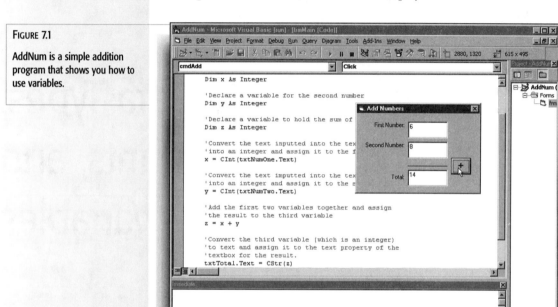

While the data is being processed in your program, it's stored temporarily in *variables*. Think of a variable as a cup that can hold various amounts of jelly beans; you never know how many jelly beans are in the cup at any given time unless you look in the cup. The same is true for a variable. A variable can hold a different value at different times. You programmatically look into it to find out its value.

You use variables when you know that you'll have to deal with a quantity at some point but don't know its present value—such as the balance of your checking account. You know the account's balance today, but you have no idea what the balance will be in a week.

Declaring Variables

You create (that is, declare) a variable by using the following form:

```
Dim VarName As DataType
```

In this syntax,

- `Dim` is the *keyword* that tells Visual Basic that you want to declare a variable.

- `VarName` is the name of the variable.

- `As` is the keyword that tells Visual Basic that you're defining the data type for the variable.

- `DataType` is the data type of the variable.

Thus, the following example creates a variable, `i`, that's of data type `Integer`:

```
Dim i as Integer
```

Listing 7.1 shows the event procedure for the `Click()` event of the `cmdAdd` button. Three variables—x, y, and z (on lines 3, 6, and 9)—are declared. These variables are of type `Integer`. (Data types are discussed later in the chapter. For now, realize that you are making variables that will accommodate numbers. Also, if you type a letter such as a in a text box, the code won't work because it's expecting a number. Preventing this sort of error is addressed at the end of this chapter.) For more information about avoiding and finding errors in your code see Chapter 21, "Debugging Your Applications."

Understanding keywords

A keyword, also known as a *reserved word*, is a word reserved for Visual Basic's exclusive use; you can't use keywords for your own programming needs. Words such as `Dim`, `As`, `New`, `ReDim`, `If`, `Then`, `Else`, `Loop`, `While`, and `End` are all Visual Basic keywords. By default, Visual Basic uses the font color blue to show all keywords that you type in a Code window.

Visual Basic has many keywords. You know a word is a keyword if the word changes color after you type it in the code window. Also, you can look in the online documentation that comes with Visual Basic to obtain a detailed list and explanation of them all.

LISTING 7.1 **07LIST01.TXT—The *cmdAdd* Event Procedure**

```
01    Private Sub cmdAdd_Click()
02        'Declare a variable for the first number
03        Dim x As Integer
04
05        'Declare a variable for the second number
06        Dim y As Integer
07
08        'Declare a variable to hold the sum of both numbers
09        Dim z As Integer
10
```

continues…

Commenting code

Notice that some lines of code begin with an apostrophe ('), which tells Visual Basic that everything on that line or following the apostrophe isn't code and should be ignored by the compiler. Such a line of text offers some remarks or information about what your programming intention is. This is called *commenting* your code. Well-written code is heavily commented. Commenting your code helps you remember your thinking when you come back to your code at a later time. It also helps those who must maintain your code after you've written it.

LISTING 7.1 Continued

```
11      'Convert the text inputted into the text box
12      'into an integer and assign it to the first variable
13      x = CInt(txtNumOne.Text)
14
15      'Convert the text inputted into the text box
16      'into an integer and assign it to the second variable
17      y = CInt(txtNumTwo.Text)
18
19      'Add the first two variables together and assign
20      'the result to the third variable
21      z = x + y
22
23      'Convert the third variable (which is an integer)
24      'to text and assign it to the text property of the
25      'TextBox for the result.
26      txtTotal.Text = CStr(z)
27  End Sub
```

Naming Variables

When you declare a variable, you must give it a name. Returning to the cup analogy, if you have two cups on a table that hold different amounts of jelly beans, you must be able to distinguish between the cups to work with them. Naming makes each variable distinct and easy to identify.

In naming a variable, you have tremendous flexibility. Variable names can be simple, or they can be descriptive of the information they contain. For example, you could name a counter variable $i\%$, or you might want to use a more descriptive name, such as NumberOfRedJellyBeansForBob or NumberOfJellyBeansForDorothy. Although you're allowed great latitude in naming, you need to know about the following restrictions:

- The name must start with a letter, not a number or other character.
- The name can't contain a period.

- The name must be unique within the current procedure or module (this restriction depends on the *scope* of the name, which you'll learn about a little later).

- The name can be no longer than 255 characters.

Some examples of incorrect variable naming are as follows:

- `1Week`—You can't begin a variable with a number.

- `Earnings.To.Data`—You can't use periods.

- `Number One`—You can't have spaces between characters.

On the other hand, the following examples work perfectly well:

```
MyNum&
```

```
i%
```

```
iNumOne
```

```
strInputValue
```

```
Number2#
```

To make your code easy to read, your variable names should describe their task but, to make your code easy to type, they should also be short. Many programmers use prefixes on their variables to indicate the type of data stored and the scope of the variable. For example, a prefix of `g_int` indicates a global or program-level variable that stores an integer. Table 7.1 describes suggested prefixes you can use with your variables.

TABLE 7.1 **Variable and Control Prefixes**

Prefix	Variable/Control	Example
b	Boolean	bLightsOn
c	Currency	cAmountDue
d	Double	dDollarPerGallon
db	Database	dbAccountsPayable
ds	Dynaset	dsOverDue
dt	Date+time	dtDateDue

continues...

TABLE 7.1   **Continued**

Prefix	Variable/Control	Example
td	TableDef	tdEmployees
h	Handle	hWnd
i	Integer	iCounter
l	Long	lNum
str	String	strMessage
s	Single	sPay
a	Array	a_iMyArray
g	Global	g_iTotal
m	Local to module or form	m_iAmount
ani	Animation button	aniMain
cbo	Combo box and drop-down list box	cboMyList
chk	Check box	chkDoctorIn
clp	Picture clip	clpEmblems
cmd	Command button	cmdFirstName
com	Communications	comLineOne
ctr	Control (used within procs when the specific type is unknown)	ctrNext
dat	Data	datEmployees
db	ODBC database	dbTaxpayers
dir	Directory list box	dirProjects
dlg	Common dialog	dlgSettings
drv	Drive list box	drvMain
fil	File list box	filPictures
frm	Form	frmMain
fra	Frame	fraTeams
gau	Gauge	gauGas

Prefix	Variable/Control	Example
gpb	Group button	gpbApps
grd	Grid	grdMain
hsb	Horizontal scroll bar	hsbText
img	Image	imgMain
key	Keyboard key status	keyASCII
lbl	Label	lblLastName
lin	Line	linRed
lst	List box	lstStooges
mdi	MDI child form	mdiMain
mnu	Menu	mnuEdit
opt	Option button	optGender
ole	OLE client	oleMain
pnl	3D panel	pnlFriends
shp	Shape	shpCircle
spn	Spin control	spnTemp
txt	Text/edit box	txtAddress
tmr	Timer	tmrBreak
vsb	Vertical scrollbar	vsbComments

Choosing the Correct Variable Type

You can store almost anything in a variable. A variable can hold a number, a string of text, or an instance of an object, including forms, controls, and database objects. This chapter looks specifically at variables that store numbers, strings, and logical values.

You can use a variable to hold any type of information, but different types of variables are designed to work efficiently with different types of information.

Returning to the earlier cup example, you might want to have a type of cup that can hold only jelly beans, only cherries, or only nails. What the cup is supposed to hold greatly influences how the cup is constructed. A cup that holds cherries might have little holes in the bottom for water to pass through. A cup to hold nails might be made of tough material so that the nails don't puncture or scratch it. The same is true of variables—the type of variable must match the data it's going to hold. When you declare a variable to be of a certain type, you're giving instructions to Visual Basic about how to build the variable to accommodate the type of data that the variable will have to hold.

Table 7.2 presents the types of variables available in Visual Basic. The table also shows the range of values that each variable can hold and the amount of memory required to store the information in the variable (sort of like the cup size). Understanding memory requirements is important if you want to optimize your code. To conserve system resources, you should use variables with smaller memory requirements whenever possible, but don't worry about optimizing code until you're comfortable with the concept of creating and using variables.

Sizing variables

At some point you may wonder whether you're using a variable of the right size, particularly with regard to numbers. A good rule of thumb is to go with the larger variable size if you don't have a very good idea of what the limit of your variable will be. For example, if you think that your program at some point might be required to use numbers with decimals or fractions, you might want to use `Double` and `Single` variable types instead of `Integer`s and `Long`s.

TABLE 7.2 **Variables Store Many Types of Information**

Type	Stores	Memory Requirement	Range of Values
Integer	Whole numbers	2 bytes	–32,768 to 32,767
Long	Whole numbers	4 bytes	Approximately +/- 2.1E9
Single	Decimal numbers	4 bytes	–3.402823E38 to –1.401298E–45 for negative values and 1.401298E–45 to 3.402823E38 for positive values
Double	Decimal numbers (double-precision floating-point)	8 bytes	–1.79769313486232E308 to –4.94065645841247E–324 for negative values and 4.94065645841247E–324 to 1.79769313486232E308 for positive values
Currency	Numbers with up to 15 digits left of the decimal and 4 digits right of the decimal	8 bytes	922,337,203,685,477.5808 to 922,337,203,685,477.5807

Type	Stores	Memory Requirement	Range of Values
String	Text information	1 byte per character	Up to 65,000 characters for fixed-length strings and up to 2 billion characters for dynamic strings
Byte	Whole numbers	1 byte	0 to 255
Boolean	Logical values	2 bytes	True or False
Date	Date and time information	8 bytes	Jan 1st 100 to December 31st 9999
Object	Pictures and any object reference	4 bytes	N/A
Variant	Any of the preceding data types	16 bytes + 1 byte per character	N/A

You know how to name a variable and what a variable can store, but how do you tell the program what you want to store? In reality, you don't have to tell Visual Basic what a variable will contain. Unlike other languages, Visual Basic doesn't require you to specifically declare a variable before it's used. If a variable isn't declared, Visual Basic uses a default data type known as a *variant*, which can contain any type of information. Read more on variants in the following section.

It's a good idea to declare your variables before they're used. Declaring variables saves you time in the long run and makes your code much more reliable.

Making Explicit Declarations

Explicit declaration means that you must use a statement to define a variable. Each of the following statements can be used to explicitly declare a variable's type:

```
Dim VarName [As VarType][, VarName2 [As VarType2]]
```

```
Private VarName[As VarType][, VarName2[As VarType2]]
```

```
Static VarName[As VarType][, VarName2[As VarType2]]
```

```
Public VarName[As VarType][, VarName2[As VarType2]]
```

Dim, Private, Static, and Public are Visual Basic keywords that define how and where the variable can be used. VarName and VarName2 represent the names of the variables that you want to declare. As indicated in the syntax, you can specify multiple variables in the same statement as long as you separate the variables by commas. (The syntax shows only two variables, but you can specify any number.)

VarType and VarType2 represent the type name of the respective variables. The *type name* is a keyword that tells Visual Basic what kind of information will be stored in the variable. The type can be one of those specified in Table 7.2 or a user-defined type.

As mentioned earlier, declaring a variable type is optional. If you include the variable type, you must include the keyword As. If you don't include a variable type, the Variant type (the default) is used. Using a variant for general information has two major drawbacks, however: it can waste memory resources, and the variable type can produce unpredictable default value behaviors, particularly with arrays.

The following code lines show the use of these declaration statements for explicitly declared variables:

```
Private iNumVal As Integer
```

```
Private iAvgVal As Integer, dInputval As Double
```

```
Static sCalcAverage As Single
```

```
Dim strInputMsg As String
```

In Visual Basic, you don't have to use the keywords Dim, Private, Static, or Public. In Visual Basic, you can use a variable name such as MyVal. If you were to put this code in your project, you would make a variable named MyVal as type Variant. MyVal would have a default value of empty. Whenever you use implicit

What's a variant?

A variant is a data type that knows how to be any data type. If you declare a variable to be of type variant, it can be an Integer, Double, String…whatever. Variables have a definite use in advanced programming. If you are a beginning programmer, however, you shouldn't use variants to avoid the labor of learning to use the proper data type for the proper situation.

declaration, Visual Basic considers that variable as type Variant. Using implicit declaration isn't recommended, however. Making a variable without a formal declaration is asking for trouble. If you use implicit declaration, then any time you make a spelling mistake or syntax error, Visual Basic will think that you're *implicitly* declaring another variable, which can lead to headaches beyond imagination. By using implicit declaration, the code below would return a zero from a "mistake" variable:

```
'Declare a variable to hold the value fo the winner
Dim iTheWinnner as Integer
'Assign a value to the winner variable
iTheWinner = 100
'This code will show you a message that says
'The winner has won: 0
'because you typed, iTheWhiner by mistake
MsgBox "The winner has won: " & CStr(iTheWhiner)
```

You can protect yourself. You can make the Visual Basic IDE force you to *explicitly* declare a variable. All you need to do is enter the keywords Option Explicit in the first line of the General section of your form or module. You can also configure the IDE to automatically do this for you whenever you add a form or module.

Configure the IDE to automatically require variable declaration

1. From the **Tools** menu, choose **Options**.

2. On the **Editor** page of the Options dialog, select the **Require Variable Declaration** check box (see Figure 7.2).

3. Click **OK**.

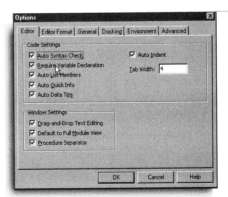

Requiring Option Explicit after you create a form or module

If you set the **Require Variable Declaration** option after starting to create a program, the option has no effect on any forms or modules already created. In this case, you need to add the Option Explicit statement as the first line of code in any existing forms or modules.

FIGURE 7.2

It's always preferable to configure the VB IDE to require you to declare your variables.

Automatic error detection

By default, VB is set to compile your code every time you run your code. Thus, if you don't change this setting and you're coding **Option Explicit**, undeclared variables will immediately appear as errors. If you want to turn off this feature, go to the Options dialog from the **Tools** menu and deselect the **Compile On Demand** check box on the **General** page.

Using uppercase letters

If you use some capital letters in your variable declarations, enter your code in all lowercase letters. Visual Basic automatically sets the capitalization of your variable to match the declaration. This gives you immediate visual confirmation that you correctly typed the name.

After you set Option Explicit, if you fail to declare a variable, you'll receive the message Variable not defined when you try to compile your code. Visual Basic's integrated debugger highlights the offending variable and halts the compilation of your program. The benefit of this is that it helps you avoid code errors possibly caused by typographical mistakes. For example, you might declare a variable with the following statement:

```
Dim strMyName As String
```

If, in a later statement, you mistype the variable name, Visual Basic will catch the error for you. For example, the following statement would cause an error:

```
strMyNme = "Clark Kent"
```

Using Type Suffixes with Variables

In previous code examples, you saw that you use the As keyword to assign a data type to a variable. You can use another method to declare a variable and assign a data type to it—*data-type suffixes*. With this type of declaration, a special character is used at the end of the variable name when the variable is first assigned a value. Doing this automatically "types" (assigns a type to) the variables. There's no need to use the As keyword. The characters for each variable type are shown in Table 7.3.

TABLE 7.3 Variable Suffixes

Variable Type	Suffix
Integer	%
Long	&
Single	!
Double	#
Currency	@
String	$
Byte	None
Boolean	None

Variable Type	Suffix
Date	None
Object	None
Variant	None

The code back in the section "Using Explicit Declarations" could be rewritten with type suffixes as follows:

```
Private NumVal%

Private AvgVal%, Inputval#

Static CalcAverage!

Dim InputMsg$
```

Using suffixes to assign a type to your variables is a quick, handy way to declare a variable. Also, using a suffix adds a new element of readability to your variable name. For example, now when you run across the variable `NumVal%` in your code, you know that the variable is of type Integer (from reading the suffix) and that its function is to be a value for a number (from reading the variable name).

Using Strings

A *string* is a collection of characters. The following are examples of different string values:

```
"Cheese"

"You have made an error!"

"a"

"July 4, 1776"

"75"
```

Notice that each collection of characters is enclosed by quotation marks (`""`). The quotation marks are very important; they tell Visual Basic that the enclosed characters are a *string value*. Characters not enclosed in quotation marks are considered to be a variable or a part of the language.

A controversy around suffixes

A controversy within the Visual Basic developer community surrounds the use of suffixes and prefixes. Some developers support the use of suffixes; others prefer the use of prefixes only. Whether to use suffixes, prefixes, or both is a decision usually made by the programming group to which you belong. Most programming groups have a document that defines the coding standard that you use during the course of a project. If you program with others, this is the standard that you should follow. The most important thing to remember is that your code must be easy to read, easy to maintain, and predictable to others with whom you work.

You might find the string value "75" a bit baffling. You might think that it's a value for an integer, but it's not. The following example illustrates the string-ness of "75":

```
strNum$ = "7" & "5"
```

Another use of strings that use numeric characters are ZIP codes and phone numbers. Notice that declaring the following ZIP code and phone number as strings allows you to use the - character:

```
strMyZipCode = "50311-0921"
strPhone = "1-515-555-1212"
```

Also, because they aren't number data types, you wouldn't and can't perform mathematical operations on them, such as addition and multiplication.

Some beginning programmers have trouble with this concept; it takes a bit of getting used to. If you look at the code in Listing 7.1, you'll see that the user's input into the text boxes is treated as numeric string characters that must be converted to integers (lines 13 and 17). Chapter 12, "Working with Strings and Typecasting," provides a more detailed look at this.

Using Variable-Length and Fixed-Length Strings

Most strings that you will use in your programs are of the type known as *variable-length strings*, which can contain any amount of text up to 64,000 characters. As information is stored in the variable, the size of the variable adjusts to accommodate the length of the string. There is, however, a second type of string in Visual Basic—the *fixed-length string*.

As the name implies, a fixed-length string remains the same size, regardless of the information assigned to it. If a fixed-length string variable is assigned an expression shorter than the defined length of the variable, the remaining length of the variable is filled with the space character. If the expression is longer than the variable, only the characters that fit in the variable are stored; the rest are discarded.

A fixed-length string variable can be declared only by using an explicit declaration of the form, such as the following:

```
Dim VarName As String * strlength
```

Therefore, to make a string, strMyString, that's always 128 characters long, you would declare it as follows:

```
Dim strMyString As String * 128
```

Notice that this declaration varies slightly from the previous declaration of a string variable. The declaration of a fixed-length string variable contains an asterisk (*) to tell Visual Basic that the string will be a fixed length. The final parameter, strlength, tells the program the number of characters that the variable can contain.

In the beginning, you probably won't have much need for fixed-length strings. As you advance, you will use them, particularly when it's time to program directly to Windows with the Windows API (Application Programming Interface).

Determining Where a Variable Can Be Used

In addition to telling Visual Basic what you want to be able to store in a variable, a declaration statement tells Visual Basic where the variable can be used. This area of use is called the *scope* of the variable. This is analogous to your phone number. You might have a phone number 555-2576, which can be reached by anyone inside your area code. However, if anyone outside your area code calls 555-2576, they will get that number as it applies within their area code. If you want to be reached from anywhere in the country, the person trying to reach you must use your area code before your local number. Conceptually, the scope of a variable is similar. You can have variables that can be seen locally only within a procedure, for instance, and you can have variables that can be seen globally from anywhere within a form, module, or even the whole program.

Scope relates to declaration location

The scope of a variable is determined by not only the type of declaration used but also the declaration's location. For instance, the Dim keyword assumes different meanings in different parts of a form's code. You can use only the Private keyword on variables in the Declaration section.

By default, a variable declared with a keyword such as Dim is local to the procedure in which it's created. For example, if you declare a variable in the event procedure for a CommandButton's Click() event procedure, it resides and is visible only within that event procedure. Therefore, to create variables that have a scope other than local, you must modify your declaration statement.

Making Variables Available Globally

In most programs, unless you have only one form and no code modules, you'll find that you need some variables that can be accessed from anywhere in the code. These are called Public variables. (Other programming languages might refer to these as global variables.) These variables are typically for holding information that's used throughout the program. They can also be used to indicate various conditions in the program.

To create a Public variable, you place a declaration statement with the Public keyword in the Declarations section of a module of your program. The following line shows the Public declaration of a variable of type Boolean (True/False):

```
Public bLightsOn as Boolean
```

In a form, the Public keyword has a special meaning. Variables defined as Public are considered to be very much like a property of the form and can be "seen" from anywhere in the program. These properties are referenced like the built-in properties of a form or control instead of like a variable. For example, you can have a string variable, strMyName, declared Public in the form frmMain, and you would access the string variable by using the following expression:

```
strSomeString = frmMain.strMyName
```

You can use the Public properties to pass information between forms and other parts of your program.

If you don't need to access a variable from everywhere in your program, you don't want to use the Public keyword in a declaration. Instead, you use the keyword Dim within a procedure. When the variable is declared inside a procedure, it can be used only within that procedure. This is typically known as a *local variable*.

The keyword `Private` is used within a form or module's Declaration section to make the variable visible only to the form or module within which it's created. This is typically known as a *form-* or *module-level variable*.

Keeping a Variable Local

At first glance, you might think that making all variables global is the easiest thing to do, but as your programs grow, this practice won't serve you well in the long run.

You saw in the preceding section that each *procedure* in a VB program can have its own variables. Each procedure can have variable names that might be common across other procedures, but because they are local to that procedure, none of the others know about them. Thus, you avoid what are called *name collisions*.

Think of it this way: You might have two procedures, `ProcA` and `ProcB`. `ProcA` creates two variables, `x%` and `y%`, and `ProcB` also creates two variables `x%` and `y%`. In `ProcA`, `x%` and `y%` are assigned values that, in turn, are passed as values to the `Left` and `Top` properties of a CommandButton, `Command1`.

In `ProcB`, the variable `y%` is assigned a value that's twice the value of `x%`. Both procedures have variables of the same name. However, because each set of variables was declared local to a distinct procedure, they are available only to the procedures in which they were declared (see Figure 7.3) .

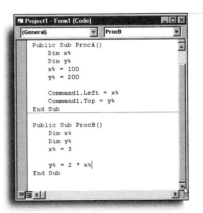

FIGURE 7.3

Properly scoping your variables makes your code more reusable.

Using Static Variables

Most variables created inside a procedure are discarded by Visual Basic when the procedure is finished. Sometimes, however, you want to preserve the value of a variable even after the procedure runs. This often is the case when you call the procedure multiple times, and the value of a variable for one call to the procedure depends on the value left over from previous calls.

Using the Static keyword when declaring a procedure

If you use the **Static** keyword to declare a procedure, all variables in the procedure are treated as static.

To create a variable that retains its value even after the procedure is through running, you use the **Static** keyword in the variable declaration. This tells Visual Basic that the variable can be referenced only within the procedure but to hold on to the value because it will be needed again. For example, to declare a static variable for an integer, you use the following:

```
Static iNumOfClicks as Integer
```

A good use of a static variable would be where you needed to know how many times somebody clicked a CommandButton. If you Dim a counting variable in a click event procedure, the variable disappears when the click event is over and the variable goes out of scope; thus, you couldn't know how many times it was clicked. If you made the variable static, however, the value persists from click to click. Thus, if you put the preceding line into a click event, you have a permanent way to keep track of the number of clicks:

```
Sub MyButton_Click()
    Static iNumOfClicks as Integer
    iNumOfClicks = iNumOfClicks + 1
    MsgBox "Number of Clicks: " & CStr(iNumOfClicks)
End Sub
```

Static variables are commonly used in timer event procedures. You will read more about this in Chapter 16, "Working with Time and Timers."

Using Constants

Variables are only one way of storing information in the memory of a computer. Another way is to use *constants*. Constants in a program are treated a special way. After you define them (or they're defined for you by Visual Basic), you can't change them later in the program by using an assignment statement. If you try, Visual Basic generates an error when you run your program.

Constants are most often used to replace a hard-to-remember value, such as the color value for the Windows title bar. It's easier to remember the constant vbActiveTitleBar than the value 2147483646. You can also use a constant to avoid typing long strings if they're used in a number of places. For example, you could set a constant such as ERR_FILE_FOUND containing the string "The requested file was not found".

Often, constants are also used for conversion factors, such as 12 inches per foot or 3.3 feet per meter. The following code example shows how constants and variables are used:

```
Const METER_TO_FEET = 3.3
Meters# = CDbl(InputBox("Enter a distance in meters"))
DistFeet# = Meters# * METER_TO_FEET
MsgBox "The distance in feet is: " & CStr(DistFeet#)
```

Using Constants Supplied by Visual Basic

Visual Basic (as of version 4.0) supplies a number of sets of constants for various activities. There are color-definition constants, data-access constants, keycode constants, and shape constants, among others. The VB-supplied constants begin with the prefix vb.

The constants that you need for most functions are defined in the help topic for the function. If you want to know the value of a particular constant, you can use the Object Browser (see Figure 7.4). Access the Object Browser by clicking its icon 📸 in the Visual Basic toolbar or pressing the F2 key. You can use the list to find the constant that you want. When you select it, its value and function are displayed in the text area at the bottom of the dialog.

FIGURE 7.4

Select the appropriate constants from the Classes list to view the constants internal to Visual Basic.

Creating Your Own Constants

Naming conventions for constants

Constants are typically named with all uppercase characters and, if necessary, with an underscore character (_) to separate the characters into words: SECRET_NUMBER = 42. Now that Visual Basic supports its own constants and constants dedicated to classes, however, it's conventional to name constants in mixed case, with a lowercase prefix: snNumber = 42.

Although Visual Basic defines a large number of constants for many activities, sometimes you need to define your own constants. Constants are defined with the Const keyword statement to give the constant a name and a value, as shown in the following syntax:

```
Const CONSTANT_NAME [As ConstantType] = value
```

This statement appears similar to the declaration of a variable. As with declaring a variable, you provide a name for the constant and optionally specify the type of data it will hold. The Const keyword at the beginning of the statement tells Visual Basic that this statement defines a constant. This distinguishes the statement from one that just assigns a value to a variable. In declaring the type of a constant, you use the same types as you did for defining variables (refer to Table 7.2). Finally, to define a constant, you must include the equal sign (=) and the value to be assigned. If you're defining a string, remember to enclose the value in quotes (" ").

What's a function?

A *function* is a named section of code that returns a value. You can reuse functions many times within your program. For calculation purposes, you can pass information into functions. The information that you pass into a function is called a *parameter*, also known as an *argument*. For more information about functions, see Chapter 18, "Writing Reusable Code with Subs and Functions."

Using the Assignment Statement

To use variables efficiently, you must also be able to assign information to the variable and manipulate that information. After you set up a variable, you need to store information in it. This is the job of the assignment statement. In the *assignment statement*, you specify a variable whose value you want to set. To assign a value to a variable, place an equal sign after the variable name and follow this with the expression that represents the value you want stored. The expression can be a literal value, a combination of other variables and constants, or functions that return a value. There's no limit on the complexity of the expression you use. However, even though Visual Basic will attempt to automatically convert mismatching data types, you should try to assign the correct type to the values that you assign to your program's variables. The following statements illustrate different assignment statements:

```
NumStudents% = 25
SumScores% = 2276
AvgScore% = SumScores% / NumStudents%
TopStudent$ = "Janet Simon"
BadStudent$ = txtStudent.Text
```

You can consider most properties of forms and controls as variables. They can be set at design time but also can be changed at runtime with an assignment statement. You can also use a property on the right side of a statement to assign its value to a variable for further processing. You saw this done in Listing 7.1. After the addition program shown in Figure 7.1 calculates the sum of the two entered numbers, it assigns the result to a third TextBox, as shown in lines 23–26:

```
'Convert the third variable (which is an integer)
'to text and assign it to the text property of the
'TextBox for the result.
txtTotal.Text = CStr(z)
```

Revisiting the Addition Program

Now that you've explored what variables are about and how to use them, you should have a better sense of what's going on in the addition program shown earlier in the chapter. If you look closely, though, you'll see that the programmer made an assump-

Understanding type mismatch errors

A type mismatch error occurs when you try to assign a value to a variable that's not the expected data type. For example, if you create a variable x% of type Integer and try to assign a string value to it, you commit a type mismatch and receive a type mismatch error:

```
Dim x%

'Next line causes

'type mismatch
error

x% = "Happy
Birthday!"
```

tion about user input, which will result in a serious error. What happens when users don't enter a number into a text box but instead another sort of string value (see Figure 7.5)?

FIGURE 7. 5

Don't assume that users will always enter the data type that your program requires.

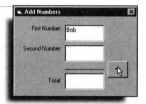

The result is a *crash*.

To prevent such an occurrence, you could use the Visual Basic IsNumeric() function to check the value to make sure that the entry is indeed a numeric value. For example, before line 13 in Listing 7.1, you would enter the following line to prevent users from assigning any non-numeric character to the variable x%:

```
If IsNumeric(txtNumOne.Text) then
    x = CInt(txtNumOne.Text)
End if
```

Obviously, making sure that the right type of data is assigned to the right type of variable (what's referred to as *data validation*) is more than an academic exercise—it's a critical programming skill. You'll find out how to solve this problem in Chapter 9, "Working with Conditional Statements"; Chapter 21, "Debugging Your Applications"; and Chapter 12, "Working with Strings and Typecasting."

Making Statements in a Program

Use assignment statements to give variables a value

Learn about the various math operations that Visual Basic supports

Build an estimation utility

Combine various strings into a single string

Continuously extend the value of a single string variable

Using the Assignment Statement

Learning the VB language

Computer programming is more than learning the Visual Basic language—it's about being able to describe and implement your ideas through the syntax of the programming language. One way to do this is by making *statements*, which are used to assign, compare, or calculate information in your programs. When you understand the steps your program must perform and can describe those steps through statements and the syntax of the Visual Basic language, you're ready to begin programming.

You learned in Chapter 7, "Using Data Types, Constants, and Variables," that you can create a variable by using the Dim keyword:

```
Dim i as Integer
```

Just because you've created a variable, however, doesn't necessarily mean that the variable has a useful value. At some point in the program, you have to give the variable an appropriate value. This is often referred to as *initializing* the variable. This job is done by the first assignment statement where the variable is the target of the assignment.

Making an *assignment statement* is easy: you specify a variable whose value you want to set, place an equal sign after the variable name, and then follow it with the expression that represents the value you want stored in the variable. The expression can be a literal value (such as the number 1 or the characters "Frank"), a combination of other variables and constants, or functions that return a value. The following statements illustrate different types of assignment statements:

```
01 i = 6
02 SumScores = 2276
03 AvgScore = SumScores / NumStudents
04 TopStudent = "Sonja Swanson"
05 PrintedInvoice = true
06 txtFirstName.Text = FirstName
```

Line 6 assigns the value of a variable, FirstName, to the value of a TextBox's Text property. This type of assignment is very common. Most properties of forms and controls are variables. They can be set at design time, but they also can be changed at runtime by using an assignment statement. You also can use a property on the right side of a statement to assign its value to a variable for further processing. For example, you could change line 6 to read a name from a text box and assign it to the variable FirstName as follows:

```
FirstName  = txtFirstName.Text
```

Using Variable Default Values

When you create a variable, Visual Basic assigns a default value to it. The actual default value depends on the variable's data type, as shown in Table 8.1.

TABLE 8.1 Default Values for a Variable

Data Type	Value
Integer	0
Long	0
Single	0
Double	0
String	" " (blank)
Boolean	False
Variant	EMPTY
Date	0
Currency	0

The assignment statement on line 3 of the previous example would be valid only if a prior assignment statement had been made for the last variable on the right side of the expression. If this variable, NumStudents, still had its default value of zero, the assignment statement would create a divide-by-zero error because we used it before we initialized it to the correct value (see Figure 8.1).

FIGURE 8.1

Unfortunately, these types of errors are usually found through testing of the program at runtime, because the values in the running program caused the error.

Using Math Operators

Math operations are used to determine customer bills, interest due on savings or credit card balances, average scores for a class test, and many other tasks. Visual Basic supports a number of different math operations that can be used in program statements. Table 8.2 summarizes these operations and the Visual Basic symbol for each operation.

TABLE 8.2 Math Operations and the Corresponding Visual Basic Operator Symbol

Operation	Operator Symbol
Addition	+
Subtraction	–
Multiplication	*
Division	/
Integer division	\
Modulus	mod
Exponentiation	^

Using Addition and Subtraction Operators

The two simplest math operations are addition and subtraction. If you've ever used a calculator, you already have a good idea how these operations are performed in a line of computer code.

A computer program, however, gives you greater flexibility than a calculator in the operations you can perform. Your programs aren't limited to working with literal numbers (for example, 1, 15, 37.63, and –105.2). Your program can add or subtract two or more literal numbers, numeric variables, or any functions that return a numeric value. Also, like a calculator, you can perform addition and subtraction operations in any combination. Now let's look at exactly how you perform these operations in your program.

As indicated in Table 8.2, the operator for addition in Visual Basic is the plus sign (+). The general use of this operator is as follows:

```
Result = iNumberOne + iNumberTwo + iNumberThree
```

Result is a variable (or control property) that contains the sum of the three numbers to the right of the equal sign (=). The equal sign indicates the assignment of a value to the variable. iNumberOne, iNumberTwo, and iNumberThree are numeric variables. As just described, you can also add literal numbers or return values rather than numeric variables from a function. You can add as many numbers together as you like, but each number pair must be separated by a plus sign.

The operator for subtraction is the minus sign (–). The syntax is basically the same as for addition:

```
Result = NumberOne - NumberTwo - NumberThree
```

Although the order doesn't matter in addition, in subtraction the number to the right of the minus sign is subtracted from the number to the left of the sign. If you have multiple numbers, the second number is subtracted from the first, the third number is subtracted from that result, and so on, moving from left to right. For example, consider the following equation:

```
Result = 15 - 6 - 3
```

The computer first subtracts 6 from 15 to yield 9. It then subtracts 3 from 9 to yield 6, which is the final answer stored in the variable Result. This left-to-right processing is used in the evaluation of expressions whenever similar operations are being performed.

If you really want to have 3 subtracted from 6 before it's subtracted from 15 for a Result of 12, you have to change the operator or force the program to evaluate the expression in the order you intended. (This order of execution is covered later in the section "Setting the Order of Precedence in Statements.") For now, consider the following statements and their resulting values:

```
1 Result = 15 "-" 3 "-" 6    'results in 6
2 Result = 15 "-" 6 + 3      'results in 12
3 Result =  3 - 6 + 15       'results in 12
```

Lines 2 and 3 show that you can also use similar operators in combination with one another. The following code lines are a few more valid math operations:

```
1 dValOne = 1.25 + 3.17              'results in 4.42
2 dValTwo = 3.21 - 1                 'results in 2.21
3 dValThree = dValTwo + dValOne      'results in 6.63
4 dValFour = dValThree + 3.75 - 2.1  'results in 8.28
5 dValFour = dValFour + 1            'results in 9.28
```

Using the Multiplication Operator

You simply use the multiplication operator—the asterisk (*)—to multiply two or more numbers. The syntax of a multiplication statement is almost identical to the ones used for addition and subtraction, as follows:

```
Result = iNumberOne * iNumberTwo * iNumberThree
```

As before, Result is the name of a variable used to contain the product of the numbers being multiplied, and iNumberOne, iNumberTwo, and iNumberThree are numeric variables. Again, you also can use literal numbers or a return value from a function.

As a demonstration of how multiplication and division might be used in a program, consider the example of a program to determine the number of rolls of wallpaper needed to cover a wall in a room. This program contains a form that lets the homeowner enter the width and height of the wall with the length, width, pattern match, and cost of the wallpaper. The program then calculates the number of wallpaper rolls required and the total cost of the project. Figure 8.2 shows an example of the form from the program; Listing 8.1 shows some of the actual code used to perform the calculations. The complete code listing for this example is in the project prjWallpaper.vbp on the MCP Web site (http://www.mcp.com/info) that supports this book.

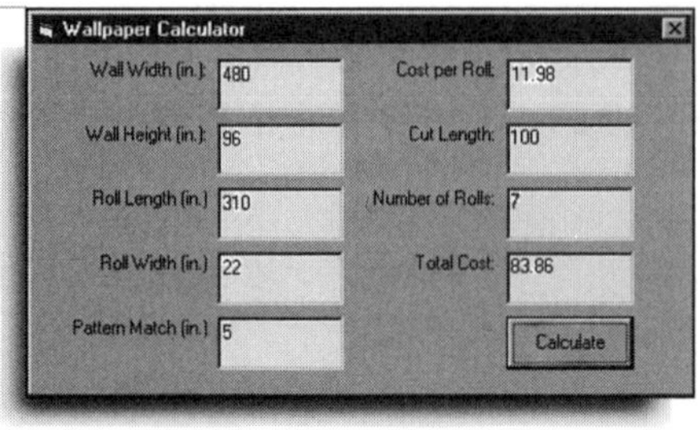

Using a variable on both sides of the assignment operator

If you aren't familiar with computer programming, line 5 may look a little funny to you. In fact, that line isn't allowed in some programming languages. In Visual Basic, however, you can enter a line of code that tells the program to take the current value of a variable, add another number to it, and then store the resulting value back in the same variable. You also can do this with string variables. (You'll see this done later in the section "Using the Concatenating String.")

Complete listings and sample programs on the Web site

After you reach our Web site, you'll be asked to enter an ISBN. You should enter 078971633x, and then click the **Search** button to go to the Book Info page for *Using VB6*, where you can download the code.

FIGURE 8.2

It's a good idea to make sure that the value contained in a string variable "looks" like a number and that the string isn't empty before you assign it to a numeric variable.

LISTING 8.1   08LIST01.TXT—Using Multiplication and Division Operators to Estimate

```
01  Private Sub cmdCalc_Click()
02  Dim WallWidth      As Integer 'Width of walls
03  Dim WallHeight     As Integer 'Height of walls
04  Dim RollLength     As Integer 'Length of the roll
05  Dim RollWidth      As Integer 'Width of the roll
06  Dim PatternMatch   As Integer 'Amount of pattern match
07  Dim CutLength      As Integer 'Length of each piece
08  Dim Remn           As Integer 'Length of remnant
09  Dim PiecePerRoll   As Integer 'Number pieces per roll
10  Dim NumofRoll      As Integer 'Number rolls needed
11  Dim dRollCost      As Double  'Cost of each roll
12  Dim dProjectCost   As Double  'Total project cost
13  Dim Msg            As String  'Message variable
14
15  'Make sure the txtWallWidth TextBox is not blank
16    If txtWallWidth.Text <> "" Then
17      'Check to make sure the text is a numeral then
18       'convert the text to the appropriate data type
19       'and assign the numeric value to the variables
20       If IsNumeric(txtWallWidth.Text) Then
21          WallWidth = CInt(txtWallWidth.Text)
22       Else
23          'It is not a number go back to the TextBox.
24          'Make a message
25          Msg = "Wall Width needs to be numeric. "
26          Msg = Msg & "Please enter a number."
27          'Display the message
28          MsgBox Msg, vbExclamation, "Data entry error"
29          'Send the mouse cursor back to the TextBox
30          txtWallWidth.SetFocus
31          'Leave the Sub
32          Exit Sub
33       End If
34    Else
35       'If it is blank, send the cursor back to the
36       'blank TextBox.
37       'Make a message
38       Msg = "You cannot leave Wall Width blank. "
39       Msg = Msg & "Please enter a number."
```

continues…

Line numbering and VB example code

The code in the listing text throughout this chapter is syntactically and operationally identical to the code in the sample programs on the Web site, except that each line of code is numbered. The code in the sample programs is fully commented to help you understand the various ideas and techniques used to create the program without having to reference back to the book.

LISTING 8.1 **Continued**

```
40        'Display the message
41        MsgBox Msg, vbExclamation, "Data entry error"
42        'Send the mouse cursor back to the TextBox
43        txtWallWidth.SetFocus
44        'Leave the Sub
45        Exit Sub
46     End If
...
213    'Make sure PatternMatch is greater than zero
214    If PatternMatch > 0 Then
215    Remn = (WallHeight Mod PatternMatch)
216    If Remn > 0 Then
217      CutLength = ((WallHeight - Remn) _
                          + PatternMatch)
218    Else
219      CutLength = WallHeight
220    End If
221    Else
222      CutLength = WallHeight
223    End If
224
225      'Make sure RollLength is greater than zero
226    If CutLength > 0 Then
227      PiecePerRoll = RollLength \ CutLength
228    Else
229      PiecePerRoll = RollLength
230    End If
231
232    'Make sure RollWidth and PiecePerRoll greater than 0
233    If RollWidth > 0 And PiecePerRoll > 0 Then
234      NumofRoll = (WallWidth / RollWidth)
235      NumofRoll = (NumofRoll / PiecePerRoll) + 0.4999
236    Else
237      NumofRoll = 0
238    End If
239
240    'Calculate the project cost
241    dProjectCost = NumofRoll * dRollCost
242
243    'Display the results in the answer boxes
244    lblCutLen.Caption = CStr(CutLength)
```

```
245  lblNumRolls.Caption = CStr(NumofRoll)
246  lblTotalCost.Caption = CStr(dProjectCost)
247  End Sub
```

Notice that line 20 of Listing 8.1 uses the `IsNumeric()` function. This function tests that the values input are numeric. The `txtWallWidth` TextBox is also checked for blank values. The purpose of lines 15 to 46 is purely for error checking this one TextBox. (In the complete listing, you'll find that each TextBox is checked in turn before the calculations are made.)

Starting at line 213 in the listing, notice that the program checks for zero values in all variables that will be used as divisors. This is to prevent the error you saw in Figure 8.1.

Using the Division Operator

Division in Visual Basic is a little more complicated than multiplication. In Listing 8.1, you saw three types of division used. The type you may find most familiar is the first one used in line 234. This type is known as *floating-point division* (the normal type of division). This type of division returns a number with its decimal portion, if one is present.

Floating-point division is the typical division you learned in school. You divide one number by another and the result is a decimal number. The floating-point division operator is the forward slash, (/), as seen in the following:

```
Result = NumberOne / NumberTwo
Result = 2.3 / 2    'result in 1.15
```

Visual Basic supports two other ways to divide numbers: *integer division* and *modulus* (or *remainder*) *division*.

Integer division divides one number into another, and then returns only the integer portion of the result. The operator for integer division is the backward slash (\):

```
Result = NumberOne \ NumberTwo
Result = 2.3 \ 2 'The value of Result is 1
```

An example in Listing 8.1 is located on line 227, where the goal is to find out the number of cut lengths that can be cut from each roll.

Error checking and documentation

Being able to make concise, robust statements is fundamental to computer programming. As your Visual Basic programming skills develop, you'll find that the functional line count in your code will shrink while the error handling and documentation line count will grow. As you can write well-behaved statements that do more with less, you will want to document and protect your programs. Getting to this point, however, takes time, practice, and experience. Right now, if you can write clear and accurate statements, you'll be in good shape.

Math operators work left to right

As with addition, subtraction, and multiplication, if you perform division on more than two successive numbers, a division operator must separate each number. Also, as with the other operations, multiple operators are handled by reading the equation from left to right.

Modulus or remainder division divides one number into another and returns what's left over after you obtain the largest integer quotient possible. The modulus operator is the word Mod, as follows:

```
Result = NumberOne Mod NumberTwo
Result = 11 Mod 3      'result in 2
                       '(11/3 = 3 with a remainder of 2)
```

Modulus is used on Line 215 to calculate the amount of additional wallpaper required on each cut length to allow for the pattern match. This remainder is then used to determine the cut length of each strip of wallpaper for the project.

Using Exponents

Exponents also are known as *powers* of a number. For example, 2 raised to the third power is equivalent to 2×2×2, or 8. Exponents are used quite a lot in computer operations, in which many things are represented as powers of two. Exponents also are used extensively in scientific and engineering work, where many things are represented as powers of 10 or as natural logarithms. Simpler exponents are used in statistics, in which many calculations depend on the squares and the square roots of numbers.

To raise a number to a power, you use the *exponential operator*, a caret (^). Exponents greater than one indicate a number raised to a power. Fractional exponents indicate a root, and negative exponents indicate a fraction. The following is the syntax for using the exponential operator:

```
Result = NumberOne ^ Exponent
```

The following equations show several common uses of exponents. The operation performed by each equation is also indicated.

Sample Exponent	Function Performed
3 ^ 2 = 9	The square of the number
9 ^ 0.5 = 3	The square root of the number
2 ^ -2 = 0.25	The fraction obtained by using a negative exponent

Setting the Order of Precedence in Statements

Consider the following statement:

```
x = 9 + 4 * 2
```

Depending on how you look at it, x could have two values—26 or 17. If you do the addition of 9 + 4 first and then multiply by 2, you get 26. However, if you multiply 4 * 2 first and then add 9, you get 17. The answer you get depends on the order in which things happen. This order is referred to as *order of precedence*.

In Visual Basic, the default order of precedence is that in a statement with multiplication/division operators and addition/subtraction operators, multiplication/division is performed *first*, before the addition/subtraction. In the preceding example, the default answer is 17. Other operators, such as comparison, logical, and string, are also affected by precedence.

When multiple types of operators are in a single statement, operator precedence controls what's performed first. Math operators are performed first, then comparison operators, and finally logical operators (see Table 8.3).

TABLE 8.3 **Precedence Order of Visual Basic Operators**

Operation	Operator Symbol
Exponentiation	^
Negation (unary)	−
Multiplication, division	*, /
Integer division	\
Modulus	mod
Addition, subtraction	+, −
Concatenation (string)	&
Comparison operators	=, <>, <, >, <=, >+
Logical operators	Not, And, Or, Xor, Eqv, Imp, Like, Is

CHAPTER 8

Controlling the order of operations

Experienced programmers use parentheses to define the ordering of operations within their programs. Using parentheses to define order of precedence removes ambiguity. You'll want to use parentheses in your code. Doing so doesn't affect the speed of your program and assures the accuracy and clarity of your code.

Parentheses are used to control specifically which parts of a statement are performed first. Without parentheses, operator precedence allows the program to determine what operation to do first. To ensure that arithmetic operations happen in the order you want them to, you can use parentheses to group operations. For example, by using the preceding statement, you could group operations as

```
x  = (9 + 4) * 2     'results in 26
```

or

```
x  = 9 + (4 * 2)     'results in 17
```

Concatenating Strings

Visual Basic supports only one string operator, the *concatenation operator*. This operator combines two or more strings of text, similar to the way the addition operator is used to combine two or more numbers. The concatenation operator is the ampersand symbol (&). When you combine two strings with the concatenation operator, the second string is added directly to the end of the first string. The result is a longer string containing the full contents of both source strings. (For more information about strings, read Chapter 12, "Working with Strings and Typecasting.")

SEE ALSO
➤ *Page 121 explains more about strings*

The concatenation operator is used in an assignment statement as follows:

```
NewString = stringOne & stringTwo & stringThree
```

In this syntax, *NewString* represents the variable that contains the result of the concatenation operation. *stringOne*, *stringTwo*, and *stringThree* all represent string expressions. These can be any valid strings, including string variables, literal expressions (enclosed in quotation marks), or functions that return a string.

The ampersand between a pair of string expressions tells Visual Basic to concatenate the two expressions. The ampersand must be preceded and followed by a space. The syntax shows an optional second ampersand and a third string expression. You can combine any number of strings with a single statement. Just remember to separate each pair of expressions with an ampersand.

Listing 8.2 shows how the concatenation of strings is used in a simple program to generate mailing labels. On line 48, the fields from the different text boxes are combined to create the different lines of the mailing label. Figure 8.3 shows the form for this program. The complete code for this example is in the project prjName.vbp on the MCP Web site (`http://www.mcp.com/info`) that supports this book.

Concatenation operator from previous versions is supported

If you're working on converting programs from an older version of Visual Basic, you may find strings combined with the plus-sign operator. This was prevalent in versions of Visual Basic prior to version 4, as well as in older BASIC languages. Although Visual Basic still supports the plus-sign operator for backward compatibility, you should use the ampersand for any work that you do to avoid confusion with the mathematical addition operation.

LISTING 8.2 08LIST02–How OptionButtons are Used to Make Exclusive Choices

```
01   Private Sub cmdShowName_Click()
02     Dim strTitle As String
03     Dim strFirst As String
04     Dim strLast As String
05     Dim strFullName As String
...
37     'Assign the value in the TextBox to a string
38     strFirst = txtFirstName.Text
39     strLast = txtLastName.Text
40
41     'Assign the Title of the selected one to a string
42     If optMr.Value Then strTitle = "Mr. "
43     If optMrs.Value Then strTitle = "Mrs. "
44     If optMiss.Value Then strTitle = "Miss "
45     If optMs.Value Then strTitle = "Ms. "
46
47     'Put the strings together
48     strFullName = strTitle & strFirst & " " & strLast
49
50     'Display the results in the answer box
51     lblFullName.Caption = strFullName
52   End Sub
```

FIGURE 8.3

A simple name-reporting program illustrates the function of the concatenation operator.

Also, you saw string concatenation used previously in the prjWallpaper example in Listing 8.1. The statement used to build a message for the error MessageBox (on lines 24 and 25) is

```
Msg  = "Wall Width needs to be numeric. "
Msg  = Msg  & "Please enter a number."
```

This is an example of concatenating a string onto a single-string variable. Another way to solve the problem above is to use the *line-continuation characters* (_), which are used on line 217 in Listing 8.1. The "space + underscore" characters allow a single program statement to extend over several contiguous lines in the program. There are limitations in its use, such as not following the line-continuation characters with a comment. The previous example would have been written as follows if the line-continuation character had been used:

```
Msg  = "Wall Width needs to be numeric. " & _
          "Please enter a number."
```

This would have eliminated the second assignment statement, which would make the code slightly more efficient.

Working with Conditional Statements

If...Then statements

If...Then...Else statements

If...Then...ElseIf statements

Select Case statements

Making Decisions in Your Program

Most statements in your programs will be assignment statements, but other statements are important for handling more complex tasks. These statements are known collectively as *control statements*. Without control statements, you couldn't write a very flexible program. Your program would start at the first line of code and proceed line by line until the last line was reached. At that point, the program would stop.

One type of control statement is the *decision statement*. These statements are used to control the execution of parts in your program, based on conditions that exist at the time the statement is encountered. Two main types of decision statements are If...Then and Select Case.

The IF Statement

Most programmers don't really understand the importance of the IF statement because it's so common in the programming environment. IF statements use comparison operators to test data values. Comparison operators or conditional operators test conditions that are either true or false. With this simple programming statement and its cousins, you can initiate complex calculations.

Writing *If...Then* Statements

In Visual Basic, you can write an If...Then statement for handling True conditions in two ways: the single-line If...Then statement and the multiline If...Then statement. Each uses the If...Then keywords to check a condition. If the condition is True, the program runs the commands associated with the If...Then statement. If the condition is False, the commands are skipped.

Writing a Single-Line *If* Statement

The single-line If statement is used to perform a single task when the condition in the statement is True. The following is the syntax of the single-line If statement:

If *condition* Then *command*

The condition represents any type of statement or function that evaluates to True. The condition can be any of the following:

- A comparison of a variable to a *literal*, another variable, or a function
- A *variable* that contains a True or False value
- Any *function* that returns a True or False value

The command represents the task to be performed if the condition is True. This can be any valid Visual Basic statement other than a variable declaration.

Look at the Simple Calculator program in Figure 9.1. The way this program works is that you enter a number in each of the two upper TextBoxes, select a math operation, and then click the CommandButton. The program performs the selected math operation on the numbers and displays the result in a third TextBox.

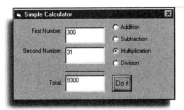

FIGURE 9.1

The Simple Calculator makes decisions in an If...Then statement, based on the value of the OptionButton.

The program decides which math operation to perform by evaluating the setting of the Value property of the OptionButton assigned to each operation. If the Value property of an OptionButton is set to True, the program does the associated math operation.

The following shows the If statement from the program. This conditional statement performs the associated math operation if True and is an example of a single-line If statement.

```
If optAddition.Value = True Then z = x + y
```

Listing 9.1 shows the entire code for the event procedure for the click of the cmdOperation CommandButton, the button that users click to perform the selected math operation.

LISTING 9.1 09LIST01.TXT—Making Decisions Based on the Value of an OptionButton

```
01   Private Sub cmdOperation_Click()
02     'Declare a variable for the first number
03     Dim x As Double
04
05     'Declare a variable for the second number
```

continues...

Download this code

The source code for this program is the project simplclc.vbp, which is available on the Web at http://www.mcp.com/info. You'll be asked to enter an ISBN; enter 078971633x and then click the **Search** button to go to the **Book Info** page for *Using Visual Basic 6*.

LISTING 9.1 Continued

```
06    Dim y As Double
07
08    'Declare a variable to hold the sum of both numbers
09    Dim z As Double
10
11    'Convert the text inputted into the text box
12    'into an integer and assign it to the first variable
13    x = CDbl(txtNumOne.Text)
14
15    'Convert the text imputted into the text box
16    'into an integer and assign it to the second variable
17    y = CDbl(txtNumTwo.Text)
18
19    'Decide what operation to do based on the
20    'value of selected option button
21    If optAddition.Value = True Then z = x + y
22
23    If optSubtraction.Value = True Then z = x - y
24
25    If optMultiplication.Value = True Then z = x * y
26
27    'For division, make sure that the second number is
28    'not equal to  zero. You cannot divide a number by
29    'zero. Blows up!
30    If optDivision.Value = True Then
31      If y <> 0 Then
32        z = x / y
33      Else
34        'Report an  error
35        MsgBox "Cannot divide by zero", vbCritical, "Error"
36      End If
37    End If
38    'Convert the third variable (which is a Double)
39    'to text and assign it to the text property of the
40    'textbox for the result.
41    txtTotal.Text = CStr(z)
42    End Sub
```

LISTING 9.1

① Single-line If statements

② Nested If statement

③ If...Then...Else statement

Executing Multiple Commands in the Conditional Statement

If you need to execute more than one command in response to a condition, you can use a block If...Then statement. A block If...Then statement bounds a range of statements between the If...Then statement and an End If statement. If the condition in the If...Then statement is True, all the commands between the If...Then and End If statements are run. If the condition is False, the program skips to the first line after the End If statement.

The structure of a multiple-command If statement is as follows:

```
If condition Then
     Command1
     Command2
     Commandn
End If
```

in which If and Then are the Visual Basic keywords that "bracket" the condition, and End If are the keywords that end the code block.

Listing 9.2 shows a portion of code that enhances the cmdOperation_Click() event procedure from Listing 9.1.

LISTING 9.2 09LIST02.TXT—Using Multiple Commands in an *If...Then* Statement

```
01    'Decide what operation to do based on the
02    'value of selected option button
03    If optAddition.Value = True Then
04        z = x + y
05        frmMain.Caption = "Addition"
06    End If
07
08    If optSubtraction.Value = True Then
09        z = x - y
10        frmMain.Caption = "Subtraction"
11    End If
12
```

continues...

LISTING 9.2 Continued

```
13   If optMultiplication.Value = True Then
14       z = x * y
15       frmMain.Caption = "Multiplication"
16   End If
```

Whereas the code in Listing 9.1 invokes only one command when an If...Then statement evaluates True (see line 21 of Listing 9.1), the code in Listing 9.2 invokes two commands when the If...Then statement evaluates True (see lines 3–6 in Listing 9.2).

Using *If...Then...Else* Statements

As you learned earlier, sometimes you might encounter this situation: If one condition exists, you do one set of commands, and if it doesn't, you do another set. For example, If you have money in your checking account, write a check; Else, transfer funds from your savings account into the checking account. This is called an If...Then...Else statement. If...Then...Else takes the following format:

```
If condition Then
    statements to process if condition is True
Else
    statements to process if condition is False
End If
```

The If and End If statements of this block are the same as before. The condition is still any logical expression or variable that yields a True or False value. The key element in this set of statements is the Else statement. This statement is placed after the last statement to be executed if the condition is True, and before the first statement to be executed if the condition is False. For a True condition, the program processes the statements up to the Else statement and then skips to the first statement after the End If. If the condition is False, the program skips the statements before the Else statement and starts processing with the first statement after the Else.

You saw the following code snippet at the end of Listing 9.1. This is an excellent example of a simple If...Then...Else statement. If the value of the variable y doesn't equal zero (line 30), the program does some division (line 31); otherwise, the program displays a Windows message box with an error message (line 34).

```
30  If optDivision.Value = True Then
31    If y <> 0 Then
32        z = x / y
33    Else
34      'Report an  error
35      MsgBox "Cannot divide by zero", vbCritical, "Error"
36    End If
37  End If
```

If you want to execute code for only the False portion of the statement, you can place code statements between the Else and End If statements; you aren't required to place any statements between the If and Else statements:

```
If x <= 1 then
Else
    MsgBox "X is not greater than 1"
End If
```

Working with Multiple *If* Statements

In the preceding sections, you saw simple If...Then statements, which evaluate one condition and can execute commands for a True or False condition. You can also evaluate multiple conditions with an additional statement in the block. If...Then...ElseIf statements let you specify another condition to evaluate whether the first condition is False. By using the ElseIf statement, you can evaluate any number of conditions.

Listing 9.3 shows a snippet of code from the program Grader.EXE (see Figure 9.2) from the project grader.vbp, available from the Web site associated with this book. The code snippet uses the ElseIf conditional structure as a way to determine the grade for a test, based on a range of correct answers.

FIGURE 9.2

The Grader program uses
If...Then...ElseIf state-
ments to determine a grade
based on correct answers.

LISTING 9.3 **09LIST03.TXT—Using *ElseIf* Statements to Evaluate Multiple Conditions**

```
01    If CorrectAnswers% >= 10 Then
02        strGrade = "A"
03    ElseIf CorrectAnswers% = 9 Then
04        strGrade = "A-"
05    ElseIf CorrectAnswers% = 8 Then
06        strGrade = "B"
07    ElseIf CorrectAnswers% = 7 Then
08        strGrade = "B-"
09    ElseIf CorrectAnswers% = 6 Then
10        strGrade = "C"
11    ElseIf CorrectAnswers% = 5 Then
12        strGrade = "C-"
13    ElseIf CorrectAnswers% = 4 Then
14        strGrade = "D"
15    ElseIf CorrectAnswers% = 3 Then
16        strGrade = "D-"
17    Else
18        strGrade = "F"
19    End If
```

This code works first by evaluating the condition in the If statement (line 1). If the condition is True, the statement (or statements) immediately following the If statement is executed (line
2), and then the program skips to the first statement after the End
If statement (line 19).

If the first condition is False, the program skips to the first
ElseIf statement (line 3) and evaluates its condition. If this condition is True, the statements following the ElseIf are executed
(line 4), and control again passes to the statement after the End
If. If the condition evaluates to False, control passes to the next

ElseIf statement. This process continues for as many ElseIf statements as are in the block.

If all the conditions are False, the program skips to the Else statement and processes the commands between the Else (line 17) and the End If statements. The Else statement isn't required.

Using Nested *If* Statements

If you need to test for a condition that depends on whether another condition is already True (such as "If it's 6:30 a.m. and if it's a weekday"), use nested If statements. A nested If statement is one that's enclosed within another If statement. The format for a nested If statement is as follows:

```
If condition Then
    If another_condition Then
        statement
    Else
        another statement
    End If
End If
```

The following code snippet demonstrates a nested If statement. You originally saw it in the cmdOperation Click() event procedure in Listing 9.1.

```
30  If optDivision.Value = True Then
31    If y <> 0 Then
32        z = x / y
33    Else
34      'Report an  error
35      MsgBox "Cannot divide by zero", vbCritical, "Error"
36    End If
37  End If
```

Using the *Select Case* Statement

Another way to handle decisions in a program is to use the Select Case statement, which enables you to run any of a series of statement groups, based on the value of a single variable. The Select Case statement identifies the variable to be evaluated, and then a series of Case statements specifies the possible values. If the value of the variable matches the value (or values) indicated in the Case statement, the commands after the Case statement are executed. If the value doesn't match, the program proceeds to the next Case statement.

The Select Case structure is similar to a series of If...Then...ElseIf statements. The following lines of code show the syntax of the Select Case block:

```
Select Case TestValue
    Case Value1
        Statement_Group_1
    Case Value2
        Statement_Group_2
End Select
```

The first statement of the Select Case block is the Select Case statement itself. This statement identifies the value to be tested against possible results. This value, represented by the TestValue argument, can be any valid numeric or string expression, including a literal, a variable, a logical expression, or a function.

Each conditional group of commands (run if the condition is met) is started by a Case statement. The Case statement identifies the expression to which the TestValue is compared. The Case statement can express a single value or a range of values. If the TestValue is equal to or within range of the expression, the commands after the Case statement are run. The program runs the commands between the current Case statement and the next Case statement or the End Select statement. If the TestValue isn't equal to the value expression or doesn't fall within a range defined for the Case statement, the program proceeds to the next Case statement.

Listing 9.4 shows you a Select Case statement that tests for equality. Listing 9.5 shows you a Select Case statement that tests for a range.

Select Case limitations

You should never use **Select Case** if a simple If...Then...Else statement will work. Sometimes using **Select Case** can be overkill and add to the confusion that complex logic statements can provide.

LISTING 9.4 **09LIST04.TXT–Testing for Equality in a *Select Case* Statement**

```
01    Select Case x%
02        Case 1:
03            MsgBox "I am 1"
04        Case 2:
05            MsgBox "I am 2"
06    End Select
```

LISTING 9.5 **09LIST05.TXT–Testing for a Range in a *Select Case* Statement**

```
01    Select Case x%
02        Case 6 To 9
03            MsgBox "I am more than 5 and less than 10"
04        Case 101 To 199
05            MsgBox "I am more than 100 and less than 200"
06        Case Else
07            MsgBox "Not in Range"
08    End Select
```

The simplest form of the Select Case block uses only a single value for the comparison expression. Listing 9.6 shows a Select Case statement that accomplishes the same thing that the If...Then...ElseIf code in Listing 9.3 does. The benefit of using a Select Case to accomplish the grading task is that the code is easier to read and easier to extend.

LISTING 9.6 **09LIST06.TXT–Rewriting an *If...Then...ElseIf* Statement as a *Select Case* Statement**

```
01    Private Sub cmdGrader_Click()
02    Dim CorrectAnswers%
03    Dim strGrade As String
04
05    'Get the correct answers from the textbox
06    CorrectAnswers% = CInt(txtNumberRight.Text)
07
08    'Assign the grade based on the correct answers
09    Select Case CorrectAnswers%
10        Case 10
11            strGrade = "A"
```

continues...

LISTING 9.6 Continued

```
12        Case 9
13            strGrade = "A-"
14        Case 8
15            strGrade = "B"
16        Case 7
17            strGrade = "B-"
18        Case 6
19            strGrade = "C"
20        Case 5
21            strGrade = "C-"
22        Case 4
23            strGrade = "D"
24        Case 3
25            strGrade = "D-"
26        Case Else
27            strGrade = "F"
28    End Select
29    'Display the grade
30    lblGrade.Caption = strGrade
31 End Sub
```

When it comes time to add another grade level—say, an A+ if the student correctly answers 11 in the following example—all you need is to add a new case, Case 11 (see Listing 9.7, line 3). If you were to use the ElseIf technique, you would have to rewrite significant portions of the If...Then...ElseIf code block.

LISTING 9. 7 09LIST07.TXT—Extending a *Select Case* Statement

```
01    Select Case CorrectAnswers%
02        'Add a case for 11 correct answers
03        Case 11
04            strGrade = "A+"
05        Case 10
06            strGrade = "A"
07        Case 9
08            strGrade = "A-"
09        Case 8
10            strGrade = "B"
11        Case 7
```

```
12          strGrade = "B-"
13      Case 6
14          strGrade = "C"
15      Case 5
16          strGrade = "C-"
17      Case 4
18          strGrade = "D"
19      Case 3
20          strGrade = "D-"
21      Case Else
22          strGrade = "F"
23  End Select
```

Using Relational Operators in *Select Case* Blocks

You can also use relational operators in a Select Case block. Sometimes you might want to test for cases within a range perhaps greater than or less than a certain number. To accomplish this with a Select Case block, you must use the Is keyword. To test within a certain range, use the To keyword as you saw earlier in Listing 9.5.

Just as you can check to see whether equality exists between two quantities with the = sign, you can also check to see whether numbers are less than, greater than, or not equal to one another. Table 9.1 shows the relational operators that you can use in your conditional statements.

TABLE 9.1 **Relational Operators**

Symbol	Meaning	Example	Result
=	Equal	8 = 9	False
>	Greater than	8 > 9	False
<	Less than	8 < 9	True
>=	Greater than or equal to	8 >= 8	True
<=	Less than or equal to	7 <= 6	False
<>	Not equal to	6 <> 7	True

Correct character order

Pay particular attention to the order of characters in the less-than and greater-than symbols. They must be ordered as shown previously. Using => or =< will produce an error.

Line 3 of Listing 9.8 shows you how to use the Is keyword to create a greater-than statement within a Select Case block. Notice that the relational operator (>) is used to make any number of correct answers greater than 11 result in a grade of A++.

LISTING 9. 8 09LIST08.TXT—Using Relational Operators with *Select Case* Statements

```
01   Select Case CorrectAnswers%
02        'Make any answer greater than 11 an A++
03        Case Is > 11
04            strGrade = "A++"
05        Case 11
06            strGrade = "A+"
07        Case 10
08            strGrade = "A"
09      Case 9
10          strGrade = "A-"
11      Case 8
12          strGrade = "B"
13      Case 7
14          strGrade = "B-"
15      Case 6
16          strGrade = "C"
17      Case 5
18          strGrade = "C-"
19      Case 4
20          strGrade = "D"
21      Case 3
23            strGrade = "D-"
24      Case Else
25          strGrade = "F"
26   End Select
```

Select Case statements are a powerful addition to your programming toolkit and take you to the next level of programming expertise. As you learn more about them, you will understand how to use If statements and Select Case statements together to make very detailed, extended decisions within your programs.

Working with Loops

Learn about the different types of loops you can use in VB6

Populate a TextBox with the *For...Next* and *Do...While* loops

See how *Do...Until* loops relate to other types of loops

Exit a loop and break an infinite loop

Use multiple loops to solve complex tasks

Putting Loops to Work

One benefit of computer programming is the capability to repeat a set of instructions reliably after they're written. The specific commands you put at the beginning and end of a set of instructions to control their repeated execution are known as *loops*. These commands tell the computer when and how often to perform the set of instructions. By using loops, you can write simpler programs that would have otherwise required redundant lines of code. Loops can be used to inspect arrays (discussed in Chapter 11, "Working with Arrays"), change properties of a program's controls, and do a set of tasks for as long as a certain condition exists, or skip a set of tasks until a certain condition is met.

Visual Basic supports two commonly used types of loops: *counter loops*, which perform a task a set number of times, and *conditional loops*, which perform a task while a specified condition exists or until a specified condition exists.

Using *For...Next* Loops

Counter loops are also known as `For` or `For...Next` loops. They're called `For...Next` loops because the beginning and end of the loop are defined by the `For` statement and the `Next` statement, respectively. The syntax of a `For...Next` loop is

```
For CounterVar = StartNum To EndNum [Step StepNum]
    statements
Next [CounterVar]
```

At the beginning of a `For...Next` loop, you define a counter variable, as well as the beginning and end points of the variable's value. The first time the loop is run, the counter variable is set to the value of the beginning point. Each time the program runs through the loop, the value of the counter increments. If the

Reading collections with loops

Visual Basic 6.0 supports other looping commands, including collection loops that use the `For Each...Next` statement. For more information about collections, see Chapter 26, "Making Object-Oriented Programs with Visual Basic."

1 Keyword that starts a loop

2 User-defined numeric variable that the loop uses as a counter

3 Number from which the loop starts

4 Keyword that separates *StartNum* from *EndNum*

5 Number at which the loop stops

6 Optional keyword that indicates that loop should **step**

7 Indicates what size step increment/decrement should be (can be negative)

8 Keyword that completes the loop

9 Identifies which *CounterVar* is updated by the `Next` keyword

Step keyword is used, the counter variable increments as dictated by the number following the Step keyword. For example, in the following statement, intCntr will increment by 2:

```
For intCntr = 0 To 10 Step 2
```

As the counter variable increments, it's checked against the value of the end point. If the counter is larger than the end point, the program skips out of the loop and onto the first statement following the loop.

If the beginning value of the loop is greater than the ending value, the loop won't execute at all, unless you set up the loop to count backward. For example, the following loop doesn't cause an error, but because the start boundary of the loop (9) is greater than the end boundary (0), the loop is ignored and the message box doesn't appear:

```
For intCntr = 9 To 0 'This loop will not run!
    MsgBox "This is loop number: " & Cstr(intCntr)
Next intCntr
```

The following loop works, however, because the loop uses the Step keyword to decrement >backward (–1) from 9 to 0:

```
For intCntr = 9 To 0 Step -1
    MsgBox "This is loop number: " & Cstr(intCntr)
Next intCntr
```

The counter variable is changed each time the loop reaches the Next statement. Unless otherwise specified with the Step keyword, the counter is increased by one for each loop.

Listing 10.1, the event handler for the For...Next button click event, shows a For...Next loop that exposes the counter variable within a larger string displayed in a TextBox (see Figure 10.1). As the loop progresses, the counter variable is converted to a string and inserted within strings, StrBegin and StrEnd. Those strings are concatenated onto a master "holding" string, StrMsg, which grows with each trip through the loop. A carriage return and line-break character is added to StrMsg at the end of the loop, and then the StrMsg is assigned to the Text property of txtDisplay. The loop then refreshes the form to repaint the TextBox.

Stepping through the loop

The default or assumed value for the **Step** in a **For...Next** loop is a positive 1, which increments the counter. Including the step value on all **For...Next** loops, even when the value is 1, improves readability and aids maintenance.

Concatenation

You concatenate a string when you add another string onto a string. An example of concatenating three strings onto one string is **FullName = First & " " & Last**, which performs two successive concatenations into the string variable **FullName**.

SEE ALSO

➤ *Find out more about the concatenation operator on page 217*

LISTING 10.1   10LIST01.TXT—Using a *For...Next* Loop to Concatenate Strings

```
01 Private Sub cmdForNext_Click()
02   Dim intCntr      As Integer
03   Dim strBegin     As String
04   Dim strEnd       As String
05   Dim strMsg       As String
06
07   'Make a phrase for the beginning of a line
08   strBegin = "This is line: "
09
10   'Make a phrase for the end of a line
11   strEnd = " of a For...Next loop"
12
13   'Make a For...Next Loop
14   For  intCntr = 0 To 20
15
16      'Put the beginning of the line in place
17       strMsg = strMsg & strBegin
18
19      'Convert the counter integer to a string
20      'and place it in the middle of the string
21      'that is being constructed
22       strMsg = strMsg & CStr(intCntr)
23
24      'Add the end of the message
25       strMsg = strMsg & strEnd
26
27      'Put in a line break constant
28       strMsg = strMsg & vbCrLf
29      'Display the resulting string in the textbox
30       txtDisplay.Text = strMsg
31       Refresh        'force a repaint of the screen
32   Next intCntr
33 End Sub
```

Documenting the end of a For...Loop

For ease of reading your program code, it's good practice to include the variable name in the `Next` statement (like on line 32 of Listing 10.1). This is especially important in *nested loops*.

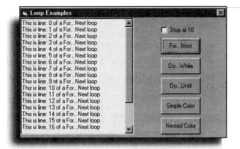

FIGURE 10.1

When you set a TextBox's MultiLine property to True, make sure that you set the TextBox's ScrollBars property accordingly. Otherwise, you may not see all the text.

An alternative method would be to only update the screen after leaving the loop. You would move the assignment statement immediately after the Next command to prevent the program from displaying any text until the loop is completed. In the case of a long-running process, you should give users a visual indication that the program is running. In long-running loops, if you wait to the end of the loop to display the results onscreen, your users may think the program has locked up.

Although you can use any numeric variable for the counter, you need to be aware of the limits of each variable type. For example, trying to run a loop 40,000 times starting from 0 with a step of 1 and an integer variable as the CounterVar causes an overrun error during execution. This is because an integer has a maximum positive value of 32,767. Using a Long integer will solve this problem when larger loop counters are required. The limitation on Long integers is negative 2,147,483,648 to positive 2,147,483,647.

Using floating-point variables such as Singles and Doubles for a CounterVar will work. There's even the capability to support fractional Step variables, although these can become difficult to maintain and should be avoided unless required by the functionality of the statements inside the loop.

You should exercise great care when manually changing the value of the counter variable inside the loop. Never reset the value of the counter variable inside a For...Next loop, because doing so may create an infinite loop or a program lockup. For

VBA constants

vbCrLf is a Visual Basic global constant that could have been substituted with the string "Chr(13) & Chr(10)". Both the VBA constant and this literal string are equivalent to a carriage return/line feed combination. For more information about using VBA constants, see Chapter 7, "Using Data Types, Constants, and Variables."

example, the following code causes the `For...Loop` to go into an infinite loop, because the end value of 4 is never reached:

```
For intCntr = 0 to 4
    intCntr = 0 ' This line causes an infinite loop
Next intCntr
```

Terminating the *For...Next* Loop Early

Typically, your `For...Next` loop should run through all the values of the counter variable, but sometimes you'll want the loop to terminate early. To do this, simply place an `Exit For` statement where you want the loop to stop. This statement is typically associated within an `If...Then` statement.

Listing 10.2 shows an enhancement to the code in Listing 10.1. Lines 16 through 22 show an added `If...Then` statement at the beginning of the `For...Next` loop. When the loop begins, the code enters the `If...Then` statement to take a look at the value of the CheckBox on the form. Selecting the CheckBox on the form tells the program that the loop needs to terminate when the value of the counting variable exceeds the quantity 10 (see Figure 10.2). Therefore, if this condition exists (the CheckBox is checked), the `Exit For` statement—contained in the `If...Then` statement within the first `If...Then` statement—forces the program out of the `For...Next` loop.

LISTING 10.2 10LIST02.TXT—Setting Many Alternative Actions Within a *For...Next* Loop

```
01  Private Sub cmdForNext_Click()
02  Dim intCntr    As Integer
03  Dim strBegin   As String
04  Dim strEnd     As String
05  Dim strMsg     As String
06
07  'Make a phrase for the beginning of a line
08  strBegin = "This is line: "
09
10  'Make a phrase for the end of a line
11  strEnd = " of a For...Next loop"
12
```

```
13   'Make a For...Next Loop
14   For intCntr = 0 To 20
15
16       'Take a look to see if the checkbox
17        'on the form is checked
18       If chkLimit.Value = 1 Then
19            'if it is, then Exit the For statement
20            'when intCntr is greater than 10
21            If intCntr > 10 Then Exit For
22       End If
23       'Put the beginning of the line in place
24       strMsg = strMsg & strBegin
25
26       'Convert the counter integer to a string
27       'and place it in the middle of the string
28       'that is being constructed
29       strMsg = strMsg & CStr(intCntr)
30
31       'Add the end of the message
32       strMsg = strMsg & strEnd
33
34       'Put in a line break constant
35       strMsg = strMsg & vbCrLf
36       'Display the resulting string in the textbox
37       txtDisplay.Text = strMsg
38       Refresh      'force a repaint of the screen
39   Next intCntr
40   End Sub
```

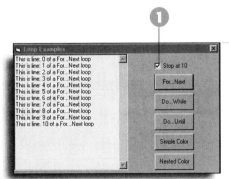

FIGURE 10.2

CheckBoxes are a good means of control when you need to set or clear a condition.

1 Check this to stop the loop at 10 counts.

Using *Do...Loop* Statements

A Do...Loop is a *conditional loop*, which is active as long or until a condition exists. The key feature of a conditional loop is, of course, the *condition* (any expression that can return a True or False value). This True/False can be a return value from a function; the value of a property, such as the Value property of an OptionButton; or an expression, such as NumVal < 15. (Chapter 18, "Writing Reusable Code with Subs and Functions," discusses functions fully.) The two basic types of conditional loops are Do...While, which repeats while the condition is True, and Do...Until, which repeats until the condition is True.

Using *Do...While* Loops

A Do...While loop works pretty much as the name implies—it does something while a certain condition is true. For example, to keep adding one to MyNum while MyNum is less than 20, you would use this:

```
Do While MyNum <20
    MyNum = MyNum + 1
Loop
```

The keyword While in the Do...While statement tells the program that the loop will be repeated while the condition expression is true. When the condition in a Do...While loop becomes false, the program moves out of the loop and onto the next statement after the Loop statement.

The syntax for a Do...While loop is

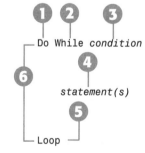

1. The keyword that denotes the beginning of the loop

2. The keyword that denotes what kind of loop it is

3. The state that ***must*** exist (for example, x = 10, MyVal <> True, or y < x)

4. The statement(s) to execute while the loop is active

5. The keyword that indicates the end of the loop block

6. Both statements must be present

Or you can use this equally valid syntax:

```
Do
    statement(s)
Loop While condition
```

As you can see in this example, the Do...While loop has two forms. The difference between the two is the placement of the condition—at the beginning of the loop or at the end.

Listing 10.3 looks similar to the For...Next loop code in Listing 10.2. When you take a closer look at Lines 13 through 41, however, you'll notice that where there was a For...Next loop, there's now a Do...While loop that runs while the value of intCntr is less than or equal to 20 (see Figure 10.3). Line 21 has also been changed from Exit For to Exit Do because the loop is now change to a Do loop. The Exit Do command is used with both types of Do loops.

Do loops will always run once if tested at the end

When the condition statement is placed after the **Loop** keyword in a **Do...While** or **Do...Until** loop, the set of instructions contained between **Do** and **Loop** is always executed once. The condition is checked only after the first iteration of the loop.

LISTING 10.3 10LIST03.TXT—A *Do...While* Loop That Does the Same Thing as a *For...Next* Loop

```
01  Private Sub cmdDoWhile_Click()
02  Dim intCntr      As Integer
03  Dim strBegin     As String
04  Dim strEnd       As String
05  Dim strMsg       As String
06
07  'Make a phrase for the beginning of a line
08  strBegin = "This is line: "
09
10  'Make a phrase for the end of a line
11  strEnd = " of a Do...While loop"
12
13  'Make a Do..While Loop
14  Do While intCntr <= 20
15
16      'Take a look to see if the checkbox
17      'on the form is checked
18      If chkLimit.Value = 1 Then
19          'if it is, then Exit the Do statement
```

continues...

LISTING 10.3 Continued

```
21              If intCntr > 10 Then Exit Do
22        End If
23
24        'Put the beginning of the line in place
25        strMsg = strMsg & strBegin
26
27        'Convert the counter integer to a string
28        'and place it in the middle of the string
29        'that is being constructed
30        strMsg = strMsg & CStr(intCntr)
31
32        'Add the end of the message
33        strMsg = strMsg & strEnd
34
35        'Put in a line break constant
36        strMsg = strMsg & vbCrLf
37        'Display the resulting string in the textbox
38        txtDisplay.Text = strMsg
39        Refresh      'force a repaint of the screen
40        intCntr = intCntr + 1
41    Loop
42 End Sub
```

FIGURE 10.3

You can us *Do...While* to loop while *intCntr* is less than or equal to 20.

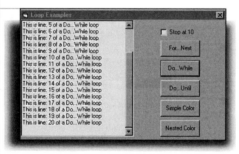

By placing the While condition clause in the Do statement, you tell the program that you want to evaluate the condition *before* you run any statements inside the loop. If the condition is True, the repetitive statements between the Do statement and the Loop statement are run. Then the program returns to the Do statement to evaluate the condition again. As soon as the condition is False, the program moves to the statement following the Loop statement.

When the form of the loop is located with the `While` keyword right after the `Do` keyword, the statements inside the loop may never be run. If the condition is `False` before the loop is run the first time, the program just proceeds to the statements after the loop. To run the `Do...While` loop at least once, use the second form of the `Do...While` loop, which places the condition after the `Loop` statement. For example,

```
Do
    Text1.Text = Text1.Text & CStr(intCntr )
    intCntr  = intCntr  + 1
Loop While intCntr  < 10
```

This form of the `Do...Loop` tells the program that you want the loop to run at least once and then evaluate the condition to determine whether to repeat the loop.

When using a `Do...While` loop, don't forget to increment the conditional variable in your code. Unlike the `For...Next` loop, the conditional or counting variables in `Do` loops are your responsibility to manage. Also, it's good practice to initialize the loop variable rather than rely on the default. For example, the following goes on infinitely because the `While` condition is never changed:

```
Dim intCntr
intCntr = 0
txtMessage.Text = ""
Do While intCntr < 10
    txtMessage.Text = txtMessage.Text _
                      & CStr(intCntr)
Loop
```

The following code loops, terminates, and displays the TextBox's text just fine:

```
Dim intCntr
intCntr = 0
txtMessage.Text = ""
Do While intCntr < 10
    txtMessage.Text = txtMessage.Text _
                      & CStr(intCntr)
    intCntr = intCntr + 1
Loop
```

Put conditional clauses in only one place

Don't put the `While` condition clause in both the `Do` and `Loop` statements because this causes an error when you try to run your program.

Replace *While...Wend* loops with *Do...While*

If you're working on code developed by someone else, you may find a loop that starts with a `While` statement and ends with a `Wend` statement. This type of loop works the same as a `Do...While` loop with the `While` clause in the `Do` statement. Visual Basic still supports a `While...Wend` loop, but it's recommended to that you use the `Do...While` type of loop because it's more flexible.

Using *Do...Until* Statements

The Do...Until loop is basically the same as the Do...While loop, except that the statements inside a Do...Until loop are run only as long as the condition is false—in other words, as long as the condition isn't met. When the condition becomes true, the loop terminates.

The syntax for a Do...Until loop is

```
Do Until condition
statement(s)
Loop
```

There are two forms of syntax for the Do...Until loop, just as there are two forms of syntax for the Do...While loop—one with the condition in the Do statement and one with the condition in the Loop statement. If you place the condition in the same line as the Do keyword, the condition is evaluated before the statements in the loop are executed. If you place the condition in the same line as the Loop keyword, the loop is run at least once before the condition is evaluated.

Listing 10.4 shows the event procedure for the cmdDoUntil button's Click event (see Figure 10.4). A Do...Until loop within the event procedure runs until the counter variable, intCntr, is greater than 20, or the Stop at 10 CheckBox is selected. This code is similar to the code for the cmdDoWhile_Click() event procedure in Listing 10.3. The only difference is that the Do...While loop is changed to a Do...Until loop (Lines 13 through 41). Also, the strEnd string on Line 11 is changed from " of a Do...While loop" to " of a Do...Until loop". As you can see, Do...While loops and Do...Until loops are closely related. Generally, which one you use is a matter of personal style.

LISTING 10.4 10LIST04.TXT–Terminating the Loop When the Condition Is True

```
01 Private Sub cmdDoUntil_Click()
02   Dim intCntr     As Integer
03   Dim strBegin    As String
04   Dim strEnd      As String
05   Dim strMsg      As String
06
```

```
07    'Make a phrase for the beginning of a line
08    strBegin = "This is line: "
09
10    'Make a phrase for the end of a line
11    strEnd = " of a Do...Until loop"
12
13    'Make a Do..Until Loop
14    Do Until intCntr > 20
...
41    Loop
42  End Sub
```

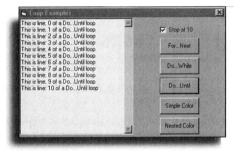

FIGURE 10.4

The *Do...Until* code still checks the value of the CheckBox.

Breaking an Infinite Loop

Getting comfortable using loops takes time. The more you use them, the better you'll get at identifying situations in which to use them. Loops can be a powerful programming tool, but they can cause enormous headaches if not properly written.

The following shows a programmer's worst nightmare—the infinite loop:

```
Dim intCntr as Integer
Do While intCntr = 0
     intCntr = 0
Loop
```

The command inside the loop sets the conditional variables and prevents the program from going beyond loop. So the code tells the program to loop *forever*. When the program enters this loop,

Terminate an infinite loop

If your program is running within the Visual Basic IDE, press Ctrl+Break. When you press these keys, the loop breaks at a line of code within the infinite loop. If your program isn't running within the IDE, the only way to terminate it is to end the program from within the Windows Task Manager. (For detailed information about the Task Manager, read the online documentation that comes with Windows.)

it's locked into the loop; everything else waits for the loop to complete, which never happens. If you run this program within the Visual Basic IDE, be aware that infinite loops will often lock it up and you may lose any program changes you made since your last update.

The best way to avoid an infinite loop is to carefully double-check any code you write that changes the conditional or counter variables in your loops. This may seem simplistic, but the power of loops is also the danger of loops. A loop can just as quickly tie up your system doing a desired productive task as it can counting to 2 billion for no reason.

Nesting Loops

In some situations, it becomes important to repeat a subtask several times during a larger task that's also being repeated. The way you write this type of program is by including a loop inside the set of instructions being repeated by a loop. This loop-within-in-a-loop structure is called *nesting*, or a nested loop. Nested loops can be a powerful programming tool, but they're confusing to understand if they're not properly written and documented.

Working with Multiple Loops

Listing 10.5 shows an example of multiple loops that change the Background Color property of the vpjLoops form and CheckBox during runtime. The main form and the CheckBox are changed to include all the visible background on the frame. This sample program is run from the Simple Color command button (refer to Figure 10.4).

LISTING 10.5 **10LIST05.TXT—An Example of Multiple *For* Loops**

```
01  Private Sub cmdForColor_Click()
02    Dim lngBlu      As Long
03    Dim lngGrn      As Long
04    Dim lngRed      As Long
05    Dim SaveBack    As Long
```

```
06   'Assign intColor Variables to initial values
07   'This will display white because all colors are 255
08   lngBlu = 255
09   lngGrn = 255
10   lngRed = 255
11
12   'Save the current background color of the form
13   SaveBack = frmLoop.BackColor
14   'Both the Form and CheckBox background are the same
15
16   'Loop 255 times reducing the Red color by 1
17   For lngRed = 255 To 1 Step -1
18       'Set the background color of the form and CheckBox
19       frmLoop.BackColor = RGB(lngRed, lngGrn, lngBlu)
20       chkLimit.BackColor = frmLoop.BackColor
21       Refresh      'force a repaint of the screen
22   Next lngRed
23
24   'Loop 255 times reducing the Green color by 1
25   For lngGrn = 255 To 1 Step -1
26       'Set the background color of the form and CheckBox
27       frmLoop.BackColor = RGB(lngRed, lngGrn, lngBlu)
28       chkLimit.BackColor = frmLoop.BackColor
29       Refresh      'force a repaint of the screen
30   Next lngGrn
31
32   'Loop 255 times reducing the Blue color by 1
33   For lngBlu = 255 To 1 Step -1
34       'Set the background color of the form and CheckBox
35       frmLoop.BackColor = RGB(lngRed, lngGrn, lngBlu)
36       chkLimit.BackColor = frmLoop.BackColor
37       Refresh      'force a repaint of the screen
38   Next lngBlu
39
40     'Loop 255 times increasing the Red color by 1
41   For lngRed = 0 To 254 Step 1
42       'Set the background color of the form and CheckBox
43       frmLoop.BackColor = RGB(lngRed, lngGrn, lngBlu)
44       chkLimit.BackColor = frmLoop.BackColor
45       Refresh         'force a repaint of the screen
46   Next lngRed
47
```

continues...

LISTING 10.5 Continued

```
48   'Loop 255 times increasing the Green color by 1
49   For lngGrn = 0 To 254 Step 1
50      'Set the background color of the form and CheckBox
51      frmLoop.BackColor = RGB(lngRed, lngGrn, lngBlu)
52      chkLimit.BackColor = frmLoop.BackColor
53      Refresh      'force a repaint of the screen
54   Next lngGrn
55
56   'Loop 255 times increasing the Blue color by 1
57   For lngBlu = 0 To 254 Step 1
58      'Set the background color of the form and CheckBox
59      frmLoop.BackColor = RGB(lngRed, lngGrn, lngBlu)
60      chkLimit.BackColor = frmLoop.BackColor
61      Refresh      'force a repaint of the screen
62   Next lngBlu
63
64   'Reset the background color on both to original
65   frmLoop.BackColor = SaveBack
66   chkLimit.BackColor = frmLoop.BackColor
67   End Sub
```

Make code easier to read

Indenting code nested inside a loop or other structure (such as an **If** statement) makes the code easier to read.

The program first saves the current background color and then proceeds to remove each of the three screen colors through a set of 255 increments. The first color removed is red, then green, and finally blue. The second set of three loops does just the opposite: first it adds in the red, then green, and finally blue. The last two lines (65 and 66) put both elements back to their original background color settings.

There are six separate loops for 67 total lines of code. These loops have many lines in common, and with a little effort, you can identify those common elements.

Using Nested Loops to Eliminate Loops

You'll notice the use of a long integer array to accomplish the function of the inner loop. Arrays are covered in depth in Chapter 11, "Working with Arrays."

Listing 10.6 shows Listing 10.5 rewritten as two nested loops.

The first loop dims the background color by color. The second, as in Listing 10.5, adds the colors back in. This sample program is run from the Nested Color command button (see Figure 10.5).

LISTING 10.6   **10LIST06.TXT–An Wxample of Two Nested Loops That Use a Long Integer Array**

```
01  Private Sub cmdNestColor_Click()
02   Dim intColorArray(1 To 3)    As Long
03   Dim SaveBack                 As Long
04   Dim intPass                  As Integer
05   Dim intHue                   As Integer
06   'Assign intColor Variables to initial values
07   'This will display white because all colors are 255
08   intColorArray(1) = 255       'Red
09   intColorArray(2) = 255       'Green
10   intColorArray(3) = 255       'Blue
11
12   'Save the current background color of the form
13   SaveBack = frmLoop.BackColor
14   'Both the Form and CheckBox background are the same
15
16   'Top Loop does each color in turn Red, Green, Blue
17   For intPass = 1 To 3
18      'Then Loop2 255 times reducing color by 1
19      For intHue = 255 To 1 Step -1
20         intColorArray(intPass) = intHue
21         frmLoop.BackColor = RGB(intColorArray(1), _
                  intColorArray(2), intColorArray(3))
22         chkLimit.BackColor = frmLoop.BackColor
23         Refresh      'force a repaint of the screen
24      Next intHue
25   Next intPass
26
27   'Top Loop does each color in turn Red, Green, Blue
28   For intPass = 1 To 3
29      'Then Loop2 255 times increasing  color by 1
30      For intHue = 0 To 254 Step 1
31         intColorArray(intPass) = intHue
32         frmLoop.BackColor = RGB(intColorArray(1), _
                  intColorArray(2), intColorArray(3))
```

continues…

LISTING 10.6 Continued

```
33          chkLimit.BackColor = frmLoop.BackColor
34          Refresh      'force a repaint of the screen
35       Next intHue
36    Next intPass
37
38    'Reset the background color on both to original
39    frmLoop.BackColor = SaveBack
40    chkLimit.BackColor = frmLoop.BackColor
41  End Sub
```

There are only 41 lines of code and only two nested loops to maintain in this new version of the program. This reduces line count by 35 percent with no loss of functionality. The key benefits that nested loops provide are consistent operation and ease of maintenance. If the same code is being used every time a loop is run, it becomes easy to make sure that it does the same tasks.

Nested loops require more effort to write and debug than simple loops. Reusable code is harder to develop than redundant code by at least a factor of 2. This topic is covered more in Chapter 18, "Writing Reusable Code with Subs and Functions."

Visual Basic's IDE makes it very tempting to write a simple loop and then cut and paste it six, seven, or 200 times in a row. Most programming tools make it very easy to copy lines of code. The challenge comes in learning to write better programs that are easier to maintain and that perform consistently.

Loading Data with Nested Loops

There are more useful examples where nested loops are invaluable. The final example in this chapter is based on the MSFlexGrid ActiveX control and how it could be loaded from a text file by using a nested loop. In this example, the control isn't bound to any data source. The example program uses a simple text file that contains one field or cell per row. The nested loop is a big help here, as it can be used to step through the rows in the grid column by column. This allows the read or input statement to appear only once in the program.

Listing 10.7 lists the setup commands for the MSFlexGrid control that are executed when the form loads. These commands set the width of the four columns used in the example. (The details of this are covered in Chapter 32, "Enhancing Your Programs Using the Advanced Data Controls.")

LISTING 10.7 10LIST07.TXT–Parameters for the MSFlexGrid Control

```
01  Private Sub Form_Load()
02    'These values are in TWIPS and set the columns on the
03    'MSFlexGrid at run time.  If you change these values
04    'you may need to also readjust the size of the Control.
05    MSFlexGrid1.ColWidth(0) = 640
06    MSFlexGrid1.ColWidth(1) = 1280
07    MSFlexGrid1.ColWidth(2) = 1280
08    MSFlexGrid1.ColWidth(3) = 1440
09  End Sub
```

> **Loading the MSFlxGrd.ocx file**
>
> An enhanced version of MSFlexGrid comes with VB6. Before you can use the MSFlexGrid control in your application, you must add the MSFlxGrd.ocx file to your Microsoft Windows System directory. For more information about adding an ActiveX control to a project, see Chapter 4, "Using the Intrinsic Controls."

By default, the Load event fires when a form is displayed. Figure 10.5 shows the grid after it has been loaded. By using this event, the program adjusts the width of the four columns to values that fit the amount of data in each column. These were identified by trial and error, but a routine could have been written to inspect the data in each grid cell and then determine the right width for each column. This function would work like the **Format** menu's **Column** and **Autofit** command in Microsoft Excel.

FIGURE 10.5

When you load the MSFlexGrid ActiveX control, you can specify runtime properties.

Now that the control is set up, the actual program is straightforward. An ASCII text file contains 24 lines or rows. Each line is read in turn and loaded into the grid. Listing 10.8 shows a partial listing of the text file; the full listing can be downloaded from the Web site, along with the sample program and the actual IMPORT.TXT file.

LISTING 10.8 **10LIST08.TXT—Part of IMPORT.TXT, Which is Read by the *cmdNextData* Subroutine**

```
01  StoreID
02  Location
03  Manager
04  Sales
05  1566
06  Minneapolis
07  James Archie
08  "$14,187,944"
...
21  1032
22  New York
23  Elmer Doren
24  "$5,437,104"
```

IMPORT.TXT is an ASCII file

The IMPORT.TXT file was created with Microsoft Notepad and can be edited. The name of the file, its location, and the number of rows is part of the program statements and must be changed to read different filenames.

Rows 1 through 4 of Listing 10.8 are used as the column headings in the grid control. There's nothing special about these rows, other than they are first, and the background and font in the MSFlexGrid control was formatted. Rows 5 though 24 are the detailed records for each of five stores, including the store ID, location, manager's name, and total sales.

The program in Listing 10.9 shows the 39 lines of code required to accomplish the task of loading the grid. Lines 21 through 34 are the nested loop that reads each line from the file and moves it into the proper cell of the grid.

LISTING 10.9 **10LIST09.TXT—Data Read Into Control a MSFlexGrid Control From a Txt File with a Nested Loop**

```
01  Private Sub cmdNestData_Click()
02    Dim strBuff As String
03    Dim intFile As Integer
04    Dim intCol As Integer
05    Dim intRow As Integer
06
07    'This message informs the user of the runtime path
08    'where the IMPORT.TXT file must be located. If
09    'the file is not found a run-time error will result.
10
```

```
11   MsgBox ("The current system path is set to: " _
          & CurDir & vbCrLf & "The program will run only" _
          & " if: IMPORT.TXT is found at the current path")
12
13   ' The next avaialble file is assigned to intFile
14   ' and file is opened for input.
15   intFile = FreeFile
16   Open CurDir & "\IMPORT.TXT" For Input As #intFile
17
18   'The MSFlexGrid was set-up for 6 rows and 4 columns
19   ' Zero(0) is the default first value
20
21   'First Loop steps through each row
22   For intRow = 0 To 5
23       ' Second Loop steps through each column
24       For intCol = 0 To 3
25           'Reads file #intFile into variable strBuff
26           Input #intFile, strBuff
27           'Set pointer to proper column
28           MSFlexGrid1.Col = intCol
29           'Set pointer tp proper row
30           MSFlexGrid1.Row = intRow
31           'Assigns the read value to the Cell text
32           MSFlexGrid1.Text = strBuff
33       Next intCol
34   Next intRow
35
36   Close #intFile     'close files as soon as you can
37 End Sub
```

Lines 7 through 18 in Listing 10.9 are for finding and opening the text file for input. The MessageBox displays the current default path of the local user's system. This is important because the default path is used with the file handler number given by the FileFree function to locate and open IMPORT.TXT. If the file isn't at this location, an error message will occur.

When the Click event on the Nested Data Read command button is fired, IMPORT.TXT is read row by row. Figure 10.6 show the grid control once the data has been read and loaded into the cells.

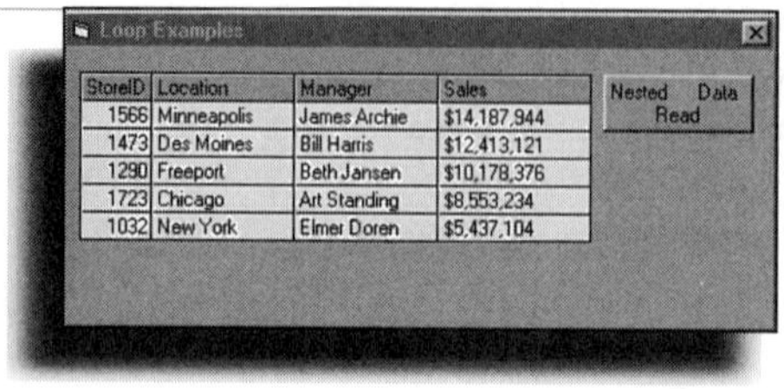

FIGURE 10.6

The nested loop reads the text file and loads the control.

Working with Arrays

Declare an array

Traverse an array with a loop

Use the ListBox and ComboBox controls

Use arrays in a sample program

What Is an Array?

A collection of similar variables, in which each has the same name and all are of the same type, is an *array*. Remember that a variable can be thought of as a cup that holds an unknown value or an always changing value (see Figure 11.1).

FIGURE 11.1

A variable is a placeholder for a specific type of value.

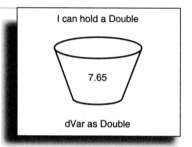

Think of an array, then, as a collection of cups. Each cup in the collection can hold the same type of data, and every cup in the collection has the same name. Each cup within the collection is an *element* and has a number assigned to it that reflects its position within the collection. The first element of an array usually has a position number of 0 (zero).

Arrays can be different sizes (see Figure 11.2). One array might have three elements, another might have 30 elements, and it's even possible for an array to have no elements at all—only the possibility of having elements that are created at a later time.

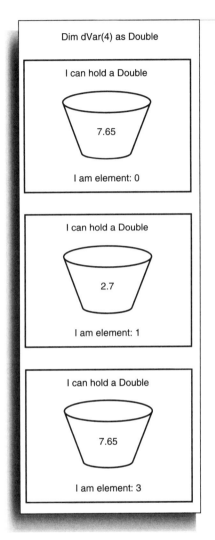

FIGURE 11.2

An array is a collection of variables.

Declaring Arrays

You can declare, or *dimension*, an array in two ways: as you would a single variable and by using the To keyword.

Declaring an Array like Declaring a Single Variable

To declare an array as you would a single variable, you use the following syntax:

```
Dim¦Public¦Private ArrayName(Subscript) As DataType
```

In this syntax,

- Dim, Public, and Private are Visual Basic keywords that declare the array and its scope. If you use Dim, the array is private to the procedure in which it is declared. Public makes the array visible from anywhere in the program, and Private (within the General section of a form or module) makes the array visible only to the form or module in which it's declared. If you use Dim within a module's procedure, the array will be available to only that procedure, but if you use Dim in the module's Declarations section, the array will be available to all procedures within the module.

- ArrayName is the name of the array.

- Subscript is the number of the highest element in the array. Remember that the first element in an array is usually zero, so if you declare an array in which Subscript is 6, you'll have seven element positions and, therefore, seven elements.

- As is the Visual Basic keyword that signifies a type declaration.

- DataType is any valid Visual Basic data type, such as Integer or Double.

Therefore, to declare an array of integers with five elements in it, you would use the following:

```
Dim iMyArray(4) As Integer
```

To assign a value to each element in the array iMyArray, you would use the following:

```
iMyArray(0) = 9
iMyArray(1) = 342
iMyArray(2) = 2746
iMyArray(3) = 0
iMyArray(4) = 8901
```

Option base

When you declare an array, the first element of the array is usually 0 (zero). It's possible, however, to force the first element of an array to be 1. To do this, insert the statement **Option Base 1** in the General section of a module within your project. You have to do this only when you want the first element of your array to be element number 1.

To change the value of the fourth element of the array `iMyArray` from 0 (zero) to 45, you would do as follows:

```
iMyArray(3) = 45
```

To declare an array of nine strings global to your entire program, you would use the code in Listing 11.1.

LISTING 11.1   **11LIST01.TXT–Assigning Values to an Array's Elements**

```
01 Public strMyArray(8) As String
02
03 strMyArray(0) = "I am a pitcher."
04 strMyArray(1) = "I am a catcher."
05 strMyArray(2) = "I play first base."
06 strMyArray(3) = "I play second base."
07 strMyArray(4) = "I play third base."
08 strMyArray(5) = "I play shortstop."
09 strMyArray(6) = "I play left field."
10 strMyArray(7) = "I play center field."
11 strMyArray(8) = "I play right field."
```

Declaring an Array with the *To* Keyword

You can also declare an array by using the `To` keyword within the subscript syntax. For example, if you want to create an array of five `Integer` variables in which the first element is number 1 and the last element is number 5, you use

```
Dim iMyArray(1 To 5) as Integer
```

This method provides an easy way to start your element numbering at a value other than 0 (zero).

Changing the Number of Elements in an Array

Although you usually set the number of elements in an array when you declare it, it's possible to alter the size of the array. When you change the number of elements in an existing array, you *redimension* it. To do so, use the ReDim keyword in the following syntax:

```
ReDim [Preserve] ArrayName(Subscript) As DataType
```

In this syntax,

- ReDim is the Visual Basic keyword denoting that the array is being redimensioned.

- Preserve is an optional Visual Basic keyword that forces all pre-existing elements in the array to hold their values. If you don't use the Preserve keyword when you redimension the array, the value of all elements will be changed to zero for numeric data types, and a zero-length string ("") for variable-length strings. Fixed-length strings will be filled with zeros, and variants will be initialized to EMPTY, which could be either zero or a zero-length string, depending on the expression.

- ArrayName is the name of the array.

- Subscript is the subscript for the highest element in the array.

- As is the Visual Basic keyword that signifies a type declaration. When redimensioning an array, the As keyword is optional.

- DataType is any valid Visual Basic data type, such as Integer or Double. When redimensioning an array, the DataType is optional and can't be changed with the Redim keyword unless the array is of type Variant.

Using ReDim in your code

The actual implementation of the ReDim statement is different from this conceptual illustration. If you create an array that you'll later redimension, you can't hard code the element size of the array when you first declare it. Therefore, in practice, the code here won't redimension the array declared in Listing 11.1.

The following code shows how, conceptually, to redimension the array strMyArray (from Listing 11.1) to contain 10 elements:

```
ReDim Preserve strMyArray(9)
strMyArray(9) = "I am the designated hitter."
```

To create an array that you'll later resize, you must first create the array without any elements. Listing 11.2 shows the proper way to create an array that you'll later redimension.

LISTING 11.2   **11LIST02.TXT—*Dim*ing an Array Without Any Elements Before *ReDim*ing It**

```
01 'Create an array without any elements
02 Dim strMyArray() as String
03
04 'Dimension the array for 9 elements
05 ReDim strMyArray(8)
06
07 'Assign values to the array elements
08 strMyArray(0) = "I am a pitcher."
09 strMyArray(1) = "I am a catcher."
10 strMyArray(2) = "I play first base."
11 strMyArray(3) = "I play second base."
12 strMyArray(4) = "I play third base."
13 strMyArray(5) = "I play shortstop."
14 strMyArray(6) = "I play left field."
15 strMyArray(7) = "I play center field."
16 strMyArray(8) = "I play right field."
17
18 'Add an element and make it so all the values
19 'of the previous elements are kept intact
20 ReDim Preserve strMyArray(9)
21
22 'Assign a value to the new array element
23 strMyArray(9) = "I am the designated hitter."
```

Notice in Listing 11.2 that the first ReDim statement (line 5) doesn't use the Preserve keyword. You can do this because initially there are no values within the array to preserve. In the second ReDim statement on line 20, however, the Preserve keyword is very important because the pre-existing elements have assigned values that you don't want to lose. If you didn't use the Preserve keyword in the second ReDim statement, strMyArray would have the following values:

```
strMyArray (0) = ""
strMyArray (1) = ""
strMyArray (2) = ""
strMyArray (3) = ""
strMyArray (4) = ""
strMyArray (5) = ""
strMyArray (6) = ""
```

```
strMyArray (7) = ""
strMyArray (8) = ""
strMyArray (9) = "I am the designated hitter."
```

Remember, arrays are tricky. Be careful!

Multidimensional Arrays

So far, the arrays in this chapter have been *one-dimensional arrays*—that is, they are a one-row collection of variables, as seen in Figure 11.2. In Visual Basic, however, you can create arrays that have up to 60 dimensions. Usually, two-dimensional arrays will suffice for most introductory programming projects, and most likely you won't need to make an array of more than three dimensions.

Think of a two-dimensional array as a tic-tac-toe board—a set of columns and rows that intersect to form a grid. Each grid cell has a location defined as *ColumnNumber*, *RowNumber*. Figure 11.3 is a conceptual illustration of iVar(2,4), a two-dimensional array of integers. Notice that each element is defined by the coordinates of the column position and the row position. For example, the array element iVar(0, 0) is 5 and the element iVar(2,2) is 49.

To create a two-dimensional array, use the following syntax:

```
Dim¦Public¦Private ArrayName(SubscriptOfCols, _
                        SubscriptOfRows) As DataType
```

In this syntax,

- Dim, Public, and Private are Visual Basic keywords that declare the array and its scope. If you use Dim, the array is private to the procedure in which it's declared. Public makes the array visible from anywhere in the program, and Private (within a form or module's General section) makes the array visible only to the form or module in which it's declared. Using Dim within a module automatically makes the array available anywhere in the program, as if the Public keyword were used.

- *ArrayName* is the name of the array.

- *SubscriptOfCols* is the number of the highest column in the array.
- *SubscriptOfRows* is the number of the highest row in the array.
- As is the Visual Basic keyword that denotes type declaration.
- *DataType* is any valid Visual Basic data type.

FIGURE 11.3

Think of a two-dimensional array as a collection of cups arranged in columns and rows.

Therefore, to declare the array shown in Figure 11.3, you would use the following syntax:

```
Dim iVar(2,4) as Integer
```

Whereas you can consider a two-dimensional array to be a rectangle, you can consider a three-dimensional array to be a rectangular block. To declare a three-dimensional array of integers, use

```
Dim iVar(1,2,1) as Integer
```

Figure 11.4 is a conceptual illustration of the three-dimensional array defined in the preceding line.

FIGURE 11.4

A three-dimensional array (1,2,1) has 12 elements. It's two columns wide by three rows tall by two planes deep.

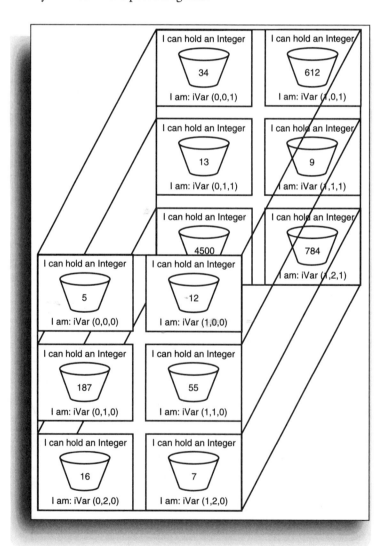

In the array iVar, the value assigned to each element, as depicted in Figure 11.4, is as follows:

```
iVar(0,0,0) = 5
iVar(0,1,0) = 187
iVar(0,2,0) = 16
iVar(1,0,0) = 12
iVar(1,1,0) = 55
iVar(1,2,0) = 7
iVar(0,0,1) = 34
iVar(0,1,1) = 13
iVar(0,2,1) = 4500
iVar(1,0,1) = 612
iVar(1,1,1) = 9
iVar(1,2,1) = 784
```

Just as with a one-dimensional array, you can use the To keyword when declaring the subscript range of each dimension in a multi-dimensional array. Thus, the line

```
Dim dMyArray(1 To 5,  3 To 8,  3 To 5) As Double
```

would declare a three-dimensional array of Double values, five columns wide by six rows tall by three planes deep.

You can also use the Redim keyword to resize a multidimensional array. If you use the Preserve keyword, however, only the last dimension of a multidimensional array can be resized, and the number of dimensions can't be changed.

Using Loops to Traverse an Array

You can use the For...Next loop that you learned about in Chapter 10, "Working with Loops," to move through, or *traverse*, an array. This can be useful when you want to change or report values in an array.

Listing 11.3 is an example of using a For...Next loop to traverse an array. The listing is the event procedure for a button click, in which an array of 20 elements is created. A For...Next loop is used twice—first to assign values to every element in the array, and then to find the value assigned to every element and make a string that reports the value of that element (see Figure 11.5).

LISTING 11.3   11LIST03.TXT—Using *For...Next* Loops to Traverse an Array

```
01 Private Sub cmdTraverse_Click()
02    Dim i%
03    Dim iMyArray%(19) As Integer
04    Dim BeginMsg$
05    Dim MidMsg$
06    Dim LoopMsg$
07    Dim FullMsg$
08
09    'Assign a value to each element in the array
10    'by using a loop to traverse to each element
11    'in the array.
12    For i% = 0 To 19
13       'Make the value of the element to be
14       'twice the value of i%
15       iMyArray%(i%) = i% * 2
16    Next i%
17
18    'Create the BeginMsg$ string
19    BeginMsg$ = "The element is: "
20    MidMsg$ = ", The value is: "
21    'Go through the array again and make
22    'a string to display
23    For i% = 0 To 19
24       LoopMsg$ = LoopMsg$ & BeginMsg$ & CStr(i%)
25       LoopMsg$ = LoopMsg$ & MidMsg$ & iMyArray(i%)
26
27       'Concatenate the loop message to the
28       'full message. Also add a line break
29       FullMsg$ = FullMsg$ & LoopMsg$ & vbCrLf
30
31       'Clean out the loop message so that
32       'new value next time through the loop
33       LoopMsg$ = ""
34    Next i%
35
36    txtTraverse.Text = FullMsg$
37 End Sub
```

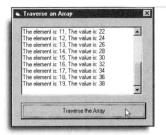

FIGURE 11.5

This program sets the value of each array element to twice its element number.

The code in Listing 11.3 is simple. Remember that a `For...Next` loop increments a counting variable as it loops. You assign this counting variable to the element position of the array. Then, set the lower bound of the array (the lowest element number) to the start point of the loop and set the upper bound of the array (the highest element number) to the end point of the loop. When you run the loop, the counting variable will always be at an element of the array.

Adding Items to ListBoxes and ComboBoxes

Of all the standard controls, the ListBox and ComboBox are best suited for categorizing and listing information from which users can make choices and selections. These controls are closely related, and the manner in which you manipulate them is almost identical. The difference is that the ComboBox combines a ListBox control with a TextBox (hence the name) and allows users to select from a list or type a new value.

Both the ListBox and ComboBox controls can handle lists. In Visual Basic, a *list* is an array of strings formally referred to with the `List` property. (The `List` property is common to the ListBox and ComboBox controls.) Most work that you do with ListBoxes and ComboBoxes involves adding and removing strings from the `List` property. You can add strings to the `List` property of a ListBox or ComboBox at design time or runtime.

Add strings to a ListBox or ComboBox at design time

1. Add a ListBox or a ComboBox control to the form.

2. Select this control on the form.

3. In the Properties window, select the **List** property (see Figure 11.6) and type the strings for the List property in the drop-down box. To add multiple lines to the List property, press Ctrl+Enter to add a new line to it (see Figure 11.7).

At design time, the strings you added to the List property will appear in the ListBox on the form (see Figure 11.8).

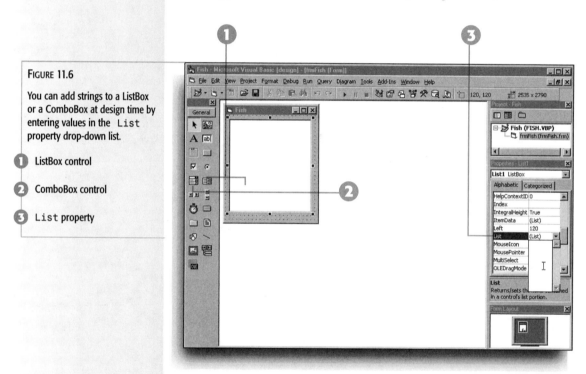

FIGURE 11.6

You can add strings to a ListBox or a ComboBox at design time by entering values in the List property drop-down list.

1 ListBox control

2 ComboBox control

3 List property

FIGURE 11.7
To add multiple items to a ListBox list at design time, press Ctrl+Enter.

FIGURE 11.8
You can view a ListBox's list at design time.

This design-time method for populating the List property is useful when your program starts up. Because the contents of a ListBox or ComboBox can change frequently while your program is running, however, you need to be able to add and remove items to and from the List property while it's running. To do this, the ListBox and CombBox controls make extensive use of the AddItem, RemoveItem, and Clear methods.

To add a string to the List of a Listbox or ComboBox during runtime, use the AddItem method, which has the following syntax:

Object.AddItem *StringToAdd*

In this syntax,

- *Object* is the Name property of the ListBox or ComboBox.
- AddItem is the Visual Basic keyword for the method.
- *StringToAdd* is the string that you want to add to the control's list.

Using methods

Remember that you can't assign a value to a method; you can only pass a value to a method. Therefore, the following statement will cause an error:
`MyList.AddItem = "Apples"`. Instead, use the `AddItem` method as follows:
`MyList.AddItem "Apples"`.

Listing 11.4 shows you how to use the `AddItem` method in a form's `Load` event procedure to add strings to the `List` of a ListBox. Figure 11.9 shows the result of the form's `Load` event.

LISTING 11.4   **11LIST04.TXT—Using the *AddItem* Method to Add Items to a ListBox Control**

```
01 Private Sub Form_Load()
02     lstHero.AddItem "Superman"
03     lstHero.AddItem "Batman"
04     lstHero.AddItem "Green Lantern"
05     lstHero.AddItem "Aquaman"
06     lstHero.AddItem "SpiderMan"
07     lstHero.AddItem "Daredevil"
08     lstHero.AddItem "Hulk"
09 End Sub
```

FIGURE 11.9

You can use the `AddItem` method in a form's `Load` event to initialize the `List` property of a ListBox control.

Selecting Items from a List

Understanding lists

This section is important! Take time to study it so that you have a good sense of what's happening. You might also want to study the documentation that comes with your copy of Visual Basic.

To understand how Visual Basic determines the value of a string selected in the `List` of a ListBox or ComboBox, you need to understand that a `List` is an array of strings. As you learned earlier in this chapter, an array is declared as follows:

```
Dim ArrayName(Subscript) As DataType
```

Therefore, if you declared a four-element array as `MyArray(3)`, you would list the elements in that array as follows:

```
MyArray(0)
MyArray(1)
MyArray(2)
MyArray(3)
```

If you want to determine the value assigned to the second element, you could use the following statement (remember, by default the first element is `MyArray(0)`):

```
MyValue = MyArray(1)
```

The ListBox and ComboBox controls use a similar format. The property `List` is the general term that Visual Basic uses to refer to the entire array of strings within a ListBox or ComboBox. Therefore, to find the value of the second string in the ListBox called `lstHero` (from Listing 11.4), you would use the following statement:

```
SecondString$ = lstHero.List(1)
```

The value of `SecondString$` is "`Batman`".

For a ListBox or ComboBox, the selected item in a list is contained in the `ListIndex` property. When you select a string in a ListBox, Visual Basic assigns the position number of that string to the `ListIndex` property of the control. Therefore, to determine the value of the selected string in `lstHero` (from Listing 11.4), you would use the following code:

```
Private Sub lstHero_Click()
    lblHero.Caption = lstHero.List(lstHero.ListIndex)
End Sub
```

This is the event procedure for the `Click` event of the `lstHero` ListBox control. When the user clicks a string in the ListBox, the code executes and reports back the value of the selection within the `Caption` property of the Label named `lblHero`. Figure 11.10 shows what happens when the user selects a string.

FIGURE 11.10

You can program the `Click`, `MouseUp`, or `MouseDown` events of a ListBox to find the value of a user's selection.

A faster way to find out the value of the string a user selects in a ListBox or ComboBox is to use the Text property. For example, you can use the following for a ListBox:

```
Dim strMyStr as String
strMyStr = List1.Text
```

For a ComboBox, use the following:

```
Dim strMyStr as String
strMyStr = Combo1.Text
```

Removing Items from a List

You remove a string from a list in a ListBox or ComboBox by using the RemoveItem method:

```
Object.RemoveItem Index
```

In this syntax

- *Object* is the Name property of the ListBox or ComboBox.

- RemoveItem is the Visual Basic keyword for the method used to remove items from a list.

- *Index* is the position in the List property of the string that you want to remove from the control. To remove a selected item from a list, use the ListIndex property of the control.

Figure 11.11 shows an enhancement to the program presented in Figure 11.10. A button has been added to remove the string that the user selects from the ListBox. Listing 11.5 shows the RemoveItem method used in code.

LISTING 11.5   **11LIST05.TXT—Using the *RemoveItem* Method to Remove a String from a ListBox**

```
01 Private Sub cmdRemove_Click()
02    lstHero.RemoveItem (lstHero.ListIndex)
03    lblHero.Caption = ""
04 End Sub
```

When you remove an item from a ListBox or ComboBox, make sure that you clear the text from the `Caption` property of the Label control `lblHero`, as shown in line 3 of Listing 11.5. If you don't do this, the user will remove the string from the ListBox, but it will remain in the Label control.

FIGURE 11.11

A CommandButton provides a way for the user to remove an item from a list.

Clearing a List

If you want to remove all the strings contained in a ListBox or ComboBox, use the `Clear` method:

```
Object.Clear
```

In this syntax

- *Object* is the `Name` property of the ListBox or ComboBox.
- `Clear` is the Visual Basic keyword for the method that removes all items from a list.

Thus, one line of code can be used to clear all the strings in the ListBox of the program shown in Figure 11.11:

```
lstHero.Clear
```

Understanding ComboBox Styles

The ListBox and ComboBox controls have much in common, but each has a distinct use. A ListBox takes up more room than a ComboBox, and when using a ListBox, you can't select or input unlisted data. A ComboBox offers more flexibility and uses a form's space more efficiently.

A ComboBox's style property enables you to change the operational characteristics and appearance of the control. Table 11.1 describes these styles, and Figure 11.12 shows the ComboBox styles applied to a form. You can also download this code from http://www.mcp.com/info. You will be asked for an ISBN. Enter 078971633x and click the **Search** button to go to the *Using Visual Basic 6* page.

Using a simple combo ComboBox

When you first add a ComboBox with the 1 - Simple Combo style to a form, the ComboBox is sized so that none of the ListBox is displayed. Increase the **Height** property to display more of the ListBox.

TABLE 11.1   Values for the ComboBox *Style* Property

Setting	Description
0 - Drop-down Combo	A drop-down list. However, users can also enter new data to the ComboBox by inputting text directly into the TextBox portion of the ComboBox.
1 - Simple Combo	A combination of a TextBox and a ListBox that doesn't drop down. Users can select data from the ListBox or type new data into the TextBox. The size of a simple ComboBox includes both edit and list portions.
2 - Drop-down List	A read-only drop-down list from which users can only select data. Users can't enter data into the control.

FIGURE 11.12

Notice that with a drop-down ComboBox style, you can add new data to the control at runtime.

1 Drop-down combo. You can enter data not on the list.

2 Simple combo. A combination ListBox and TextBox.

3 Drop-down list combo. You can only select data.

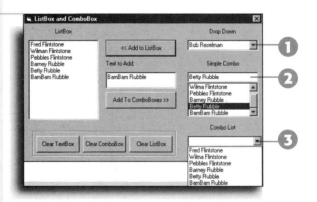

The most common ComboBox styles are `0` - `Drop-down Combo` and `2` - `Drop-down List`. As mentioned earlier, you use a drop-down ComboBox style when you want to let users add new data that's not in the ComboBox's list. You use the drop-down list style when you want users to choose from data that's only in the drop-down list of the ComboBox.

Using Arrays, ComboBoxes, and ListBoxes in a Sample Program

The Baseball ScoreKeeper program uses many things you've just learned. It uses arrays to keep track of each inning's score throughout the game and uses `For...Next` loops to traverse arrays to set and get particular values of an array's elements. It also uses arrays with a ListBox to present a team's roster and to display which player is now at bat.

To use the program, users pick the team now at bat by clicking the appropriate OptionButton at the left of the form. Then users can select the current player from a ListBox that lists the players on the team. At the end of an inning, users enter the inning number and the number of runs scored into two TextBoxes at the bottom of the form. Then users click the Add Runs button to display the runs scored during the inning and the total score in the appropriate scoreboard and total score Label controls (see Figure 11.13).

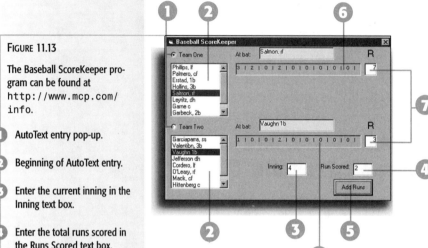

FIGURE 11.13

The Baseball ScoreKeeper program can be found at
`http://www.mcp.com/
info`.

1   AutoText entry pop-up.

2   Beginning of AutoText entry.

3   Enter the current inning in the
Inning text box.

4   Enter the total runs scored in
the Runs Scored text box.

5   Click the Add Runs button.

6   The score appears in the
Scoreboard.

7   The total runs show up in the
Total Runs Label control.

Examining ScoreKeeper's Event Procedures

The bulk of the work in the Baseball ScoreKeeper program takes
place within the code of two event procedures, Form_Load() and
cmdAddRun_Click().

How the *Form_Load()* procedure initializes the program

1. It declares local variables for scorekeeping and the scoreboard string and declares one array for each team's roster.
Finally, it redimensions the two global scorekeeping arrays
(these are declared in the module modBaseBall, one for each
team) to nine elements. The elements of these arrays will
hold the score for each inning.

2. It uses a For...Next loop to traverse each element in the
Team One scorekeeping array, gTeamOneInnings(). Within
each iteration of the loop, it takes the value in each element
and adds it to the variable TotalScore%, which holds the total
score for all the innings. Then Form_Load converts the value
in each element to a character by using the CStr() function

and combines this converted character with the ¦ character to form a larger scorekeeping string variable, InningString$ (you'll learn more about this in Chapter 12, "Working with Strings and Typecasting"). Next, the value of the InningString$ variable is assigned to the Caption property of the Scoreboard label, and the value of the TotalScore% variable is assigned to the Caption property of the total runs Label. Finally, the InningString$ variable is reset, and this step is repeated for Team Two.

3. It redimensions the team roster arrays for both teams to have nine elements. Then it adds the names and playing positions of each player to the element that corresponds to the player's position in the batting order.

4. It uses a For...Next loop with the AddItem method of each team's ListBox to traverse the roster arrays of each team and add the value of each element in the array (player name and playing position) to the respective ListBox.

Listing 11.6 shows these steps within the code of the Form_Load() event procedure.

LISTING 11.6   11LIST.06.TXT—Initializing the Main Form of the Baseball Scorekeeper Application with the *Form_Load()* Event Procedure

```
01 Private Sub Form_Load()
02 '====================STEP ONE====================
03 Dim i% 'Counter variable
04 Dim TotalScore%
05 Dim InningsString$ 'String to display score for inning
06 Dim TeamOneRoster$() 'Array to hold players' names
07 Dim TeamTwoRoster$() 'Array to hold players' names
08 'Redimension the global score arrays
09 'DEFAULT_INNINGS is a constant declared in the module,
10 'modBaseBall
11 ReDim gTeamOneInnings(DEFAULT_INNINGS - 1)
12 ReDim gTeamTwoInnings(DEFAULT_INNINGS - 1)
13
14 '====================STEP TWO====================
15 'Initialize the default score for Team One
16
```

continues...

LISTING 11.6 Continued

```
17  TotalScore% = 0
18  For i% = 0 To DEFAULT_INNINGS - 1
19
20      InningsString$ = InningsString$ _
                & CStr(gTeamOneInnings(i%)) & " ¦ "
21  Next i%
22
23  'Display the concatenated string in the score label
24  lblTeamOne.Caption = InningsString$
25  'Display the total score for Team One
26  lblTeamOneScore.Caption = CStr(TotalScore%)
27
28  'Clean out score string for new trip through
29  'Team Two's score
30  InningsString$ = ""
31
32  'Initialize the default score for Team Two
33  For i% = 0 To DEFAULT_INNINGS - 1
34  InningsString$ = InningsString$ _
                & CStr(gTeamTwoInnings(i%)) & " ¦ "
35  Next i%
36  'Display the concatenated string in the score label
37  lblTeamTwo.Caption = InningsString$
38  'Display the total score for Team Two
39  lblTeamTwoScore.Caption = CStr(TotalScore%)
40  '====================STEP THREE====================
41  'Make room in the roster arrays for 9 players
42  ReDim TeamOneRoster$(8) 'Array elements begin at zero
43  ReDim TeamTwoRoster$(8)
44
45  'Add the players for Team One to the roster array
46  TeamOneRoster$(0) = "Phillips, lf"
47  TeamOneRoster$(1) = "Palmero, cf"
48  TeamOneRoster$(2) = "Erstad, 1b"
49  TeamOneRoster$(3) = "Hollins, 3b"
50  TeamOneRoster$(4) = "Salmon, rf"
51  TeamOneRoster$(5) = "Leyritz, dh"
52  TeamOneRoster$(6) = "Garne, c"
53  TeamOneRoster$(7) = "Gerbeck, 2b"
54  TeamOneRoster$(8) = "DiScensa, ss"
55
```

```
56   'Add the players for Team Two to the roster array
57   TeamTwoRoster$(0) = "Garciaparra, ss"
58   TeamTwoRoster$(1) = "Valentibn, 3b"
59   TeamTwoRoster$(2) = "Vaughn, 1b"
60   TeamTwoRoster$(3) = "Jefferson, dh"
61   TeamTwoRoster$(4) = "Cordero, lf"
62   TeamTwoRoster$(5) = "O'Leary, rf"
63   TeamTwoRoster$(6) = "Mack, cf"
64   TeamTwoRoster$(7) = "Hittenberg, c"
65   TeamTwoRoster$(8) = "Frey, 2b"
66
67   '====================STEP FOUR====================
68   'Traverse the roster arrays and add the contents
69   'the the roster listboxes.
70   For i% = 0 To 8
71       lstTeamOne.AddItem (TeamOneRoster(i%))
72       lstTeamTwo.AddItem (TeamTwoRoster(i%))
73   Next i%
74
75   End Sub
```

The cmdAddRun_Click() event procedure is the code that adds the runs scored in a given inning to the Scoreboard when the user clicks the Add Runs button.

How the *cmdAddRun_Click()* procedure works

1. It creates variables that reflect the current inning and current score. It also creates a counter variable and variables that hold the total score and the scoreboard string.

2. It takes the text entered in the Inning TextBox, inspects it to make sure that it's a number by using the IsNumeric() function, and makes sure that the user didn't enter a number higher than the number of innings in the game so far. If this value is acceptable, the procedure assigns it to the current inning variable, CurrentInning%. cmdAddRun_Click() does the same sort of IsNumeric() check on the text in the Runs Scored TextBox, txtRuns. If this is acceptable, the procedure assigns it to the current score variable, CurrentScore%.

3. The procedure checks the value of the OptionButton for Team One. If the OptionButton is selected, its value will be

Using *IsNumeric()*

IsNumeric() is a Visual Basic function that checks a string number to see whether it looks like a number. If the string looks like a number, IsNumeric() returns True; otherwise, it returns False. IsNumeric() is often used to validate user input.

True and the value in the current score variable, CurrentScore%, will be assigned to an element in gTeamOneInnings(), the global array that holds the values for Team One's per-inning score. The current score is assigned to the element position that's one less than the value of the current inning variable, CurrentInning%. This is because the first element in the gTeamOneInnings array is zero. If the value of the OptionButton for Team One is False, the OptionButton for Team Two must have been selected and this step should be done in terms of Team Two.

4. It traverses the global arrays that hold the value of every inning's score for each team to determine the total runs scored for each team. Then the procedure constructs the scoreboard string and assigns the results to the appropriate controls. (This is an exact repeat of the work done in the fourth step of the Form_Load() event procedure.)

Listing 11.7 shows the event procedure for the cmdAddRuns_Click event.

LISTING 11.7 11LIST07.TXT—Determining the Team and Inning to Which the Scored Runs Apply

```
01 Private Sub cmdAddRun_Click()
02     '====================STEP ONE====================
03     Dim CurrentInning%
04     Dim CurrentScore%
05     Dim i%
06     Dim TotalScore%
07     Dim InningsString$
08
09     '====================STEP TWO====================
10     'Convert the text in the txtInning to an Integer if
11     'indeed the text looks like a number
12     If IsNumeric(txtInning.Text) Then
13         CurrentInning% = CInt(txtInning.Text)
14     Else
15         CurrentInning% = 1
16     End If
17
18     'Make sure the inning number is not more than 9
```

```
19    If CurrentInning% > DEFAULT_INNINGS Then
20        CurrentInning% = DEFAULT_INNINGS
21    End If
22
23    'Convert the text in the txtRuns to an Integer if
24    'indeed the text looks like a number
25    If IsNumeric(txtRuns.Text) Then
26        CurrentScore% = CInt(txtRuns.Text)
27    Else
28        CurrentScore% = 0
29    End If
30    '=====================STEP THREE===================
31    'Set the score to the designated inning for the team
32    'identified by the check option box.
33 If opTeamOne.Value = True Then
34    gTeamOneInnings(CurrentInning% - 1) = CurrentScore%
35  Else
36   'If TeamOne.Value is not true, then TeamTwo.Value must
37   'be True. It's a logic thing!
38    gTeamTwoInnings(CurrentInning% - 1) = CurrentScore%
39 End If
40
41    'Set the new score for Team One
42    For i% = 0 To DEFAULT_INNINGS - 1
43        TotalScore% = TotalScore% + gTeamOneInnings(i%)
44        InningsString$ = InningsString$ _
                & CStr(gTeamOneInnings(i%)) & " ¦ "
45    Next i%
46    '=====================STEP FOUR===================
47    'Display the concatenated string in the score label
48    lblTeamOne.Caption = InningsString$
49    'Display the total score for Team One
50    lblTeamOneScore.Caption = CStr(TotalScore%)
51
52    'Clean out score string for new trip through
53    'Team Two's score
54    InningsString$ = ""
55    'Clean out the total score integer variable
56    TotalScore% = 0
57
58    'Set the new score for Team Two
59    For i% = 0 To DEFAULT_INNINGS - 1
```

continues...

LISTING 11.7   Continued

```
60       TotalScore% = TotalScore% + gTeamTwoInnings(i%)
61       InningsString$ = InningsString$ _
            & CStr(gTeamTwoInnings(i%)) & " ¦ "
62   Next i%
63
64   'Display the concatenated string in the score label
65   lblTeamTwo.Caption = InningsString$
66   'Display the total score for Team One
67   lblTeamTwoScore.Caption = CStr(TotalScore%)
68
69 End Sub
```

The last thing that the program does is report who is at bat. This occurs in the Click event of the ListBox for each team's roster whenever the user selects a player. Listing 11.8 shows the code for Team One's ListBox Click event procedure. This code uses the List and ListIndex properties that you learned about in the section "Selecting Items from a List."

LISTING 11.8   11LIST08.TXT—Code for the *lstTeamOne_Click* Procedure

```
01 Private Sub lstTeamOne_Click()
02    'Have the name that the user clicks appear in the
03    'at bat label
04    lblTeamOneAtBat.Caption = lstTeamOne.List(lstTeamOne.ListIndex)
05 End Sub
```

The only difference between the lstTeamOne_Click and lstTeamTwo_Click event procedures is that the first references the Team One at bat Label and ListBox, and the other references the Team Two at bat Label and ListBox.

Some potential problems still exist:

- What happens if the user enters a letter character such as "a" in the Runs Scored or Inning text box? You need to provide an error check on these text boxes, possibly using the IsNumeric() function.

- What if a game goes into extra innings? You need to Redim

the scorekeeping arrays.

■ How do you remind users to change the player at bat if they forget, and what happens if users forget to change the team at bat? You might set a variable that tracks the most recently accessed player or team and provide a message box if this variable matches the new player or team when the Add Runs button is clicked.

You can easily solve these and other problems; for the most part, you possess the tools you need to address them. All that's required is a little thought and some experimentation.

Working with Strings and Typecasting

Learn how to parse and manipulate strings

See how to use the new Visual Basic string array functions

Learn how to validate user input

Learn how Visual Basic typecasts and converts variables

Manipulating Strings

Visual Basic 6's string functions

Visual Basic 6 comes with a lot of new string functions, many of them vast functional enhancements to the native language. Seasoned VB programmers can now replace entire custom functions in their programs with a single line of code. Because of VB6's numerous new string functions, expect to refer to this chapter several times before you uncover all that can be accomplished with these new functions.

The first task when working with strings is to be able to locate parts of a string and then rearrange them as required.

Reversing the Order of Characters in Strings

Visual Basic's new StrReverse() function enables you to completely reverse the order of a string. Its syntax is as follows:

```
strResult = StrReverse(strMyString)
```

In this syntax,

- *strResult* is the string returned from the function.

- StrReverse is the function name.

- *strMyString* is the string to be reversed.

The TextBoxes shown in Figure 12.1 were initialized during the form's load event. Notice that line 3 of the following code is an empty string of length zero. It's important to distinguish this from a null string. Most databases, such as Microsoft Access and SQL Server, allow fields to be null or undefined until they're initialized. These null values will cause problems for the string functions.

```
01 Private Sub Form_Load()
02 txtMyString.Text = "It's raining cats and dogs."
03 txtResult.Text = ""
04 End Sub
```

Visual Basic defaults all internal variables to valid values—numeric variables default to zero, and strings default to empty. The problem happens when you take a null data field from a database and assign it to an internal variable or when you perform a string function on the null data field.

The sample program in Figure 12.1 uses two ways of reversing a string. Listing 12.1 shows the code required for Visual Basic 5. In this version, a loop was required to step through each character in the string and then build the new string in reverse order. The code in Listing 12.2 delivers the same result with the new StrReverse() function, with no loops and only one simple command.

LISTING 12.1   **12LIST01.TXT—A VB5** *For...Loop* **That Reverses a String by Using the** *Len()* **Function**

```
01   Private Sub OldVersion_Click()
02   Dim intLength   As Integer 'Length of the string
03   Dim intCntr     As Integer 'Loop counter
04
05   'Initialize the txtResult.Text string and then
06   ' determine the length of txtMyString.Text
07   intLength = Len(txtMyString.Text)
08   txtResult.Text = ""
09
10   'Loop through the first string one character at a time.
11   'Concatenate each character to the beginning.
12   For intCntr = 1 To intLength
13   txtResult.Text = Mid(txtMyString.Text, intCntr, 1) _
                 & txtResult.Text
14   Next intCntr
15 Refresh
16
17   End Sub
```

LISTING 12.2   **12LIST02.TXT—Using the New** *StrReverse()* **Function**

```
01   Private Sub NewVersion_Click()
02   'This new function works on strings.
03
04   txtResult.Text = StrReverse(txtMyString.Text)
05   Refresh
06
07   End Sub
```

Download this chapter's code

You can find all the code for the examples in this chapter on the Web at http://www.mcp.com/info. At the prompt, enter 078971633x (for the book's ISBN) and then click **Search** to go to the Book Info page for *Using Visual Basic 6.*

Listing 12.2's seven code lines are more for contrast than function. Only lines 4 and 5 perform any actions. Notice, however, that because a simple assignment statement could be used, the value of txtResult.Text didn't have to be initialized, further reducing the lines of code required.

Replacing Characters Within Strings

The next new function to introduce is Replace(), which can find and then replace or remove the found string within the target string. Find operations also can either consider or ignore capitalization. If you've ever used the replace feature in a word processing program, you have a good understanding of how this function works.

The syntax for the Replace() function is as follows:

```
strResult = Replace(strMyString, strFind, strRplWith, _
                     intStart, intCnt, intCompare)
```

In this syntax,

- *strResult* is the string returned from the function.
- Replace is the function name.
- *strMyString* is the string to be changed.
- *strFind* is the string to find in *strMyString*.
- *strRplWith* is the string to be used to replace *strFind*.
- *intStart* is an optional position parameter within *strMyString* at which to begin looking for *strFind*.
- *intCnt* is an optional parameter for the maximum number of times to replace *strFind* in *strMyString*.
- *intCompare* is an optional integer parameter that indicates case sensitivity for the function.

The *intCompare* argument has several settings (see Table 12.1). The first option enables the function to be driven by the global compare option, which can be set in the general declaration section of the program. This makes changing the case sensitivity for all Replace() functions in a program as simple as changing one line of code.

Replace() can return a partial string

A feature of the **Replace()** function is that it returns only the portion of the string to which the function was directed to work on. When you specify the optional parameter **intStart** with a value greater than 1, the return string won't contain the characters before the **intStart** position.

TABLE 12.1   **Options for the *intCompare* Argument**

Constant	Value	Description
`vbUseCompareOption`	-1	Performs a comparison as set in the `Option Compare` statement
`vbBinaryCompare`	0	Performs a case-sensitive comparison
`vbTextCompare`	1	Performs a comparison that is not case sensitive

The program in Figure 12.2 uses the string contained in the first TextBox as the target of a search-and-replace operation.

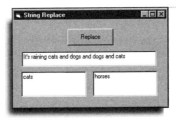

FIGURE 12.2
The word *cats* is replaced with the word *horses* in both locations in the string.

As with the example for reversing a string, the sample program in Figure 12.2 initializes the TextBox Text properties when the form is loaded. In the following code, lines 3 and 4 show the values of the *strFind* and *strRplWith* arguments, respectively.

```
01 Private Sub Form_Load()
02 txtMyString.Text = "It's raining cats and dogs" _
            & "and dogs and cats"
03 txtFind.Text = "cats"
04 txtRplWith.Text = "horses"
05 End Sub
```

When the click event is fired, the assignment statement takes the return value from the Replace() function and assigns it to the Text property of TextBox1. Line 3 in the following code uses the continuation symbol (_) to allow the statement to extend to the next line.

```
01 Private Sub cmdReplace_Click()
02 'The Replace function works on strings.
03 txtMyString.Text = Replace(txtMyString.Text, _
```

```
                      txtFind.Text, txtRplWith.Text)
04 Refresh
05 End Sub
```

When the TextBoxes are updated (see Figure 12.3) with horses as the *strFind* value and "" (the zero-length string) as the *strRplWith* value, the function will replace the found string with nothing. This is how you can use the function to remove only the found values, but notice again that both locations in the string were changed.

FIGURE 12.3

The Replace() function can also remove characters.

Replace() won't always work

It's important to be able to process the return values of the Replace() function when an error has occurred. This function can err in several ways that are important to capture in your program.

The power of Replace also offers the opportunity to create errors. Table 12.2 lists six conditions that, when you're writing programs, you need to understand and check for. Each condition identifies a return value when the function is given a certain input to work with.

TABLE 12.2   Return Values from Errors in the *Replace*() Function

When...	Replace() Returns...
strMyString is zero length	A zero-length string of ""
strMyString is null	An error
strFind is zero length	A copy of *strMyString*
strRplWith is zero length	A copy of *strMyString* with all occurrences of *strFind* removed
intStart > Len(*strMyString*)	A zero-length string of ""
intCnt is 0	A copy of *strMyString*

When the value of *strFind* or *strRplWith* is a zero-length string, an unwanted result might occur that you can trap with a simple If...Then statement around the function. The following code and Figure 12.4 show how the function on line 3 of the preceding example could be changed to check for this condition. This would be important if you wanted to prevent any replacement of characters when the *strFind* or *strRplWith* string is empty.

```
01 Private Sub cmdReplace_Click()
02 'Test for Empty String; then Replace the strings.
03 If txtFind.Text = "" Or txtRplWith = "" Then
04     MsgBox "You Found the Error", vbExclamation, _
         " Empty String data error"
05 Else
06     txtMyString.Text = Replace(txtMyString.Text, _
         txtFind.Text, txtRplWith.Text)
07 End If
08 Refresh
09 End Sub
```

There are many other techniques for finding and processing errors. Chapter 21, "Debugging Your Applications," covers these more extensively.

FIGURE 12.4

The Replace() function parameters should be checked for unwanted values.

Concatenating Strings

Concatenating one string to another means combining both strings. In Visual Basic, you concatenate two strings by using the & operator. In Listing 12.3, the value of strResult will be blueberry.

More efficient code

This example helps you understand the role of variables and literals. The same result could be achieved in one line: `cmdBerry.Caption = "blue" & "berry"`.

LISTING 12.3   **12LIST03.TXT–Simple Concatenation of Two Strings**

```
01    Private Sub cmdBerry_Click()
02        Dim strMine As String
03        Dim strYours As String
04        Dim strResult As String
05
06        strMine = "blue"
07        strYours = "berry"
08        strResult = strMine & strYours
09
10        cmdBerry.Caption = strResult
11    End Sub
```

You can also concatenate more than two strings together with the & operator. For example, you might want to add a space character between a first name and last name, as shown in Listing 12.4. Figure 12.5 shows Listing 12.4's code in action.

LISTING 12.4   **12LIST04.TXT–Concatenating More Than Two Strings**

```
01    Private Sub cmdFullName_Click()
02        Dim strFirst As String
03        Dim strLast As String
04        Dim strFull As String
05
06        'Get the first name for the textbox
07        strFirst = txtFirst.Text
08
09        'Get the last name from another textbox
10        strLast = txtSecond.Text
11
12        'Concatenate the first and last name, putting
13        'a space character between them.
14        strFull = strFirst & " " & strLast
15
16        'Display the Full Name
17        lblResult.Caption = strFull
18
19    End Sub
```

FIGURE 12.5

Using the + character to concatenate strings is a holdover from
earlier versions of Visual Basic and
can produce unwanted results if
your string variables have numbers in them. See the sample
program later in the section
"Controlling Data Types with
Typecasting."

Determining a String's Length with *Len()*

You use the Visual Basic Len() function to determine how many
characters are in a given string. You'll use this function often,
particularly with the other string-manipulation functions.

The syntax of the Len() function is as follows:

intResult = Len(*strMyString*)

In this syntax,

- *intResult* is an integer that contains the number of characters returned by the function.
- Len is the name of the function.
- *strMyString* is the string, the length of which you want to
  determine.

Listing 12.5 shows how to use the Len() function. Figure 12.6
shows the result of Listing 12.5 in action.

LISTING 12.5   **12LIST05.TXT—Using the *Len()* Function**

```
01   Private Sub cmdFindLen_Click()
02       Dim strFind As String
03       Dim intLen As Integer
04
05       'Assign a string to find to the local variable
06       strFind = txtFirst.Text
07
08       'Find the length of the string
09       intLen = Len(strFind)
```

continues…

LISTING 12.5   **Continued**

```
10
11     'Report the results
12     lblResult.Caption = CStr(intLen)
13  End Sub
```

FIGURE 12.6

You can also use `Len()` to find the size (in bytes) of a nonstring variable.

Truncating Strings with *Left()* and *Right()*

You use the `Left()` and `Right()` functions to truncate strings. Informally, to *truncate* a string means to cut off part of it to make the string smaller. The `Left()` function returns a certain number of characters from the left side of a given string to a buffer string. (A *buffer string* is a holding string.)

The `Right()` function is similar to the `Left()` function, but rather than return characters from the left side of a string, `Right()` returns a given number of characters from the right side of a string.

The following is the syntax for the `Left()` and `Right()` functions:

```
strResult = Left(MyString, lNumToReturn)
strResult = Right(MyString, lNumToReturn)
```

In this syntax,

- *strResult* is the string returned from the function.
- `Left` and `Right` are the function names.
- *MyString* is the string on which you want to perform the function.
- *lNumToReturn* is a `Long` that indicates the number of characters that you want to return. The least amount of characters you can return is 1. Using 0 (zero) will produce an error.

Listing 12.6 shows how to use the Left() and Right() functions to truncate a given amount of characters from a string. Figure 12.7 shows the result of this code.

LISTING 12.6   12LIST06.TXT—Using the *Left()* and *Right()* Functions

```
01   Private Sub cmdLeft_Click()
02       Dim intChrCnt As Integer   'Number of characters
03       Dim strBuffer As String    'String buffer
04       Dim strMyString As String  'String to truncate
05
06       'Convert the numeral for the number of
07       'characters to truncate to a number
08       intChrCnt = CInt(txtSecond.Text)
09
10       'Get the string to truncate
11       strMyString = txtFirst.Text
12
13       'Truncate the string by using the Left() function
14       strBuffer = Left(strMyString, intChrCnt)
15
16       'Display the results
17       lblResult.Caption = strBuffer
18   End Sub
19
20   Private Sub cmdRight_Click()
21       Dim intChrCnt 'Number of characters to return
22       Dim strBuffer  'string buffer
23       Dim strMyString As String 'string to truncate
24
25       'Convert the numeral for the number of
26       'characters to truncate to a number
27       intChrCnt = CInt(txtSecond.Text)
28
29       'Get the string to truncate
30       strMyString = txtFirst.Text
31
32       'Truncate the string by using the Right() function
33       strBuffer = Right(strMyString, intChrCnt)
34
35       'Display the results
36       lblResult.Caption = strBuffer
37   End Sub
```

FIGURE 12.7

Left() returns a given number of characters from the left side of a string; Right() returns a given number of characters from the right side.

Using *Mid()* to Return Characters from Inside a String

The Mid() function returns a string of a given number of characters from a specified location in another string. For example, if you want to return the string "Allen" from the string "Edgar Allen Poe", you use the Mid() function.

The syntax for the Mid() function is as follows:

```
strResult = Mid(MyString, lngStart[, lngSize])
```

In this syntax,

- *strResult* is the string returned from the function.

- Mid is the function name.

- *MyString* is the string from which to extract the return string.

- *lngStart* is a value of type Long that reflects the position on which the characters to extract begin. If this number is larger than the size of *strMyString*, the return will be an empty string (""). This number can't be less than 1.

- *lngSize* is an optional value of type Long that reflects the number of characters to return from *strMyString*. If you don't specify a length, Mid() returns all the characters starting from the position determined by *lngStart* to the end of the string *strMyString*. For example, in the following code, the value of strResult is r All:

```
MyString = "Edgar Allen Poe",
strResult = Mid(MyString, 5, 5)
```

In the following example, the value of strResult is r Allen Poe:

```
MyString = "Edgar Allen Poe",
strResult = Mid(MyString, 5)
```

Listing 12.7 shows you how to use the Mid() function to extract a substring from a string.

continues…

LISTING 12.7   12LIST07.TXT—Using the *Mid()* Function

```
01  Private Sub cmdSimpleMid_Click()
02      Dim strBuffer     As String 'String Buffer
03      Dim strMyString  As String 'The string on which
04                        'to perform the Mid() function
05
06      Dim lngStart As Long    'The starting position
07                              'of the Mid()function
08
09      Dim lngSize As Long   'Size of the string to return
10
11      'Assign the text in the first textbox to the
12      'MyString variable
13      strMyString = txtFirst.Text
14
15      'Convert the numeral in the second textbox to a
16      'LONG and assign it to the starting position
17      'variable.
18      lngStart = CLng(txtSecond.Text)
19
20      'Convert the numeral in the third textbox to a
21      'LONG and assign it to the return size variable.
22      lngSize = CLng(txtThird.Text)
23
```

The space character occupies a character position

Notice in this example that the space clearly occupies position 6 and **Allen** doesn't start until position 7.

LISTING 12.7 Continued

```
24      'Run the Mid() function and assign the result to
25      'the buffer variable.
26      strBuffer = Mid(strMyString, lngStart, lngSize)
27
28      'Display the result in a textbox.
29      txtHold.Text = strBuffer
30  End Sub
```

The Mid() function is powerful. It takes some practice to get accustomed to using it. Remember the following helpful hints:

- The value of the start position variable must be at least 1.

- Characters in strings start at 1, unlike array indices, which start at 0.

- If you don't specify a return size variable for the return string, the Mid() function returns all characters from the value of the start position variable to the end of the string.

Using *InStr()* to Search for Characters Within a String

You use the InStr() function to determine whether a character or string exists within another string. If it does, the function returns a Long that reflects the position of the located string. For example, if you want to know whether a decimal character is in a string, 123.345, you use the Instr() function. The syntax for the InStr() function is

```
lngResult = InStr([intStart, ]strMyString, strFind[, intCompare])
```

In this syntax,

- *lngResult* is the returned Long value that indicates the position of the first found instance of the *strLookedFor* string in the string *strMyString*.

- InStr is the function name.

- *lngStart* is an optional number that indicates where to start looking. If you omit it, the function starts searching at the beginning of the string *strMyString*.

- *strMyString* is the string in which the function searches for the substring *strFind*.

- *strFind* is the string or character for which you're searching.

- *intCompare* is the number that indicates how to look for the string *strFind*. If you omit this argument or set it to zero, InStr() does a case-sensitive search. If you include *intCompare* with the value 1, the search won't be case sensitive.

Listing 12.8 shows you how to use the InStr() function; Figure 12.8 shows the code in action.

LISTING 12.8   12LIST08.TXT–Using the *InStr()* Function

```
01   Private Sub cmdInStr_Click()
02       Dim lngResult As Long
03       Dim strMyString As String
04       Dim strFind As String
05       Dim lngStart As Long
06
07       'Assign the value for the string in which you are
08       'going to look for your character or string.
09       strMyString = txtFirst.Text
10
11       'Get the string you want to look for from the
12       'TextBox
13       strFind = txtSecond.Text
14
15       'If the TextBox is not empty, get the starting
16       'position for the search
17       If txtThird.Text <> "" Then
18           lngStart = CLng(txtThird.Text)
19       Else
20           'If it is empty, set the starting position to
21           'the first character
22           lngStart = 1
23       End If
24       lngResult = InStr(lngStart, strMyString, strFind)
25
26       'Display the answer
27       txtHold.Text = CStr(lngResult)
28   End Sub
```

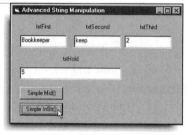

Using Strings and Arrays of Strings

One of the more time-consuming parts of working with strings
and arrays of strings is the extensive programming required to
manipulate and prepare lists. Many extensive programs have
been written to handle the tasks. The following three new functions provide easy control over any long string of words and provide for the creation of arrays from those lists.

The sample program used in this section reads a long string of
modem filenames from a text file and then demonstrates the use
of each new function. Listing 12.9 details the declarations and
the first command button that loads the list of filenames into a
public string variable; Figure 12.9 shows the initial screen.

**LISTING 12.9   12LIST09.TXT—Declarations and Load Statements for the
Filter.vbp Program**

```
01   Public strModems As String
02   Public varFull As Variant
03   Public varFilter As Variant
04
05   Public Sub Form_Load()
06     'When the form is loaded, display the current path
07     ' and the filename. Clear the two ListBoxes
08     txtDir.Text = CurDir & "\MODEM.TXT"
09     lstFull.Clear
10     lstFilter.Clear
11   End Sub
12
13   Private Sub cmdLoad_Click()
```

```
14   Dim intFile As Integer
15   ' Find the next free File handle
16   intFile = FreeFile
17     ' Open the modem file for input and then read
18     ' the first and only row into Public strModem
19     Open CurDir & "\MODEM.TXT" For Input As #intFile
20     Input #intFile, strModems
21     Close #intFile
22     'Display the String in the TextBox
23     txtList.Text = strModems
24   End Sub
```

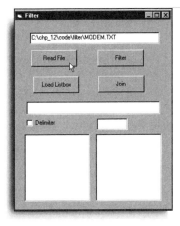

FIGURE 12.9

The Filter.vbp program starts with the Load File command, which reads a text file for a list of modem filenames.

Line 23 in Listing 12.9 displays the contents of strModems in the second TextBox on the form. This is the data used throughout the sample program and is a public string variable. The program also uses two variant-type variables to hold the array of strings for the Split() and Filter() examples.

Splitting a String into an Array of Strings with *Split()*

Visual Basic's new Split() function takes a list of words or numeric values stored in a string and breaks them into individual elements of an array of strings. In past versions of Visual Basic, this function would require several complex programming steps

Delimiters can be more than one character

Delimiters aren't limited to a single character, such as a space or a comma. Any valid string of characters can be used. The important feature to remember is that the delimiter isn't returned with the substring. If the only distinguishing separator is an important part of the word or data field, you can add the delimiter back after creating the array.

to walk through the string and build the array. The key to using this function is knowing how the string to be separated is constructed. In the case of a sentence, a space acts as the delimiter. A row from a data file can contain numbers and words separated by a comma. Either option will work with this function.

The syntax for Split() is as follows:

```
varResult = Split(strList, strDelimiter, intElemCnt, intCompare)
```

In this syntax,

- *varResult* is the variant that contains a one-dimensional array of strings returned from the function.

- Split is the function name.

- *strList* is the string list that's to be separated by the function.

- *strDelimiter* is the character or string of characters used to identify the separate elements of the string. Delimiters are used to find the end point of the current element and the starting point for the next element in the array. The delimiters are dropped and not returned with the substrings. The default value is the space character, which is the ASCII character code 32. If a zero-length string is used for the delimiter, the entire string is loaded into the first element of the array.

- *intElemCnt* is the number of string array elements to create from the *strList*.

- *intCompare* is the integer that indicates case sensitivity for the function when identifying the delimiters in the *strList*. The default value is zero, which indicates a case-sensitive search. *intCompare* uses the following values:

Constant	Value	Description
vbUseCompareOption	-1	Performs a comparison by using the setting of the Option Compare statement
vbBinaryCompare	0	Performs a binary comparison
vbTextCompare	1	Performs a textual comparison
vbDatabaseCompare	2	Performs a comparison based on information in your database (for Microsoft Access only)

Listing 12.10 shows the Split() function being used to turn a long string into a array of strings. Lines 21–23 detail the For...Loop that's used to add the elements of the array of strings to the ListBox. The lstFull ListBox contains all the values in the strModems string unless the delimited CheckBox is selected. Lines 7–14 check this condition, and if checked, the list is built with only six values from the original.

LISTING 12.10   12LIST10.TXT–String Splitting with an Optional Delimiter

```
01   Private Sub cmdList_Click()
02   Dim intRecCnt As Integer
03   Dim intCntr As Integer
04
05   'Check if the String is to be split with the default
06   'delimiter.
07   If chkDelimit.Value Then
08      'If checked, use the value in the txtFilter
09      'TextBox and limit the number of elements to 6
10      varFull = Split(strModems, txtFilter.Text, 6)
11   Else
12      'If not checked, use the default values for Split()
13      varFull = Split(strModems)
14   End If
15
16   'Determine the number of elements in the array
17   intRecCnt = UBound(varFull)
18
19   lstFull.Clear
```

continues...

LISTING 12.10 Continued

```
20   'Add Elements to ListBox for each element in array
21   For intCntr = 0 To intRecCnt _
22       lstFull.AddItem varFull(intCntr)
23   Next intCntr
24
25   Refresh
26   End Sub
```

Creating a Sublist from an Array of Strings with *Filter()*

The Filter() function builds on the power of the Split() function. When you have your list in an array of strings, the Filter() function lets you create a new list that's a filtered version of your first list. This function, like the Split() function, returns an array of strings.

The syntax for Filter() follows:

varResult = Filter(*varlist*, *strFind*, *bolInclude*, *intCompare*)

In this syntax,

- *varResult* is the variant that contains a one-dimensional string array returned from the function.
- Filter is the function name.
- *varList* is the variant that contains the string array that the function is to filter.
- *strFind* is the string of characters used to identify which elements to include in the new string array.
- *bolInclude* is the Boolean flag used to indicate whether elements containing the *strFind* value are included or excluded. By default, the elements are included.
- *intCompare* is the integer that indicates case sensitivity for the function when matching a *strFind* with the *varList* element. The default value is zero and performs a case-sensitive search.

If no matches of *strFind* are found within the string array *varList*, the function returns an empty array. If *varList* is null or isn't a one-dimensional array, an error is returned. Listing 12.11 shows the code used to select from an array with the Filter() function.

LISTING 12.11   12LIST11.TXT—Using *Filter()* to Select from an Array

```
01   Private Sub CmdFilter_Click()
02   Dim intRecCnt As Integer
03   Dim intCntr As Integer
04
05   'Create the Filtered array from the Full array
06   varFilter = Filter(varFull, txtFilter.Text)
07
08   'Determine the number of elements in the array
09   intRecCnt = UBound(varFilter)
10
11   lstFilter.Clear
12   'Add Elements to ListBox for each element in the array
13   For intCntr = 0 To intRecCnt _
14       lstFilter.AddItem varFilter(intCntr)
15   Next intCntr
16
17   Refresh
18   End Sub
```

Combining an Array of Strings with *Join()*

The new Join() function is the counterpart to the Split() function. This function combines all the elements in an array of strings into one single string. The optional delimiter enables the delineation of the separate elements on the string, which allows for enhanced processing in the future.

The syntax for Join() is as follows:

```
strResult = Join(varList, strDelimiter)
```

In this syntax,

- *strResult* is the string that contains the concatenation of the array and the delimiters returned by the function.
- Join is the function name.
- *varList* is a variant that contains a one-dimensional string array that the function will combine.
- *strDelimiter* is the character, or string of characters, that's placed between the separate elements of the array when combined into the *strResult*. The delimiter is used to mark the end point of each element and the starting point for the next element in the string. The default delimiter is the space character. If a zero-length string is used for the delimiter, the string is built without delimiters.

Line 9, or line 12, performs the join in Listing 12.12. If the delimited CheckBox has been marked, the join will use the value in the txtFilter.Text property (line 9) for the delimiter. The sample program lets you try various combinations of characters for delimiters. The resulting new string is placed in the txtListBox, which is the highlighted ListBox in Figure 12.10. Notice that in this example, two characters (**) are used as a delimiter.

LISTING 12.12   12LIST12.TXT—Putting Together an Array of Strings

```
01   Private Sub CmdJoin_Click()
02   Dim intRecCnt As Integer
03   Dim intCntr As Integer
04
05   'Check if the Join will use the default delimiter
06   If chkDelimit.Value Then
07      'If checked, use the value in the txtFilter
08      'TextBox to separate the Sub-strings
09      txtList.Text = Join(varFilter, txtFilter.Text)
10   Else
11      'If not checked, use the default values for Join()
12      txtList.Text = Join(varFilter)
13   End If
14   Refresh
15   End Sub
```

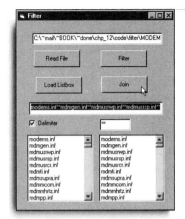

FIGURE 12.10

You can join an array of strings by using any character as the delimiter.

Changing a String's Case with *UCase()* and *LCase()*

The UCase() and LCase() functions affect the case of a given string or character. The UCase() function returns a string in which all the characters are set to uppercase, whereas the LCase() function returns a string in which all the characters are set to lowercase. The following is the syntax for the UCase() and LCase() functions:

```
strResult = UCase(strMyString)
strResult = LCase(strMyString)
```

In this syntax,

- *strResult* is the string returned from the function.
- UCase¦LCase are the function names.
- *strMyString* is the string to set to uppercase (or lowercase).

Listing 12.13 shows you how to use UCase() and LCase() to set a given string to uppercase and lowercase; Figure 12.11 shows the code example in action.

LISTING 12.13 **12LIST13.TXT—Using the *UCase()* and *LCase()* Functions**

```
01    Private Sub cmdUpper_Click()
02        Dim strBuffer As String   'string buffer
03        'Assign the characters in the first textbox
04        'to the buffer variable
05        strBuffer = txtFirst.Text
06
07        'Set all the characters in the buffer to
08        'uppercase and display the result
09        lblResult.Caption = UCase(strBuffer)
10    End Sub
11
12    Private Sub cmdLower_Click()
13        Dim strBuffer As String    'String buffer
14        'Assign the characters in the first textbox
15        'to the buffer variable
16        strBuffer = txtFirst.Text
17
18        'Set all the characters in the buffer to
19        'lowercase and display the result
20        lblResult.Caption = LCase(strBuffer)
21    End Sub
```

FIGURE 12.11

UCase() and LCase() are
closely related functions.

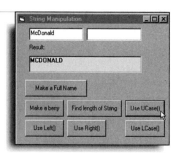

Using String-Parsing Functions

Now that you've seen how to do basic string manipulation with the Len(), Left(), Right(), Mid(), and InStr() functions, you're going to put what you've learned to more detailed use.

String parsing—the activity of stripping and manipulating strings—is a common activity among programmers. One of the most common parsing requirements that programmers encounter is retrieving the first-name string and the last-name string from a full-name string. You'll now study a set of user-defined functions that do this: GetFirstName(), which returns the first name from the full name, and GetLastName(), which returns the last name from the full name. Both functions take one argument: a string indicating the full name. These functions are designed around a central conceptual principle (and assumption) that within a full-name string, the first name is separated from the last name by a space character and that if you know the location of the space character in the full-name string, you can strip out the first-name characters and the last-name characters.

Figure 12.12 illustrates the logic of determining the first-name and last-name strings from a full-name string. In Listing 12.14, you can see the code for the functions GetFirstName() and GetLastName().

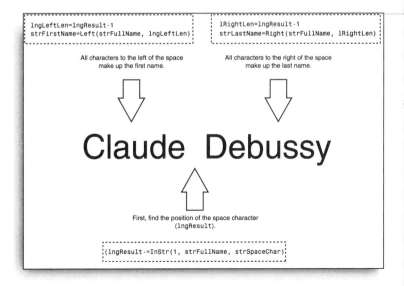

FIGURE 12.12

The most important thing that you need to know in order to parse names from a string is the position of the space characters.

LISTING 12.14 **12LIST14.TXT—Using *GetFirstName()* and *GetLastName()* to Parse Strings**

```
01  Public Function GetFirstName(strFullName As String) _
        As String

...

20      Dim lSpacePos As Long        'Position of space char
21                                   'in a string
22      Dim strSpaceChar As String   'Space character
23      Dim strFirstName As String   'Buffer for First Name
24      Dim lngResult As Long        'Result variable
25      Dim lngLeftLen As Long       'Number of characters
26                                   'Name
27
28      'Use the IsValid function to make sure that the
29      'Full Name string has only one space character in it
30      If IsValid(strFullName) = False Then
31          'If it doesn't, return the error string
32          GetFirstName = "Error"
33          'And exit the function
34          Exit Function
35      End If
36
37      'Define space character
38      strSpaceChar = " "
39
40      'Find the position of the space character within the
41      'full-name string.
42      lngResult = InStr(1, strFullName, strSpaceChar)
43
44      'The position of the space character is also
45      'the length to extract for the left side (First Name)
46      lngLeftLen = lngResult
47
48      'Extract the First Name and assign it to the
49      'First Name variable
50      strFirstName = Left(strFullName, lngLeftLen)
51
52      'Return the value of the first name
53      GetFirstName = strFirstName
54  End Function
55
56  Public Function GetLastName(strFullName As String) _
```

```
       As String
...
75     Dim lSpacePos As Long 'Position of space
76                           'character in a string
77     Dim strSpaceChar As String  'Space character
78     Dim strLastName As String   'Buffer string
79     Dim lngResult As Long       'Result variable
80     Dim lRightLen As Long 'Num of chars in Last Name
81
82     'Use the IsValid function to make sure that the
83     'Full Name string has only one space character.
84     If IsValid(strFullName) = False Then
85         'If it doesn't, return the error string
86         GetLastName = "Error"
87         'And exit the function
88         Exit Function
89     End If
90
91     'Define space character
92     strSpaceChar = " "
93
94     'Find the position of the space character
95     lngResult = InStr(1, strFullName, strSpaceChar)
96
97     'Define the number of characters to extract from
98     'the right of the space character, (Last Name).
99     'If you subtract the position of the space character
100    'for the total number of characters in the Full Name
101    'string, this will yield the number of characters to
102    'extract from the right side of the Full Name string.
103    'This technique avoids including the space character
104    'itself by accident.
105    lRightLen = Len(strFullName) - lngResult
106
107    'Extract the right side of the Full Name string and
108    'assign it to the Last Name Buffer
109    strLastName = Right(strFullName, lRightLen)
110
111    'Return the value of the Last Name string out of the
112    'function.
113        GetLastName = strLastName
114 End Function
```

You might have a full name that contains a middle name or middle initial or have a last name made up of two strings, such as Von Beethoven. In this case, the function wouldn't be valid. You build a *validation* function, IsValid(), to determine whether the string can be parsed into a first name and last name. Figure 12.13 illustrates the logic for the user-defined function IsValid(), and Listing 12.15 shows the code for the function.

FIGURE 12.13

Loops are an excellent way to traverse a string, provided you know the string's length.

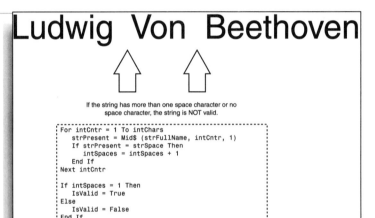

Ludwig Von Beethoven

If the string has more than one space character or no space character, the string is NOT valid.

```
For intCntr = 1 To intChars
    strPresent = Mid$ (strFullName, intCntr, 1)
    If strPresent = strSpace Then
        intSpaces = intSpaces + 1
    End If
Next intCntr

If intSpaces = 1 Then
    IsValid = True
Else
    IsValid = False
End If
```

LISTING 12.15   12LIST15.TXT—Testing to Verify Only One Space Character Per String

```
01  Public Function IsValid(strFullName) As Boolean
02  '*****************************************
03  'Sub/Function: IsValid
04  '
05  'Arguments: strFullName   A string representing a full
06  '                         name to validate
07  '
08  'Return:                  True, if the string has only 1
09  '                         character
10  '
11  'Remarks:          This function is used to
12  '                  determine if more than one
13  '                  space character exists in a string.
14  '
15  'Programmer: Bob Reselman
```

```
16  '
17  'Copyright 1998, Macmillan Publishing
18  '*****************************************
19
20      Dim intSpaces  As Integer  'Hold the count of the
21                                 'number ofspaces in a string
22      Dim intChars   As Integer  'Number of characters
23      Dim intCntr    As Integer  'Counter variable
24      Dim strSpace   As String   'The space character
25      Dim strPresent As String   'A buffer to hold one
26                                 'character to examine
27      'Define the space character
28      strSpace = " "
29
30      'Find out how many characters are in the full name
31      intChars = Len(strFullName)
32
33      'Loop through the entire string, strFullName
34      For intCntr = 1 To intChars
35          'Look at each character one at a time
36          strPresent = Mid$(strFullName, intCntr, 1)
37          'If the character that you are inspecting is a
38          'space....
39           If strPresent = strSpace Then
40              '...Increment the space counter variable by 1
41              intSpaces = intSpaces + 1
42          End If
43      Next intCntr
44
45      'If there is only one space in the Full Name string...
46      If intSpaces = 1 Then
47          '...return True
48          IsValid = True
49      Else
50          'If not, return False
51          IsValid = False
52      End If
53  End Function
```

If you want to see this code in action, go to the project AdvncStr.VBP, which you can download from http:// www.mcp.com/info. When you run the code, you'll see buttons for the GetFirstName() and GetLastName() functions, as well as one to test the IsValid() function. Enter a full name in the txtHold TextBox and then click the buttons to see the results.

Controlling Data Types with Typecasting

When you *typecast* a variable, you transform its value from one type to another. As you read earlier, Visual Basic is so highly automated that it hides many mundane chores of typecasting from you. Consider the following code:

```
Private Sub cmdAutoType_Click()
    txtFirst.Text = 5
End Sub
```

The data type that the Text property expects is a String, but it's being assigned an Integer. However, it works! Visual Basic automatically takes the Integer 5 and converts it to a String type. You would have to do a lot to get this code to work in a more *type-safe* language such as C++.

Now consider the following code (Figure 12.14 shows this code in action):

```
Private Sub cmdError_Click()

    lblResult.Caption = txtFirst.Text + txtSecond.Text
End Sub
```

FIGURE 12.14

Concatenating string variables yields a different result than adding integers.

Notice that Visual Basic's automated nature has now broken down. If you type 5 and 2 in the TextBoxes, the result is the string 52, not the integer 7. VB will convert 5 to an integer only if you try to add it to a value or variable of type Integer; the + operator works just like & for strings.

Therefore, to ensure that integer addition does indeed happen as you plan it to, you must convert at least one TextBox Text value to an integer by using the CInt() function. For example, in the following code snippet, if txtFirst.Text and txtSecond.Text hold numeric strings, the value of lblResult's Caption property will be the result of integer addition:

```
lblResult.Caption = CInt(txtFirst.Text) + txtSecond.Text
```

Letting Visual Basic do most of the work with regard to data types might serve you well, but as you can see from the preceding example, gaining control of data types and typecasting is a skill that you need to develop over the long term.

Changing Data Types with the Conversion Functions

Throughout this book you've seen the functions CStr() and CInt() used liberally with no real explanation. These functions are conversion functions. A *conversion function* transforms a value from one data type to another. In Visual Basic, you use the conversion functions to typecast.

Because experienced Visual Basic programmers try to impose as much type safety on their code as they can, among seasoned programmers it's not unusual to find the value of an object's property typecast before it's applied to a variable. Of course, before you try to convert a value from one type to another, make sure that the value is appropriate to the type. For example, the following would be erroneous:

```
strMyString = "Batman"
intCounter - CInt("Batman")

intCounter = strMyString$
```

Table 12.3 shows the type conversion functions and provides a discussion and example of each function.

Testing for proper data in your programs

Ensuring that data type conversion is possible is where validation functions such as IsNumeric(), IsValue(), and IsDate() come in handy. For a detailed discussion of these functions, read Visual Basic's online help.

TABLE 12.3 **Type Conversion Functions**

Function	Comments	Example
CBool()	Converts a value to a Boolean	CBool(-1)
CByte()	Converts values between 0 and 255 to a Byte	Cbyte(254)
CCur()	Converts a value to Currency	CCur("$23.98")
CDate()	Converts a date expression to a Date data type	CDate("July 4, 1776")
CDbl()	Converts a value to a Double	CDbl(MyInt%)
CDec()	Used only with variants	N/A
CInt()	Converts a value to an Integer	CInt("4")
CLng()	Converts a value to a Long	CLng(Form1.hWnd)
CSng()	Converts a value to a Single	CSng("23.1")
CVar()	Converts a value to a Variant	CVar(Text1.Text)
CStr()	Converts a value to a String	CStr(MyInt%)

Validating Data with *IsNumeric()*

As your programs rely more on valid user input, you must address the issue of users inputting text strings when you need them to enter numeric strings. Visual Basic has a built-in function that will help: IsNumeric(). IsNumeric() checks a string to see whether it "looks" like a number. If a string looks like a number, IsNumeric() returns True; otherwise, it returns False. The syntax for IsNumeric() is as follows:

bResult = IsNumeric(*MyString*)

In this syntax,

- *bResult* is a return value of type Boolean.
- IsNumeric is the function name.
- *MyString* is the string that you want to check.

Listing 12.16 shows code that uses IsNumeric() to check whether user input can be assigned to variables of type Integer.

LISTING 12.16   **12LIST16.TXT—Using *IsNumeric()* to Validate User Input**

```
01   Private Sub cmdIsNumeric_Click()
02       Dim intAnswer  As Integer
03       Dim intX       As Integer
04       Dim intY       As Integer
05
06       If IsNumeric(txtFirst.Text) = True Then
07           intX = CInt(txtFirst.Text)
08       Else
09           MsgBox "Type Error", vbCritical
10           Exit Sub
11       End If
12
13       If IsNumeric(txtSecond.Text) = True Then
14           intY = CInt(txtSecond.Text)
15       Else
16           MsgBox "Type Error", vbCritical
17           Exit Sub
18       End If
19
20       intAnswer = intX + intY
21
22       lblResult.Caption = CStr(intAnswer)
23   End Sub
```

Table 12.4 lists all the Visual Basic validation functions.

TABLE 12.4   **Visual Basic's Validation Functions**

Function	Test Condition
IsArray()	Returns True if the variable is an array
IsDate()	Returns True if the expression is a valid date
IsEmpty()	Returns True if the variable hasn't been initialized or has been set to empty
IsError()	Returns True if a numeric expression represents an error
IsMissing()	Returns True if no value has been passed to a function
IsNull()	Returns True if the expression is null or has been set to null
IsNumeric()	Returns True if the entire expression is a number
IsObject()	Returns True if the expression is an object

PART

III

The Elements of Visual Basic 6

13 **Creating Menus in Your Programs** 247

14 **Enhancing Your Programs with Forms and Dialog Boxes** 267

15 **Handling Keyboard and Mouse Input in Your Programs** 291

16 **Working with Time and Timers** 317

17 **Adding Graphics to Your Programs** 333

18 **Writing Reusable Code with Subs and Functions** 347

19 **Saving and Retrieving Your Data with Visual Basic** 365

20 **Deploying Your Visual Basic Applications** 385

Creating Menus in Your Programs

Use the Application Wizard to make a menu for your program

See what's required in Windows standard menus

Use the Menu Editor to make or change menus

Place access keys in your menus

Assign shortcut keys to your menus

Change a menu's properties and methods

Understanding the Windows Standard Menus

Any program with more than a few simple functions or features can benefit from the addition of a well-built menu. When you design your program, the goal is to make your features as easy to use as possible. A well-designed menu will accomplish this goal.

The menu will be one of the most visible features of your application. A good menu will make using your program easy. Your program will seem natural and familiar to the user. A bad menu at best will confuse your users and could actually keep them from understanding how your program works.

Many programs have file functions that let users create and save files. Programs that use any common Windows features, such as opening and saving files or copying and pasting text, have the additional requirement of complying with the expected standards for Window application menus. You handle this expectation of your programs by building Windows standard menus.

Microsoft's goal is to make all the main Windows features standard across the entire Windows graphical user interface (GUI). This basically means that no matter what program you are in—whether it be Word, Excel, or Access—the main features will look and work the same. For instance, the way you access the Printer feature in one program will be the same in all programs across the entire platform. These standards are documented in many places, such as in the help systems within Windows, on Microsoft's Web page, and in countless books, magazines, and articles.

The expected location and function of the common Windows menu features have evolved through habit. The most common features are the **File**, **Edit**, and **Help** menus. The first two are usually the first choices on the left side of the menu bar; the **Help** menu is usually the last choice on the main menu bar. Don't use >> to indicate submenus.

The individual elements of Windows standard menus also follow a standard, as listed in Table 13.1.

When to break tradition

Unless there's a powerful reason to go against the tradition of using the **File**, **Edit**, and **Help** menus in your application, it's better to observe this tradition. One example of when it would be important to break with tradition is when your functions are significantly different from the standard functions. The new location alerts your users that something is different from what they would normally expect to do.

TABLE 13.1 **Windows Standard Menu Conventions**

Feature	Convention
Caption	Use one or two short specific words.
Organization	Menu items should be grouped logically by function and allow for a minimal number of levels to access each feature.
Access keys	Each menu item should be assigned an access key (the underlined letter in a menu or menu selection) to allow for keyboard access to the menu choices. The key should be unique in each section of the menu and is normally the first letter of the caption.
Shortcut keys	Any menu features that are frequently used or need to be available from any part of the program should be assigned a shortcut key. Each shortcut key can be assigned to only one menu item.
Check box	Menu items that simply set or clear a single program option should contain a checked feature directly in the menu.
Ellipsis	Each menu item that opens a dialog should be followed by an ellipsis (...).

Using Visual Basic's Application Wizard

Visual Basic 6 has improved the Application Wizard to allow for the creation of fully customized menus directly in the wizard. In the earlier versions of the wizard, you could select from only a limited set of standard menu options to include in your application. This improvement makes the wizard a useful tool and a good starting point for building and understanding your first menu.

The primary benefit of VB's Application Wizard is that it can make menus that have the Windows standard features already loaded. You simply select the features you want from the template provided. They're also already arranged in the Windows standard layout.

Application Wizard options

Most programmers don't know all the standard features they want to use in an application until later in the development process. For this reason, if you use the Application Wizard, you should select any option you think you might use in your program. You can always delete it later.

Limitations of the Application Wizard

You can't use the Application Wizard to modify existing projects. Many third-party support programs add more functionality to your project without having you do more programming. You can also use the add-ins that come with Visual Basic, such as the Menu Editor.

The Application Wizard is a straightforward tool for building a new application. This means that the Application Wizard is used to build a functional application shell with standard features. If you want additional features, you have to program them yourself or use the Menu Editor to add them. After you click **Finish** in the Application Wizard and the base program is generated, you're on your own to make changes to the program by using the Menu Editor (discussed later in this chapter).

Build a simple menu with the Application Wizard

1. Start the Application Wizard through the default dialog that opens when Visual Basic 6.0 starts or by choosing **New Project** from the **File** menu (see Figure 13.1).

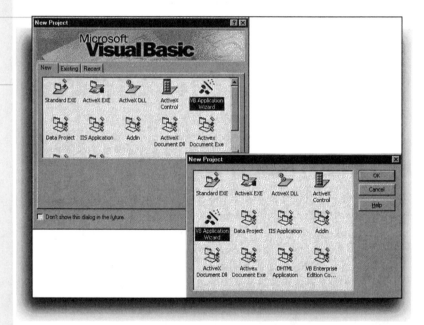

FIGURE 13.1

Double-click the Application Wizard icon to start the wizard.

2. The wizard's Introduction dialog allows you to reuse the answers you saved during a previous Application Wizard session (see Figure 13.2). Leave the default choice and choose **Next**.

3. In the Interface Type dialog, select the type for the initial application screen (see Figure 13.3). For this sample application, select **S̲ingle Document Interface**. Leave the default project name and choose **N̲ext**.

4. A Windows standard default menu is created for you to begin to modify. Not all possible choices have been selected in the initial menu, as shown in Figure 13.4. After you make your modifications, choose **N̲ext**.

5. The Application Wizard allows for the customization of a toolbar, resource file, browser, database connectivity, and other templates. For this example, skip these dialogs; choose **N̲ext** five times to get to the final dialog.

Save some time in building the program menu

By saving your settings in the Application Wizard, you can save time re-entering choices you've already made. The Application Wizard saves the menu and toolbar settings in a profile file (.RWP). Profiles also provide a basis for a consistent look and feel to your programs while reducing duplicate effort in building the menus. This allows for a common starting point in the development of an application, which is helpful in large projects in which many teams of developers might be working on separate parts of a single large application.

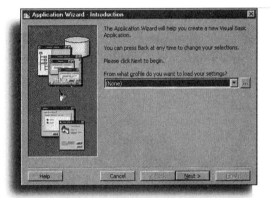

FIGURE 13.2

Profiles allow for the reloading of choices from previously completed and saved Application Wizard sessions.

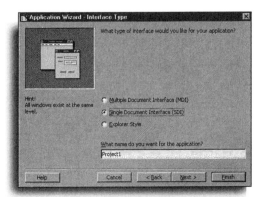

FIGURE 13.3

Selection of interface types is based on how the application will be used. Multitask applications often use MDI.

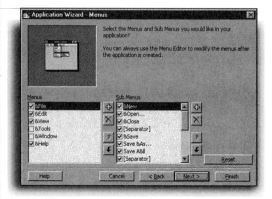

6. In the last dialog, you can save your profile (see Figure
13.5). Enter a name for your profile that will be easy to
relate to your application. After you enter the name, choose
Finish to complete the Application Wizard. (Clicking
Finish on any of the earlier dialogs in the wizard bypasses
the option to save the profile for future use.)

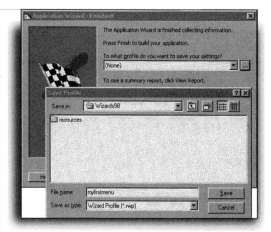

SEE ALSO

➤ *Find more information on the Application Wizard on page 582*

Using Visual Basic's Menu Editor

The Menu Editor allows you to create menu bars from scratch or modify already created menus. As with the Application Wizard, these menus are located at the top of a form, with associated drop-down submenus or pop-up menus that users typically access by right-clicking.

Make a simple menu with the Menu Editor

1. Open a new project. Save the project with a new filename. Rename the default form (with a name such as `frmMenu`) and save it to a new filename, such as frmMenu.frm.

2. Open the Menu Editor by clicking the Menu Editor button 📄 on the Standard toolbar. If the form doesn't have the focus, the Menu Editor icon is grayed out.

3. In the Menu Editor dialog, type `&File` in the **Caption** text box and `mnuFile` in the **Name** text box. Click **Next**.

4. Click the button with the arrow pointing to the right. This is the indent button.

5. Type `E&xit` in the **Caption** text box and `itmExit` in the **Name** text box. Your menu should appear in the dialog as shown in Figure 13.6.

6. Click **OK.**

7. The menu you created is embedded in the form (see Figure 13.7). Drop down the **File** menu that you just created and click **Exit**. The code window for the `itmExit_Click()` event procedure appears.

8. Add the `Unload Me` statement to the `itmExit` event procedure, as shown in Figure 13.8.

9. Press F5 to run the code.

Don't press Enter yet!

Press Tab or use the mouse to move between text boxes in the Menu Editor; otherwise, you cause the Menu Editor to create a new menu item.

Using ampersands

Including an ampersand in the menu caption forces the character that comes after it to be underlined when it appears in the menu. The underlined character becomes the hot key, which users can press (combined with the Alt key) to make a selection. For example, with the F underlined on the **File** menu, users can press Alt+F to pull down that menu.

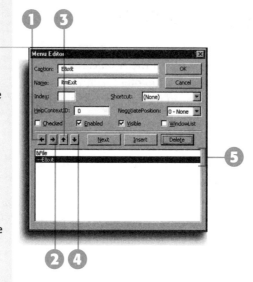

FIGURE 13.6

The arrow buttons allow you to indent and rearrange items in the menu list.

1. Moves the selected item out one level.

2. Moves selected entry in one level. You can have up to four levels (submenus).

3. Moves the selected item up one position but maintains the same level.

4. Moves the selected item down one position but maintains the same level.

5. Menu entries. Indented levels represent submenus.

FIGURE 13.7

An entry item in a menu is like any other Visual Basic control. It has properties and one event: the click event.

Granted, this exercise is simple, but it demonstrates the fundamental techniques for making a menu with the Menu Editor. You've added a **File** menu to the main form. Your menu has a submenu item, **Exit**, that allows users to terminate the program. You accomplished program termination by putting the End statement in the event procedure for the **Exit** menu item's click event.

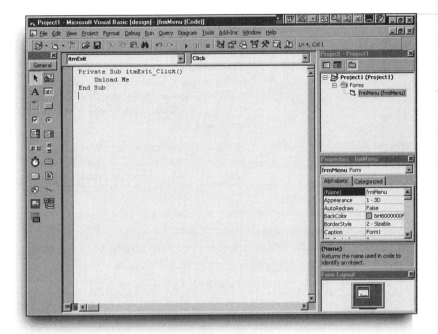

FIGURE 13.8

You write code in menu-item event procedures as you would for any other Visual Basic control.

Setting Menu Properties

As mentioned earlier, a menu is a control with its own set of properties and one event, the Click() event. Table 13.2 shows the most commonly used properties for a Menu object.

TABLE 13.2 **Commonly Used Properties of the *Menu* Object**

Property	Value/Type	Description
Caption	String	The text that appears on the menu bar.
Checked	Boolean	Puts a check mark before the Caption string of a menu item.
Enabled	Boolean	Doesn't gray out the Caption string if True.
Name	String	The name of the object—available only at design time.

continues...

TABLE 13.2   Continued

Property	Value/Type	Description
Shortcut	N/A	A key combination that allows you to access the menu item's functionality. You can choose this setting only at design time from a list that appears in the **Shortcut** drop-down list in the Menu Editor.
WindowList	Boolean	Makes a top-level menu in an MDI form display a list of windows open in that MDI form—available only at design time.

As with any control, you assign a value to the Name property when you create a menu or menu item. Failing to set the Name value results in an error. Another common mistake is to leave the value of the Caption property set to null (""), which results in a functional menu item that shows up in the menu bar as a blank line.

Adding Access Keys to Menu Items

In addition to clicking a menu item to perform a task, you can access a menu item's functionality by using *access keys*. Access keys allow users to perform menu selections by pressing Alt and then the assigned letter of the access key. After a menu is open, users select from the menu by pressing the access key for the desired menu choice.

An access key is denoted by an underlined character in a menu item's Caption—for example, the F in **File** on a standard Windows menu bar. When you press Alt+F, the result is the same as if you had clicked **File** on the menu bar.

To denote an access character, put an ampersand before the character you want to use. In Figure 13.9, the ampersand indicates that the letter F in File will be underlined.

FIGURE 13.9

Shortcut keys are assigned in the Menu Editor before compiling the program and can't be changed in the runtime environment.

1 Allows you to choose a key or key combination

2 Allows you to add a new menu item at the level of the preceding one

3 Adds a menu item above the selected item

4 Removes a selected menu item

Access keys are grouped according to menus. You can have different access keys with the same letter—**Save** and **Paste Special**, for instance—as long as they appear in different menus. (In Microsoft Word, these commands would appear under the menus **File** and **Edit**, respectively.) If you put two access keys with the same letter in the same part of the submenu, the first key in the hierarchy will be the first one executed. When the access key is pressed for the second time, the next menu item with the same matching key is selected.

Access keys are especially helpful in programs that require a lot of keyboard entry. If an access key is assigned, your users don't have to break their typing position and reach for the mouse to perform a function.

Don't do this!

Putting two access keys with the same letter in the same part of the submenu is bad programming practice and should be avoided. Doing so just complicates things for users; however, the purpose of using GUIs is to simplify things.

Adding Shortcut Keys to Menu Items

Adding shortcut keys with the Menu Editor

In the Application Wizard, you aren't given a chance to enter any shortcut keys for your custom menu items; the standard Windows menu shortcuts are added. You have to use the Menu Editor to go back in and add shortcut keys to your custom menu elements.

Using *shortcut keys* (also known as *accelerator keys*) is another way of performing menu functions from the keyboard. You set a shortcut key combination by choosing a combination from the Menu Editor's **Shortcut** drop-down list (see Figure 13.10).

Shortcut keys work anywhere in the program, whether or not the menu item is visible. That's why they're called shortcuts—they're active all the time, and users can jump to the function without going through the menu selection process.

FIGURE 13.10

Each application can have only one instance of an accelerator key combination. If you use Ctrl+N for **New**, you can't use Ctrl+N for **Open** too.

You can assign a shortcut key or key combination to only one menu element; redundancies aren't accepted. The Visual Basic IDE catches the error when you attempt to enter a duplicate entry (see Figure 13.11). In this situation, Visual Basic doesn't enforce uniqueness when editing menus.

FIGURE 13.11

Visual Basic's Menu Editor catches the error when you click **OK**.

Creating Pop-Up Menus

There are two types of menus: menu bars and pop-up menus. A *menu bar* is the type that you made with the wizard and edited in the Menu Editor—a sequence of menus embedded on a form. A *pop-up menu* is, as the name implies, a menu that pops up from somewhere on a form. When you right-click in the Windows Explorer, for example, a pop-up menu appears. You can make any menu appear as a pop-up menu by using a form's PopupMenu method:

1
```
PopupMenu mnuFile
```
2

A menu command can exist within a menu bar and as a pop-up menu, if you want (see Figure 13.12). You need to create a form to go with the pop-up menu because the PopupMenu method must be part of a form. The following code demonstrates how this feature works:

1 The method

2 A valid menu object

```
Private Sub Form_MouseDown (Button As Integer, _
  Shift As Integer, X As Single, Y As Single
   If Button = 2 Then
      PopupMenu mnuFile
   End If
End Sub
```

For this code to work, you need to create a form that includes a Menu control to be named mnuFile, which must have at least one submenu. You need to program this code into the form's Declarations section and press F5 to run it.

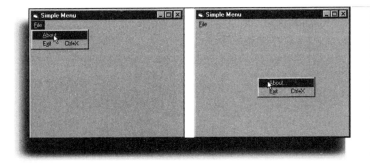

FIGURE 13.12

When you use the PopupMenu method as shown in the form on the right, only the submenu items of a menu will appear.

Creating Complex Menus

Now that you have an overview of how to use the Menu Editor to make a menu, the following example creates a menu system for a simple text editor.

The Amazing Text Editor, the code for which is in the project TextEdit.vbp on the Web site at `http://www.mcp.com/info`, can do the following tasks:

- Create a new file
- Open an existing file
- Save a file
- Reverse the editor's font and background color setting
- Provide copyright notification
- Exit the program
- Undo the preceding action
- Cut, copy, and paste text
- Select all text

Before you start coding, take some time to review the program's features to make a properly designed and categorized menu system. As mentioned earlier in the section "Understanding the Windows Standard Menus," most menu bars begin with a **File** menu and are followed by an **Edit** menu.

The following is a viable menu categorization for the feature set of the Amazing Text Editor.

File Menu	**Edit Menu**
New	Undo
Open	Cut
Save	Copy
Settings	Paste
About	Select All
Exit	

Now that you have a categorized menu system, you can implement it in the Menu Editor. Table 13.3 shows the menu hierarchy and `Name` and `Caption` properties, as well as accelerator and shortcut keys for each menu object.

TABLE 13.3 **Menu Objects for the Amazing Text Editor Application**

Name	Caption	Level	Shortcut
mnuFile	&File	0	None
itmNew	&New	1	None
itmOpen	&Open	1	None
itmSave	&Save	1	None
sepOne	- (a hyphen)	1	None
itmSettings	Se&ttings	1	None
itmBlackOnWhite	Black On White	2	None
itmWhiteOnBlack	White On Black	2	None
itmAbout	&About	1	None
sepTwo	-	1	None
itmExit	E&xit	1	Ctrl+X
mnuEdit	&Edit	0	None
itmUndo	&Undo	1	Ctrl+Z
sepThree	-	1	None
itmCut	Cu&t	1	Ctrl+X
itmCopy	&Copy	1	Ctrl+C
itmPaste	&Paste	1	Ctrl+V
sepFour	-	1	None
itmSelectAll	Select &All	1	Ctrl+A

Standard functionality of shortcut keys

The shortcut keys used in Table 13.3 adhere to the established convention that Windows programmers use for menu items with the demonstrated functionality.

Adding Separator Lines to Menus

You add separator lines to a menu by typing a single hyphen (-) in the Menu Editor's **Caption** text box. Notice that Table 13.3 lists some entries that have a `Caption` value of - and begin with the prefix `sep` in the object name. When you run the program,

Separator line limits

You can't use separator lines at the 0 (zero) level of a menu's hierarchy. You must be at least one indent level in.

separator lines appear in the drop-down menus where the hyphens are used (see Figure 13.13). I use the sep prefix to denote that the name of the menu item reflects a separator line.

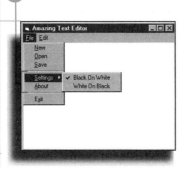

FIGURE 13.13

If a submenu item has another submenu associated with it, you'll see a right-pointing arrow to the right of the submenu item's caption.

1 Separator lines

Using the *Checked* Property

You use a menu's Checked property to communicate that some state exists or that a choice has been made. The Amazing Text Editor uses check marks in its menu system to communicate the current choice made for font/background color layout (refer to Figure 13.13). If users choose the Black on White menu item, a check mark will appear next to the selection, the font color will be set to black, and the background client area will be set to white.

You can set the value of a menu item's Checked property at run-time or design time. If you want to set its value at design time, you can set it within the Menu Editor by selecting the **Checked** check box. You also can set the value of the Checked property at design time within code, as follows:

```
MyMenuItem.Checked = True
```

When the value of the a menu item's Checked property is set to True, a check mark appears to the left of the menu item's caption.

Listing 13.1 shows the event procedure for the itmBlackOnWhite_Click() event. This is an example of how to set the Checked property of a menu item at runtime.

LISTING 13.1 **13LIST01.TXT–Setting the *Checked* Property at Runtime**

```
01 Private Sub itmBlackOnWhite_Click()
02     'Set the color scheme for Black on White
03     txtMain.BackColor = vbWhite
04     txtMain.ForeColor = vbBlack
05
06     'Set the menu checks accordingly
07     itmBlackOnWhite.Checked = True
08     itmWhiteOnBlack.Checked = False
09 End Sub
```

The *Checked* property isn't exclusive

You can set multiple checked events to **True**, if you want.

Cutting, Copying, and Pasting with the *Clipboard* Object

One of the more important features that the Windows operating system brought to computing was the capability to transfer data from one application to another via the Clipboard. The Clipboard is an area of memory reserved by Windows to which you send and from which you retrieve data. All applications have access to the Clipboard. Over time, the type of data that you can save to the Clipboard has become complex. You can save any registered Windows object, as well as simple text and numeric values.

Visual Basic allows your applications to access the Windows Clipboard through the Clipboard object. This object has no properties, but it does have a number of methods. Table 13.4 describes the various Clipboard methods.

TABLE 13.4 *Clipboard* **Methods**

Method	Description
Clear	Clears all data from the Clipboard
GetData	Returns a graphic from the Clipboard
GetFormat	Returns an integer that references the type of data in the Clipboard
GetText	Retrieves ASCII text from the Clipboard
SetData	Sends a graphic to the Clipboard
SetText	Sends ASCII text to the Clipboard

The **Cut**, **Copy**, and **Paste** items on the Amazing Text Editor's **Edit** menu (see Figure 13.14) use the Clipboard object to set and retrieve text to and from the Clipboard. The following is the code for itmCopy_Click(), the event procedure that copies selected text to the Clipboard:

```
01 Private Sub itmCopy_Click()
02     Clipboard.SetText txtMain.SelText
03 End Sub
```

FIGURE 13.14

The **Edit** menu items use the conventional Windows shortcut keys.

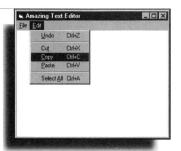

The code takes the value of the SelText property of the TextBox and uses the Clipboard's SetText method to send the text to the Clipboard (line 2).

Listing 13.2 shows you how to retrieve text from the Clipboard. The listing is a snippet of code from the **Paste** menu item's Click event procedure.

LISTING 13.2 **13LIST03.TXT—Retrieving Text from the Clipboard**

```
01 Private Sub itmPaste_Click()
02 Dim Temp$                 'Text from clipboard
03 Dim strLeft As String     'Holds text from left of cursor
04 Dim strRight As String    'Holds text from right of cursor
05 Dim strFull As String     'Full text
06
07     'Get the text from the clipboard
08     Temp$ = Clipboard.GetText(vbCFText)
...
32 End Sub
```

Selecting Text in a TextBox

The Cut and Paste code in the Amazing Text Editor makes extensive use of copying selected text to and from the Clipboard. The code determines which text to copy by using the SelText property of the TextBox.

The TextBox control has many standard Windows text-selection features built in to it. When you double-click a word that has been written into a TextBox, the TextBox automatically knows enough to highlight that word's characters. If you drag the mouse pointer across a line of text, that line will be highlighted automatically. When you click a TextBox, the text cursor will automatically be positioned between the characters you clicked.

The TextBox has three selection properties: SelStart, SelLength, and SelText. The value of SelStart is the string position of the cursor within a TextBox's contents. The value of SelLength is the number of characters highlighted during a selection process. The value of SelText is the characters highlighted during the selection process. The following code shows how to use the SelStart and SelLength properties to select a block of text (see Figure 13.15):

```
01 Private Sub Form_Click()
02     Text1.SelStart = 3
03     Text1.SelLength = 6
04 End Sub
```

Using text boxes with menus

Although TextBoxes really don't have much to do with menus, this discussion is included simply to help you complete the Amazing Text Editor application.

FIGURE 13.15

The SelStart and SelLength properties make the TextBox a powerful control.

Not only can you read these properties, but you can also set them at runtime. SelStart and SelLength are pretty straightforward. If you set SelText at runtime, however, Visual Basic automatically inserts the string value of SelText into the contents of the TextBox at the cursor position, moving the existing text to accommodate this (see Figure 13.16):

```
01 Private Sub Command1_Click()
02     Text1.SelText = "Dog "
03 End Sub
```

FIGURE 13.16

SelText is a good property to use if you want to insert text into a TextBox repeatedly.

The code for the Amazing Text Editor also contains the Right(), Left(), and Len() functions, and the MsgBox statement. Chapter 12, "Working with Strings and Typecasting," discusses these functions in more detail, and Chapter 14, "Enhancing Your Programs with Forms and Dialog Boxes," explains how to use the MsgBox statement, as well as the MsgBox() function.

SEE ALSO

➤ *Details on the* Right(), Left(), *and* Len() *functions start on page 219*

➤ *Learn more about the* MsgBox *statement and the* MsgBox() *function on page 271*

Enhancing Your Programs with Forms and Dialog Boxes

Use message boxes for fast response to users

Develop rapidly with the Forms Repository

Save time with the Visual Basic CommonDialog ActiveX control

Work effectively with MDI forms

Creating Message Boxes with the *MsgBox()* Function and the *MsgBox* Statement

Message boxes are simple forms that display messages and at least one CommandButton that's used to acknowledge the message (see Figure 14.1). Optionally, a message box can display an icon or use multiple buttons to let users make a decision. You can use a message box to display information or to obtain a decision from the user.

FIGURE 14.1

A message box is *task modal*, meaning that the application can't continue until the message box is closed.

You can display a message box by using the MsgBox statement or the MsgBox() function. The difference between them is that the function displays the message box and returns a value, but the statement only displays the message box. Also, there's a slight syntactical difference—the use of parentheses and a return value are required for the MsgBox() function.

Using the MsgBox() function is valuable if you need your program's users to make a decision and you want to respond to that decision. For example, if you want to ask users if they want to proceed with a process, you would use the following statements:

Visual Basic constants

Visual Basic has many predefined constants that you can use when programming with message boxes. For instance, you use **vbYesNo** to display a message box with Yes and No buttons. Using these internal constants is discussed in detail later in the section, "Retrieving a Value from the **MsgBox( )** Function."

```
Dim iResponse as Integer
iResponse = MsgBox("Do you want to proceed", vbYesNo,
App.Name)
If iResponse = vbYes then
    'Place your proceed code here
End If
```

The syntax for a MsgBox statement is

```
MsgBox strMessage, [Options][, strTitle][, strHelpFile][, _
       HelpContextID]
```

The following MsgBox statement displays the message box shown in Figure 14.1:

```
Private Sub Command1_Click()
    MsgBox "I am a Message Box"
End Sub
```

The syntax for a MsgBox() function is

```
RetInt = MsgBox(strMessage[, Options][, strTitle][, _
              strHelpFile][, HelpContextID])
```

In both sets of syntax, the following options and keywords are used:

- *RetInt* is an integer that stores the value of the return from the MsgBox() function.

- MsgBox is the statement/function name.

- *StrMessage* is a string expression to display in the message area of the message box.

- *Options* indicates an optional integer constant(s) that determines what button (or combination of buttons) and icons to display in the message box.

- *StrTitle* is an optional string expression to display in the title bar of the message box.

- *strHelpFile* is an optional string that is the path of the help file that provides additional information about the message box's topic.

- *HelpContextID* is an optional help context ID constant that references a topic in the help file as determined by *strHelpFile*.

The simple message box is acceptable for many types of messages, but you will probably want to dress up your messages a little more as you progress into more complex programming. You can specify two optional arguments for the MsgBox statement and the MsgBox() function: *Options* and *strTitle*. The *Options* argument is an integer that specifies the icon to display in the message box, the CommandButton(s) set to display, and which of the CommandButtons is the default. The *strTitle* argument is a text string that specifies a custom text to be shown in the title bar of

Using message boxes for error messages

If you decide to use a message box to report an error, remember the three fundamental rules for reporting an error: State the error, inform users of what they most likely did to cause the error, and suggest a way to correct the error.

the message box. Figure 14.2 shows a simple message box that has been enhanced to show an icon and additional buttons. The following code displays this message box:

```
Private Sub Command2_Click()
    MsgBox "I am a Fancy Message Box", _
           vbInformation + vbYesNoCancel, _
           "Message Box Title"
End Sub
```

FIGURE 14.2

You can add icons and additional buttons to a message box.

1 Title

2 Icon

3 Additional CommandButtons

Adding Icons to Message Boxes

You have a choice of four icons to display in a message box. These icons and their purposes are summarized in Table 14.1.

TABLE 14.2   Icons and Icon Constants

Icon	Constant	Purpose
⊗	vbCritical	A critical message indicates that a severe error has occurred. Often, a program is shut down after this message.
⚠	vbExclamation	A warning message indicates that a program error has occurred that requires user correction or might lead to undesirable results.
?	vbQuestion	A query indicates that the program requires additional information from users before processing can continue.
ⓘ	vbInformation	An information message informs users of the status of the program. This is most often used to notify users of a task's completion.

If you're wondering how you're going to remember the syntax of the MsgBox statement/function and the constants to be used for the options, don't worry. The statement completion capabilities of Visual Basic's Code Editor help tremendously. When you type the space after the MsgBox statement/function name in the code window, a pop-up shows you the syntax of the command (see Figure 14.3).

Using multiple constants

When you use the pop-up constants list, you can select a second constant by entering a plus sign (+) after the first constant.

FIGURE 14.3

The statement completion feature of Visual Basic lets you select the constants appropriate to your needs.

As you type in the function name, after you enter the message to be displayed and enter a comma, Visual Basic pops up a list of constants that can be used to add an icon to the message box or to specify the button set to be used. You can select a constant from the list by pressing Ctrl+Enter or typing it yourself.

Retrieving a Value from the *MsgBox()* Function

The MsgBox statement works fine for informing users of problems or prompting them to take an action. If you need to obtain a decision from users, however, you must return a value by using the MsgBox() function.

You can use six sets of CommandButtons in the `MsgBox()` function:

- **OK**—Displays a single button with the caption OK. This asks users to acknowledge receipt of the message before continuing.

- **OK, Cancel**—Displays two buttons in the message box, letting users choose between accepting the message and requesting a cancellation of the operation.

- **Abort, Retry, Ignore**—Displays three buttons, usually along with an error message. Users can choose to abort the operation, retry it, or ignore the error and continue with program execution.

- **Yes, No, Cancel**—Displays three buttons, typically with a question. Users can answer yes or no to the question or choose to cancel the operation.

- **Yes, No**—Displays two buttons for a simple yes-or-no choice.

- **Retry, Cancel**—Displays the two buttons that allow users to retry the operation or cancel it. A typical use is to indicate that the printer isn't responding. Users can retry the print job after turning on the printer (for example) or cancel the printout.

To specify the CommandButtons that will appear in the message box, you need to specify a value for the *Options* argument of the `MsgBox()` function. Table 14.2 lists the values for each CommandButton set.

TABLE 14.2 **Setting the *Options* Argument of the *MsgBox()* Function**

Button Set	Value	Constant
OK	0	vbOKOnly
OK, Cancel	1	vbOKCancel
Abort, Retry, Ignore	2	VBAbortRetryIgnore
Yes, No, Cancel	3	vbYesNoCancel
Yes, No	4	vbYesNo
Retry, Cancel	5	vbRetryCancel

The MsgBox() function is designed so that any combination of the icon constant and the CommandButton constant creates a unique value. This value is then broken down by the function to specify the individual pieces. The code used to create Figure 14.2 combines an icon constant and CommandButton constant to create an information message box with **Yes**, **No**, and **Cancel** buttons.

Setting a Default Button in a Message Box

If you're using more than one CommandButton in the message box, you can also specify which button is the default. The *default button*—which has the focus when the message box is displayed—is the one that users will most likely choose or that will be clicked if users automatically press Enter.

To specify which button is the default, you need to add another constant to the *Options* argument of the MsgBox() function:

Default Button	Value	Constant
First	0	vbDefaultButton1
Second	256	vbDefaultButton2
Third	512	vbDefaultButton3
Fourth	768	vbDefaultButton4

Evaluating a Return Value from the *MsgBox()* Function

You can choose from seven buttons, with the selection depending on the button set used in the message box. Each button, when clicked, returns a different value to your program (see Table 14.3).

TABLE 14.3   **Return Values from the *MsgBox()* Function**

Button	Return Value	Constant
OK	1	vbOK
Cancel	2	vbCancel
Abort	3	vbAbort
Retry	4	vbRetry

continues...

TABLE 14.3 Continued

Button	Return Value	Constant
Ignore	5	vbIgnore
Yes	6	vbYes
No	7	vbNo

After you know which button the user clicked, you can use the information in your program. Listing 14.1 shows you code that uses the MsgBox() function to confirm whether to delete a file.

Hands-on project

The code for the **MsgBox** examples can be found in the project SimplMsg.vbp on the Web site dedicated to this book (**http://www.mcp.com/info**). When you find that URL, enter **078971633x** as the ISBN and then click **Search** to go to the Book Info page for *Using Visual Basic 6*.

LISTING 14.1   14LIST01.TXT–Deleting a File According to the Return from the MsgBox() Function

```
01 Private Sub Command4_Click()
02 Dim strTextFile As String    'path of file to delete
03     Dim Msg$                 'Message box message
04     Dim OpVal%               'Option value variable
05     Dim RetVal%              'variable for return value
06     Dim TitleMsg$            'Title message variable
07
08     'Set the file to delete
09     strTextFile = "MYDATA.TXT"
10
11     'Create a message for the message box
12     Msg$ = "Do you really want to delete file: '"
13     Msg$ = Msg$ & strTextFile & "'?"
14
15     'Create a custom value for the Option parameter
16     OpVal% = vbExclamation + vbYesNo + vbDefaultButton2
17
18     'Create a title string
19     TitleMsg$ = "Delete Confirmation"
20
21     'Display the message box and get a return value
22     RetVal% = MsgBox(Msg$, OpVal%, TitleMsg$)
```

```
23
24    'If the value is Yes, set the commandButton
25    'caption to report that the Kill function has
26    'been selected
27    If RetVal% = vbYes Then
28        Command4.Caption = "Kill " & strTextFile
29    End If
30
31 End Sub
```

Using Predefined Forms

Visual Basic 6 comes with a number of predefined forms that can save you time in your coding activity. Visual Basic has predefined forms for data access, an About box, splash screens, and logins, to name a few.

Choose **Add** **Form** from the **Project** menu to display the dialog that contains the various predefined forms that ship with Visual Basic. Select the form that you want to use from this dialog (see Figure 14.4).

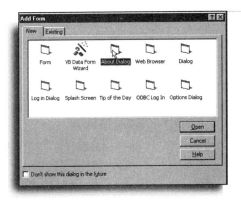

FIGURE 14.4
You can choose from predefined forms or a Form Wizard in the Add Form dialog.

If you need to add an About dialog to your project, click About Dialog in the Add Form dialog. (Figure 14.5 shows an About Dialog form.) Not only does Visual Basic add the form to your project, it also provides a substantial amount of code that covers the fundamental functionality of the form. The About Dialog provides code that reports that application's name and version information, as shown in the following code:

```
Private Sub Form_Load()
    Me.Caption = "About " & App.Title
    lblVersion.Caption = "Version " & App.Major & "." _
                          & App.Minor & "." & App.Revision
    lblTitle.Caption = App.Title
End Sub
```

The About dialog also provides all the code, including the external Windows API calls, that you need to report the user's system information. (If you want to review the system information code, add the About Dialog form to a new project and look at the code under the **System Info** button.)

FIGURE 14.5

The About dialog that ships with VB6 automatically provides code that reports your program's name and version information as well as the user's system information.

Need the code?

The code for the CommonDialog control examples is in the project SimpleCD.VBP on the Web site dedicated to this book.

Getting User Input from the CommonDialog Control

At some point you'll probably want to write a program in which your users can specify filenames, select fonts and colors, and control the printer. Although you could create your own dialogs to handle these tasks, you don't need to. Visual Basic provides you with the CommonDialog control, with which you can easily display predefined dialogs to obtain user information. Although the ease of setup is a great benefit, an even bigger bonus is that these dialogs are already familiar to users because they are the same dialogs used by Windows itself.

By using a single CommonDialog control, you have access to the following four Windows dialogs:

- *File* lets users select a file to open or choose a filename in which to save information.
- *Font* lets users choose a base font and set any desired font attributes.
- *Color* lets users choose from a standard color or create a custom color for use in the program.
- *Print* lets users select a printer and set some printer parameters.

To use the CommonDialog control, you first have to add it to your project by selecting **Microsoft Common Dialog Control 6.0** from the Components dialog (choose **Components** from the **Project** menu). After you add the CommonDialog control to your ToolBox, click the control and draw it on the form, like any other control. The CommonDialog control appears on your form as an icon; the control itself isn't visible when your application is running. However, when the code calls the CommonDialog, the specific dialog becomes visible.

SEE ALSO

➢ *See about adding controls to the ToolBox on page 57*

The following sections discuss each type of dialog that can be accessed with the CommonDialog control. For each dialog, you must set the control's properties through the Properties window or through the CommonDialog control's Property Pages dialog. The Property Pages dialog provides you easy access to the specific properties necessary for each common dialog type (see Figure 14.6). You access the Property Pages dialog by clicking the ellipsis button in the Custom property of the CommonDialog control in the Properties window.

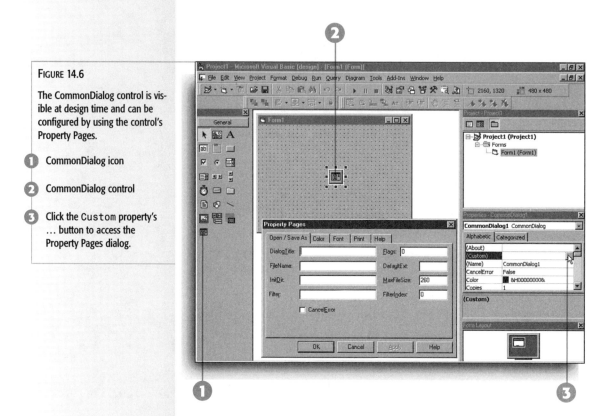

Retrieving File Information with the File Dialog

A key use of the CommonDialog control is to obtain filenames from users in two ways: file open and file save. File-open mode lets users specify a file to be retrieved and used by your program. File-save mode lets users specify the name of a file to be saved (the equivalent of the Save As dialog for many programs). Figure 14.7 shows a dialog with the major components indicated.

The dialogs for the Open and Save functions are similar. To open an existing file, you use the ShowOpen method of the CommonDialog control. (This method displays the dialog shown in Figure 14.7.) You use this method by specifying the name of the CommonDialog control and the method name, as follows:

```
CommonDlg1.ShowOpen
```

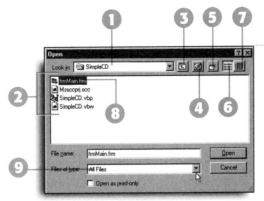

Running the CommonDialog control for saving a filename is essentially the same as for opening a file. In this case, however, the name of the method is ShowSave. There are a few subtle differences between the dialogs shown for the Open and Save functions, such as the title of the dialog and the captions on the buttons.

So far, you've learned how to display the File dialogs with all files shown in a folder. You might, however, want to specify that only certain file types, such as text or document files, be shown. The file types shown in the dialog are specified by using the CommonDialog control's Filter property. You set this property in design mode from the Property Pages dialog or set it at run-time with an assignment statement, as shown here:

```
controlname.Filter = "description¦filtercond"
```

In this syntax,

- *controlname* is the assigned name of the CommonDialog control.

- Filter is the name of the property.

- *description* is a text description of the file types to be shown. Examples of the description are "Text Files", "Word Documents", and "All Files". The vertical line, ¦ (the *pipe symbol)* must be present.

- *filtercond* is the actual filter for the files. You typically express the filter as an asterisk followed by a period and the

Be careful with filter syntax

Don't include spaces before or after the pipe symbol. If you do, you might not get the file list that you want.

extension of the files that you want to display. The filters that correspond to the preceding descriptions are `*.txt`, `*.doc`, and `*.*`, respectively.

If you specify the `Filter` property with an assignment statement, you must enclose the filter in double quotation marks. Omit the quotation marks if you specify the filter from the Property Pages dialog.

You can specify multiple *description¦filtercond* pairs within the `Filter` property. Each pair must be separated from the other pairs by the pipe symbol, as shown in the following example:

```
cdlgGetFile.Filter = "Text Documents¦*.txt ¦All Files
(*.*)¦*.*"
```

The `FileType` combo box in Figure 14.7 shows the preceding code applied to the CommonDialog.

Finally, when all your filtering is set, you use the CommonDialog control's `FileName` property to retrieve the name of the file that users selected:

```
MyFileName$ = cdlgGetFile.FileName.
```

Retrieving a filename from a file

1. Open a <u>N</u>ew Visual Basic project.

2. Add CommonDialog controls as described earlier.

3. Add a CommondDialog control, CommandButton, and Label to the form.

4. Align the Label control so that it's above the CommandButton. Place both controls in the upper left corner of the form.

5. Double-click the CommandButton on the form to expose the `Command1_Click` event procedure.

6. Add the following code to the event procedure (leave out the line numbers):

```
01 CommonDialog1.Filter = "All Files (*.*)¦*.*"
02 CommonDialog1.ShowOpen
03     If CommonDialog1.FileName <> "" Then
04         Label1.Caption = CommonDialog1.FileName
```

```
05    Else
06        Label1.Caption = "No file selected"
07    End If
```

This code works as follows:

- Line 1 sets the filter of the CommonDialog to show all the files in a given folder.

- Line 2 displays the CommonDialog box in open file mode. At this point, users can select a file and click **Open** or not choose a file and click **Cancel**. Regardless of their choice, Visual Basic assigns a value to the CommonDialog's FileName property.

- Lines 3–7 check the value of that assignment within an If...Then statement. If users didn't select a file, the value of the FileName property is an empty string. Thus, if the string isn't empty, users must have selected a file (Line 3). The program assigns the value of the FileName property to the Caption property of the Label control (Line 4). If the value of the FileName property is empty, the program tells users that no file has been selected (Line 6).

Selecting Font Information with the Font Dialog

Setting up the CommonDialog control to show the Font dialog is as easy as setting it up for file functions. In fact, you can use the same CommonDialog control to handle file, font, color, and printer functions.

The first step in using the CommonDialog control to handle font selection is to set a value for the Flags property. This property tells the CommonDialog control whether you want to show screen fonts, printer fonts, or both. The Flags property can be set to one of three constants:

Using flags with the CommonDialog control

If you're using the CommonDialog control to select fonts and don't set a value for the **Flags** property, you will receive an error message stating that no fonts are installed.

Font Set	Constant	Value
Screen fonts	cdlCFScreenFonts	1
Printer fonts	cdlCFPrinterFonts	2
Both sets	cdlCFBoth	3

Figure 14.8 shows a Font dialog that contains only screen fonts.

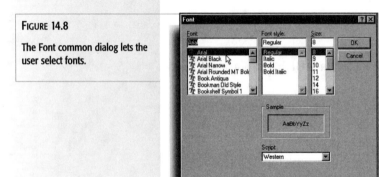

You can set the value of the Flags property from the design environment by using the Property Pages dialog or from your program by using an assignment statement. After you set the Flags
property, you can run the Font dialog from your code by using
the ShowFont method, which has the same syntax as the ShowOpen
method described earlier.

The information about the fonts chosen from the
CommonDialog control is contained in the control's properties.
Table 14.4 shows the control's properties and the font attributes
that each manipulates.

TABLE 14.4   **Control Properties That Store Font Attributes**

Property	Attribute
FontName	The name of the base font
FontSize	The height of the font in points
FontBold	Whether boldface is selected
FontItalic	Whether italic is selected
FontUnderline	Whether the font is underlined
FontStrikethru	Whether the font has a line through it

The font information can be used to set the font of any control in your program or even to set the font for the `Printer` object. The following code shows how the font information would be retrieved and used to change the fonts in the `txtSample` TextBox.

```
'cdlGetFont is the name of a common dialog
cdlGetFont.ShowFont
txtSample.FontName = cdlGetFont.FontName
txtSample.FontSize = cdlGetFont.FontSize
txtSample.FontBold = cdlGetFont.FontBold
txtSample.FontItalic = cdlGetFont.FontItalic
txtSample.FontUnderline = cdlGetFont.FontUnderline
txtSample.FontStrikethru = cdlGetFont.FontStrikethru
```

Selecting Colors with the Color Dialog

The CommonDialog control's Color dialog lets users select colors for the foreground or background of your forms or controls (see Figure 14.9). Users can choose a standard color or create and select a custom color.

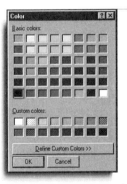

FIGURE 14.9

The Color common dialog lets your users choose a color to use in the program.

Setting up the CommonDialog control for colors is basically the same as for fonts. You set the `Flags` property to the constant `cdlCCRGBInit` and then call the `ShowColor` method.

When users select a color from the dialog, its color value is stored in the control's Color property. The following code shows how to change a form's background color through the Color dialog:

```
CommonDlg1.Flags = cdlCCRGBInit
CommonDlg1.ShowColor
Myform.BackColor = CommonDlg1.Color
```

Setting Printer Options with the Print Dialog

The CommonDialog control's Print dialog lets users select which printer to use for a print job and specify options for the print process. These options include specifying all pages, a range of pages, or the selection to print. There's also an option to specify the number of copies to be printed, as well as an option to print to a file.

To run the Print dialog, call the CommonDialog control's ShowPrinter method. No flags are set before the call.

In the Print dialog, users can select the printer from the Name list, which contains all printers installed in Windows. Below the Name list is the Status line, which tells you the current status of the selected printer.

The Print dialog returns the information from users in the dialog's properties. The FromPage and ToPage properties tell you the starting and ending pages of the selected printout. The Copies property tells you how many copies users want printed.

This is provided only as information. The Print dialog doesn't automatically set up the desired printout. In the Windows environment, the printer is considered to be nothing more than another output device and is treated programmatically the same as your computer monitor; there's no intelligence within your monitor that knows how to make a form or window. Your program does this and passes that output onto the monitor. The same is true with printing. Your program makes the output and then passes it onto the printer.

Making a Simple MDI Application

MDI is an acronym for Multiple Document Interface. An MDI application is one in which all windows of the application are enclosed in one containing window. Examples of an MDI application are Microsoft Word and Microsoft Excel (see Figure 14.10).

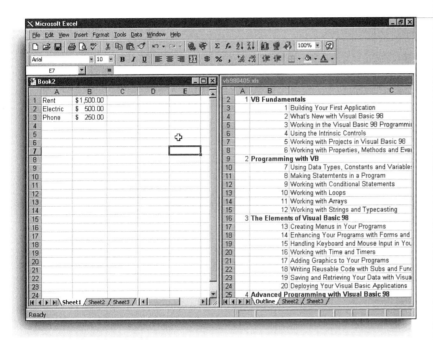

FIGURE **14.10**
Microsoft Excel is an example of an MDI application.

Visual Basic has defined an MDI object named the MDIForm. A given VB application can contain *only* one MDIForm object but can have a multitude of other forms, some of which can be children of the MDIForm object and some of which can be independent, standalone windows. The child windows of an MDIForm don't contain their own menu. Instead, the child windows are controlled by the menu of their parent MDI form. If you add a menu to an MDI child form, at runtime it won't be visible within the MDI child form. The active child's menu appears on the parent window in place of the parent's menu.

Form and component naming

The forms and other components of the sample application have suggested names, but feel free to experiment and tailor the program to your needs.

Make a simple MDI application

1. Open a new project and name it SimplMDI.VBP.

2. Rename the project's default form to `frmChild`. Save the form file with the name frmChild.vbp.

3. From the **Project** menu, choose **Add MDI Form** to add an MDI form to your project. Rename the MDI form as `mdiMain`. Save the form file with the filename mdiMain.frm.

4. Set `frmChild`'s `MDIChild` property to `True` to make the form a child of `mdiMain`.

5. Press Ctrl+E or click 🗐 to open the Menu Editor.

6. Create a menu for the `mdiMain` form, as shown in Figure 14.11. Set the values of the `Name` and `Caption` properties of the menu and menu items, as shown in Table 14.5. Make sure that you select the `WindowList` CheckBox (on the middle right of the Menu Editor) for `mnuWindow`.

FIGURE 14.11

You make menus for an MDI application by using the Visual Basic Menu Editor.

TABLE 14.5   Object Captions and Names for the SimplMDI Menu

Caption	Name	Indent
&File	mnuFile	0
&Add	itmAdd	1
E&xit	itmExit	1
&Window	mnuWindow	0
&Cascade	itmCascade	1
&Tile	itmTile	1

7. From the **Project** menu, choose **SimplMDI Properties**. On the **General** page of the Project Properties dialog, select **mdiMain** from the **Startup Object** drop-down list (see Figure 14.12).

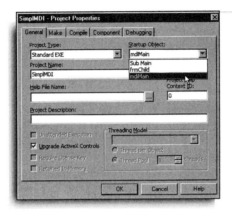

FIGURE 14.12
Choose the MDI form to be the startup form.

8. Between the lines `Private Sub itmAdd_Click()` and `End Sub`, add the code in Listing 14.2 (lines 2–9).

LISTING 14.2   14LIST02.TXT–The *itmAdd_Click()* Event Procedure

```
01 Private Sub itmAdd_Click()
02   Dim NewForm As New frmChild ' Declare another new form
03   Dim FormNum%
04   'Add it to the new form
05   Load NewForm
06   'Get a number for the new form, less the MDI parent
07   FormNum% = Forms.Count - 1
08   'Set its caption
09   NewForm.Caption = "I am MDI child: " + CStr(FormNum%)
10 End Sub
```

9. Between the lines `Private Sub itmExit_Click()` and `End Sub`, add the following code:
```
Un Load Me
```

10. Between the lines `Private Sub itmCascade_Click()` and `End Sub`, add the following code line:
```
Arrange vbCascade
```

11. Between the lines `Private Sub itmTile_Click()` and `End Sub`, add the following code line:

```
Arrange vbTileHorizontal
```

12. Compile and run the code.

The code for SimplMDI works this way: First you create a standard VB project and do some renaming. Then you add an MDI form to the project. You go back to the default form created when you originally made the project. You make it a child of the `mdiMain` MDI form by changing its `MDIChild` property to `True`. Then you open the Menu Editor and make a menu for the `mdiMain` form. You check the WindowsList check box for `mnuWindow` to enable the menu to list all open windows of an MDI form object. After the menu is created, you change the startup form. Then you add the event handlers for the menu items. Finally, you compile and run (see Figure 14.13).

FIGURE 14.13

The project SimplMDI shows you child forms within a MDI form.

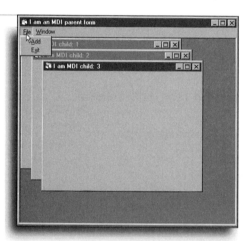

The `itmAdd_Click()` event procedure dynamically creates a new form by using the `New` operator. The new form's caption has a number, `FormNum%`—added to the end of the string assigned to it—to indicate the order in which the child form was created. `FormNum%` is determined by polling the application to report all its forms using the `Forms.Count` property. After all the forms are determined, 1 is subtracted to account for the uniqueness of the application-only MDIForm object. Therefore, within the scope of this application, the resulting number must be the number of child forms the MDIForm object contains.

The application uses the MDIForm object's Arrange method in the itmCascade_Click() and itmTile_Click() event handlers. The Arrange method automatically positions child windows within an MDI window. The Arrange method takes an argument, *arrangement*, which can be set to one of the values in Table 14.6.

TABLE 14.6 Windows *Arrange* Settings

Constant	Value	Description
vbCascade	0	Cascades all nonminimized MDI child forms
vbTileHorizontal	1	Tiles all nonminimized MDI child forms horizontally
vbTileVertical	2	Tiles all nonminimized MDI child forms vertically
vbArrangeIcons	3	Arranges icons for minimized MDI

The *Appearance* Property

Users respond positively to forms with a three-dimensional (3D) style. Visual Basic allows you to make 3D forms by changing the Appearance property of an MDI form to 1 - 3D.

The *AutoShowChildren* Property

By default, the AutoShowChildren property is set to False. For this reason, unless you remember to use the Show method in your code to display the form after you load it, users will have to go through some sort of process to make the form visible. This can be a potential headache for you if you forget to use the Show method to display a newly loaded form. When you set AutoShowChildren to True, an MDI child form becomes visible when displayed through the Load statement. Doing this saves you programming time while also making your code more reliable.

Using the Show method

If you have a form that loads data into itself, set the AutoShowChildren property to False and use the Show method. First, load the data into the form. Second, make sure that all the data loaded correctly. Last, show the form. If your form depends on the integrity of data, this process offers you the highest degree of reliability.

MDI applications have become a very popular way to give a uniform appearance to applications. It wasn't too long ago that Visual Basic was an SDI (single-document interface) application in which all windows of the Visual Basic IDE existed independent of one another. Although making the VB IDE to be SDI is a configuration option, many developers find the MDI configuration an easier alternative and more in line with the rest of the Visual Studio initiative. Also, with more and more applications taking on the look and feel of Web browsers, making your program an MDI application might serve you well for applications that require more than one window.

SEE ALSO

➤ *For more information about configuring the Visual Basic IDE for MDI or SDI, see page 64*

Handling Keyboard and Mouse Input in Your Programs

See how Windows controls the computer hardware devices to make programming easier

Use event procedures to process keyboard and mouse input

Learn about the ASCII character set and Visual Basic KeyCode constants

Understanding Device Input

Microsoft supports device independence

In the Windows NT operating system, one part of the Executive Services is the *Hardware Abstraction Layer (HAL)*. The presence of this distinct architecture element demonstrates the distinct support for device independence in the current Microsoft operating systems.

Windows is a *device-independent* operating system. The Windows operating system separates independent operating-system hardware (devices) such as the keyboard, mouse, monitor, and printer from the application programs. This separation—or *abstraction*, as it's called in object-oriented programming—enables programmers to work with general categories of hardware devices from which they can accept data and to which they can send data (see Figure 15.1). In other words, programmers never know the exact type of hardware connected to a given system; all they know is that a particular category of hardware is out there. Programmers code for a printer in general, not a specific model of printer. The same is true for the keyboard and mouse. What particular brand of input device is attached to a computer is the responsibility of the Windows operation system and the specific device drivers installed on the system. Device independence enables you to treat hardware devices as nothing more than event generators.

FIGURE 15.1

The device independence of Windows frees VB programmers from the difficult task of writing code for a particular piece of hardware.

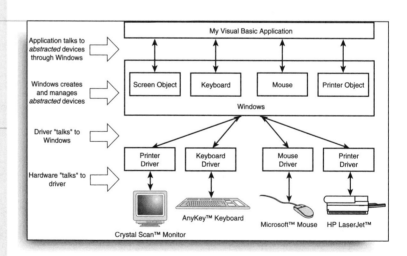

Most Visual Basic controls support three keyboard input events—KeyPress(), KeyUp(), and KeyDown()—and five mouse events—(Click(), DblClick(), MouseUp(), MouseDown(), and MouseMove().

Working with the *KeyPress* Event

When users press a key within your program, Windows fires a KeyPress event to the form with the focus and then to the control with the focus. The KeyPress event has this syntax:

```
Private Sub ControlName_KeyPress(KeyAscii as Integer)
```

In this syntax,

- Private denotes the scope of the event.
- Sub denotes a procedure.
- *ControlName* is the name of the control from which the event is being fired.
- KeyPress is the name of the event.
- *KeyAscii* is the ASCII code of the character being pressed.

KeyPress is associated with the character of the key being pressed. When the event is fired, Visual Basic passes the ASCII code of the character being input to the *KeyAscii* argument and thus makes it available to the event procedure for use. If having a parameter attached to an event handler is new to you, take a minute to think about it. You will be seeing many of these in the KeyPress, KeyDown, and KeyUp events.

An ASCII code is a number assigned, by formal convention, to each letter in the alphabet (separate numbers exist for uppercase and lowercase letters) as well as number characters and punctuation characters. Table 15.1 shows the more often used characters with their associated ASCII code numbers.

Function keys don't generate a KeyPress event

Only numeric, alphabetic, and select command keys generate a **KeyPress** event. You can test which keys work with this event by using the sample program in the project KeyPress.vbp on the Web site devoted to this book.

TABLE 15.1   **The Popular ASCII Characters**

Number	Character	Number	Character	Number	Character
32	space	64	@	96	`
33	!	65	A	97	a
34	"	66	B	98	b
35	#	67	C	99	c
36	$	68	D	100	d
37	%	69	E	101	e
38	&	70	F	102	f
39	'	71	G	103	g
40	(	72	H	104	h
41	)	73	I	105	i
42	*	74	J	106	j
43	+	75	K	107	k
44	,	76	L	108	l
45	-	77	M	109	m
46	.	78	N	110	n
47	/	79	O	111	o
48	0	80	P	112	p
49	1	81	Q	113	q
50	2	82	R	114	r
51	3	83	S	115	s
52	4	84	T	116	t
53	5	85	U	117	u
54	6	86	V	118	v
55	7	87	W	119	w
56	8	88	X	120	x
57	9	89	Y	121	y
58	:	90	Z	122	z
59	;	91	[	123	{
60	<z	92	\	124	|
61	=	93	]	125	}
62	>	94	^	126	~
63	?	95	_		

Figure 15.2 shows you the output from a program that reports the value and the corresponding character of the *KeyAscii* parameter passed during the *KeyPress* event for a TextBox. Listing 15.1 shows the code for the *KeyPress* event procedure for the TextBox. In this case, the ASCII code number 103 was passed to the TextBox, along with the lowercase character *g*. You will find this is the correct value, as listed in Table 15.1.

FIGURE 15.2

The *KeyPress* event is associated with the character sent to the control.

LISTING 15.1   15LIST01.txt–Converting a Character's ASCII Code into a String

```
01   Private Sub txtSimpl_KeyPress(KeyAscii As Integer)
02       Dim strKeyPressed As String 'inputted character
03       Dim strAscii      As String 'Ascii number
04       Dim Msg           As String 'Message string
05
06       'Convert KeyAscii to a character
07       strKeyPressed = Chr(KeyAscii) 'VB function Chr
08
09       'Convert the actual number to a string
10       strAscii = CStr(KeyAscii)     'VB function CStr
11
12       'Build the Message display string
13       Msg = "ASCII Number: " & strAscii
14       Msg = Msg & ", " & "Character: " & strKeyPressed
15       MsgBox Msg
16   End Sub
```

Download the code

You can find the code in Listing 15.1 in the project simplKey.VBP on the Web site devoted to this book (http://www.mcp.com/info). Also on this Web site is the sample project KeyPress.vbp, which you can use to test the key combinations in Table 15.2.

The ASCII code convention also includes 32 special command or control codes that were extremely important in the era of character-based terminals (see Table 15.2). Several of these codes are still used for their original purpose in Visual Basic.

Select command keys generate KeyPress events

Under Windows 95, the Backspace, Enter, and Esc keys generate ASCII values that can be trapped by the **KeyPress** event's *KeyAscii* parameter. These values are 8, 13, and 27, respectively. You also can combine the Backspace and Enter keys with the Ctrl key to produce 127 and 10 for ACSII values. These key combinations are in addition to those listed in Table 15.2.

TABLE 15.2   **The ASCII Control Characters**

Number	Key Combinations	Control Code	Control Name
0	Ctrl+Shift+@	NUL	Null
1	Ctrl+A	SOH	Start of heading
2	Ctrl+B	STX	Start of text
3	Ctrl+C	ETX	End of text
4	Ctrl+D	EOT	End of transmit
5	Ctrl+E	ENQ	Inquiry
6	Ctrl+F	ACK	Acknowledgement
7	Ctrl+G	BEL	Bell
8	Ctrl+H	BS	Backspace
9	Ctrl+I	HT	Horizontal tab
10	Ctrl+J	LF	Line feed
11	Ctrl+K	VT	Vertical tab
12	Ctrl+L	FF	Form feed
13	Ctrl+M	CR	Carriage feed
14	Ctrl+N	SO	Shift out
15	Ctrl+O	SI	Shift in
16	Ctrl+P	DLE	Data line escape
17	Ctrl+Q	DC1	Device control 1
18	Ctrl+R	DC2	Device control 2
19	Ctrl+S	DC3	Device control 3
20	Ctrl+T	DC4	Device control 4
21	Ctrl+U	NAK	Negative acknowledgment
22	Ctrl+V	SYN	Synchronous idle
23	Ctrl+W	ETB	End of transmit block
24	Ctrl+X	CAN	Cancel
25	Ctrl+Y	EM	End of medium
26	Ctrl+Z	SUB	Substitute
27	Ctrl+[	ESC	Escape

Number	Key Combinations	Control Code	Control Name
28	Ctrl+\	FS	File separator
29	Ctrl+]	GS	Group separator
30	Ctrl+Shift+^	RS	Record separator
31	Ctrl+Shift+_	US	Unit separator

It's important that you be aware of these codes and their uses. Consider a program that needs to disable the entry of an escape command. Although you might remember to program your application to ignore the pressing of the Esc key, a user could also press Ctrl+[and send the program an unwanted command. On the other hand, if a program disallowed the entry of any ASCII values less than 32, it might prevent the Tab and Enter keys from working properly.

Working with the *KeyUp* and *KeyDown* Events

Every time a user presses a key on the keyboard, a KeyDown event is fired to the control that has the focus. When the key is released, a KeyUp event is fired.

The KeyUp/KeyDown event procedures use this syntax:

```
Private Sub ControlName_KeyUp(KeyCode as Integer, _
                        Shift as Integer)
Private Sub ControlName_KeyDown(KeyCode as Integer, _
                        Shift as Integer)
```

In this syntax,

- Private denotes the scope of the event.
- Sub denotes a procedure.
- ControlName is the name of the control from which the event is being fired.
- KeyUp and KeyDown are the event names.
- KeyCode is an integer that reports the KeyCode constant of the key being pressed or released.
- Shift is an integer that reports whether the Shift, Control, or Alt keys are also being held down (see Table 15.3).

Detection of keystrokes versus character codes

The important distinction between the **KeyUp** and **KeyDown** events and the **KeyPress** event is that **KeyPress** is associated with characters, whereas **KeyUp** and **KeyDown** are associated with keys on the keyboard. Remember, most keys can input one of two characters, depending on the state of the Shift key (a and A, for example). If it's important to your program to know which character has been input, use the **KeyPress** event. However, if it's important that you know which *key* has been pressed, use the **KeyUp/KeyDown** event.

TABLE 15.3 The Different Values for the *Shift* Parameter

Combination Key(s) Held Down	Value
Shift	1
Ctrl	2
Alt	4
Shift+Ctrl	3
Shift+Alt	5
Ctrl+Alt	6
Shift+Ctrl+Alt	7

The trick to using the KeyUp/KeyDown event handlers is working with the *KeyCode* and *Shift* parameters. In addition to reporting which alphabetic key has been struck, the *KeyCode* parameter also can report whether users pressed a function key (F1–F12), a key on the numeric keypad, the arrow keys, or any other key. When a key is pressed, Visual Basic sends a value to the *KeyCode* parameter that's reporting the key in question. The number sent to *KeyCode* is represented by a constant value, as shown in Table 15.4.

TABLE 15.4 Visual Basic 6.0 *KeyCode* Constants

Constant	Key
vbKeyLButton	Left mouse button
vbKeyRButton	Right mouse button
vbKeyCancel	Cancel
vbKeyMButton	Middle mouse button
vbKeyBack	Backspace
vbKeyTab	Tab
vbKeyClear	Clear
vbKeyReturn	Enter
vbKeyShift	Shift
vbKeyControl	Ctrl

Constant	Key
vbKeyMenu	Menu
vbKeyPause	Pause
vbKeyCapital	Caps Lock
vbKeyEscape	Esc
vbKeySpace	Spacebar
vbKeyPageUp	Page Up
vbKeyPageDown	Page Down
vbKeyEnd	End
vbKeyHome	Home
vbKeyLeft	♦
vbKeyUp	↑
vbKeyRight	∅
vbKeyDown	¬
vbKeySelect	Select
vbKeyPrint	Print Screen
vbKeyExecute	Execute
vbKeySnapshot	Snapshot
vbKeyInsert	Insert
vbKeyDelete	Delete
vbKeyHelp	Help
vbKeyNumlock	Num Lock
vbKeyA through vbKeyZ	A through Z, respectively
vbKey0 through vbKey9	0 (zero) through 9, respectively
vbKeyNumpad0 through vbKeyNumpad9	0 through 9 on number pad, respectively
vbKeyMultiply	Multiplication sign (*) on number pad
vbKeyAdd	Plus sign (+) on number pad
vbKeySeparator	Enter on number pad
vbKeySubtract	Minus sign (–) on number pad

Help keys come in two flavors

Many applications use the F1 key as their Help key, because most keyboard manufactures don't provide a separate key labeled Help. Windows, however, supports a Help key, so you may want to support both in your applications. The actual keyboard BIOS scan codes for these two keys are `vbKeyHelp = 0x2F` and `vbKeyF1 = 0x70`.

continues…

TABLE 15.4 **Continued**

Constant	Key
vbKeyDecimal	Decimal point (.) on number pad
vbKeyDivide	Division sign (/) on number pad
vbKeyF1 through vbKeyF16	F1 through F16, respectively

Listing 15.2 shows a piece of code from the project KeyEvent.vbp, which you can find on the Web site dedicated to this book (http://www.mcp.com/info). This code reports which function key has been pressed. It also reports the state of the Shift, Ctrl, and Alt keys. Figure 15.3 shows the code in action.

LISTING 15.2   **15List02.TXT—Checking Whether a Function Key Has Been Pressed**

```
01   Private Sub Form_KeyDown(KeyCode As Integer, _
                          Shift As Integer)
02   Dim strKey As String 'variable to hold key string
03
04       'Pass Keycode parameter through Case statement.
05       'If the key up/down is a function key, the case
06       'statement will catch it.
07       Select Case KeyCode
08           Case vbKeyF1
09               strKey = "F1"
10           Case vbKeyF2
11               strKey = "F2"
12           Case vbKeyF3
13               strKey = "F3"
14           Case vbKeyF4
15               strKey = "F4"
16           Case vbKeyF5
17               strKey = "F5"
18           Case vbKeyF6
19               strKey = "F6"
20           Case vbKeyF7
21               strKey = "F7"
22           Case vbKeyF8
23               strKey = "F8"
```

```
24          Case vbKeyF9
25              strKey = "F9"
26          Case vbKeyF10
27              strKey = "F10"
28          Case vbKeyF11
29              strKey = "F11"
30          Case vbKeyF12
31              strKey = "F12"
32          Case vbKeyF13
33              strKey = "F13"
34          Case vbKeyF14
35              strKey = "F14"
36          Case vbKeyF15
37              strKey = "F15"
38          Case vbKeyF16
39              strKey = "F16"
40          Case Else
41              strKey = "Some other key"
42       End Select
43       'Check to see if Shift, Ctrl or Alt key is down
44       Select Case Shift
45          Case 0
46            frmKeyEvent.Caption = "No key down"
47          Case 1
48            frmKeyEvent.Caption = "Shift down"
49          Case 2
50            frmKeyEvent.Caption = "Ctrl down"
51          Case 3
52            frmKeyEvent.Caption = "Shift and Ctrl down"
53          Case 4
54            frmKeyEvent.Caption = "Alt down"
55          Case 5
56            frmKeyEvent.Caption = "Shift and Alt down"
57          Case 6
58            frmKeyEvent.Caption = "Ctrl and Alt down"
59          Case 7
60            frmKeyEvent.Caption = "Shift,Ctrl,Alt down"
61       End Select
62       'Report which key is down
63       txtKeyEvent.Caption = "Key Down, Key: " & strKey
64    End Sub
```

FIGURE 15.3

The KeyUp/KeyDown event procedures enable access to all keys on the keyboard.

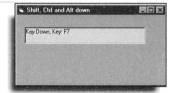

Using the *KeyPreview* Property

Sometimes you want a form to process keyboard input, even if a control on a form has the focus. You use the form's KeyPreview property to do this.

When you create a form, the default value of the KeyPreview property is False. Thus, any keyboard input that you send to a control on the form (a TextBox, for instance) goes directly to that control. If you set the value of KeyPreview property to True, however, the form intercepts all keyboard input. You can then access the input through the form's keyboard event procedures. After the form handles the input, it's passed to the control with the focus.

At http://www.mcp.com/info is a sample project, KeyPress.vbp, in which the form's KeyPress event procedure intercepts all keyboard input headed for a TextBox and manipulates it into a backward string, and then ASCII reads it out (see Figure 15.4). It then sends each respective string to its own TextBox control. The form can intercept and distribute all the keyboard input to the various TextBoxes because the value of the KeyPreview property is set to True. Listing 15.3 shows the code for the Form_KeyPress() event procedure.

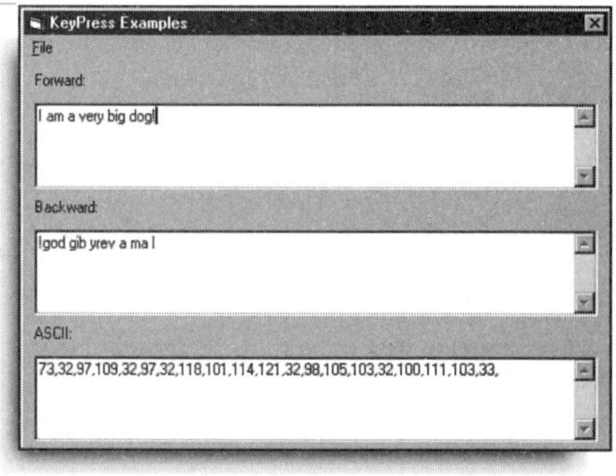

FIGURE 15.4

If the value of the form's KeyPreview property were set to False, only the Forward TextBox would receive data.

LISTING 15.3   15LIST03.TXT–The Form's *KeyPress* Event Procedure

```
01  Private Sub Form_KeyPress(KeyAscii As Integer)
02        'Send the mouse cursor to the first textbox
03        txtForward.SetFocus
04
05        'Convert the KeyAscii parameter to a character and
06        'put it in front of the existing text
07        txtBackward.Text = Chr(KeyAscii) & txtBackward.Text
08
09        'Turn the KeyAscii value to a numeral and
10        'concatenate it to the end of the existing string
11        txtAscii.Text = txtAscii.Text & CStr(KeyAscii) & ",
12  End Sub
```

Understanding Mouse Input

Every time you do something with the mouse, a mouse event is fired in your Visual Basic application. If you click the mouse, a Click event is fired. When you double-click, a DblClick event is fired. When you press a mouse button down, a MouseDown event is fired, whereas letting the mouse button up causes a MouseUp event. Every time the mouse moves, a MouseMove event occurs. Where and when a given event occurs depends on the position of the mouse pointer.

Most controls support the event procedures just described. Some controls, however, such as the ComboBox, have no support for the MouseDown, MouseUp, and MouseMove events.

Sometimes one gesture with a mouse fires many events. When you click a mouse, not only is a Click event fired, but MouseDown and MouseUp events are also fired. Taking control of the interactions among all the different events requires some getting used to.

Using the *Click* Event

Program a click event procedure

1. Start a new project. Name the project and the form TClick and frmTClick, respectively. Add a TextBox to the form as shown in Figure 15.5.

FIGURE 15.5

The TextBox supports the click
event procedure.

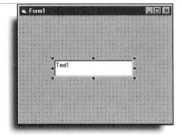

2. Assign a name to the TextBox, such as txtClick.

3. Double-click the TextBox to open the code window. Go to
   the event procedure drop-down list and change the event
   procedure from the Change event to the Click event (see
   Figure 15.6).

FIGURE 15.6

The default event procedure for
the TextBox control is the
Change event. Some people
mistakenly program this event,
thinking it's the click event.

4. In the Properties window, clear the value of txtClick's Text
   property from "Text1" to an empty string (see Figure 15.7).

5. Add the lines of code between Private Sub txtClick_Click()
   and End Sub (lines 2–21) in Listing 15.4 to the
   txtClick_Click() event procedure.

6. Compile and run the code (see Figure 15.8).

FIGURE 15.7

Deleting the Text property string value in the Properties window deletes text from the TextBox.

LISTING 15.4   **15LIST4.TXT—Displaying a Message, in the TextBox, That Reports How Many Times You've Clicked It**

```
01   Private Sub txtClick_Click()
02       'Make this static so it keeps its
03       'value from click to click
04       Static intCntr As Integer
05
06       'Make a variable to hold a message string
07       Dim Msg As String
08
09       'Begin a message
10       Msg = "This is click number "
11
12       'Convert the counter variable from an
13       'integer to a string and concatenate it
14       'to the preceding string
15       Msg = Msg & CStr(intCntr) & "."
16
17       'Display the string in the text box
18       txtClick.Text = Msg
19
20       'Increment the counter variable
21       intCntr = intCntr + 1
22   End Sub
```

FIGURE 15.8

Programming the click event in a TextBox control is atypical. Although meaningful for demonstration purposes, it confuses users when they try to input text.

As you can see, the Click event is a simple event procedure to program. In fact, you can follow the same process to program the DblClick event procedure. Remember, however, that variables declared in a Click event procedure go out of scope when the procedure is completed. Therefore, if you want to maintain a state or value from click to click, you're required to reference a Static variable or a variable from the parent form within the Click event procedure. Static variables are covered in Chapter 7, "Using Data Types, Constants, and Variables."

Working with *MouseDown* and *MouseUp* Events

The MouseDown and MouseUp event procedures use this syntax:

```
Private Sub ControlName_MouseDown(Button As Integer, _
            Shift As Integer, x As Single, y As Single)
Private Sub ControlName_MouseUp(Button As Integer, _
            Shift As Integer, x As Single, y As Single)
```

In this syntax,

- Private denotes the scope of the event.
- Sub denotes a procedure.
- ControlName is the name of the control from which the event is being fired.
- MouseUp and MouseDown are the event procedures.
- Button is an integer that reports the mouse button or combination of mouse buttons pressed (see Table 15.5).
- Shift is an integer that reports whether the Shift, Control, or Alt keys also are being held down (refer to Table 15.3).

- *x* is the horizontal position of the mouse pointer.
- *y* is the vertical position of the mouse pointer.

TABLE 15.5 **Mouse Button Values**

Mouse Button(s) Pressed	Button Parameter Value
Left	1
Right	2
Left and right	3
Middle	4
Left and middle	5
Right and middle	6
All	7

In many ways, working with the MouseDown and MouseUp event procedures is very similar to working with the KeyDown and KeyUp procedures. The difference is that MouseDown and MouseUp have a few different parameters passed into them. When a MouseDown event is fired, Visual Basic passes information about what mouse button was pressed and whether the Shift, Ctrl, or Alt key is being held down. VB also passes in the location of the mouse pointer within the control firing the event. The same is true when working with the MouseUp event.

Although you might think that the MouseDown and MouseUp events are a complication of the Click event procedure, you ought to consider them an enhancement. For instance, you can take advantage of the value of the *Shift* parameter of the MouseDown event procedure to do things that you can't do within a Click event procedure. Suppose that you want to have a secret way to display an *Easter egg*. Listing 15.5 shows how to use the *Shift* parameter with a form's MouseDown event procedure to accomplish this. Only someone holding down the Shift key, when the mouse is clicked, can display the message box and the hidden image of an Easter egg.

LISTING 15.5   **15LIST05.TXT–If the *Shift* Parameter Is Equivalent to 1, the Shift Key Is Being Held Down**

```
01   Private Sub Form_MouseDown(Button As Integer, _
            Shift As Integer, X As Single, Y As Single)
02      If Shift = 1 Then
03         imgEgg.Visible = True
04         MsgBox "I am a secret Easter Egg"
05      End If
06      imgEgg.Visible = False
07   End Sub
```

Examples available for download

The code for Listing 15.5 is in the project MouseBut.vbp, and the code for Listing 15.6 is in the project Mouse.vbp. Both projects are available for download from http://www.mcp.com/info.

On the Web site set up for this book is the project Mouse.vbp, which demonstrates programming the MouseDown and MouseUp event procedures as well as the Click and DblClick event procedures. The project reports all the mouse activity that takes place within a PictureBox control named Picture1. When users press a mouse button (thus firing a MouseDown event), the MouseDown event procedure reports which button and which combination of Shift, Ctrl, and Alt have been pressed. The event procedure uses two Select Case statements to create a string that reports the status of the *Shift* and *Button* parameters. The event procedure also reports the position of the mouse pointer (see Figure 15.9). Listing 15.6 shows the code for the MouseDown and MouseUp event procedures.

LISTING 15.6   **15LIST06–The *MouseDown* Event Procedure for the *Picture1* PictureBox Control**

```
01   Private Sub Picture1_MouseDown(Button As Integer, _
            Shift As Integer, X As Single, Y As Single)
02      Dim strButton As String  'holds value of Button param
03      Dim strShift As String   'holds value of Shift param
04      Dim strX As String       'holds value of X param
05      Dim strY As String       'holds value of Y param
06
07      'Convert X , Y parameters from integers to a string
08         strX = CStr(X)
09         strY = CStr(Y)
10
11         'Run the SHIFT parameter through a Select Case
```

```
12      'statement in order to figure out what combination
13      'of Shift, Ctrl or Alt keys are depressed.
14
15      'Assign the result to the Shift string variable
16      Select Case Shift
17          Case 0
18              strShift = ""
19          Case 1
20              strShift = "Shift"
21          Case 2
22              strShift = "Ctrl"
23          Case 3
24              strShift = "Shift + Ctrl"
25          Case 4
26              strShift = "Alt"
27          Case 5
28              strShift = "Shift + Alt"
29          Case 6
30              strShift = "Ctrl + Alt"
31          Case 7
32              strShift = "Shift + Ctrl + Alt"
33      End Select
34
35      'Run the BUTTON parameter through a Select Case
36      'statement to determine what combination of the
37      'Mouse Buttons have been pushed. Assign the
38      'result to the Button string variable
39      Select Case Button
40          Case 0
41              strButton = ""
42          Case 1
43              strButton = "Left"
44          Case 2
45              strButton = "Right"
46          Case 3
47              strButton = "Left + Right"
48          Case 4
49              strButton = "Middle"
50          Case 5
51              strButton = "Left + Middle"
52          Case 6
53              strButton = "Right + Middle"
```

continues...

LISTING 15.6   Continued

```
54          Case 7
55              strButton = "All"
56      End Select
57
58      'Diplay the event fired
59      lblMouse.Caption = "Mouse Down"
60
61      'Display the combination of keys pressed
62      lblShift.Caption = strShift
63
64      'Display the mouse buttons pressed
65      lblButton.Caption = strButton
66  End Sub
```

FIGURE 15.9

The mouse click event fires
`Click`, `MouseDown`, and
`MouseUp` events.

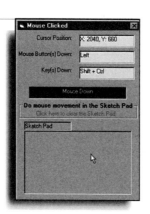

Notice in Figure 15.9 that the position of the mouse pointer is reported in *twips*. This number might be confusing at times. If you need to report the position of the mouse in pixels, replace lines 7–9 of Listing 15.6 with the following code:

```
'Report the X and Y position in pixels by dividing the
'value of X and Y by the TwipsPerPixelX(Y) property of
'the Screen object. Convert the X and Y parameters from
'integers to a string
    strX = CStr(x/Screen.TwipsPerPixelX)
    strY = CStr(y/Screen.TwipsPerPixely)
```

Notice also that the following code for the `MouseUp` event is minimal compared with the `MouseDown` event. This minimalism is intentional. When users release a mouse button, the `MouseUp` and

MouseMove events are both fired. If the code in each event procedure is trying to affect the same controls, you run into a conflict because you must ensure that each event procedure's scope of activity is relatively exclusive. In the Mouse.vbp project, the MouseUp event sets a Label control's caption, on line 3 below , whereas the MouseMove event reports the mouse pointer's position in another Label control and uses the Line method to draw on the PictureBox.

```
01 Private Sub Picture1_MouseUp(Button As Integer, _
          Shift As Integer, X As Single, Y As Single)
02      'Diplay the event fired
03      lblMouse.Caption = "Mouse Up"
04 End Sub
```

Working with the *MouseMove* Event

The syntax for the MouseMove event procedure is as follows:

```
Private Sub ControlName_MouseMove(Button As Integer, _
          Shift As Integer, x As Single, y As Single)
```

It's identical to the MouseDown and MouseUp event procedures. Whenever you move the mouse, a MouseMove event is fired.

The Mouse.vbp project used in the preceding section demonstrates programming the MouseMove event. This event procedure is programmed to report the location of the mouse within the PictureBox control (see Figure 15.10).

FIGURE 15.10

Most controls support the MouseMove event procedure.

As shown in Listing 15.7, the MouseMove event procedure of the Picture control takes the value of the x and y parameters passed to it and displays those values in a Label control. Every time the mouse moves, the new value is reported. Also, the parameters are used to draw lines in the PictureBox by using the Line method of that control. Line 10 in Listing 15.7 performs the drawing that's shown in Figure 15.10.

LISTING 15.7   **15LIST07.TXT—Reporting the Mouse Pointer's Value with the** *MouseMove* **Event Procedure**

```
01  Private Sub Picture1_MouseMove(Button As Integer, _
        Shift As Integer, X As Single, Y As Single)
02      Dim strX As String 'holds  converted value of  X
03      Dim strY As String 'holds  converted value of  Y
04
05      'Convert X , Y parameters from integers to string
06      strX = CStr(X)
07      strY = CStr(Y)
08
09      'Draw line in the Sketch Pad
10      Picture1.Line -(X, Y)
11
12  'Display the mouse pointer position
13  lblCursor.Caption = "X: " & strX & ", " & "Y: " & strY
14  End Sub
```

When programming with the MouseMove event, remember that the event is fired every time the mouse moves. This might sound simplistic, but the implications are important. If the code you write in the MouseMove event handler takes longer to execute than the amount of time before the next MouseMoves is fired, your program will display some very strange, possibly fatal behaviors. In Listing 15.8, for example, every time the mouse moves, the code creates a new For...Next loop, thus creating a queue of loops waiting to execute. The loops could go on forever. This unanticipated behavior will affect the integrity of your program.

LISTING 15.8   **15LIST08.TXT—Using the** *MouseMove* **Event Procedure with Loops**

```
01  Private Sub Form_MouseMove(Button As Integer, _
        Shift As Integer, X As Single, Y As Single)
```

```
02      Dim intCntr As Integer
03      'Loop could go on forever under certain conditions
04      'depending on the frequency of mouse movement.
05      For intCntr = 0 To 10000
06          frmMouse.Caption = CStr(intCntr)
07      Next intCntr
08  End Sub
```

Recognizing VB's Limitations with Mouse Input

Visual Basic has two significant shortcomings when it comes to handling mouse input. The first is that the mouse event procedures are control specific. In other words, there's no easy way for a form's mouse-movement event procedures to override a contained child control's event procedure. If you have a PictureBox control on a form or a separate form in the same application and then move the mouse pointer over the PictureBox, the control's MouseMove event procedure is executed. The parent form's MouseMove event procedure is ignored, and control is passed to the PictureBox that now has focus. This is important because the event procedure's *x* and *y* mouse pointer location parameters are relative to the control on which the mouse pointer is being moved.

Going back to the PictureBox control scenario, if you place the mouse pointer in the upper left corner of the PictureBox control, the *x* and *y* parameters passed to the form's MouseMove event procedure are 0,0. If you put your mouse pointer in the upper left corner of the Picture, the *x* and *y* parameters passed to the PictureBox's MouseMove event procedure also are 0,0. (This assumes that the PictureBox isn't in the upper left corner of the form.) Although the Picture is a contained child to the form, it doesn't report back the coordinates of the form; instead, it reports back coordinates relative to its internal Top and Left 0,0 position (see Figure 15.11).

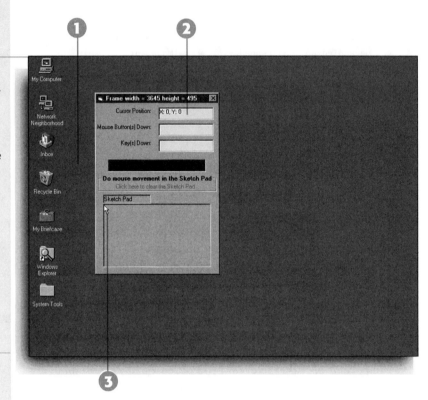

FIGURE 15.11

Keeping track of the mouse pointer's location relative to the form can be difficult.

1   A Visual Basic application can't detect mouse movement outside itself unless the MouseDown event was initiated and held down outside the control.

2   The upper x, y coordinates reported in the Form's MouseMove event procedure are 0,0.

3   The upper x, y coordinates reported in the PictureBox's MouseMove event procedure also are 0,0.

Draping the mouse outside the form

Use the Mouse.exe application to find the relative offset of the SketchPad PictureBox from its parent form. You can check your answers by looking at the Top and Left properties of the SketchPad PictureBox in the sample Mouse.vbp application on the dedicated Web site.

The second shortcoming is that Visual Basic doesn't report the mouse pointer's location outside its application, unless the MouseDown event has been initiated while under the control of the application and held down during the MouseMove event. (This is often referred to as *dragging the mouse*.) While the mouse is being dragged, it continues to report its relative position to the control through the MouseMove event; however, you have one final chance to process this information. When the mouse button is released and the MouseUp event fires, you can process the last x and y values, remembering that these are relative to the initiating control's location. These values could easily be negative.

This all means that after the mouse pointer leaves your Visual Basic application, VB normally has no idea where it is. Thus, writing a program that needs to know the location of the mouse pointer anywhere onscreen at anytime is very difficult to accomplish. You can use Visual Basic to access functions in the

Windows API (Application Programming Interface) that enable you to use an advanced programming technique called *subclassing* to accomplish this task. However, this type of API programming is very advanced and very delicate. An error in a Visual Basic application that implements subclassing can cause serious problems not only in the VB application but also throughout the entire system.

SEE ALSO

➤ *For more information about using the Windows API, see page 535*

Working with Time and Timers

Use the Timer control

Use the *Format()* and *DateDiff()* functions

Work with the *Date* data type

Understanding Serial Time

Visual Basic deals with time differently than you might be accustomed: It uses the Date data type, which uses the day as the basic unit of time. Thus, an hour is 1/24 of a day, and a second is 1/86,400 of a day. You would represent a week as 7 because a week contains seven days. The Date data type displays dates according to how your computer's time format is set: by 12-hour or 24-hour format.

In Julian time, Day 1 is January 1, 0000. Visual Basic, on the other hand, considers Day 1 to be December 31, 1899. Thus, Day 2 is January 1, 1900, and June 12, 1968, is Day 25001 or simply 25001, the 25001st day from December 31, 1899. The serial date 25001.5 translates to noon, June 12, 1968. Dates before December 31, 1899 are represented by negative numbers; for instance, July 4, 1776, is –45103—45,103 days before December 30, 1899.

You can assign literal date values to Date variables by enclosing the literal within a pair of number signs (#)—for example,

```
Dim MyDate as Date
MyDate = #May 15, 1998#
```

Year 2000 compliance

Although Visual Basic 6 is Year 2000 compliant, realize that programs you write won't automatically be compliant. When using dates in an application, be careful to validate user input to make sure that you're using the appropriate date. Also be sure to test your application thoroughly before deployment.

The Date data type can be converted into any other data type. For example, 2 p.m. May 15, 1998, would be 35390.58333 as a Double. Everything to the left of the decimal point is the day; everything to the right of it is the time or the portion of the day: hours, minutes, seconds, and milliseconds. Notice that decimal values less than 1 can be used to specify only a time; for example, 0.12345 represents 2:57:46 a.m.

Understanding the Timer Control

In Visual Basic, the Timer control enables you to track time. Think of a Timer as a clock that fires a programmable event at an interval you specify (see Figure 16.1). The event the Timer fires is called a Timer event, and the event procedure that you program is *TimerName*_Timer(), in which *TimerName* is the value of the Name property of the Timer control.

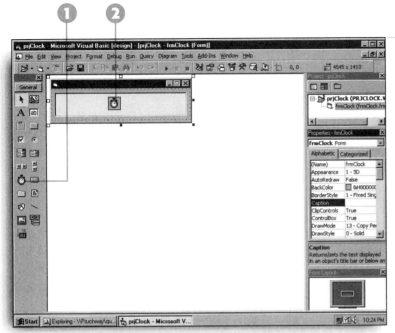

FIGURE 16.1

The Timer control is an invisible control. You don't see it at run-time.

1️⃣ The Timer control in the Toolbox

2️⃣ The Timer control added to a form

You can set the interval at which the Timer event fires by assigning a value to the Timer control's Interval property. The unit of measure for the Interval property is a millisecond, so if you want the Timer event to fire every half second, you would use the following:

```
Timer1.Interval = 500
```

The Interval can be as small as once every thousandth of a second or as large as your program requires. However, the shortest interval is 55ms because the system clock ticks only 18 times per second.

Because all the Timer control does is fire a Timer event, the control doesn't have many properties (see Table 16.1).

Counting long intervals

The maximum value for Interval is 65,535, which means that the maximum interval you can set is just over 65.5 seconds. To use a longer interval, such as 10 minutes, you must actually count 10 intervals of 60,000 milliseconds.

TABLE 16.1   Timer Control Properties

Property	Description
Name	Defaults to Timer1 if you have one Timer control, Timer2 if you have two Timer controls, and so on.

continues...

TABLE 16.1   Continued

Property	Description
Enabled	Turns a Timer on and off. The default is True, or on.
Index	Reports the position of a specific Timer control within a control array.
Interval	Determines, in milliseconds, when a Timer event will fire (1 second = 1000).
Left	The position of the left edge of a Timer.
Tag	The Tag property is like having a variable built right into the control. It's a catch-all property to which you can assign any necessary data to your program and that you want to persist throughout the life of your program.
Top	The position of the top edge of a Timer.

Timers are invisible

The Left and Top properties are irrelevant because a Timer isn't shown on the form at runtime.

Using the *Time, Date,* and *Now* Functions

Although you can program a Timer to fire a Timer event, the Timer doesn't know what time it is at any given point during its operation. For the Timer to report the time of day, it must check the computer's system clock and report back the time that the system clock passes to it.

When accessing a computer's system clock, you use the Time function to obtain the system time and use the Date function to obtain the system date. If you want to find out both the time and date on the system clock, use the Now function.

To see how these functions work, create a project and add three CommandButtons to a form. Name these buttons cmdTime, cmdDate, and cmdNow and add the appropriate code from Listing 16.1 to the event procedure for each button. (You can download this code from http://www.mcp.com/info.) Figure 16.2 shows the data that each function returns.

LISTING 16.1   **16LIST01—Event Procedures That Use the *Time, Date,* and *Now***
Functions

```
01   Private Sub cmdTime_Click()
02      'Get the time and convert it to a string
03      cmdTime.Caption = CStr(Time)
04   End Sub
05
06   Private Sub cmdDate_Click()
07      'Get the date and convert it to a string
08      cmdDate.Caption = CStr(Date)
09   End Sub
10
11   Private Sub cmdNow_Click()
12      'Get the date and time. Convert them to a string
13      cmdNow.Caption = CStr(Now)
14   End Sub
```

FIGURE 16.2

The Time, Date, and Now functions return a variant (Date) data type, which can be converted to a string with the CStr() function.

Use a Timer to Build a Clock Program

Let's create a clock program to see how a Timer works. This program shows the running time on the client area of the form and the current date in the form's title bar. When you minimize the form, the running time appears in the form's caption on the taskbar. (Keep in mind that you can customize this program to your specifications.)

Create a clock program

1. Start a standard EXE project and size the default form as shown earlier in Figure 16.1 or as you see fit.

2. Place a Label control and Timer control on the form, as shown in Figure 16.1. (In Figure 16.1, the Label takes up the entire form. Also, you can put the Timer anywhere because it isn't visible at runtime.)

3. Name the form `frmClock` and the label `lblTimeDisplay`. Leave the value of the Timer's `Name` property as the default, `Timer1`.

4. Set the value of the `BorderStyle` property of the form to `1 - Fixed Single`. Set the value of the `MinButton` property of the form to `True`.

5. From Listing 16.2, add the code between the lines `Private Sub Form_Load()` and `End Sub` into the `Form_Load()` event procedure.

6. Set the value of the Timer's `Interval` property to 500 (one-half second). Set the value of the Timer's `Enabled` property to `True`.

7. From Listing 16.3, add the code between the lines `Private Sub Timer1_Timer()` and `End Sub` into the `Timer1_Timer()` event procedure.

8. Save and run the code (see Figure 16.3).

Changing the `BorderStyle` property

When you change the `BorderStyle` property, the values of the button properties can change automatically. Keep this in mind when you design your application so that you choose a `BorderStyle` that contains the appropriate buttons.

LISTING 16.2   **16LIST02.TXT–The *Form_Load()* Event Procedure**

```
01   Private Sub Form_Load()
02       'Set the position and size of the Label control
03       'to the form's client area.
04       lblTimeDisplay.Top = ScaleTop
05       lblTimeDisplay.Left = ScaleLeft
06        lblTimeDisplay.Width = ScaleWidth
07       lblTimeDisplay.Height = ScaleHeight
08   End Sub
```

LISTING 16.3   **16FIG03.TXT–The *Timer1_Timer()* Event Procedure**

```
01   Private Sub Timer1_Timer()
02       'If the form is diplayed as a window, show
03       'the time in the client area and the date
04       'in the window's title bar.
05       If frmClock.WindowState = vbNormal Then
```

```
06          lblTimeDisplay.Caption = CStr(Time)
07          frmClock.Caption = Format(Date, "Long Date")
08      Else
09          'If the form is minimized into the Task Bar,
10          'set the caption to show the time. This will
11          'make the time appear in the Task Bar.
12          frmClock.Caption = CStr(Time)
13      End If
14  End Sub
```

FIGURE 16.3
Setting the form's MaxButton property to False disables it.

The Clock program uses a few things that you might not have seen before. The Format() function sets the string that displays the date to show the complete day, month, and year. (You'll find a detailed discussion of the Format() function in the following section.) You also set the form's MinButton property to True to enable the minimize button on the title bar, thus allowing the form to be minimized to the taskbar.

Forms have three properties—MinButton, MaxButton, and ControlBox—that affect the three buttons on the right side of the title bar. MinButton and MaxButton are used to turn on (value set to True) or off (value set to False) the Maximum and Minimum buttons on a form. These properties are available only at design time, when the BorderStyle of the form is set to 1 - Fixed Single or 2 - Sizable, and when the ControlBox property of the form must be set to True.

The ControlBox property turns on (value set to True) or off (value set to False) the control-menu box, located in the left side of the title bar. You can turn on the control-menu box only when the form's BorderStyle property is set to 1 - Fixed Single, 2 - Sizable, or 3 - Fixed Dialog.

The WindowState property

Be careful when you set the WindowState property. You might run into a situation in which you accidentally set the BorderStyle to be **Fixed Single** and the WindowState to be **Maximized**. This will result in a nonsizable splash screen type of window that fills the entire screen, which users can't control.

The program also checks the value of the form's WindowState property to determine whether the form is minimized. The WindowState property has three values: 0 - Normal (vbNormal), 1 - Minimized (vbMinimized), and 2 - Maximized (vbMaximized). You can read the value of the WindowState property to determine whether a window is sized regular, full screen, or in the taskbar. You can also set the value of the WindowState property to make a window full screen, restore it to normal, or minimize it to the taskbar.

Using the *Format()* Function

The Format() function is a powerful Visual Basic function that allows you to control the way strings present themselves. The function is used primarily to display time/date values and numbers, although you can use it to give string values a consistent look.

The Format() function takes the following syntax:

```
MyString$ = Format(Expression[, Format_String[, _
            FirstDayofWeek[, FirstWeekOfYear]]])
```

In this syntax,

Creating new format settings

The Format() function has many levels of complexity. You can use its intrinsic settings, or you can make up your own user-defined settings. For more information, refer to the online documentation that comes with Visual Basic.

- MyString$ is the return value.
- Format is the name of the function.
- *Expression* is any expression that returns a string, date, or numeric value.
- *Format_String* is the string template that tells the function how you want the result string to appear.
- FirstDayOfWeek is an optional constant that sets the first day of the week. The default is Sunday, but if you want Monday to be considered the first day of the week, you need to reset this argument.

- `FirstWeekOfYear` is an optional constant expression that specifies the first week of the year. By default, the week in which January 1 falls is the first week of the year. However, you can have other settings—the first full week, for example. (If you want more details about these last two arguments, read the online documentation that comes with Visual Basic.)

The key to working with the `Format()` function is understanding the `Format_String` parameter. This parameter tells the value (as described by the `Expression` parameter) how to appear as a string. Table 16.2 shows you how to use the settings that come built into the `Format()` function to manipulate the appearance of time and date strings.

TABLE 16.2 **Using the *Format()* Function for the Time and Date**

Format String	Example	Result
`"Long Date"`	`Format(36000, "Long Date")`	Friday, July 24, 1998
`"Medium Date"`	`Format(36000, "Medium Date")`	24-Jul-98
`"Short Date"`	`Format(36000, "Short Date")`	7/24/98
`"Long Time"`	`Format(0.874, "Long Time")`	8:58:34 p.m.
`"Medium Time"`	`Format(0.874, "Medium Time")`	08:58 p.m.
`"Short Time"`	`Format(0.874, "Short Time")`	20:58

Table 16.3 shows how to use the `Format()` function to manipulate numeric values into a desired string display.

TABLE 16.3 **Using the *Format()* Function for Numbers**

Format String	Example	Result
`"General Number"`	`Format(36000, "General Number")`	36000
`"Currency"`	`Format(36000, "Currency")`	$36,000.00
`"Fixed"`	`Format(36000, "Fixed")`	36000.00
`"Standard"`	`Format(36000, "Standard")`	36,000.00
`"Percent"`	`Format(36000, "Percent")`	3600000.00%
`"Scientific"`	`Format(36000, "Scientific")`	3.60E+04

continues...

Using the `Format_String` parameter

You must put the `Format_String` parameter between quotation marks because the function is looking for the literal string. When learning to use the `Format()` function, many people forget to do this, in which case the function will fail. For example, the statement `MyString$ = Format(.50, Percent)` will generate an error, but this line is correct: `MyString$ = Format(.50, "Percent")`

TABLE 16.3 **Continued**

Format String	Example	Result
"Yes/No"	Format(36000, "Yes/No")	Yes
"True/False"	Format(36000, "True/False")	True
"On/Off"	Format(36000, "On/Off")	On

You also can create other format strings to fit your specific needs. For example, if you want to make sure user input always includes two decimal places, use the line Format(235.6, "###,##0.00"), which would return the value 235.60.

Calculating Date Differences

Use the DateDiff() function when you need to know the amount of time between two dates. The DateDiff() function has the following syntax:

```
MyLong = DateDiff(Interval, Start_Date, End_Date[, _
          FirstDayOfWeek[, FirstWeekOfYear]])
```

In this syntax,

- MyLong is the return value of type Long.
- DateDiff is the function name.
- *Interval* is a string describing the interval of time by which the date difference will be measured (see Table 16.4).
- *Start_Date* is the date from which to start measuring (of data type Date).
- *End_Date* is the date from which to end measuring (of data type Date).
- FirstDayOfWeek is an optional constant that sets the first day of the week (similar to the constant used in the Format() function).
- FirstWeekOfYear is an optional constant expression that specifies the first week of the year (similar to the constant used in the Format() function).

The DateDiff() function works by taking the first date, represented by the parameter *Start_Date*, and subtracting it from the second date, represented by the parameter *End_Date*. After the subtraction takes place, the function returns a number of data type Long, which is the difference between the dates. The unit of measure by which the difference is reported is dictated by the string value of the *Interval* parameter (see Table 16.4).

TABLE 16.4   The Different Values for the *DateDiff()* Interval Parameter

Value	Interval	Usage	Return Value
"yyyy"	Year	DateDiff("yyyy", "7/4/76", "7/4/86")	10
"q"	Quarter	DateDiff("q", "7/4/76", "7/4/86")	40
"m"	Month	DateDiff("m", "7/4/76", "7/4/86")	120
"y"	Day of year	DateDiff("y", "7/4/76", "7/4/86")	3652
"d"	Day	DateDiff("d", "7/4/76", "7/4/86")	3652
"w"	Weekday	DateDiff("w", "7/4/76", "7/4/86")	521
"ww"	Week	DateDiff("ww", "7/4/76", "7/4/86")	521
"h"	Hour	DateDiff("h", "7/4/76", "7/4/86")	87648
"n"	Minute	DateDiff("n", "7/4/76", "7/4/86")	5258880
"s"	Second	DateDiff("s", "7/4/76", "7/4/86")	315532800

The project DateDff.vbp (which you can find on the Web site set up for this book) illustrates how to use the DateDiff() function to report the age of a person in days and in years. It works by having users enter their birthday in a text box, and then click the **Start Counting** button. Within the Click event procedure for that button, code verifies that the entry looks like a valid date string by using the IsDate() function. If the string is valid, the birthday text is converted to a date and assigned to a global date variable, gf_dtBirthday (gf_ is a prefix denoting that the variable is global to the form), and the Timer is enabled. If the string isn't valid, an error message is shown. After users close the message box, the code sets the cursor back to the text box, highlights the problematic text, and exits the event procedure.

Day and day of year, week, and weekday intervals

Although the day ("d") and day of year ("y") intervals are generally interchangeable, the week ("ww") and weekday ("w") intervals can return different results in specific cases. For more information, see the online documentation that comes with Visual Basic.

Using IsDate()

IsDate() is a VB function that checks a string or date value to see whether it's a valid date. If the string or date looks like a valid date, IsDate() returns True; otherwise, it returns False. For example, IsDate("September 16, 1998") and IsDate(#9/16/98#) return True, but IsDate("Birthday") returns False.

Within the `Timer1_Timer()` event procedure, which fires every half second (`Interval = 500`), the Timer control looks at the system date and time by using the `Now` function. The event procedure uses the `DateDiff()` function twice—once to measure the difference between the instantaneous time and the birthday time (as assigned to the global birthday variable) in terms of days and once to measure the difference in dates in terms of years. The different return values are assigned to their respective local variables, `lYourAgeInDays` and `lYourAgeInYears`. Listing 16.4 shows the `Click` event procedure and `Timer` event procedure from the code; Figure 16.4 shows the program displaying calculated values.

LISTING 16.4   **16LIST04.TXT–Source Code That Uses *DateDiff()***

```
01   Private Sub cmdStart_Click()
02
03      'Check to make sure that the string "looks"
04      'like a date.
05      If IsDate(txtBDate.Text) Then
06         'If it is a date, convert the text to a date data
07         'type and assign it to the global birthday date
08         'variable
09         gf_dtBirthday = CDate(txtBDate.Text)
10      Else
11         'If it isn't, then report an error
12         MsgBox "You must enter a proper date!", _
                  vbCritical, "Data error"
13         'Set the cursor back to the textbox
14         txtBDate.SetFocus
15         'Set the cursor to the beginning of the text box
16         txtBDate.SelStart = 0
17         'Highlight the erroneous text
18         txtBDate.SelLength = Len(txtBDate.Text)
19         'Leave the sub
20         Exit Sub
21      End If
22
23      'Turn on the timer
24      Timer1.Enabled = True
25   End Sub
```

Highlighting text in a text box

The code in lines 13 through 18 highlight the user's input by setting the focus to the text box (line 15), selecting the beginning of the string (line 17), and then selecting the entire string (line 19). This technique makes a nice addition because it helps your users locate the spot where they need to re-enter information.

```
26
27   Private Sub Timer1_Timer()
28       Dim lYourAgeInSecs As Long
29       Dim lYourAgeInDays As Long
30       Dim lYourAgeInYears As Long
31
32       'Calculate the date difference in seconds
33       lYourAgeInSecs = DateDiff("s", gf_dtBirthday, Now)
34
35       'Calculate the date difference in days
36       lYourAgeInDays = DateDiff("d", gf_dtBirthday, Now)
37
38       'Calculate the date difference in years
39   lYourAgeInYears = DateDiff("yyyy", gf_dtBirthday, Now)
40
41       'Report the date differences
42       lblAgeSecs.Caption = CStr(lYourAgeInSecs)
43       lblAgeDays.Caption = CStr(lYourAgeInDays)
44       lblAgeYears.Caption = CStr(lYourAgeInYears)
45   End Sub
```

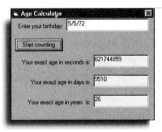

FIGURE 16.4

Using the Format() function makes the days and seconds values easier to read.

Using Static Variables with a Timer

Suppose you need to write a program that attempts to do an activity every half second for no more than 10 tries. To do this, you would need to create a variable that keeps track of the number of times the Timer control fires the Timer event. If you create a counter variable within the Timer event, however, every time the Timer event procedure terminates, the variable will go out of scope and reset its value to zero.

Clearly, you can't accomplish what you need to do by using this method. However, there are two alternative methods. First, you can set a global variable, and then increment and check the value of the variable within the Timer event, as shown in Listing 16.5.

LISTING 16.5   16List05.TXT—Using a Global Variable to Keep Track of *Timer* Events

```
01   Sub Timer1_Timer()
02       If g_TimeLimit% > 10 Then
03           MsgBox "Attempts exceeded!"
04       Else
05           'Attempt to do something
06       End if
07
08       g_TimeLimit% = g_TimeLimit% + 1
09
10   End Sub
```

Although this code will work, it's not optimal because creating a global variable creates a dependency external to the Timer control. If you decided to eliminate the Timer from the code for some reason, this global variable would still be hanging around with no real purpose and at some point would come back to haunt you.

A better strategy for keeping track of the number of times the Timer event procedure executes is to declare a counter variable with the Static keyword, as in Listing 16.6.

Be careful with Static variables!

Using **Static** variables doesn't mean that you should abandon declaring global variables within the General section of a form or module. Actually, you should be judicious in your use of **Static** variables. Nothing is more frustrating than finding a bug in your program that might be caused by a misbehaving global value, and then having to search through your code to determine whether a wrongly assigned **Static** variable is the culprit. If you need to create variables that will be shared among many areas of your code, you should declare them as **Public** or **Private** variables in the General section.

LISTING 16.6   16LIST06.TXT—Using a Static Variable to Keep Track of *Timer* Events

```
01   Private Sub Timer1_Timer()
02       'Make a static variable that will retain value even
03       'after the event procedure terminates
04       Static i%
05
06       'Report the present value of i%
07       frmMain.Caption = "Present value of i%: " & CStr(i%)
08
09       'Report the running time
10       lblTime.Caption = Format(Time, "Long Time")
```

```
11
12      'Check to see if the counter has exceeded 10 loops
13      If i% >= 10 Then
14          'If the counter is exceeded, send a notice
15          lblLimitNotice.Caption = "Limit Exceeded!"
16      Else
17          'If not, keep the reporting label blank
18          lblLimitNotice.Caption = ""
19      End If
20
21      'Increment the counter
22      i% = i% + 1
23  End Sub
```

When you create a Static variable, it keeps its value even after the procedure in which it's declared goes out of scope. The advantage of doing this is that the variable is *encapsulated* within the control on which it depends. The value of the variable persists, regardless of the state of the procedure in which you created it. You can find a program that uses a static variable in the StatVar.vbp project at http://www.mcp.com/info.

Adding Graphics to Your Programs

Use the PictureBox and Image controls

Use the *LoadPicture()* function

Use the FileListBox control

Create custom buttons

Change the size of pictures

Remember to experiment

Although the projects, forms, and so on, have specific names in this chapter, you can experiment with naming convention and with other parts of the code to fit your needs.

Adding Graphics to a Form

Add graphics to a form

1. Open a Standard EXE project and name it SmplGrfx. Name the default form frmMain. Set the form's Caption property to Simple Graphics.

2. Add a PictureBox to the form by double-clicking the PictureBox icon in the toolbox or by selecting the PictureBox and then drawing the control on the form. Name the PictureBox picMain.

3. Add an Image control to the form by using the same procedures as those described in step 2 for the PictureBox. Name the Image control imgMain.

4. Size and place the PictureBox and Image controls where you want them on the form, as shown in Figure 17.1.

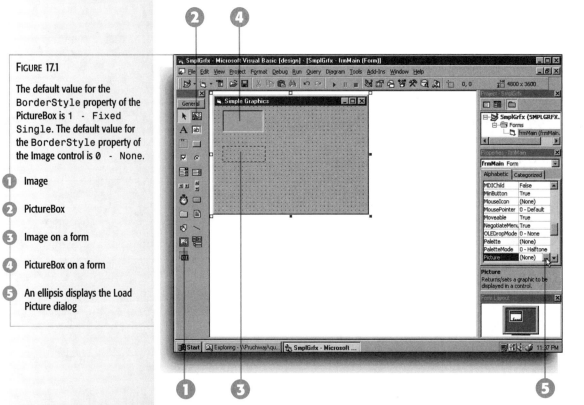

FIGURE 17.1

The default value for the BorderStyle property of the PictureBox is 1 - Fixed Single. The default value for the BorderStyle property of the Image control is 0 - None.

1 Image

2 PictureBox

3 Image on a form

4 PictureBox on a form

5 An ellipsis displays the Load Picture dialog

5. Select the `picMain` PictureBox. Go to the `Picture` property in the Properties window and open the Load Picture dialog by clicking the ellipsis button (see Figure 17.2).

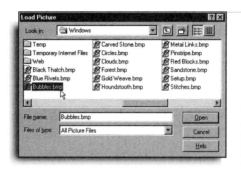

FIGURE 17.2
The Windows directory on your system ships with many different types of graphics files.

6. Go to the Windows directory and select **Bubbles.bmp**. When you click the **Open** button, this bitmap will appear in the PictureBox.

7. Set the value of the `AutoSize` property of the `picMain` PictureBox to **True**. This enlarges the area of the PictureBox to accommodate the size of the bitmap Bubbles.bmp.

8. Select the Image control and set the value of the `Picture` property to the bitmap **Triangles.bmp**. (This file is also in the Windows directory.) Do this the same way you added a picture to the PictureBox. You can't set the `AutoSize` property, however, because it isn't supported by the Image control.

9. Save and run your code (see Figure 17.3).

Many graphics files will work

Bubbles.bmp is a bitmap that ships with Windows. If for some reason this file isn't present in your Windows directory, choose another bitmap or choose any icon, metafile or enhanced metafile, JPEG, or GIF file. All these formats can be contained within a PictureBox.

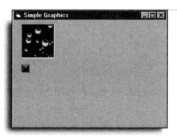

FIGURE 17.3
The Image control doesn't support an *AutoSize* property. It automatically resizes itself to the dimensions of the assigned picture when the graphic is added.

Changing a Picture at Runtime

You can change the graphic assigned to the Picture property of a PictureBox or Image control at runtime by changing the value of the control's Picture property.

Change a control's *Picture* property at runtime

1. Reopen the SmplGrfx.vbp project that you created earlier.

2. Add a CommandButton to the form and name it cmdChange. Set the value of the Caption property to Change the graphic.

3. Add the following code to the cmdChange_Click() event procedure:

    ```
    picMain.Picture = imgMain.Picture
    ```

4. Save and run the code (see Figure 17.4).

FIGURE 17.4

Setting the PictureBox control's *AutoSize* property to *True* resizes the control's area to the same size as the image.

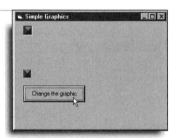

Making a Custom Button

You can use the process of setting a Picture property at runtime to make a custom button that looks different but works the same as a CommandButton.

Make a custom button

1. Open a Standard EXE project and name it CustBut.vbp. Change the name of the default form to frmCust and set the form's Caption property to Custom Button.

2. Add three Image controls to the form. Set the Name property of one to imgMain, another to imgUp, and the last to imgDown.

3. Assign the icon file cbUp.ico to imgUp and assign cbDown.ico to imgDown. (You can find these files at http://www.mcp.com/info.) Don't assign a picture to imgMain.

4. Arrange the Image controls on the form as shown in Figure 17.5.

5. Add the event procedure code shown in Listing 17.1 for the Form_Load(), imgMain_MouseDown(), and imgMain_MouseUp() event procedures to the General section of frmCust.

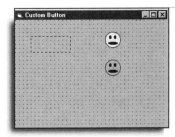

FIGURE 17.5

Creating a custom button requires three Image controls. When you don't add an image to an Image control, it appears as a dashed box on your form.

LISTING 17.1   17LIST01.TXT—Settings for the Custom Button Image Control

```
01 Private Sub Form_Load()
02     imgMain.Picture = imgUp.Picture
03 End Sub
04
05 Private Sub imgMain_MouseDown(Button As Integer, _
06             Shift As Integer, X As Single, Y As Single)
07     imgMain.Picture = imgDown.Picture
08 End Sub
09
10 Private Sub imgMain_MouseUp(Button As Integer, _
11             Shift As Integer, X As Single, Y As Single)
12     imgMain.Picture = imgUp.Picture
13 End Sub
```

6. Set the value of the Visible property for the Image controls imgDown and imgUp to **False**.

7. Set the following code in the Click event procedure of the Image control imgMain:

```
MsgBox "I am a custom button!"
```

8. Save and run the code (see Figure 17.6).

When you run the code in the project CustBut.vbp, the Image control imgMain becomes a custom button with an associated Click event procedure. The key to the construction of the custom button is to have the Image control's MouseDown and MouseUp behavior resemble general button down and button up graphical behaviors of a CommandButton. For example, when you click a CommandButton, notice that it shows a slightly different picture when the mouse button is down compared to when the mouse button is up. The custom button you just made does the same thing (see Figure 17.7). You can program the Click event procedure of the Image control custom button without interfering with other mouse behaviors because the imaging behavior of that control is relegated only to the MouseDown and MouseUp event procedures.

FIGURE 17.7

MouseDown and MouseUp images vary slightly to indicate state changes.

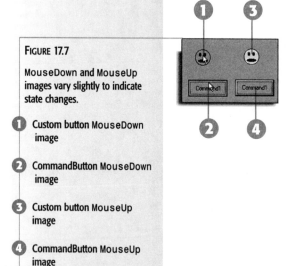

1 Custom button MouseDown image

2 CommandButton MouseDown image

3 Custom button MouseUp image

4 CommandButton MouseUp image

Adding Graphics to Forms with *LoadPicture()*

If you want to load a graphic file into a PictureBox or Image control from your hard disk, you use the LoadPicture() function:

MyPicture = LoadPicture(strFilePath)

In this syntax,

- *MyPicture* is a picture for a PictureBox or Image control.
- *LoadPicture* is the function name.
- *strFilePath* is a string that references the exact location on the hard disk of the graphics file that you want to load. This string must be in quotation marks.

Load a file from disk

1. Open a standard EXE project and name it LoadPrj.vbp. Rename the default form frmLoad. Set the form's Caption property to Load File.

2. Add a PictureBox to the form and name it picLoad. Set the value of the AutoSize property of the PictureBox to **True**.

3. Add a CommandButton to the form and name it cmdLoad. Set the Caption property of cmdLoad to Load from File.

4. Size and place the controls on the form as shown in Figure 17.8.

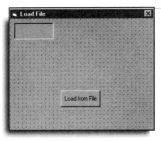

You can download this example

The code for this example can be found at
http://www.mcp.com/
info. When prompted, enter
078971633x for the ISBN
and click the **Search** button.

FIGURE 17.8

When you set the AutoSize property of a PictureBox to True, be sure to leave enough expansion room for the PictureBox to accommodate a large picture.

5. Add the following code to the Click event procedure of the CommandButton cmdLoad. (If you want to use a bitmap from a different folder or if circles.bmp is in a different folder on your system, use that path instead.)

```
picLoad.Picture = LoadPicture("c:\windows\circles.bmp")
```

6. Save and run the code. Figure 17.9 shows the program in run mode.

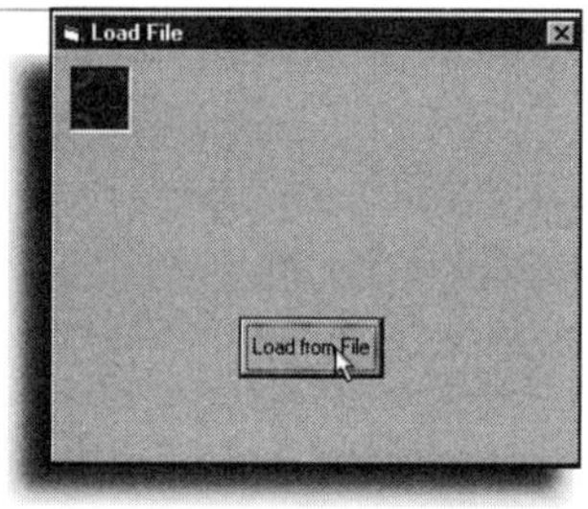

FIGURE 17.9

To clear a PictureBox or Image control, call LoadPicture without any arguments:
picLoad.Picture = LoadPicture.

Making a Form Icon

Windows programs commonly have an icon embedded within the executable file (.exe) to graphically represent the given program. When you create a program, Visual Basic automatically assigns one of your form's icons to your executable. Unless you change it, Visual Basic will use the default form icon (see Figure 17.10).

FIGURE 17.10

You set the unique properties of your program within the Project Properties dialog.

1 Default Visual Basic program icon

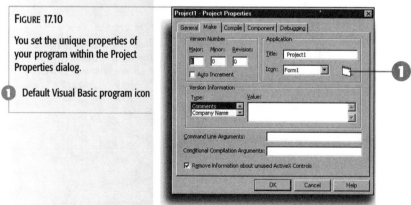

You can embed a custom icon into your program's executable file, however, by assigning an icon to the Icon property of a form in your project. Visual Basic contains many icons for you to use in the \VB\Graphics\Icons folder within the Visual Basic folder on your hard drive.

Change a form's icon

1. Select the Icon property of the form.

2. Click the ellipsis button to display the Load Icon dialog and browse for your custom icon (see Figure 17.11).

3. Click the **Open** button to add the icon to the form.

FIGURE 17.11

In Windows, icon files show their image in all views.

If your project has only one form, adding a custom icon to the Icon property of the form will automatically assign the same icon to the program. If your project has multiple forms, you must set the application icon from the Project Properties dialog.

Set the icon for your application

1. Set the icon for each form in your application.

2. Open the Project Properties dialog and select the **Make** tab.

3. From the **Icon** drop-down list, select the form that has the icon you want to use as your program's icon (see Figure 17.12).

Creating a new icon

You can't create an icon within Visual Basic or with the MS Paint program that ships with Windows. However, the Visual Basic 6 CD-ROM does contain a program for making icons. It's called the Microsoft Image Editor (imagedit.exe), located in the directory \Tools\Imagedit. If you can't find this program on your system, it probably wasn't installed; run Visual Basic setup again to install it.

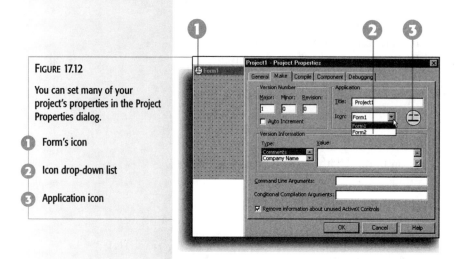

FIGURE 17.12

You can set many of your project's properties in the Project Properties dialog.

1️⃣ Form's icon

2️⃣ Icon drop-down list

3️⃣ Application icon

Loading Files with a File List Box

Look at the project MoreGrfx.vbp (from
http://www.mcp.com/info). This program sums up the techniques
you've learned thus far to display graphics (see Figure 17.13). It
enables you to display icon or bitmap images embedded in the
form and to select a file from disk to display in the main
PictureBox control picDisplay.

FIGURE 17.13

The application More Graphics uses OptionButtons to determine which technique the program should use to display images.

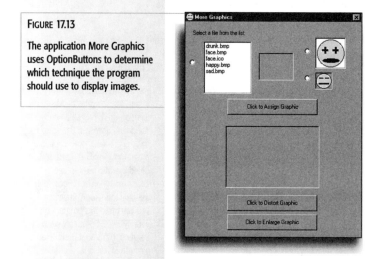

MoreGrfx uses a FileListBox (similar to a ListBox) to display the available graphic files. However, whereas the ListBox must be programmed to load string values to display, the FileListBox automatically displays strings that reflect the files of a specific folder. All you need to do is tell the FileListBox which folder by setting the value of the Path property of the FileListBox to the exact location of the folder containing the files you want to display.

Listing 17.2 shows the Form_Load() event procedure for the project MoreGrfx.vbp. This event procedure is where the value of the Path property for the FileListBox File1 is set.

LISTING 17.2   17LIST02.TXT—Using the *Pattern* Property of the FileListBox

```
01 Private Sub Form_Load()
02     'Set the path of the FileListbox to be the
03     'directory in which the application resides.
04     File1.Path = App.Path
05
06     'Make it so the FileListbox only displays
07     'bitmap and icon files.
08     File1.Pattern = "*.bmp;*.ico"
09 End Sub
```

Notice that the value of the FileListBox's Path property is set to the value of the Path property of the App object, which holds information about your application. The value of the App object's Path property reports the directory in which the application executable file resides. Thus, the FileListBox displays the files in the folder from which the application was started.

After a file is selected in the FileListBox File1, the user clicks the CommandButton cmdAssign. Listing 17.3 shows the Click event procedure for this CommandButton.

Study this code closely

Many of this program's nuances can be understood only by working directly with the program and looking at the entire code.

LISTING 17.3   **17LIST03.TXT—The *Click()* Event Procedure of the CommandButton**

```
01 Private Sub cmdAssign_Click()
02     Dim strFilePath As String
03
04     'Query the option buttons to see which one
05     'has been checked.
06     If optBitmap.Value = True Then
07       'Show the bitmap graphic
08       picDisplay.Picture = picBitmap.Picture
09     ElseIf optIcon.Value = True Then
10       'Show the icon graphic
11       picDisplay.Picture = picIcon.Picture
12     ElseIf optList.Value = True Then
13       'Assign the exact path of the graphic in the file
14       'list box to the strFilePath string variable.
15       'Don't forget, to get the string in a list box
16       'you must identify the Listindex selected within
17       'a List Control's List array.
18       strFilePath = File1.Path & "\" _
                           & File1.List(File1.ListIndex)
19       'Load the picture from disk and assign it to the
20       'picture property of the Picture control.
21       picDisplay.Picture = LoadPicture(strFilePath)
22
23     End If
24 End Sub
```

As shown in Listing 17.3, if the OptionButton optList is checked (line 12), the application loads the selected file from disk into the PictureBox picDisplay by using the LoadPicture() function.

SEE ALSO

➤ *For more information about ListBoxes, see page 193*

Creating Special Graphic Effects

In the project MoreGrfx.vbp, after users assign a picture to the PictureBox picDisplay, they can decide to distort the picture by clicking the CommandButton cmdDistort. When this button is clicked, the picture in the PictureBox is assigned to the Picture property of the Image control imgDistort with the following statements:

```
imgDistort.Width = picDisplay.Width * 1.5
imgDistort.Picture = picDisplay.Picture
```

The Image control distorts the picture because the value of the Stretch property of imgDistort is set to True and the value of the Width property of the Image control is modified to be irregular relative to the PictureBox picDisplay. The PictureBox must have the value of its AutoSize property set to True to resize itself and accommodate the area of pictures assigned to it. The Image control resizes itself by default to accommodate the area of assigned pictures. However, when the value of the Image control's Stretch property is set to True, Visual Basic resizes the assigned picture to the dimensions of the Image control, regardless of the size of the Image control. This can make for some unusual distortions (see Figure 17.14).

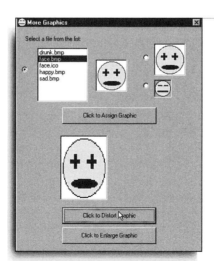

FIGURE 17.14

You can use the *Stretch* property of the Image control to distort pictures. To enlarge a picture, size the Image control to the same ratio as the original picture.

However, you can use the Stretch property to enlarge a picture within an Image control. Listing 17.4 shows the code for the cmdEnlarge_Click() event procedure. The cmdEnlarge CommandButton allows users to enlarge the picture displayed in the smaller PictureBox picDisplay. The trick to enlarging a picture is to maintain the width-to-height (aspect) ratio of the picture when sizing the Image control to which the picture will be stretched. The code in Listing 17.4 determines the ratio of the PictureBox picDisplay by calculating the control's width over its height (line 4). Then the code applies that ratio to the Height of the Image control imgDistort (line 8). As a result, the value of imgDistort.Width is reset, and the aspect ratio is maintained.

LISTING 17.4   17LIST04.TXT–The Code to Enlarge a Picture

```
01 Private Sub cmdEnlarge_Click()
02    Dim dSizeRatio As Double
03    'Figure out the ratio
04    dSizeRatio = picDisplay.Width / picDisplay.Height
05
06    'Apply the ratio to Image control's Height to
07    'get the new Width
08    imgDistort.Width = imgDistort.Height * dSizeRatio
09 End Sub
```

Writing Reusable Code with Subs and Functions

Make subs

Return values with functions

Use procedures that take arguments

Start programs from *Sub Main()*

Using Procedures in Visual Basic

You might not be aware of it, but you've been working with subs and functions for a while. Event procedures such as Click() and Load() are subs, and Visual Basic comes with many predefined functions built right into it, such as LoadPicture() and Len().

Visual Basic is a *procedural* language—that is, you can make blocks of code that can be referred to by a name. After a block of code has a name, it can be *called* and executed. In other words, you can write some lines of code, enclose them in a code block, give the block a name, and then call the block when you need it. It's almost like having a program within a program. These little programs that live within larger programs are called "functions" if they return a value and "subs" if they don't.

Programmers have written user-defined subs and functions for years. (In fact, the term "sub" is a shortened form of "subroutine" that gradually became its own word.) They make coding easier, faster, and more *robust*. Also, making your own subs and functions puts you on the road to writing *encapsulated* and reusable code. *Encapsulation* is simply the methods and properties of an object enclosed behind a public interface.

Making and Calling a Simple Sub

Making code changes easily

Subs enable you to change code easily. If you have a body of code that you need to use repeatedly, put the code in a sub. Then, if you need to make a change in the code, simply go to the sub to make changes. If you don't put the code in a sub, you will have to go to every instance of the code in your program to make the required change. The more dispersed your code is, the harder it is to make changes effectively and efficiently.

A sub is a procedure that executes the lines of code within its block but doesn't return a value. The syntax for a simple sub is as follows:

```
[Private¦Public] Sub SubName()
.....lines of code
End Sub
```

In this syntax

- [Private¦Public] are the optional Visual Basic keywords that define the scope of the sub.
- Sub is the Visual Basic keyword that denotes the type of procedure.

- *SubName* is the name that you assign to your sub.
- End Sub are the Visual Basic keywords that denote the end of a code block.

The following code snippet is an example of a simple sub:

```
Public Sub DataNotFound()
    MsgBox "Data Not Found", vbInformation
End Sub
```

When you call this sub from other areas of your code, the sub displays a Windows message box with the string Data Not Found. The message box will display whatever text is used for the string constant.

Listing 18.1 shows the sub being called with the Visual Basic Call statement (line 2). Using the Call statement is optional. Although you can call a Sub by using only its name, using the Call keyword makes your code more readable.

LISTING 18.1   **18LIST01.TXT—Calling a Sub from an Event Procedure**

```
01    Private Sub itmOpen_Click()
02        Call DataNotFound
03    End Sub
```

Making Subs by Using Add Procedure

You can add a sub to your project in two ways:

- By writing the code directly into the General Declarations section of a form or module.
- By using the **Tools** menu's **Add Procedure** option.

Add a sub to your project with Add Procedure

1. From the **Tools** menu, choose **Add Procedure** to display the Add Procedure dialog.
2. Enter the sub **Name** (see Figure 18.1).
3. Click **OK** to add the sub's code block to the form or module (see Figure 18.2).

Enabling the Add Procedure menu item

For the **Add Procedure** menu item to be enabled, you must be in Code window view of the form or module into which you want to add the procedure.

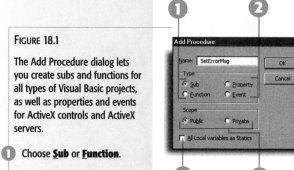

FIGURE 18.1

The Add Procedure dialog lets you create subs and functions for all types of Visual Basic projects, as well as properties and events for ActiveX controls and ActiveX servers.

1 Choose **Sub** or **Function**.

2 Used when you make objects.

3 Set the procedure to be **Public** or **Private**.

4 Makes all variables in the procedure hold their values, even when the procedure goes out of scope.

FIGURE 18.2

You'll find the new sub in the General section of the form or module.

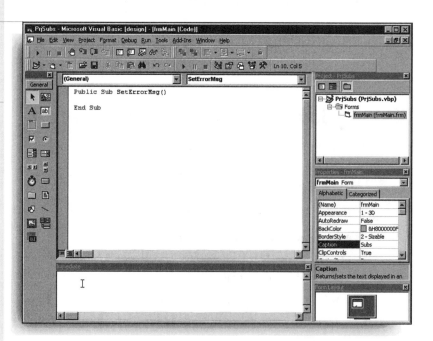

After you create the sub code block with the Add Procedure dialog, you add the procedure's code within the code block. Don't enter any code for the Sub after the End Sub keywords; this is illegal and generates syntax errors when you compile the code.

Making a Simple Function

A function is a procedure that executes lines of code and returns a value. The syntax for declaring a simple function is as follows:

```
[Private¦Public] Function FunctionName() As DataType
...lines of code
 FunctionName = ReturnValue
End Function
```

In this syntax

- Private¦Public are the optional Visual Basic keywords that define the scope of the function.

- Function is the Visual Basic keyword that denotes the procedure is a function.

- FunctionName is the name that you assign to your function.

- As is the Visual Basic keyword that denotes a data type assignment.

- DataType is the data type of the value that the function will return.

- ReturnValue is the value that you pass back from the function by assigning it to the function's name. (This is very important!)

- End Function are the Visual Basic keywords that denote the end of a code block.

The code snippet in Listing 18.2 shows a function, GetNumber(), the purpose of which is to return a number defined within the function itself.

LISTING 18.2   18LIST02.TXT—A Simple Function

```
01  Public Function GetNumber() As Integer
02      Dim a%
03      Dim b%
04      Dim c%
05      'Assign values to some variables
06      a% = 7
07      b% = 12
08
09      'Add them together
10      c% = a% + b%
11
12      'Pass the result out of the function by assigning
13      'it to the function name.
14       GetNumber = c%
15  End Function
```

You add a function to your project by using the same two methods that you use to add a sub—by putting it directly into the General Declarations section of the form or module or by using the Add Procedure dialog. However, be advised that you have to manually add a little code when you add a function to your code by using the Add Procedure dialog (see Figure 18.3).

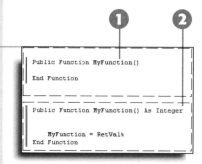

FIGURE 18.3

Add the code block in the Add Procedure dialog.

 The code block created with the Add Procedure dialog

2 The code block after you make the necessary manual additions

Passing Arguments into Subs and Functions

You can enhance the power and versatility of subs and functions by using *arguments*. An argument, also referred to as a *parameter*, is a variable that acts as a placeholder for a value that you'll pass into the sub or function. You create arguments by placing them within the parentheses of the declaration statement of the sub or function. The following snippet of code shows the declaration for the function EndDay(), which takes two arguments: one of type Integer and one of type String.

```
EndDay(NumOne As Integer, strName As String) As Integer
```

Using arguments greatly increases the reusability of your code. For example, imagine that in many places of your code you need to figure out the greater of two numbers. Every time you need to do this calculation, you could write out the code, line for line, or you could write out a function that does this for you and then call the function when you need to do the calculation. The advantage of the latter method is twofold:

- One call satisfies many needs throughout your code.
- If you need to enhance this functionality, you don't have to go through your code and make enhancements line by line; you simply go back to the function and make the changes within the function's code block.

Listing 18.3 shows the *user-defined function* GetGreaterNum(), which returns the greater of two numbers passed to it.

LISTING 18.3   **18LIST03.TXT–A Simple Function That Takes Arguments**

```
01   Public Function GetGreaterNum(NumOne As Integer, _
                     NumTwo As Integer) As Integer
02       'If the first number is greater than the second
03       If NumOne > NumTwo Then
04           'return the first number
05           GetGreaterNum = NumOne
06       Else
07           'if not, return the second number
08           GetGreaterNum = NumTwo
09       End If
10   End Function
```

Listing 18.4 shows the GetGreaterNum() function called from within a Click() event procedure.

LISTING 18.4   18LIST04.TXT—Using a Function Within an Event Procedure

```
0 1 Private Sub cmdGreaterNum_Click()
02     Dim i%
03     Dim j%
04     Dim RetVal%
05
06 'Get the input in txtNumOne and convert it to an integer
07   i% = CInt(txtNumOne.Text)
08
09 'Get the input in txtNumTwo and convert it to an integer
10   j% = CInt(txtNumTwo.Text)
11
12   RetVal% = GetGreaterNum(i%, j%)
13
14   'Take the result from the function, convert it to a
15   'string and assign it to the caption of the button.
16   cmdGreaterNum.Caption = CStr(RetVal%)
17 End Sub
```

It's very important when you use subs or functions that the argument's type and order match up. If you have a procedure that has three arguments of type Integer, you must pass in three integers; if you pass in two Integers and a String, the compiler will throw an error. For example, if you have a function EndDay() declared as follows,

```
Public Function EndDay(iNum As Integer, dAccount _
                        As Double) As Double
```

and call the function by using the following line of code,

```
dMyResult = EndDay(6, "D56R")
```

this call generates an error. "D56R" is of type String, but the function is expecting the second argument to be of type Double. For this reason, a variable type declaration error appears.

Also, the argument count must match up. For example, you have a function declared as follows:

```
Public Function Bar(iNum as Integer, dNum as Double, _
strName as String) as Integer
```

and you call the function by using the following line of code:

```
iMyResult = Bar(6, 7)
```

This call also causes an error. The function expects three arguments, but you've passed in only two. Again, an error occurs.

It's possible to make an argument optional by using the Optional keyword before an argument when you declare the function. If there's an upper limit on the number of arguments that you're going to pass, you should use the Optional keyword. These arguments must be declared as Variant.

Using Named Arguments

You can use named arguments to make passing arguments to a procedure easier. A named argument is the literal name of an argument in a procedure. For example, if you have a function EndDay() that takes two arguments, NumOne and NumTwo, of type Integer, you define it as follows:

```
EndDay(NumOne as Integer, NumTwo as Integer) as Integer
```

To pass a value to the function by using named arguments, you use the names of the arguments and assign values to them by using the := characters. Thus, to pass actual values into EndDay() by using named arguments, you do the following:

```
X = EndDay(NumOne:=3, NumTwo:=4)
```

> **Avoid problems with named arguments**
>
> Using named arguments enables you to avoid problems that might arise in function use because of the ordering of arguments.

Exiting Subs and Functions

Sometimes you need to leave a procedure before it finishes. You do this by using the Exit keyword. Listing 18.5 shows the function ExitEarly(), which takes two arguments: an Integer used to determine the upper limit of a loop and an Integer that flags the function when a special condition exists that requires the function to be exited early.

LISTING 18.5 **18LIST05.TXT—Using the *ExitEarly()* Function**

```
01   Public Function ExitEarly(iLimit As Integer, _
                          iFlag As Integer) As Integer
02       Dim i%
03       Dim Limit%
04       Dim Flag%
```

continues...

LISTING 18.5 **Continued**

```
05
06        'Assign the limit argument to a local variable
07        Limit% = iLimit
08
09        'Assign the state argument to local variable
10        Flag%= iFlag
11
12        'Run a For...Next loop to Limit%
13        For i% = 0 To Limit%
14
15            'If the passed in state is one
16            If Flag% = 1 Then
17
18                'Check to see if i% equals half the value of
19                'the Limit variable
20                If i% = Limit% / 2 Then
21
22                    'If it does, pass out the value of i%
23                    'at that point
24                    ExitEarly = i%
25
26                    'Terminate the function; there is no
27                    'reason to go on
28                    Exit Function
29                End If
30            End If
31        Next i%
32
33        'If you made it this far, the flag variable does not
34        'equal one, so pass the value of i% out of the
35        'function by assigning the value of i% to the
36        'function name.
37        ExitEarly = i%
38
39    End Function
```

The ExitEarly() function works by taking the iLimit argument, assigning it to a variable local to the function (line 7) and then using that local variable to be the upper limit of a For...Next loop (line 13). The function also takes the iFlag argument and assigns that variable to one that's also local to the function (line 10). Then the `For...Next` loop is run. Within the loop, if the value of the local `Flag` variable is 1 (line 16), an `If...Then` statement checks the value of the counting variable, `i%`, to see whether it's equal to half the value of the variable `Limit` (line 20). If it is, the value is assigned to the function's name (line 24) to be passed back to the call, and the `Exit` keyword terminates the execution of the function (line 28). If the value of the local variable `Flag` is other than 1, the loop continues until it reaches its limit (line 31). Then the value of `i%` is assigned to the function's name, and control is returned to the calling code (line 36).

When you create a user-defined function, the Visual Basic IDE treats it as though it were an intrinsic function. This means that the function is listed in the Object Browser and appears in the Quick Info window (see Figure 18.4).

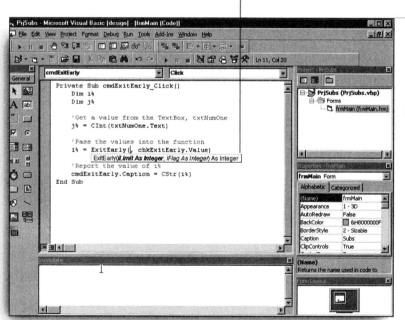

FIGURE 18.4

One nice feature of Visual Basic 6 is that the Quick Info window pops up even for user-defined subs and functions.

❶ Shows the arguments for a function and bolds the argument to be entered

Understanding Scope

Scope is the capability of two different variables to have the same name and maintain different values and lifetimes. Listing 18.6 shows two functions, EndDay() and Bar().

LISTING 18.6   18LIST05.TXT—Two Variables with Different Scope

```
01   Public Function EndDay() as Integer
02       Dim x as Integer
03       Dim y as Integer
04
05       x = 2
06       y = 7
07       EndDay = x + y
08   End Function
09
10   Public Function Bar() as Integer
11       Dim x as Integer
12       Dim y as Integer
13
14       x = 12
15       y = 34
16       Bar = x * y
17   End Function
```

Notice that each function declares variables x and y. Also notice that those variables are assigned different values within each function (lines 5–6 and 14–15). This is possible because each set of variables exists only where it's created. In the function EndDay(), the variables x and y are created in lines 2 and 3. When the function ends in line 8, the variables are removed from memory and no longer exist. (This is known as going *out of scope*.) The same is true of the x and y variables in the Bar() function. Neither variable set can see the other. If you wanted to create variables i and j, the values of which could be seen by both functions, you would create the variables higher in scope in the General Declarations section of a form or module, using the Public or Private keywords when declaring them.

Documenting Subs and Functions

Although the EarlyExit()function is functionally adequate, it's difficult to implement from project to project. If other programmers wanted to use it, they would have to take more than a passing glance to figure out what the function is about and how to put it to good use. Proper documentation addresses this deficiency.

All subs and functions should have a *header*, a section of commented code that appears at the top of a code block. The header usually gives a synopsis of the procedure: the procedure name, a description of the arguments and return value if any, and some remarks as to what the procedure is about, with any special instructions. Also in the header is a history of when and who created the code. If any changes are made to the code, a description and date of the changes are added to the header. Finally, the header contains the appropriate copyright information.

You should also comment each task within the procedure. This saves time for others who will maintain your code. Commenting your code will save you a lot of effort when it comes time to revisit the code later. Listing 18.7 shows the ExitEarly() function commented in a professional manner (line numbering has been omitted for the sake of clarity).

LISTING 18.7   18LIST06.TXT–A Well-Documented Function

```
01  Public Function ExitEarly(iLimit As Integer, _
02                              iFlag As Integer) As Integer
03  '******************************************
04    'Sub/Function: ExitEarly
05    '
06    'Arguments: iLimit   The upper limit of the For..Next Loop
07    '           iFlag    An integer indicating early exit from
08    '                    the function. 1 = Exit.
09    '                    Other values are ignored.
10    '
11    'Return: The value of the For...Next loop counter
12    '
```

continues…

LISTING 18.7 Continued

```
13    'Remarks:    This function is used to demonstrate the way
14    '                to use arguments within a function
15    '
16    'Programmer: Bob Reselman
17    '
18    'History: Created 4/20/98
19    '
20    'Copyright 1998, Macmillan Publishing
21    '*****************************************
22
23    Dim i%        'Counter variable
24    Dim Limit%  'Internal variable for the upper limit of the
25                    'For...Next loop
26    Dim Flag%   'Internal variable for the exit flag
27
28    'Assign the limit argument to a local variable
29    Limit% = iLimit
30
31    'Assign the state argument to local variable
32    Flag% = iFlag
33
34    'Run a For...Next loop to Limit%
35    For i% = 0 To Limit%
36
37        'If the passed in state is one
38        If Flag% = 1 Then
39
40            'Check to see if i% equals half the value of
41            'the Limit variable
42            If i% = Limit% / 2 Then
43
44                'If it does, pass out the value of i%
45                'at that point
46                ExitEarly = i%
47
48                'Terminate the function; there is no reason
49                'to go on
50                Exit Function
51            End If
52        End If
53    Next i%
```

```
54
55    'If you made it this far, the state variable does not
56    'equal one, so pass the value of i% out of the function
57    'by assigning the value of i% to the function name.
58    ExitEarly = i%
59
60 End Function
```

Determining Your Entry Point with *Sub Main()*

By default, when you start a Visual Basic project, the first form created will be the first form that the project loads. This is adequate if you have a one-form project. What if you have a project with many forms or a project with no forms at all? For the multiple-form problem, you could "chain" Form_Load() event procedures—have one form's Load event procedure Load another form—as follows:

```
Private Sub Form_Load()
     Load frmAnotherForm
End Sub
```

This would work adequately for projects with a limited amount of forms, but it's not the best programming practice, particularly if you have projects that require the presentation of many forms.

For projects that have no forms (and there are such projects, particularly in server-side Internet programs that use Visual Basic), there's nothing to load. What do you do for an *entry point* (or starting point) for your program? Visual Basic provides a nonform-based entry point for your program—the Sub Main() procedure. Sub Main() is a special procedure reserved by Visual Basic as the startup procedure for any given project. Sub Main() must be declared in a module, and there can be only one Sub Main() per project.

Set *Sub Main()* to be the startup point for a project

1. From the **Project** menu, choose *ProjectName* **Properties**.

2. Select **Sub Main** from the **Startup Object** drop-down list on the **General** page of the Project Properties dialog (see Figure 18.5).

3. Click **OK**.

FIGURE 18.5

You can choose Sub Main() or any form in your project as the startup object.

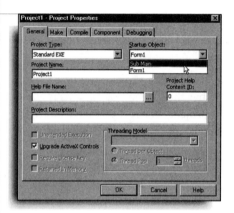

After you define Sub Main() to be the startup object for your project, you need to create Sub Main in a module. You can use the Add Procedure dialog that you've used to create user-defined procedures, or you can manually enter the declaration in the General section of your chosen module. Remember, a project can have only one Sub Main(). After you create Sub Main(), you need to fill in some startup code.

Listing 18.8 shows a Sub Main() that displays two forms by using the Show method (lines 4 and 5) and then displays a message box after all the forms are visible (line 8).

LISTING 18.8   **18LIST07.TXT–A Simple *Sub Main()***

```
01   Sub Main()
02        'Use the Show method to display both
03        'forms upon startup
04        frmMain.Show
05        frmOther.Show
06
```

```
07        'Report that all forms are shown
08        MsgBox "Everything shown"
09   End Sub
```

The code for some versions of `Sub Main()` can be simple, but some `Sub Main()` procedures can be complex. Listing 18.9 shows how `Sub Main()` is used to invoke a comprehensive startup routine that calls other procedures. This listing is the `Sub Main()` procedure for the VBScheduler program that you can download from `http://www.mcp.com/info`.

LISTING 18.9   18LIST09.TXT—A More Complex *Sub Main()*

```
01   Sub Main()
02   'Load the form and let it run the code in the
03   'Form_Load event handler
04   Load frmMain
05   'Intialize the contact list combo box
06   Call InitComboAsDb(frmMain.cboName, frmMain.DataMain)
07   'Fill the appointment list with today's appoinments
08   Call GetDailyAppointments(CDbl(Cdate _
                          (frmMain.FormDateString())), _
                          frmMain.lstSchedule, _
                          frmMain.DataMain, _
                          gAppointmentDelta%)
09   'Show the main form
10   frmMain.Show
11   'Set the mouse pointer back to an arrow
12   frmMain.MousePointer = 0
13   End Sub
```

Saving and Retrieving Your Data with Visual Basic

Save and retrieve text data from your hard drive

Save and retrieve graphical data by using *SavePicture* and *LoadPicture()*

Use the Registry to store information

Work with the FileSystemObjects

Understanding Persistence

For your program to keep information from session to session, you must be able to store data on the hard drive. Otherwise, when your application terminates, all the program's data in memory will vanish. Therefore, to have any sort of data *persistence*, your program must be able to save data to and retrieve data from the hard disk.

You can save data to and retrieve data from disk in several ways. You can use a *binary* or text file to work with information of varying size and formats. You can read from and write to the Windows Registry to accommodate small bits of binary or text information. Also, you can use a database for more complex persistence issues.

Working with Files to Store and Retrieve Data

Data lives in computer memory, and a file lives on the hard drive. Your program never works directly with a file on a hard drive. The program asks the operating system to mediate between the hard drive and your program.

You find the location of a file on a hard drive by asking the operating system for a *file handle*. You use the FreeFile function to obtain a file handle number from the operating system. After you have a file handle, you use the Open statement to assign the handle to the file that you want to write to or read from. When your program hooks up a file handle to a file, it can write data to the file by using the Print (or Write) statement or read lines of data from a file on disk by using the Line Input statement. Figure 19.1 illustrates this concept.

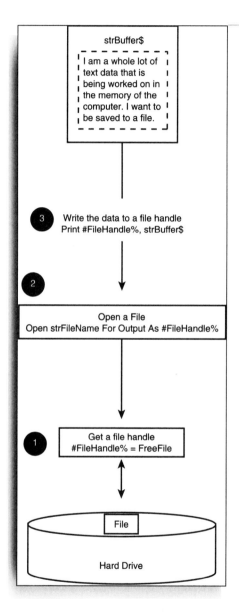

FIGURE 19.1

Writing to a file is the inverse of reading from a file. You still need a file handle, and you need to use the Open statement.

Saving Data with the *Open* Statement

Look at the project AdvTedit.vbp, which you can download from http://www.mcp.com/info. This program is a text editor that uses the Open statement to save and retrieve data from a file on your hard disk.

To use the program, when you want to save data, you click the File menu's **Open** command. A common dialog appears, into which you enter a filename and select a location on the hard disk. Then you click the common dialog's **Save** button to commit the data to disk (see Figure 19.2).

SEE ALSO

➤ *For more information about common dialogs, see page 276*

FIGURE 19.2

Using the common dialog is an easy way to create a filename and location for your data.

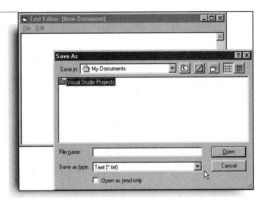

Behind the scenes you're using the Open and Print statements.

The syntax for the Open statement is as follows:

```
Open FilePath [For Mode] [Access AcessType [LockType] As
[#]FileNumber [Len=CharInBuffer%]
```

In this syntax,

- Open is the statement name.
- *FilePath* is the exact location of the file to read or save, with the drive and directory included.
- For is the keyword that specifies the file mode to follow.
- *Mode* is the file access type (see Table 19.1).

TABLE 19.1   **File Modes**

Mode	Description
Append	Add data to the end of an existing file. If the file doesn't exist, it will be created.
Binary	Open a file as pure binary—bits and bytes. If the file doesn't exist, it will be created.
Input	Open file for reading.
Output	Open file for writing. If the file doesn't exist, it will be created.
Random	Open file for random access. This is used for simple record storage. If the file doesn't exist, it will be created.

- `Access` is the optional keyword that specifies access type to follow.

- *`AccessType`* is the choice of `Read`, `Write`, or `Read Write`.

- *`LockType`* (optional) specifies whether others can read the file while your program is working with the file. The values supported are `Shared`, `Lock Read`, `Lock Write`, and `Lock Read Write`. Normally, these values relate to use of a data file in a networking environment. When the value is shared, specified users can access the file; however, if the value is specified as `Lock Read`, users can only read data from the file. The same holds true for `Lock Write`, in which case users can write to the file, whereas `Lock Read Write` allows Read and Write access. These values also could be used on a single PC environment, but it's more common in networking situations.

- `As` is a keyword that signifies the file handle is about to follow.

- `#` is the symbol that denotes that the *`FileNumber`* integer is a file handle.

- *`FileNumber`* is the file handle.

- `Len` is the optional keyword that introduces the record-length parameter.

- *`CharInBuffer%`* is the optional record length for a file opened for random access.

You open a file for reading as follows:

```
'Get a free file handle and assign it to
'the file handle variable
FileHandle% = FreeFile

'Open a file for writing
Open strFileName For Output As #FileHandle%
```

Listing 19.1 shows the Click() event procedure for the **Save** menu item. The procedure opens a file with the Open statement (line 28) and saves the contents of a TextBox to the file by using the Print method (line 34). After the write takes place, the event procedure closes the file by using the Close statement (line 40). The Close statement takes the file handle as an argument.

LISTING 19.1   19LIST01.TXT—Saving the Contents of a TextBox to a File on Disk by Using a Common Dialog

```
01    Private Sub itmSave_Click()
02    Dim strFileName As String 'String of file to open
03    Dim strText As String      'Contents of file
04    Dim strFilter As String    'Common Dialog filter string
05    Dim strBuffer As String    'String buffer variable
06    Dim FileHandle%            'Variable to hold file handle
07
08     'Set the Common Dialog filter
09     strFilter = "Text (*.txt)¦*.txt¦All Files (*.*)¦*.*"
10     cdMain.Filter = strFilter
11
12     'Open the common dialog in save mode
13     cdMain.ShowSave
14
15    'Make sure the retrieved filename is not a blank string
16     If cdMain.filename <> "" Then
17         'If it is not blank, open the file
18         strFileName = cdMain.filename
19
20         'Assign a value to the text variable
21         strText = txtMain.Text
22
23         'Get a free file handle and assign it to the file
24         'handle variable
```

```
25        FileHandle% = FreeFile
26
27        'Open a file for writing
28        Open strFileName For Output As #FileHandle%
29
30   'Set an hour glass pointer just in case it takes a while
31        MousePointer = vbHourglass
32
33        'Do the write
34        Print #FileHandle%, strText
35
36        'Reset the pointer to the Windows default.
37        MousePointer = vbDefault
38
39        'Close the file when completed
40        Close #FileHandle%
41     End If
42
43   End Sub
```

Closing a file

It's important to remember to **Close** a file when you're finished with it. The **Close** statement frees the file handle from memory.

Retrieving Data with Input Statements

You retrieve data from disk much the same way you write data to disk. The only difference is that, rather than use Append, Output, Binary, or Random mode, you use Input mode. Also, rather than use the Print or Write method to write the data, you read the lines of data in the file, line by line, by using the Line Input statement. The syntax for the Line Input statement is as follows:

```
Line Input #FileHandle, strBuffer
```

In this syntax

- Line Input are the keywords for the statement.
- # is the character denoting a file handle.
- *FileHandle* is a valid file handle of an open file.
- *strBuffer* is the string into which to put the data retrieved by the statement.

Simple text files are saved to disk in lines. If you were to do some data entry in NotePad and never press the Enter key, you would have entered one line of code. Every time you press Enter, VB adds the string Chr(13) & Chr(10) (carriage return and line feed) to the TextBox to mark the end of a line; when you save the file, these characters are also written to the file. VB has a constant defined for this string: vbCrLf. The Line Input statement will read into a file until it encounters the end-of-line sequence (vbCrLf). At the end of a line, the statement will take the characters it finds and send them to the string buffer argument, discarding the vbCrLf.

To traverse all the lines in the entire file, use a Do While loop. You use the Visual Basic EOF() function to determine whether the end of the file has been reached. This function takes the file handle number as an argument. As long are you aren't at the end of the file, the Line Input statement continues reading the lines of the file from within the Do While loop.

Listing 19.2 shows the event procedure for the **Open** menu item from the AdvTedit.vbp project. The user clicks this menu item to open a file into the text editor. The event procedure uses a common dialog to enable the user to identify a file to open.

Learning from the AdvTEdit.vbp project

You might want to take some time to study the AdvTEdit.vbp project. You can use many useful programming techniques in the code in many situations where you have to accommodate user input and save it to disk.

LISTING 19.2 19LIST02.TXT–Using the _Line Input_ Statement to Read a Text File

```
01  Private Sub itmOpen_Click()
02  Dim strFileName As String  'String of file to open
03  Dim strText As String      'Contents of file
04  Dim strFilter As String    'Common Dialog filter string
05  Dim strBuffer As String    'String buffer variable
06  Dim FileHandle%            'Variable to hold file handle
07
08    'Set the Common Dialog filter
09    strFilter = "Text (*.txt)¦*.txt¦All Files (*.*)¦*.*"
10    cdMain.Filter = strFilter
11
12    'Open the common dialog
13    cdMain.ShowOpen
14
15  'Make sure the retrieved filename is not a blank string
16    If cdMain.filename <> "" Then
17
18      'If it is not blank, open the file
```

```
19      strFileName = cdMain.filename
20
21      'Get a free file handle and assign it to the file
22      'handle variable
23      FileHandle% = FreeFile
24
25      'Open the file
26      Open strFileName For Input As #FileHandle%
27
28      'Make the mouse pointer an hourglass
29      MousePointer = vbHourglass
30
31      'Traverse the lines of the file
32      Do While Not EOF(FileHandle%) 'Check for end of file
33
34         'Read a line of the file
35         Line Input #FileHandle%, strBuffer.
36
37         'Add the line from the output buffer
38         strText = strText & strBuffer & vbCrLf
39      Loop
40
41      'Change the mousepointer back to the arrow
42      MousePointer = vbDefault
43
44      'Close the file when completed
45      Close #FileHandle%
46
47      'Assign the retrieved text to the text box
48      txtMain.Text = strText
49
50      'Put the filename in the form caption
51      frmMain.Caption = "Text Editor- [" & strFileName & "]"
52   End If
53 End Sub
```

Manipulating Graphics with _LoadPicture()_ and _SavePicture()_

As well as save and retrieve text from a file, you can also save and retrieve graphics. You use the LoadPicture() function to load a bitmap or icon file from disk and assign it to the Picture property of a PictureBox or Image control. The syntax for LoadPicture() is as follows:

```
ImageCtrl.Picture = LoadPicture(FilePath)
```

In this syntax,

- *ImageCtrl* is a PictureBox control, Image control, or form.
- *Picture* is the Picture property of that object.
- LoadPicture is the function name.
- *FilePath* is the exact location on disk of the file to load.

You save a picture that has been assigned to a PictureBox control, Image control, or form by using the SavePicture statement. The syntax for SavePicture is as follows:

```
SavePicture Picture, strFilePath
```

In this syntax,

- SavePicture is the name of the statement.
- *Picture* is the picture assigned to or embedded in the Picture property of a PictureBox control, Image control, or form.
- *StrFilePath* is the exact location and filename on disk to which you want to save the file.

Listing 19.3 shows the SavePicture statement used to save a Picture in an Image control to a location on disk. The program uses a common dialog to determine what to name the file and where to store it. The complete code for this program is in project SaveGrfx.vbp, which you can download from http://www.mcp.com/info.

SavePicture has an elementary use

Because of the graphics environment on the Internet and in Windows, you may find yourself using more and more graphics. The SavePicture statement allows you to manipulate, control, and save graphic elements from within your programming code. Manipulating them requires advanced programming skills as well as knowledge of the way Windows handles graphical device contexts. If you want to do advanced graphics work in Visual Basic—even just saving graphic files in multiple formats—you can use many third-party ActiveX controls.

LISTING 19.3   19LIST03.TXT—Using the *SavePicture* Statement

```
01   Private Sub cmdImgSave_Click()
02       Dim strFilter As String 'common dialog filter
03       Dim strFileName As String 'Filename variable
04
05       'Set the CommonDialog filter
06       strFilter = "Bitmaps (*.bmp)¦*.bmp"
```

```
07
08       'Assign the filter
09       cdMain.Filter = strFilter
10
11       'Show the dialog
12       cdMain.ShowSave
13
14       'Make sure a value was entered in the
15       'common dialog.
16       If cdMain.filename <> "" Then
17           strFileName = cdMain.filename
18
19           'Save the Picture in the image control
20           SavePicture imgMain.Picture, strFileName
21
22           'Tell the user the file's been saved
23           MsgBox strFileName & " saved."
24       End If
25   End Sub
```

Saving and Retrieving Data with the Visual Basic Registry Functions

You can use the Windows Registry to store small pieces of information custom to your program. You can use the Registry to store information about the location and size of your program's forms or user preferences. Some programmers use the Registry to store a list of the last files used. No matter what the need is, as long as the information is relatively small, you'll find that using the Registry is a fast, easy way to persist information.

Visual Basic comes with four easy-to-use procedures for accessing the Windows Registry: DeleteSetting, GetSetting, GetAllSettings, and SaveSetting. These internal Registry functions have one major drawback, however—Visual Basic can get and write data only to a specific key in the Registry, MyComputer\HKEY_CURRENT\USER\Software\VB and VBA Program Settings. This process is automatic to VB; Visual Basic can't write to or read from any other keys in the Registry without the aid of the Win32 API functions.

Figure 19.3 shows the location of the Visual Basic applications keys in the Windows Registry.

FIGURE 19.3

When you use the Registry functions internal to VB, data is saved in a key dedicated to all VB and VBA applications.

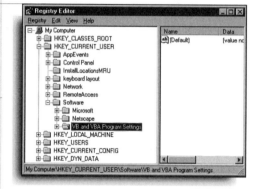

Retrieving Values with *GetSetting()*

You use the GetSetting() function to retrieve a value from a particular section in Visual Basic key of the Windows Registry:

```
MyString = GetSetting(VBKeyName, Section, Key[, Default])
```

In this syntax,

- *MyString* is the string value returned by GetSetting().
- GetSetting is the name of the function.
- *VBKeyName* is a string value that's the name of the key within the VB/VBA area of the Registry.
- *Section* is a string value representing the section or subkey for the specific applications setting.
- *Key* is a string value that represents the name of a specific entry within the section. A section can have many keys.
- The optional *Default* argument is a string value that represents the value to return if GetSettings() fails or encounters an error. If the function is successful, it returns the string found at the key setting; if it's unsuccessful, it returns the string value assigned to the *Default* argument.

Thus, the following code snippet

```
Return$ = GetSetting(App.Title, "FormInit", "Left",
DefaultLeft$)
```

looks for a Registry entry as shown in Figure 19.4. If it fails, it returns the value assigned to the sample string, DefaultLeft$.

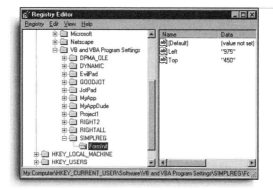

FIGURE 19.4

The VB Registry functions can save your data under your program's key.

Saving Values to the Registry with the *SaveSetting* Statement

If you want to save a value to the MyComputer\HKEY_CURRENT\USER\Software\VB and VBA Program Settings key in the Registry, you use the SaveSetting statement:

SaveSetting *VBKeyName, Section, Key, Setting*

In this syntax,

- SaveSetting is the statement name.
- *VBKeyName* is a string value that's the name of the key within the VB/VBA area of the Registry.
- *Section* is a string value representing the section or subkey for the specific applications setting.
- *Key* is a string value that represents the name of a specific entry within the section. A section can have many keys.
- *Setting* is a string value that you want to set to a given key.

This procedure relates closely to the GetSetting() function—it's the inverse. Whereas you use GetSetting() to retrieve a VB value from a specified key in the Registry, you use SaveSetting to set a value to the given VB key. All arguments, except for the last one, are identical.

Hands-on code

For a detailed look at how to use the **SaveSetting** statement and the **GetSetting()** function, look at the user-defined procedures **SetFormPos** and **GetFormPos** in the module modAlign.bas in the project Dynamic.vbp, which you can download from http://www.mcp.com/info.

378

Thus, the following code snippet

```
SaveSetting App.Title, "FormInit", "Left", "975"
```

produces the Registry setting shown in Figure 19.4.

Retrieving an Array of Settings with *GetAllSettings()*

You use the Visual Basic function GetAllSettings() to retrieve an array from the Registry that contains all the key settings and those keys' respective values of a particular section within MyComputer\HKEY_CURRENT\USER\Software\VB and VBA Program Settings. The syntax for GetAllSettings() is as follows:

```
MyVariant = GetAllSettings(VBKeyName, Section)
```

In this syntax

- *MyVariant* is an array of values returned by the function, of type Variant.
- GetAllSettings is the function name.
- *VBKeyName* is a string value that's the name of the key within the VB/VBA area of the Registry.
- *Section* is the string value representing the section to query.

When you use GetAllSettings(), the function returns a two-dimensional array in the form of a variant. To obtain the values, you transverse the array as you would any other.

SEE ALSO

➤ *For more information about how to traverse an array, see page 191*

Deleting a Key Section with the *DeleteString* Statement

If you want to delete an entire section from a key, you use the DeleteSetting statement:

```
DeleteSetting VBKeyName, Section[, Key]
```

In this syntax,

- `DeleteSetting` is the statement name.

- *VBKeyName* is a string value that's the name of the key within the VB/VBA are of the Registry.

- *Section* is the string value representing the section to delete.

- *Key* is the string value representing a specific subkey to delete. If you don't set this optional parameter, all the subKeys of the section will be deleted.

Thus, the following code snippet

```
DeleteSetting App.Title, "FormInit
```

deletes the Registry setting shown in Figure 19.4.

Using File System Objects

New to Visual Basic 6 are the file system objects, which *encapsulate* the objects, methods, and data that you use to work with files, directories, and drives within a computer's file system. Before you can use the file system objects, you must add the DLL that contains the object into the Visual Basic IDE. After you open the References dialog (choose **References** from the **Project** menu), select **Microsoft Scripting Runtime** (SCRRUN.DLL). This process is similar to adding any COM object to the VB IDE (see Figure 19.5).

File system objects versus FileSystemObjects

The file system objects are all the objects that enable you to work with the file system of a computer: the Drive, Folder, File, TextStream, and FileSystemObject objects. The FileSystemObject is a central object that gives you access to the various file system objects by way of a return from the various methods of the FileSystemObject.

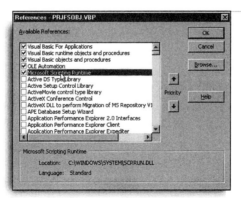

FIGURE 19.5

You can use the file system objects to access methods and objects necessary to work with files on your hard drive.

Table 9.2 shows the various file system objects.

TABLE 19.2 **The File System Objects**

Name	Description
Drive	Enables you to access various drives on a system. These drives can be CD-ROM drives, RAM disks, or mapped network drives.
Folder	Enables you to work with folders (directories) on a system. You can find out names and location. You also can create and delete folders with methods of the Folder object.
File	Enables you to open, create, or move files.
FileSystemObject	The central file system object. You use the FileSystemObject to access other file system objects.
TextStream	Enables you to read, write, and append text files.

Working with objects

To receive the full benefit of the FileSystemObject, you need to have a basic knowledge of object-oriented programming (OOP). For an overview of OOP, read Chapter 26, "Making Object-Oriented Programs with Visual Basic."

You declare a FileSystemObject by using the New keyword. Thus, to make the fso FileSystemObject, you use the following code:

```
Dim fso As New FileSystemObject
```

When you have a FileSystemObject, you can use that object to access other file system objects, such as the TextStream object (line 15 of Listing 19.4). The TextStream object enables you to treat the contents of text files as a very big string of text. Thus, you can avoid having to read the contents of the file a line at a time. Listing 19.4 shows you how to use a TextStream object to read the contents of a text file. Notice that line 21 uses the Read method of the TextStream object ts to read the contents of a text file from within a loop that traverses the entire contents of the TextStream object (lines 20 and 22).

LISTING 19.4 **19LIST04.TXT—Reading the Contents of a TextStream Object**

```
01   Dim fso As New FileSystemObject
02   Dim ts As TextStream
03   Dim strData As String
04
05   'Set a common dialog filter to show only
06   'text files
```

```
07   cdlgMain.Filter = "Text (*.txt)¦*.txt"
08
09   'Open the common dialog in Show Open mode
10   cdlgMain.ShowOpen
11   gf_strOpenFile = cdlgMain.FileName
12
13   'Get a Text Stream Object using the
14   'OpenTextFile method of the FileSystemObject
15   Set ts = fso.OpenTextFile(gf_strOpenFile)
16
17   'Traverse to the end of the TextStream
18   'concatenating the contents onto a string
19   'buffer variable.
20   Do While ts.AtEndOfStream <> True
21     strData = strData & ts.Read(1)
22   Loop
23
24   'Close the TextStream
25   ts.Close
26
27   'Assign the contents of the string buffer
28   'to the Text property of a TextBox.
29   txtData.Text = strData
```

You can use the CreateTextFile() method of the
FileSystemObject to create a file. Then you can use the Write
method of the TextStream object to write data to that created
file. Listing 19.5 shows you the code to do this. Notice the Write
method is at line 15.

LISTING 19.5   **19LIST05.TXT–Saving Data with the *Write* Method in a TextSteam
Object**

```
01   'Set a common dialog filter for text
02   cdlgMain.Filter = "Text (*.txt)¦*.txt"
03   'Open a save dialog
04   cdlgMain.ShowSave
05   'Get a filename for saving the data
06   gf_strOpenFile = cdlgMain.FileName
07   'Create a TextStream objet to the
08   'filename
```

continues…

LISTING 19.5 **Continued**

```
09   Set ts = fso.CreateTextFile(gf_strOpenFile, True)
11   'Get the text to write to the file from
12   'the Text property of the TextBox
13   strData = txtData.Text
14   'Do the write
15   ts.Write (strData)
16   'Close the TextSteam
17   ts.Close
```

In addition to using the file system objects to manipulate files and data, you can query properties of the objects to get information. Listing 19.6 shows you how to use various properties of the File object file to report statistics about a file. Figure 19.6 shows you the result of the code.

LISTING 19.6 **19LIST06.TXT—Using File Object Properties to Report File Information**

```
01   Dim fso As New FileSystemObject
02   Dim fil As File
03   Dim strData As String
04
05   'Get a file by using the global variable filename
06   Set fil = fso.GetFile(gf_strOpenFile)
07   'Get the filename
08   strData = "Name: " & fil.Name & vbCrLf
09   'Get the date created
10   strData = strData & "Created: " & fil.DateCreated _
                      & vbCrLf
11   'Get the date last modified
12   strData = strData & "Modifed: " _
                            & fil.DateLastModified & vbCrLf
13   'Get the date last accessed
14   strData = strData & "Last Access: " _
                            & fil.DateLastAccessed & vbCrLf
15   'Get the size in bytes
16   strData = strData & "Size: " & CStr(fil.Size) & _
                          " characters" & vbCrLf
17   'Get the file type
18   strData = strData & "Type: " & fil.Type & vbCrLf
```

```
19   'Get the parent folder
20   strData = strData  & "Parent: " _
                        & fil.ParentFolder.Name & vbCrLf
21   'Get the file path
22   strData = strData & "Path: " & fil.Path & vbCrLf
23   'Report the findings
24   MsgBox strData, vbOKCancel, "File Statistics"
```

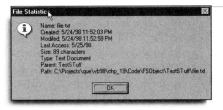

The file system objects make coding a computer's file system easier over the long term. In the beginning, however, becoming accustomed to them might seem difficult. The sample project prjFSObj.vbp that you can download shows you how to open a file for reading and writing with file system objects. The code also shows how to create files and obtain file statistics. The code in Listings 19.4 through 19.6 comes from that code. You also might find it useful to take an in-depth look at the File System Object model on the Help files that accompany your copy of VB6. File system objects are powerful, but they take time to master. You will find it time well spent.

Deploying Your Visual Basic Applications

Use the *App* object

Compile your application

Use the Package and Deployment Wizard

Using revision numbers

The revision number is also known as the build number because it signifies how many times the application has been compiled by its creator. This is often helpful in technical support issues because the revision number is how bugs can be tracked.

Working with Version Information

One of the first professional touches you can add to your application is to provide commonly requested application information. This information includes the company name, the version number, the revision (or build) number, and other similar information. Visual Basic enables you to store all this information through the use of the App object, a predefined object in Visual Basic that doesn't need to be specifically created by your application.

Most properties of the App object are used to provide general information about your application. Table 20.1 shows the most commonly used properties.

TABLE 20.1 **Commonly Used *App* Object Properties**

Property	Description
Comments	Returns a string containing comments about the application. Read only at runtime.
CompanyName	Returns company or creator. Read only at runtime.
EXEName	Returns filename of .EXE without extension. Read only.
FileDescription	String that briefly describes the application's purpose. Read only at runtime.
HelpFile	Specifies the help file associated with the application. Read and write at runtime.
LegalCopyright	Returns copyright notification string. Use the Character Map program to add special symbols in this box. Read only at runtime.
LegalTrademarks	Returns trademark information, if necessary. Use the Character Map program to add special symbols in this box. Read only at runtime.
Major	Returns major version number (for example, the 4 in 4.3). Read only at runtime.
Minor	Returns minor version number (for example, the 3 in 4.3). Read only at runtime.
Path	Returns the directory from which the application started. Read only at runtime.

PrevInstance	Returns a value if an instance of the application is running. Read only at runtime.
Product Name	Returns the assigned product name of the application. Read only at runtime.
Revision	Returns the revision number of the application. Read only at runtime.

You can use these properties to communicate important information about your application to those who will be using it. These properties are set in the Project Properties dialog (see Figure 20.1).

You can read the values of these properties at runtime within your VB code (see Listing 20.1). You can also set the value for the version information properties of the App object by right-clicking the compiled EXE file and selecting **Properties** from the pop-up menu (see Figure 20.2).

LISTING 20.1   Reading an *App* Object's Properties in Code

```
01   Private Sub cmdCopyright_Click()
02     lblMain.Caption = App.LegalCopyright
03   End Sub
04
05   Private Sub cmdPath_Click()
06     lblMain.Caption = App.Path
07   End Sub
08
09   Private Sub cmdProductName_Click()
10     lblMain.Caption = App.ProductName
11   End Sub
12
13   Private Sub cmdVersionNum_Click()
14     Dim strVerNum
15
16     strVerNum = CStr(App.Major) & "." _
         & CStr(App.Minor) & "." _
         & CStr(App.Revision)
17
18     lblMain.Caption = strVerNum
19   End Sub
```

Read-only App properties

The values of the **App** object's version information properties are embedded within the binary format of your Visual Basic executable. They can't be changed at runtime.

FIGURE 20.1

To access the Project
Properties dialog, choose
ProjectName Properties
from the **Project** menu.

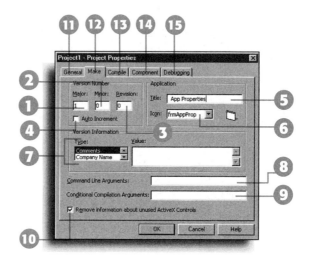

① Set the major release number.

② Set the minor release number.

③ Set the revision number.

④ Select to increase the **Revision** number each time you run a make.

⑤ Give the application a formal name (you can use spaces here).

⑥ Select the form that contains the icon that you want to represent the application.

⑦ Assign values for the different Version Information properties.

⑧ Pass values to the application when you run the executable for Windows Explorer's Run dialog.

⑨ Set constants that will be used during a conditional compilation.

⑩ Remove references to controls in your Toolbox but not used in your application

⑪ Determine what type of application to make on this page.

⑫ Set App object properties and select application icons here.

⑬ Set up native or interpreted compilation and optimization on this page.

⑭ Use this page when you make ActiveX components.

⑮ Offer options for debugging component-based and Internet-based applications.

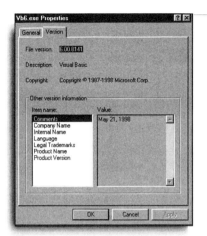

FIGURE 20.2

Select the **Version** tab in Windows Explorer to see the version properties.

Working with the App object's properties is important because through these properties you and your users can manage multiple releases of your code. Also, using the version properties of the App object, such as LegalCopyright and LegalTrademark, is the way by which users can verify that the program you made is really yours, thus avoiding potential incidents of piracy.

Compiling Your Project

After you set the values for the properties of your project's App object, you can compile your code. Up to this point in your programming activity, your project has been a collection of text and graphic files, which you've built with the Visual Basic IDE. Now it's time to transform these files into an executable file that will run independently of the IDE. This process is called *compiling your code* or *making an executable*.

Visual Basic 6.0 supports two formats into which you can compile your code: P-code or native code. When you compile your code into P-code, the resulting executable file runs as

P-code versus native code

A native code executable file tends to be bigger in size than its P-code cousin. Thus, if you want to deploy the smallest possible executable file, you should use P-code. However, if you want the fastest code possible, you should distribute your application in Native code.

interpreted code, just as it did in previous versions of Visual Basic. (P-code isn't the same thing as pseudocode.) Interpreted code is read by a runtime engine that determines the instructions to run. It's like giving someone an instruction sheet to build a product instead of giving them the product directly. The person receiving the instructions has to put all the pieces together correctly to create the end product.

If you compile the code as native code, the project files are transformed into more efficient binary code that uses your computer processor's full capabilities. This code tends to execute much faster. However, native code still requires the runtime DLLs—the only difference is that the DLLs are accessed and used differently by the EXE.

Compile your code into a standard EXE

1. Open the project that you want to compile.

2. Choose **Make *ProjectName*.exe** from the **File** menu. The Make Project dialog appears (see Figure 20.3).

FIGURE 20.3

Enter the name of the executable in this dialog. Click the **Options** button to change some of the App object's properties.

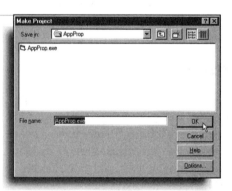

3. Rename the executable file in the **File Name** text box, if you want.

4. Click the **Options** button to open the Project Properties dialog. On the **Compile** page, choose between **P-Code** or **Native Code** compilation (see Figure 20.4).

5. Click **OK** in the Project Properties and Make Project dialogs to compile the code.

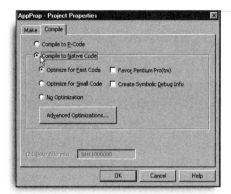

FIGURE 20.4

You can select from many options for native code compilation. Generally, the faster code option creates a larger file size for the executable.

Completing this process produces an executable file that runs outside the Visual Basic IDE. However, your application isn't fully ready for deployment. To deploy the application, you need to run the Application Setup Wizard for the executable to be able to run on a system on which Visual Basic is *not* installed.

Using the Package and Deployment Wizard

Because Visual Basic applications can be created in many different forms and used on different platforms, including the Internet, the old Application Setup Wizard has been replaced by the Package and Deployment Wizard in Visual Basic 6. You can use this tool to create installation packages for any type of application you build in Visual Basic. This section concentrates on creating an installation package for a standalone application.

To begin, start the Package and Deployment Wizard (shown in Figure 20.5). It should be listed on the **Visual Basic** submenu of your **Start** menu because it's installed by default. If not, you might have to install the tool on your system.

If you have ever used a previous version of the Setup Wizard included with Visual Basic, this tool will amaze you. Microsoft finally listened to programmer complaints and included a respectable installation tool. It doesn't do everything, but it can handle most of the simple installations required for Visual Basic applications.

Creating other project types

The make process that you've just completed pertains to standard EXE projects. You can make many other types of projects with Visual Basic 6.0, including ActiveX controls and ActiveX DLLs. This chapter is focusing on making standalone executables, however; building ActiveX controls is covered in Chapter 27, "Creating Your Own ActiveX Controls with Visual Basic."

FIGURE 20.5

The Package and Deployment Wizard is new with Visual Basic 6.0. It replaces the Setup Wizard.

Create an installation package

1. Select the project file at the top of the dialog.

2. To build a self-extracting setup program, click the **Package** button.

3. If you haven't compiled your application, the wizard will ask to compile the application for you (see Figure 20.6). Click the **Compile** button to continue.

Selecting a sample project

For these steps, you can use any Visual Basic project you have, or you can use a sample from Visual Basic. This section uses the ATM sample project included with VB.

FIGURE 20.6

The wizard needs to bundle an EXE file with the setup program, so it automatically compiles the application for you from the VB project file.

4. After the wizard compiles your application, it will ask you what type of package you want to build (see Figure 20.7). Select **Standard Setup Package** and click the **Next** button.

5. Indicate where you want to place the installation files that the wizard will create. These files will eventually be copied to your distribution media, whether it be a disk or CD-ROM. Select a directory (see Figure 20.8) and click **Next** to continue.

Save installation files to hard drive

Don't tell the wizard to save your files to floppy or CD-ROM at this point in the process; the wizard needs to modify the files several times before completing the process. Store the files on your hard drive and create the CD when the process is all done.

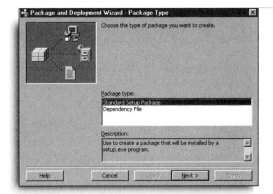

FIGURE 20.7

Select the type of package you want to build with the wizard.

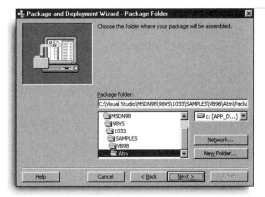

FIGURE 20.8

The wizard needs a temporary holding location for the files involved in the installation.

6. As mentioned earlier, Visual Basic applications consist of more files than just the executable. The next dialog (see Figure 20.9) lists the files that need to be installed with your executable. If you have other files (such as help files, as discussed in Chapter 24, "Adding Help to Your Programs") that should be installed, you can add them at this point. Because you don't have any other files in this case, click **Next** to continue.

7. The next step in the wizard deals with the size of the distribution media you want to use. If you plan to put your application on disks, the biggest file that the wizard can produce is the maximum size of the disk. Because you're not actually going to copy these files to floppy for this example, select the **Single Cab** option and click **Next** to continue.

Working with CAB files

The files that the wizard will produce are called CAB, or cabinet files. These files are a special type of archive file designed by Microsoft, much like a ZIP file. If you use the popular utility WinZIP, the 7.0 release will have support for viewing the contents of CAB files. CAB files are used by various tools, including Windows 98, for storing installation files.

FIGURE 20.9

This dialog shows a complete list of the files required to make this application run on another computer.

8. Next, specify the title of your application (see Figure 20.10). This title will be shown during installation. Enter an appropriate title and click **Next** to continue.

FIGURE 20.10

Enter the title of your application in this dialog.

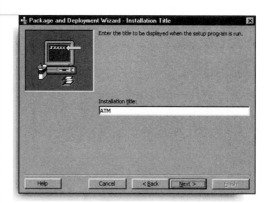

9. For your application to be used, it needs to have an icon on the Start menu. The next step in the wizard (see Figure 20.11) is a unique way to specify the icon groups and icons to create. The default settings are to create a group with the application's name and then to create an icon to start the program.

Because the application has only a single icon, the standard is to create that icon under Programs. Click the ATM group and then click the **Remove** button. Next, click the **New Item** button, enter the name of the application, and click **OK** in the dialog that appears (see Figure 20.12). Click **Next** when you're finished adding groups and icons.

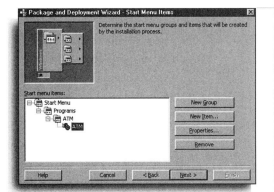

FIGURE 20.11

Pick the icons and groups you want created for your application.

FIGURE 20.12

Specify certain options about each icon you want to create.

10. The next dialog (see Figure 20.13) enables you to change the installation location of each file that's not required by the system. All system files are automatically installed in the \Windows\System directory; everything else is up to you. Because the specified directory is correct for this example, click **Next**.

11. Certain files, such as DLLs and OCXs, are considered shared files. If you were adding any of these files as part of your installation, they should be marked as shared so that when users uninstall your application, the shared files are verified before removal. The dialog shown in Figure 20.14 lets you mark any files as shared. Standalone executables like this one normally aren't shared, however, so click **Next**.

FIGURE 20.13

If you need to change the installation directory for files you've added, this dialog lets you do it.

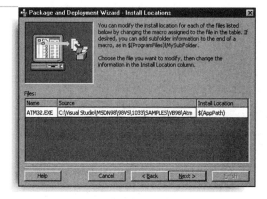

FIGURE 20.14

Mark any shared files as such in this dialog.

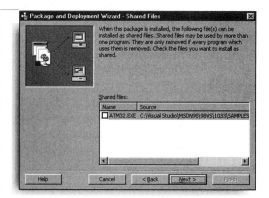

12. Give your script a name (see Figure 20.15) and click the **Finish** button to build your installation package.

FIGURE 20.15

The last step in the wizard enables you to give your script a name for later use.

13. After the wizard finishes building the installation package, it generates a report with some important messages about what was accomplished. Read the report and then click **Close** on the report and the wizard.

Advanced Programming
with Visual Basic 6

21   **Debugging Your Applications** 399

22   **Creating Controls On-the-Fly Using Control Arrays** 401

23   **Programming Beyond Visual Basic Using the Windows API** 421

24   **Adding Help to Your Programs** 437

25   **Using VBA to Connect Your VB Programs with Microsoft Office** 457

26   **Making Object-Oriented Programs with Visual Basic** 475

27   **Creating Your Own ActiveX Controls with Visual Basic** 529

28   **Creating VB Programs for the Internet** 543

29   **Making Programming Easier with Visual Basic Add-Ins** 579

Debugging Your Applications

Catch missing variables with *Option Explicit*

Find bugs with breakpoints

Check a variable's value at runtime

Step through your code

Use the Search and Replace feature

Design for debugging by using conditional compilation

Catching Undeclared Variables with *Option Explicit*

As you're coding, the Visual Basic IDE captures most statement syntax errors you make (see Figure 21.1). Syntax errors are considered spelling or keyword placement errors. These errors are normally easy to find and easy to fix.

FIGURE 21.1

The Visual Basic IDE catches If statements without the Then keyword as you type. However, it catches missing End If keywords only when you compile the code.

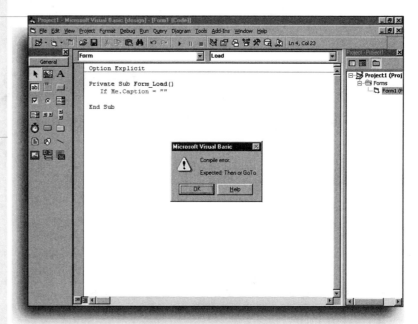

If you type like I do, you probably make spelling errors all the time. If you don't want VB to stop and display a message for each error, you can tell VB to highlight the line and allow you to keep typing. To change this option, choose **Options** from the **Tools** menu and clear the **Auto Syntax Check** check box (see Figure 21.2). Clearing this box doesn't prevent the compiler from finding errors when you attempt to run your program—it simply suppresses the normal syntax error messages that become highly annoying when you're typing lots of code.

FIGURE 21.2

Disable **Auto Syntax Check** if you don't want to see messages about your syntax errors while you're typing.

When you run your code within the IDE, Visual Basic reports errors such as type mismatches and incomplete code blocks (see Figure 21.3). Unless you have Option Explicit set, however, Visual Basic allows your code to run with undeclared variables. When you enter the keyword Option Explicit in a form or module's general section, all variables in your code must be declared explicitly by using one of the following keywords: Public, Private, Dim, or Static.

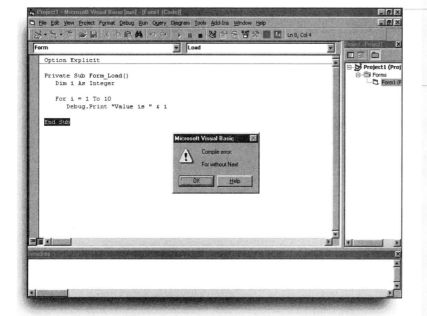

FIGURE 21.3

The IDE reports an incomplete Loop block when you compile the code.

Simple typing mistakes can lead to major errors in your code when you don't use `Option Explicit`. In Listing 21.1, you can see a typing error on line 6. The variable is declared with the name `intMyNum`, but line 6 attempts to use `intMyNim` instead. Because `Option Explicit` isn't declared, VB automatically creates a new variable called `intMyNim` and automatically initializes that variable to zero. Figure 21.4 shows the result. Had this code used `Option Explicit`, the IDE would have picked up the typing error when the code was run.

LISTING 21.1   A Bug Caused by a Typing Mistake

```
01  Private Sub cmdUnWit_Click()
02      Dim intMyNum As Integer
03
04      intMyNum = 2 + 2
05
06      MsgBox CStr(intMyNim)
07  End Sub
```

FIGURE 21.4

If you had used `Option Explicit`, you would have received an error message indicating that `intMyNim` was not defined.

Checking Code Segments with Breakpoints

You can easily stop your Visual Basic code at any point in its execution and examine it with breakpoints. A *breakpoint* is a place in your code at which you stop (break) your code during execution. You can set a breakpoint in four ways:

- Click the code line on which you want to break and press the F9 key.
- Click the Breakpoint icon in the standard toolbar.

- Toggle the breakpoint from the **Debug** menu.
- Click in the margin of the Code window.

When you set a breakpoint, notice that the line on which the break is set turns red. For your code to break, run the code. When the code breaks, the line on which you set the break turns yellow. Also, an arrow in the left margin of the Code window points to the line of code where execution has halted (see Figure 21.5).

Clearing breakpoints

To clear all the breakpoints in your code, choose **Clear All Breakpoints** from the **Debug** menu. You can also clear all breakpoints by pressing Ctrl+Shift+F9.

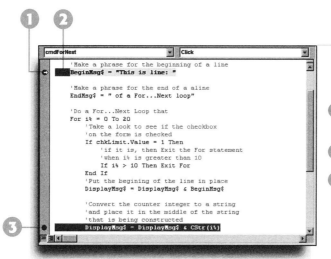

FIGURE 21.5

To go to the next breakpoint, press the F5 key.

①   An arrow indicates the currently executing line

②   The present breakpoint line

③   A stop sign points out a break

Not all bugs are caused by errors in code syntax; most bugs are caused by an error in code logic or faulty design. These types of bugs are hard to find. You use breakpoints to narrow down the area of code where you think a bug is occurring. After you determine a line of code in which you know your bug occurs, you set a breakpoint and look at the erroneous area by using *watches*.

Monitoring Variable Values with Watches

Look again at Listing 21.1 and Figure 21.3. This code has a bug, and the reason is obvious—a typo. For educational purposes, however, suppose that you have no idea why the bug occurred.

All you know is that the message box is reporting the wrong answer. This is a good opportunity to use breakpoints and watches.

Set a watch to inspect the value of the displayed variable

1. Set a breakpoint at the line of code that shows the message box.

2. Start your program.

3. Drag the mouse pointer over the variable whose value you want to view and let it stay there for a moment. A small window with the value of the variable appears.

When you watch the variables in question, you can see a discrepancy in values. Thus, you find that the code did assign the value properly to the variable intMyNum and that the second occurrence of the variable somehow lost the assigned value. Therefore, the addition logic is sound. The next step is to compare the spelling of the variables, which will lead you to the spelling mistake and the creation of the unwanted variable.

Monitoring Additional Variables with Add Watch

At times you need to watch more than one variable. To do so, you use the Watch window.

Add variables to the Watch window

1. Set a breakpoint or two to the variables you want to add. Press F5.

2. At each breakpoint, highlight the variable that you want to add.

3. Right-click and choose **Add Watch** from the pop-up menu.

4. Make the proper settings in the Add Watch dialog (see Figure 21.6) and then click **OK**.

5. To display the Watches window (see Figure 21.7), choose **Watch Window** from the **View** menu. This window also appears when you add a watch.

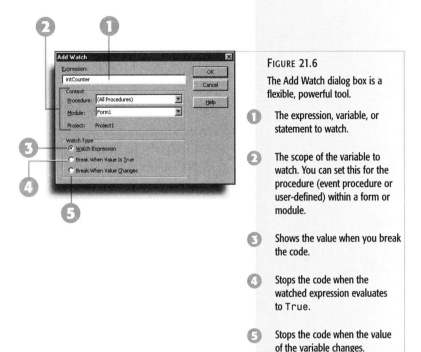

FIGURE 21.6

The Add Watch dialog box is a flexible, powerful tool.

1. The expression, variable, or statement to watch.

2. The scope of the variable to watch. You can set this for the procedure (event procedure or user-defined) within a form or module.

3. Shows the value when you break the code.

4. Stops the code when the watched expression evaluates to True.

5. Stops the code when the value of the variable changes.

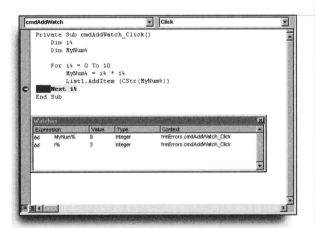

FIGURE 21.7

In Break mode, make sure that you are at a place in your code where the variables listed in the Watch window are in scope.

Keeping track of many interdependent variables that change continuously can be very difficult. The Watch window is an effective tool for inspecting values in these dynamic situations, particularly in loops or arrays.

Examining Code Line by Line with Step Into and Step Over

You can step through your code to examine every line of code as it executes and in the order that it executes. You can step in two ways: step into and step over.

When you step into code, you move through your code line by line. If one line of code happens to call another procedure—an event procedure or one that's user defined—you step into that procedure (see Figure 21.8).

FIGURE 21.8

You can step into code by pressing F8 or by choosing **Step Into** from the **Debug** menu.

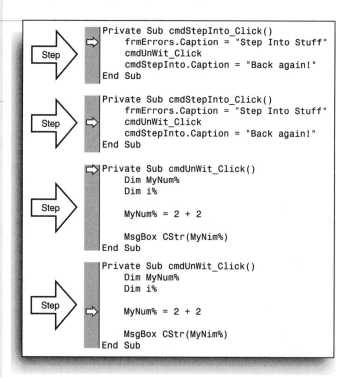

```vb
Private Sub cmdStepInto_Click()
    frmErrors.Caption = "Step Into Stuff"
    cmdUnWit_Click
    cmdStepInto.Caption = "Back again!"
End Sub
```

```vb
Private Sub cmdStepInto_Click()
    frmErrors.Caption = "Step Into Stuff"
    cmdUnWit_Click
    cmdStepInto.Caption = "Back again!"
End Sub
```

```vb
Private Sub cmdUnWit_Click()
    Dim MyNum%
    Dim i%

    MyNum% = 2 + 2

    MsgBox CStr(MyNim%)
End Sub
```

```vb
Private Sub cmdUnWit_Click()
    Dim MyNum%
    Dim i%

    MyNum% = 2 + 2

    MsgBox CStr(MyNim%)
End Sub
```

If you start your code with a step into, you might be surprised sometimes to see nothing happen. This is perfectly logical. If you have no code in the Form_Load() event procedure, there's no event to execute. Remember, Windows is an event-driven operating system; some event must fire for code to execute. The only real default startup code you have is a `Form_Initialize()`, `Form_Load()`, or `Sub Main()` procedure. If there's no code behind these events, your program will sit stagnant until an event is fired.

To step into some code, it's better to set a breakpoint where you want to begin to step and then run your code as you normally would. When you come to the breakpoint, invoke the step into feature to proceed. If you've used step into to enter a procedure and want to quickly exit that procedure, you can step out of the procedure by pressing Ctrl+Shift+F8 or by choosing **Step Out** from the **Debug** menu.

When you step over code, you also move through your code line by line. When you encounter a code line that calls another procedure, however, you don't enter the called procedure—instead, you execute that code as if it were solely a single line of code (see Figure 21.9).

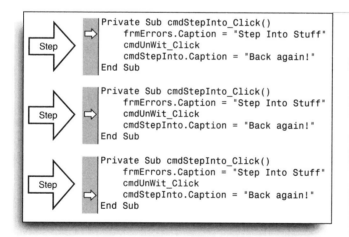

FIGURE 21.9

If you don't want to debug the internal code of an event procedure, such as `cmdUnWit_Click()`, step over it by pressing Shift+F8.

You might find it faster and easier to perform these debugging techniques by using the Debug toolbar (see Figure 21.10).

SEE ALSO

➤ *To find out how to display the Debug toolbar, see page 52*

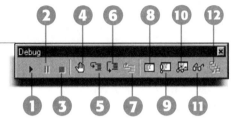

Stopping at Selected Lines with Run to Cursor

Every time you set a breakpoint, it stays in force until you return to your code and clear it or until you clear all the breakpoints by choosing **C**lear All Breakpoints (Ctrl+Shift+F9) from the **D**ebug menu. Too many breakpoints make debugging slow and bothersome. You can make things easier by using Run to Cursor to stop your code at arbitrary points.

You click the code line on which you want to halt execution and then press Ctrl+F8 or choose **Run to Cursor** from the **D**ebug menu. Then press F5 to run your code. The Visual Basic IDE stops execution of your code at the line that you clicked.

Using Advanced Debugging Tools

In addition to watching your code and moving through it by using the various step techniques, you can use the tools shown in Figures 21.11 through 21.14. Visual Basic provides these tools to do advanced debugging.

The Locals window (see Figure 21.11) is an easy way to view all the variables now in scope. Simple variables are listed with their values. Objects have a plus sign next to them, which you can click to view an object's properties. If a property is actually an object, you'll see another plus sign. In this window, you can easily see all variables at the same time without having to click each one.

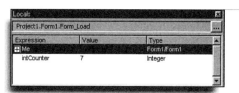

FIGURE 21.11

The Locals window shows all the variables now in scope and their values. You access this window by choosing **Locals Window** from the **View** menu.

The Immediate window (see Figure 21.12) can be used to test lines of code without having to run your program. To try it out, enter the following in the Immediate window:

```
Print 2 * 3
```

Below the Print statement will be the answer 6.

The Immediate window works fine for one-line statements. You can't declare new variables in the window, but you can use any variable that's now in scope. For instance, if you stopped your program in a subroutine that had an intCounter variable defined, you could put this line of code in the Immediate window to see its value:

```
Print intCounter
```

You can also modify values in the Immediate window and execute methods on objects. Anything that requires a single line of code can be run here.

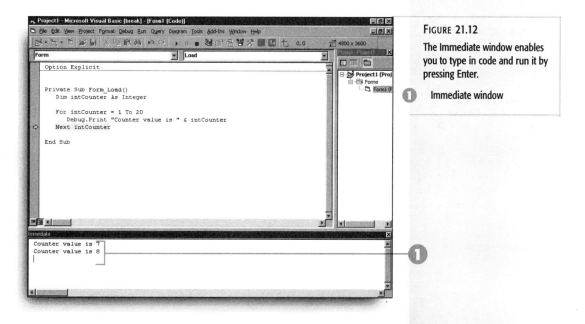

FIGURE 21.12

The Immediate window enables you to type in code and run it by pressing Enter.

① Immediate window

The Call Stack dialog is useful if you're using many procedures and events. This dialog (see Figure 21.13) shows all currently active procedures, functions, and event handlers. The item listed at the top of the dialog is the current procedure, the one below it is the one that called it, and so on. This dialog is opened by clicking the **Call Stack** button on the Debug toolbar or by pressing Ctrl+L.

FIGURE 21.13

The Call Stack dialog shows you all the active procedures. This is functional only in Break mode.

To show the Quick Watch dialog (shown in Figure 21.14), put a break in your code, click a variable, or highlight an expression and choose **Quick Watch** from the **Debug** menu.

FIGURE 21.14

You can also invoke the Quick Watch dialog by pressing Shift+F9.

1 Set the breakpoint and run the code

2 Highlight a variable

3 Click the **Add** button to add the variable to the Watch window

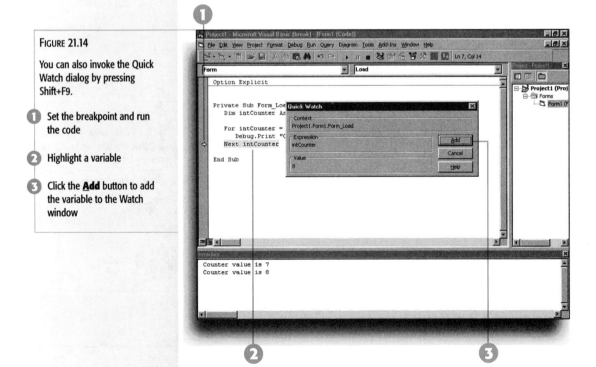

Using Find and Replace

If you've used any type of word processor, at some point you've probably done a Find and Replace. Find and Replace is a technique by which you search a document or portion of a document for a collection of characters and substitute as marked that collection with another—find all occurrences of *Bob* and change them to *Joe*, for example.

Find and Replace is a useful debugging tool that lets you make changes over a large expanse of code with relative ease. For the most part, the code you've seen in this book doesn't have a large line count, so finding and fixing something such as the misspelled variable encountered earlier isn't a difficult task. However, if you have a piece of code that runs more than 10,000 lines (which, by the way, isn't unusual for production code), the amount of work that you would have to do throughout the code to make a change—x + 2y to x * 2y, for example—would be considerable. Find and Replace makes things a bit easier.

Find and Replace works much as it does in a word processor. You select a set of characters that you want to locate and then invoke the process.

Find a set of characters

1. Choose **Find** from the **Edit** menu (Ctrl+F) to display the Find dialog.

2. Enter the word or characters you want to find in the **Find What** combo box.

3. Click the **Find Next** button (see Figure 21.15).

4. To display the Replace dialog, click the **Replace** button (see Figure 21.16).

FIGURE 21.15

The Find dialog has many logical search features built in.

1️⃣ Searches the current procedure

2️⃣ Searches the current module

3️⃣ Searches the entire project

4️⃣ Finds words that match, inclusive of case sensitivity (for example, MyVar doesn't match myvar)

5️⃣ Lets you search with pattern wildcards

6️⃣ Displays the Replace dialog

7️⃣ Continues a search

8️⃣ Lets you search up or down in the code

9️⃣ Searches for a word not included as part of another word

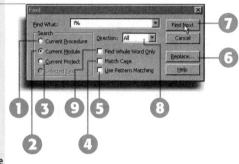

FIGURE 21.16

You can access the Replace dialog by choosing **Replace** from the **Edit** menu or by pressing Ctrl+H.

1️⃣ The word or characters to substitute

2️⃣ The word or characters to find

3️⃣ Substitutes only the highlighted word

4️⃣ Traverses the entire code, the scope of which is determined by the selection of the particular Search option, and replaces all the words entered in the **Find What** text box

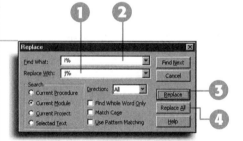

Designing Applications for Debugging

If you're planning to do much programming, chances are you'll end up writing some large programs that have many changes in them. The problem with debugging by using breakpoints and watch windows is that they aren't permanent. For instance, if you know about a problematic piece of code that causes errors each time you modify it, wouldn't it be nice to permanently embed some debugging code nearby so that you could quickly diagnose your error? You can make this work in Visual Basic in a number of ways, the easiest and most efficient being conditional compilation. *Conditional compilation* is the process through which VB can exclude pieces of code if certain conditions aren't met. C/C++ programmers have had this for years with `#ifdef` and related statements. VB made this feature available in a previous version of the product, but it hasn't been widely used yet.

This section shows you how to use conditional compilation to embed permanent debugging code in your application. The debugging code will never actually make it to the client, however—VB will leave it out.

Listing 21.2 is a simple piece of code that sums the numbers from 1 to 20 and displays the result.

LISTING 21.2   Simple Addition Code

```
01  Private Sub Form_Load()
02     Dim intCounter As Integer
03     Dim intSum As Integer
04     intSum = 0
05
06     For intCounter = 1 To 20
07        intSum = intSum + intCounter
08     Next intCounter
09     MsgBox "Sum is " & intSum & "."
10
11  End Sub
```

Suppose that you're unsure whether the addition is working right. An easy way to test it is to add a `Debug.Print` statement, as shown on line 8 of Listing 21.3.

LISTING 21.3   Simple Addition Code with Output

```
01  Private Sub Form_Load()
02      Dim intCounter As Integer
03      Dim intSum As Integer
04      intSum = 0
05
06      For intCounter = 1 To 20
07          intSum = intSum + intCounter
08          Debug.Print "Value: " & i & ", New Sum: " & intSum
09      Next intCounter
10      MsgBox "Sum is " & intSum & "."
11
12  End Sub
```

The results of the Debug.Print statement will show up in the Immediate window when this program runs in the VB environment. Whenever you compile this program for distribution, however, those Debug.Print statements won't do anything because there's no Immediate window to print to. For this reason, it makes sense to leave them out by using conditional compilation. To do this, the Debug.Print statement must be wrapped with conditional operators, as shown on lines 9–11 in Listing 21.4.

LISTING 21.4   Output Wrapped in Conditional Compilation Tags

```
01  Private Sub Form_Load()
02      Dim intCounter As Integer
03      Dim intSum As Integer
04      intSum = 0
05
06      For intCounter = 1 To 20
07          intSum = intSum + intCounter
08
09  #If DEBUG_ON Then
10          Debug.Print "Value: " & intCounter & ", New Sum: " _
                            & intSum
11  #End If
12
13      Next intCounter
14      MsgBox "Sum is " & intSum & "."
15
16  End Sub
```

The code between #If and #End If is evaluated only if the #If condition is True. If not, the code essentially doesn't exist in the VB environment. You can't do any normal debugging tasks on code wrapped in this manner when the condition isn't met. For the code to work, you have to add the following line to the form's declarations section:

```
#Const DEBUG_ON = True
```

This special definition causes the DEBUG_ON compilation constant to be True. The Debug statement will now print out properly.

Creating an Error Handler

If you've ever used a software package and had it crash on you, you were the victim of one of the biggest problems in programming: error handling. Every program needs to be responsible for itself and any errors that can occur. In this section, you see how to use VB's built-in error-handling capabilities. You also will build a simple error handler that can be expanded for your own applications.

See what happens when you don't handle errors

1. Start a new project.

2. In the Form_Load event handler, add this code:

   ```
   Dim intTest as Integer
   intTest = 100 / 0
   ```

3. Run your project.

Because division by zero is an error, VB stops and generates an error message. If your program had been running as an executable, users would receive the same error message you did, and the program would immediately exit. This isn't good programming style.

Luckily, you have a few ways to deal with runtime errors through Visual Basic's error handling. The first of these is the On Error Resume Next command. This statement, used as part of an error handler, causes Visual Basic to skip the error and go on. This type of error handler is useful when you don't necessarily need to resolve the error. For instance, if an error occurs while

> **Why use conditional compilation?**
>
> The best part about the conditional compilation code is that all the conditional parts are removed before the executable is built. If a condition was True when the code was compiled, the code within the If...Then is left in the resulting VB code. If the condition was False, the wrapped code is completely removed. This way, your code can be smaller and faster, especially because the processor doesn't have to do any work at runtime to evaluate debug flags.

you're exiting the program, there isn't any point in handling the error, because you're exiting anyway.

To try out On Error Resume Next, replace your Form_Load code with the following code:

```
Dim intTest As Integer
On Error Resume Next
intTest = 100 / 0
Debug.Print "Program is past the error."
```

Because you now have an error handler, VB can detect the error and skip the line that the error occurs in. In the Immediate window, you will see the results of the Print statement you created.

In this case, the error handler will save your program from crashing. However, not solving this error here can cause other errors later in the program. Farther on, some code that needs the value of the intTest variable might not work, and you will end up with an even bigger error, known as a *cascading error*.

A cascading error is much like multiple-car pileups that occur on interstate freeways: The first car crashes into something, the next car can't stop and runs into the first, and so on, until you have a real mess.

To help prevent these types of nightmares, Visual Basic provides additional error-handling features, such as the capability to create a more specific error handler. For instance, you want to let users reattempt to open their CD-ROM drive but don't want to continue if a division-by-zero error occurs. To do this, replace your Form_Load code with the following (minus the line numbers, of course):

```
01 Private Sub Form_Load()
02    Dim intTest As Integer
03    Dim intRet As Integer
04    On Error GoTo EH
05    intTest = 5 / 0
06    Exit Sub
07
08 EH:
09    If Err.Number = 11 Then
10       MsgBox "Division by zero error occurred.", _
             vbCritical
```

Looking at all the errors

You can find other trappable errors for VB by searching for **Trappable Errors** in your VB help file. Literally hundreds of errors can happen. Also, each control or library that you add can have its own errors defined. Refer to each library/control's documentation for information about errors that can occur.

```
11     End
12   ElseIf Err.Number = 71 Then
13       intRet = MsgBox("That drive is not ready.", _
             vbExclamation + vbAbortRetryIgnore)
14       Select Case intRet
15       Case vbRetry
16          Resume
17       Case vbAbort
18          End
19       Case vbIgnore
20          Resume Next
21       End Select
22   '
23   ' more conditions follow
24   '
25   End If
26 End Sub
```

First, the On Error statement now uses the GoTo statement (line 4) to tell VB where to go in case of an error. In this case, you want to go to a block of code labeled with EH (line 8). Labels are used almost exclusively for error handling and are simply text followed by a colon, like the EH: just above the error-handling code.

This error-handling section (lines 9–25) checks the Number property of the Err object. This number determines what the error is. This particular block checks for a division-by-zero error, which obviously will occur. When it does, the programmer has decided that it is serious enough to require the program to shut down. The End statement (line 18) will immediately shut down the program.

The next error to check for is the Drive Not Ready error, which happens frequently when you try to access a CD-ROM or floppy drive without a disk in it. This particular case offers users three choices:

- Abort—Stop the program immediately.
- Retry—Try the drive again.
- Ignore—Skip the statement and move on.

You can see the code for each value of the MsgBox function in the preceding example. After the Drive Not Found error, you typically would have more error-handling blocks to handle other types of errors that might occur during the operation of your program. You can use Select Case to handle groups of errors in a similar way, because the errors are numbered. For instance, all the Drive Not Ready error types should be handled in the way used here—that is, allow users to abort, retry, or ignore. Other error types, such as division by zero and other critical errors, will normally cause the program to fail—maybe not immediately but possibly later.

The most important thing to remember about error handling is that every procedure with significant code in it needs an error handler. You can name all the error-handling blocks the same—that is, they can all be labeled EH. This makes it easier for you to duplicate code and drop in as you need it.

Creating Controls On-the-Fly Using Control Arrays

Create control arrays with Cut and Paste

Create control arrays with the *Load* statement

Build event procedures for control arrays

Destroy controls by using *For...Next* loops

What Is a Control Array?

In Visual Basic, you can create arrays of any data type you want. You can also create an array of controls. Control arrays are a distinctive feature of Visual Basic that brings efficiency and power to the language. You can use them to create a common event procedure that's shared among all the controls in the control array. You also can use them to add and remove controls and forms to your program dynamically at runtime. This chapter shows you all you need to know to be able to work effectively with them.

All the intrinsic controls can be used in control arrays. These controls all have an Index property that's used to identify a particular control in a control array.

Can I create a control array?

The name **Index** is used for other purposes, so check the online help before assuming that a control can be added to a control array.

Creating a Control Array at Design Time

Many control arrays that you create will be built at design time. As you add controls to your form, you will need to group some of them into control arrays. This example shows you how to do that.

Create a control array of CommandButtons

1. Add a CommandButton to the center of the form frmMain and name it cmdMyButton. Set the value of cmdMyButton's Caption property to Action.

2. Make sure that cmdMyButton is selected. Choose **Copy** from the **Edit** menu ⧉ to copy the CommandButton to the Clipboard.

3. Choose **Paste** from the **Edit** menu ⧉. You're presented with a dialog box asking whether you want to create a control array. Click **Yes** to create the control array.

Now that the control array is created, if you go to the Properties window and display the Object drop-down list, notice that there are now two CommandButtons with the name cmdMyButton, each with its own subscript (see Figure 22.1).

Double-click either CommandButton to look at the Click event procedure. Notice that it now has an Index argument (see Figure 22.2). This argument is an Integer that indicates the subscript of the control to which the event procedure applies. Because all controls of a control array share the same event procedure, you differentiate between controls by the value of Index—0 is the first control, 1 is the second control, 2 is the third, and so on.

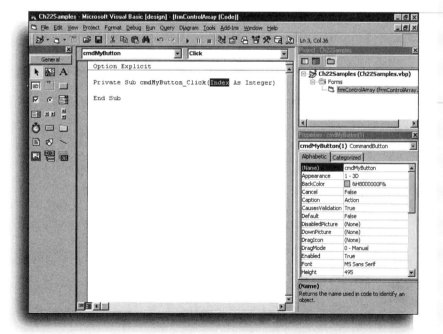

The code in Listing 22.1 displays a string in the titlebar of the form frmMain that reports which CommandButton of the control array cmdMyButton() the user clicked. Copying this code to the cmdMyButton_Click(Index as Integer) event procedure can give you a sense of how to work with the Index argument. Figure 22.3 shows this code in action.

LISTING 22.1

1 Refers to the form in which this code resides

LISTING 22.1   **The CommandButton's *Click* Event Handler**

```
01  Private Sub cmdMyButton_Click(Index As Integer)
02    ' Change the form's caption to indicate which
03    ' button in the control array generated an event.
04    Me.Caption = "You clicked button #" & Index & "."
05  End Sub
```

FIGURE 22.3

After the user clicks the button on the right, the form's title changes accordingly.

Extending Control Arrays at Runtime

Making a control array at design time will suffice if you know how many controls you will need in the array. But what do you do if you don't know how many controls you will need in your control array until the program is running? You solve this problem by adding controls to your control array at runtime by using the Load statement.

Add a control to a control array at runtime

1. Add a CommandButton to the upper-left corner of the form frmDArry and name it cmdCtrlArray.

2. In the Properties window, set the value of the CommandButton's Index property to 0.

3. So you can tell the controls apart at runtime, set the CommandButton's caption to Button #0.

Creating a control array

This action creates a control array with one element. The Index must be set to zero initially, so that controls loaded later will be added to the control array correctly.

PART **IV**

What Is a Control Array?   CHAPTER **22**   **425**

4. Add the code in Listing 22.2 to the form's `Form_Load()` event.

5. Save and run the code.

LISTING 22.2   Adding a New CommandButton

```
01   Private Sub Form_Load()
02      'Create a new command button
03      Load cmdCtrlArray(1)
04
05      'Move it directly underneath the old one
06      cmdCtrlArray(1).Left = cmdCtrlArray(0).Left
07      cmdCtrlArray(1).Top = cmdCtrlArray(0).Top _
                             + cmdCtrlArray(0).Height
08      cmdCtrlArray(1).Caption = "Button #1"
09
10      'Make the new button visible
11      cmdCtrlArray(1).Visible = True
12
13   End Sub
```

When you run the code, notice that the program makes a new CommandButton on the form and places it just below the first (see Figure 22.4).

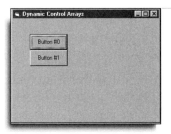

FIGURE 22.4

Using the Load statement creates another CommandButton on the form. The rest of the code takes care of positioning the control correctly.

You must do a certain amount of tweaking to get a newly created control to be operational in your program. New controls are exact duplicates of the first control element of the control array. The values of all properties except Index and Visible are identical—including the values of Left and Top. Thus, when you create a new control, it will be placed right over the first control in the

Where did the control go?

All newly created elements of a control array have a Visible value of False. When you make your new controls at run-time, don't forget to put a line of code in that sets the value of the Visible property to True. Otherwise, you can't see the control.

array. For the new control to be able to coexist with other controls in the control array, you must move the control to a new position.

Working with a Common Event Handler

As you saw in the preceding example, one benefit of control arrays is the ability to have a common event handler. This section features a program that allows users to input some numbers into a numeric telephone touch pad to place a call. Users also can set whether the call should be made by pulse or tone and can choose to send a fax or a simple voice call.

Don't worry if you don't know anything about telephony programming—you won't be writing any. This example is simply designed to show how control arrays could be used in this application.

This program uses a control array of CommandButtons to handle user input. Each keypad button is part of the cmdNum control array. Using a control array greatly simplifies matters. In this project, if you didn't use a control array, you would have 12 event procedures to program—not a very pleasant undertaking. However, when you use a control array, you have only one event procedure to program. You use the Index argument within the control array's one event procedure to figure out which control fired the event procedure (see Figure 22.5).

Listing 22.3 shows the code for the Click() event procedure of the control array. Notice that the control array's event procedure uses a Select Case statement to provide different responses depending on which button has been clicked.

LISTING 22.3 **Keypad Event Handler**

```
01 Private Sub cmdNum_Click(Index As Integer)
02    Dim strChar As String
03
04    'Find out which button was clicked by analyzing
05    the Index argument. Depending on which button
06    'you push, set the other string variable accordingly.
```

```
07   Select Case Index
08      'This button has the "*" character
09      Case 10
10         strChar = "*"
11      'This button has the "#" character
12      Case 11
13         strChar = "#"
14      'All the buttons have captions that match
15      'their index value.
16      Case Else
17         strChar = CStr(Index)
18   End Select
19
20   ' Add the new digit to the phone number.
21   lblNumber.Caption = lblNumber.Caption & strChar
22
23 End Sub
```

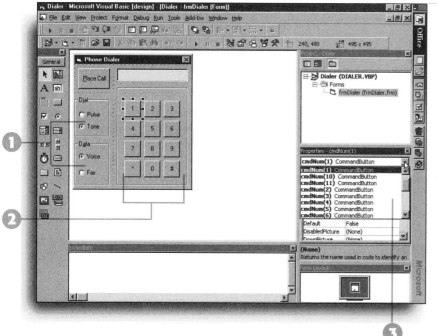

FIGURE 22.5

Every element of a control array is listed in the Properties window with its subscript.

1. By grouping OptionButtons in a Frame control, you can have sets of options from which to choose

2. Control array of CommandButtons

3. Control elements listed in Properties window

The only issue with this code is that each CommandButton's Index property must match exactly with its Caption property. For instance, this code assumes that the button marked as the one digit has a control array index of 1, the two button has an index of 2, and so on. If these buttons were deleted and re-created, they would have to be put back in order exactly or the code wouldn't work.

Listing 22.4 shows a revised version of this code, which still uses a single event handler but doesn't rely on the value of Index. Instead, it simply uses the value of the Caption property. It's also quite a bit shorter and more reliable.

LISTING 22.4   Revised Keypad Event Handler

```
01 Private Sub cmdNum_Click(Index As Integer)
02    lblNumber.Caption = lblNumber.Caption _
         & cmdNum(Index).Caption
03 End Sub
```

Grouping Objects with the Frame Control

In earlier chapters, you learned that within a group of OptionButtons, only one OptionButton can have a value of True (see Figure 22.6). But as you saw in the dialer application in the last section, sometimes you need to have sets of OptionButtons so that you can return many different sets of choices.

FIGURE 22.6

If you don't group your OptionButtons in containers, they all work as one big group.

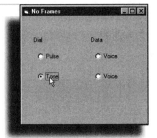

You group OptionButtons by using a container control such as a frame. After a set of OptionButtons is pasted into a frame, the members of the set are exclusive to one another.

You add a Frame control to a form as you would any other control. After a control is pasted into a frame, the frame becomes that control's container. Thus, all coordinates of the child controls are relative to the frame. When you move a frame, all the controls within the frame move with it.

There's a trick to adding controls to the Frame control.

Add a control to a frame

1. If the control is already on the form, select it and choose **Cut** from the **Edit** menu.

2. Select the Frame control and choose **Paste** from the **Edit** menu. The control will be placed inside the frame.

Before you add or paste a control into a frame, make sure that the frame is selected. If you don't have the frame selected, the control is really not being added to the frame. Also, after a control is added or pasted into a frame, it can't be moved out of the frame except by pressing Delete or choosing **Cut** from the **Edit** menu. (See Figure 22.7.)

> **Frames aren't the only containers**
>
> PictureBox controls can also be used as containers, as can the 3D Panel control.

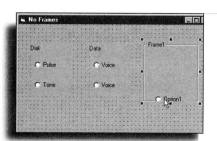

FIGURE 22.7

Make sure that the frame is selected before you add controls to it.

Using the Scroll Bar Controls

The standard scroll bar controls, HScrollBar and VScrollBar, allow you to move through data or a range of values by clicking the up and down scroll arrows or by moving the scrollbar's scroll box (the little button between the scroll arrows). The scroll bar controls have a few special properties that you should know about, as described in Table 22.1.

TABLE 22.1   **Special Properties for the HScrollBar and VScrollBar Controls**

Property	Description
Min	Sets the lowest possible value of the control when the scroll box is positioned at the topmost or leftmost of the respective scroll bar. The default value is 0, but negative numbers can also be used.
Max	Sets the highest possible value of the control when the scroll box is at the bottommost or rightmost of the respective scroll bar. The default value is 32,767.
Value	The position of the scroll box relative to the Max and Min properties.
LargeChange	Sets the amount of change of the Value property when users click between the scroll box and scroll arrow.
SmallChange	Sets the amount of change of the Value property when users click the scroll arrow.

Make a form with VScrollBar and HScrollBar controls

1. Create a new project and name it SmpScrll.vbp. Rename the default form frmMain. Set the value of the Caption property to Simple Scroll Bars.

2. Add VScrollBar and HScrollBar controls to the form. Name the VScrollBar control vscrNS and the HScrollBar control hscrWE.

3. Add two TextBox controls. Name one txtNS and the other txtWE. Set the Text property for both TextBoxes to an empty string (see Figure 22.8).

4. Set the properties for the VScrollBar and HScrollBar controls as listed in Table 22.2.

TABLE 22.2   **Property Settings for ScrollBar Controls**

Property	Setting
Min	0
Max	20
SmallChange	1
LargeChange	2

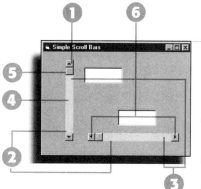

FIGURE 22.8

The only difference between the HScrollBar and VScrollBar controls is their orientation.

1. Click scroll arrows to make a SmallChange

2. Min position

3. Max position

4. Click area between the scroll arrows and the scroll box to make a LargeChange

5. Moving the scroll box fires a Scroll event

6. Moving the scroll box or clicking the scroll arrows fires a Change event

5. Add the following code to the General section of frmMain:

```
Private Sub hscrWE_Change()
    txtWE.Text = CStr(hscrWE.Value)
End Sub

Private Sub vscrNS_Change()
    txtNS.Text = CStr(vscrNS.Value)
End Sub
```

6. Save and run the code.

When you run the code, notice that when you click the scroll arrows of the HScrollBar or VScrollBar control, the value of the respective TextBox changes by 1, the value of the SmallChange property. If you click the area between the scroll box and the scroll arrow, the amount in the TextBox changes by 2, the value of the LargeChange property (see Figure 22.9).

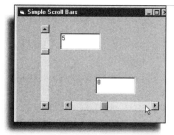

FIGURE 22.9

Because the Max property is set to 20, when you move the scroll bars, the values shown in the TextBoxes will never exceed 20.

Using *For...Next* Loops with Control Arrays

Using For...Next loops is an efficient way to traverse and manipulate elements in a control array. Listings 22.5 and 22.6 show you two ways to create and manipulate elements in a control array. Listing 22.5 illustrates the old-fashioned way—creating the controls one at a time by using the Load statement. Listing 22.6 shows you a way to make the controls by using a For...Next loop. Compare the two.

LISTING 22.5 **Dynamically Making and Manipulating a Control Array One Element at a Time**

```
01 Private Sub cmdMakeArray_Click()
02    'Create additional controls in the
03    'imgFace control array.
04    Load imgFace(1)
05    Load imgFace(2)
06    Load imgFace(3)
07    Load imgFace(4)
08
09    'Set the top new elements of the control array
10    'to the top of the one before it.
11    imgFace(1).Top = imgFace(0).Top
12    imgFace(2).Top = imgFace(1).Top
13    imgFace(3).Top = imgFace(2).Top
14    imgFace(4).Top = imgFace(3).Top
15
16    'Set the left starting position of the new
17    'control to the left plus the width of the control
18    'before it
19    imgFace(1).Left = imgFace(0).Left + imgFace(0).Width
20    imgFace(2).Left = imgFace(1).Left + imgFace(1).Width
21    imgFace(3).Left = imgFace(2).Left + imgFace(2).Width
22    imgFace(4).Left = imgFace(3).Left + imgFace(3).Width
23
24    'Set ALL of the controls in the control array
25    'and make them visible
26    imgFace(0).Visible = True
27    imgFace(1).Visible = True
```

```
28   imgFace(2).Visible = True
29   imgFace(3).Visible = True
30   imgFace(4).Visible = True
31 End Sub
```

LISTING 22.6   **Using *For...Next* Loops to Make and Manipulate Elements in a Control Array**

```
01 Private Sub cmdLoopArray_Click()
02   Dim i As Integer            'Counter variable
03
04   'Set the picture of the first element of the
05   'imgFace control array to the picture in the control,
06   'imgHappy face.
07   imgFace(0).Picture = imgHappy.Picture
08
09   For i = 1 To 4
10      'Create a new control in the array
11      Load imgFace(i)
12      'Set the top of the new control to top of the
13      'one before it.
14      imgFace(i).Top = imgFace(i - 1).Top
15      'Set the left starting position of the new
16      'control to the left plus the width of the control
17      'before it
18      imgFace(i).Left = imgFace(i - 1).Left _
            + imgFace(i - 1).Width
19      imgFace(i).Visible = True
20   Next i
21
22 End Sub
```

As you compare the two, notice that everything you can do one at a time, with regard to control array elements, you can do with much more elegance by using a For...Next loop. For...Next loops can also control an unknown number of elements in any control array, giving you versatility and extensibility.

Figure 22.12 shows the results of the application. The upper portion of the project's form shows an implementation of the code in Listings 22.5 and 22.6. The bottom portion of the form shows a way to use the VScrollBar control to dynamically generate a varying number of controls in a control array of ImageBoxes.

FIGURE 22.10

The number of controls shown will be one more than the scroll position because the zero element is the first element in the control array.

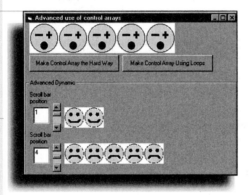

Don't try this at home... or work

In a real-world production environment, unloading and re-creating control array elements each time you need them is a grossly inefficient programming practice. It's done here to demonstrate this Visual Basic feature.

When you closely study the code in Listing 22.7 (the Change event procedure for one of the VScrollBar controls), notice that not only does the code dynamically create new elements of the ImageBox control array through the Load statement, but it also dynamically destroys all but the zero value element of the control array through the Unload statement.

LISTING 22.7   **Creating and Destroying Elements of a Control Array**

```
01 Private Sub vscrFirst_Change()
02    'This sub removes all the existing elements of
03    'the control array, imgFirst(), except for the
04    'first one, and then creates a new set of elements
05    'as determined by the value of the vertical scrollbar
06    'position.
07
08    'Number of images in
09    'ImageBox Control array
10    Static intNumOfImage As Integer
11    Dim i As Integer   'Counter variable
12
13    'Report the value of the scrollbar position
14    'in a TextBox. Don't forget to convert to an integer.
15    txtFirst.Text = CStr(vscrFirst.Value)
16
```

```
17   'Set the Picture property of the first element of
18   'the ImageBox control array to the picture in the
19   'happy face image box.
20   imgFirst(0).Picture = imgHappy.Picture
21
22   'Unload all pre-existing elements of the ImageBox
23   'control array.
24
25   'Make sure the previous value of the Static variable
26   'is greater than zero. If the value is zero, you would
27   'be trying to the zero element control array element.
28   'This is bad!
29   If intNumOfImage > 0 Then
30     'If the number is over zero, there are elements left
31     'over from your last time uses of this event
32     'procedure.
33
34     '(Remember, a the value of a Static variable holds
35     'value after the event procedure goes out of scope.)
36     For i = 1 To intNumOfImage
37         'Nuke all the elements of the control array
38         Unload imgFirst(i)
39     Next i
40   End If
41
42   'Set a new value for the static variable, intNumOfImage
43   'based upon the value of the scroll bar position.
44   intNumOfImage = vscrFirst.Value
45
46   'Traverse the intended number of new controls for the
47   'control array.
48   For i = 1 To intNumOfImage
49     'Make a new ImageBox for the control array
50     Load imgFirst(i)
51     'Set the top of the new control to top of the
52     'one before it.
53     imgFirst(i).Top = imgFirst(i - 1).Top
54     'Set the left starting position of the new
55     'control to the left plus the width of the control
56     'before it
57     imgFirst(i).Left = imgFirst(i - 1).Left _
                        + imgFirst(i - 1).Width
```

...continues

LISTING 22.7   Continued

```
58    Next i
59
60    'Traverse ALL of the controls in the control array
61    'and make them visible
62    For i = 0 To intNumOfImage
63        imgFirst(i).Visible = True
64    Next i
65 End Sub
```

One note about this application: If you try to Load a control in a control array by using a subscript for an already loaded control, you will get an error. If you click the Make Control Array the Hard Way button and then click the Make Control Array Using Loops button, an error will be generated (see Figure 22.11). This is because the first button's Click event procedure creates a control array, and the second button's Click event procedure tries to re-create the same control array by using the same subscripts. Be careful when you work with control arrays and For...Next loops.

FIGURE 22.11

Using a Load statement on an array element that already exists will cause an error.

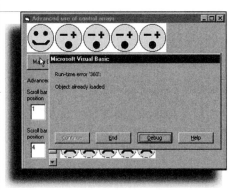

Programming Beyond Visual Basic Using the Windows API

Understand the Application Programming Interface (API)

Work with the API Viewer

Use the API to monitor mouse movement

Keep windows on top with the API

Enhance ListBox controls with the API

Understanding the Windows API

The Windows *Application Programming Interface (API)* is a set of hundreds of predefined functions built into the DLLs that make up the Windows operating system. *End users* can't access these functions. However, programmers can access the code written in the DLLs through the API and use this code in their programs (see Figure 23.1). This allows you to use existent code in the DLLs and save you time in the programming development cycle.

FIGURE 23.1

The most often used DLLs in the API for 32-bit Windows operating systems are Kernel32.DLL, User32.DLL, and GDI32.DLL.

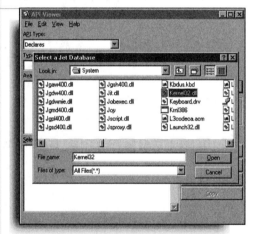

You can program any type of Visual Basic project to access the Windows API by using the Declare statement in the General Declarations section of a module. For example, one function that you can access is GetCursorPos, which locates the onscreen cursor position. You define it for use within Visual Basic as follows:

```
Declare Function GetCursorPos Lib "user32" _
    Alias "GetCursorPos" (lpPoint As POINTAPI) As Long
```

In this syntax,

- `Declare`   A keyword indicating an external procedure declaration
- `Function`   The procedure type
- `GetCursorPos`   The name of this particular external procedure
- `Lib`   A keyword indicating the DLL in which to locate the function
- `"user32"`   The DLL (must be enclosed in quotation marks, no file extension required and must be in the path—that is, the program must know where to find the DLL)
- `Alias`   A keyword that indicates a friendly name by which you can refer to the function
- `"GetCursorPos"`   The friendly name
- `lpPoint`   An argument variable
- `As POINTAPI/As Long`   A keyword indicating argument type
- `POINTAPI`   An argument type
- `Long`   A function return type

As you can see, `GetCursorPos` resides in the DLL User32.DLL. The function takes one argument, `lpPoint`, which is a Windows-defined type, `POINTAPI`. The function returns a `Long`. (Listing 23.1 shows you how to define the `POINTAPI` Windows-defined type.)

LISTING 23.1   23LIST01.TXT–The API and Subsequent Windows-Type Declaration for *GetCursorPos*

```
01   Declare Function GetCursorPos Lib "user32" _
         (lpPoint As POINTAPI) As Long
02
03   Type POINTAPI
04      x As Long
05      y As Long
06   End Type
```

You don't need any tools other than VB itself to use the Windows API. Working with the API requires a lot of extra knowledge, however. If you plan to do any coding with the

---

Windows-defined types

A *type* is also known in C(++) as a *structure*. A structure is a group of variables organized under one name. When they're grouped, you can create instances of the type, as you would create a variable. (See Chapter 26, "Making Object-Oriented Programs with Visual Basic.") When you program directly in Windows by using the API, sometimes you have to use Windows-defined types, such as **POINTAPI**. You can find the definition of these Windows-defined types within the API Viewer tool provided with your copy of VB or within the documentation of the Windows Software Development Kit (SDK), which comes on the Developers Network CD-ROM included in your copy of VB.

Windows API, you need a copy of The Microsoft Developers Network CD-ROM, which ships with the Professional and Enterprise versions of Visual Basic and documents all the available Windows API functions. It's an extensive work that provides a lot of sample code. Sadly, most of the code is in C, so you might need a good third-party Visual Basic book that deals with the Windows API. One such resource is Macmillan's Web site at http://www.mcp.com, where you can view many books about Windows programming in the library and even purchase a book from the online catalog.

Working with the API Viewer

Although you don't need any additional tools to work with the Windows API (Application Programming Interface), Visual Basic ships with a tool, the *API Viewer*, that enables you to cut and paste API functions, constants, and Windows-defined types right into your code. You access the API Viewer from the Visual Basic Start menu. Also, you can add the API Viewer to your VB IDE in the form of an Add-In, thus having it readily available to you while you work.

Simply put, the API lets you access the DLLs in the Windows environment for programming purposes. Microsoft wisely put all reusable code into DLLs (dynamic link libraries) so they can be used over and over. This not only saves valuable programming time but also standardizes the programming community, as it allows the same code to be used repeatedly. This may not seem very important in some instances, but with the same code running in many similar applications, they become more compatible.

Add the API Viewer to the Add-In menu

1. Choose **<u>A</u>dd-In Manager** from Visual Basic's **<u>A</u>dd-Ins** menu.

2. Select **VB 6 API Viewer** from the **Available Add-Ins** list.

3. In the Load Behavior section in the lower right corner of the Add-In Manager dialog, select **Load on <u>S</u>tartup**. (If this option is already checked, the API Viewer should already be available in the Add-Ins menu.)

4. Click **OK**.

5. Close Visual Basic and restart it.

6. Choose **API Viewer** from the **Add-Ins** menu to open the API Viewer window.

In the following sections, you'll build a small program that shows you how to use some API functions to do things you normally can't do in VB. You'll use the API Viewer to retrieve functions, constants, and Windows-defined types to help you accomplish this. You'll also build a function that reports back the position of the cursor anywhere onscreen. To do this, you need to use the API function GetCursorPos.

To use the API Viewer to retrieve GetCursorPos, you first need to configure the viewer for first-time use.

Configure the API Viewer

1. Start the API Viewer.

2. Choose **Load Text File** from the **File** menu (see Figure 23.2).

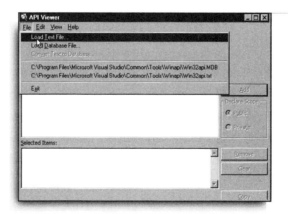

FIGURE 23.2

You load API definition data into the API Viewer from either a text file or a database file.

3. Select the file **Win32API.txt** from the Open File dialog.

4. When the text file is loaded into the API Viewer (this takes about 15 seconds), choose **Convert Text to Database** from the **File** menu.

5. Save the database file with the filename suggested by the API viewer, Win32API.mdb.

The API Viewer doesn't have API data definition built into it; you must load the data at the beginning of every session. After you configure the API Viewer to read its API definition data from a database file, you select the database file whenever you need to use the API Viewer. Although you can use the provided text file, Win32API.txt, using the database file makes the API Viewer perform faster.

After you configure the API Viewer, you can use it to select functions, constants, and Windows-defined types associated with the Windows API.

Select the API function *GetCursorPos*

1. Select **Declares** from the **API Type** drop-down list (see Figure 23.3).

2. Type GetCursorPos in the text box below the **API Type** drop-down list (See Figure 23.4).

3. When the GetCursorPos function is located in the **Available Items** list, click the **Add** button to add the function to the **Selected Items** list.

4. From the **API Type** drop-down list, select **Types**.

5. Type the word POINTAPI in the search text box.

6. Click the **Copy** button to send the entire function and type definitions to the Clipboard (see Figure 23.5).

7. Exit and start a new session of Visual Basic.

8. Choose **Add Module** from Visual Basic's **Project** menu.

9. Paste the function definition for GetCursorPos and the type definition for POINTAPI from the Clipboard to the General Declaration section of the module (see Figure 23.6).

API Viewer auto-searching

The API Viewer auto-searches input made in the search TextBox against items listed in the **Available Items** list. However, it takes time for the API Viewer to do a search. Therefore, if you type slowly, the API Viewer performs more accurately.

FIGURE 23.3

You can locate constants, declares (API functions), and types in the API Viewer.

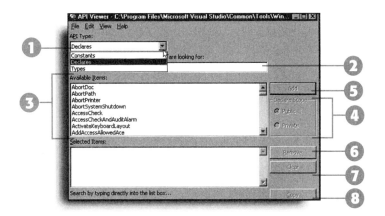

① Enables you to filter the available items in terms of constants, declares, or types

② Type the item you're looking for in the search text box.

③ Displays items according to constants, declares, or types. You can scroll through the list, type a few letters in the text box above, or type directly into the list to do a search.

④ Select whether you want a selected item to be **Public** or **Private** in scope

⑤ When you find what you want, click to add the item to the **Selected Items** list

⑥ Removes a selected item from the **Selected Items** list

⑦ Clears the **Selected Items** list of all items

⑧ Copies all items in the **Selected Items** list onto the Clipboard for pasting into your project

FIGURE 23.4

When you enter a word in the search text box, the API Viewer looks through the available items on a letter-by-letter basis.

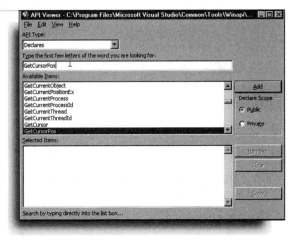

FIGURE 23.5

The Selected Items list holds selected constants, declares, and types that you can copy to the Clipboard in one process.

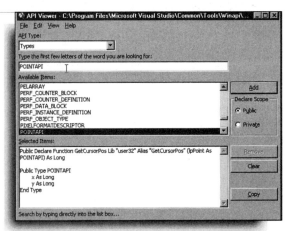

Notice that GetCursorPos takes a Windows-defined type, POINTAPI, as an argument. You need to include the type definition in your VB project for the code to work.

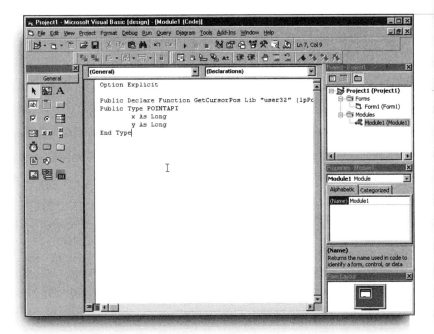

FIGURE 23.6

You must copy API declarations into the General Declarations section of a module.

Monitoring Mouse Movement with *GetCursorPos*

Now that you've seen how to use the API Viewer to work more easily with the Windows API, let's put the function GetCursorPos to work in a real-world example.

GetCursorPos reports the position of the mouse pointer anywhere onscreen. Normally, a Visual Basic application is limited to reporting the position of the mouse pointer with the boundaries of itself, so when the mouse pointer is moved beyond a Visual Basic application's form, the application has no idea where the cursor is. Windows always knows where the mouse pointer is, however, and reports the location through the GetCursorPos API function.

Wrapper function

A wrapper function is one that primarily uses the functionality of another function, as if the function were wrapping itself around another.

This use of GetCursorPos is illustrated in the project prjAPIStuff.vbp (see Figure 23.7), which you can download from http://www.mcp.com/info. At the prompt for the book's ISBN, enter 078971633x and then click the **Search** button to access the book Info page for Using VB6. You can then download the code. Within the project, in the module modAPIStuff is a user-defined function, ReportMousePos(), which returns a string that reports back the location of the mouse pointer in *friendly language*. The function is a *wrapper function* for GetCursorPos. Listing 23.2 shows the structure of ReportMousePos().

FIGURE 23.7

The APIStuff project demonstrates various API functions.

LISTING 23.2   **23LIST02.TXT–*ReportMousePos()* Wraps *GetCursorPos***

```
01    Public Function ReportMousePos() As String
02
03        Dim MyPointAPI As POINTAPI
04        Dim l As Long
05        Dim strReport As String
06
07        'Call the API function
08        l = GetCursorPos(MyPointAPI)
09
10      'Make a report string
11      strReport = "X=" & CStr(MyPointAPI.X) & ", "
12      strReport = strReport & "Y= " & CStr(MyPointAPI.Y)
13
14      'Return the value of the report string
15      If l > 0 Then
16          ReportMousePos = strReport
17      Else
```

```
18          ReportMousePos = "Error"
19      End If
20
21  End Function
```

Notice that line 3 initializes POINTAPI. The actual declaration of the type and the GetCursorPos function were done in the General Declarations section of the module. Line 8 calls the GetCursorPos function, using the type instance MyPointAPI as an argument. Windows passes back the x and y location of the mouse pointer to the elements of MyPointAPI. If the value of l (the return buffer) is greater than 0, the call was successful. Lines 11 and 12 *concatenate* a string that reports back the pixel location of the mouse pointer with some "x:" and "y:" labeling. If the operation was successful (line 15), the reporting string is returned by the ReportMousePos() function. Otherwise, an error string is returned (line 18).

This function is called from within a Timer control's Timer() event procedure. The Timer() event procedure assigns the function's return value to the Caption property of a Label control. The event procedure is as follows:

```
Private Sub Timer1_Timer()
    lblMousePos.Caption = ReportMousePos()
End Sub
```

GetCursorPos doesn't report back the mouse pointer position unless called. Therefore, the Timer control is used to *poll* Windows every 1/10 of a second for the location of the mouse pointer.

For more information about timers, see Chapter 16, "Working with Time and Timers."

Keeping a Window Always on Top by Using *SetWindowPos*

Sometimes you might want to write an application that has an "always-on-top" feature. An always-on-top feature ensures that your application's window isn't covered by another active

ByRef versus ByVal

By default, Visual Basic passes arguments to a function **ByRef** (by reference), which means that VB passes the address of the location in a computer's memory where the argument lives. When you're working within the usual confines of Visual Basic, this is no cause for concern; when you move into API programming, however, passing memory locations to an external procedure can cause a problem. Therefore, most of the time you pass only the value of the argument to a function, not the address of the memory location—hence, the use of the keyword **ByVal** (by value).

What's an hWnd?

Part of the Windows operating system's job is to make windows. Therefore, whenever you start a program, Windows makes all the windows the program needs on invocation. On creation, every window that Windows makes is assigned a number, called the *window handle* and referred to as an *hWnd*. Some windows contain other windows. Most of the intrinsic controls are considered windows and have their own window handles. Windows assigns the value of a control's **hWnd** to the control's **HWnd** property.

application's window. This sort of feature is typical among utilities such as clocks that need to be visible at all times, whether or not they're running in the background.

To make your application always-on-top, you use the Windows API function SetWindowPos. The definition for SetWindowPos, which is put in the General Declarations section of a module, is as follows:

```
Public Declare Function SetWindowPos Lib "user32" _
        (ByVal hWnd As Long, _
        ByVal hWndInsertAfter As Long, _
        ByVal X As Long, _
        ByVal Y As Long, _
        ByVal cx As Long, _
        ByVal cy As Long,_
        ByVal wFlags As Long) As Long
```

The arguments for this function are as follows:

- hWnd is the handle of the window to place.

- hWndInsertAfter is the preceding window or (as in cases of always on top) the Windows constant that sets the window as topmost. These constants can be retrieved from the API Viewer.

- X is the new left position of the window.

- Y is the new top position of the window.

- cx is the new width of the window measured in pixels.

- cy is the new height of the window measured in pixels.

- wFlags is the numeric "flag" that tells Windows to consider certain things about window sizing and placement.

These constants can be retrieved from the API Viewer. For a full description of the constants and other associated values for SetWindowPos, see the documentation that comes with your copy of VB.

The way you use SetWindowPos to make a window always on top is straightforward. First, you have to use SetWindowPos only once a session. When you call the function, Windows will juggle or adjust the bits in memory to tell the window in question whether to be on top all the time. After you set the always-on-top bit, you don't have to do anything else, unless (of course) you want to reset the window to not be on top all the time.

The way you set the always-on-top bit is to use the constant HWND_TOPMOST for the argument hWndInsertAfter. When you pass this value, Windows automatically knows how to set the window to be on top all the time. To avoid resizing or repositioning issues, you need to combine the constants SWP_NOMOVE and SWP_NOSIZE and pass them as the wFlags argument. Combining the values effectively tells Windows to keep the size and position that the user determines.

To use this API function for your coding needs, you must retrieve the function's description as well as the values for the constants associated with the function, using the API Viewer. Figure 23.8 shows the retrieved functions and constants included in the **Selected Items** list.

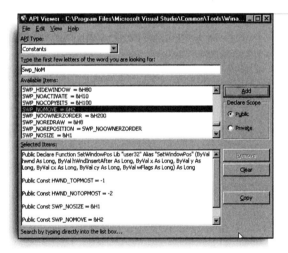

FIGURE 23.8

You can add API and associate functions to the **Selected Items** list before you copy them to the Clipboard.

Listing 23.3 shows an abridged version of the user-defined function SetWinPos() from the module of the prjAPIStuff.vbp project. SetWinPos() is a wrapper function for the SetWindowPos API function.

LISTING 23.3   23LIST03.TXT–*SetWinPos()* Wraps *SetWindowPos*

```
01   Public Function SetWinPos (iPos As Integer, _
                              lHWnd As Long) As Boolean
02   Dim lWinPos As Long 'A variable to hold the value of
03                        'the API window position constant
```

continues...

LISTING 23.3 Continued

```
04    Dim l As Long
05
06    'Use a SELECT CASE to set the value of the
07    'API Window constant
08
09    Select Case iPos
10        'The window is set to its regular position
11        Case 0
12            lWinPos = HWND_NOTOPMOST
13        'Set the window always on top
14        Case 1
15            lWinPos = HWND_TOPMOST
16        'You have a bad value; leave the function
17        Case Else
18            Exit Function
19    End Select
20
21    'Run the API SetWindowPos function
22    If SetWindowPos(lHWnd, lWinPos, 0, 0, 0, 0, SWP_NOMOVE _
                                    + SWP_NOSIZE) Then
23    'If the function is greater than 0 (FALSE), the operation
24    'was successful. Return a True to indicate such.
25            SetWinPos = True
26        End If
27    End Function
```

The user-defined SetWinPos function takes two arguments: iPos, an integer that determines whether the function will set a window always on top or not, and lHWnd, the handle of the window to process. Lines 9–19 are a Select Case statement that determines which value to pass to the hWndInsertAfter parameter of the SetWindowPos API function. If iPos is 0, the window to be processed isn't always on top (HWND_NOTOPMOST); if iPos is 1, the window is always on top (HWND_TOPMOST). Any value greater than 1 is considered an error, and the function is terminated, returning the default value of False.

Line 22 is the core of the user-defined function—this is where the API function is called. SetWindowPos takes it the value of its HWnd (window handle) argument from lHwnd, the value passed into the user-defined function SetWinPos (line 1). lWinPos is determined within the Select Case statement in lines 9–19. The size and position arguments x, y, cx, and cy are all set to 0 because the window being affected retains its original values. The combined values of the constants SWP_NOMOVE and SWP_NOSIZE are passed to the wFlags argument, effectively telling Windows to not change any of the original size and position settings of the window. If the API function is successful, a True value is passed out of SetWinPos (line 25). You can see a more fully commented version of this code on the Web at **http://www.mcp.com**.

The way end users select whether they want the window in project prjAPIStuff to be always on top at runtime is to check the Keep on Top check box (refer to Figure 23.7). When the user checks the check box, the Click() event procedure for the control is called, which in turn calls the user-defined wrapper function SetWinPos. Listing 23.4 shows the code for the event procedure.

LISTING 23.4   **23LIST04.TXT—Using a Wrapper Function to Set a Window Always on Top**

```
01    Private Sub chkOnTop_Click()
02        Dim b As Boolean
03        If chkOnTop.Value = 1 Then
04            b = SetWinPos(1, Me.hWnd)
05            Me.Caption = "Always on Top"
06        Else
07            b = SetWinPos(0, Me.hWnd)
08            Me.Caption = "Not Always on Top"
09        End If
10
11    'If b returns false, the API function was unsuccessful
12        If Not b Then
13    MsgBox "Positioning Error", vbCritical, "Program Error"
14        End If
15    End Sub
```

The keyword Me

Me is a Visual Basic keyword that refers to the current form or class object in which the word is used.

If the value of the check box is set to 1 (checked), the wrapper function sends the API function instructions to set the window (as determined by the argument Me.hWnd) to always on top (line 4). Also, end users are sent a notification in the form's title bar that the window is set to always on top (line 5). If it's not checked, the window is set to not always on top (line 7) and an associated notification is sent to the end user (line 8).

Dragging a Window by Using *SendMessage*

Usually, you drag a window around the computer screen by clicking while the mouse pointer is over a window's title bar and then dragging. To move a window without using the title bar, you trick Windows into thinking that your mouse is over the title bar—by using the API function SendMessage.

Windows is an operating system that uses messaging extensively. Every time something happens in Windows—for example, a mouse movement, a key press, or a window creation—a message is sent. Every second, thousands of numeric messages are sent to all the windows through the Windows environment, sort of like a very fast, internal mail delivery system. Not only are messages sent by the internals of Windows, but you, the programmer, also can send messages to Windows by using the SendMessage API function. The structure of SendMessage is as follows:

```
Public Declare Function SendMessage Lib "user32" _
    Alias "SendMessageA" (ByVal hWnd As Long, _
    ByVal wMsg As Long, _
    ByVal wParam As Long, _
    lParam As Any) As Long
```

❶ The handle of the window to which the message is being sent

❷ The numeric message

❸ A packet of numeric data specific to the message being sent

The return value of SendMessage also is specific to the message being sent.

To manipulate Windows into thinking that when you do a mouse move on a form, you're doing a mouse move on the form's title bar, you must send Windows a message by means of

WM_NCLBUTTONDOWN in the form's MouseMove event procedure. WM_NCLBUTTONDOWN is a numeric message that Windows translates to mean that the left mouse button is down in the *nonclient area* of a window. Before you can send Windows the new message, however, you must nullify the message that Windows receives when you initially move your mouse over the form. You do so by using the ReleaseCapture() API call.

Make your form movable by dragging from anywhere on the form

1. Copy the ReleaseCapture and SendMessage API functions from the API Viewer to a module's Declarations section (see Figure 23.9).

Client area

The client area of a window is where end users enter data. Formally, the client area is the region of a window that doesn't include the title bar, menus, toolbars, status bars, or window borders. In Visual Basic, the width and height to the client area can be determined by examining the value of a form's ScaleWidth and ScaleHeight properties, respectively.

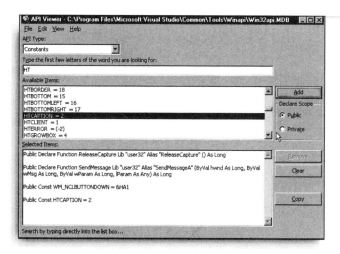

FIGURE 23.9

Use the Windows API to copy the ReleaseCapture and SendMessage functions from the API Viewer to a module's declarations section.

2. Copy the constants WM_NCLBUTTONDOWN and HTCAPTION for the API Viewer to the same module's Declarations section.

3. Copy the code in Listing 23.5 to the MouseMove event procedure of a project's form. Omit the line numbers.

LISTING 23.5   23LIST05.TXT–The Code for Dragging a Window from a Form

```
01  Dim l As Long     'Buffer for function return
02  'If the left button has been pressed
03  'and the Drag checkbox is checked
04  If Button = 1 And chkMove.Value = 1 Then
```

continues...

LISTING 23.5 Continued

```
05      'terminate the mouse move message to the form
06      ReleaseCapture
07      'Send a new message to trick Windows into thinking
08      'that the user is dragging around the form's title
09      'bar
10      l = SendMessage(Me.hwnd, WM_NCLBUTTONDOWN, _
                              HTCAPTION, 0)
11  End If
```

Using the logical AND

You can combine two conditions into one If...Then statement by using the logical AND operator, which compares the two conditions. If both evaluate to True, the entire If...Then statement is True. If either condition evaluates to False or both are False, the entire statement is False.

When you move a mouse over a form, the form's MouseMove event is raised, thus allowing you to program the form's MouseMove event procedure. The code in Listing 23.5 checks whether the left mouse button is pressed during movement. The code also checks whether the Drag from Form check box (refer to Figure 23.7) has a check mark (chkMove in line 4). If these conditions are True, the program invokes the API function ReleaseCapture to nullify the default mouse action (line 6). Then, the program sends a new message to Windows, making Windows think that the mouse is being dragged over the form's title bar (lines 10–11). The constant HTCAPTION is a parameter associated with the WM_NCLBUTTONDOWN message that tells Windows that the mouse button is down over the menu bar. By default, when the mouse is dragged on a window's title bar, the window moves. For this reason, Windows moves the form because it believes the mouse is being dragged from the title bar.

Enhancing a List Box with *SendMessage*

Extended study of the Windows messaging system

Going into the details of each Windows message is well beyond the scope of this book. If you're interested in pursuing extended study of Windows messages, you should read the documentation in the Software Development Kit on the Microsoft Developers Network Library CD-ROM that accompanies your copy of VB.

As mentioned earlier, the API function SendMessage is very versatile. Windows has hundreds of different messages that you can master to alter your program's or another program's behavior within the Windows environment. To demonstrate the versatility of the SendMessage function, however, another use of the function is provided in the prjAPIStuff project created for this chapter.

When you run the code for the project, notice that a ToolTip window appears as you move your mouse over items in the form's list box (see Figure 23.10).

FIGURE 23.10

You can use the Windows API to help display the contents of a ListBox item in a ToolTip window.

The code uses the LB_ITEMFROMPOINT message to determine which item a mouse pointer is moving over within a list box. After the ListIndex is determined, the text of that item is assigned to the list box's ToolTipText property. For a detailed account of the process, look at the MouseMove event procedure of the list box lstFiles in the project prjAPIStuff.vbp, which you can download from the Web at http://www.mcp.com/info.

Adding Help to Your Programs

Learn to use the Help Workshop

Construct files that help users learn your program

Add context-sensitive help to your programs

Providing Help for Your Programs

Professionally programmed applications provide online help. Whether your Visual Basic application is intended for general deployment to a wide variety of users or is a specialized corporate application to be used within a limited enterprise, you owe it to your users to provide detailed and understandable online documentation. Also, the documentation should be as *context sensitive* as possible so that when users press the F1 key, they arrive at the exact topic in the help documentation that addresses the particular need at hand.

Learning to create useful, appropriate online help is a profession in itself. There's more to creating good help documentation than learning the mechanics of making help files. A good help system allows users to find the information they need, when they need it. That information should be clear, concise, and instructive.

Use this chapter's sample project

This chapter is simply an overview. For a more detailed description of the process of creating help files, take the time to read the Help Workshop's online documentation and study the sample Composer.hpj project provided for this chapter. You can find this project at http://www.mcp.com/info. When you locate this Web site, you'll be asked to enter an ISBN; enter **078971633x** and then click the **Search** button to go to the Book Info page for *Using Visual Basic 6*.

Using the Help Workshop

The Microsoft Help Workshop 4.0 is a set of tools, separate from Visual Basic, that you use to create help files for applications that run under 32-bit Windows systems. The Help Workshop is shipped on the same CD-ROM on which you received your copy of Visual Basic 6.0, in the directory \Tools\Hcw. You invoke Setup.exe to install the Help Workshop on your computer.

You use the tools in the Help Workshop to make a set of help files for your application. Generally, the help files that you make for your application's online help documentation are a contents file (.cnt—see Figure 24.1) and associated help files (.hlp—see Figure 24.2).

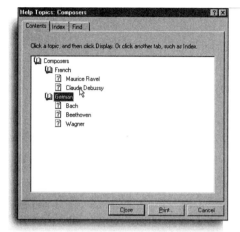

FIGURE 24.1

Content files (.cnt) list the topics of your application's help documentation in a hierarchy.

FIGURE 24.2

A help file (.hlp) contains various topics' text and hypertext.

A content file is similar to a global table of contents for your help documentation. Users click a topic description on the Contents page to find a specific topic within a help file. For example, when users choose Claude Debussy in Figure 24.1, they're presented with the help topic for Claude Debussy, as shown in Figure 24.2.

You create your help data by using any word processor that supports footnotes and the Rich Text Format (.rtf). Then you "compile" the RTF files and the help project file (.hpj) with the Help compiler to create the help file (.hlp—see Figure 24.3). Table 24.1 shows the different data and executable files used within this process. You make the contents file within the Help Workshop environment (see Figure 24.4).

FIGURE 24.3

You create the help project file (.hpj) and the help document's content file (.cnt) in the Help Workshop. You make help data in any word processor that supports Rich Text Format (.rtf).

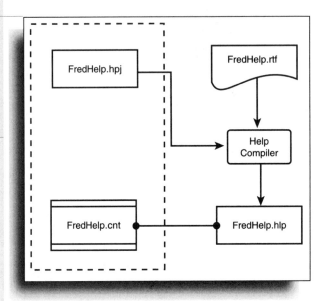

TABLE 24.1   **Parts of the Help Workshop**

File	Name	Description
Hcw.exe	Help Workshop	Online documentation workspace
Hcrtf.exe	Help Compiler	Transforms an .rtf file into an .hlp file
Shed.exe	Hotspot Editor	Creates hypertext jump regions on bitmaps
Dbhe.exe	Dialog Box Help Editor	Makes context-sensitive help dialogs
Hcw.hlp		The help file for the Help Workshop
Shed.hlp		The help file for the Hotspot Editor
Dbhe.hlp		The help file for the Dialog Box Help Editor
MyProject.hpj	Help project file	Project-specific data created by the Help Workshop

File	Name	Description
*.rtf	Rich text format files	RTF files that will be transformed into an .hlp file
MyProject.hlp	Help file	The help file made from the .rtf file
MyProject.cnt	Contents file	The contents file associated with given online help
MyProject.log	Log file	The file that lists compilation errors

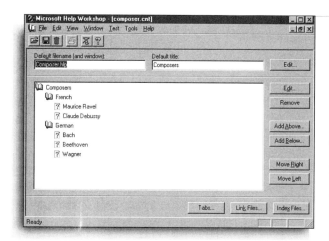

FIGURE 24.4

You set the topic hierarchy of a content file within the Help Workshop environment.

Third-party tools

Third-party tools, such as RoboHelp, also are available to automate the creation of content and help files. These tools work just as well as, if not better than, the Help Workshop.

You can have help documentation that references more than one distinct help file through a content file (see Figure 24.5). This sort of configuration is useful if you have a large program with many categories of help topics. Breaking up help files into numerous smaller ones makes the development process easier to distribute among many documentation developers. Also, smaller help files load faster, making the overall performance of your program better.

FIGURE 24.5

You can have your content file reference more than one help file.

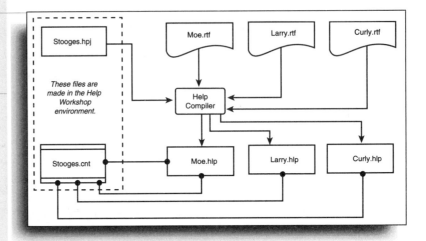

Making a Help File

You make a help file by using a special footnote markup language in Rich Text Format. The RTF file is constructed in three sections: the jump text, the topic text, and the footnote tags (see Figure 24.6).

FIGURE 24.6

You use footnote tags to set up the hypertext jump structure of a help file.

1. Topics are written and tagged in the text portion of the RTF document

2. The jump locations, topic indexing, and topic subjects are entered in the footnote section

3. Jump text

4. Jump location ID

5. Footnote tags

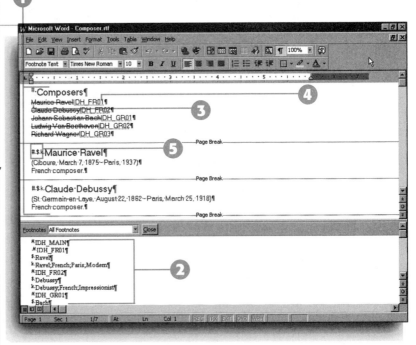

The heart of the help document structure is the topic, a section of Rich Text bounded with a page break. The first line of the section is footnoted with at least the special footnote character #. You enter the topic ID of the topic section next to this character in the footnote area of the RTF file. (A topic ID is a location address of the given topic within the RTF file.) You also use the characters $ and k as footnote characters at the beginning of each topic section. The $ character represents a tag for subject. The k character is used to denote index keywords that will show up when you look at the Index page in the Help Topics dialog, as shown in Figure 24.7. Words entered in the subject footnote appear in the History window of the help documentation.

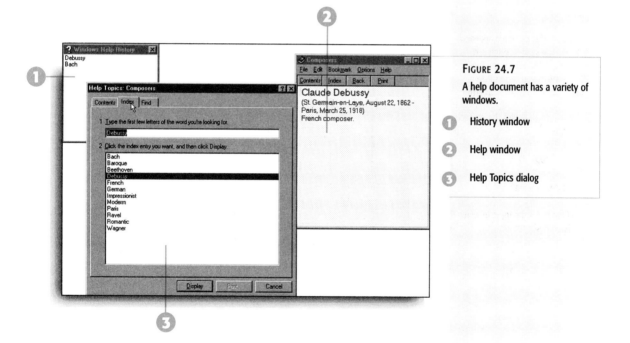

FIGURE 24.7

A help document has a variety of windows.

1. History window

2. Help window

3. Help Topics dialog

The sections interact by the use of strikethrough text to indicate that the characters of that text are hypertext. You place text formatted as hidden after the strikethrough text. The text formatted as hidden is the jump-to address that will be referenced by the strikethrough text. The contents of the jump-to address is formally known as the Topic ID. When you run the RTF file through the Help Workshop's Help Compiler, the strikethrough text is transformed into hypertext. When users click the hypertext, the Help runtime engine (WinHelp.exe) looks to the text that was formatted as Hidden and placed after the strikethrough characters for the address of where to jump. Then, after the engine knows the address, it looks in the footnote section for the location of that address within the help file. The engine then goes to the topic at that address and displays the information (see Figure 24.8).

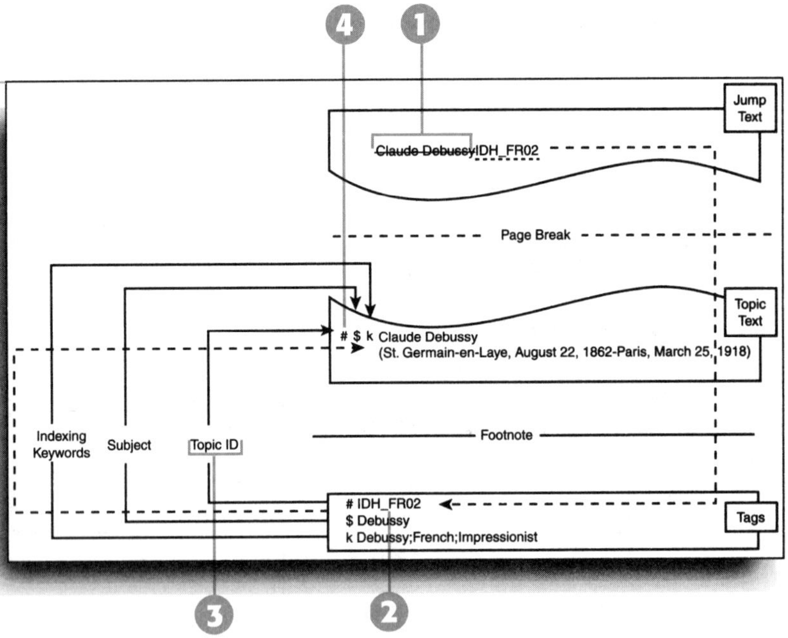

FIGURE 24.8

Make sure that no space appears between the strikethrough text and the hidden text for the topic ID. If there is, you can't make a jump, and you'll receive an error.

❶ Strikethrough makes the characters hypertext.

❷ Call this topic ID...

❸ ...at this location

❹ Hidden text is the topic to which the strikethrough text jumps.

Make a simple RTF help file

1. Open a **New** document from the **File** menu in Microsoft Word.

2. Enter the following:
   ```
   Moe
   Larry
   Curly
   ```

3. Enter a blank line following the last line above.

4. Enter a page break by choosing **Break** from Word's **Insert** menu and then selecting **Page Break**, or by pressing Ctrl+Enter.

5. Enter the following line of text, followed by a page break:
    `Moe is a bossy stooge.`

6. Enter the following line of text, followed by a page break:
    `Larry has funny hair.`

7. Enter the following line of text, followed by a page break:
    `Curly is roly-poly.`

8. Go back to the first three lines of text. Enter `IDH_MOE` after the word `Moe`. Be sure to enter the text directly after the word; don't insert a space.

9. Select the word `Moe` and select **Strikethrough** in the Font dialog (choose **Font** from the **Format** menu). Make sure that the word isn't marked as **Hidden**.

10. Select `IDH_MOE` with your mouse. In the Font dialog, select **Hidden**. (Hidden format doesn't hide the text onscreen.) Repeat this step for the `IDH_LARRY` text on the next line.

11. Format `Larry` as **Strikethrough**. Again, make sure that the word isn't marked as **Hidden**.

12. Enter `IDH_CURLY` after `Curly` on the third line.

13. Format Curly as **Strikethrough** (make sure that the word isn't marked as **Hidden**). Format `IDH_CURLY` as **Hidden**.

14. Place the text cursor at the beginning of the line `Moe is a bossy stooge`. Choose **Footnote** from the **Insert** menu.

15. In the Footnote and Endnote dialog (see Figure 24.9), select **Custom Mark** and enter # in the text box. Click **OK**. The footnote section of the Word document appears.

FIGURE 24.9

Use the # character within an RTF document's footnote to apply a Topic ID to a topic.

16. Enter IDH_MOE next the # character in the footnote section.

17. Place the text cursor at the beginning of the Larry has funny hair line. Enter a custom footnote as explained in steps 14 and 15.

18. Enter IDH_LARRY after the newly inserted # character in the footnote section.

19. Place the text cursor at the beginning of the Curly is roly-poly line. Enter a custom footnote.

20. Enter IDH_CURLY after the newly inserted # character in the footnote section.

21. Save the document as an RTF file, stooges.rtf (select **Rich Text Format** from the **Save as Type** drop-down list of the Save As dialog).

Compiling an RTF file into an .hlp file

1. Launch the Help Workshop by choosing **Microsoft Help Workshop** from the **Programs** submenu of the **Start** menu, or by finding and double-clicking **HCW.EXE** in Windows Explorer.

2. Choose **New** from the **File** menu.

3. In the New dialog, select a new help project. Save the new project as stooges.hpj (see Figure 24.10).

FIGURE 24.10

You can make either a help file (.hlp) or a content file (.cnt) with the Help Workshop.

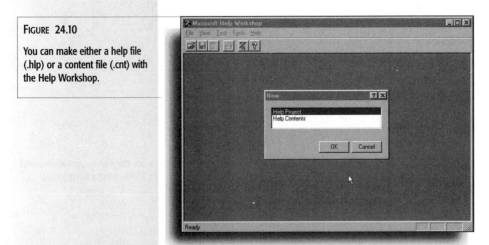

4. Click **File** on the right side of the Workshop to access the Topic File dialog. Click **Add** to display the Open File dialog.

5. Select the stooges.rtf and click **OK** to add it to the Help Workshop (see Figure 24.11).

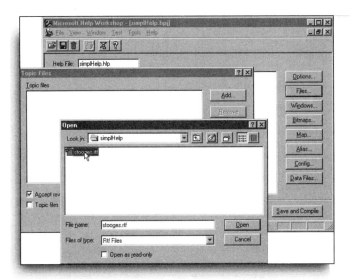

FIGURE 24.11

The content for a help file is an RTF file, which the Help Workshop compiles an HLP file.

6. To compile the .RTF file into an .HLP file, click **Save and Compile** at the bottom right of the Help Workshop.

7. Choose **Run WinHelp** from the **File** menu.

8. In the View Help File dialog, click **View Help** to view the compiled help file, stooges.hlp (see Figure 24.12). You also can go to the project's working directory within Windows Explorer and double-click stooges.hlp to view the file.

The mechanics of the markup language are difficult to understand at first pass. The purpose of this discussion is to give you a sense of how the help files work. You should read the detailed set of online help files that comes with the Help Workshop. You also can download the example files for this chapter from `http://www.mcp.com/info`.

The Help Workshop is an extensive development environment. You can add custom bitmaps to your files and associate certain topics with certain custom windows. It even has a complete

HTML help

In addition to the Help Workshop, Microsoft is beginning to support a newer technology called HTML Help. HTML Help uses documents written in HTML and viewed through Internet Explorer to implement the features seen in the Help Workshop. The help system for VB6 is written in HTML Help. HTML Help ships in the Windows NT 4.0 Service Pack 3, available on MSDN. As of this writing, however, the Help Workshop is still the authoring environment that ships with VB6. Be advised, however, that HTML help is destined to be the help authoring environment of the very near future.

built-in macro language that allows you to make conditional decisions and use functionality from other programs. If you want, you can access the WinHelp API, a powerful tool with many levels of complexity that will take you a while to master.

FIGURE 24.12

You can view help files from within the Help Workshop.

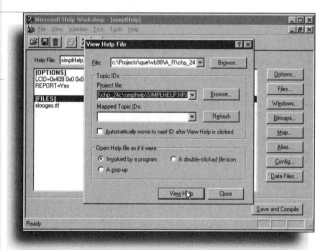

Adding Help Files to Your Application

After you make your help documentation, you need to integrate it in your program. You associate a help file to your program at design time from the Project Properties dialog.

Associate a help file to a program

1. Open the project Composer.vbp, which is available from the vb6ch24.zip file on http://www.mcp.com/info.

2. Choose **Composer Properties** from the **Project** menu.

3. Click the **...** button to the right of the Help File Name text box.

4. From the Help File dialog, browse to find the help file **Composer.hlp**, which also available from vb6ch24.zip.

5. Click the **Open** button in the Help File dialog to add the filename to the Project Properties dialog.

6. Click **OK** in the Project Properties dialog (see Figure 24.13).

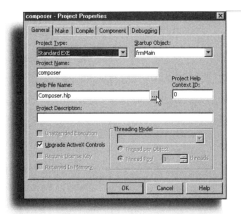

FIGURE 24.13

You can associate a help file with a project at design time from the Project Properties dialog.

You can associate a help file to an application at runtime by using the HelpFile property of the App object:

```
Private Sub Form_Load()
    App.HelpFile = "Composer.hlp"
End Sub
```

When you associate a help file to an application with the Project Properties dialog, if you put the help file in the same directory as the application, you can truncate the drive and directory path from the filename. This eliminates a possible runtime error.

After a help file is associated with an application, if you press F1 when your application has the focus, the associated help file will always appear.

Making Context-Sensitive Help

Context-sensitive help means that your application can call up a specific topic in a help file based on the area from which your program is making the call for help. For example, if you are in a message box that has a Help button, clicking the button displays a help file specific to the message box (see Figure 24.14).

You make your application and your application's help context-sensitive by assigning a topic ID's numeric value to the HelpContextID property of a given control or object. As you learned earlier, the topic ID is the string that identifies the location of a given topic within the structure of a help file. Generally, topic IDs follow a naming convention that begins with the characters IDH_, which loosely stands for "identification for help file." You follow the underscore character with some additional naming logic. (In the sample file, Composer.rtf, French composers start with the characters FR followed by serialization numbers, and German composers follow the underscore with the characters GR, which are also serialized—GR01, GR02, and GR03. The composer prefix naming convention is programmer defined.) After the help file is tagged with topic IDs, you assign a number that corresponds to a topic ID's string.

FIGURE 24.14

Applications with context-sensitive help are much easier to use.

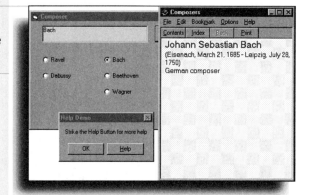

You assign the topic ID a number in the Map dialog of the Help Workshop (see Figure 24.15). After the topic IDs are assigned a unique number, you compile the help project file. The number assigned to the topic ID is the value that you'll assign to the HelpContextID property in your Visual Basic application.

The Composer.vbp project illustrates assigning a value to the HelpContextID property. The project is a control array of five OptionButtons. The HelpContextID property of each OptionButton is assigned a unique value that corresponds to a related topic ID within the help file Composer.hlp (see Figure 24.16). When users select a specific OptionButton and then press F1, the help file Composer.hlp automatically opens to the topic related to the OptionButton (see Figure 24.17).

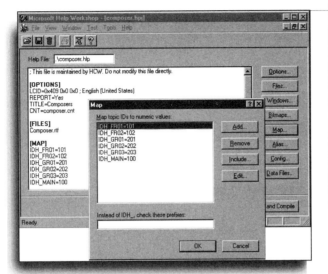

FIGURE 24.15
You access the Map dialog by clicking the Map button of the Help Workshop window.

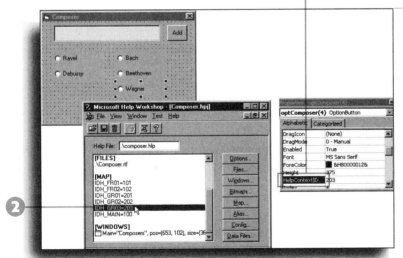

FIGURE 24.16
The value for `HelpContextID` is created when you make the help file in the Help Workshop.

❶ OptionButton being assigned a `HelpContextID` value

❷ `TopicID` is assigned a numeric value in the Help Workshop

In addition to using the `HelpContextID` property to make your program react in a context-sensitive manner when users press F1, you can also make message boxes display context-sensitive <u>H</u>elp buttons. Listing 24.1 shows you how to take advantage of the last two arguments of the `MsgBox()` function, `HelpFile` and

HelpContextID, which assign a help file and topic to the message box. Notice that the HelpFile argument is assigned the value of the App object's HelpFile property (line 20). The HelpContextID of the given OptionButton is assigned to the HelpContextID argument of the MsgBox() function on line 21. Assigning the specific HelpContextID of the OptionButton to the HelpContextID argument of the MsgBox() function displays the exact topic for that OptionButton when users click the **Help** button. Figure 24.10 shows the listed code in action.

FIGURE 24.17

When users select the OptionButton and press F1, the appropriate topic appears in the help window.

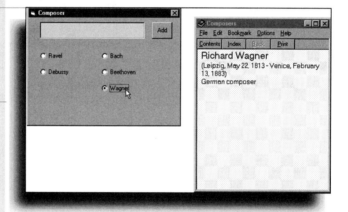

LISTING 24.1   24LIST01.TXT–Assigning Context-Sensitive Help to a Message Box

```
01 Private Sub cmdAdd_Click()
02     Dim i%
03     Dim Result%
04     Dim Msg$
05     'Make a message for the Message Box
06     Msg$ = "Strike the Help Button for more help"
07
08     'Traverse all the OptionButtons in the control array
09     'to find the one that is true. (Count is a property
10     'of the control array collection that reports the
11     'number of items in the control array.)
12     For i% = 0 To optComposer.Count - 1
13       If optComposer(i).Value = True Then
14         lblComposer.Caption = optComposer(i%).Caption
15
```

```
16          'Display a Message Box with a Help button. Also
17          'assign a Help file and Help topic to the
18          'Message Box
19          Result% = MsgBox(Msg$, vbMsgBoxHelpButton, _
                            "Help Demo", App.HelpFile, _
                            optComposer(i).HelpContextID)
20       End If
21    Next i%
22 End Sub
```

A good prompting scheme not only notifies users that an error has occurred or a decision must be made, but also provides details about what the issue is and suggestions on how to resolve it. By assigning a help file and `HelpContextID` to a message box, you greatly increase the amount of information that you provide to users at key decision points or when they need to address errors.

You can never offer your users too much help. A good, easy-to-use and easy-to-understand help system will distinguish your program for the better. If you are so inclined, study other programs' help documentation. Many companies devote a great deal of resources to making quality help systems, and taking advantage of their efforts will help you in your own endeavors.

Usable error reporting

A message box that reports an error should convey three points of information: what the error is, what probably caused the error, and what users can do to correct the error.

Using VBA to Connect Your VB Programs with Microsoft Office

Program Microsoft Office with VBA

Use the Microsoft Office code-generation tools

Work with the Microsoft Word Object Model

Create a document search program

Create a spelling checker

Create an Access-to-Excel conversion utility

Working with VBA

Visual Basic for Applications (VBA) is the superset language from which all other flavors of Visual Basic are derived. For the most part, the Visual Basic that you're accustomed to is VBA. For instance, VBA holds the math functions, such as `Sqr()`, `Sin()`, and `Tan()`. It has the common string functions, including (but not limited to) `Format()`, `Mid()`, `Left()`, `Right()`, and `Instr()`. VBA is also where you find the conversion functions, such as `CStr()`, `CInt()`, and `CDbl()`. The ability to declare and manipulate different types of variables (standard and object) is part of VBA. Again, apart from the graphical elements of the programming environment and the ability to create standalone programs, most of the functionality that you've come to know as VB is really VBA.

As of the Office 97 version, all applications in the Microsoft Office suite have VBA built in to them. Microsoft Project also contains VBA. Other software vendors have licensed VBA to be the underlying scripting language for their applications. One such prominent non-Microsoft application with built-in VBA is Visio, a popular program for making technical drawings and schematics.

You might wonder what having VBA "built in" to an application means in a hands-on sense. When VBA is built in to an application, the application is enabling itself to be scripted by VBA. The application is also exposing its functionality in a way that allows other applications access to it via VBA.

An application exposes its functionality through *objects*. Applications such as Word and Excel have hundreds of objects that they expose and that can be manipulated via VBA. For example, if you want to work with a Word table—either within Word or through another application—you use the `Table` object within Word. If you want to work with the grammar engine in Word, you use the `CheckGrammar()` method of the Word `Document` object. Getting a grasp on all these objects can be a chore, but you can use some tricks and tools to make working with objects a bit easier.

Using VBA with Microsoft Office

All Microsoft Office applications have VBA built in. You work with VBA just as you would with VB, through an Integrated Development Environment (IDE). In Office, the IDE is called the Visual Basic Editor. You can access the Visual Basic Editor for Word 97, Excel, and PowerPoint by choosing **Macro** from the **Tools** menu or by pressing Alt+F11 (see Figure 25.1). To get to the Visual Basic Editor in Access 97, you create a new module by selecting **Module** from the **Insert** menu.

FIGURE 25.1

In MS Office, you access the Visual Basic Editor as a macro tool.

Inside the Visual Basic Editor, you can code objects within the application or in other applications just as you would in a standard Visual Basic IDE. All the editing tools that you're accustomed to in the Visual Basic IDE—such as automatic word completion, parameter help, and Quick Info—are readily available to you in the Microsoft Office Visual Basic Editor.

Using the Record Macro Tool

As mentioned earlier, VBA allows you to do some very sophisticated programming to Microsoft Office after you have a grasp of the different objects residing within the various Microsoft Office applications. However, learning to manipulate all the properties, methods, and events of the various objects is difficult for the inexperienced. Luckily, Microsoft Office comes with a tool that not only gives you a quick introduction to the mysteries of the various objects and *object models* within Microsoft Office, but also writes code for you as you go along. This tool is known as the Macro Recorder.

Writing *macros* in Microsoft Office is the same as writing a *procedure* in VBA. When you use the Macro Recorder, you're required to declare a name for the macro that you want to record. This process is the same as naming a procedure in VBA. When you look at the resulting code generated by the Macro Recorder, you'll see that the name you assigned to the resulting VBA procedure is the same as the one that you assigned to the macro that you recorded.

Write a simple macro that automatically inserts a blank line

1. Open a new Word document.

2. From the **Tools** menu, choose **Macro** and then **Record New Macro**.

3. In the Record Macro dialog, type in the **Macro Name** text box the name of the macro that you plan to record. For now, leave the name as the default, Macro1 (see Figure 25.2).

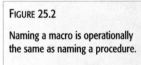

FIGURE 25.2

Naming a macro is operationally the same as naming a procedure.

4. Select the new document—*Document#* (document)—from the **Store Macro In** drop-down list. (This prevents this new macro from being a permanent addition to the normal.dot template, thus keeping the macro from becoming forever part of your Microsoft Word working environment.)

5. Click **OK** in the Record Macro dialog. The small Macro Recorder toolbar appears onscreen.

6. Press **Enter** to insert a line in the new document.

7. Click the **Stop Recording** button in the Macro Recorder toolbar (see Figure 25.3).

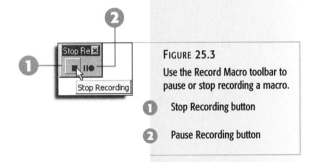

FIGURE 25.3
Use the Record Macro toolbar to pause or stop recording a macro.

1. Stop Recording button

2. Pause Recording button

View the code that you've generated

1. From the **T**ools menu, choose **M**acro and then **M**acros, or press Alt+F8.

2. From the list in the Macros dialog, select the macro that you've just recorded. Click the **E**dit button to display the macro procedure in the Visual Basic Editor (see Figure 25.4).

Although this use of the Macro Recorder is somewhat simplistic, it's a practical way to show how to use it as a tool to generate and understand VBA code as it pertains to the Word object model. The Microsoft Office object model is tricky and takes some getting use to. If you don't know that within the Word object model, you use the TypeParagraph method of the Selection object to insert a blank line, you will be hacking VBA and Office for a long time, trying to figure out how to do a simple line insert. Clearly, the Macro Recorder is a good tool for learning how to manipulate the Word object model with VBA.

FIGURE 25.4

You access the Visual Basic code for a macro through the Macros dialog.

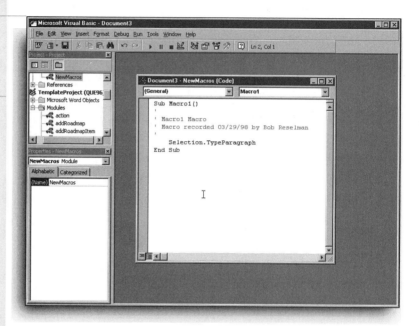

Using the Object Browser

Microsoft Office is composed of hundreds of objects. The relation between these objects can be complex. Microsoft understood that having a detailed understanding of and operational facility with the properties, methods, and events of each object in the applications suite are nearly impossible tasks for the average programmer. To simplify working with objects, Microsoft made a tool that allows you to look at the different objects that reside within the various applications, *ActiveX controls*, and *ActiveX components* that you use when you program with VB and VBA. This tool is the Object Browser.

The Object Browser shows you all the properties, methods, and events for all objects contained in the ActiveX controls included in the project on which you're working. If your project references *VB class libraries* or *ActiveX components*, these also appear in the Object Browser. In addition to showing you various objects, the Object Browser allows you to access a description of an object's various properties, methods, and events. If you need more detailed information, the Object Browser lets you access

Access the Object Browser

You access the Object Browser by pressing F2 from within the Visual Basic Editor in Microsoft Office or the Visual Basic IDE.

the help file for a particular item. The Object Browser also allows you to search the various components for a specified object, property, method, or event.

The Object Browser displays only the ActiveX controls, ActiveX components, and class libraries added to a given project. If your project contains a class module in the Project Explorer, the methods, properties, and events of that class module will also appear in the Object Browser. If an ActiveX control or ActiveX component is *referenced* in your project, it too will appear in the Object Browser (see Figure 25.5).

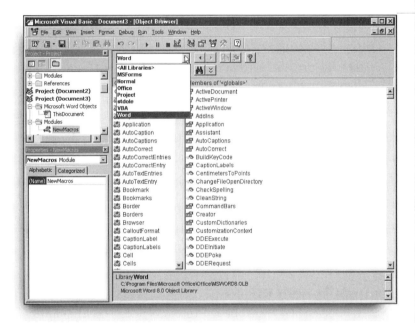

FIGURE 25.5

You can see all the libraries accessible to the Object Browser from the Libraries drop-down list.

If you want to work within an ActiveX control that doesn't appear in the Object Browser, you must add it to your project by choosing **Components** from the **Project** menu (within the Visual Basic IDE) or by pressing Ctrl+T. If you're in the Visual Basic Editor of Microsoft Office, choose **Additional Controls** from the **Tools** menu. In the Component dialog, you can select the ActiveX control that you want to add.

If you want to add an ActiveX component to your project from within the VB IDE, choose **References** from the **Project** menu.

If you are in the Microsoft Office Visual Basic Editor, choose **References** from the **Tools** menu. The References dialog shows all the ActiveX components registered on your computer. You select a component from this dialog.

Granted, the terminology can be confusing—going to the Components dialog to choose an ActiveX control and going to the References dialog to choose an ActiveX component—but you'll grow accustomed to it after a while. In the next section, where you interact with Word, you learn how to add ActiveX components to your project.

Making a Simple VB/Microsoft Office Application

Now that you have a fundamental understanding of the concepts and tools that you need in order to work with VBA and Microsoft Office applications, it's time to build a simple VB/Microsoft Office application. The application that you'll build allows you to take some textual data from a standalone Visual Basic program and insert that data into a Word document.

The tasks of this program are straightforward. When users click a button, the program will open a Word document, write a simple sentence (the contents of which come from a text box on a form in the VB application), save the document to a file with a serialized naming convention, close the document, and quit Word.

Create the sample application

1. Open a new Visual Basic Project. Name the startup form frmMain. (This is only a suggestion. You can name the form whatever you like, but be mindful of the naming differences when you're coding or adding pre-existing code.)

2. Choose **References** from the **Project** menu. In the References dialog, select **Microsoft Word 8.0 Object Library** from the **Available References** list, as shown Figure 25.6. (This is very important. The code won't run unless you select this ActiveX component.)

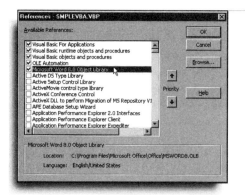

FIGURE 25.6
The References dialog shows all the ActiveX components registered on your computer.

3. Add two CommandButtons, a Label, and a TextBox, as shown in Figure 25.7. Name one CommandButton cmdWordApp and the other cmdQuit. Name the label lblMain. Set the Caption property of the form, CommandButtons, and Label as shown in Figure 25.7. Name the TextBox txtMain. Set the Text property of the TextBox so that no text appears in it.

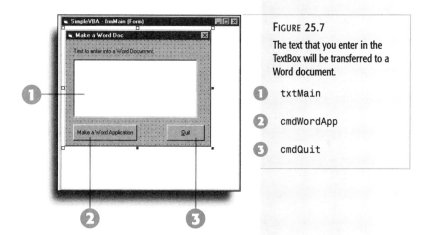

FIGURE 25.7
The text that you enter in the TextBox will be transferred to a Word document.

1 txtMain

2 cmdWordApp

3 cmdQuit

4. Enter the statement End in the cmdQuit_Click() *event handler*. This causes the application to terminate when the button is clicked.

5. Add the code in Listing 25.1 to the cmdWordApp_Click() event handler.

6. Save the code and run the program (see Figure 25.8).

LISTING 25.1 25LIST01.TXT–Adding Text to a Word Document by Using VBA Code in a VB Application

```
01 Static i As Integer
02 Dim strMsg As String
03 Dim w As New Word.Application
04
05 cmdWordApp.Enabled = False
06
07 If txtMain.Text = "" Then
08  MsgBox "You cannot use a blank TextBox", vbCritical, _
          "Entry Error"
09  txtMain.SetFocus
10  cmdWordApp.Enabled = True
11  Exit Sub
12 Else
13
14  strMsg = txtMain.Text
15 End If
16
17 w.Documents.Add
18
19 w.Selection.TypeText (strMsg)
20
21 w.ChangeFileOpenDirectory (App.Path)
22
23 w.ActiveDocument.SaveAs filename:="VBAsmpl_" & _
   CStr(i) & ".doc", _
   FileFormat:=wdFormatDocument, _
   LockComments:=False, Password:="", _
   AddToRecentFiles:=True, WritePassword:="", _
   ReadOnlyRecommended:=False, EmbedTrueTypeFonts:=False, _
   SaveNativePictureFormat:=False, SaveFormsData:=False, _
   SaveAsAOCELetter:=False
24
25  w.ActiveDocument.Close SaveChanges:=wdDoNotSaveChanges
26  w.Application.Quit
27  Set w = Nothing
28
29 strMsg = "The document, " & "VBAsmpl_" & CStr(i) & _
          ".doc" & vbCrLf
30 strMsg = strMsg & "has be saved in the directory, " & _
          App.Path & "."
```

```
31  MsgBox strMsg
32
33  cmdWordApp.Enabled = True
34
35  i = i + 1
```

FIGURE 25.8

The simple VBA program connects Visual Basic to Word.

The key to understanding the code is to understand the Word Application object. Look at line 3 of the code:

```
Dim w As New Word.Application
```

Line 3 declares an object variable, w, that references a Word.Application object with the New keyword. The Word.Application object is, for all intents and purposes, a fully functional instance of Microsoft Word. After you create this object variable, you can access nearly all the functionality of Word through that object, provided that the user has Word installed on his or her computer.

Lines 7–15 are error-checking code to make sure that the user has typed in some text to enter into Word.

Line 17 is important; it adds a new document to the Word session. Just because you've opened an instance of a Word application, it doesn't automatically follow that you have a document on which to work. You don't. This line addresses this issue. (If you go to Word, you can close all the documents in Word and still have the application running without a document in it. You can't do much, but the application is running.)

Line 19 inserts the text from the text box into the Word document by using the Word.Application's Selection child object's TypeText method. Line 21 changes the Word's save directory to be the same as the VB application's.

Confirm that MS Office is on the computer

Don't be misled into thinking that because you reference the Word Object Library at design time, Word magically goes with your program to the end user's system when he or she runs your program. It doesn't. You should provide some functionality in your code that confirms that Word is indeed installed on the user's computer.

Line 23 saves the document by using the ActiveDocument object's SaveAs method. ActiveDocument is a *child object* of the Word.Application object. (If you save a document in Word while running the Macro Recorder, you'll see this code generated.)

Line 25 closes the document. Line 26 closes the Word application. Line 27 clears the object variable's value. Lines 29–31 create and report a message to users, informing them where the saved Word document is located.

Line 35 increments the counter variable. This variable is concatenated to new filenames to accommodate the creation and addition of new Word document files should the user want to keep making documents, as shown in line 23.

Making a Spelling Checker with VB and Word

Let's develop the techniques for having VB "talk to" Word a little further. Now, no edition of Visual Basic comes with an ActiveX control that enables you to check the spelling of a word. You can buy an ActiveX control from a third party to do spell checking, or you can use Word to accomplish this task.

One of Word's most commonly used features is the ability to check spelling. Word *encapsulates* this functionality into two methods: CheckSpelling and GetSpellingSuggestions. The GetSpellingSuggestions method is a *member function* of the Application and Range objects in Word. CheckSpelling is a member function of the Application, Range, and Document objects. You use CheckSpelling to determine whether a word is spelled correctly. If a word is misspelled, you use the GetSpellingSuggestions method to return a *collection* of SpellingSuggestion objects for the misspelled word. The SpellingSuggestion object has a number of properties that describe the object (see Figure 25.9).

SEE ALSO

➤ *For more information about encapsulating objects with Visual Basic, see page 512*

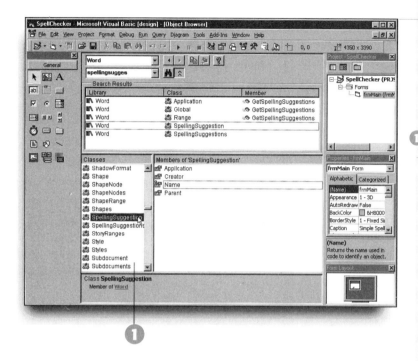

FIGURE 25.9

You use the search area of the Object Browser to locate an object such as SpellingSuggestion, in addition to a property, method, or event for any object.

① Object Browser search box

The Name property is a string that represents a suggested word to replace the misspelled word. Thus, if you want to find out whether a word is correctly spelled and obtain a list of suggested corrections in case of error, you pass the word in question to the CheckSpelling method as a *parameter*. If the method returns False, you pass the misspelled word to GetSpellingSuggestions. As described earlier, you'll receive a SpellingSuggestions collection. When you have the SpellingSuggestions collection in hand, you cycle through the collection, examining the Name property of each SpellingSuggestion object in the collection to determine which string is the suggestion.

Create a SpellCheck program

1. Open a new Visual Basic project.

2. Add a TextBox, two CommandButtons, two Label controls, and a ListBox to the startup form, as shown in Figure 25.10. Name the form frmMain, the CommandButtons cmdCheck and cmdQuit, and the TextBox txtMain. Name the Label controls lblMsg and lblSugs and name the ListBox lstSuggestions.

View the sample code

The sample code for this exercise is in the project prjSplCk.vbp, which you can find on the Web at http://www.mcp.com/info. This code is fully commented.

Set the Caption property of the CommandButtons, Labels, and form as shown in Figure 25.10. (The names are merely suggestions. You can name the controls what you like; just be mindful of your naming as you enter code.)

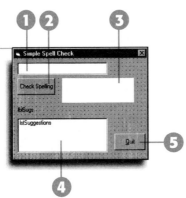

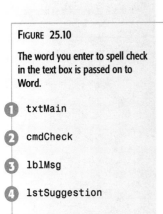

FIGURE 25.10

The word you enter to spell check in the text box is passed on to Word.

1 txtMain

2 cmdCheck

3 lblMsg

4 lstSuggestion

5 cmdQuit

3. Add the following code to the Declaration section of the form:

```
Private Const NUM_OF_SUGS = _[sr]
    "Number of Spelling Suggestions: "
```

4. Add the following code to the Form_Load() event handler so that the label caption shows the number of suggestions to be zero:

```
lblSugs.Caption = NUM_OF_SUGS & CStr(0)
```

5. Add the following code to the cmdQuit_Click() event handler:

```
End
```

6. Add the code in Listing 25.2 to the cmdCheck_Click() event handler.

7. Save the project and run the code (see Figure 25.11).

LISTING 25.2   **25LIST02.TXT—The Core Code for Accessing Word's Spell-Checking Functionality with VB**

```
01 Dim wd As New Word.Application
02 Dim wdsp As Word.SpellingSuggestions
```

```
03 Dim i%
04 Dim strBuffer As String
05
06 On Error GoTo cmdCheckErr
07
08 lblSugs.Caption = NUM_OF_SUGS & CStr(0)
09 lblMsg.Caption = ""
10 lstSuggestions.Clear
11
12 strBuffer = txtMain.Text
13
14 cmdCheck.Enabled = False
15 cmdQuit.Enabled = False
16
17 frmMain.MousePointer = vbHourglass
18
19 If Not wd.CheckSpelling(strBuffer) Then
20     txtMain.ForeColor = vbRed
21     lblMsg.Caption = "Spelling Incorrect!"
22     wd.Documents.Add
23     Set wdsp = wd.GetSpellingSuggestions(strBuffer)
24     lblSugs.Caption = NUM_OF_SUGS & CStr(wdsp.Count)
25
26     For i% = 1 To wdsp.Count
27         lstSuggestions.AddItem wdsp(i%).Name
28     Next i%
29
30     wd.Documents.Close
31 Else
32     lblMsg.Caption = "Spelling OK"
33 End If
34
35 wd.Quit
36 set wd = nothing
37 txtMain.ForeColor = vbBlack
38 frmMain.MousePointer = vbDefault
39 cmdCheck.Enabled = True
40 cmdQuit.Enabled = True
41 Exit Sub
42 cmdCheckErr:
43 MsgBox Err.Description
44 wd.Quit
```

FIGURE 25.11

The Spell Check utility uses Word's *SpellingSuggestions* collection to report back corrections to the misspelled word.

With regard to declaring variables, line 1 declares an object variable, wd, that creates an instance of the Word.Application object. Line 2 declares an instance of the Word.SpellingSuggestions collection. Line 3 is a counter integer, and line 4 is a string buffer that holds message-box message strings. Line 6 puts some fundamental error checking in place through the On Error keywords. Lines 8–17 initialize the GUI for the Click() event procedure and disable the CommandButtons (Lines 14 and 15) so that users can't reinvoke the process until the spelling check is complete. (Hooking up to Word can take a bit of time—hence, the need to set the mouse pointer to an hourglass and disable the CommandButtons.)

Line 19 begins the spelling check. Embedded in the If...Then...Else statement in lines 29–33 is a call to the Word.Application's CheckSpelling method (line 19), by way of the object variable wd. The string strBuffer assigned from the Text property of txtMain is passed as a parameter to CheckSpelling. If the return is True, flow of the program passes to line 32; if CheckSpelling returns False, the program offers some suggested spellings in the lstSuggestions ListBox (lines 26–28).

A document is added to the Word application as shown in line 23. This is important because the GetSpellingSuggestions method won't work if the instance of the Word.Application object doesn't have a document in its Documents collection. The collection variable wdsp is set to *reference* the SpellingSuggestions collection returned by the method GetSpellingSuggestions, as shown in line 24. After you set the collections variable, you cycle through each SpellingSuggestion in the collection by using a For...Next statement and add the suggestion to the ListBox, lstSuggestions. You find out how many SpellingSuggestion objects are in the SpellingSuggestions collection by examining the Count property of the collection. This is done on lines 23–29.

Setting an object variable to Nothing

An object variable doesn't hold a value the way data variables (such as Integer and Double) do. A variable of type Integer or Double actually contains the value you assign to it. When you assign a value to an object variable by using the Set keyword, you're assigning the location of the object in computer memory to be the value of the object variable. This is somewhat similar to the use of pointers in C++. When you're through with an object variable, it's good practice to reset it so that it doesn't contain any object's memory location as its value (this is called garbage collection). You do this with the keyword Nothing. The following code creates an object variable, sets it to a Word application object, and then releases the object variable from Word:

```
Dim wd As New
   Word.Application

Set wd = Nothing
```

After this process, it's pretty much cleaned up. You close the document on line 30, quit the Word application on line 35, release the object variable its reference in line 36, reset the user interface on lines 37 and 38, and enable the CommandButtons in lines 39 and 40. You then Exit the click event handler in line 41 to avoid flow-through to the Error label in the line below.

Making a Word Search Program

You can use VBA with objects in Microsoft Word to find a word within one or more Word documents. Finding a word in a document is similar to checking the spelling of a word, except that you use some previously unused objects and a few different method calls.

To find a word within a Word document, you use the Range object and its *child object*, the Find object. The Range object can be thought of as a continuous area of a Word document, very similar to dragging your mouse pointer across a portion of a page or pages within Word. A Range object can contain a few words, a few sentences or paragraphs, or the entire contents of a document. In this case, the Range object will be the entire contents of an active document.

The Find object is almost identical to the Find dialog in Word. The Find object has many different properties—Font, ParagraphFormat, and Style, to name a few. With the proper amount of forethought, you can program the Find object to do anything that you would do within the Find (and Replace) dialog, were you working directly in Word.

For this WordSearch application, you'll program the Find object's Execute method and Found property to search multiple documents for a word. Then, if the sought-after word is found, the WordSearch program adds the document's filename to a ListBox control.

Create the WordSearch program

1. Open a new Visual Basic project.

2. On the left side of the startup form, add a Frame control. Within this control, add DriveListBox, DirListBox, and FileListBox controls.

3. On the right side of the form, add three CommandButtons, a TextBox, and a ListBox, as shown in Figure 25.12.

FIGURE **25.12**

Numbering the steps necessary to utilize the Word Find program makes it easier for end users to use.

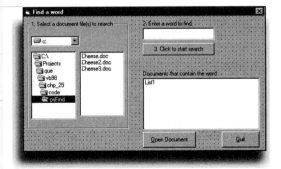

4. Name the frame `frMain`. Leave the DirListBox, DriveListBox, FileListBox, and ListBox with their default names. Name the TextBox `txtWord`. Name one CommandButton `cmdFind`, the second CommandButton `cmdOpenDoc`, and the third CommandButton `cmdQuit`.

5. Add two Label controls to the form. Name one `lblWord` and the other `lblDocs`.

6. Set the **MultiSelect** property of the FileListBox to **2-Extended**. This allows you to select more than one file within the FileListBox.

7. Arrange the controls on the form and set the Label, CommandButtons, and form `Caption` property as shown in Figure 25.12.

8. To make the DirListBox react to a change of drives in the DriveListBox, add the following line of code to the `Drive1_Change()` event handler:
```
Dir1.Path = Drive1.Drive
```

9. To make the FileListBox react to a change of directories in the DirListBox, add the following line of code to the `Dir1_Change()` event handler:
```
File1.Path = Dir1.Path
```

10. To have the application terminate when the user clicks the Quit CommandButton, add the following line of code to the `cmdQuit_Click()` event handler:
```
End
```

11. Add the code in Listing 25.3 to the `cmdFind_Click()` event handler.

LISTING 25.3   25LIST03.TXT—Doing a Document Word Search by Using Word Objects with VB

```
01 Dim wd As New Word.Application
02 Dim myRange As Word.Range
03 Dim i%, j%, k%
04 Dim strPath As String
05 Dim NumOfFiles%
06 Dim strFileBuff() As String
07 Dim strMsg As String
08
09 If txtWord.Text = "" Then
10   strMsg = "No word has been entered for a seach." & _
       bCrLf & vbCrLf
11   strMsg = strMsg & "Please enter a word."
12   MsgBox strMsg, vbCritical, "Missing Search Word"
13   txtWord.SetFocus
14   Exit Sub
15 End If
16
17 i% = File1.ListCount
18
19 For j% = 0 To i% - 1
20   If File1.Selected(j%) = True Then
21     NumOfFiles% = NumOfFiles% + 1
22   End If
23 Next j%
24
25 If NumOfFiles = 0 Then
26   strMsg = "A document file has not been selected." & _
       vbCrLf & vbCrLf
27 strMsg = strMsg & "Please select one or more document "
28   strMsg = strMsg & "files."
29   MsgBox strMsg, vbCritical, "File Selection Error"
30   File1.SetFocus
31   Exit Sub
32 End If
33
```

continues…

LISTING 25.3 Continued

```
34 ReDim strFileBuff(NumOfFiles% - 1)
35
36 For j% = 0 To i% - 1
37     If File1.Selected(j%) = True Then
38      strFileBuff(k%) = File1.Path & "\" & File1.List(j%)
39      k% = k% + 1
40     End If
41 Next j%
42
43 i% = 0
44 j% = 0
45 k% = 0
46
47 For j% = 0 To UBound(strFileBuff)
48     strPath = strFileBuff(j%)
49     cmdFind.Enabled = False
50     frmMain.MousePointer = vbHourGlass
51     frmMain.Caption = "Searching " & strPath
52     wd.Documents.Open (strPath)
53     wd.Documents(1).Activate
54     Set myRange = wd.ActiveDocument.Content
55     myRange.Find.Execute FindText:=txtWord.Text, _
     Forward:=True
56
57     While myRange.Find.Found = True
58         i% = i% + 1
59         myRange.Find.Execute FindText:=txtWord.Text
60     Wend
61
62     If i% > 0 Then
63         List1.AddItem strPath
64         i% = 0
65     End If
66 Next j%
67
68 wd.Quit
69 set wd = nothing
70 frmMain.Caption = "Search Complete"
71 frmMain.MousePointer = vbDefault
72 cmdFind.Enabled = True
```

12. Add the code in Listing 25.4 to the `cmdOpenDoc_Click()` event handler.

LISTING 25.4   **25LIST04.TXT—Opening a Word Document by Using the Object's *Open* Method in VBA *Document***

```
01   Dim wd As New Word.Application
02
03   On Error GoTo cmdOpenDocErr
04
05   If List1.Selected(List1.ListIndex) = True Then
06       wd.Documents.Open (List1.List(List1.ListIndex))
07       wd.Visible = True
08   End If
09   Exit Sub
10
11 cmdOpenDocErr:
12   Select Case Err.Number
13     Case 381
14       MsgBox "Please select a document.", vbCritical, _
             "Document Selection Error"
15       List1.SetFocus
16
17   End Select
```

13. Add the code in Listing 25.5 to the `List1_DblClick()` event handler.

LISTING 25.5   **25LIST05.TXT—Opening a Word Document by Using the *Document* Object's *Open* Method in VBA**

```
01 Dim wd As New Word.Application
02
03 If List1.Selected(List1.ListIndex) = True Then
04     wd.Documents.Open (List1.List(List1.ListIndex))
05     wd.Visible = True
06 End If
```

14. Save the project and run the code (see Figure 25.13).

FIGURE 25.13

The Word Search program allows
you to open the Word documents
in which the sought-after word is
located.

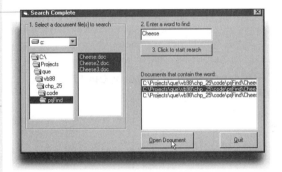

Let's examine how the program works. The code behind the
CommandButton cmdQuit, the DriveListBox, and the DirListBox
was explained as you built the code. The areas of code that need
detailed review are Listings 25.3 and 25.4, the cmdFind_Click()
and cmdOpenDoc_Click() event handlers.

The cmdFind_Click() event handler in Listing 25.3 first ensures
that there is indeed a search word entered in the TextBox (line
9). If there isn't, some error messages and behaviors are generated, and the event handler is terminated (lines 10–14). If a word is
in the TextBox, the program figures out how many document
files are in the FileListBox by using the FileListBox's ListCount
property (line 17). Then, it cycles through the FileListBox to
determine which files have been selected (lines 19–23). Another
error trap is inserted to make sure that filenames have been
selected (lines 25–32). The selected files are added to a string
array for further manipulation (lines 34–41). The counting variables i%, j%, and k% reinitialize on lines 43–45.

The purpose of the code at this point is to set up for the subse-
quent work of opening an instance of a Word Document object.
All the filenames for the files to be searched are stored in the
string array strFileBuff(). Lines 47–66 are a For...Next loop in
which one file at a time is opened as a Word.Document object (line
52) and set to be the document with the focus (line 53). The
contents of the open document are set to the object variable for
the Range object myRange (line 54). The Range object variable then
implements the Execute method of its child object, the Find
object. The Execute method takes two *named parameters*,
FindText (the word to search for) and Forward (a Boolean value
that directs Word to search forward). A While loop is set up

around the condition of the Find object's Found property (line 57). If the word being sought is found, the Found property is automatically set to True. While the Found property is True (line 57), a counter variable is incremented (line 58) and the Execute method is reinvoked (line 59), keeping the While loop in force. After the counter variable i% is incremented, this means that the sought-after word has been identified within the document and that the document's filename should be added to the ListBox (line 63).

The For...Next loop continues for all the filenames in the string array strFileBuff (line 66). When the upper bound of the string array strFileBuff is reached, the For...Next loop is exhausted. Then the Quit method of the Word.Application object wd is invoked, terminating the Word session (line 68). The user interface is reset. The user is notified that the search is complete (line 70). The mouse pointer resets to default (line 71), and the cmdFind CommandButton is enabled to allow the user to search other documents (line 72).

SEE ALSO

> *For more information about* For...Next *loops, see page 191*

Listing 25.4 is the code for the CommandButton cmdOpenDoc_Click() event handler. This event handler opens the document selected in the ListBox that denotes a list of files in which a sought-after word was found.

The code in Listing 25.4 creates an object variable, wd, which is an instance of the Word.Application object (line 1). An error handler is inserted at line 3 in case the ListBox doesn't have any document filenames or one hasn't been selected. After the document is selected, the Open method of the Window.Application's Documents collection is invoked on the file selected in the ListBox (line 6). When the document is opened, the Word application running in memory is brought forth to the user. This is done by setting the Word.Application's Visible property to True (line 7).

Listing 25.5 is similar to Listing 25.4, except that the error-handling code has been omitted. Logic dictates that the Dbl_Click() event handler of the ListBox wouldn't be invoked unless there were files listed in it.

LBound() and Ubound()

You use the **LBound()** and **UBound()** functions to determine the lower and upper elements of an array, respectively. For example, if you have the array **MyArray(25)**, **LBound(MyArray)** evaluates to zero and **UBound(MyArray)** evaluates to 25.

Word can run unseen

Remember, one tricky thing about accessing Word through VBA by using **Word.Application** object variables is that although Word is working hard in memory, it doesn't appear on the taskbar or onscreen unless the **Visible** property of the object is set to **True**. The only evidence that Word is active is the **Winword** entry in the task list that shows itself when you press Ctrl+Alt+Delete.

Working with Visual Basic, Access, and Excel

Data access

We won't cover the basics of data access using DAO here. If your DAO is rusty, you might want to review Chapter 30, "Database Basics and the Data Control," and Chapter 32, "Enhancing Your Programs Using the Advanced Data Controls."

Until now, all the work you've done to make VB work with Office has centered on using Microsoft Word. Let's move on to two other applications in the Microsoft Office suite: Excel and Access. In this section, you'll build a utility named DBTransporter, which opens an Access database file, reads the tables and associated fields within the file, and then transports records from selected fields into an Excel spreadsheet.

You locate the data in the Access database .MDB file by using Data Access Objects (DAO). After you obtain the data from the Access database, use the Excel Application, Workbook, Worksheet, and Range objects to insert the retrieved data into an Excel spreadsheet.

Create the DBTransporter Utility

Download the project's code

Again, the sample code for this exercise (in the project DBtoXLS.vbp) is available on the Web at http://www.mcp.com/info.

1. Open a new Visual Basic project.

2. On the startup form, add three CommandButtons, a ComboBox, a ListBox, a CommonDialog control, and two Label controls. (If the CommonDialog control isn't visible in the toolbox, press Ctrl+T to open the Components dialog and select **Microsoft Common Dialog Control 5.0** from the **Controls** list.)

3. Name the startup form frmMain, the ComboBox cboTables, and the ListBox lstFields. Name the first CommandButton cmdOpenDB, the second CommandButton cmdSave, and the last CommandButton cmdQuit. Name the CommonDialog control cdlgMain. Let the Label controls keep their default names.

4. Arrange the controls and set their Caption and Text properties as shown in Figure 25.14. Set the value of the MultiSelect property of the ListBox to 2 - Extended so that users can choose more than one line.

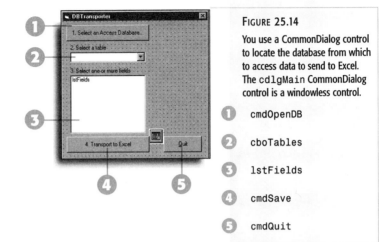

FIGURE 25.14

You use a CommonDialog control to locate the database from which to access data to send to Excel. The `cdlgMain` CommonDialog control is a windowless control.

① `cmdOpenDB`

② `cboTables`

③ `lstFields`

④ `cmdSave`

⑤ `cmdQuit`

5. To have the application terminate when users click the Quit CommandButton, add the following line of code to the `cmdQuit_Click()` event handler:

```
End
```

6. Add the following code to the Declarations section of the startup form:

```
Private Const ACCESS_SYSTEM_PREFIX = "MSYS"
Private Const MAXIMUM_RECS = 20
Private Const TRANS_MSG = "DBTransporter is _
transporting..."
Private Const DEFAULT_XLS_FILENAME = "DBTrans"
Private gf_strDbPath As String
```

7. Add the code in Listing 25.6 to the `cmdOpenDB_Click()` event handler.

Getting commented code

The code in the sample application, although completely identical in syntax and operation to the code listed here, is more highly commented. Much of what you'll read in this section is built in to the comments in that code.

LISTING 25.6   25LIST06.TXT—Finding Table Names in a Database by Using DAO

```
01  Dim ws As Workspace
02  Dim db As Database
03  Dim strTblName As String
04  Dim strFilter As String
05  Dim strMsg As String
06  Dim iReturn As Integer
07  Dim i%
```

continues...

LISTING 25.6 Continued

```
08
09 strFilter = "Access DB (*.mdb)¦*.mdb"
10 cdlgMain.Filter = strFilter
11
12 cdlgMain.ShowOpen
13
14 While gf_strDbPath = ""
15    gf_strDbPath = cdlgMain.filename
16    If gf_strDbPath = "" Then
17       strMsg = "You have not selected a file."
18       strMsg = strMsg & vbCrLf & vbCrLf
19       strMsg = strMsg & "Do you want to select one now?"
20       iReturn = MsgBox(strMsg, vbCritical + vbYesNo, _
             "Selection Error")
21       If iReturn = vbNo Then
22          Exit Sub
23       Else
24          cdlgMain.ShowOpen
25       End If
26    End If
27 Wend
28
29 Set ws = DBEngine.Workspaces(0)
30 Set db = ws.OpenDatabase(gf_strDbPath)
31
32 cboTables.Clear
33
34 For i% = 0 To db.TableDefs.Count - 1
35    strTblName = db.TableDefs(i%).Name
36    If Left(UCase(strTblName), 4) <> _
          ACCESS_SYSTEM_PREFIX Then
37       cboTables.AddItem strTblName
38    End If
39 Next i%
40
41 db.Close
42 ws.Close
```

LCase() and UCase()

Use the **LCase()** and **UCase()** functions to change all characters in a given string to lowercase or uppercase, respectively. Suppose that you have the string **strFirstName**, containing the characters "**Dorothy**". **LCase(strFirstName)** evaluates to "**dorothy**" and **UCase(strFirstName)** evaluates to "**DOROTHY**". **LCase()** and **UCase()** are useful functions to use to avoid user typing errors. If you want to ensure that users enter the correct characters into your program, regardless of case, you can convert all the characters to either lowercase or uppercase and then check them. If, however, you require the data to be case-sensitive correct (a password, for example), you should check the characters as is.

8. Add the code in Listing 25.7 to the cboTables_Click() event handler.

LISTING 25.7   **25LIST07.TXT—Finding the Field Names in a Table by Using DAO**

```
01 Dim ws As Workspace
02 Dim db As Database
03 Dim tdef As TableDef
04 Dim i%
05 Dim strFieldName As String
06
07 lstFields.Clear
08 Set ws = DBEngine.Workspaces(0)
09 Set db = ws.OpenDatabase(gf_strDbPath)
10 Set tdef = _
   db.TableDefs(cboTables.List(cboTables.ListIndex))
11 For i% = 0 To tdef.Fields.Count - 1
12     lstFields.AddItem tdef.Fields(i%).Name
13 Next i%
14
15 db.Close
16 ws.Close
```

9. Add the code in Listing 25.8 to the cmdSave_Click() event
   handler.

LISTING 25.8   **25LIST08.TXT—Taking Data from Access and Sending It to Excel by
Using VBA**

```
01 Dim xla As New Excel.Application
02 Dim xlb As New Excel.Workbook
03 Dim xls As New Excel.Worksheet
04 Dim xlr As Excel.Range
05 Dim ws As Workspace
06 Dim db As Database
07 Dim rs As Recordset
08 Dim strSQL As String
09 Dim i%, j%, k%
10 Dim rc%
11 Dim r%, c%
12 Dim strFields() As String
13 Dim strTable As String
14 Dim strMsg As String
15 Dim strBuffer As String
```

continues…

LISTING 25.8 **Continued**

```
16 Dim strFilter As String
17
18 For i% = 0 To lstFields.ListCount - 1
19     If lstFields.Selected(i%) = True Then
20         j% = j% + 1
21     End If
22 Next i%
23
24 If j% - 1 = -1 Then
25     strMsg = "You must select at least one field."
26     strMsg = strMsg & vbCrLf & vbCrLf
27     strMsg = strMsg & _
            "Please select a field in the Field Listbox"
28     MsgBox strMsg, vbCritical, "Field Selection Error"
29     lstFields.SetFocus
30     Exit Sub
31 End If
32
33 ReDim strFields(j% - 1)
34
35 cmdQuit.Enabled = False
36 cmdOpenDB.Enabled = False
37 cboTables.Enabled = False
38 lstFields.Enabled = False
39
40 frmMain.MousePointer = vbHourGlass
41 strBuffer = frmMain.Caption
42 frmMain.Caption = TRANS_MSG
43
44 j% = 0
45
46 For i% = 0 To lstFields.ListCount - 1
47     If lstFields.Selected(i%) = True Then
48         strFields(j%) = lstFields.List(i%)
49         j% = j% + 1
50     End If
51 Next i%
52
53 strTable = cboTables.Text
54
55 Set ws = DBEngine.Workspaces(0)
```

```
56  Set db = ws.OpenDatabase(gf_strDbPath)
57
58  Set xlb = xla.Workbooks.Add
59  Set xls = xlb.Worksheets.Add
60
61  xls.Activate
62
63  For i% = 0 To UBound(strFields)
64      strSQL = "SELECT " & strTable & ".[" _
                    & strFields(i%) & "]"
65      strSQL = strSQL & " FROM " & strTable
66      Set rs = db.OpenRecordset(strSQL)
67
68      rs.MoveLast
69      rs.MoveFirst
70
71      c% = i% + 1
72      j% = 0
73      'Set the column name
74      xls.Cells(1, c%) = strFields(i%)
75      Set xlr = xls.Cells(1, c%)
76      'Make the top row bold
77      xlr.Select
78      xlr.Font.Bold = True
79
80      If rs.RecordCount > MAXIMUM_RECS Then
81          rc% = MAXIMUM_RECS
82      Else
83          rc% = rs.RecordCount
84      End If
85
86      For r% = 2 To rc% + 1
87          xls.Cells(r%, c%) = rs(strFields(i%))
88          rs.MoveNext
89      Next r%
90  Next i%
91
92  frmMain.MousePointer = vbDefault
93  frmMain.Caption = strBuffer
94
95  strMsg = "Access file: " & vbCrLf & vbCrLf
96  strMsg = strMsg & gf_strDbPath & vbCrLf & vbCrLf
97  strMsg = strMsg & "has been successfully transported."
```

continues...

LISTING 25.8 Continued

```
 98 MsgBox strMsg, vbExclamation, "Transport successful"
 99
100 cmdQuit.Enabled = True
102 cmdSave.Enabled = True
103 cmdOpenDB.Enabled = True
104 cboTables.Enabled = True
105 lstFields.Enabled = True
106
107 strMsg = "DBTransporter has transported " _
           & "the Access data "
108 strMsg = strMsg & "to an Excel spreadsheet."
109 strMsg = strMsg & vbCrLf & vbCrLf
110 strMsg = strMsg & "Do you want to save " _
                   & "the Excel spreadsheet?"
111
112 If MsgBox(strMsg, vbQuestion & vbYesNo) = vbYes Then
113    strFilter = "Excel Spreadsheet (*.xls)¦*.xls"
114    cdlgMain.Filter = strFilter
115    cdlgMain.filename = DEFAULT_XLS_FILENAME
116    cdlgMain.ShowSave
117
118    If cdlgMain.filename <> "" Then
119      xls.SaveAs (cdlgMain.filename)
120      strMsg = "Access data has been saved to file:"
121      strMsg = strMsg & vbCrLf & vbCrLf
122      strMsg = strMsg & cdlgMain.filename
123      MsgBox strMsg, vbExclamation, "Spreadsheet saved"
124    End If
125  End If
126
127 xlb.Saved = True
128
129 xla.Quit
```

10. Save the project and run the code (see Figure 25.15).

The code for DBTransporter is divided into three areas. The first area is the code that allows users to select a database and then automatically populates the ComboBox cboTables with the tables from the database. The second area is the code that populates the ListBox lstFields with the fields of a selected table. The last part is the code that does the actual transporting of data between the Access and Excel.

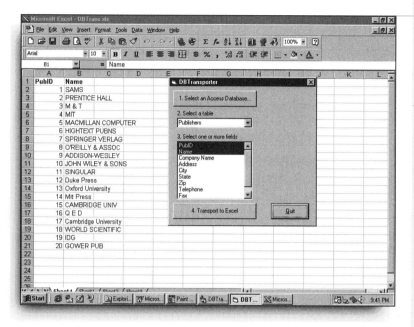

FIGURE 25.15
DBTransporter boldfaces the first row of the Excel sheet to distinguish the field names from the data.

Listing 25.6 is the code that presents a CommonDialog to users for selecting a database from which to transport data. Lines 1–7 set up the variables that you'll use throughout the event handler. For users to see only Access database files (.MDB), the code sets a file *filter* string to the string variable strFilter (line 9). That string is assigned to the Filter property of the CommonDialog control (line 10). The CommonDialog is shown in line 12, using the ShowOpen method.

SEE ALSO

➤ *For more information about the CommonDialog control, see page 276*

An error trap loop is set up on lines 14–27 with a While loop. When users select a valid .MDB file, the program flow will move out of the loop. However, should users not choose a valid file, they will be prompted with a message box asking them whether they want to try again or discontinue the process (line 20). If they choose not to go on, the event handler is exited (line 22).

After an .MDB file is selected, the Workspace and Database object variables are set (lines 29 and 30), and the contents of the ComboBox are cleared (line 32). The database is examined for all the tables within it. The examination is done by running the

counter variable i% from the For...Next loop as the index parameter of the database's TableDefs collection (line 35). As each
TableDef is determined, it's checked to make sure that it isn't an
Access system table (line 36). Access system tables begin with the
letters Msys. These letters have been assigned to the constant
ACCESS_SYSTEM_PREFIX in the Declarations section of the form. If
a table isn't a system table, it's added to the ComboBox (line 37).
Having exhausted the For...Next loop, the code disconnects
from the database (lines 41 and 42).

The next order of business is getting all the field names from a
chosen table listed in the lstFields ListBox (Listing 25.7). Lines
1–5 declare variables, some of which are DAO object variables,
as you've seen before. Line 7 uses the Clear method to eliminate
any field names that might exist in the ListBox because of a previous inspection.

Collections within databases are hierarchical

To get a handle on the hierarchy of
collections of a database, remember
this: All databases contain a collection of tables, and each table contains a collection of fields.

Lines 8 and 9 open the database that the user has previously
chosen. Line 10 determines the string that the user has clicked,
using the ListBox's ListIndex property as the index of the
ListBox's List property, and uses that string to determine which
TableDef in the TableDefs collection should be set to the
TableDef object variable tdef. After a table is determined, a
For...Next loop is used to cycle through the Fields collection of
the TableDef object and to add the field names to the ListBox
lstFields by using the AddItem method (line 12). Having cycled
through all the fields of a given table, the event handler disconnects the database from the program (lines 15 and 16).

The work of moving the data from Access to Excel begins after a
database is chosen, a table is determined, and a set of fields is
chosen to transport. This activity takes place in Listing 25.7.

Lines 1–16 declare many variables; most you've seen before, but
a few are new. The new ones are Excel objects. To make this
whole procedure more comprehensible, let's take a moment to
review the hierarchy of objects in Excel. The base object is
Excel.Application, which can hold multiple Workbooks during a
session. Each Workbook can hold one or more Worksheets. Each
Worksheet contains cells. A collection of geometrically contiguous cells is a Range. Lines 1–4 declare object variables for an
Application, Workbook, Worksheet, and Range.

After the variables are declared, the program cycles through all the field names listed in the lstField ListBox to determine how many have been selected. If none have been selected (line 24), a message is sent to users, informing them of such (lines 25–28). The focus is returned to the ListBox (line 29), and the event handler is then terminated (line 30). If a field name or set of field names is selected, the string array that holds the field names for further manipulation is redimensioned (line 33). The CommandButtons are disabled on lines 35–38. The mouse pointer is set to an hourglass icon (line 40). Also, users are told that data is about to be transported by using the string constant TRANS_MSG, defined in the Declarations section of the form, as the value of the form's Caption property (lines 35–42).

The program cycles through the strings in the lstFields ListBox a second time, adding the selected strings to the string array strFields (lines 46–51). The database object variables are set, as are object variables for an Excel workbook and worksheet (lines 55–59). This effectively has Access and Excel open so that data can be passed between them. The added worksheet is brought to the foreground on line 61.

A For...Next loop is set up to accommodate each field listed in the strFields string array (line 63). The logic is that for each field in the For...Next loop, a SQL statement will be created, asking the table for all the records for that field (lines 64 and 65). The request is made on line 66, and a quick move is made through the returned *recordset* to figure out how many records were retrieved (lines 68 and 69). Data in hand, the appropriate column of the Excel worksheet in which to list the retrieved records of the field is determined (line 71). The program moves to the first row of the Excel worksheet (line 74) where the field name in the strFields() array is inserted as a column heading. A cell is assigned to the Excel Range object variable xlr (line 75) to take advantage of the Range object's Font.Bold property. The font in the first row of the column is set to boldface (lines 77 and 78).

For the program to execute more quickly, a limit has been placed on the number of records that the program will write to a given column. This limit is determined by the constant MAXIMUM_RECS,

---

Resizing arrays

You can resize an array by using the ReDim keyword. If you have MyArray(25), you can increase the size of the array to 50 by using Redim MyArray(50). When you resize an array, however, all its elements lose their values. To resize an array and allow its elements to keep their values, use the Preserve keyword:
Redim Preserve MyArray(50).

as defined in the Declarations section of the startup form. The Count of the retrieved recordset is compared with the maximum constant (lines 80–84).

When the column header has been written and set to boldface, the program proceeds through another For...Next loop, which retrieves the pertinent data from the recordset, writes the data to the cell, and then moves to the next recordset and next cell (lines 86–89). When the original For...Next loop cycle for the field is completed (line 90), the program repeats the cycle again, moving to the next column and using the next field name in the strFields() string array.

After the Excel sheet is filled with all data retrieved from the fields of a given table, the user interface is reset (lines 92 and 93), and users see a message box that tells them that the process has been successful (lines 95–98). The CommandButtons are enabled on lines 100–105. Then users are asked whether they want to save the newly created spreadsheet (lines 107–110). If they answer yes, the CommonDialog is presented again by using the ShowSave method to get a filename (line 116). The spreadsheet is saved by using the Worksheet object's SaveAs method. A message is sent to users, informing them that the file is saved. The Workbook object's SaveAs property is set to True (line 127) so that the Excel application object doesn't prompt users when DBTransporter quits Excel (line 129).

Making Object-Oriented Programs with Visual Basic

Work with user-defined types

Make classes and objects

Learn about the role that encapsulation plays in the creation of Visual Basic classes

Learn how to share your classes with other applications by using an ActiveX DLL

Understanding User-Defined Types

Before you dive into the complexities of classes and objects, you need to understand user-defined types. As you go along, you'll learn that user-defined types and classes are very similar.

Throughout this book you've been using the intrinsic Visual Basic data types such as Integer, Double, and String. One advanced feature of VB is that it enables you to take the use of data types further by creating your own custom data type, known as a *user-defined data type*. You can think of a user-defined type as a variable that's broken into pieces for each part of the UDT that can be used repeatedly throughout your program.

Consider a program that stores the names of musical pieces and of the composer of each piece. You could keep track of everything by declaring variables grouped by a naming convention, as shown in Listing 26.1.

LISTING 26.1   26LIST01.TXT—Using Variable Naming to Keep Track of Related Data

```
01   Public g_ComposerOne As String
02   Public g_PieceOne As String
03
04   Public g_ComposerTwo As String
05   Public g_PieceTwo As String
06
07   Public g_ComposerThree As String
08   Public g_PieceThree As String
```

This might work well in the short run, if you don't have many pieces to track. No matter what size your program is, however, you're relying on the naming of variables to define a structure that your program's data needs. An easier way would be to make a "package" of variables and give that package a name. This package is formally called a user-defined type. Then, you would create variables for your user-defined types by using the Dim, Public, or Private keywords.

You create a user-defined type by using the Type keyword in the General section of a module:

```
Type TypeName
    Elements as DataType
    ...
End Type
```

In this syntax,

- Type is the Visual Basic keyword that denotes the beginning of a type block.

- *TypeName* is the name that you give to the type.

- Elements as *DataType* is each member of the type.

- End Type denotes the end of the Type statement.

You reference elements in the user-defined type by using the following syntax:

```
VarName.ElementName
```

In this syntax,

- *VarName* is the name that you give to the variable (an instance of the type).

- *ElementName* is the name of the specific element in the type.

Listing 26.2 shows you how to create a user-defined type, Music, which encapsulates the composer and the piece. (If you want to follow along, this code is in project UserType.vbp, which you can download from http://www.mcp.com/info. At this site, enter the book's ISBN (078971633x) and then click the Search button to go to the Book Info page for Using Visual Basic 6. Listing 26.3 shows you how to create a variable of the Music user-defined type, named MyMusic (line 1).

LISTING 26.2   26LIST02.TXT—Creating a User-Defined Type

```
01  'Make a user-defined type that has
02  'elements for the composer and the piece
03  Type Music
04      Composer As String
05      Piece As String
06  End Type
```

LISTING 26.3   26LIST03.TXT—Implementing a User-Defined Type

```
01  Dim MyMusic As Music
02  Dim Msg$
03  'Assign values to each element in the user-
04  'defined type. Values come from TextBoxes on a form.
05  MyMusic.Composer = txtComposer.Text
06  MyMusic.Piece = txtPiece.Text
07
08  'Create a string that displays all of the
09  'values in the type
10  Msg$ = "Composer: " & MyMusic.Composer & vbCrLf
11  Msg$ = Msg$ & "Piece: " & MyMusic.Piece
12
13  'Display the string
14  MsgBox Msg$
```

Using user-defined types in Windows API programming

If you decide to pursue Windows API programming with Visual Basic, you can expect to be using user-defined types often. The Windows API is filled with hundreds of them.

Keep this in mind: Variables that are instances of user-defined types are subject to the same rules of scope as any other variable. Therefore, you might want to think about where your type will be used. Always plan ahead before declaring variables. You need to ask yourself if the variables will be local or global. If different areas of your program will share it, you need to make it global. However, if only certain areas of your program will need access to your variables, don't make them global.

Making Objects from Classes

Definitions of a data element

In the world of object-oriented programming, a data element is also known as a *property*, and a procedure is also know as a *method*. Other terms for property and method are *attribute* and *behavior*, respectively.

A class is similar to a user-defined type, except that in addition to having data, a class has procedures. A class is a collection of properties and procedures. An *object* is an instance of a class. For example, the user-defined type Music is defined as follows:

```
Type Music
    Composer As String
    Piece As String
End Type
```

Consider a procedure named Report:

```
Sub Report()
    Dim Msg$
```

```
    Msg$ = "Composer: " & Composer & vbCrLf
    Msg$ = Msg$ & "Piece: " & Piece

    'Display the string
    MsgBox Msg$
End Sub
```

Now consider that you could add the procedure to be an element of the user-defined type `Music`:

```
Type Music
    Composer As String
    Piece As String
    Report()
End Type
```

Next, you declare an instance of the type:

```
MyMusic as Music
```

Then you assign the values:

```
MyMusic.Composer = "Prince"
MyMusic.Piece = "Nothing Compares 2 U"
```

Thus, if you want to display the elements' values, you could call

```
MyMusic.Report()
```

Theoretically, this is what a class is about. However, things are trickier than this conceptual example illustrates: Scope plays a larger role, and the mechanics of Visual Basic demand that you create a class's properties and methods in a specific way.

Creating a Class in Visual Basic

A class is like an ActiveX control without a graphical user interface—you can use it, but you can't program it visually as you would an ActiveX control. As discussed earlier, you create objects from a class. The building block of a class is the class module.

Make a class with properties and a method that lets you add a number to a grand total

   1. Create a new project and name it SmplMath.vbp. Rename the default form to `frmMain`. Set the value of the form's `Caption` property to Simple Math Class.

Download this project

The code for this example is in the project smplmath.vbp, which you can download from `http://www.mcp.com/info`, as explained earlier in this chapter.

2. Choose **Add Class Module** from the **Project** menu.

3. Choose to begin a new project.

4. Set the class module's Name to CSmplMath. Make sure the Properties window is available and then save the class to the file CSmplMath.cls (see Figure 26.1).

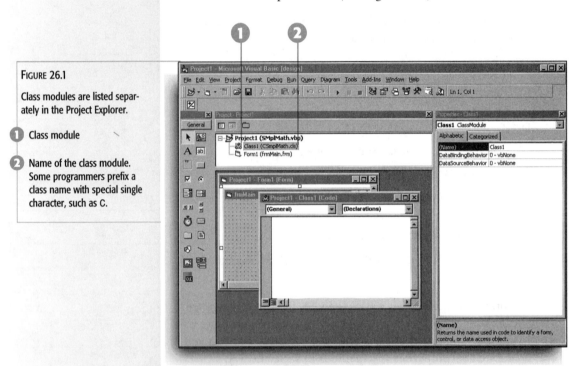

FIGURE 26.1

Class modules are listed separately in the Project Explorer.

1 Class module

2 Name of the class module. Some programmers prefix a class name with special single character, such as C.

5. Add a TextBox, CommandButton, and Label control to the form frmMain. Set the Name and Caption properties of the controls as shown in Table 26.1, and size and position the controls as you want them (see Figure 26.2).

TABLE 26.1   **Control Names and Captions**

Control	Name	Text Property Value
TextBox	txtNum	(leave blank)
CommandButton	cmdAdd	Add
Label	lblAnswer	(leave blank)

FIGURE 26.2

You enter data to be passed to a CSmplMath object through a form.

Adding Properties to a Class

So far, you've created the project structure of a form and a class module. You created an object as an instance of the class represented by the class module. Now you need to create the properties for the class. The class CSmplMath has two properties, NumToAdd and Total, both of type Integer. Figure 26.3 shows a diagram of the class CSmplMath and its properties. It also shows one internal Let and two internal Get procedures for the class, which will be discussed in a moment.

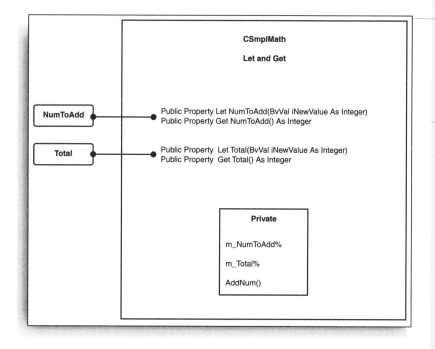

FIGURE 26.3

The scope of data and procedures is crucial when making a class. The only data that should be visible outside the class are the properties of the class.

Add properties to a class

1. Select the class module in the **Code** window.

2. Choose **Add Procedure** from the **Tools** menu.

3. Select the **Property** option in the Add Procedure dialog.

4. Add the property NumToAdd in the **Name** text box (see Figure 26.4). Click **OK**.

Notice that the Add Procedure dialog adds the Property methods Get NumToAdd and Let NumToAdd to the Code window, as shown in Figure 26.5.

FIGURE 26.4

When you use the Add Procedure dialog to add a property to a class, the Visual Basic IDE creates a Let and Get procedure for that property.

FIGURE 26.5

You set and access a class's internal data for a property by using the Let and Get procedures, respectively.

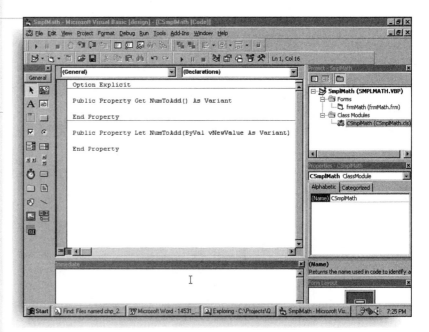

5. Add the property Total to your class module through the Add Procedure dialog, the same way you added the property NumToAdd.

6. Add the sub AddNum to the class module by using the Add Procedure dialog (see Figure 26.6). Make sure that the **Sub** option is selected.

7. Add the following code to the General section of the class module:

```
Private As Integer m_NumToAdd%
Private As Integer m_Total%
```

8. Complete the Get and Let procedures of the class module as well as the sub AddNum, as shown in Listing 26.4.

LISTING 26.4   Code for the *CSmplMath* Class Properties and Methods

```
01    Public Property Get NumToAdd() As Integer
02        NumToAdd = m_NumToAdd%
03    End Property
04
05    Public Property Let NumToAdd(ByVal iNewValue As Integer)
06        m_NumToAdd% = iNewValue
07        AddNumbers
08    End Property
09
10    Public Property Get Total() As Integer
11        Total = m_Total%
12    End Property
13
14    Public Property Let Total(ByVal iNewValue As Integer)
15        m_Total% = iNewValue
16    End Property
17
18    Private Sub AddNumbers()
19        m_Total% = m_NumToAdd% + m_Total%
20    End Sub
```

9. Go back in the class's Get and Let procedures in the code and change the Variant data types to Integers.

10. Save the code.

A lot is going on in this code. First, consider the functionality of the class CSmplMath, which has two properties, NumToAdd and Total. When you assign an Integer to NumToAdd, it's assigned through the internals of the class to a grand total. Then that grand total is internally transferred to the property Total.

Now consider the internals. In a class, you have Public data and procedures and Private data and procedures. Public data and procedures are what you've come to know as properties and methods. Private data and procedures are called *member variables* and *member functions*. This Public/Private schema is called *encapsulation*, a fundamental principle of object-oriented programming (OOP).

Specific ways of accessing Private data and functions

Get and Let are specific to Visual Basic. Other object-oriented languages use different ways of accessing Private data and functions.

In object-oriented programming, the program using the class doesn't work directly with Private data members or member functions. Instead, the program asks the class's Public procedures to access the data. The Public access procedures used by Visual Basic to access private data and functions are the Get and Let functions. Note that Visual Basic automatically handles property procedures differently from most object-oriented languages—they must be in a particular format with only certain arguments, or they won't work.

As you saw when you created the property NumToAdd, Get and Let property procedures were created to accommodate the property. Internal to the class are two private member variables, m_NumToAdd% and m_Total%, which you created in the General section. These variables hold the real data for class. The Let property procedure NumToAdd(iNewValue as Integer) passes in the runtime value of the property NumToAdd to the Private member variable m_NumToAdd% in line 6 of Listing 26.4. The runtime value is passed to the Let property procedure NumToAdd() as the argument iNewValue:

```
05 Public Property Let NumToAdd(ByVal iNewValue As Integer)
06     m_NumToAdd% = iNewValue
07     AddNumbers
08 End Property
```

The Get property procedure of the property NumToAdd is Get NumToAdd() As Integer. This property procedure, which is a function, passes on the value of the associated private member variable m_NumToAdd% in line 2 to the property NumToAdd:

```
01 Public Property Get NumToAdd() As Integer
02     NumToAdd = m_NumToAdd%
03 End Property
```

The same principles apply for the property Total. The private member variable associated with Total is m_Total%. The Get and Let property procedures are Get Total() As Integer and Let Total(ByVal iNewValue As Integer), respectively. The internal works are

```
10 Public Property Get Total() As Integer
11     Total = m_Total%
12 End Property
13
14 Public Property Let Total(ByVal iNewValue As Integer)
15     m_Total% = iNewValue
16 End Property
```

The sub AddNum() is a procedure private to the class. This procedure adds the member variable m_NumToAdd% to m_Total%:

```
19 Private Sub AddNumbers()
20     m_Total% = m_NumToAdd% + m_Total%
21 End Sub
```

This procedure is called within the Let property procedure Let NumToAdd(ByVal iNewValue As Integer) in line 7. In reality, this means that every time the program sets a number to the class's AddToNum property, the class sets the property's value to the private member m_NumToAdd%, as shown in line 6. Then the class calls AddNum() (line 7), which adds the member variable m_NumToAdd% to m_Total% (line 20).

When the program calls the class's Total property, the property procedure Get Total() As Integer returns the now incremented private member variable m_Total% to the class's Total property, as shown in line 11.

Private member variables assignments

By convention, private member variables are assigned by the prefix m.

Calling the class's property

When you set a value to an object's property, internally the object's class calls the associated Let property procedure. When you ask an object for a property's value, the internals call the Get property procedure.

Creating an Object from a Class

Now that you've created a class, you can use an instance of it in your program as an object.

Create an object based on the class *CSmplMath*

1. Select the form **frmMain** from Project Explorer and then click the **View Code** button 🔳.

2. Add the code shown here to the General section of the form frmMain (see Figure 26.7).

```
Public gf_MyMath As New CSmplMath
```

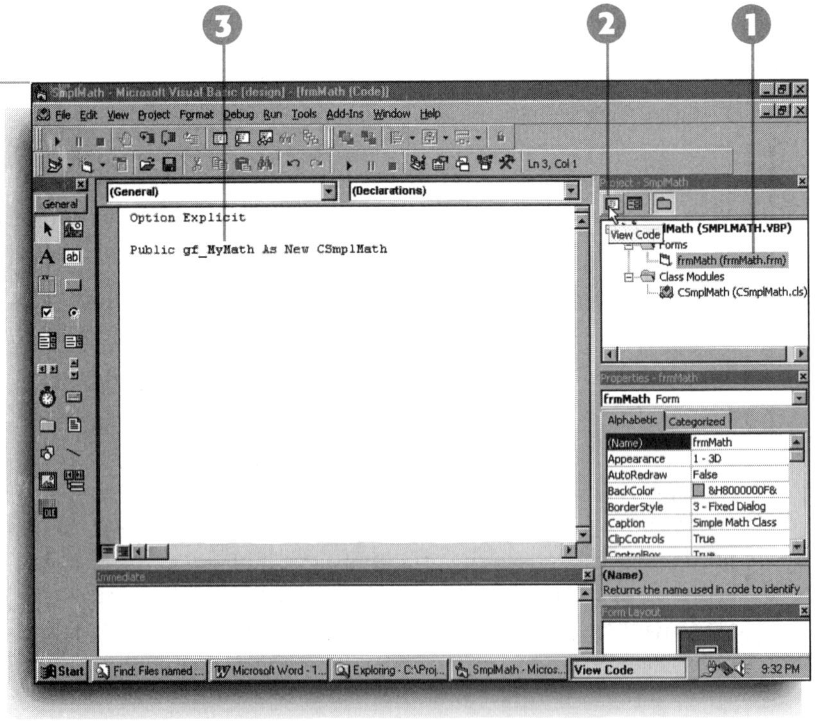

FIGURE 26.7

If you want an object to persist throughout the life of the program, you must create it in the General section.

1 Select the form in Project Explorer.

2 Select the code view.

3 Declare an object by using the New keyword.

3. Add the following code to the cmdAdd_Click() event procedure:

```
gf_MyMath.NumToAdd = CInt(txtNum.Text)
    lblAnswer.Caption = CStr(gf_MyMath.Total)
```

4. Save and run the code.

You created your first object when you declared the variable gf_MyMath in the General section of the form frmMain. The syntax for creating an object is

```
Dim¦Public¦Private MyObject As New MyClass
```

In this syntax,

- Dim¦Public¦Private are the keywords that define the object's scope.
- *MyObject* is the name of the object.
- As is the keyword indicating type definition.
- New is the keyword that creates an instance of an object.
- *MyClass* is the class from which to instantiate an object.

Thus, the statement

```
Public gf_MyMath As New CSmplMath
```

creates an object that you can use in your code, based on the class you made in the class module.

If you want to use this class in other projects, all you need to do is add the class module file CSmplMath.cls to the new project and then instantiate an object within the project's form or module by using the New keyword.

Making an ActiveX DLL

The class that you made earlier can be used only within the project if the .cls file is one of the project's files. If you want to make this class available to other programs at runtime as a separate DLL, you can do this by making the class an ActiveX DLL.

An ActiveX DLL can be complex, with implications far beyond this introductory exercise. The goal here is to give you a sense of what an ActiveX DLL is about by transforming the Visual Basic class that you made previously into one. If you want to know more about ActiveX DLLs, you can read about them in the Visual Basic Books Online documentation that comes with your copy of Visual Basic.

ActiveX DLLs are language independent

ActiveX DLLs are language independent. They can be written in any language that supports the Component Object Model (COM).

Make an ActiveX DLL by using your *CSmplMath* class

1. Create a new project. Select **ActiveX DLL** as the project type (see Figure 26.8).

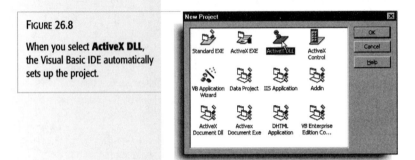

FIGURE 26.8

When you select **ActiveX DLL**, the Visual Basic IDE automatically sets up the project.

2. Select the project in Project Explorer and name it CMathSrvr (see Figure 26.9). Save it to the file CMathSrvr.vbp.

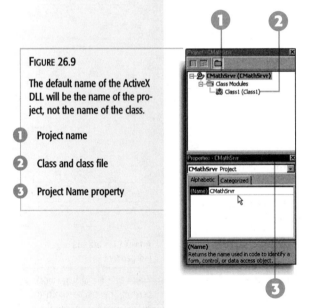

FIGURE 26.9

The default name of the ActiveX DLL will be the name of the project, not the name of the class.

❶ Project name

❷ Class and class file

❸ Project Name property

3. Right-click in the Project Explorer window. Choose **Add** from the context menu and then choose **Add File**.

4. Add the file CSmplMath.cls for your class, CSmplMath. (You can download the file from http://www.mcp.com/info.)

5. Right-click the default class file in the Project Explorer Class1.cls and choose **R̲emove Class1.cls** from the context menu.

6. From the **P̲roject** menu, choose **CMathSrvr P̲roperties**.

7. Enter Simple ActiveX DLL Demo in the **Project Description** text box (see Figure 26.10).

> **Don't use the default class file**
>
> When you create an ActiveX DLL, you're provided with a default class file. If you want to make your class part of the project, you must add your class's .cls file.

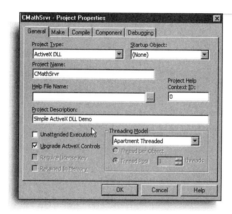

> **FIGURE 26.10**
>
> The **Project Description** text box describes your class to others when it's viewed in the Object Browser and the Tools/References dialog.

8. Select the class **CSmplMath** in Project Explorer. In the Properties window, set the Instancing property to **5 - MultiUse** (see Figure 26.11).

You compile an ActiveX DLL as you would an executable. When you deploy it, use the Setup Wizard to ensure that all the accompanying runtime files are shipped with the DLL.

9. Choose **Ma̲ke CMathSrvr.dll** from the **F̲ile** menu.

FIGURE 26.11

You can have many different
types of Automation Servers.
"MultiUse" means that all objects
created from this class will share
a single instance of the server.

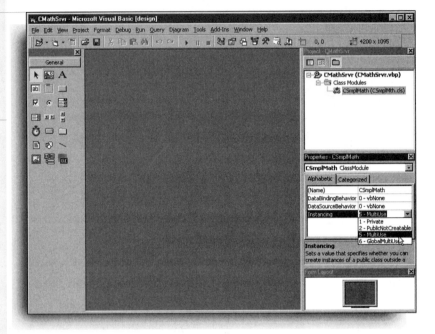

You've just made an ActiveX DLL. Your class, CSmplMath, now
resides in that DLL and can be used in Visual Basic just like any
other ActiveX component. Before you can use the class, however, you must add the DLL to the Visual Basic IDE.

Add an ActiveX DLL to Your Visual Basic code

1. Create a new project and name it UserActvX. Rename the
   default form frmMain. Set the value of the form's Caption
   property to Using an ActiveX DLL.

2. Add a TextBox, CommandButton, and Label control. Set the
   Name and Caption properties as shown earlier in Table 26.1.
   Position the controls as you did for the form shown in
   Figure 26.2.

3. From the **Project** menu, choose **Refere_nces**.

4. Make sure that the ActiveX DLL is listed in the Reference
   dialog by its description (see Figure 26.12). If it's not, click
   the **Browse** button to open the Add Reference dialog, navigate to the location where you saved the DLL
   CMathSrvr.DLL, and select the file.

**Automated features of ActiveX
in Visual Basic**

Visual Basic automates a lot of the
labor required to use ActiveX DLLs.
In other languages such as C++, to
use an ActiveX DLL, you must first
find the DLL's *type library* (which
describes the DLL to other programs). Visual Basic automatically
makes and subsequently finds your
custom ActiveX DLL's type library.
Then VB presents the ActiveX DLLs
to you in the References dialog.

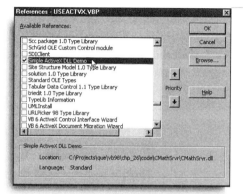

FIGURE 26.12

If an ActiveX DLL is registered with your system, the classes in the DLL will appear in the References dialog. Otherwise, you need to select the DLL directly by using the Browse button. If you install the DLL using a Setup.EXE, the Setup process will register the DLL to your system.

5. To make the new classes in the ActiveX DLL available to your project, select the check box of the `CMathSrvr` class (it will be listed by its description, as in Figure 26.12). Then click **OK**.

6. Press **F2** to display the Object Browser. Select the `CMathSrvr` class library from the drop-down list at the top left corner (see Figure 26.13).

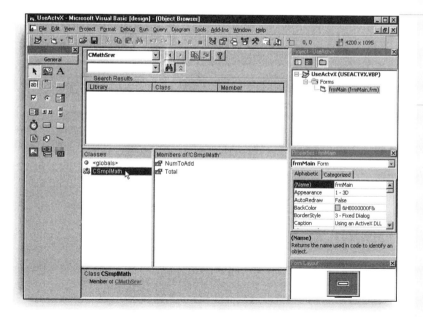

FIGURE 26.13

The Object Browser enables you to look at all of a class's properties and methods within an ActiveX component.

7. Select the class **CSmplMath** from the classes list. Click the Copy icon 🖻 at the top of the Object Browser.

8. Enter the following code into the General section of the project's only form, frmMain:

```
Public gf_MyMath As New
```

9. Paste the classname from the Clipboard to complete the line of code. If you don't want to paste the object from the Object Browser, you can select the object **CSmplMath** from the auto-complete drop-down list (see Figure 26.14).

FIGURE 26.14

When you add a class to the project, it automatically appears in the Methods/Objects drop-down list of the Visual Basic IDE.

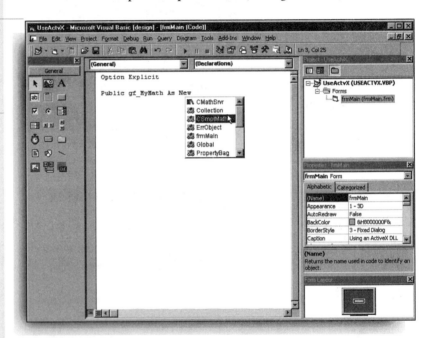

10. Add the following code to the cmdAdd_Click() event procedure:

```
gf_MyMath.NumToAdd = CInt(txtNum.Text)
lblAnswer.Caption = CStr(gf_MyMath.Total)
```

11. Save and run the code (see Figure 26.15).

FIGURE 26.15

This program might seem identical to the one you made earlier, but it's not. This code is calling a class that's part of an external DLL, whereas the previous code compiled the class right into the executable.

Working with Components

On the Web site at http://www.mcp.com/info is a project named MthFuncs.vbp, which is the source code for an ActiveX component named SimpleMathFunctions. *ActiveX component* is a term for an Active DLL that contains one or more classes.

The SimpleMathFunctions component is an enhancement of the work you did with CSmplMath. SimpleMathFunctions contains the class CMathFunc. CMathFunc publishes three properties: NewValue, Operation, and TotalValue. It also publishes one method, DoOperation.

The way the class works is that you set a numeric value to the property NewValue, and then you set a value to the property Operation. Operation can take one of four values:

- 0 - Addition
- 1 - Subtraction
- 2 - Multiplication
- 3 - Division

After the NewValue and Operation properties are set with appropriate values, you invoke the DoOperation method. The result will be displayed in the read-only property TotalValue.

This ActiveX component is an advanced demonstration of ActiveX DLLs. Remember when you use this code to make sure that the DLL is registered to your system or included in the Visual Basic IDE. Remember to use the Add Reference dialog to make the component available to your program.

Mastering OOP with ActiveX DLLs

Making ActiveX DLLs requires mastery of object-oriented programming. You might want to start by making a few class modules first to get the hang of things. Then, when you have a clear understanding and facility in that arena, you can expand these skills by working with ActiveX DLLs.

ActiveX DLLs are a key part of Microsoft's Distributed Computing Technology. Not only can you design ActiveX DLLs to reside on a desktop computer and to be used by applications on that desktop computer, but you can make ActiveX DLLs that reside on remote computers and are accessed by local computers. You can even make Active DLLs that can run on Microsoft's Internet Information Server as components or IIS applications.

Creating Your Own ActiveX Controls with Visual Basic

Create an ActiveX control

Work with the different parts of an ActiveX control

Enhance your ActiveX controls with the Windows API

Organize your work with project groups

Deploy your ActiveX controls for use by others

Creating an ActiveX Control

Save some time and effort

Whenever you need a control, especially in a work environment, you should always check to see first if the control is available as a commercial product. The last resort should be to program or create it yourself. Building your own controls requires a lot of time and effort.

It used to be that the ability to make custom ActiveX controls was the sole domain of C++ programmers. This is no longer true. With Visual Basic 6, you can make full-fledged ActiveX controls for use not only in Visual Basic programming but also within other programming environments such as C++ and Delphi. If you're involved with Internet programming, the ActiveX controls that you make with Visual Basic can bring a new level of functionality and interactivity to your Web pages.

Make an ActiveX control with Visual Basic

1. Create a new project. Select **ActiveX Control** in the New Project dialog (see Figure 27.1).

FIGURE 27.1

You make an ActiveX control within a separate project.

2. Name the project CursorReporter and save the project to the file rptcursr.vbp.

3. Change the name of the UserControl from UserControl1 to CursorReport (see Figure 27.2). (To avoid a *name collision*, be sure to name the control CursorReport, not CursorReporter.)

4. Add a Label control to the UserControl Designer. Set the control's properties to values such as those shown in Table 27.1.

What is a UserControl?

The UserControl is the name by which Visual Basic refers to the palette on which you apply intrinsic controls to make a custom control. If you use non-intrinsic controls, be sure you secure a license for them.

Download the code for this project

The code for this chapter is in the project rptcursr.vbp, which you can find at http://www.mcp.com/info. Also included with the project is the bitmap necessary to complete this example.

TABLE 27.1 **The Label Control Property Settings**

Property	Value
Name	lblMain
BorderStyle	1 - Fixed Single

Property	Value
BackColor	&H0000FFFF
Caption	(blank)
Height	375
Left	0
Top	0
Width	1215

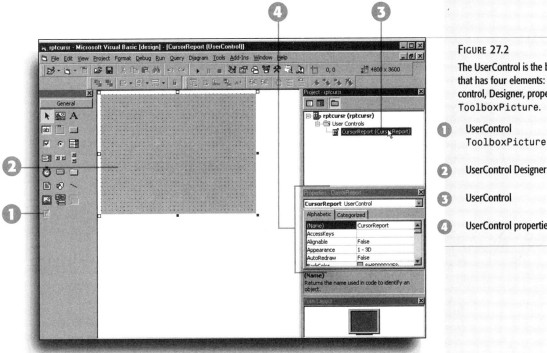

FIGURE 27.2
The UserControl is the base object that has four elements: the User control, Designer, properties, and ToolboxPicture.

① UserControl
   ToolboxPicture

② UserControl Designer

③ UserControl

④ UserControl properties

5. Select the **ToolboxBitmap** value of UserControl CursorReport in the Properties window. Click the value's ... button and assign the bitmap cursor.bmp (which you can download from http://www.mcp.com/info) to the ToolboxPicture property (see Figure 27.3).

FIGURE 27.3

The `ToolboxBitmap` is the image that will represent your control in the Visual Basic toolbox.

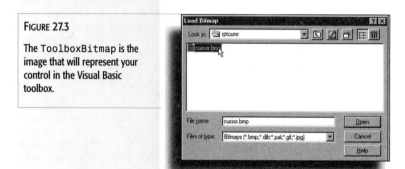

6. Resize the UserControl container so that it's just a little bigger than the perimeter of the Label control (see Figure 27.4).

FIGURE 27.4

When you add your ActiveX control to an application's form, the control's initial dimensions are the size of the UserControl Designer.

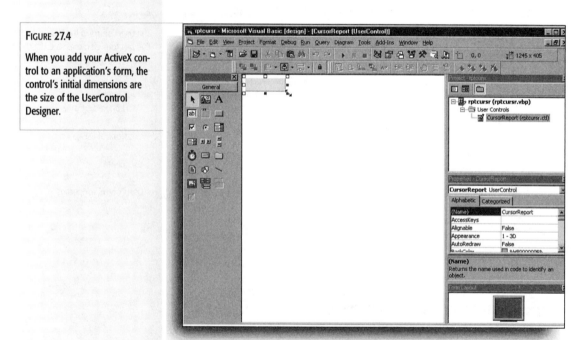

7. Save the project. Make sure that the files are named as follows:

Type	Name	File Name
Project	CursorReporter	rptcursr.vbp
UserControl	CursorReport	rptcursr.ctl

8. Choose **C**lose from the control menu (the icon on the menu bar).

Your ActiveX control's `ToolBoxPicture` now appears in the Visual Basic Toolbox (see Figure 27.5).

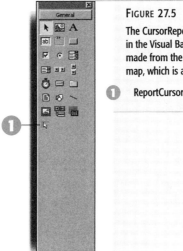

FIGURE 27.5

The CursorReport ActiveX control in the Visual Basic ToolBox was made from the cursor.bmp bitmap, which is a Windows cursor.

1 ReportCursor Toolbox icon

You've just performed the basics of creating an ActiveX control. You add the control to a form as you would any other ActiveX control. Granted, the control doesn't do much, but you'll find that even when you create controls with more useful functionality, you'll use these same steps.

Understanding the UserControl Object

At the heart of every ActiveX control that you make with Visual Basic is the UserControl object. The UserControl object is the base on which you can add other Visual Basic ActiveX controls to create a uniquely new control. Controls that you add to a UserControl object are called *constituent controls*. In the example created earlier, the UserControl is CursorReport, and the constituent control is the Label control `lblMain`.

One more object is important with regard to making ActiveX controls—the AmbientProperties object, which is a set of

Using the ActiveX Control Interface Wizard

Visual Basic 6 ships with the ActiveX Control Interface Wizard, which allows you to easily define the properties and methods of constituent controls that you want to expose in your custom control. The wizard also allows you to create properties and methods specific to your custom control. You access the ActiveX Control Interface Wizard by attaching it to the IDE as a Visual Basic add-in. You normally use the ActiveX Control Interface Wizard when you want to create simple ActiveX controls. Generally, the wizard will meet all your needs. Sometimes when you want a specific control that the Wizard can't produce, you would want to custom program your own. You can do this as described previously.

Using project groups

Visual Basic allows you to work with multiple projects at one time. The collection of projects can be managed as a project group within a .vbg file. You also can work with multiple projects independent of a project group by opening multiple instances of Visual Basic. For more information about working with project groups, see Chapter 5, "Working with Projects in Visual Basic 6." You can save all open projects in the IDE into a project group file, which has the extension .vbg.

properties that represent the state of the form or other container object that's using your ActiveX control. The AmbientProperties object is accessed by referencing the UserControl object's `Ambient` property. For example, if you want to set the value of your UserControl's `BackColor` property to the same value as the `BackColor` property of the container that's using your control, you use the following code:

```
UserControl.BackColor = Ambient.BackColor
```

In this code,

- `UserControl` is the keyword reference to the ActiveX control. You must use the keyword whenever you're referring to your project's UserControl control, regardless of the name of the UserControl.

- `BackColor` is the property that refers to the background color of the control.

- `Ambient` is the UserControl property that references the AmbientProperties object. Operationally, to reference properties of the containing form, you use the word `Ambient`.

Adding a UserControl to a Form

Add the CursorReport ActiveX control to a new project's form

1. Return to the project rptcursr.vbp that you made in the preceding steps. Make sure that the UserControl Designer window is closed and the CursortReport icon is enabled in the toolbox.

2. Choose **A̲dd Project** from the **F̲ile** menu; don't select **N̲ew Project**.

3. Select a **Standard EXE** from the Add Project dialog.

4. Select the CursorReport custom ActiveX control from the toolbox and add it to the main form in the new project (see Figure 27.6).

5. Choose **Sa̲ve Project Group** from the **F̲ile** menu. Save the added project with the default names and save the project group to the file MyGroup.vbp.

6. Press F5 to run the new project.

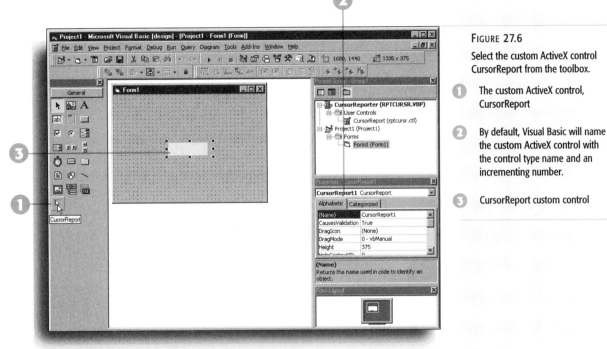

FIGURE 27.6

Select the custom ActiveX control CursorReport from the toolbox.

① The custom ActiveX control, CursorReport

② By default, Visual Basic will name the custom ActiveX control with the control type name and an incrementing number.

③ CursorReport custom control

Adding Functionality to an ActiveX Control

So far, you've seen how you can adapt an intrinsic control to be a part of your custom ActiveX control. Now you can add some functionality to your control to make your control useful to other programmers.

You're going to enhance the control that you started to create in the preceding section so that it reports back the location of the mouse pointer anywhere on the computer screen. The ActiveX control will also be resizable.

Normally, applications written in Visual Basic can't determine the location of the mouse pointer anywhere other than within the boundaries of forms that are part of the given application. To enable your control to report the location of the mouse pointer onscreen, you use the Windows API GetCursorPos.

Adding Projects to the IDE

When you add more than one project to the IDE, Visual Basic will automatically try to create a project group for all the projects.

The Application Programming Interface

API stands for the Application Programming Interface. The Windows API is a collection of hundreds of functions that make up the Windows operating system. For a detailed discussion of the Windows API in relation to Visual Basic, refer to Chapter 23, "Programming Beyond Visual Basic Using the Windows API."

Using GetCursorPos

The ActiveX control that you make in this chapter is an enhancement of the APIStuff project that you saw in Chapter 23. The project APIStuff.vbp in Chapter 23 also uses the API function GetCursorPos. You can download APIStuff.vbp from http://www.mcp.com/info.

To allow your ActiveX control to determine the location of the cursor onscreen at any time, you add a Timer control to the UserControl and program the Timer event procedure to call the Windows API function GetCursorPos. GetCursorPos returns the location of the cursor anywhere onscreen. After the call to the function, you assign a string containing the returned location of the cursor to the Caption property of the constituent control lblMain.

Set up your ActiveX control to display the screen location of the mouse pointer

1. Return to the project group MyGroup.vbg, which contains the custom ActiveX control CursorReport (rtpcursr.vbp).

2. Add a Timer control to the custom ActiveX control. Set the value of the Interval property to **100**.

3. Select the custom ActiveX control, **CursorReport** (which is saved to the file rtpcursr.vbp) in the Project Explorer window.

4. Click the View Code icon 🔲 in the Project Explorer to display the Code window for the ActiveX control (see Figure 27.7).

FIGURE 27.7

You view code for any control or module by clicking the View Code icon in the Project Explorer.

1 Shows the Code window for the selected item

2 Shows the Form Designer for a form or user controy

3 Displays the Project Explorer tree with or without folders

5. Add the following code to the General Declarations section of the custom ActiveX control:

```
Private Declare Function GetCursorPos _
    Lib "user32"

(lpPoint As POINTAPI) As Long

Private Type POINTAPI
```

```
          x As Long
          y As Long
     End Type
```

6. Add the code in Listing 27.1 to the `Timer1_Timer()` event procedure.

LISTING 27.1   27LIST01.TXT—Code to Report the Location of the Mouse Pointer Anywhere Onscreen

```
01 'Return variable for the API function
02 Dim l As Long
03
04 'Variable of the Windows defined type, POINTAPI.
05 'This is the structure to which the API function
06 'will return the coordinates of the cursor
07 Dim pt As POINTAPI
08
09 'Get the mouse pointer coordindates
10 l = GetCursorPos(pt)
11
12 'Get the x and y elements from the POINTAPI type
13 'and create a display string. Assign that string
14 'to the constituent label's Caption property.
15 lblMain.Caption = CStr(pt.x) & " ," & CStr(pt.y)
```

---

7. Add the following code to the `UserControl_Resize()` event procedure:

```
lblMain.Width = UserControl.Width
lblMain.Height = UserControl.Height
```

8. Close the UserControl window.

9. Open the Form Designer window for the main form of the other project in the project group, the one that uses the custom ActiveX control. Notice that the custom ActiveX control now reports back the location of the mouse in the custom ActiveX control (see Figure 27.8).

10. Save all projects within the project group, as well as the project group itself.

FIGURE 27.8

Resize the Label control within the UserControl's Resize event procedure.

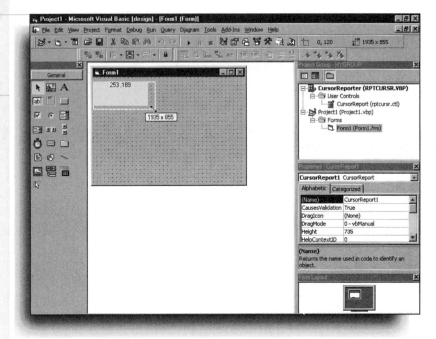

You now have a fully functional ActiveX control that displays the location of a cursor anywhere onscreen. It can be added to any program, whether the program is written in Visual Basic or Visual C++. The control also can be used in a Web page. Before it can be incorporated into these various environments, however, it must be compiled into an OCX file.

Compiling Custom ActiveX Controls

Before you can deploy your custom ActiveX control, you must compile it into an OCX file.

Compile your ActiveX control into an OCX

1. Select the project **CursorReporter** (rptcursr.vbp) in the Project Explorer.

2. Select **Make RPTCURSR.OCX** from the **File** menu to display the Make Project dialog.

3. Click **OK** in the Make Project dialog (see Figure 27.9).

4. Save the project and close the project group.

OCX filename defaults

The OCX filename is, by default, the same name as the project filename.

FIGURE 27.9

The Make process for an OCX is similar to the Make process for an EXE file. If you click the **Options** button, you can set version numbers and other particulars.

After you compile your custom ActiveX control into an OCX, you no longer need to use the "two-project" technique to work with the ActiveX control; you can simply use the control as you would any other ActiveX control. You can use the Package and Deployment Wizard to distribute the OCX to other programmers.

Use the control in your projects

1. Choose **Components** from the Projects menu.

2. In the Components dialog, click **Browse**.

3. In the Add ActiveX Control dialog, navigate to the folder that contains your ActiveX control.

4. Select the control by marking it in the Components list (see Figure 27.10).

FIGURE 27.10

You add a custom ActiveX control made in Visual Basic to the IDE as you would any other ActiveX control.

Deploying Custom ActiveX Controls

Licensing and copyright issues

If you use commercial controls, all the licensing agreements you made with the control vendor when you bought the control are in force. It's illegal to repackage third-party ActiveX controls as constituent controls and call them your own. Check the documentation that comes with all the ActiveX controls that you plan to use with your custom ActiveX controls to see how the licensing agreements apply.

After you compile your ActiveX project into an OCX file, you're ready to deploy it. To deploy the OCX, you must use the Setup Wizard. As with any other Visual Basic project, certain runtime files must ship with the OCX. The OCX also must be registered to the user's system. The Package and Deployment Wizard automatically takes care of all this in the setup process. If you make a special ActiveX control that uses controls other than the standard Visual Basic controls, those controls also must be included by the Package and Deployment Wizard and shipped with your special control.

Practically all Windows programs must be formally installed. Being able to simply copy and invoke executable files from a hard disk—although valid under older DOS programs—is very rare with Windows programs. Recent architectural developments in Windows over the past few years require that a lot of information about a program be entered into the Windows Registry. This is particularly true for custom ActiveX controls. This information is entered when you run a program's or ActiveX control's Setup.exe.

It's also a good idea to always use the Uninstall version of a setup program when you want to remove a program from your system. The Visual Basic Package and Deployment Wizard automatically leaves an uninstall option for your program in the Add/Remove Program Control Panel applet.

SEE ALSO

➤ *For more information about using the Package and Deployment Wizard, see page 391*

If you plan to use your ActiveX control in a Web page on the Internet, you'll have to do a certain amount of programming in VBScript and HTML. You'll also have to embed your OCX files in a .cab file that will reside on the Internet server. The Package and Deployment Wizard is a very useful tool for this process.

Being able to make your own ActiveX controls brings a whole new dimension to the scope of your programming. Using Visual Basic to make ActiveX controls makes your code truly reusable, with little or no dependence on extraneous source code file. Be advised that making an ActiveX control requires a lot of detail work. Many properties, methods, and events take a long while to master, even for the more experienced programmers. However, if you take it slowly, you will discover some very challenging programming opportunities.

Custom control runtime files

Custom ActiveX controls made with Visual Basic require more than the OCX file at runtime. The Package and Deployment Wizard automatically adds these files to your deployment when it comes time to distribute your ActiveX control. However, be advised that the size of these associated files can add up to approximately 2MB. On a desktop application this isn't a big imposition, but for ActiveX controls used over the Internet, this could cause a significant increase in download time. The good news is that the runtime download happens only once, not every time you download an ActiveX control.

Creating VB Programs
for the Internet

Programming with VBScript

Understanding HTML elements

Working with DHTML

Using ActiveX Controls on a Web page

Working on the Internet

Advantages of using VB and VBScript on the Internet

More than likely, you already have a general idea of what the Internet is, and you use it every day for email, Web browsing, and downloading files. Also, many of you probably already develop Internet applications with C++ or Java. You can use any document on the Internet, including spreadsheets and databases, but sometimes you need to do a little programming to force the application to do what you want it to do. Learning Visual Basic and VBScript in relation to Internet programming puts you one step ahead, and your Web pages will work and look much better.

Before you look at how to use Visual Basic to do Internet programming, it's useful to have a fundamental concept of how the Internet works. In a nutshell, the *Internet* is a very large network with millions of users and computers interacting with each other. To expand on this concept, the entire Internet is nothing more than millions of computers communicating with each other by means of special documents. These documents are written in special code that all computers can understand. Some of these documents are *interactive*, meaning that any user can change the information that the document contains. One example of this is the *Web page*, which is one or many documents in which users can add or change information.

As complex and unwieldy as the Internet is, its fundamental dynamics concern the relationship between a client PC and server computer. A *client* is something that needs a service, and a *server* is something that provides a service. In the case of the Internet, the client is the computer in your home or at your office, and the server is a computer somewhere on the Web that provides data to the client.

The way by which the client can talk to the server is via protocols. A *protocol* is a set of rules by which the client knows how to pass requests for data to the server. Likewise, the server knows how to send responses back to the calling client. Protocols are useful because they don't rely on platform specifics. A client doesn't need to know whether a server is an HP running an operating system such as UNIX or an IBM running OS/2; the server doesn't need to know whether the client computer is a Macintosh or a Gateway PC.

The protocol used most often on the Internet is HTTP (Hypertext Transfer Protocol). Another widely used protocol is FTP (File Transfer Protocol), and there are others. Any computer that can talk HTTP or FTP can communicate with servers on the Internet, and vice versa.

For a computer to be a server on the Internet, it must have two things: an address by which other computers can locate it and the capability to understand and process the various protocols. A server is assigned a unique numeric ID called an *IP* (Internet Protocol) *address*. Normally, however, you don't use the numeric address when calling a server on the Internet; instead, you use the server's associated *domain name*. The domain name is the friendly addressing format, www.domainname.com, that you've come to know from using the World Wide Web (see Figure 28.1).

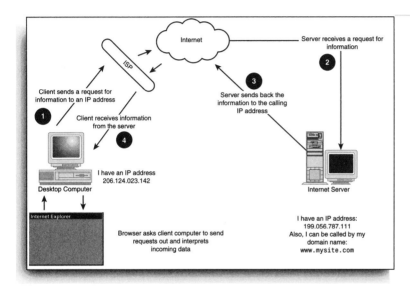

FIGURE 28.1

The Internet is based on discrete conversations between a client computer and an Internet server.

The software used on the physical computer to make it a server that can speak the protocols of the Internet and respond accordingly is called *Internet server software*. The particular Internet server software manufactured by Microsoft is Internet Information Server (IIS).

For a client computer to be able to communicate with a server on the Internet, it must have a connection to the Internet. Then, when connected, it must have a way to contact and receive data from Internet servers through the various protocols. The connection is accomplished via an Internet service provider (ISP), such as America Online, CompuServe, MSN, AT&T Worldnet, MCI, or Sprint. The tool to communicate to the server and decipher the data returned by the Internet server is handled by the Internet browser, such as Microsoft's Internet Explorer or Netscape Navigator.

Many ISPs out there

The ISP that you use might depend on your local area. This book doesn't recommend any particular service because they all provide one basic function—connecting you to the rest of the world. Each ISP is unique because each has a slightly different format. You might try several before settling on one. Some services, such as AT&T Worldnet and America Online, offer trial memberships in which you can "try before you buy."

Client side versus server side

If you write a program that resides and executes on a client computer, that program is called a *client-side* program. If you create a program that runs on an Internet server, that program is called a *server-side* program. Microsoft Word is considered a client-side program. Yahoo Search, a program that searches for articles on the Web, is a server-side program.

Where does Visual Basic fit in all this? Microsoft has positioned Visual Basic to play an important role on the client side and the server side. On the client side, you can use a derivative of Visual Basic, VBScript, to create Web page programs that can run from within Internet Explorer. You also can use Visual Basic to create custom ActiveX components that you can embed in Web pages and run as any custom ActiveX component would.

On the server side, you can use VBScript to create Active Server Pages (ASP) in order to create logic that enables IIS to respond to various input from client computers. Also, you can use Visual Basic to create custom ActiveX components designed to work as extensions and enhancements to the IIS environment. These components are called *server-side components*.

You can use VBScript with server-side ActiveX components to access databases connected to the Internet server to return data to the client. You can keep track of the various activities of the users accessing your server. You can handle mail and deliver files. You can create responses custom-tailored to the specific requester. You can transact business.

On the client side, you can use VBScript to make decisions about what information to send back to the server, to create animation effects, and to interact with other programs on the client computer, to name a few examples.

Microsoft is very serious about the Internet and is trying to position Visual Basic as *the* language by which to program for the Internet, provided that you use Internet Explorer as the client browser and Internet Information Server as the Internet server software on the back end. Therefore, using Visual Basic or VBScript within the context of the Internet is a skill that's more and more expected of programmers.

Making a Simple Program with VBScript

When you install Internet Explorer on your computer, you have access to some benefits of the Visual Basic programming environment. Although IE isn't a complete programming environment, you still have a lot of programming potential at your disposal. Most commands, statements, and functions available to you in Visual Basic are also accessible to you in Internet Explorer.

When used to its full potential, VBScript is a useful but not really powerful script language that lets you write programs to control the way things happen on the Internet and in other environments. There has never been a script language that can compete with a programming language such as Visual Basic. You could probably achieve the most power by combining the two environments and using both VBScript and Visual Basic. Other VBScript limitations include the following:

- VBScript is bound to the interpreter that lives with Internet Explorer.
- VBScript has only one data type, `Variant`.

Also, you can't do the advanced things that Visual Basic enables you to do, such as create custom controls and classes or access the Windows API. However, with VBScript you can access ActiveX controls. The more you use VBScript, the more ways you will discover to make it work to your benefit.

Because VBScript is a text-based programming language, you don't need to have a copy of Visual Basic to program in VBScript. All you need is a text editor such as Notepad to create HTML pages with VBScript embedded in it. Advanced tools such as Visual InterDev offer the benefit of visual programming enhancements and editing capabilities that enable you to write VBScript more easily.

VBScript executes as a Web page loads into Internet Explorer. For example, you can use VBScript to write text to a browser window, thus avoiding the need to write the page in HTML. Although it's far from being a replacement for HTML, VBScript does most of the same functions, providing you with a quick solution to some Web programming problems.

Programs versus scripts

Most often you can think of a *script* as a small program. However, there are subtle differences between a program and a script. In the traditional sense, you can think of a script as a set of tasks performed in sequence. On a Web page, a script is a set of tasks that the page executes as it loads. *Programs*, on the other hand, are a collection of sets of tasks that can be performed sequentially or at random. For instance, you can have a program that runs a set of tasks on startup and another set of tasks when a user clicks a button (event-driven). As scripting languages such as VBScript become more powerful, however, the boundary between where a script ends and a program begins becomes more and more complicated.

Creating an Hello World program in VBScript

1. Open Notepad or another text editor and enter the following text:

```
<SCRIPT LANGUAGE="VBScript">
    document.write "Hello World"
</SCRIPT>
```

2. Save the text as Test.htm.

3. Open Internet Explorer.

4. Drag the Test.htm file from Windows Explorer to the client area of Internet Explorer (see Figure 28.2).

FIGURE 28.2

VBScript enables you to control output to Internet Explorer.

Using VBScript with Internet Explorer

You can use VBScript with HTML to make Web pages that appear and behave like Visual Basic programs. This is possible because, as you read earlier, much of Visual Basic functionality is built into Internet Explorer. Figure 28.3 shows a simple page of HTML, 28htm01.htm (see Listing 28.1), presented in Internet Explorer. If users enter Fred Flintstone in the top text box, the bottom text box returns the validation string You are in!. Any other text produces the response You are out. If you're interested in more information on HTML programming, look into some of the books on the subject at http://www.mcp.com.

FIGURE 28.3
You can process data by using VBScript and HTML.

LISTING 28.1   **28HTM01.HTM—A Simple Page of HTML That Processes Data**

```
01  <HTML>
02  <TITLE>Using VB6: VBScript</TITLE>
03  <HEAD>
04  <!--This is how you make a commented line in HTML-->
05  <SCRIPT LANGUAGE=VBSCRIPT>
06  <!--
07  'This is a commented line in VBScript. You only use
08  'the apostrophe within the SCRIPT tag.
09
10  Sub cmdValidate_OnClick()
11      'This Sub examines the value of the text
12      'entered in the first TEXT element.
13      If txtName.Value = "Fred Flintstone" Then
14          'If TRUE, then ALLOW Login
15          txtValidate.Value = "You are in!"
16      Else
17          'If NOT, then DISALLOW Login
18          txtValidate.Value = "You are out!"
19      End if
20  End Sub
21  -->
22  </SCRIPT>
23  </HEAD>
24
25  <BODY>
```

Placing VBScript on a Web page

You place VBScript between the <SCRIPT></SCRIPT> tags on a Web page. As the script is loaded from the Web page, script is executed as each line is encountered. If you have script at the top of a page, that script executes even if the page is still loading. If the script is a procedure, however, it's not executed until it's called from other areas in the page. Usually, procedures are placed within the <HEAD></HEAD> tags at the beginning of the page.

continues...

LISTING 28.1   Continued

```
26 <!--Create heading using the heading
27     H1 tag and center the heading    -->
28 <CENTER>
29 <H1>Secret Login</H1>
30 </CENTER>
31
32 <!--Put in a paragraph break; create a
33     textbox using the INPUT TYPE= HTML
34     element. Make sure to put some labeling
35     text above the textbox.            -->
36 <P>
37 Name:
38 <BR>
39 <INPUT TYPE=Text Size=40 ID=txtName>
40
41 <!--Put in a paragraph break; create another
42     textbox using the INPUT TYPE= HTML
43     element. Make sure to put some labeling
44     text above the textbox.            -->
45 <P>
46 Authentication:
47 <BR>
48 <INPUT TYPE=Text Size=40 ID=txtValidate>
49
50 <!--Put in a paragraph break; create a
51     button. Give it an ID of cmdValidate
52     so that it will call the event handler
53     coded in the above SCRIPT tag. The
54     event handler is cmdValidate_OnClick. -->
55 <P>
56 <INPUT TYPE=Button Value="Validate" ID=cmdValidate>
57 </BODY>
```

Download this code

A fully commented, unnumbered version of this code is available from http://www.mcp. com/info. The code for this chapter is in the file VB6CH28.zip.

What are HTML elements?

Think of HTML elements as controls embedded in the Internet Explorer browser and accessed via HTML. HTML elements are covered in more detail in the following section.

What's interesting about this program is that although it appears to be using an intrinsic Visual Basic ActiveX control, it's not; it's made completely from HTML and HTML elements.

The way the program works is that two HTML <INPUT TYPE=Text> elements (lines 39 and 48) and an <INPUT TYPE=Button> HTML element (line 56) are created. When users click the button, a click event handler written in VBScript (lines 10–20) processes the data input into the first text element (line 13). A response is output in line 15 or 18.

Working with HTML Elements

If you don't have a working knowledge of HTML, this code might be difficult to grasp. A fundamental understanding of HTML and HTML elements is a prerequisite for working with VBScript on the Internet. HTML, the language of the Internet, is a *tagged language*, which means that tags are used to issue instructions to the HTML interpreter about how to process data sent from the server to the calling client. For instance, the following piece of HTML instructs the browser to make the words `Hello World` boldface.

```
<B>Helllo World</B>
```

In addition to tags that tell the browser how to handle text are tags that tell the browser about the structure of the HTML page. Also, some tags create elements very similar to the intrinsic ActiveX controls. Table 28.1 lists these elements.

TABLE 28.1   HTML Elements Compared to Intrinsic ActiveX Controls

HTML Element	ActiveX Intrinsic Control
`<INPUT TYPE=CHECKBOX>`	CheckBox
`<SELECT>`	ComboBox
`<INPUT TYPE=BUTTON>`	CommandButtons
`<FRAME>`	Frame
`<INPUT TYPE=IMAGE>`	Image
`<SELECT MULTIPLE>`	ListBox
`<INPUT TYPE=RADIO>`	OptionButton
`<INPUT TYPE=TEXT>`	TextBox
`<TEXTAREA>`	TextBox with multiple lines and scrollbars
`<INPUT TYPE=BUTTON>`	CommandButton
`<SELECT>`	DropDownCombo or ListBox

HTML elements have properties that you can set at design time, as you would an ActiveX control. HTML element properties are called *arguments*. The syntax for these arguments is a bit different from properties of ActiveX controls. To create an <INPUT TYPE=TEXT> element with the text Hello World in it, you would use the following:

```
<INPUT TYPE=TEXT SIZE=40 VALUE="Hello World">
```

In this syntax,

- INPUT TYPE=TEXT tells the browser to make a text element.
- SIZE=40 tells the browser to make the element 40 characters wide.
- VALUE="Hello World" tells the browser to set Hello World as the text element's string.

The following sections provide a more detailed description of the HTML elements that you use with VBScript.

The *<FORM>* element

HTML forms begin with the tag <FORM> and ends with the tag </FORM>. The <FORM> element takes the following format:

```
<FORM ACTION = URL METHOD= post¦get NAME=aname>
...
</FORM>
```

In this syntax,

- ACTION is the server-side uniform resource locator to which the form's data will be passed. Typically, this is a CGI script.
- METHOD is the way that the data is passed. You can choose between the post (moves everything into the URL) and get (sends behind the scenes, in the background) methods. These methods evolve from CGI programming.
- NAME is a user-defined ID that identifies the form. This is particularly useful when you have Web pages that contain more than one form.

Therefore,

```
<FORM ACTION=http://www.mysite.com/cgi-bin/myscript.exe
 METHOD=post NAME-myform>
```

Working with CGI

The *common gateway interface* (CGI) is a specification that defines a set of standards by which data consistently and predictably enters and leaves an Internet Server. Originally developed for the UNIX environment, CGI is used for Internet-based data-processing and decision-making routines such as queries and lookups. Programs that do this sort of server-side processing are called *CGI scripts* and are usually written in a language such as Perl or C++.

```
. . .
</FORM>
```

denotes a form that will pass its data to a CGI script, myscript.exe, on the server www.mysite.com. The form will use the post method. The name of the form is myform.

Forms are *parent elements*, which means that the information gathered is generated by other HTML elements living between the <FORM> and </FORM> tags. An element that lives within a <FORM> is called a *child element*.

You can think of the <FORM> element as a nongraphical version of a Visual Basic form. A VB form can contain buttons, text boxes, labels, and a host of other controls. When you reference a control within a VB form, you do so through the form. For instance, if you had a CommandButton named Command1 on a form named Form1, you would reference the CommandButton with the following piece of code:

```
Form1.Command1.
```

The same is true of an HTML <FORM>. You can have <INPUT>, <TEXTAREA>, and <SELECT> elements that reside with a <FORM>. Therefore, if you have a <FORM NAME=MyForm> element that contains an <INPUT TYPE=TEXT NAME=MyText> element, you would reference it with VBScript as

```
MyForm.MyText
```

This notion of parent and child elements becomes very important when you work with VBScript and the Internet Explorer Document Object Model (DOM).

The *<INPUT>* Element

The <INPUT> elements are what you provide for users to enter in form data and trigger a submission of the form's data onto a server on the Internet.

HTML has a standard set of <INPUT> types, just as VB has a standard set of controls that you adapt to a particular purpose. Also, as with VB control properties, each <INPUT> element has attributes that you configure to accommodate a particular layout need.

The Document Object Model (DOM)

The Document Object Model is the hierarchical relationship of data in a Web page. For example, the window object contains the document object, which can contain a form object. Modern VB Internet programming is about using the DOM. In earlier versions of HTML, the DOM was much less complex. Now the DOM has hundreds of objects, attributes, and methods. For an in-depth look at the DOM, visit Microsoft's Web page at http:// www. microsoft.com/msdn/s dk/inetsdk/help/ dhtml/references/ domrefs.htm.

The <INPUT> element attributes are as follows:

Attribute	Description
NAME	Defined name of <INPUT>'s data, similar to a variable name
VALUE	<INPUT>'s data, similar to the value of a variable
TYPE	Defines the type of <INPUT> element, such as Text, Radio, Checkbox, and so on
MAXLENGTH	Specifies the maximum number of characters that may be entered in an <INPUT> field
SIZE	Defines the size (width) of the <INPUT> field, is used for Text or Password
CHECKED	Marks a check box or sets a radio button to True

The <INPUT> element types are as follows:

- Text—You use the Text type to enable users to enter textual data:
```
<INPUT TYPE=Text SIZE=40 NAME=txtName>
```

- Password—A Password type is similar to a Text <INPUT> element type, but the characters that users enter are masked with asterisks. Although the type offers some measure of security, the type's security can be breached with little difficulty if you don't have a secure transaction.
```
<INPUT TYPE=Password NAME=pswMain>
```

- Submit—The Submit button is the <INPUT> type that you use to create a button that, when clicked, triggers the submission of a form's data to a server on the Internet. The browser will show the caption of the Submit type to be the string Submit unless the VALUE is assigned another string.
```
<INPUT TYPE=Submit Value="Submit Profile"
 NAME=Submit>
```

- Reset—This <INPUT> type creates a button that clears the data from all fields on an HTML form when clicked:
```
<INPUT TYPE=Reset Value="Clear Profile"
 NAME=Reset>
```

- Button—This <INPUT> type creates a button that can be referenced with VBScript:
```
<INPUT TYPE=Button NAME=cmdValidate
 Value="Validate">
```

- Radio—Radio buttons are used to make exclusive choices, very much in the same way that you use an OptionButton control in VB. The tricky thing is to understand that for a set of Radio types to be exclusive of one another, all Radio types to be grouped must have the same value attached to their NAME attribute:

```
<INPUT TYPE=RADIO NAME=opFlintstones
 VALUE="Fred">Fred<BR>
<INPUT TYPE=RADIO NAME=opFlintstones
 VALUE="Wilma">Wilma<BR>
<INPUT TYPE=RADIO NAME=opFlintstones
 VALUE="Betty">Betty<BR>
<INPUT TYPE=RADIO NAME=opFlintstones
 VALUE="Barney">Barney<BR>
```

When you submit the form, only the VALUE of the chosen Radio type will be sent to the server.

- Checkbox—Check boxes are used to make inclusive choices. The value of the NAME attribute for each check box must be different. When you add the parameter CHECKED, you put a check mark in the check box.

```
<INPUT TYPE=CHECKBOX NAME=chkCartoon
 VALUE=IsCartoon CHECKED>
```

- Hidden—Hidden <INPUT> types are never shown on the form. Using hidden types is a good way to send some data from the form to the server without users knowing about it. It's as though you have a piece of data embedded in the form, which you can return to the server on a free-ride basis. For the following code example, I attached this name to a HIDDEN input type:

```
<INPUT TYPE=Hidden NAME=hidAuthor
 VALUE="Bob Reselman">
```

When the data is sent back to the server, my name will also be sent to the server without users ever having chosen to have such data sent.

- Image—An IMAGE <Input> type displays a GIF image that has the behavior of a SUBMIT <INPUT> type:

```
INPUT TYPE=image NAME=imgMain SRC=gifs/gifbut.gif>
```

The *<SELECT>* Element

A <SELECT> element is similar to an <INPUT> element in that it enables users to input data to be submitted to a server on the Internet. The <SELECT> element is a little more powerful, however, in that it has the behavior of a Visual Basic ListBox or ComboBox.

The tag begins with <SELECT> and ends with </SELECT>. Between the tags, you place <OPTION> elements:

```
<SELECT NAME="lstUser">
<OPTION VALUE="Admin">Admin
<OPTION VALUE="Employee">Employee
<OPTION VALUE="Guest">Guest
</SELECT>
```

If you use the MULTIPLE attribute in the tag definition, the element will appear as a list, similar to the Visual Basic ListBox. When the element appears as a list, you can submit multiple <OPTION> elements to the server. If you omit the MULTIPLE attribute, the element will appear as a drop-down box, similar to a VB ComboBox, from which you can choose only one <OPTION>.

The *<TEXTAREA>* Element

The <TEXTAREA> element is similar to a TEXT <INPUT> type, except that a <TEXTAREA> element can accept multiple lines of text. The tag definition begins with <TEXTAREA> and ends with </TEXTAREA>:

```
<TEXTAREA NAME=txtComments ROWS=5 COLS=30>
</TEXTAREA>
```

Any text that appears between the tags will show up in the field of the <TEXTAREA>. These tags will also accept a default value.

The <TEXTAREA> element has three attributes:

Attribute	Description
NAME	The name of the element (required)
ROWS	The number of rows in the <TEXTAREA> field
COLS	The width of the field in characters

Some things in common

Although various HTML elements have common arguments, the behavior associated with these elements is different. Fortunately, the VB6 IDE has created a way to set HTML elements just as you would an ActiveX control. This topic is covered later in the section "Using DHTML with ActiveX Components."

More on Scripts

From the browser's point of view, the only difference between Web pages that contain a script and those than don't is the presence of the `<SCRIPT>` tag in the page's HTML. A `<SCRIPT></SCRIPT>` tag indicates that everything between the tags is VBScript or JavaScript. The syntax of the `<SCRIPT>` tag is

`<SCRIPT LANGUAGE = scripting language>...</SCRIPT>`

When a browser sees the `<SCRIPT>` tag, it says to itself, "I have some script stuff coming up to consider." When the browser sees the `</SCRIPT>` tag, it stops that consideration. Unless the script is code for an event handler, sub, or function, the script will be executed in the order in which it's encountered.

The `<SCRIPT>` tag has a `LANGUAGE` attribute that indicates the scripting language used. The `<SCRIPT>` tag supports VBScript, Jscript, and JavaScript.

You code VBScript between the `<SCRIPT></SCRIPT>` tags just as you would code VB within the Visual Basic IDE. You `Dim` variables, write code, and use apostrophes to begin comment lines. If you declare a variable within a `Sub` or `Function`, that variable is local to the `Sub` or `Function`; variables declared outside a `Sub` or `Function` are global. As mentioned earlier, all variables are variants, but you can typecast values by using the conversion functions of `Cint()`, `CLng()`, `CStr()`, and so forth.

SEE ALSO

➢ *For more information on typecasting, see page 240*

As mentioned earlier, scripts can run from a server on the Internet or from your local hard drive. The browser considers only the structure of the script, not its source. Therefore, you load and run client-side scripted HTML as you load any other Web page. This might not be entirely true in all cases if you're trying to run scripts by using objects that will run on the client or the server based on where the page resides.

In Listing 28.1, lines 5–22 are the `<SCRIPT>` portion of the page. The script contains the code for a click event handler for the `Button` element `cmdValidate`. The code for the event handler starts at line 10 and ends at line 20.

Incorporating VBScript with HTML

Figure 28.4 shows a Web page that contains the <TABLE>, Form, CheckBox, Radio, Text, <TEXTAREA>, <SELECT>, Password, and Button HTML elements. At the bottom of the page is a button that, when clicked, displays the Internet Explorer Alert dialog. If users enter the correct password, the Alert dialog—the HTML equivalent of a MessageBox—reports back the type of user, any comments from the Comment text area, the selected Radio elements, and an indication of which check boxes have been selected. The code that executes this logic is written in the VBScript click event procedure cmdValidate_OnClick. Listing 28.2 shows the HTML and VBScript for this page.

FIGURE **28.4**

The <TABLE> element, part of the HTML 3.0 standard, creates a table that contains a caption (<CAPTION>) and any number of rows (<TR>). More new tags are being added to this element every day.

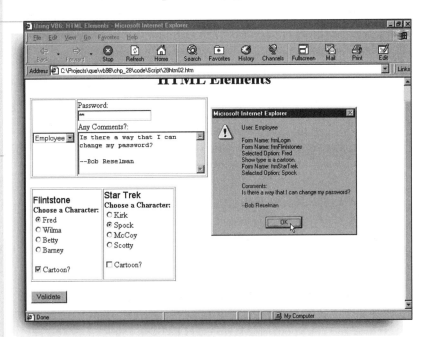

LISTING 28.2   **28HTM02.HTM—A Web Page with the HTML elements**

```
01    <html>
02    <!--Created by Bob Reselman
03        Copyright 1998 Macmillan Publishing -->
04    <head>
05    <title>Using VB6: HTML Elements</title>
06    </head>
```

```
07
08    <body>
09    <script language="VBScript"><!--
10    Sub cmdValidate_OnClick()
11      Dim br            'Line Break variable'
12      Dim strBuffer     'String buffer to hold
13                        'alert message
14      Dim i             'Counter variable
15      Dim j             'Another counter variable
16
17      'Set the line break var to the line break chars
18      br = Chr(10) & Chr(13)
19
20      'Set the string buffer to report who is entering
21      'by getting the value from the SELECT element.
22      strBuffer = strBuffer + "User: " & _
                 frmLogin.lstUser.Value + br + br
23    'Cycle through all the forms in the document in the
24    'browser window
25    For i = 0 to document.forms.length - 1
26                  + document.forms(i).name + br
27    strBuffer = strBuffer + "Form Name: " _
      For j = 0 to document.forms(i).elements.length - 1
28        'Within each form, check all the child elements
29        'to see if the type is a RADIO
30        If document.forms(i).elements(j).type = "radio" Then
31          'If you find a RADIO, see if it is checked
32          If document.forms(i).elements(j).checked Then
33            'Concatenate the string by adding an indication
34            'of which RADIO has been checked.
35            strBuffer = strBuffer + "Selected Option: "
36            strBuffer = strBuffer _
                        + document.forms(i).elements(j).value
37            'Put in a line break
38            strBuffer = strBuffer + br
39          End If
40        ElseIf _
          'check to see if the element is a checkbox
41        document.forms(i).elements(j).type = "checkbox" Then
42          If document.forms(i).elements(j).Checked Then
43            'If the checkbox is checked, concatenate the string
44            'buffer to indicate the check means the show is
```

continues…

Commenting HTML

You comment HTML code by putting comments between the characters, <!-- and -->. For example, the code <!-- _Created by Bob Reselman --> indicates that the string **Created by Bob Reselman** won't be interpreted as HTML; it will be ignored as comments. You can have as many lines between the begin and end comment characters as you want.

LISTING 28.2 Continued

```
45        'a cartoon.
46        strBuffer = strBuffer + "Show type is a cartoon." _
                          + br
47      End If
48    End If
49  Next
50 Next
51 'Concatenate the string buffer to line break and
52 'report the comment that is entered.
53 strBuffer = strBuffer + br + "Comments: " + br
54 'in the TEXTAREA element of the FORM, frmLogin (read
55 'the value property)
56  strBuffer = strBuffer + frmLogin.txtComments.Value
57 'Check to see if the user entered the proper password
58 '("TV") in the PASSWORD element.
59 If frmLogin.pswMain.Value = "TV" Then
60   'If the entry is valid, display the string buffer
61   Alert strBuffer
62 Else
63    'If not, report an error message
64    Alert "You did not login correctly"
65 End If
66 End Sub
67 -->
68 </script>
69 <!--Create heading using the H1 tag and
70     center the heading    -->
71
72 <H1 align="center">HTML Elements</H1>
73
74 <!--Make a table 1 row by 2 colswhich creates
75    a layout structure for the FORM, frmLogin.
76    Set the Border value to one so that the lines
77    show up.-->
78 <TABLE BORDER="1">
79 <!-- Create a form using the <FORM> tag. -->
80 <FORM NAME="frmLogin">
81 <TR>
82 <!--Put the user drop-down in the first cell of the
83    first row. -->
84 <TD>
```

```
85   <SELECT NAME="lstUser" SIZE="1">
86     <OPTION VALUE="Admin">Admin </OPTION>
87     <OPTION VALUE="Employee">Employee </OPTION>
88     <OPTION VALUE ="Guest">Guest </OPTION>
89   </SELECT >
90   </TD>
91   <!--Add the Password element and the TextArea
92     Comment box to the second cell in the first row of
93     the table. -->
94   <TD>
95   Password:<BR>
96   <INPUT TYPE="PASSWORD" SIZE="20" NAME="pswMain"><BR>
97   Any Comments?: <BR>
98   <TEXTAREA NAME ="txtComments" ROWS="5" 102:COLS="30">
99   </TEXTAREA >
100  <!--Put in the closing tags for the Table and the
101    form. -->
102  </TD>
103  </TR>
104  </FORM>
105  </TABLE>
106
107  <P>
108  <!-- Create another table, 1 row by 2 cols to
109    hold all the TV radio elements and the checkbox
110    elements. -->
111  <TABLE BORDER="1">
112  <TR>
113  <TD>
114  <!-- Put the form to hold the elements for the
115    Flintstones in the first row, first column. -->
116  <FORM Name="frmFlintstones">
117  <!-- Make the font for the heading of these groups
118    larger, bold and Arial. Put a line break at the end
119    of the heading-->
120  <FONT SIZE="4" FACE="ARIAL">Flintstone</FONT><BR>
121  <!-- Make the label bold and put a space after the
122    end of the label and then a line break. -->
123  <B>Choose a Character: </B><BR>
124  <!-- Create some radio buttons for the
125    Flintstones. Put a page break between
126    each radio button.-->
```

continues...

Case sensitivity

Because VBScript and HTML aren't case-sensitive languages, `<INPUT TYPE=Text>` is the same as `<input type=text>`. However, JavaScript is case-sensitive.

LISTING 28.2 Continued

```
127 <INPUT TYPE="radio" NAME="opFlintstones"
128                       VALUE="Fred">Fred<BR>
129 <INPUT TYPE="radio" NAME="opFlintstones"
130                       VALUE="Wilma">Wilma<BR>
131 <INPUT TYPE="radio" NAME="opFlintstones"
132                       VALUE="Betty">Betty<BR>
133 <INPUT TYPE="radio" NAME="opFlintstones"
134                       VALUE="Barney">Barney<P>
135 <!--Put in a checkbox to denote a cartoon. -->
136 <INPUT TYPE="checkbox" CHECKED NAME="chkCartoon"
137                           VALUE ="IsCartoon">Cartoon?
138 <!-- Close off the Flintstone form -->
139 </FORM>
140 <!-- Close off the first cell -->
141 </TD>
142 <!-- Make the next cell in the first row hold
143     the Star Trek stuff. -->
144 <TD>
145     <!-- Make the form name, frmStarTrek >
146 <FORM NAME="frmStarTrek">
147 <!-- Set the heading font as above -->
148 <FONT SIZE="4" FACE="ARIAL">Star Trek</FONT><BR>
149 <!-- Bold and line break as before. -->
150 <B>Choose a Character: </B><BR>
151 <INPUT TYPE="radio" NAME="opStarTrek"
152                       VALUE="Kirk">Kirk<BR>
153 <INPUT TYPE="radio" NAME="opStarTrek"
154                       VALUE="Spock">Spock<BR>
155 <INPUT TYPE="radio" NAME="opStarTrek"
156                       VALUE="McCoy">McCoy<BR>
157 <INPUT TYPE="radio" NAME="opStarTrek"
158                       VALUE="Scotty">Scotty<P>
159 <!--Put in a checkbox to denote a cartoon. -->
160 <INPUT TYPE="checkbox" NAME="chkCartoon"
```

```
161                        VALUE="IsCartoon">Cartoon?
162  <!-- Close off the Form and Table -->
163  </FORM>
164  </TD>
165  </TR>
166  </TABLE>
167  <!--Make a button; put the word Validate in the button
168    face. Make the name of the button cmdValidate. -->
169  <P><INPUT TYPE ="button" VALUE="Validate"
170  NAME="cmdValidate">
171  <!-- Close off the Body of the page. -->
172  </BODY>
173  </HTML>
```

This VBScript code shows you how to program the various standard HTML elements. Notice on line 26 that the code uses the length property of the document.forms element to determine how many forms are within the HTML document. In HTML, the length property is similar to the Visual Basic count property for collections. The use of the length property on line 26 and again on line 29 for the elements collection should give you a sense that an HTML document is a series of collections within collections (or arrays within arrays, to use non–language-centric terminology). As you program more with HTML and DOM, you will find yourself traversing and manipulating the various collections of elements in a document. Therefore, an understanding of the different collections and parent-child hierarchies with the DOM is fundamental for developing more complex Web pages with VBScript. The SideNote titled "The Document Object Model (DOM)" earlier in this chapter shows you the URL for the Microsoft site that provides documentation for the DOM.

Static versus dynamic Web pages

A static Web page is one in which the content is hard-coded in HTML and not subject to quick change. For instance, if you wanted to make a Web page that presents the works of Shakespeare, you could type up all the plays in a word processor, save the document as HTML, and put it on a Web site. You probably wouldn't expect the data to change at all after you posted it on the site. Dynamic data, on the other hand, changes all the time and is usually written using an HTML script. For instance, if you wanted to have a Web page that reports the current price of your favorite stock, you would do it by writing a small program in a scripting language such as VBScript. The program would go to a stock-reporting server, ask for the current price of your stocks, and then forward those prices to you.

As you can see, making the page in Figure 28.4 (refer to Listing 28.2) is a laborious effort because of manipulating the HTML elements necessary to organize the page into an acceptable presentation and writing the VBScript to handle the events and actions within the page. DHTML is much more difficult and time-consuming in this respect. Before Visual Basic 6, this sort of scripting was the only way that you could make dynamic Web pages. Although powerful, scripting of this sort is tedious and exposed. The code that you write is open for the world to see—not advantageous if you are at all concerned with protecting your intellectual property. However, Visual Basic 6 lets you write VBScript with HTML in a way that's less burdensome and more protective of your code—using dynamic HTML.

Handling Events with VBScript

You write an event procedure for an HTML element or ActiveX control in VBScript by using the standard Visual Basic syntax. The only difference is that, whereas the Visual Basic IDE creates the event-procedure code block for you, in VBScript you must create the code block yourself. Therefore, if you want to write a click event procedure for the element <INPUT TYPE=BUTTON NAME=MyButton>, you write

```
<SCRIPT Language=VBScript>
Sub MyButton_OnClick()
'Enter code here.
...
End Sub
</SCRIPT>
```

Plenty more information on VBScript and ActiveX controls is available. The Internet contains so much on subjects related to Internet programming that it would probably take a normal person several thousand years to research only a small percentage of it. I make this statement with the intention of motivating you to discover how huge the resources are. Some of these resources can be found at Microsoft's Knowledge Base (http://www.microsoft.com) and at Netscape (http://www.netscape.com). You also can refer to http://www.mcp.com, particularly for *Java 97 Unleashed*, *FrontPage 97 Unleashed*, and other books on HTML.

FIGURE 28.5
You select a DHTML application project from the New Project dialog.

Understanding a DHTML Application

Visual Basic has a new project type, the DHTML application (see Figure 28.5). A DHTML application is a program that you design within the DHTML Page Designer in the Visual Basic IDE (see Figure 28.6) and program in Visual Basic (see Figure 28.7), but it runs as HTML in Internet Explorer (see Figure 28.8).

Working with designers

A *designer* is a helper application that you load into the Visual Basic IDE. Designers automate many programming functions that you need for a particular activity or type of program. VB6 has introduced numerous new designers, including designers for data projects and add-ins. The DHTML Page Designer provides a visual way to lay out, format, and code DHTML pages. As of this writing, designers are written in C++.

FIGURE 28.6

The DHTML Page Designer for a DHTML application is very similar to the standard Visual Basic IDE.

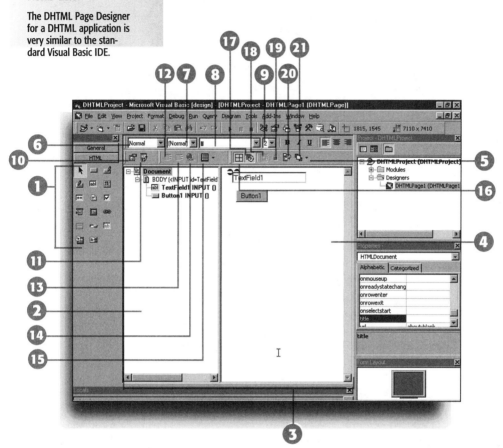

1	HTML Element Toolbox	8	Font Face drop-down	15	Table Operations
2	Object Hierarchy pane	9	Font Size drop-down	16	Show Table Borders
3	DHTML Page Designer Form	10	DHTML Page Designer Properties	17	Show Details
4	Page View pane	11	Launch HTML Editor	18	Absolute Position
5	DHTML Page Designer toolbar	12	Wrap Selection in `<DIV></DIV>`	19	Lock Elements and Controls
6	HTML Font Element drop-down	13	Wrap Selection in `<SPAN></SPAN>`	20	Absolute Position Mode
7	Styles drop-down	14	Create HyperLink	21	ZOrder

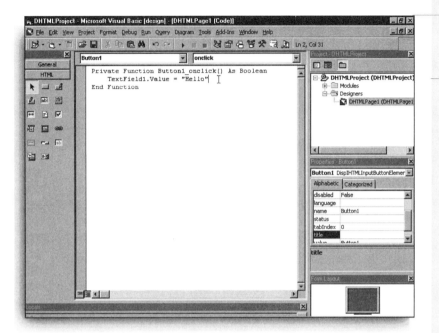

FIGURE 28.7

You code DHTML applications as you would a standard VB program.

FIGURE 28.8

DHTML applications run within Internet Explorer as HTML.

There's a slight twist, however—the code that you write for your DHTML application is compiled into a DLL that's embedded in a Web page that the Visual Basic IDE creates as part of the DHTML project. All the code—event procedures, variables, functions, subs, and so on—is contained in that DLL. The only thing exposed is the HTML that defines and positions the HTML elements (see Figure 28.9).

FIGURE 28.9

The DHTML application compiles into a DLL that the Visual Basic IDE embeds in a Web page and references with a class ID.

Programming a Simple DHTML Application

You create a DHTML program as you would a standard Visual Basic application. The only difference is that the IDE for a DHTML application contains a Toolbox for HTML elements. Rather than use intrinsic ActiveX controls on a form, you use HTML elements within a Web page. For example, rather than call the Text property to find out the contents of a TextBox control, you call value. This is because DHTML uses the <INPUT TYPE=Text> element instead of a TextBox. You can use ActiveX controls within a DHTML application, but you use only those ActiveX controls that ship as an OCX or ActiveX DLL. You can't use the intrinsic controls in the VB6 runtime DLL.

Another noteworthy difference between standard VB and a DHTML application is the use of the property id instead of Name. You use the id property for an element or ActiveX control in DHTML as you would use the Name property for a control in VB. This use is particular to Microsoft's enhancement of DHTML as it relates to use under Internet Explorer. You can use the Name property when scripting standard HTML.

If you're unfamiliar with the DOM and the properties associated with DHTML elements, you might have a little period of adjustment ahead of you. The Microsoft Web site is an excellent learning resource. Also, you can use the Books Online reference that comes on your Visual Basic CD-ROM.

Using multiple browsers

As of this writing, DHTML applications aren't supported by any browser other than Internet Explorer. Although Netscape supports a version of DHTML, it's not officially recognized by the W3C consortium and isn't compatible with Microsoft's Internet Explorer.

Create a simple DHTML application

1. Open a New DHTML application project.

2. Double-click the **DHTMLPage Designer** in the Project window to open the DHTML form (see Figure 28.10).

Download this project's code

The code for this project is in the file VB6CH28.zip, which you can download from http://www.mcp.com/info. The project file is DHTMLProject.vbp.

FIGURE 28.10
The DHTML Page Designer automates code generation.

3. Double-click the `TextField` element to add it to the form.

4. Double-click the `Button` element to add it to the form (see Figure 28.11).

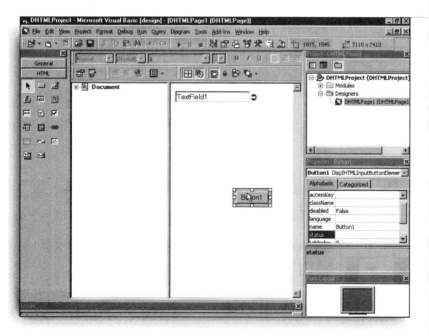

FIGURE 28.11
You can drag and drop HTML elements around a form just as you would in the standard Visual Basic IDE.

5. Position the `TextField` and `Button` elements one on top of the other.

6. Select Button1's value property in the Properties window. Change the value property from Button1 to Click Me.

7. In the page view pane, double-click the **Button1** element to open a code pane to the Button1_onclick() event procedure.

8. Enter the code shown in Figure 28.12 in the Button1_onclick() event procedure.

9. Save the project and press the F5 key to run the code.

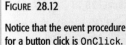

FIGURE 28.12

Notice that the event procedure for a button click is OnClick.

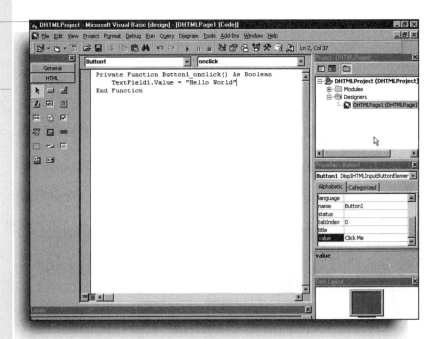

When you run the code for this simple application, Visual Basic compiles the code into a temporary DLL, generates the HTML around the DLL, and automatically embeds the DLL on the page. Then the code is run in Internet Explorer. When you look at the source HTML that loads into the browser, you see no VBScript of any kind—the code is embedded in the DLL, and your intellectual property is safe.

Rapid Development with DHTML Applications

The capability to quickly create powerful, interactive Web pages is a major benefit of VB6's DHTML application feature. Figure 28.13 shows a simple login page with a validation button.

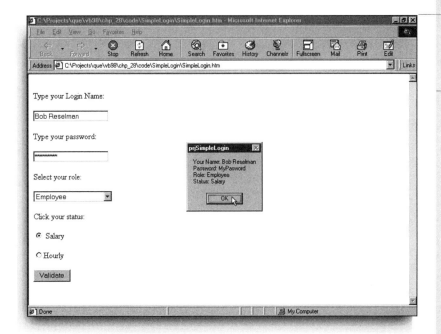

FIGURE 28.13
DHTML applications present the
same appearance as HTML pages
in a Web browser.

Listing 28.3 shows the HTML/VBScript code for the login
page. Listing 28.4 shows the same login page, only generated as
part of the Visual Basic DHTML application project. (I've
altered the text layout of both listings for the code to be more
readable; the syntax of the code hasn't been altered in any way.)

LISTING 28. 3   28HTM03.HTM—A Login Screen That Uses VBScript with HTML

```
01   <!--Copyright 1998 Macmillan Publishing
02       by Bob Reselman -->
03   <HTML>
04   <TITLE>Simple Login in Standard HTML</TITLE>
05   <HEAD>
06   <SCRIPT LANGUAGE=VBScript>
07   <!--
08   Sub cmdValidate_OnClick()
09       'Declare variables to which to assign
10       'the values of each element
11     Dim strName
12     Dim strPWD
13     Dim strRole
14     Dim strStatus
```

Download this project's code

The code for this project can be
found in the file VB6CH28.zip,
which you can download from
the Web site dedicated to this
book. The project file is
prjSimpleLogin.vbp.

continues...

LISTING 28.3 **Continued**

```
15    Dim strMsg
16      Dim br
17
18      'Set the line break var to the line break chars
19      br = Chr(10) & Chr(13)
20
21      'Assign the values
22      strName = txtName.Value
23      strPWD = pwdMain.Value
24      strRole = selectMain.Value
25      If Option1.Checked Then
26          strStatus = Option1.Value
27      Else
28          strStatus = Option2.Value
29      End If
30
31      'Make a string that reports all
32      'the values of the various elements
33      strMsg = strMsg & "Your Name: " & strName & vbCrLf
34      strMsg = strMsg & "Password: " & strPWD & vbCrLf
35      strMsg = strMsg & "Role: " & strRole & vbCrLf
36      strMsg = strMsg & "Status: " & strStatus & vbCrLf
37
38      'Show the string
39      window.alert(strMsg)
40    End Sub
41    -->
42    </SCRIPT>
43    </HEAD>
44
45    <P>Type your Login Name:</P>
46    <P>
47    <INPUT TYPE=TEXT NAME=txtName></P>
48    <P>Type your password:</P>
49    <P>
50    <INPUT TYPE=PASSWORD NAME=pwdMain></P>
51    <P>Select your role:</P>
52    <P><SELECT NAME=selectMain>
53          <OPTION SELECTED VALUE=Guest>Guest
54          <OPTION VALUE=Employee>Employee
55          <OPTION VALUE=Contractor>Contractor
56    </SELECT>
57
58    </P>
59    <P>Click your status:</P>
```

```
60   <P><INPUT NAME=Option1
61           TYPE=RADIO
62           VALUE=Salary CHECKED> Salary</P>
63   <P><INPUT NAME=Option2
64           TYPE=RADIO
65           VALUE=Hourly>Hourly</P>
66
67   <P><INPUT NAME=cmdValidate
68           TYPE=button
69           VALUE=Validate></P>
70   </BODY>
71   </HTML>
```

Notice that lines 6–42 in Listing 28.3 show the script that captures the button click event procedure, whereas Listing 28.4 shows no script whatsoever. This is because the button click event procedure for Listing 28.4 is encapsulated within a DLL referenced by the classid, as shown on line 3.

LISTING 28.4 **SIMPLELOGIN.HTM–DHTML Code Generated by a VB DHTML Application**

```
01   <!--METADATA TYPE="MsHtmlPageDesigner" startspan-->
02   <object id="DHTMLPage1"
03   classid="clsid:9318A4D8-12D7-11D2-A58E-B6A734C6C111"
04   width=0 height=0>
05   </object>
06   <!--METADATA TYPE="MsHtmlPageDesigner" endspan-->
07   <BODY>
08   <P>Type your Login Name:</P>
09   <P>
10   <INPUT id=txtName name=txtName ></P>
11   <P>Type your password:</P>
12   <P>
13   <INPUT id=pwdMain name=PasswordField1 type=password></P>
14   <P>Select your role:</P>
15   <P><SELECT id=selectMain
16           name=selectMain
17           style="HEIGHT: 22px; WIDTH: 161px"
18           value = Select1>
19       <OPTION selected value=Guest>Guest
```

Class ID

DHTML references functionality that's created within a DHTML application DLL through a *class ID*. A DHTML project compiles into a DLL. When you compile the code, VB assigns a unique number—a class ID—to the DLL. When you deploy your DHTML application to Internet Explorer via the Internet, the browser automatically registers the class ID of the DLL in the Windows Registry. Then, when Internet Explorer encounters the class ID in the page, it automatically looks up the classid in the Registry to find the location of the DLL and other particulars.

continues...

LISTING 28.4 **Continued**

```
20        <OPTION value=Employee>Employee
21        <OPTION value=Contractor>Contractor</SELECT>
22   </P>
23   <P>Click your status:</P>
24   <P><INPUT id=Option1
25             name=Option1
26             type=radio
27             value=Salary CHECKED> Salary</P>
28
29   <P><INPUT id=Option2
30             name=Option2
31             type=radio
32             value=Hourly>Hourly</P>
33   <P><INPUT id=cmdValidate
34             name=cmdValidate
35             type=button
36             value=Validate></P>
37   </BODY></HTML>
```

Making an interactive page like this login page by using HTML with VBScript requires paying a lot of attention to the detail of HTML and how it interacts with VBScript. The programming experience isn't at all visual. Everything is character based, thus giving you ample opportunity to make time-consuming syntax errors. On the other hand, making the same page as a DHTML application enables you to use your existing VB programming skills and visually create pages. Also, because you're using the Visual Basic IDE, you can take advantage of VB's debugging capabilities. You'll find that VB DHTML applications enable you to make more robust dynamic pages for the Web in half the time it takes using HTML, VBScript, and a text editor.

Using DHTML with ActiveX Components

Add a Slider ActiveX control to a DHTML application

1. Open a new DHTML application project.

2. Open the Components dialog by choosing **Components** from the **Project** menu.

Download the code for this project

The code for this project can be found in the file VB6CH28.zip, which you can download from http://www.mcp.com/info. The project file is prjSlider.vbp.

3. Select the Microsoft Windows Common Controls 6.0 ActiveX control to add Common Control icons to the Toolbox.

4. Select the **DHTMLPage Designer** in the **Project** window.

5. Click the 📧 icon to view the DHTML Designer Form (see Figure 28.14).

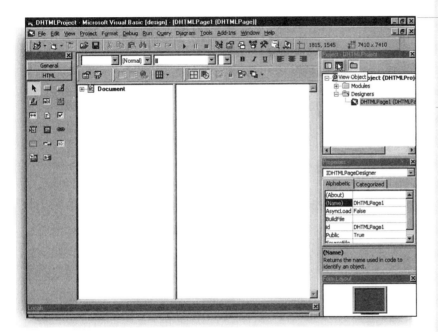

FIGURE 28.14

The DHTML Designer Form contains the page view pane on the right and the HTML element hierarchy on the left.

6. Click the page view pane of the DHTML Designer Form. Type This is a slider control and then press Enter to create a new line.

7. Select the **General** tab in the Toolbox and then drag the Slider control to the new line in the page view pane.

8. Press Enter to create a new line.

9. Type This is the value of the slider control: and then press Enter to create a new line.

10. Select the **HTML** tab in the Toolbox and then drag the TextField element to the new line in the page view pane.

11. In the Properties window, set the id of the TextField to txtMain. Also, set the name to txtMain and the value to blank (no text).

12. Double-click the Slider control to expose its code.

13. Select the **Scroll** event from the event procedure drop-down (see Figure 28.15).

FIGURE 28.15

You code event procedures in DHTML applications just as you do in standard VB programs.

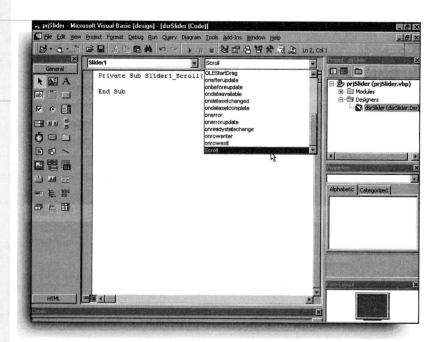

14. Add the following line of code in the scroll event procedure:

```
txtMain.Value = Slider1.Value
```

15. Save the project and run it by pressing F5 (see Figure 28.16).

Saving DHTML application projects

You name and save a number of files when you save a DHTML application. You save the designer, the default module, and the project file. Designers end with the extension .dsr, whereas modules have the familiar .bas extension and projects have the .vbp extension.

FIGURE 28.16
ActiveX controls can interact
with HTML elements in a DHTML
application.

Compiling a DHTML Application

You compile a DHTML application as you would for any other
ActiveX DLL—you choose **Make MyDLLName.DLL** from
the **File** menu. However, behind the scenes a little more work
happens; in addition to making the DLL, Visual Basic generates
the Web page for the DHTML application. You will be prompted to name this HTM page. Remember that DHTML is an
integration of HTML with an ActiveX DLL that contains the
interactive code for the page. Therefore, the page needs the class
ID of the DLL to find the DLL and subsequently the interactive
functionality of the page. The class ID is automatically added to
the HTML within the Web page as you compile your project.

After you complete your Web page, you can make it available to
other users on the Web in the following ways:

- Take advantage of your ISP's services. Most of these services
  provide you with a limited amount of disk space on which
  you can have one or more Web pages. Also, most ISPs provide information on how to upload your file to their servers,
  from which your application or Web page will be available
  to other users on the Internet.

  You must have all your files in a specific directory on your
  hard drive. This is one of the most common problems when

Compiling your project

When you compile your project,
it's a good idea to save the project files, the DLL, and the
HTML page to the same folder.
When it comes time to deploy
your DTHML application, you
can more easily find the files
you need. Pay particular attention to this situation because
when you want to deploy your
application, you will know
where all your project files are
located. It's important to keep
them all in the same directory.

you are uploading these types of files to another server. Most servers also require Web directories to have an index file, such as index.html. If the requesting server doesn't find this file, you will normally have problems.

- Check each Web search engine, such as Yahoo, to determine what you need to do in order to register your site so that other users can find your Web page. In most cases, this involves giving your URL or Web address and the name of your site. Some search engines require a little more information, but most don't. It usually takes several weeks for your Web page to appear on their search list. Some common Web search engine registration locations are as follows:

Search Engine	URL
Yahoo	http://www.yahoo.com
Infoseek	http://www.infoseek.com
WebCrawler	http://www.webcrawler.com
Apollo	http://www.apollo.com
Lycos	http://www.lycos.com
World Wide Web Yellow Pages	http://www.yellow.com

Making Programming Easier with Visual Basic Add-Ins

Include add-ins within the IDE

Use the more popular add-ins

Use the Visual Basic IDE Object Model

Create your own add-in by using the Add-In Designer

Working with Add-Ins

An add-in is a design-time tool that you attach to the Visual Basic IDE. Generally, an add-in simplifies, enhances, or automates some aspect of your programming activity. You can use add-ins to build classes; view API functions, structures, and constants; or help create deployment packages of your applications or custom ActiveX controls.

Attaching Add-Ins to the Add-Ins Menu

Visual Basic 6 ships with a number of add-ins, which you attach to the IDE by using the Add-In Manager.

Attach an add-in to the VB programming environment

1. Choose **Add-In Manager** from the **Add-Ins** menu.

2. In the Add-In Manager dialog, select an add-in from the list (see Figure 29.1).

3. Select one or more of the **Load Behavior** check boxes.

4. Click **OK**.

FIGURE 29.1

You use the Add-In Manager to attach an add-in to the IDE.

1 Adds the add-in to the IDE when you select it in the add-in list

2 Loads the add-in every time you start Visual Basic

3 Loads the add-in when Visual Basic is started from the WindowsRun menu, a command prompt, or a startup script

4 Shows a brief description of the add-in

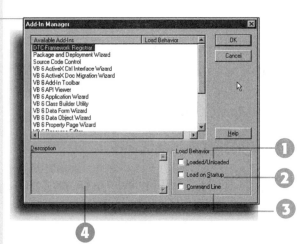

If you select **Loaded/Unloaded** as a load behavior, the add-in appears immediately in the IDE as an item in the **Add-Ins** menu (see Figure 29.2). If you selected **Load on Startup**, you need to close Visual Basic and restart it.

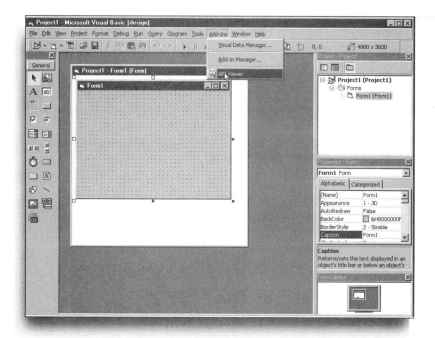

FIGURE 29.2

Some tools that ship with Visual Basic, such as the API Viewer, can be attached to the IDE as an add-in.

Attaching Add-Ins to the Add-Ins Toolbar

In addition to attaching add-ins to Visual Basic's **Add-Ins** menu, you can display an add-in toolbar to which you can insert buttons for various add-ins. This toolbar itself is an add-in, so you first must attach it to the IDE. After you insert the toolbar, you insert buttons representing different add-ins.

Display the Add-In toolbar

1. Choose **Add-In Manager** from the **Add-Ins** menu.

2. Select **VB 6 Add-In Toolbar** from the **Available Add-Ins** list.

3. Select the **Loaded/Unloaded** check box.

4. Click **OK** to insert the toolbar in the Visual Basic IDE (see Figure 29.3).

Insert add-ins in the toolbar

1. Click the Add/Remove Add-In button ▣ on the add-in toolbar to display the Add/Remove Toolbar Items dialog (see Figure 29.4).

FIGURE 29.3

The add-in toolbar is blank until you insert some add-ins except for the Add/Remove icon.

FIGURE 29.4

The add-ins that you insert in the add-in toolbar won't be displayed on the Add-Ins menu.

2. Select the add-ins that you want to add to the toolbar.

3. Click **OK** to close the dialog and insert the add-ins into the toolbar (see Figure 29.5).

FIGURE 29.5

The add-in toolbar is really a *coolbar* control.

1 Add/Remove Add-In

2 Application Wizard

3 Data Form Wizard

Third-party tools

A third-party tool is one made by one developer to support another developer. For instance, Microsoft is the maker of Visual Basic, but another company may make a control or an add-in designed to work with and add value to Visual Basic. The company that makes the tool to support VB is considered a third party, whereas you, the user of the product, are considered the first party and Microsoft is considered the second party.

Using Add-Ins

As mentioned, Visual Basic ships with a number of third-party add-ins. Some of these add-ins are advanced. Most are provided to make your day-to-day programming much easier. Let's look at two: the Application Wizard and the Data Form Wizard.

Using the VB6 Application Wizard

The Application Wizard add-in allows you to quickly create a framework for your application. The Application Wizard is a great tool for creating simple applications and also for implementing front ends (menus) for your programs.

Create a Multiple Document Interface application with a File menu

1. Click the  icon on the add-in toolbar.

2. Let the profiles setting stay at **(None)** in the Application Wizard dialog (see Figure 29.6). Click the **Next** button.

The wizard creates a shell program

If you really want to do specific things with a program created with the Application Wizard, you may have to do more programming. The Application Wizard can create programs that handle information very well, but you may have to do more programming if you want to do much more. It at least provides you with basic code to start with and gives you some learning experience if you have never programmed before.

FIGURE 29.6

Eventually you'll have a number of preset profiles from which you automatically create different types of applications. You can save these profiles at the end of the creation process in the Application Wizard.

3. Select the **Multiple Document Interface (MDI)** option button and enter a name for your application in the text box at the bottom of the dialog (see Figure 29.7). Click **Next**.

4. Deselect all menu items except **&File** in the **Menus** list. Deselect all submenu items except **&New**, **&Open**, **&Close**, and **E&xit** in the **Sub Menus** list (see Figure 29.8). Click **Next**.

5. Remove all toolbar buttons from the application's toolbar except for **New** and **Open** by selecting the button in the list on the right and clicking the left-arrow button (see Figure 29.9). Click **Next**.

Separating menu items

You use separator bars in menus for several reasons. For example, if you have several categories of icons (such as programming, applications, and databases), you could separate these items and make it easier to find what you're looking for.

FIGURE 29.7

You can choose an MDI, SDI, or Explorer interface for your application. A visual and descriptive hint appears in the upper left of the dialog.

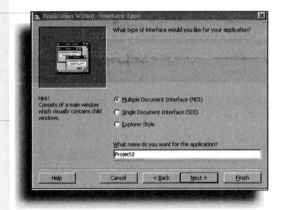

FIGURE 29.8

Select menu items you want to include in your application and then select which submenu items to include.

① Add a menu item

② Delete a menu item

③ Move a menu item within the menu bar to the left

④ Move a menu item within the menu bar to the right

⑤ Add a submenu item

⑥ Delete a submenu item

⑦ Promote a submenu item

⑧ Demote a submenu item

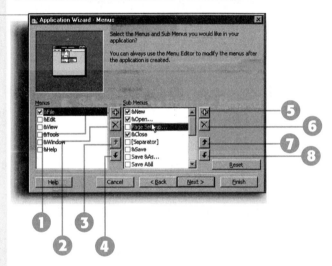

6. Select **No** to avoid adding a resource string to the project (see Figure 29.10). Click **Next**.

7. Select **No** again to avoid adding a Web page and default URL to your project (see Figure 29.11). Click **Next**.

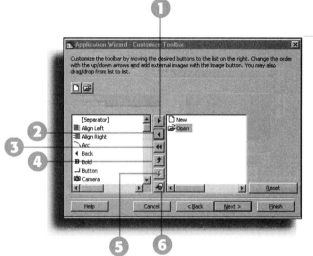

FIGURE 29.9

You add or remove the various images that you want to associate with an application's toolbar in the Customize Toolbar page of the Application Wizard. An example of the toolbar is shown at the top of the dialog.

1. Move button onto the toolbar

2. Move button off the toolbar

3. Move all buttons onto the toolbar

4. Move a button on the toolbar to the left.

5. Move a button on the toolbar to the right

6. Add a new image

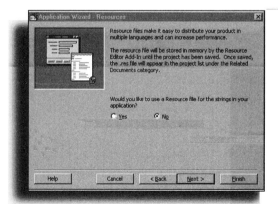

FIGURE 29.10

You can embed a table of string directly into your executable if you decide to make a string resource file.

FIGURE 29.11

If you want, you can auto-matically make your application Web enabled.

8. Leave all the check boxes deselected on the Standard Forms page of the wizard (see Figure 29.12). Click **Next**.

FIGURE 29.12

You can add a splash screen, login, custom settings, and an About box form to your applica-tion.

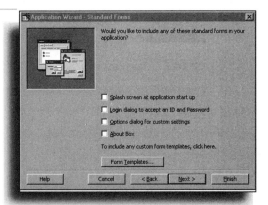

Working with resource files

With resource files, you can distrib-ute your application in multiple lan-guages and increase the performance of the application. The Resource Editor add-in will store the resource file in memory until the project is saved. After it's saved, the resource file will appear in the pro-ject but under the Related Documents category.

9. Don't add any data forms to your application (see Figure 29.13). Click **Next**.

10. Don't save this application configuration as a profile (see Figure 29.14). Click **Finish**.

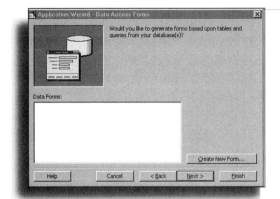

FIGURE 29.13

You can create or add forms that reference a database to your application.

FIGURE 29.14

You can save the application's framework configuration as a profile so that the next time you want to create this type of application, you load the profile within the wizard.

As you can see in Figure 29.15, the Application Wizard has created a project according to the settings provided. Because you chose to make an MDI project, you have an MDI form and a child form. The wizard created a module as well as named and saved the forms and project. The wizard also added an ImageList control and a CommonDialog control to the project to provide images and functionality for the menus and toolbar.

FIGURE 29.15

The Application Wizard makes a full-fledged MDI application project with little effort.

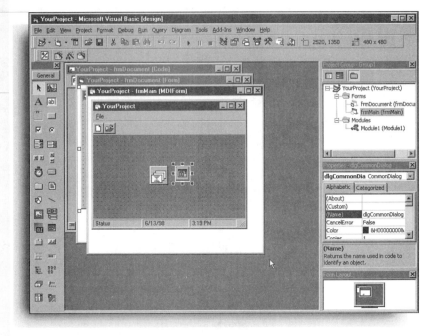

Using the VB6 Data Form Wizard

The Biblio and Northwind databases

Microsoft ships two Access databases with every copy of Visual Basic: Biblio.mdb and Nwind.mdb. These databases are fictitious. Biblio represent a database of books and publishers. Northwind is a database of an imaginary food company, Northwind Traders. These databases are provided so that you have formal data on which to test your data-access tools and routines. These are also great resources to learn from.

Many Visual Basic applications involve accessing and working with data on a database or some other type of data source. Therefore, having a tool that allows you to quickly make forms that map to a given database is a useful addition to your programming toolbox. The Data Form Wizard is such a tool.

The Data Form Wizard is an add-in that ships with Visual Basic 6. You attach the Data Form Wizard to the VB IDE by using the Add-In Manager to add it to the **Add-Ins** menu. Alternatively, you can attach the add-in toolbar to the IDE and then add the Data Wizard to the add-in toolbar. Both techniques are described earlier in the section "Working with Add-Ins."

After you attach the Data Form Wizard to the IDE, you take the following steps to create a Data Form for the Access database Biblio.mdb.

1. Invoke the Data Form Wizard by selecting it from the **Add-Ins** menu or by clicking the 🔲 icon on the add-in toolbar. The Data Wizard – Introduction dialog appears (see Figure 29.16).

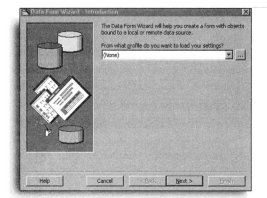

FIGURE **29.16**

The Data Form Wizard allows you to load a predefined profile from a prior use.

2. Let the profile setting stay at the default, **(None)**. Click **Next**.

3. Select **Access** from the list of the wizard's Database Type dialog (see Figure 29.17). Click **Next**.

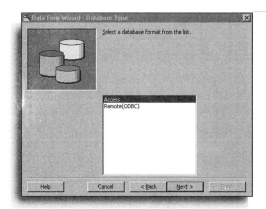

FIGURE **29.17**

You can choose between ODBC and Access databases.

4. Click the **Browse** button to browse for an Access database. Select **Biblo.mdb** from the dialog (see Figure 29.18) and click **Open**. Click **Next**.

5. Enter a name for the data form, keep the form layout as **Single Record**, and keep the binding type as **ADO Data Control** (see Figure 29.19). Click **Next**.

FIGURE 29.18

When you choose an access database, you need to provide the database filename and location.

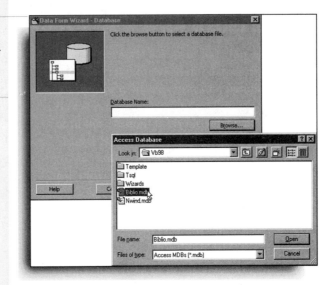

FIGURE 29.19

You can view a thumbnail of the layout type in the upper left corner of the wizard's Form dialog.

1 Shows the data of each field one at a time

2 Shows the data in a table format

3 Combines the Single Record and Grid layouts

4 Shows the data in a hierarchical table

5 Shows the data as a graph or within a graphic

6 Connects your program to the data via an ActiveX control

7 Creates code that connects your program to the data via ActiveX Data Objects (ADO)

8 Encapsulates the ADO code that connects your program to data into a custom class module that you call from code

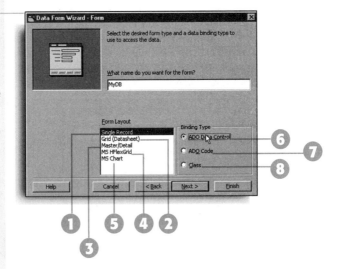

6. Select the **Titles** table from the **Record Source** drop-down list (see Figure 29.20). Select the **Subject**, **Title**, and **Year Published** fields in the **Available Fields** list and click the 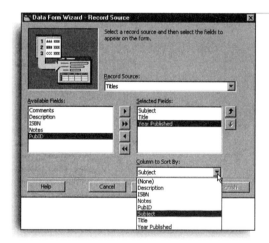 button to move the fields into the **Selected Fields** list. Select **Subject** from the **Column to Sort By** drop-down list and then click **Next**. (For more information on ADO, see Chapter 30, "Database Basics and the Data Control," and Chapter 32, "Enhancing Your Programs Using the Advanced Data Controls.")

7. Click **Next** to accept the defaults (all available controls) on the wizard's Control Selection dialog (see Figure 29.21).

8. Leave the profile settings drop-down list set to **(None)** on the wizard's last dialog (see Figure 29.22). Click **Finish**. You may want to save the profile of this file so it will be available to you next time around.

FIGURE 29.20

You decide the precise data you want to view by selecting tables and fields from within the wizard's Record Source dialog.

FIGURE 29.21

You can use Add, Update, Delete, Refresh, and Close buttons on your data forms.

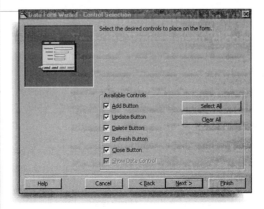

FIGURE 29.22

You can save the Data Form Wizard's settings to a custom profile as you can in the Application Wizard.

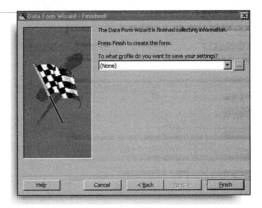

After you click **Finish**, the wizard creates a form that's bound to the database of your choice by the method that you've chosen. By following the preceding steps, you create a database that's connected to the Titles table of the Bibli.mdb database. The form shown in Figure 29.23 includes the **Subject**, **Title**, and **Year Published** fields, as well as all the buttons that you selected to be included.

Clearly, if you do much data-access work, the Data Form Wizard is a tool that saves you a significant amount of time. As you become a more developed programmer, you'll create a set of profiles within the wizard that you can use repeatedly.

FIGURE 29.23

The Data Form Wizard creates a data-bound form in seconds, as opposed to the hours you'd have to spend creating the form on your own.

Creating a Custom Add-In

Visual Basic 6 is created in such a way as to make writing a custom add-in feasible for less experienced programmers. Although making a custom add-in was possible in prior versions of Visual Basic, it was difficult even for the more experienced programmer. Visual Basic 6 ships with an add-in project type that you can select when you start a new project. The add-in project uses the Add-In Connect Designer to automatically do many of the fundamental tasks associated with creating an add-in (see Figure 29.24). The Add-In Connect Designer is included as a module within the add-in project, as is a starting form on which you create a graphical user interface for your add-in.

Let's look at a custom add-in that every programmer needs: an automatic procedure-header generator. Good code is well commented. In the heat of programming, however, many developers forget to put in the all-important procedure header that describes what a particular procedure is about and what it does. The add-in ProcHeader is a custom add-in that allows programmers to generate the code that declares a procedure, either Sub or Function. When the procedure is declared, the add-in inserts a predefined procedure header template into the code.

First, you need to generate the framework for the add-in. Then, you code the specifics for the add-in.

Designers

A *designer* is a programming tool written in C++ that Visual Basic programmers use to generate code for a specific functionality. Designers present a graphical user interface to programmers. Programmers enter programming information into the designer, and the designer in turn generates the appropriate code. VB6 ships with designers for data access, add-ins, Internet components, and DHTML pages, to mention a few. In this chapter, you use the Add-In Connect Designer.

FIGURE 29.24

The Add-In Connect Designer automatically generates code for your custom add-in.

1 Add-In Connect Designer in Form view

2 Click the View Code icon to see the code the Designer generates.

3 Click the View Object icon to see the Designer form.

4 Add-In Connect Designer in Project window

5 Startup form in Project window

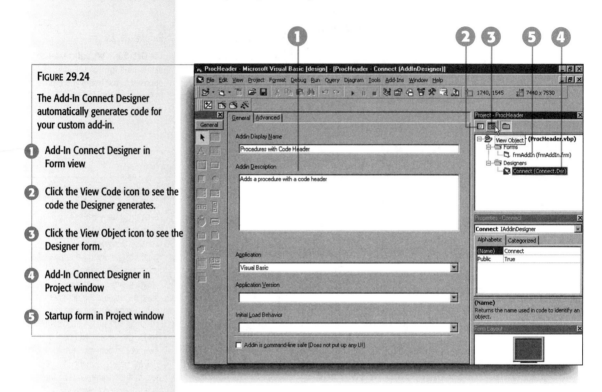

Create the framework

1. Choose **New Project** from Visual Basic's **File** menu.

2. Select **Addin** in the New Project dialog (see Figure 29.25).

3. Select the **Connect Designer** in the Project window. Then click the View Form icon to display the Designer form (refer to Figure 29.24).

4. Enter the data in the Designer form as shown in Figure 29.24.

FIGURE 29.25
The Addin project automatically creates a framework on which you can make a custom add-in.

An add-in—even one made by using the designer built in to the add-in project—generates a volume of code that's beyond the breadth of an introductory chapter. Therefore, the code that you need in order to work with the following can be found at http://www.mcp.com/info. To gain the most from the following, you might want to open the code in the VB6 IDE and follow along.

How the Add-In Works

The way the custom add-in works is that you choose an option from the **Add-Ins** menu to display the add-in's form. You select whether the procedure is to be a Sub or Function and Private or Public in scope (see Figure 29.26). When you click **OK**, the add-in goes to the bottom of the code pane and adds a procedure declaration with a code header. The code header text is defined in an external text file, header.txt. Last, the add-in moves the text cursor in the code pane to the location of the newly inserted lines of code so that the code pane displays the declaration for the new procedure.

FIGURE 29.26

The Procedure with Code Header add-in allows you to declare a Sub or Function and automatically include a procedure header.

Error traps are put in to ensure that there are no errors when accessing the external text file or when writing to the code pane.

The add-in is an ActiveX DLL and compiled as such. When you compile the code, the project automatically includes the newly compiled add-in to the list of available add-ins in the Add-In Manager.

When you deploy the add-in to other programmers, you deploy it as you would any other ActiveX DLL or EXE. For more information about deploying an ActiveX DLL, see Chapter 20, "Deploying Your Visual Basic Applications."

Understanding the Visual Basic 6 IDE Object Model

Making custom add-ins is possible because Visual Basic exposes itself as a set of interrelated objects that you can manipulate. You manipulate the VB object model to make an add-in very much in the same way that you manipulate the Microsoft Word object model when you write a macro that manipulates the user interface for the word processing application.

(For more information about object models, see Chapter 25, "Using VBA to Connect Your VB Programs with Microsoft Office," Chapter 26, "Making Object-Oriented Programs with Visual Basic," and Chapter 27, "Creating Your Own ActiveX Controls with Visual Basic.")

The object model is complex and comprehensive. Luckily, the Connect Designer add-in (Connect.dsr) does most of the preliminary work for you. After the designer sets up the framework for you, you have to manipulate only a few objects in the model to get the behaviors that you need in order to declare a procedure and insert a code header within the procedure block.

The objects that you manipulate are CodePane and CodeModule. The CodePane object represents the code window in which you add the code; the CodeModule object is the code that appears in the code window, similar to a module or class file.

The core code that creates the procedure declaration and inserts the code header is found in the function AddHeaderProc() (see Listing 29.1). AddHeaderProc() is a procedure of the frmAddIn form.

LISTING 29.1   29LIST01.TXT—Excerpts from the *AddHeaderProc* Function

```
01   Public Function AddHeaderProc(strHeaderFile As String, _
                      strProcName As String, _
                      strProcType As String, _
                      strProcScope As String) As Boolean
02   '***********************************
03   'Function Name:AddHeaderProc
04
05   '
06   'strHeaderFile The path and filename of the file has
07   '              the header template
08   'strProcName:  The name of the procedure to make
09   '
10   'strProcType:  The type of procedure, Sub or Function
11   '
12   'strProcScope: The scope of the procedure, Private or
13   '              Public
14   'Remarks:      If the function is successful, it returns
15   '              True. On an error, this function will
16   '              return a message box reporting the error
17   '              number and description. In addition, the
18   '              function returns False.
19   'History:
20   'Programmer: Bob Reselman
21   'Created: 6/14/98
22   '***********************************
23
24   Dim cm As CodeModule          'Code Module Object var
25   Dim cp As VBIDE.CodePane      'Code Pane Object var
26   Dim strHeader As String       'Header string
27   Dim strBuffer As String       'Concatenation buffer
```

continues...

LISTING 29.1 Continued

```
28   Dim strFileName As String          'Header template filename
29   Dim strBorder As String            'Border characters
30   Dim strProcDim As String           'Declaration statement
31   Dim strCreated As String           'Created date statement
32   Dim strFirstProcLine As String 'First line of the code
33                                      'header
34   Dim strTemp As String              'Another string buffer
35   Dim FileHandle As Integer          'File handle var
36
37     On Error GoTo AddHeaderProcErr:
38
39       'Create an object variable for the code pane
40       Set cp = VBInstance.ActiveCodePane
41
42       'Create an object variable for the code module
43       '!!!Remember, the code pane only shows lines of the
44       'code module. The code module is where the actual
45       'code lives!!!!!
46       Set cm = cp.CodeModule
47
48       'Start building the procedure declaration
49       strProcDim = strProcScope & " " & strProcType & " "
50       strProcDim = strProcDim & " " & strProcName & "()"
51       strProcDim = strProcDim
52

...

67       'Get the header template filename
68       strFileName = strHeaderFile
69       FileHandle = FreeFile()
70
71       'Open the file
72     Open strFileName For Input As #FileHandle%
73
74     'Make the mouse pointer an hourglass
75       MousePointer = vbHourglass
76
77     'Traverse the lines of the file
78       Do While Not EOF(FileHandle%) ' Check for end of file.
79         'Read a line of the file
80          ' Read line of data.
81          Line Input #FileHandle%, strTemp
```

```
82    'Add the line from the output buffer to the text string
83          strHeader = strHeader & strTemp & vbCrLf
84      Loop
...
89      'Close the file once you have had your way with it
90      Close #FileHandle%
91
92      'Add the header file template to the string buffer
93      strBuffer = strBuffer & strHeader
...
103     'Add the End statement for the end of the procedure
104     strBuffer = strBuffer & "End " & strProcType
105
106     'Insert the procedure and header into the code page
107     Call cm.InsertLines(cm.CountOfLines + 1, strBuffer)
108
109     'Hide the Add-In
110     Connect.Hide
111
112     'Set the top line of the pane to the last line
113     cp.TopLine = cm.ProcStartLine(strProcName, _
                                   vbext_pk_Proc)
114
115     'Return a success value
116     AddHeaderProc = True
117
118     'Exit the function; things are good!
119      Exit Function
120 AddHeaderProcErr:
..
126      MsgBox ErrMsg$, vbCritical, Err.Source
127 End Function
```

Notice that line 40 sets a CodePane object variable to the active code pane. Line 46 assigns the CodeModule object variable to the code module associated with the active code pane by calling CodePane's CodeModule property.

After all the *object variables* are set, the function goes about constructing the code procedure declaration and code header. Lines 48–52 construct the declaration lines of the procedure. Code that isn't shown (but is available on the Web site) adds the header border and constructs the first line of the header.

Lines 53–72 open the text file that has the header template, cycles through all the lines within the text file, and concatenates the retrieved lines (strTemp) onto the header string (strHeader). Line 75 concatenates the constructed header (strHeader) onto the overall string buffer, strBuffer. Line 77 creates the End procedure line.

SEE ALSO

➤ *Find more information about opening and reading the contents of text files on page 380*

After the procedure declaration and procedure header are constructed, they must be inserted in the code module. The procedure declaration and procedure header are one very big string. This string is inserted one line beyond the last line of code in the code module. Inserting the code is accomplished by using the InsertLines() method of the CodeModule object variable on line 80. InsertLines() takes two arguments: the location of the line in which to insert the code and the string to insert. The location is determined by going one line beyond the total number of lines in the code module, as determined by the value returned by the CodeModule's CountOfLines property (CountOfLines +1, as shown on line 80). The string to insert is the buffer that contains the procedure declaration and procedure header (strBuffer).

Line 80 inserts the procedure and procedure header, but you might not be able to see it if the code pane is set to the top lines or some other spot outside the viewing area of the code pane. Therefore, the code pane needs to be adjusted to show the first line of code of the newly inserted procedure. Line 86 resets the top line of the code pane to be the first line of code in the newly inserted procedure. The CodeModule object has a method, ProcStartLine(), that allows you to determine the starting line of a procedure. ProcStartLine() takes two arguments: the name of the procedure from which to determine the first line and a constant that communicates the procedure kind. The method returns a Long that's the first line of the procedure within the code pane. On line 86, the add-in passes in the string variable that represents the procedure and the constant vbext_pk_Proc, which communicates that the procedure kind is a procedure. (You can use the Object Browser to look up all the values that go with the *Enum*, vbext_ProcKind.)

If everything is successful, the function returns True. If for some reason an error occurs, control is passed to the AddHeaderProcErr code label for error processing.

Granted, this discussion is very high level for creating a custom add-in. You might want to take some time to make a detailed study of all the code involved in making such a tool. As you study the code, you'll see how to use the Office.CommandBarControl object's PasteFace method to add an icon bitmap to the submenu entry, as shown in Figure 29.27. You'll also learn how to test to make sure that a code window is indeed open. Otherwise, you'll be blindly adding procedures to code panes you can't see. Finally, you'll see how to build on the code and graphical framework that the add-in's Connect Designer provides. For an exhaustive discussion of the Visual Basic Object Model (also known as the VB IDE Extensibility Model), look at the documentation that comes with your copy of Visual Basic.

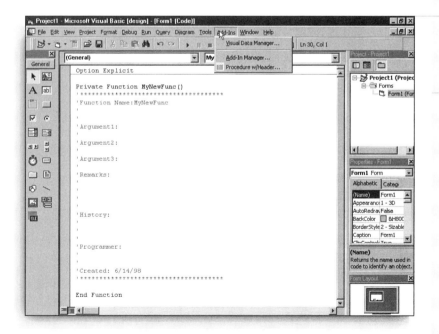

FIGURE 29.27

The ProcHeader add-in submenu item has a bitmap icon that identifies it.

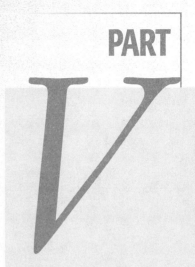

PART

V

Database Programming
with Visual Basic 6

30 Database Basics and the Data Control 605

31 Making Reports in Visual Basic 6 621

**32 Enhancing Your Programs Using the Advanced
Data Controls 631**

Database Basics and the Data Control

Learn the difference between flat and relational databases

Use the Data control to work with databases

Use Visual Basic's Data Form Wizard to create database-bound forms

Understanding Databases

In simplest terms, a database is a collection of information. The most common example of a database is a phone book, which is a collection of names, addresses, and phone numbers. Each line in a phone book is a *record* that contains the information for a single person or family. The entire set of records—that is, all the listings in the book—is a *table*. Another important characteristic a phone book has in common with most databases is that information is presented in a specific order—in the case of the phone book, alphabetically by last name.

Computer databases are similar in concept to phone books in that they provide a way to store and retrieve information easily and quickly. Computers actually can use two basic types of databases—*flat-file* and *relational*. A phone book is an example of a flat-file database. This means that a single record stores all the *fields*, or discrete data, for each entry, and a single table contains all the records for the database (see Figure 30.1).

FIGURE 30.1

Each unique instance of a collection of fields is called a *record*.

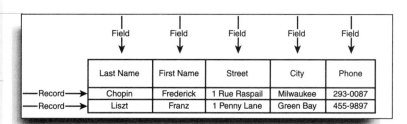

By contrast, a relational database stores information in a number of tables related by a common field known as the *primary key*. For instance, you might have a Customer Information table that contains specific information about your customers, and you might have another table called Loans Outstanding that contains information about outstanding loans. Both tables contain a common field—Social Security Number. In a relational database, by keying on the Social Security Number field, you could produce a third table, Average Days to Pay, that's made of data from each of the other tables (see Figure 30.2).

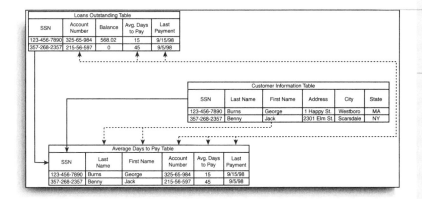

FIGURE 30.2

Relational databases are commonly used for large-scale applications.

Understanding Database Terminology

Thus far, you've seen a few terms, such as *record* and *field*, used to refer to different parts of a database. It's important that you understand a few more terms before learning about databases. Table 30.1 defines the key parts of a database.

TABLE 30.1 **The Basic Elements of a Database**

Element	Description
Database	A group of data tables that contain related information.
Table	A group of data records, each containing the same type of information. In the phone book example, the book itself is a table.
Record	A single entry in a table, consisting of a number of data fields. In a phone book, a record is one of the single-line entries.
Field	A specific piece of data contained in a record. In a phone book, at least four fields can be identified: last name, first name, address, and phone number.
Index	A special type of table that contains the values of a key field or fields and contains pointers to the location of the actual record. These values and pointers are stored in a specific order and can be used to present data in that order. For the phone book example, one index might be used to sort the information by last and first name; another index might be used to sort the information by street address; and a third might be used to sort the information by phone number.

continues...

TABLE 30.1   Continued

Element	Description
Query	A command, based on a specific set of conditions or criteria, designed to retrieve a certain group of records from one or more tables or to perform an operation on a table. For example, you would write a query that could show all the students in a class whose last name begins with *S* and who have a grade point average of more than 3.0.
Recordset	A group of records, created by a query, from one or more tables in a database. The records in a recordset are typically a subset of all the records in a table. When the recordset is created, the number of records and the order in which they're presented can be controlled by the query that creates the recordset.

The Microsoft Jet database engine provides the means by which Visual Basic interacts with databases. You use it with Visual Basic to access databases and database functionality. The Jet engine is shared by Visual Basic, Microsoft Access, and other Microsoft products, and it lets you work with a wide variety of data types, including several types of text and numeric fields. These different data types give you a great deal of flexibility in designing database applications. Table 30.2 lists the data types available.

TABLE 30.2   Many Data Types Are Available with the Jet Database Engine

Type	Description	Size/Range
Text	Character strings	255 characters maximum
Memo	Long character strings	Up to 1.2GB
Byte	Integer (numeric data)	0 to 255
Integer	Integer (numeric data)	–32,768 to 32,767
Long	Integer (numeric data)	–2,147,483,648 to 2,147,483,647
Counter	Long integer, automatically incremented	
Single	Real (numeric data)	–3.402823E38 to –1.401298E–45 for negative values and from 1.401298E–45 to 3.402823E38 for positive values

Type	Description	Size/Range
Double	Real (numeric data)	–1.79769313486232E308 to –4.94065645841247E–324 for negative values and from 4.94065645841247E–324 to 1.79769313486232E308
Currency	Real (numeric data)	–922,337,203,685,477.5808 to 922,337,203,685,477.5807
Yes/No	Logical/Boolean	
Date	Date and time values	
Binary	Binary data	Up to 1.2GB
OLE	OLE objects	Up to 1.2GB

As your database programming skills develop, you will be inter-acting with the Jet database engine on an abstract level. For now, the Jet engine will be relatively transparent to you because you will use the Data control to do your database work. This control works with the Jet database engine, which in turn works with the database. Whether a database is flat or relational isn't important for the time being because using the Data control during design time hides most of the inner workings of the database from you.

Working with the Intrinsic Data Control

The Data control is a link between the information in your data-base and the Visual Basic control that you use to display the information. As you set the Data control's properties, you tell it which database and what part of that database to access. By default, the Data control creates a *dynaset-type* recordset from one or more of the tables in your database. This means that the recordset is dynamic so that records within it are updated when the data from the original table is modified.

The Data control also provides the navigation functions that your application will need to switch between records. By using these buttons, users can move to the first or last record in the recordset or to the next or previous record (see Figure 30.3). The design of the buttons is somewhat intuitive in that they're similar to the buttons you might find on a VCR or CD player.

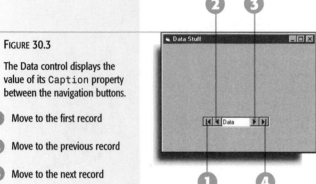

FIGURE 30.3

The Data control displays the value of its Caption property between the navigation buttons.

① Move to the first record

② Move to the previous record

③ Move to the next record

④ Move to the last record

Download this project's code

You can find the code for all the examples in this chapter at http://www.mcp.com/info. When prompted, enter 078971633x for the ISBN and click the **Search** button.

Use the Data control

1. Create a new project and name it DataProj. Name the default form frmMain.

2. Select the Data control from the Toolbox and draw a Data control on the form.

3. Retain the default name of the Data control, Data1.

4. Add two TextBox controls to the form. Name one txtFirst and the other txtLast. Position the Data and TextBox controls as shown in Figure 30.4.

5. Save the project as DataProj.vbp.

FIGURE 30.4

Use the Data control to access a database and to bind controls on a form to the fields of a database.

① Data control

② Data control icon

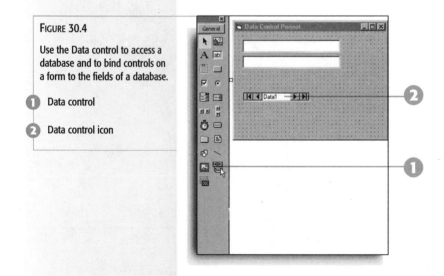

Connecting the Intrinsic Data Control to a Database

After the Data control is on your form, you need to make the connection between it and the information in your database. This is done by setting the properties of the Data control.

Although several properties can affect the way a Data control interacts with the database, only two properties are required to establish the link to a Jet database: DatabaseName and RecordSource. Specifying DatabaseName "connects" a Data control to a specific database, whereas RecordSource specifies a table within that database. After you set these two properties, the Data control is ready to retrieve, create, and edit information.

Attach a Data control to a database and table

1. Select the Data control on the form frmMain in the project DataProj.vbp created earlier.

2. Select the **DatabaseName** property in the Properties window (see Figure 30.5).

3. Select the database **Composer.mdb** from the DatabaseName dialog.

4. Select table **tblComposers** from the RecordSource property drop-down list (see Figure 30.6).

The DatabaseName and Name properties

The DatabaseName property isn't the same as the Name property. The Name property specifies the name of the data control object and is used to reference the object in code. The DatabaseName property, on the other hand, specifies the name of the database file that the data control is accessing.

Creating Databases

Creating a database from scratch in Visual Basic is an advanced skill. For now, you're going to work with pre-existing database files made in the Microsoft Access environment. The demonstration items in this chapter will reference the Access database file Composer.mdb, available for download from http://www.mcp.com/info. You can also use Biblio.mdb or Nwind.mdb, both included with Visual Basic, with minor modifications to the steps in this chapter.

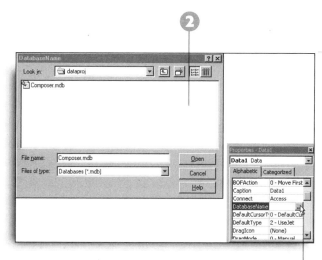

FIGURE 30.5

When you select the DatabaseName property in the Properties window, an ellipsis appears to the right of the value area. Click the ellipsis to open the DatabaseName dialog.

❶ Click to display the DatabaseName dialog

❷ Select the database from the DatabaseName dialog

FIGURE 30.6

Assigning a database file to the Data control's DatabaseName property populates the RecordSource property's drop-down list with all the tables and queries in that database.

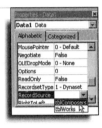

Assign a RecordSource **before a** DataField

Be sure to have a table assigned to the Data control's RecordSource property before you select a value for another control's DataField. If you don't have a table assigned to the RecordSource property, you will get an error.

5. Select the **txtFirst** TextBox on the form.

6. For the TextBox's DataSource property, select **Data1** in the Properties window (see Figure 30.7).

7. For the TextBox's DataField property, select **FirstName** (see Figure 30.8).

FIGURE 30.7

The DataSource property lists all the Data controls on a form.

FIGURE 30.8

All fields from the table assigned to the Data control's RecordSource property are displayed in the DataField drop-down list.

8. Assign the Data control Data1 to the DataSource property of the txtLastName TextBox, just as you did for the txtFirstName TextBox.

9. In the Properties window, select **LastName** for the DataField property of the TextBox txtLastName (see Figure 30.9).

10. Save and run the code (see Figure 30.10).

FIGURE 30.9

When you assign a field from a table to the DataField property of a TextBox, the contents of that field will appear in that TextBox on a record-by-record basis.

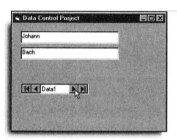

FIGURE 30.10

You can move through the data-base's table by using the Data control's navigation buttons.

In the preceding steps, you "connected" a database to a Data control and then selected a RecordSource for the control. Then you assigned that Data control to be a DataSource for two TextBoxes. You *bound* each TextBox to a field in the database (the Data control's RecordSource) by selecting a field for the TextBox's DataField property.

If you want to add and bind more TextBoxes to the Data control, or if you want to add and bind a Label control, you follow the process enumerated earlier. Controls such as CheckBoxes and ListBoxes can also be bound to a Data control; however, the fields to which a CheckBox or ListBox is bound must contain data of type Boolean (see Table 30.3).

TABLE 30.3 Some Controls That Can Be Bound Only to Specific Data Types

Control	Available Data Types
TextBox	Any data types. Editing is allowed.
Label	Any data types. Editing isn't allowed.
Image	Displays graphics stored in the database but doesn't allow editing of the image.

continues...

TABLE 30.3   **Continued**

Control	Available Data Types
Picture	Displays graphics stored in the database and allows editing of the image.
CheckBox	`Boolean` data type only. This allows updating of the record.
ListBox	Text data types. Editing is allowed on the selected record.
ComboBox	Text data types. Editing is allowed on the selected record.

Bound controls such as the TextBox can also be used to edit a record. To do this, the user simply edits the contents of the control while your program is running. When a different record is selected with the Data control's navigation buttons (or the form is closed), the information in the database is automatically updated to reflect the user's changes.

Creating Database-Bound Forms with the Data Form Wizard

Visual Basic provides a tool that lets you easily make forms that have controls bound to a database. Called the VB Data Form Wizard, it can be accessed from the **Add-Ins** menu. The Data Form Wizard creates a form that lets you browse a database, complete with text boxes, labels, and the ADO Data control. The ADO Data control is slightly different from the intrinsic Data control you used in the preceding section but will appear to work the same to users.

When you installed the Visual Basic programming environment on your computer, the VB Data Form Wizard wasn't installed. You must attach it to the **Add-Ins** menu.

SEE ALSO

➤ *For more details on the ADO Data control, see page 632*

Install the Data Form Wizard

1. Choose **Add-In Manager** from the **Add-Ins** menu.

2. In the Add-In Manager dialog, select **VB 6 Data Form Wizard** from the list and select the **Loaded/Unloaded** check box (see Figure 30.11). Click **OK**.

Don't need the wizard anymore?

To remove the wizard from the **Add-Ins** menu, select **VB 6 Data Form Wizard** in the Add-In Manager dialog and deselect the **Loaded/Unloaded** and **Load on Startup** check boxes.

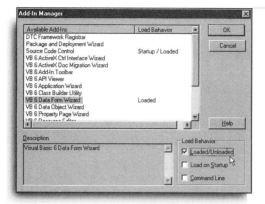

FIGURE 30.11

If you select **Load on Startup**, the VB Data Form Wizard will be added to the **Add-Ins** menu after the installation process.

Now that you've attached the VB 6 Data Form Wizard to the Visual Basic IDE, you can use it in all your projects. You can now use the VB Data Form Wizard to create a form for the table tblWorks in the database file Composer.mdb.

Create a bound form for a database table

1. Choose **Data Form Wizard** from the **Add-Ins** menu.

2. Click **Next** in the Introduction dialog (see Figure 30.12).

Download this project's code

The form that these steps create is frmWorks, which is part of the project DataProj.vbp. It's located at http://www. mcp.com/info.

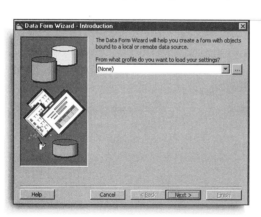

FIGURE 30.12

The Introduction dialog lets you load a profile of your common Data Form Wizard settings.

3. In the Database Type dialog, select Access and click **Next**.

4. In the Database dialog, click the **Browse** button to see the Access Database dialog. You can now select the database for which you want to make a form. Locate Composer.mdb and click **Next**.

5. Name the form `frmWorks`. Select **Single Record** from the **Form Layout** list, select **ADO Data Control** from the **Binding Type** options, and click **Next** (see Figure 30.13).

FIGURE 30.13

You select the layout that you want the data form to take by choosing an option from the **Form Layout** list.

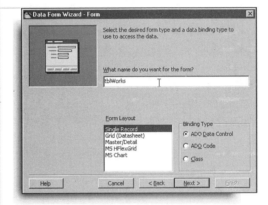

6. Select `tblWorks` from the **Record Source** drop-down list (see Figure 30.14).

FIGURE 30.14

All tables and queries of the selected database are listed in the **Record Source** drop-down list. After you select the record source, the fields of the record source will appear in the **Available Fields** list.

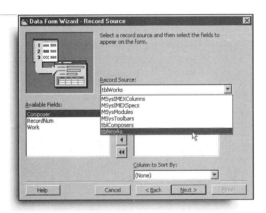

7. Click the >> button and click **Next** (see Figure 30.15).

8. Don't deselect any of the check boxes so that all data manipulation controls are made available on your form (see Figure 30.16). Click **Next**.

9. Save the settings you've just made by clicking the ellipsis button (see Figure 30.17).

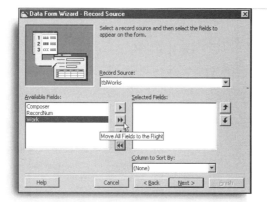

FIGURE 30.15
Any fields you select will appear on the data form. If you want only some fields, select them one at a time and click the > button. To remove fields from the data form, click the < and << buttons.

FIGURE 30.16
You can select a limited number of buttons to be on the data form by selecting or clearing the appropriate check boxes.

FIGURE 30.17
Saving your settings in a profile can save you time during database program development.

10. Click **Finish**. A final Data Form Created dialog will appear; click the **Don't Show This Dialog in the Future** check box if you don't want to see this confirmation message in the future. Click **OK**.

11. Save the code, remembering to change the name of the form to `frmWorks.frm` to follow the Visual Basic naming convention for forms.

12. Open the Project Properties dialog by selecting **DataProj Properties** from the **Project** menu.

13. Select the `frmWorks` form from the **Startup Object** drop-down list (see Figure 30.18).

14. Save and run the code (see Figure 30.19).

FIGURE 30.18

If you want a newly added form to be the startup form for your application, you must reset the Startup object.

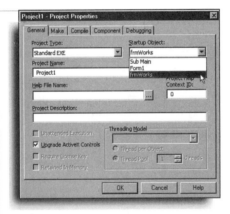

FIGURE 30.19

The data form created by the wizard allows you to add, update, delete, and refresh data from the table assigned to the value of the Data control's RecordSource property.

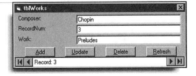

You can use multiple Data controls on a form. Each Data control can be assigned a RecordSource from the same database or from different databases. You can also change a Data control's properties at runtime, but be advised that you will probably also have to change properties of the controls bound to the Data control.

The Data control makes working with databases simple, but this is partly because it's rather limited. Database programming is a complete discipline itself. As data structures and business requirements become more complex, so will the programming. After a time, you might outgrow the Data control in favor of a more advanced technology known as ActiveX Data Objects (ADO). Regardless of your future plans, the Data control will serve you well in most aspects of your database programming activity, especially for simpler applications.

Making Reports in Visual Basic 6

Learn about the new reporting tools in VB

Build a data environment

Build a simple report

What's New with Reporting?

Creating reports is a main function of any good business application. You might have useful data in the system, but without a coherent way to present it, the numbers are meaningless. Visual Basic's primary reporting tool wasn't even a Microsoft product until this version. Previous versions of VB included a version of Seagate Software's Crystal Reports tool. With the release of VB 6, Microsoft has integrated a good report writer into VB that will provide most users an alternative to purchasing another tool.

The VB Data Report Designer will look familiar to developers who have built reports in Microsoft Access, because the layout of the tools is almost identical. However, the Data Report for VB can actually be compiled into your executable, which means no format files need to be installed on a user's machine. This also means that the format files can't be corrupted by users who decide to go exploring.

Your VB reporting workspace has a few new additions. The first is the Report Layout window (shown in Figure 31.1). You learn more about its different sections later in this example.

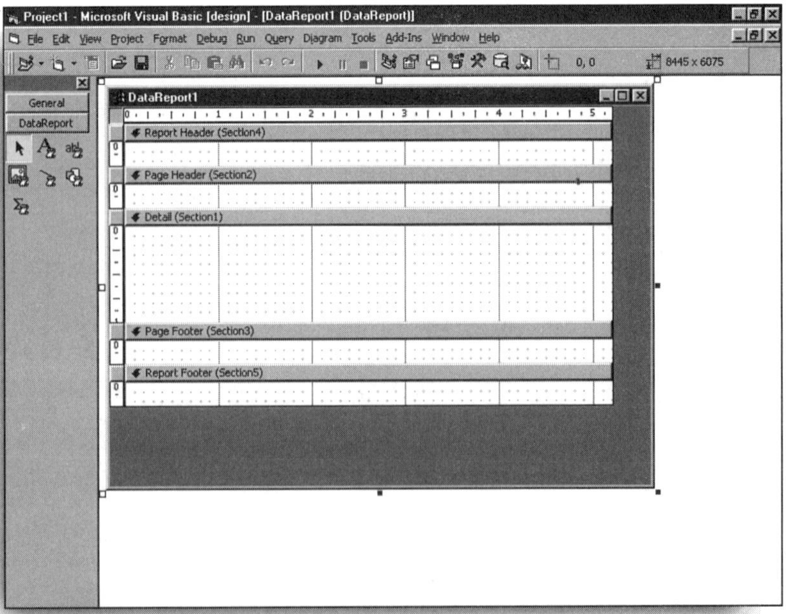

FIGURE 31.1

The Report Layout window looks similar to the Report Designer used in Microsoft Access.

The next change is the addition of six new controls to the Toolbox, as described in Table 31.1.

TABLE 31.1 Data Report Designer Controls

Control Type	Description
RptTextBox	Any data that will be supplied at runtime— through code or through a command—needs to be put in a RptTextBox. RptTextBox controls can be configured to look like plain text without any borders.
RptLine	Use this control to draw a variety of lines on the report.
RptFunction	This control performs functions on data groups in the report and can be used only in a group footer section of the report. It supplies functions such as row and value counting, sums, and so on.
RptLabel	The RptLabel control is used to add static text to the report.
RptImage	Use the RptImage control to add a picture to your report. This control, like the standard Image control, can hold bitmaps (BMP), icons, metafiles, or GIF or JPEG files.
RptShape	You can use the RptShape control to add a variety of graphical shapes to your report, including rectangles, circles, and variations of them.

Data Report Designer ToolBox controls

These six controls aren't interchangeable with their counterparts you've always used for form design. Likewise, you can't use form design controls in Data Report Designer.

Building a Simple Report

As its name implies, the Data Report Designer builds reports from database tables. The example in this chapter uses the Northwind Traders database (Nwind.mdb), which is included in the main Visual Basic directory.

Start building your report

1. From the <u>P</u>roject menu, choose **Add Data Report**.

2. You need a title for your report. This title can be either in the Report Header, and only on the first page of the report, or in the Page Header and on the top of every report. Add a RptLabel control or two to create a title for your report, as shown in Figure 31.2. Simply draw the RptLabel control where you want it and set at least the Caption property to change the text that should be displayed.

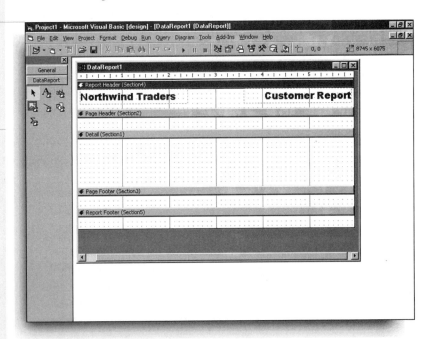

FIGURE 31.2

RptLabel controls enable you to add static text anywhere on your report. The text in the Report Header section repeats on every page in your report.

Cleaning up the report

You can also set the Caption property of the Report itself by using the Properties window when the Report is selected. Also, any blank space you leave around the controls will be repeated whenever the report is shown, so be sure to place the controls correctly and to close up any blank space around them.

You can add other labels or graphics to the report as you want. The next step is to connect the report to a data source by using the Data Environment Designer. A data environment contains all the connections and queries that you're using in your application. In this example, you need a query to generate a list of customers for your report.

Using the Data Environment Designer

1. From the <u>P</u>roject menu, choose **More ActiveX Designers** and then choose **Data Environment**.

2. To make a connection to the Northwind Traders database, right-click **Connection1** and select **Properties** from the popup menu.

3. Because you're connecting to an Access database, select **Microsoft Jet 3.51 OLE DB Provider** (see Figure 31.3) and then click **Next**.

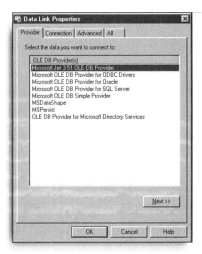

FIGURE 31.3

Always use the Jet OLE DB Provider when connecting to Access databases in a data environment.

4. Enter or select the database filename to use for this connection. The Northwind Traders database is located in the VB installation directory. For the other options in the window (see Figure 31.4), you don't need to specify any user ID (other than Admin) because no access control is set up on the Nwind.mdb file. If you were using another database that had security, you would have to specify a user ID and password here or at runtime.

5. To verify that the connection is correct, click the **Test Connection** button. If you receive a message indicating a successful test, click **OK** to continue. Otherwise, go back and make sure that you followed the steps correctly.

6. Because a name like Connection1 isn't useful, click the **Connection1** item and hover for a few seconds. VB will allow you to rename the connection at this point. Pick a useful name, such as dcnNWind, which is the name used throughout this example.

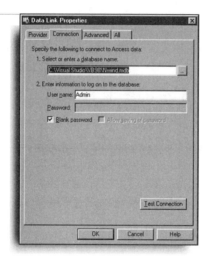

7. Repeat step 6 and give the data environment a useful name, such as denvNWind. If you have multiple data environments in your project, it's imperative that you keep the names straight.

You've successfully created a data environment. Be sure to save your work but don't shut the window just yet. With the data environment created, you can now create the query that will retrieve customer information from the database.

Create the query to retrieve information from the database

1. Right-click **Commands** and select **Add Command** from the popup menu. The Data Environment Designer will add a new command to the environment. Right-click it and select **Properties**.

Quite a few properties are available for the command, but the ones you need to set are on the first page, **General** (see Figure 31.5).

2. Give the command a useful name, such as qryGetCustomerList.

3. Pick the connection to use. Select **dcnNWind** from the **Connection** drop-down list.

FIGURE 31.5
All the properties you need to set
for this query are on the **General**
page.

4. Because the database can understand SQL, type the following **SQL Statement** to specify how to retrieve the data:
```
SELECT CompanyName, City, Region, Country, Phone
FROM Customers ORDER BY CompanyName
```

5. Click **OK**.

Be sure to save your work because you have now finished building your data connections.

Finish building the report

1. Before adding the data fields, you need to set a few properties on the report itself so that it knows where to obtain its
data. Set the DataSource property to the name of your data
environment; set the DataMember property to the name of
your customer list query. If you don't set these properties,
you'll receive errors when you try to run the report.

2. To add data to the report, take a field from the Data
Environment Designer window, such as CustomerName, and
drag it to the Detail section of your report. VB will automatically draw a RptTextBox, along with a RptLabel, control
on the report.

Use the SQL Builder

You can use the SQL Builder if
you want to create complex
joins and don't want to type the
SQL yourself.

Finding the Properties window

If you can't see the Properties
window (where these properties can be set), press F4 to
open it.

Using repeating rows

The Detail section is very narrow because any blank space in this section will be repeated for every row in the report. Also notice that a line is drawn beneath the column headers. You can use the RptLine control to create this graphic, if you like.

FIGURE 31.6

You can move your controls between sections to create a column-based report.

3. To make this report column-based, drag the RptLabel into the PageHeader section. Place the RptTextBox beneath the RptLabel but leave the RptTextBox in the Detail section. Repeat this process for all the fields. Your window will look like Figure 31.6.

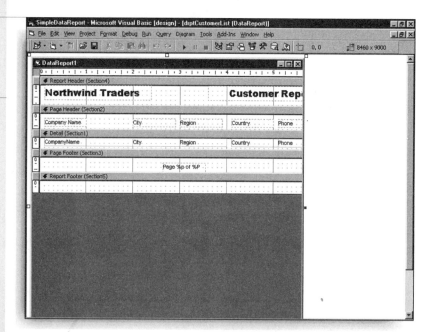

4. To include a page number and total number of pages (as in Page 3 of 5), create a page footer. This is very easy to do with a RptLabel control, which supports a number of substitutions so that you don't have to write code to put page numbers in your report. The RptLabel control supports these substitutions:

%p	Current page number
%P	Total number of pages
%d	Current date (short format)
%D	Current date (long format)
%t	Current time (short format)
%T	Current time (long format)
%i	Report title

If, for instance, you wanted to include a page number, the `Caption` for the RptLabel control would be as follows:

`Page %p of %P`

VB will automatically substitute the page number and number of pages on each page of the report.

Now that the report is complete, you can run it just like any other module in your project. Choose **Prop**_e_**rties** from the **Project** menu and use this report as your startup form. When you run your program, your report will be displayed as shown in Figure 31.7.

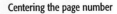

Centering the page number

To center the page number, right-click the RptLabel, select **Center in Section**, and then select **Horizontally** from the pop-up menu.

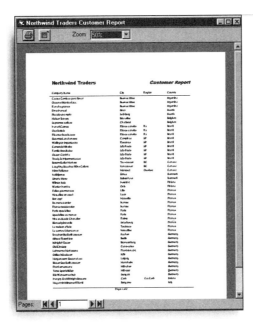

FIGURE 31.7

The report is shown in its final form in run mode.

With the report viewer, users can print or export the report to plain text or HTML. As shown in Figure 31.7, you also can shrink or enlarge the report by using the Zoom feature available on the viewer.

To show this report from code, use the standard `Show` method. You can use the `PrintReport` method to instruct the report to print through code. Adding a `True` or `False` to the `PrintReport` call tells VB whether to display a Print dialog. You don't even have to have a CommonDialog control in your project—VB will automatically create the Print dialog.

Enhancing Your Programs Using the Advanced Data Controls

Create and configure an ADO Data control

Use the DataGrid, DataList, and DataCombo controls

Learn about the Data Form Wizard

What Are Advanced Data Controls?

In Chapter 30, "Database Basics and the Data Control," you learned how to use the Data control to link automatically to a database. The Data control is good for browsing records and allowing you to edit existing records one at a time. With the data binding possible with the Data control, you can build a simple data entry form quickly.

However, very few applications can use a data-entry form as simple as the one you built. Most forms enable users to choose values from various lists, such as state or country codes. In other cases, it's more helpful for users to see multiple records at the same time, especially when dealing with financial data.

For these and other reasons, Visual Basic includes three other specialized controls that bind to data in different ways for more flexibility. This chapter will show you how to use these three controls: DataGrid, DataList, and DataCombo. These new controls use Active Data Objects (ADO) to communicate with the database. Visual Basic 6 makes extensive use of ADO in advanced database programming. Rather than use the Data control that you learned about in Chapter 30, these new controls make use of the ADO Data control. This control works similar to a Data control in that it handles the database access. However, it's much more flexible than a standard Data control because it uses ADO to communicate with the database instead of the older Data Access Objects (DAO).

Active Data Objects (ADO)

ADO is Microsoft's long-term data access strategy. Instead of the alphabet soup that exists now (DAO, RDO, ODBC, and so on), ADO will replace all of them. ADO also can read data from sources other than databases. For instance, ADO can read data from Microsoft Index Server, which is used to search the contents of a Web site. ADO uses OLE DB and OLE DB providers to actually connect to a data source. Just like DAO can be used to connect to Access' Jet engine, ADO is used to connect to the OLE DB engine. Microsoft has already released OLE DB providers for Access/Jet, ODBC, and others. Visit `http://www.microsoft.com/data` for more information on Microsoft's strategic plans for ADO.

Adding and Configuring the ADO Data Control

Before you can use these new controls, you have to create at least one ADO Data control on the form.

Create and configure an ADO Data control

1. From the **Project** menu, choose **Components**.

2. From the list, select **Microsoft ADO Data Control 6.0 (OLE DB)** and then click **OK** (see Figure 32.1). The ADO Data control will now be shown in your Toolbox (see Figure 32.2).

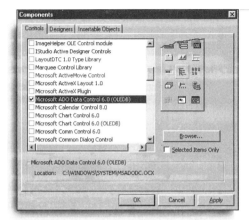

FIGURE 32.1
Add the ADO Data control to your Toolbox by selecting it from this dialog.

FIGURE 32.2
The ADO Data control is now part of your Toolbox.

3. Double-click the ADO Data control 🔲 to add one to your form. Set the control's name to adcCustomers, because it will be showing customer information from the sample database.

4. With the control added to the form, it's time to configure it to talk to the database. Click the ellipsis button in the ConnectionString property and then click the **Bu**ild button on the Property Pages dialog (see Figure 32.3).

Sample databases

The examples in this chapter all use several sample Access databases included with Visual Basic. These databases are located in Visual Basic's installation directory. You can modify these databases to your heart's content. Before you do, however, make a copy of them—you may want to reuse the database later.

FIGURE 32.3

The Property Pages dialog lets you specify how to connect to the data source.

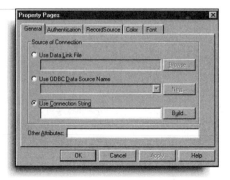

5. Select an OLE DB provider to use. Because the sample database is an Access database, select the **Microsoft Jet 3.51 OLE DB Provider** to connect to it (see Figure 32.4). Click **Next** to continue.

FIGURE 32.4

The ADO Data control can connect to a data source by using any of these OLE DB providers. Use the Jet provider for any Access database.

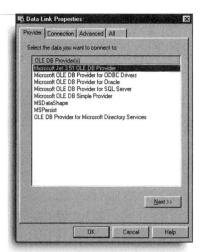

6. Select the database file to use with this connection. Click the ellipsis button next to the database name text box to select the Nwind.mdb file in the main VB directory. The database filename will be filled in the Database Name field on the dialog (see Figure 32.5).

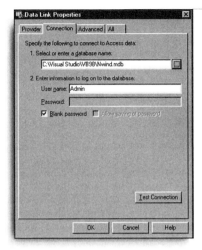

FIGURE 32.5

After you select a database, its filename will appear in this dialog.

Notice that a user ID has been entered in this dialog. That user ID should be left as is for now. Every Access database has a default user ID of Admin created. You need to specify this when you're building the connection.

7. Click the **Test Connection** button to make sure that the connection will work. If you get a good result (see Figure 32.6), click **OK** to continue. If not, follow the steps again to make sure that all the information is filled in properly.

FIGURE 32.6

If you see this message, you correctly configured your ADO Data control.

8. With the connection to the database working, you can specify which table to load. Click the Custom property's ellipsis button and then select the **RecordSource** tab (see Figure 32.7). From the **Command Type** drop-down list, select **2 - adCmdTable**. Then, from the **Table or Stored Procedure Name** drop-down list, select **Customers**. Click **OK**.

FIGURE 32.7

The **RecordSource** tab lets you specify the data to use in your ADO Data control.

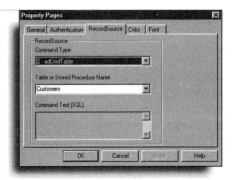

That's all you have to do to configure the ADO Data control. It may seem like a lot of steps, but after a few times it will become second nature to you.

Using the DataGrid Control

The first control you'll be using is the DataGrid, which lets users see and edit multiple rows of data simultaneously. The DataGrid is also useful for rapid entry of large amounts of data. To use this control, you have to add it to the Visual Basic Toolbox.

Add the DataGrid control

1. From the **Project** menu, choose **Components**.

2. From the list, select **Microsoft DataGrid Control 6.0** and then click **OK**. The DataGrid control will now be shown in your Toolbox window.

You can now add a DataGrid to your form. Double-click the DataGrid icon 🎛 in your Toolbox. Enlarge the control so that it fills most of the form.

If you were to run your program now, the DataGrid would be completely empty because you haven't linked it to the ADO Data control yet.

Linking a DataGrid to the ADO Data control

1. Click the DataGrid control on your form. Set its Name property to dgrdCustomers because it will be showing customer information.

2. From the DataSource property's drop-down list, select adcCustomers, which is the ADO Data control you created earlier.

After you specify the DataSource for the DataGrid, the DataGrid can configure itself automatically with the appropriate number of columns and rows. To see the form in action, choose **Start** from the **Run** menu ▶ . The window will show data from the Customers table (see Figure 32.8).

FIGURE 32.8

The DataGrid control can automatically configure itself to show the data from the source you specify.

Because the default settings aren't always the best, the DataGrid is fully configurable and lets you specify which columns are shown, the format, and the color of each. You also can split the DataGrid into multiple parts that each scroll independently of the other parts. This functionality is common to Microsoft Excel and other spreadsheets.

Selecting Grid Columns

Because database tables can grow quite large, you won't always want to show users every single column in the table. At other times, you will want to show every column so that users can add more records. This section will show you how to specify the columns to show in a DataGrid control. Before you start, however, you have to decide which columns to show in the DataGrid. For this example, the DataGrid will show the Company Name, the Contact Name, the Phone Number, and the Country.

Specify columns in a DataGrid

1. Right-click the DataGrid and select **Retrieve Fields** from the pop-up menu. Answer **Yes** when VB asks if you want to replace the existing grid layout. All the fields from the selected RecordSource (in this case, the Customers table) will be loaded into the DataGrid control (see Figure 32.9).

FIGURE 32.9

The DataGrid control loads all the fields from the table so that you can select the ones you want to see.

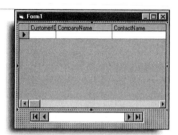

2. Right-click the DataGrid and select **Edit** from the pop-up menu. You won't see any changes to the control when you choose Edit; however, you now can click individual columns and edit them.

3. To delete columns from this list, right-click the **CustomerID** field and choose **Delete**. The CustomerID field will no longer be shown (see Figure 32.10).

FIGURE 32.10

When the DataGrid is in Edit mode, you can add and remove columns visually.

4. Delete the ContactTitle, Address, City, Region, PostalCode, and Fax columns by using the same technique used in step 3.

5. The control won't quite let you rearrange the columns by using drag-and-drop. If, for instance, you wanted to swap the ContactName and CompanyName columns, you would first cut the ContactName column and then right-click CompanyName and select Paste. The DataGrid will keep all the settings you've made for a column. Feel free to rearrange the columns as you see fit.

6. When showing the data in this DataGrid, the column headers don't necessarily have to be the same as the field names. For instance, **CompanyName** should be written **Company Name**. To make this change, right-click a column and select **Properties**. On the **Columns** page, enter the new name for the column in the **Caption** text box (see Figure 32.11).

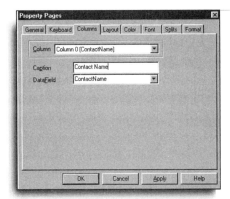

FIGURE 32.11

The Caption property on the **Columns** page controls what will be shown in each column's header.

7. Repeat step 6 for each column header whose caption you want to change. You can pick each column without leaving the Properties window.

Cleaning Up the Form

You can do some fine-tuning to this form to make it look more finished. First, the ADO Data control doesn't need to be visible. It's used automatically by the DataGrid, and it isn't necessary to allow users to see it. Set the ADO Data control's Visible property to False.

You also can cause the DataGrid to always fill the form. First, set the Align property to 1 - vbAlignTop to cause the DataGrid to sit at the top of the form and fill the form left to right. Then add the following code to force the DataGrid to fill top to bottom:

```
Private Sub Form_Resize()
    dgrdCustomers.Height = Me.ScaleHeight
End Sub
```

A final polish is to add a title to your form, such as Customer Viewer, through the form's `Caption` property. When you're done, your form will have a more professional look (see Figure 32.12).

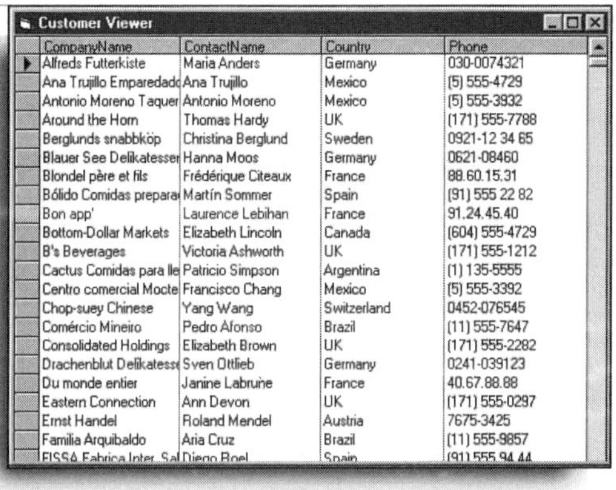

FIGURE 32.12

Your DataGrid is complete and even includes a few professional touches.

Configuring Other DataGrid Properties

You can configure quite a few other properties on the DataGrid. As they're all fairly easy to use, Table 32.1 explains the purpose of each property.

TABLE 32.1   DataGrid Properties

Property	Explanation
`Align`	Specifies whether the DataGrid should be aligned with the top, left, right, or bottom of the form.
`AllowAddNew`	If set to `True`, new records can be added at the bottom of the DataGrid.
`AllowArrows`	If set to `True`, navigation can be performed by using the arrow keys.
`AllowDelete`	If set to `True`, rows can be deleted from the DataGrid by pressing the Delete key.
`AllowUpdate`	If set to `True`, rows can be edited and have their changes saved automatically.

Be careful with `AllowDelete`

If your record is linked to other tables in any type of relationship, deleting the record won't be allowed and the resulting error message could confuse your users. Deletions can normally take place only if all other related records have been removed.

Property	Explanation
CausesValidation	If set to True, the Validate event will trigger when focus shifts to another control.
ColumnHeaders	Turns column headers on or off.
HeadLines	Specifies the number of vertical lines for the column headers.
RowDividerStyle	Supplies various options for the format of the row dividers.
TabAcrossSplits	Performs the Tab key shift between the split portions of the DataGrid
TabAction	Specifies the response to a Tab keypress
WrapCellPointer	Specifies whether the cursor should shift to the next row and first column when reaching the end of a row.

Using the DataList Control

The DataList control is much simpler than the DataGrid control. It's used to show a single column list of entries from a database table. Because it's data-bound, there's no memory limit as to how many items you can show. However, the more you add, the harder it is for users to find a particular item. Like the DataGrid, the DataList also uses an ADO Data control.

Create and use a DataList control

1. On a new form, add a new ADO Data control that accesses the Customers table in the Nwind.mdb database, as explained earlier in this chapter.

2. Add the DataList control to your Toolbox window by choosing **Components** from the **Project** menu.

3. From the list, select **Microsoft DataList Controls 6.0** and then click **OK**.

4. The DataList control 🔳 will now be shown in your Toolbox window. Double-click it to add it to your form with the ADO Data Control.

5. Name the DataList control dlstCustomers. This example will list the customer names in the DataList control so you can see the differences in presentation.

Editing rows in a grid

When you're designing your application and think about using a grid, you can edit data in a grid only if you store the data in a single table. If you need to put data into more than one table for a single record, you must use a different type of form. For example, an order will have both information about the order and information about the items on the order. You couldn't edit an order in a single grid because the data would be stored in at least two different tables. However, the DataGrid can show lists of items, such as shippers or state codes. If you just need to view data from other tables, the DataGrid may still be an option for you.

6. Set the RowSource property to adcCustomers. This property specifies the data source that will provide the list of data to show. To specify which field to show, set the ListField property to CompanyName.

Those are the only properties you have to set to make this form work. Make sure that the DataList is large enough for you to see the contents, and then choose **Start** from the **Run** menu ▸. The companies will be listed in the DataList control (see Figure 32.13).

FIGURE 32.13

The DataList control shows a single column of data from the data source.

You can also apply the same cleanup techniques to this form. To automatically resize the DataList to fill the whole form, simply add the following code to the form:

```
Private Sub Form_Resize()
    dlstCustomers.Height = Me.ScaleHeight
    dlstCustomers.Width = Me.ScaleWidth
End Sub
```

Configuring DataList Control Properties

As mentioned earlier, the DataList control has far fewer properties than the DataGrid. However, it does have some interesting features that the DataGrid doesn't, as listed in Table 32.2.

TABLE 32.2   **Selected DataList Properties**

Property	Explanation
CausesValidation	If set to True, the Validate event will trigger when focus shifts to another control.
IntegralHeight	Specifies whether the DataList control will show portions of items if the control isn't large enough.
MatchEntry	As users type, the DataList jumps based on the characters entered. This property determines how that matching works.

Using the DataCombo Control

The DataCombo control is nearly identical to the DataList except in its appearance. Rather than take up a lot of vertical space, the DataCombo's list portion can drop down as necessary. This is especially helpful in cases where the form needs to stay small. The DataCombo, like a standard ComboBox, should be used for small numbers (less than 100) of items.

Create and use a DataCombo control

1. On a new form, add a new ADO Data control that accesses the Customers table in the Nwind.mdb database, as explained earlier in this chapter. Because the DataList and DataCombo controls are packaged together, the DataCombo control ▦ is already in your Toolbox.

2. Double-click the DataCombo control. Name it dcboShippers because it will be used to hold the names of available shippers.

3. Add an ADO Data control that accesses the Shippers table in the Nwind.mdb table, as explained earlier in the chapter. Name the control adcShippers.

4. Set the DataCombo's RowSource property to adcShippers and ListField property to CompanyName, like you did with the DataList control.

When you run your program now, you'll see the available shippers listed in the DataCombo control (see Figure 32.14).

FIGURE 32.14

The DataCombo control loads the CompanyName field from the rows in the Shippers table.

The configurable properties for the DataCombo are basically the same as the ones available for the DataList control. One difference is the `Style` property, which functions in a similar fashion to the ComboBox's `Style` property. The DataCombo can be read-only or editable, which gives users a chance to add their own record to the available list. Because the DataCombo is used most often for selecting values from a set list, you normally want to leave the `Style` property at `2 - Dropdown List`.

Working with the Data Form Wizard

If all the preceding material looks a little daunting, don't fear because Visual Basic 6 comes with an all-new Data Form Wizard that can create most of these controls and data entry forms for you. In this section, you'll learn a little bit about what types of forms the Data Form Wizard can build and how you can make the most of this helpful tool.

SEE ALSO
➤ *You can see how to use the Data Form Wizard on page 614*

After selecting the database you want to use in the Data Form Wizard, you'll be presented with several options for what you want your form to do (see Figure 32.15).

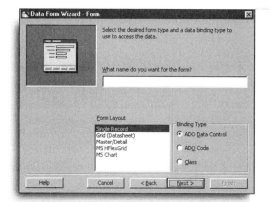

FIGURE 32.15
Select the type of form the wizard should build.

As you select each type of form, the graphic in the upper-left corner will show a sample of what the form will look like. The Binding Type section shows how the form will work:

- **ADO <u>D</u>ata Control** uses the techniques you just learned in this chapter.

- **AD<u>O</u> Code** doesn't use any ADO Data controls. Instead, the wizard generates code that operates the controls. If you want examples of how ADO code works, let the wizard generate a sample for you.

- **<u>C</u>lass** creates a class module that provides the data-access functionality.

Feel free to try out all three methods with any of the form types and see what you get. In most cases, you'll have to adjust the output a bit to get what you want, but the Data Form Wizard is certainly a major timesaver for these types of forms.

Later in the process of answering the wizard's questions, you'll select a table or query to use, pick the fields for the form, select a sorting order, and even select which actions are allowed for the form. The wizard can automatically build code to handle adding new records, editing existing ones, deleting records, and refreshing the existing data.

Command Syntax

Visual Basic provides more than 200 built-in statements and functions. Some are used frequently; some are seldom used at all. Even experienced programmers sometimes happen upon a statement or function they didn't know about.

This appendix can be considered a quick-reference guide to all of VB's built-in statements and functions. It offers the syntax for each, as well as a brief description of what it does and how its arguments (if any) are used. This is by no means a complete reference. Microsoft's *Visual Basic 6.0 Language Reference* is probably the best source for in-depth information on VB's statements and functions. If you have any questions about syntax or use of a particular statement or function, then you are strongly urged to consult that reference to obtain additional information.

Functions and Statements

Abs Function

```
Abs(number)
```

Returns the absolute value of *number*. The data type returned is the same as the data type of the *number* argument.

AppActivate Statement

```
AppActivate title[,wait]
```

Activates the application window that has the string *title* in its title bar or, alternatively, the task ID specified by *title*. The optional *wait* argument (Boolean) can be used to specify whether the calling application should wait until it has the focus before the application window is activated.

Array Function

```
Array(arglist)
```

Returns a Variant data item that contains an array. *arglist* refers to a comma-delimited list of values that make up the elements of the array, with the first value corresponding to the first element of the array, the second value corresponding to the second element of the array, and so on.

Asc Function

```
Asc(string)
```

Returns an Integer value that represents the ASCII code for the first character in the *string*.

Atn Function

```
Atn(number)
```

Returns a Double value that is the arctangent of *number*.

Beep Statement

```
Beep
```

Sounds a tone through the PC's speaker. Frequency and duration of the tone may vary from system to system.

Call Statement

```
[Call] name [argumentlist]
```

Executes a sub, function, or DLL procedure. The *name* argument specifies the name of the procedure to call, and *argumentlist* is an optional list of arguments that will be passed to the called procedure. The Call keyword is optional, but if it is included, then at least one or more arguments for *argumentlist* must also be included.

CBool Function

CBool(*expression*)

Converts the value of *expression* to a Boolean data type. The argument *expression* can be any valid string or numeric expression.

CByte Function

CByte(*expression*)

Converts the value of *expression* to a Byte data type. The argument *expression* must be a numeric value between 0 and 255.

CCur Function

CCur(*expression*)

Converts the value of *expression* to a Currency data type. The argument *expression* must be a numeric value between –922,337,203,685,477.5808 and 922,337,203,685,477.5807.

CDate Function

CDate(*expression*)

Converts the value of *expression* to a Date data type. The argument *expression* must be a valid date expression.

CDbl Function

CDbl(*expression*)

Converts the value of *expression* to a Double data type. The argument *expression* must be a numeric value between –1.79769313486232E308 and –4.94065645841247E-324 for negative values, or between 4.94065645841247E-324 and 1.79769313486232E308 for positive values.

CDec Function

CDec(*expression*)

Converts the value of *expression* to a Decimal data type. The argument *expression* must be a numeric value of +/–79,228,162,514,264,337,593,543,950,335 for zero-scaled numbers (numbers with no decimal places), or +/–7.9228162514264337593543950335 for numbers with 28 decimal places.

ChDir Statement

ChDir *path*

Changes the current directory to the one specified by the *path* argument. Note that although ChDir changes the default directory, it does not change the default drive as well.

ChDrive Statement

ChDrive *drive*

Changes the current drive to the one specified by the *drive* argument.

Choose Function

Choose(*index*, *choice-1*[, *choice-2*, ... [, *choice-n*]])

Returns a value from a list of choices (specified by the arguments *choice-1* through *choice-n*) based on the value of the *index* argument. If *index* is 1, then the value returned by the Choose function will be the value represented by *choice-1*; if *index* is 2, then the value returned will be that of *choice-2*; and so on.

Chr Function

Chr(*charcode*)

Returns a one-character String value that represents the ASCII character of the number specified by the *charcode* argument.

CInt Function

```
CInt(expression)
```

Converts the value of *expression* to an Integer data type. The argument *expression* must be a numeric value from –32,768 to 32,767. Fractions are rounded.

CLng Function

```
CLng(expression)
```

Converts the value of *expression* to a Long data type. The argument *expression* must be a numeric value from –2,147,483,648 to 2,147,483,647. Fractions are rounded.

Close Statement

```
Close [filenumberlist]
```

Closes any files opened with the Open statement that correspond to the file numbers specified by *filenumberlist*. The *filenumberlist* argument can contain a single file number (for example, #1) or multiple file numbers (for example, #1, #4, #5). If the *filenumberlist* argument is omitted, all open files will be closed.

Command Function

```
Command
```

Returns any command-line arguments specified when launching Visual Basic. For compiled programs, Command returns the command-line arguments specified when the program was launched.

Const Statement

```
[Public ¦ Private] Const constname [As type] = expression
```

Declares a constant with the name *constname* and the value represented by *expression*. The Public and Private keywords define the constant's scope, and the optional As *type* specifies the constant's data type. If the As *type* is omitted, the constant will be declared as the data type most appropriate for *expression*.

Cos Function

`Cos(number)`

Returns a `Double` value that is the cosine of the angle specified by the *number* argument.

CreateObject Function

`CreateObject(class)`

Creates and returns a reference to an ActiveX object of type *class*. The *class* argument should use the syntax *appname.objecttype*, where *appname* is the name of the application providing the object, and *objecttype* is the class of the object to be created.

CSng Function

`CSng(expression)`

Converts the value of *expression* to a `Single` data type. The argument *expression* must be a numeric value from –3.402823E38 to –1.401298E-45 for negative values, or from 1.401298E-45 to 3.402823E38 for positive values.

CStr Function

`CStr(expression)`

Converts the value of *expression* to a `String` data type. The string that `CStr` returns depends on the data type of the *expression* argument: For `Booleans`, `CStr` returns either `True` or `False`; for `Dates`, `CStr` returns a date based on the short date format on your system; for `Errors`, `CStr` returns the word `Error` followed by the error number. *expression* values that are `Empty` return a zero-length string, and numeric *expression* values return a string containing the number. A `Null` *expression* value will cause a runtime error.

CurDir Function

CurDir[(*drive*)]

Returns a String value that represents the full path of the current directory. If the *drive* argument is given, then CurDir returns the directory path of the current directory for that drive.

CVar Function

CVar(*expression*)

Converts the value of *expression* to a Variant data type. The argument *expression* can be either numeric or a string.

CVErr Function

CVErr(*errornumber*)

Returns a Variant of subtype Error that contains the error number specified by the *errornumber* argument.

Date Function

Date

Returns a Variant of subtype Date that contains the current system date.

Date Statement

Date = *date*

Sets the current system date as specified by the *date* argument. For Windows 95 systems, *date* must be a valid date between January 1, 1980 and December 31, 2099. For Windows NT systems, *date* must be a valid date between January 1, 1980 and December 31, 2079.

DateAdd Function

```
DateAdd(interval, number, date)
```

Returns a Variant of subtype Date calculated by taking the date specified by the *date* argument and adding or subtracting the amount of time specified by *interval* and *time*. The *interval* argument contains a code that represents a unit of time (for example, *yyyy* for years, *m* for months, *d* for days), and *number* is the number of units to be added to *date*.

DateDiff Function

```
DateDiff(interval, date1, date2[,firstdayofweek[,
firstweekofyear]])
```

Returns a Variant of subtype Long that represents the number of time units between two dates (*date1* and *date2*). The *interval* argument contains a code that represents the unit of time (for example, *yyyy* for years) that will be returned by the function. The optional *firstdayofweek* and *firstweekofyear* arguments are used to specify how the time difference should be calculated when certain codes are used for *interval*.

DatePart Function

```
DatePart(interval, date[,firstdayofweek[,firstweekofyear]])
```

Returns a Variant of subtype Integer that contains the part of *date* specified by *interval*. The *interval* argument contains a code that represents the unit of time (for example, *ww* for weeks) that will be returned by the function. The optional *firstday-ofweek* and *firstweekofyear* arguments are used to specify how the date should be calculated when certain *interval* codes are used.

DateSerial Function

```
DateSerial(year, month, day)
```

Returns a Variant of subtype Date that represents a date as specified by the *year*, *month*, and *day* arguments.

DateValue **Function**

```
DateValue(date)
```

Returns a Variant of subtype Date that is derived from the date value specified by the *date* argument.

Day **Function**

```
Day(date)
```

Returns a Variant of subtype Integer that represents the day of the month (1[nd]31) for the date value specified by the *date* argument.

DDB **Function**

```
DDB(cost, salvage, life, period[, factor])
```

Returns a Double value that represents the depreciation of an asset for a specified amount of time using a given method of depreciation. The *cost* argument represents the initial cost of the asset, *salvage* represents the value of the asset at the end of its working lifetime, *life* represents the lifetime of the asset, and *period* represents the period (in months) for which the depreciation is calculated. The optional *factor* argument specifies the rate at which the balance declines. If it is omitted, then the double-declining depreciation method is used.

Declare **Statement**

```
[Public ¦ Private] Declare Sub name Lib "libname" [Alias _
"aliasname"][([arglist])]
```

or

```
[Public ¦ Private] Declare Function name Lib "libname"
[Alias "aliasname"][([arglist])][As type]
```

Declares references to Sub or Function procedures in an external DLL (dynamic-link library). The optional Public and Private keywords define the procedure's scope. The *name* argument is the name of the procedure, and the *libname* argument specifies the DLL that contains the procedure. The optional *aliasname* argument specifies an alternate name for the procedure in the DLL. *arglist* is a list of arguments passed to the procedure. For Function procedures, the As *type* specifies the data type of the value returned by the Function. Declare statements can only be used at module level.

DefBool Statement

DefBool *letterrange*[, *letterrange*]...

Specifies that all variables and function return values that begin with the letters specified by the *letterrange* arguments are automatically defined to be of the Boolean data type. The *letterrange* arguments should be constructed as *letter1*[-*letter2*], where *letter1* is the first (or only) letter in the range, and *letter2* is the last letter in the range. DefBool can only be used at module level.

DefByte Statement

DefByte *letterrange*[, *letterrange*]...

Specifies that all variables and function return values that begin with the letters specified by the *letterrange* arguments are automatically defined to be of the Byte data type. The *letterrange* arguments should be constructed as *letter1*[-*letter2*], where *letter1* is the first (or only) letter in the range, and *letter2* is the last letter in the range. DefByte can only be used at module level.

DefCur Statement

DefCur *letterrange*[, *letterrange*]...

Specifies that all variables and function return values that begin with the letters specified by the *letterrange* arguments are automatically defined to be of the Currency data type. The *letterrange* arguments should be constructed as *letter1* [-*letter2*], where *letter1* is the first (or only) letter in the range, and *letter2* is the last letter in the range. DefCur can only be used at module level.

DefDate Statement

```
DefDate letterrange[, letterrange]...
```

Specifies that all variables and function return values that begin with the letters specified by the *letterrange* arguments are automatically defined to be of the Date data type. The *letterrange* arguments should be constructed as *letter1*[-*letter2*], where *letter1* is the first (or only) letter in the range, and *letter2* is the last letter in the range. DefDate can only be used at module level.

DefDbl Statement

```
DefDbl letterrange[, letterrange]...
```

Specifies that all variables and function return values that begin with the letters specified by the *letterrange* arguments are automatically defined to be of the Double data type. The *letterrange* arguments should be constructed as *letter1*[-*letter2*], where *letter1* is the first (or only) letter in the range, and *letter2* is the last letter in the range. DefDbl can only be used at module level.

DefDec Statement

```
DefDec letterrange[, letterrange]...
```

Specifies that all variables and function return values that begin with the letters specified by the *letterrange* arguments are automatically defined to be of the Decimal data type. The *letterrange* arguments should be constructed as *letter1*[-*letter2*], where *letter1* is the first (or only) letter in the range, and *letter2* is the last letter in the range. DefDec can only be used at module level.

DefInt Statement

```
DefInt letterrange[, letterrange]...
```

Specifies that all variables and function return values that begin with the letters specified by the *letterrange* arguments are automatically defined to be of the Integer data type. The *letterrange* arguments should be constructed as *letter1*[*-letter2*], where *letter1* is the first (or only) letter in the range, and *letter2* is the last letter in the range. DefInt can only be used at module level.

DefLng Statement

DefLng *letterrange*[, *letterrange*]...

Specifies that all variables and function return values that begin with the letters specified by the *letterrange* arguments are automatically defined to be of the Long data type. The *letterrange* arguments should be constructed as *letter1*[*-letter2*], where *letter1* is the first (or only) letter in the range, and *letter2* is the last letter in the range. DefLng can only be used at module level.

DefObj Statement

DefObj *letterrange*[, *letterrange*]...

Specifies that all variables and function return values that begin with the letters specified by the *letterrange* arguments are automatically defined to be of the Object data type. The *letterrange* arguments should be constructed as *letter1*[*-letter2*], where *letter1* is the first (or only) letter in the range, and *letter2* is the last letter in the range. DefObj can only be used at module level.

DefSng Statement

DefSng *letterrange*[, *letterrange*]...

Specifies that all variables and function return values that begin with the letters specified by the *letterrange* arguments are automatically defined to be of the Single data type. The *letterrange* arguments should be constructed as *letter1*[*-letter2*], where *letter1* is the first (or only) letter in the range, and *letter2* is the last letter in the range. DefSng can only be used at module level.

DefStr Statement

```
DefStr letterrange[, letterrange]...
```

Specifies that all variables and function return values that begin with the letters specified by the *letterrange* arguments are automatically defined to be of the String data type. The *letterrange* arguments should be constructed as *letter1*[-*letter2*], where *letter1* is the first (or only) letter in the range, and *letter2* is the last letter in the range. DefStr can only be used at module level.

DefVar Statement

```
DefVar letterrange[, letterrange]...
```

Specifies that all variables and function return values that begin with the letters specified by the *letterrange* arguments are automatically defined to be of the Variant data type. The *letterrange* arguments should be constructed as *letter1*[-*letter2*], where *letter1* is the first (or only) letter in the range, and *letter2* is the last letter in the range. DefVar can only be used at module level.

DeleteSetting Statement

```
DeleteSetting appname, section[, key]
```

Deletes an application's section or key setting entries from the System Registry. The *appname* argument specifies the name of the application, and *section* is the name of the section to be deleted. If the optional *key* argument is used, then only that key (and not the whole section) will be deleted.

Dim Statement

```
Dim [WithEvents] varname[([subscripts])] [As [New] type]
[,[WithEvents]
varname[([subscripts])] [As [New] type]]...
```

Declares one or more variables or objects. The *varname* argument is the name of the variable, and the optional As [New] *type* indicates its data type. If the New keyword is used, then an implicit creation of the object is made. The optional WithEvents keyword (valid only when the Dim statement is used in class modules) indicates that *varname* is an object variable as is used to respond to events triggered by an ActiveX object. The optional *subscripts* are the dimensions of an array variable.

Dir Function

```
Dir[(pathname[, attributes])]
```

Returns a String value containing the name of a file, directory, or folder that matches a pattern (specified in the *pathname* argument) and/or a file attribute (specified in *attributes*). The first time the Dir function is called, it returns the name of a file based on the *pathname* and *attributes* arguments. If the function is called again and no arguments are given, then it returns the second file name for the given *pathname* and *attributes*, and so on.

Do...Loop Statement

```
Do [{While ¦ Until} condition]
    [statements]
    [Exit Do]
    [statements]
Loop
```

or

```
Do
    [statements]
    [Exit Do]
    [statements]
Loop [{While ¦ Until} condition]
```

Repeats one or more *statements* while a *condition* is True or until a *condition* becomes True. The optional Exit Do keywords pass control to the line of code immediately following the Do...Loop structure.

DoEvents Function

```
DoEvents( )
```

Temporarily gives control to the operating system so that it can process other events. The DoEvents function is typically used inside loops so that a program does not tie up system resources for a long period of time.

End Statement

```
End
End Function
End If
End Property
End Select
End Sub
End Type
End With
```

Ends a program (`End`), procedure (`End Function`, `End Property`, or `End Sub`), type structure (`End Type`), or program block (`End If`, `End Select`, or `End With`).

Enum Statement

```
[Public ¦ Private] Enum name
    membername [= constantexpression]
    membername [= constantexpression]
        . . .
End Enum
```

Declares an enumeration type named *name* that is composed of one or more members specified by *membername*. Members can be assigned values using *constantexpression*. The optional `Public` and `Private` keywords define the enumeration's scope.

Environ Function

```
Environ({envstring ¦ number})
```

Returns the `String` value of the operating system variable specified by *envstring* or, alternatively, the numeric order of the environment string in the environment-string table specified by *number*.

EOF Function

```
EOF(filenumber)
```

Returns a True or False value (Integer) that indicates whether the end of file marker has been reached for the Random or Input file associated with the *filenumber* argument.

Erase Statement

```
Erase arraylist
```

Reinitializes the elements in one or more fixed-size array and frees up the dynamic-array storage space that was taken up by the array(s). The *arraylist* argument is one or more comma-delimited array names.

Error Function

```
Error[(errornumber)]
```

Returns a String value that contains the error message that corresponds to the *errornumber* argument.

Error Statement

```
Error errornumber
```

Causes an error to occur. The *errornumber* argument indicates the type of error that should occur.

Event Statement

```
[Public] Event procedurename [(arglist)]
```

Declares a user-defined event with the name *procedurename*. The optional Public keyword indicates that the Event should be visible throughout the project, even though that is the default. The optional argument list (*arglist*) should contain one or more arguments defined using the syntax:

```
[ByVal ¦ ByRef] varname[()] [As type]
```

where *varname* is the name of the argument, As *type* indicates the data type of the argument, and the optional ByRef or ByVal keywords specify whether the argument should be passed by reference (`ByRef`) or by value (`ByVal`). If `ByRef` and `ByVal` are not specified, then the argument will be passed by reference.

Exit Statement

```
Exit Do
Exit For
Exit Function
Exit Property
Exit Sub
```

Exits a procedure (`Exit Function`, `Exit Property`, or `Exit Sub`) or looping structure (`Exit Do` or `Exit For`).

Exp Function

```
Exp(number)
```

Returns a `Double` value that is `e` (the base of natural logarithms) raised to the power specified by `number`.

FileAttr Function

```
FileAttr(filenumber, returntype)
```

Returns a `Long` value that indicates the file mode for a file opened using the `Open` statement. The argument `filenumber` is the file number for the open file, and `returntype` indicates the type of information to be returned. Although `returntype` can be set to 2 to return the operating system file handle for the open file, it only works on 16-bit systems and should be avoided in VB5. Instead, use a value of 1 for `returntype` to return the open file type. The possible values returned by the `FileAttr` function for indicating file type are: 1 for `Input`, 2 for `Output`, 4 for `Random`, 8 for `Append`, and 32 for `Binary`.

FileCopy Statement

```
FileCopy source, destination
```

Copies the filename and path specified by the `source` argument to the filename and path specified by the `destination` argument.

FileDateTime Function

```
FileDateTime(pathname)
```

Returns a Variant of subtype Date that indicates the date and time when the file specified by the *pathname* argument was last modified.

FileLen Function

```
FileLen(pathname)
```

Returns a Long value that contains the file size (in bytes) of the file specified by the *pathname* argument.

Fix Function

```
Fix(number)
```

Returns the integer portion of the number specified by the *number* argument. If *number* is negative, then Fix returns the first negative integer greater than or equal to *number*.

For Each...Next Statement

```
For Each element In group
    [statements]
    [Exit For]
    [statements]
Next [element]
```

Executes one or more *statements* for each *element* in the array or collection specified by *group*. The optional Exit For can be used to immediately exit the looping structure.

For...Next Statement

```
For counter = start To end [Step step]
    [statements]
    [Exit For]
    [statements]
Next [counter]
```

Executes one or more *statements* a specified number of times.

The *counter* argument is a variable used to increment from *start* to *end*. By default, *counter* is incremented by 1 each time the loop is executed, although the optional *step* argument can be used to specify a different increment. The optional Exit For can be used to immediately exit the looping structure.

Format Function

```
Format(expression[, format[, firstdayofweek[, _
firstweekofyear]]])
```

Returns a Variant of subtype String that contains the value specified by *expression* using a format defined by the *format* argument. The *format* argument uses codes (for example, *d* for days or *#* for numbers) to determine how *expression* will be formatted. The optional *firstdayofweek* and *firstweekofyear* arguments are used when formatting certain values.

FreeFile Function

```
FreeFile[(rangenumber)]
```

Returns an Integer value the represents the next file number available for use with the Open statement. The optional *rangenumber* argument can be used to specify which range of file numbers should be used: 0 (the default) for file numbers in the range of 1–255, or 1 for file numbers in the range of 256–511.

Function Statement

```
[Public ¦ Private ¦ Friend] [Static] Function name _
[(arglist)] [As type]
    [statements]
    [name = expression]
    [Exit Function]
    [statements]
    [name = expression]
End Function
```

Declares the various parts of a Function procedure. The optional Public, Private, and Friend keywords can be used to define the Function's scope, and the optional Static keyword indicates that the procedure's local variables are preserved between calls to the

Function. The *name* argument specifies the name of the Function procedure and can be assigned a value (*name = expression*) that will be returned by the procedure. The data type of the return value can be specified using the As *type* clause. The optional Exit Function can be used to exit the Function procedure immediately.

The optional list of arguments (*arglist*) defines the arguments that will be passed to the procedure. The arguments should use the following syntax:

```
[Optional] [ByVal ¦ ByRef] [ParamArray] varname[()] [As _
type] [= default value]
```

where the Optional keyword can be used to specify that the argument is not required (*default value* assigns the argument's default value), ByVal and ByRef determine whether the argument should be passed by value or by reference (the default), and the ParamArray keyword specifies that the argument is an Optional array of Variant elements. ParamArray can only be used with the last argument in the argument list.

FV Function

```
FV(rate, nper, pmt[, pv[, type]])
```

Returns a Double value that indicates the future value of an annuity based on a number (*nper*) of periodic fixed payment amounts (*pmt*) and a fixed interest rate (*rate*). The optional *pv* argument specifies a present value or lump sum of a series of future payments, and the optional *type* argument specifies when payments are due (0 for end of the payment period, the default; 1 for beginning of the payment period).

Get Statement

```
Get [#]filenumber,[ recnumber,] varname
```

Reads data from the open disk file corresponding to the *filenumber* argument into a variable (*varname*). Get works with files open as Random or Binary, and a record number (*recnumber*) can be specified when retrieving data from a Random file. When using Binary files, *recnumber* can alternatively be used to specify the byte position from which the data is to be read.

GetAllSettings Function

GetAllSettings(*appname, section*)

Returns a list of key settings and their values from a specific application (*appname*) entry and section (*section*) in the System Registry.

GetAttr Function

GetAttr(*pathname*)

Returns an Integer value that represents the attributes for the file, directory, or folder specified by the *pathname* argument. The value returned can be compared bitwise with several VB constants (vbNormal, vbReadOnly, vbHidden, vbSystem, vbDirectory, and vbArchive) to determine which attributes are set.

GetAutoServerSettings Function

object.GetAutoServerSettings([*progid*], [*clsid*])

Returns a Variant array that contains information concerning the state of an ActiveX *object*'s registration. The optional *progid* and *clsid* can be included to specify the object's ProgID and CLSID, respectively. The values of the elements of the Variant array that are returned by GetAutoServerSettings are, in order: local/remote registration of object (True if the object is registered remotely), the remote machine name, the RPC network protocol name, and the RPC authentication level.

GetObject Function

GetObject([*pathname*] [,*class*])

Returns a reference to an object of type *class*. The *pathname* argument can be included to specify the path and filename from which the object should be retrieved; however, if it is omitted, then the *class* name must be specified.

GetSetting Function

```
GetSetting(appname, section, key[, default])
```

Returns a single key setting value from a specific application (*appname*) entry and section (*section*) in the System Registry. If no value is set for the key setting specified, then the optional *default* value can be returned. If default is omitted, then the default value returned will be a zero-length string.

GoSub...Return Statement

```
GoSub line
    ...
    line
    ...
Return
```

Transfers program control to the subroutine indicated by the line label or line number *line* until the Return statement is reached; then returns control to the line of code immediately following the GoSub statement.

GoTo Statement

```
GoTo line
```

Transfers program control to the line of code specified by the line label or line number *line*. The line must be inside the procedure that contains the GoTo statement.

Hex Function

```
Hex(number)
```

Returns a String value that represents the hexadecimal value of the argument *number*.

Hour Function

```
Hour(time)
```

Returns a Variant of subtype Integer that represents the hour (0[nd]23) of the time value specified by the *time* argument.

If...Then...Else Statement

```
If condition Then [statements] [Else elsestatements]
```

or

```
If condition Then
    [statements]
[ElseIf condition-n Then
    [elseifstatements] ...
[Else
    [elsestatements]]
End If
```

Conditionally executes one or more *statements* if the value expressed by *condition* is True. One or more ElseIf clauses can be included to test other conditions and execute other statements (*elseifstatements*) if the preceding condition is False. An Else clause can also be included to execute other statements (*elsestatements*) if none of the preceding conditions are True.

IIf Function

```
IIf(expression, truepart, falsepart)
```

Returns one of two values based on whether *expression* evaluates to True or False. If True, then IIf returns the *truepart* value; if False, then the *falsepart* value is returned.

IMEStatus Function

```
IMEStatus
```

Returns an Integer value that represents Windows' current Input Method Editor (IME) mode. IMEStatus is only available in Far East versions.

Implements Statement

```
Implements [interfacename ¦ class]
```

Specifies an interface (*interfacename*) or class (*class*) that will be implemented in the class module in which the Implements statement is used.

Input # Statement

```
Input #filenumber, varlist
```

Reads data from the open file associated with the *filenumber* argument and places it in the variables in the *varlist* argument. The *varlist* argument should contain one or more comma-delimited variables.

Input Function

```
Input(number, [#]filenumber)
```

Returns a String value containing characters read in from the open file that corresponds to the *filenumber* argument. The number of characters to be read in are specified by the *number* argument.

InputBox Function

```
InputBox(prompt[, title][, default][, xpos][, _
ypos][,helpfile, context])
```

Displays a dialog box and waits for the user to enter text or click a button; then returns what the user entered in a String value. The *prompt* argument specifies the message to be displayed in the dialog box, *title* specifies an optional caption for the dialog box's title bar, and *default* specifies the optional default value returned by the InputBox function if no value is entered by the user. The optional *xpos* and *ypos* arguments specify (in twips) the horizontal and vertical position of the dialog box on the screen. The optional *helpfile* and *context* arguments are used to provide context-sensitive Help for the dialog box.

InStr Function

```
InStr([start, ]string1, string2[, compare])
```

Returns a Variant of subtype Long that specifies the starting position of the first occurrence of a substring (*string2*) within another string (*string1*). The optional *start* argument specifies from which character in *string2* to start searching; the default is 1 (first character). The optional *compare* argument specifies the type of string comparison that will be made (0 for binary or 1 for textual noncase-sensitive).

Int Function

```
Int(number)
```

Returns the integer portion of the number specified by the *number* argument. If *number* is negative, then Int returns the first negative integer less than or equal to *number*.

IPmt Function

```
IPmt(rate, per, nper, pv[, fv[, type]])
```

Returns a Double value that indicates the interest payment for a fixed-period annuity based on a number (*nper*) of periodic fixed payments (*per*) and a fixed interest rate (*rate*). The *pv* argument specifies the present value of a series of payments or receipts. The optional *fv* argument specifies the future value or cash balance left after the final payment. The optional *type* argument specifies when payments are due (0 for end of the payment period, the default; 1 for beginning of the payment period).

IRR Function

```
IRR(values()[, guess])
```

Returns a Double value indicating the internal rate of return for an array of *values* that represent cash flow. The *values()* array must contain at least one negative value (payment) and one positive value (receipt). The optional *guess* argument specifies an estimate value to be returned by IRR (default estimate is .1).

IsArray Function

```
IsArray(varname)
```

Returns a Boolean value that indicates whether the variable specified by *varname* is an array.

IsDate Function

```
IsDate(expression)
```

Returns a Boolean value that indicates whether *expression* is capable of being converted to a date value.

IsEmpty Function

```
IsEmpty(expression)
```

Returns a Boolean value that indicates whether a numeric or string *expression* has been initialized.

IsError Function

```
IsError(expression)
```

Returns a Boolean value that indicates whether a given *expression* is an error value.

IsMissing Function

```
IsMissing(argname)
```

Returns a Boolean value that indicates whether an optional Variant argument (*argname*) has been passed to a procedure. IsMissing returns True if no value has been provided for the specified argument.

IsNull Function

```
IsNull(expression)
```

Returns a Boolean value that indicates whether a given *expression* contains no data and is Null.

IsNumeric Function

```
IsNumeric(expression)
```

Returns a Boolean value that indicates whether a given *expression* can be evaluated as a numeric value.

IsObject Function

```
IsObject(identifier)
```

Returns a Boolean value that indicates whether a given *identifier* represents an object variable.

Kill Statement

```
Kill pathname
```

Deletes the file(s) or directory represented by the *pathname* argument. Filenames in the *pathname* argument can contain wildcards, allowing multiple files to be deleted.

LBound Function

```
LBound(arrayname[, dimension])
```

Returns a Long value that represents the smallest subscript for a dimensioned array (*arrayname*). For multidimensional arrays, the *dimension* argument can be included to specify which dimension should be used.

LCase Function

```
LCase(string)
```

Converts a *string* to all lowercase characters and returns a new String value.

Left Function

```
Left(string, length)
```

Returns a String value *length* characters long that is taken from the left side of a given *string*.

Len Function

```
Len(string ¦ varname)
```

Returns a Long value that indicates the number of characters in a *string* or, alternatively, the number of bytes required to store a particular variable (*varname*).

Let Statement

```
[Let] varname = expression
```

Assigns the value of an *expression* to a variable (*varname*). The Let keyword is usually omitted and is assumed by Visual Basic.

Line Input # Statement

```
Line Input #filenumber, varname
```

Reads a line of data (ending with a carriage return or carriage return-linefeed) from an open disk file corresponding to the *filenumber* argument. The data is placed in the String or Variant variable specified by *varname*.

Load Statement

```
Load object
```

Loads an *object*, such as a form or control, into memory.

LoadPicture Function

```
LoadPicture([stringexpression])
```

Loads the image specified by the *stringexpression* argument and returns it. This allows pictures to be loaded in and assigned to a Form's Picture property, a PictureBox control, or an Image control. If no *stringexpression* argument is given, then LoadPicture returns an empty picture.

LoadResData Function

```
LoadResData(index, format)
```

Loads data from the resource (.RES) file with the identifier of the *index* argument. The *format* argument specifies the format of the data (1 for cursors, 2 for bitmaps, 3 for icons, 4 for menus, 5 for dialog boxes, 6 for strings, 7 for font directories, 8 for fonts, 9 for accelerator tables, 10 for user-defined resources, 12 for group cursors, and 14 for group icons). The data returned by the LoadResData function can be assigned to a variable or object of the appropriate type.

LoadResPicture Function

```
LoadResPicture(index, format)
```

Loads a bitmap, icon, or cursor from the resource (.RES) file with the identifier of the *index* argument. The *format* argument specifies the format of the data (0 for bitmaps, 1 for icons, and 2 for cursors). The data returned by the LoadResPicture function can be assigned to an object of the appropriate type.

LoadResString Function

```
LoadResString(index)
```

Loads a string from the resource (.RES) file with the identifier of the *index* argument. The string that is returned can be assigned to a variable of String or Variant data type.

Loc Function

```
Loc(filenumber)
```

Returns a Long value that indicates the current byte position within the open file that corresponds to the *filenumber* argument.

Lock Statement

```
Lock [#]filenumber[, recordrange]
```

Prevents another process from accessing all or part of the open file that corresponds to the *filenumber* argument. The *recordrange* argument refers to a range of records (or bytes) that are to be locked and should use the syntax:

```
recnumber ¦ [start] To end
```

where *recnumber* is the record number (for Random files) or byte position (for Binary files) where locking should begin. Alternatively, the starting and ending record numbers or bytes to be locked can be specified using the *start* and *end* arguments.

LOF Function

```
LOF(filenumber)
```

Returns a Boolean value that represents the byte size of the open file that corresponds to the *filenumber* argument.

Log Function

```
Log(number)
```

Returns a Double value that represents the natural logarithm of a specified *number*.

LSet Statement

```
LSet stringvar = string
```

or

```
LSet varname1 = varname2
```

In the first syntax, LSet assigns a *string* value to a String variable (*stringvar*), left-aligning the string to the String variable. In the second syntax, LSet copies a variable (*varname2*) from one user-defined type to a variable (*varname1*) in another user-defined type.

LTrim Function

```
LTrim(string)
```

Returns a Variant of subtype String that contains a copy of a given *string* with any leading spaces removed.

Mid Function

```
Mid(string, start[, length])
```

Returns a String value of one or more characters, taken from the String variable specified by the *string* argument. The *start* argument specifies the character position within *string* where the new String is to be obtained, and the optional *length* argument specifies how many characters are to be taken from *string*. If no *length* is specified, then all the characters in *string* (starting at the position given in the *start* argument) are used.

Mid Statement

```
Mid(stringvar, start[, length]) = string
```

Replaces one or more characters in a String variable (*stringvar*) with another *string*. The *start* argument specifies the character position within *stringvar* to place the new *string*, and the

optional *length* argument specifies how many characters of
string should be used. If *length* is omitted, then the entire
string is used.

Minute Function

```
Minute(time)
```

Returns a Variant of subtype Integer that represents the minute
(0–59) of the time value specified by the *time* argument.

MIRR Function

```
MIRR(values(), financerate, reinvestrate)
```

Returns a Double value that represents the modified internal rate
of return for an array of *values* that represent cash flow. The
values() array must contain at least one negative value (payment) and one positive value (receipt). The *financerate* argument
specifies the interest rate paid as a cost of financing, and the
reinvestrate argument specifies the interest rate received on
gains from cash reinvestment.

MkDir Statement

```
MkDir path
```

Creates the new directory or folder specified by the *path* argument.

Month Function

```
Month(date)
```

Returns a Variant of subtype Integer that represents the month
(1[nd]12) for the date value specified by the *date* argument.

MsgBox Function

```
MsgBox(prompt[, buttons][, title][, helpfile, context]
```

Displays a message in a dialog box with one or more buttons and
waits for the user to respond. MsgBox then returns an Integer
value that represents the button that was clicked. The *prompt*

argument specifies the message to be displayed in the dialog box, and *title* specifies an optional caption for the dialog box's title bar. The optional *buttons* argument specifies which buttons will be displayed. The optional *helpfile* and *context* arguments are used to provide context-sensitive Help for the dialog box.

Name **Statement**

```
Name oldpathname As newpathname
```

Renames the file, directory, or folder specified by the *oldpathname* argument to the name specified by *newpathname*.

Now **Function**

```
Now
```

Returns a Variant of subtype Date that contains the current system date and time.

NPer **Function**

```
NPer(rate, pmt, pv[, fv[, type]])
```

Returns a Double value that indicates the number of periods for an annuity based on periodic fixed payments (*pmt*) and a fixed interest rate (*rate*). The *pv* argument specifies the present value of a series of payments or receipts. The optional *fv* argument specifies the future value or cash balance left after the final payment. The optional *type* argument specifies when payments are due (0 for end of the payment period, the default; 1 for beginning of the payment period).

NPV **Function**

```
NPV(rate, values())
```

Returns a Double value that represents the present value of an investment based on a discount rate (*rate*) and an array of *values* that represent cash flow. The *values()* array must contain at least one negative value (payment) and one positive value (receipt).

Oct Function

```
Oct(number)
```

Returns a `String` value that represents the octal value of the argument *number*.

On Error Statement

```
On Error GoTo line
On Error Resume Next
On Error GoTo 0
```

Enables or disables the use of an error-handling routine. The `On Error` statement can specify a line label or line number (specified by the *line* argument) to branch to when an error occurs, allowing error-handling to be enabled. Alternatively, using `On Error Resume Next` causes program control to be transferred to the line of code immediately following the line of code that causes an error. Finally, `On Error GoTo 0` disables all error-handling.

On...GoSub Statement

```
On expression GoSub destinationlist
```

Evaluates a given *expression* and, depending on its value, transfers program control to a certain subroutine. The possible subroutines are contained in the *destinationlist* argument, which contains one or more comma-delimited line labels or line numbers. If *expression* evaluates to 1, then the first subroutine in the *destinationlist* is used; if it evaluates to 2, then the second subroutine in the *destinationlist* is used; and so on. Control is transferred to the line of code immediately following the `On...GoSub` line when a `Return` statement is encountered.

On...GoTo Statement

```
On expression GoTo destinationlist
```

Evaluates a given *expression* and, depending on its value, transfers program control to a certain line label or line number. The possible transfer points are contained in the *destinationlist* argument, which contains one or more comma-delimited line labels or line numbers. If *expression* evaluates to 1, then the first line label in the *destinationlist* is used; if it evaluates to 2, then the second line label in the *destinationlist* is used; and so on.

Open Statement

```
Open pathname For mode [Access access] [lock] As _
[#]filenumber [Len=reclength]
```

Opens a file for input/output and assigns it to the given *filenumber*. The *pathname* argument specifies the name of the file to open, and *mode* indicates the file mode (Append, Binary, Input, Output, or Random). The optional Access clause can be used to specify permissions for the file (Read, Write, or Read Write). The optional *lock* argument can specify the operations that can be performed on the file by other processes (Shared, Lock Read, Lock Write, or Lock Read Write). The *reclength* argument can be used to specify the record size for random files or the buffer size for sequential files.

Option Base Statement

```
Option Base [0 ¦ 1]
```

Declares the default lower bound of array subscripts. Option Base can only be used at module level.

Option Compare Statement

```
Option Compare [Binary ¦ Text ¦ Database]
```

Declares the default method used for string comparisons. Option Compare can only be used at module level.

Option Explicit Statement

```
Option Explicit
```

Forces explicit declaration of all variables in a module. If Option Explicit is not used, undeclared variables are automatically typed as Variants. Option Explicit can only be used at module level.

Option Private Statement

```
Option Private Module
```

Prevents a module's contents (that is, variables and objects) from being used outside its project. Option Private is only necessary when working with host applications that allow variables and objects to be referenced across multiple projects.

Partition Function

```
Partition(number, start, stop, interval)
```

Returns a Variant of subtype String that describes a range of numbers in which the *number* argument falls. The *start* and *stop* arguments specify the overall range of numbers, which is split up into smaller ranges as specified by the *interval* argument. The Partition function returns a string representation of the smaller range in which the number can be found, such as " 1: 10" for a *number* that falls in the range of 1 to 10.

Pmt Function

```
Pmt(rate, nper, pv[, fv[, type]])
```

Returns a Double value that indicates the payment for an annuity based on a number (*nper*) of periodic fixed payments and a fixed interest rate (*rate*). The *pv* argument specifies the present value of a series of payments or receipts. The optional *fv* argument specifies the future value or cash balance left after the final payment. The optional *type* argument specifies when payments are due (0 for end of the payment period, the default; 1 for beginning of the payment period).

PPmt Function

```
PPmt(rate, per, nper, pv[, fv[, type]])
```

Returns a Double value that indicates the principle payment for a given period (*per*) of an annuity based on a number (*nper*) of periodic fixed payments and a fixed interest rate (*rate*). The *pv* argument specifies the present value of a series of payments or receipts. The optional *fv* argument specifies the future value or cash balance left after the final payment. The optional *type* argument specifies when payments are due (0 for end of the payment period, the default; 1 for beginning of the payment period).

Print # Statement

```
Print #filenumber, [outputlist]
```

Writes data to the open sequential file that corresponds to *filenumber*. The optional *outputlist* argument can consist of one or more comma-delimited expressions to be written and should use the following syntax:

```
[{Spc(n) ¦ Tab[(n)]}] [expression][charpos]
```

where Spc is optionally used to write *n* spaces, and Tab is optionally used to advance to the *n*th column number. The *expression* argument can specify the data to be written, and the *charpos* argument can specify the insertion point for the next character. If *charpos* is omitted, the next character will be written on the next line. If it is a semicolon, the next character will be written immediately following the last character.

Private Statement

```
Private [WithEvents] varname[([subscripts])] [As [New]
type][,[WithEvents]
varname[([subscripts])]        [As [New] type]]...
```

Declares one or more private variables. The *varname* argument specifies the name of the variable being declared, and *subscripts* are the dimensions for an array variable. The optional As [New] *type* clause can be used to specify the variable's data type, with the New keyword enabling implicit creation of an object. The optional WithEvents keyword specifies that the variable being declared is an object variable used to respond to events triggered by an ActiveX object. The Private statement can only be used at module level, and variables declared with it cannot be used outside their own module.

Property Get **Statement**

```
[Public ¦ Private ¦ Friend] [Static] Property Get name
[(arglist)] [As type]
    [statements]
    [name = expression]
    [Exit Property]
    [statements]
    [name = expression]
End Property
```

Declares the various parts of a Property Get procedure, which is used to obtain the value of a property. The optional Public, Private, and Friend keywords can be used to define the procedure's scope, and the optional Static keyword indicates that the procedure's local variables are preserved between calls to the procedure. The *name* argument specifies the name of the property to be retrieved and can be assigned a value (*name* = *expression*) that will be returned as the property's value. The data type of the property can be specified using the As *type* clause. The optional Exit Property can be used to exit the Property Get procedure immediately.

The optional list of arguments (*arglist*) defines the arguments that will be passed to the procedure. The arguments should use the following syntax:

```
[Optional] [ByVal ¦ ByRef] [ParamArray] varname[()]     [As
type] [= default value]
```

where the Optional keyword can be used to specify that the argument is not required (*default value* assigns the argument's default value), ByVal and ByRef determine whether the argument should be passed by value or by reference (the default), and the ParamArray keyword specifies that the argument is an Optional array of Variant elements. ParamArray can only be used with the last argument in the argument list.

Property Let Statement

```
[Public ¦ Private ¦ Friend] [Static] Property Let name
([arglist,] value)
    [statements]
    [Exit Property]
    [statements]
End Property
```

Declares the various parts of a Property Let procedure, which is used to assign a value to a property. The optional Public, Private, and Friend keywords can be used to define the procedure's scope, and the optional Static keyword indicates that the procedure's local variables are preserved between calls to the procedure. The *name* argument specifies the name of the property being referenced, and *value* indicates the value to be assigned to the property. The optional Exit Property can be used to exit the Property Let procedure immediately.

The optional list of arguments (*arglist*) defines the arguments that will be passed to the procedure. The arguments should use the following syntax:

```
[Optional] [ByVal ¦ ByRef] [ParamArray] varname[()]    [As
type] [= default value]
```

where the Optional keyword can be used to specify that the argument is not required (*default value* assigns the argument's default value), ByVal and ByRef determine whether the argument should be passed by value or by reference (the default), and the ParamArray keyword specifies that the argument is an Optional array of Variant elements. ParamArray can only be used with the last argument in the argument list.

Property Set Statement

```
[Public ¦ Private ¦ Friend] [Static] Property Set name
([arglist,] reference)
    [statements]
    [Exit Property]
    [statements]
End Property
```

Declares the various parts of a Property Set procedure, which is used to set a reference to an object. The optional Public,

Private, and Friend keywords can be used to define the procedure's scope, and the optional Static keyword indicates that the procedure's local variables are preserved between calls to the procedure. The *name* argument specifies the name of the property being used, and *reference* indicates the object reference to be set to the property. The optional Exit Property can be used to exit the Property Set procedure immediately.

The optional list of arguments (*arglist*) defines the arguments that will be passed to the procedure. The arguments should use the following syntax:

```
[Optional] [ByVal ¦ ByRef] [ParamArray] varname[()] [As
type] [= default value]
```

where the Optional keyword can be used to specify that the argument is not required (*default value* assigns the argument's default value), ByVal and ByRef determine whether the argument should be passed by value or by reference (the default), and the ParamArray keyword specifies that the argument is an Optional array of Variant elements. ParamArray can only be used with the last argument in the argument list.

Public Statement

```
Public [WithEvents] varname[([subscripts])] [As [New]
type][,[WithEvents]
varname[([subscripts])] [As [New] type]]...
```

Declares one or more public variables. The *varname* argument specifies the name of the variable being declared, and *subscripts* are the dimensions for an array variable. The optional As [New] *type* clause can be used to specify the variable's data type, with the New keyword enabling implicit creation of an object. The optional WithEvents keyword specifies that the variable being declared is an object variable used to respond to events triggered by an ActiveX object. The Public statement can only be used at module level, and variables declared with it can be used outside their own module.

Put Statement

`Put [#]filenumber, [recnumber], varname`

Writes data to the open disk file corresponding to the *filenumber* argument from a variable (*varname*). Put works with files open as Random or Binary, and a record number (*recnumber*) can be specified when writing data to a Random file. When using Binary files, *recnumber* can alternatively be used to specify the byte position at which the data is to be written.

PV Function

`PV(rate, nper, pmt[, fv[, type]])`

Returns a Double value that indicates the present value of an annuity based on a number (*nper*) of periodic fixed payments (*pmt*) and a fixed interest rate (*rate*). The optional *fv* argument specifies the future value or cash balance left after the final payment. The optional *type* argument specifies when payments are due (0 for end of the payment period, the default; 1 for beginning of the payment period).

QBColor Function

`QBColor(color)`

Returns a Long value that represents the RGB color code that corresponds to a given color *number* (0[nd]15) of the color palette used in Microsoft QuickBasic.

RaiseEvent Function

`RaiseEvent eventname [(argumentlist)]`

Triggers an event. The optional *argumentlist* specifies one or more comma-delimited arguments to be passed to the event procedure. The event procedure must be declared in the same module as the RaiseEvent function or an error will occur.

Randomize Statement

`Randomize [number]`

Initializes the random number generator, using the optional *number* argument as a seed value.

Rate Function

```
Rate(nper, pmt, pv[, fv[, type[, guess]]])
```

Returns a Double value that indicates the fixed interest rate per period for an annuity based on a number (*nper*) of periodic fixed payments (*pmt*). The optional *fv* argument specifies the future value or cash balance left after the final payment. The optional *type* argument specifies when payments are due (0 for end of the payment period, the default; 1 for beginning of the payment period). The optional *guess* argument specifies an estimate value to be returned by Rate (default estimate is .1).

ReDim Statement

```
ReDim [Preserve] varname(subscripts) [As type] [,
varname(subscripts) [As type]]...
```

Redimensions one or more dynamic array variables and reallocates their storage space. The optional Preserve keyword can be used to keep the contents of the array intact when it is being redimensioned. The *varname* argument is the name of the variable, and the optional As *type* clause indicates its data type. The *subscripts* are the dimensions of the array variable.

Rem Statement

```
Rem comments
```

Allows *comments* to be added to a program. Everything on the line after the Rem statement is ignored by Visual Basic. An apostrophe (') can also be used in lieu of the Rem statement.

Reset Statement

```
Reset
```

Closes all files opened with the Open statement and writes any file buffer contents to disk.

Resume Statement

```
Resume [0]
Resume Next
Resume line
```

Resumes execution of a program when an error-handling routine is finished. Resume by itself causes execution to resume with the statement that caused the error or, if the error occurred in a called procedure, the statement that last called out of the error-handling procedure. Resume Next causes execution to resume with the statement immediately following the one that caused the error. Resume *line* transfers control to the line label or line number specified by the *line* argument.

RGB Function

```
RGB(red, green, blue)
```

Returns a Long value that represents an RGB color value as specified by the *red*, *green*, and *blue* color components passed to the RGB function. All color components should be Integers in the 0[nd]255 range.

Right Function

```
Right(string, length)
```

Returns a String value *length* characters long that is taken from the right side of a given *string*.

RmDir Statement

```
RmDir path
```

Removes the directory or folder specified by the *path* argument.

Rnd Function

```
Rnd[(number)]
```

Returns a Single value that contains a randomly generated number less than 1 but greater than or equal to zero. The optional *number* argument can be used to determine how Rnd generates the random number.

RSet Statement

```
RSet stringvar = string
```

Assigns a *string* value to a String variable (*stringvar*), right-aligning the string to the String variable.

RTrim Function

```
RTrim(string)
```

Returns a Variant of subtype String that contains a copy of a given *string* with any trailing spaces removed.

SavePicture Statement

```
SavePicture picture, stringexpression
```

Saves an graphic image from an object's Picture or Image property to a file. The *picture* argument specifies the control from which the graphics file is to be created (Picture or Image), and *stringexpression* specifies the path and filename to which the image is saved.

SaveSetting Statement

```
SaveSetting appname, section, key, setting
```

Saves or creates an application (*appname*) entry, section (*section*), key setting (*key*), and value (*setting*) in the System Registry.

Second Function

```
Second(time)
```

Returns a Variant of subtype Integer that represents the second (0[nd]59) of the time value specified by the *time* argument.

Seek Function

```
Seek(filenumber)
```

Returns a Long value that specifies the current record or byte position for the open file associated with *filenumber*. When dealing with Random files, Seek returns the number of the next record to be read or written. For all other file types, Seek returns a byte position.

Seek Statement

```
Seek [#]filenumber, position
```

Sets the record or byte *position* of the open file associated with *filenumber*.

Select Case Statement

```
Select Case testexpression
    [Case expressionlist-n
        [statements-n]] ...
    [Case Else
        [elsestatements]]
End Select
```

Evaluates an expression (*testexpression*) and, depending on the result, executes one or more statements (*statements-n*) that correspond to the expression's value (*expressionlist-n*). In other words, the value of *testexpression* is compared with one or more other values (*expressionlist-n*), and whichever matches gets its statements (*statements-n*) executed. If there are no matches, an optional Case Else set of statements (*elsestatements*) is executed.

SendKeys Statement

Generates one or more keystrokes as if they came from the keyboard. The *string* argument determines which keystrokes to send, and the optional Wait argument (Boolean) specifies whether keystrokes must be processed before control is returned to the procedure. False, the default value, means that control is returned to the procedure immediately after the keystrokes are sent.

Set Statement

```
Set objectvar = {[New] objectexpression ¦ Nothing}
```

Assigns an object reference (*objectexpression*) to a variable or property (*objectvar*). The optional New keyword can be used to indicate that the object should be created implicitly. To disassociate *objectvar* with a specific object and free up the resources it is using, assign it the Nothing keyword.

SetAttr Statement

```
SetAttr pathname, attributes
```

Sets attributes for the file or directory specified by the *pathname* argument. The *attributes* argument can use several VB constants (vbNormal, vbReadOnly, vbHidden, vbSystem, vbDirectory, and vbArchive) that can be combined bitwise to determine which attributes are set.

Sgn Function

```
Sgn(number)
```

Returns a Variant of subtype Integer that represents the sign of a given *number*.

Shell Function

```
Shell(pathname[, windowstyle])
```

Runs the executable program specified by the *pathname* argument and returns a Variant of subtype Double that represents the program's task ID. If Shell is unsuccessful, it returns zero. The optional *windowstyle* argument determines the style of the window in which the shelled program runs.

Sin Function

```
Sin(number)
```

Returns a Double value that represents the sine of a given angle (as specified by the *number* argument).

SLN Function

```
SLN(cost, salvage, life)
```

Returns a Double value that represents the straight-line depreciation of an asset when given its initial *cost*, *salvage* value at the end of its useful life, and *life* span.

Space **Function**

Space(*number*)

Returns a Variant of subtype String that contains a *number* of spaces.

Spc **Function**

Spc(*n*)

Inserts a specified number of spaces (*n*) when writing or displaying text using the Print # statement or the Print method.

Sqr **Function**

Sqr(*number*)

Returns a Double value that represents the square root of a given *number*.

Static **Statement**

Static *varname*[([*subscripts*])] [As [New] *type*] [, *varname*[([*subscripts*])]
[As [New] *type*] ...

Declares one or more static variables, which retain their values as long as the program is running. The *varname* argument is the name of the variable, and the optional As [New] *type* indicates its data type. If the New keyword is used, then an implicit creation of the object is made. The optional *subscripts* are the dimensions of an array variable.

Stop **Statement**

Stop

Suspends program execution.

Str **Function**

Str(*number*)

Returns a Variant of subtype String that is a representation of a given *number*.

StrComp Function

```
StrComp(string1, string2[, compare])
```

Returns a Variant of subtype Integer that indicates the result of a comparison between two strings (*string1* and *string2*). The optional *compare* argument specifies how strings are to be compared, with 0 for a binary comparison and 1 for a noncase-sensitive textual comparison.

StrConv Function

```
StrConv(string, conversion)
```

Returns a Variant of subtype String that has been converted from an original *string* as specified by the *conversion* argument. The *conversion* argument can use several VB constants to specify the type of conversion, such as vbUpperCase, vbLowerCase, and vbProperCase.

String Function

```
String(number, character)
```

Returns a Variant of subtype String that is of the length specified by *number* and is filled with a given *character*.

Sub Statement

```
[Public ¦ Private ¦ Friend] [Static] Sub name [(arglist)]
    [statements]
    [Exit Sub]
    [statements]
End Sub
```

Declares the various parts of a Sub procedure. The optional Public, Private, and Friend keywords can be used to define the Sub's scope, and the optional Static keyword indicates that the procedure's local variables are preserved between calls to the Sub. The *name* argument specifies the name of the Sub procedure. The optional Exit Sub can be used to exit the Sub procedure immediately.

The optional list of arguments (*arglist*) defines the arguments that will be passed to the procedure. The arguments should use the following syntax:

```
[Optional] [ByVal ¦ ByRef] [ParamArray] varname[()] [As _
type] [= default value]
```

where the Optional keyword can be used to specify that the argument is not required (*default value* assigns the argument's default value), ByVal and ByRef determine whether the argument should be passed by value or by reference (the default), and the ParamArray keyword specifies that the argument is an Optional array of Variant elements. ParamArray can only be used with the last argument in the argument list.

Switch Function

```
Switch(expr-1, value-1[, expr-2, value-2 ... [, expr-n, _
value-n]])
```

Evaluates a list of expressions (*expr-1*, *expr-2*...*expr-n*) and returns a Variant value that corresponds to the first expression that evaluates as True. If *expr-1* is True, then Switch returns the value indicated by *value-1*; if *expr-2* is True, then Switch returns the value indicated by *value-2*; and so on.

SYD Function

```
SYD(cost, salvage, life, period)
```

Returns a Double value that represents the sum-of-years' digits depreciation of an asset when given its initial *cost*, *salvage* value at the end of its useful life, *life* span, and *period* for which depreciation is calculated.

Tab Function

```
Tab(n)
```

Positions output to a given column (*n*) when writing or displaying text using the Print # statement or the Print method.

Tan Function

```
Tan(number)
```

Returns a Double value that represents the tangent of a given angle (specified by the *number* argument).

Time Function

```
Time
```

Returns a Variant of subtype Date that contains the current system time.

Time Statement

```
Time = time
```

Sets the system time to the time specified by the *time* argument.

Timer Function

```
Timer
```

Returns a Single value that represents the number of seconds that have elapsed since midnight.

TimeSerial Function

```
TimeSerial(hour, minute, second)
```

Returns a Variant of subtype Date that represents a time as specified by the *hour*, *minute*, and *second* arguments.

TimeValue Function

```
TimeValue(time)
```

Returns a Variant of subtype Date that is derived from the time value specified by the *time* argument.

Trim Function

```
Trim(string)
```

Returns a Variant of subtype String that contains a copy of a given *string* with any leading and trailing spaces removed.

Type Statement

```
[Private ¦ Public] Type varname
    elementname [([subscripts])] As type
    [elementname [([subscripts])] As type]
    ...
End Type
```

Defines a user-defined type (UDT) structure that contains one or more elements (*elementname*). The optional Public and Private keywords specify the UDT's scope, and *varname* specifies the UDT's name. Elements can be arrays (by specifying *subscripts*), and their data type must be defined using the As *type* clause. The Type statement can only be used at module level.

TypeName Function

```
TypeName(varname)
```

Returns a String value that indicates the data type of a given variable (*varname*). Possible return values are: Byte, Integer, Long, Single, Double, Currency, Decimal, Date, String, Boolean, Error, Empty, Null, Object, Unknown, Nothing, or an object type.

UBound Function

```
UBound(arrayname[, dimension])
```

Returns a Long value that represents the largest subscript for a dimensioned array (*arrayname*). For multidimensional arrays, the *dimension* argument can be included to specify which dimension should be used.

UCase Function

UCase(*string*)

Converts a *string* to all uppercase characters and returns a new String value.

Unload Statement

Unload *object*

Unloads an *object* (such as a form or control) from memory and frees up any resources being used by the object.

Unlock Statement

Unlock [#]*filenumber*[, *recordrange*]

Removes locking that prevents another process from accessing all or part of the open file that corresponds to the *filenumber* argument. The *recordrange* argument refers to a range of records (or bytes) that are to be unlocked and should use the syntax:

recnumber ¦ [*start*] To *end*

where *recnumber* is the record number (for Random files) or byte position (for Binary files) where unlocking should begin. Alternatively, the starting and ending record numbers or bytes to be unlocked can be specified using the *start* and *end* arguments.

Val Function

Val(*string*)

Returns the numeric value of a *string*. The data type that is returned by Val depends on the kind of numeric value the string contains. If the string does not contain a numeric value, then Val returns zero.

VarType Function

```
VarType(varname)
```

Returns an Integer value that represents the subtype of the variable specified by *varname*. Several VB constants are used to define the data type values returned by the VarType function, including: vbEmpty, vbNull, vbInteger, vbLong, vbSingle, vbDouble, vbCurrency, vbDate, vbString, vbObject, vbError, vbBoolean, vbVariant, vbDataObject, vbDecimal, vbByte, and vbArray.

Weekday Function

```
Weekday(date, [firstdayofweek])
```

Returns a Variant of subtype Integer that represents the day of the week for a given *date*. Weekday returns a 1 for Sunday, 2 for Monday, and so on. The optional *firstdayofweek* argument can be used to specify the first day of the week. If *firstdayofweek* is not specified, then Sunday (1) is assumed.

While...Wend Statement

```
While condition
    [statements]
Wend
```

Repeats one or more *statements* while a *condition* remains True. When the *condition* becomes False, then control is passed to the line of code immediately following the While...Wend structure.

Width # Statement

```
Width #filenumber, width
```

Assigns an output line *width* (in characters) for the open file associated with *filenumber*.

With Statement

```
With object
    [statements]
End With
```

Executes one or more *statements* on a single *object* or user-defined type.

Write # Statement

```
Write #filenumber, [outputlist]
```

Writes data to the open sequential file associated with the *filenumber* argument. The *varlist* argument should contain one or more comma-delimited variables that contain the data to be written to the file.

Year Function

```
Year(date)
```

Returns a Variant that represents the year for the date value specified by the *date* argument.

Summary

This chapter is designed to be a quick-reference for all of VB's built-in functions and statements, providing syntax and a brief description for each. For more information about particular functions and statements, consult Visual Basic's online Help system or Microsoft's *Visual Basic 5.0 Language Reference*.

Control Syntax: Properties, Events, and Methods

Visual Basic relies heavily on components, such as ActiveX controls and objects. Each component often has dozens of properties, events, and methods by which it can be modified or manipulated. It's often difficult to remember the details of a control or object's interface, especially if it is an object that is seldom used.

This appendix provides a quick reference to the properties, events, and methods of Visual Basic's many components. Not only are all the ActiveX controls detailed here, other important objects (such as Screen, Printer, and UserControl) are also included. Although this is not meant to be a complete reference, it may prove useful because it allows you to see all the properties, events, and methods for a control within the space of a page or two. It also provides pertinent information about each, such as the data types of properties, the syntax of methods, and the arguments of events. If you require a more in-depth source of information, Microsoft's *Visual Basic 6.0 Language Reference* and *Visual Basic 6.0 ActiveX Controls Reference* are highly recommended.

Each control or object in this appendix shows the full list of properties, events, and methods. A few notes about the way the information is presented are listed here:

- Properties, events, and methods that are common to many controls or objects are detailed at the beginning of this chapter. Any applicable common properties, events, and methods are also listed for each control and object in the chapter, but they are not detailed.

- Property listings give the data types, or the appropriate object type, collection name, or enumeration name for each property. Properties with an asterisk to the left of their names are read-only at runtime.

- Event listings show the arguments returned by the events, as well as each argument's data or object type.

- Method listings show the arguments that may be passed to the method, but they do not show the arguments' data or object type. Optional arguments are enclosed in brackets.

- In some cases, a control will utilize an object that has its own set of properties, events, and methods. The object's interface elements are not included in this reference.

Common Properties, Events, and Methods

Many properties, events, and methods are common to many controls. For example, the BorderStyle property is used in several different controls. In some, it is implemented as an Integer value. Others use the BorderStyleConstants enumeration type.

This section lists many common properties, events, and methods used in Visual Basic. The information here portrays the most commonly used formats. However, some controls may use slightly different implementations. For example, an event may return different arguments, or a method may have a different syntax.

Common Properties

The following list includes properties that are common to several different controls.

*Appearance	Integer
BackColor	Long
*BorderStyle	Integer or BorderStyleConstants Enum
Container	Object
DataBindings	DataBindings Collection
DataChanged	Boolean
DataField	String
DragIcon	IPictureDisp Object
DragMode	Integer
Enabled	Boolean
Font	StdFont Object or IFontDisp Object
FontBold	Boolean
FontItalic	Boolean
FontName	String
FontSize	Single
FontStrikethru	Boolean
FontTransparent	Boolean
FontUnderline	Boolean
ForeColor	Long
*hDC	Long
Height	Single
HelpContextID	Long
*hWnd	Long
*Index	Integer
Left	Single
LinkItem	String
LinkMode	Integer
LinkTopic	String
LinkTimeout	Integer
MouseIcon	IPictureDisp Object

MousePointer	Integer
*Name	String
*Object	Object
OLEDragMode	Integer
OLEDropMode	Integer
*Parent	Form Object or Object
RightToLeft	Boolean
ScaleHeight	Single
ScaleLeft	Single
ScaleMode	Integer
ScaleTop	Single
ScaleWidth	Single
TabIndex	Integer
TabStop	Boolean
Tag	String
ToolTipText	String
Top	Single
Visible	Boolean
WhatsThisHelpID	Long
Width	Single

Common Events

The following list includes events that are common to several different controls.

```
Click()
```

```
DblClick()
```

```
DragDrop(source As Control, x As Single, y As Single)
```

```
DragOver(source As Control, x As Single, y As Single, state
As Integer)
```

```
GotFocus()
```

```
KeyDown(keycode As Integer, shift As Integer)
```

```
KeyPress(keyascii As Integer)
```

KeyUp(*keycode* As Integer, *shift* As Integer)

LinkClose()

LinkError(*linkerr* As Integer)

LinkExecute(*cmdstr* As String, *cancel* As Integer)

LinkNotify([*index* As Integer])

LinkOpen(*cancel* As Integer)

LostFocus()

MouseDown(*button* As Integer, *shift* As Integer, *x* As Single, *y* As Single)

MouseMove(*button* As Integer, *shift* As Integer, *x* As Single, *y* As Single)

MouseUp(*button* As Integer, *shift* As Integer, *x* As Single, *y* As Single)

OLECompleteDrag(*effect* As Long)

OLEDragDrop(*data* As DataObject, *effect* As Long, *button* As Integer, *shift* As Integer, *x* As Single, *y* As Single)

OLEDragOver(*data* As DataObject, *effect* As Long, *button* As Integer, *shift* As Integer, *x* As Single, *y* As Single, *state* As Integer)

OLEGiveFeedback(*effect* As Long, *defaultcursors* As Boolean)

OLESetData(*data* As DataObject, *dataFormat* As Integer)

OLEStartDrag(*data* As DataObject, *allowedeffects* As Long)

Common Methods

The following list includes methods that are common to several different controls.

Drag	*object*.Drag(*action*)
LinkExecute	*object*.LinkExecute(*cmdstr*, *cancel*)
LinkPoke	*object*.LinkPoke
LinkRequest	*object*.LinkRequest
LinkSend	*object*.LinkSend
Move	*object*.Move(*rows*, *start*)
OLEDrag	*object*.OLEDrag

Refresh	*object*.Refresh
Scale	*object*.Scale(*x1*, *y1*)-(*x2*, *y2*)
ScaleX	*object*.ScaleX(*width*, *fromscale*, *toscale*)
ScaleY	*object*.ScaleY(*height*, *fromscale*, *toscale*)
SetFocus	*object*.SetFocus
ShowWhatsThis	*object*.ShowWhatsThis
ZOrder	*object*.ZOrder(*position*)

Animation

Properties

Common Properties: BackColor, Container, DragIcon, DragMode,
Enabled, Height, HelpContextID, hWnd, Index, Left, Name, Object,
OLEDropMode, Parent, TabIndex, TabStop, Tag, ToolTipText, Top,
Visible, WhatsThisHelpID, Width

AutoPlay	Boolean
BackStyle	Integer
Center	Boolean

Events

Common Events: Click, DblClick, DragDrop, DragOver, GotFocus,
LostFocus, MouseDown, MouseMove, MouseUp, OLECompleteDrag,
OLEDragDrop, OLEGiveFeedback, OLESetData, OLEStartDrag

Methods

Common Methods: Drag, Move, OLEDrag, SetFocus,
ShowWhatsThis, ZOrder

Close	*object*.Close
Open	*object*.Open (*file*)
Play	*object*.Play ([*repeatcount*], [*startframe*],
[*endframe*])	
Stop	*object*.Stop

CheckBox

Properties

Common Properties: Appearance, BackColor, Container, DataChanged, DataField, DragIcon, DragMode, Enabled, Font, FontBold, FontItalic, FontName, FontSize, FontStrikethru, FontUnderline, ForeColor, Height, HelpContextID, hWnd, Index, Left, MouseIcon, MousePointer, Name, OLEDropMode, Parent, RightToLeft, TabIndex, TabStop, Tag, ToolTipText, Top, Visible, WhatsThisHelpID, Width

*Alignment	Integer
Caption	String
DisabledPicture	IPictureDisp Object
DownPicture	IPictureDisp Object
MaskColor	Long
Picture	IPictureDisp Object
*Style	Integer
UseMaskColor	Boolean
Value	Integer

Events

Common Events: Click, DragDrop, DragOver, GotFocus, KeyDown, KeyPress, KeyUp, LostFocus, MouseDown, MouseMove, MouseUp, OLECompleteDrag, OLEDragDrop, OLEDragOver, OLEGiveFeedback, OLESetData, OLEStartDrag

Methods

Common Methods: Drag, Move, OLEDrag, Refresh, SetFocus, ShowWhatsThis, ZOrder

ComboBox

Properties

Common Properties: Appearance, BackColor, Container, DataChanged, DataField, DragIcon, DragMode, Enabled, Font, FontBold, FontItalic, FontName, FontSize, FontStrikethru, FontUnderline, ForeColor, Height, HelpContextID, hWnd, Index, Left, MouseIcon, MousePointer, Name, OLEDragMode, OLEDropMode, Parent, RightToLeft, TabIndex, TabStop, Tag, ToolTipText, Top, Visible, WhatsThisHelpID, Width

*IntegralHeight	Boolean
ItemData	Long Array
List	String Array
*ListCount	Integer
ListIndex	Integer
Locked	Boolean
*NewIndex	Integer
SelLength	Long
SelStart	Long
SelText	String
*Sorted	Boolean
*Style	Integer
Text	String
TopIndex	Integer

Events

Common Events: Click, DblClick, DragDrop, DragOver, GotFocus, KeyDown, KeyPress, KeyUp, LostFocus, OLECompleteDrag, OLEDragDrop, OLEDragOver, OLEGiveFeedback, OLESetData, OLEStartDrag

Change()

DropDown()

Scroll()

Methods

Common Methods: Drag, Move, OLEDrag, Refresh, SetFocus, ShowWhatsThis, ZOrder

AddItem	*object*.AddItem(*item* [, *index*])
Clear	*object*.Clear
RemoveItem	*object*.RemoveItem(*index*)

CommandButton

Properties

Common Properties: Appearance, BackColor, Container, DragIcon, DragMode, Enabled, Font, FontBold, FontItalic, FontName, FontSize, FontStrikethru, FontUnderline, Height, HelpContextID, hWnd, Index, Left, MouseIcon, MousePointer, Name, OLEDropMode, Parent, RightToLeft, TabIndex, TabStop, Tag, ToolTipText, Top, Visible, WhatsThisHelpID, Width

Cancel	Boolean
Caption	String
Default	Boolean
DisabledPicture	IPictureDisp Object
DownPicture	IPictureDisp Object
MaskColor	Long
Picture	IPictureDisp Object
*Style	Integer
UseMaskColor	Boolean
Value	Boolean

Events

Common Events: Click, DragDrop, DragOver, GotFocus, KeyDown, KeyPress, KeyUp, LostFocus, MouseDown, MouseMove, MouseUp, OLECompleteDrag, OLEDragDrop, OLEDragOver, OLEGiveFeedback, OLESetData, OLEStartDrag

Methods

Common Methods: Drag, Move, OLEDrag, Refresh, SetFocus, ShowWhatsThis, ZOrder

Common Dialog

Properties

Common Properties: FontBold, FontItalic, FontName, FontSize, FontStrikethru, FontUnderline, hDC, Index, Name, Object, Parent, Tag

Action	Integer
CancelError	Boolean
Color	OLE_COLOR
Copies	Integer
DefaultExt	String
DialogTitle	String
FileName	String
FileTitle	String
Filter	String
FilterIndex	Integer
Flags	Long
HelpCommand	Integer
HelpContext	Long
HelpFile	String
HelpKey	String
InitDir	String
Max	Integer
MaxFileSize	Integer
Min	Integer
PrinterDefault	Boolean
ToPage	Integer

Events

No events

Methods

ShowColor	*object*.ShowColor
ShowFont	*object*.ShowFont
ShowHelp	*object*.ShowHelp
ShowOpen	*object*.ShowOpen
ShowPrinter	*object*.ShowPrinter
ShowSave	*object*.ShowSave

Data

Properties

Common Properties: Appearance, BackColor, DragIcon, DragMode, Enabled, Font, FontBold, FontItalic, FontName, FontSize, FontStrikethru, FontUnderline, ForeColor, Height, Index, Left, MouseIcon, MousePointer, Name, OLEDropMode, Parent, RightToLeft, Tag, ToolTipText, Top, Visible, WhatsThisHelpID, Width

Align	Integer
BOFAction	Integer
Caption	String
Connect	String
*Database	Database Object
DatabaseName	String
DefaultCursorType	Integer
DefaultType	Integer
*EditMode	Integer
EOFAction	Integer
Exclusive	Boolean
Options	Integer

ReadOnly	Boolean
Recordset	Recordset Object
RecordsetType	Integer
RecordSource	String

Events

Common Events: DragDrop, DragOver, MouseDown, MouseMove, MouseUp, OLECompleteDrag, OLEDragDrop, OLEGiveFeedback, OLESetData, OLEStartDrag, Resize

Error(*dataerr* As Integer, *response* As Integer)

Reposition()

Validate(*action* As Integer, *save* As Integer)

Methods

Common Methods: Drag, Move, OLEDrag, Refresh, ShowWhatsThis, ZOrder

UpdateControls
object.UpdateControls

UpdateRecord   *object*.UpdateRecord

DBCombo

Properties

Common Properties: Appearance, BackColor, Container, DataBindings, DataChanged, DataField, DragIcon, DragMode, Enabled, Font, ForeColor, Height, HelpContextID, hWnd, Index, Left, MouseIcon, MousePointer, Name, Object, OLEDragMode, OLEDropMode, Parent, RightToLeft, TabIndex, TabStop, Tag, Text, ToolTipText, Top, Visible, WhatsThisHelpID, Width

BoundColumn	String
BoundText	String
IntegralHeight	Boolean

ListField	String
Locked	Boolean
*MatchedWithList	Boolean
MatchEntry	MatchEntryConstants Enum
RowSource	IRowCursor Object
*SelectedItem	Variant
SelLength	Long
SelStart	Long
SelText	String
Style	StyleConstants Enum
*VisibleCount	Integer
*VisibleItems	Variant Array

Events

Common Events: Click, DblClick, DragDrop, DragOver, GotFocus, KeyDown, KeyPress, KeyUp, LostFocus, MouseDown, MouseMove, MouseUp, OLECompleteDrag, OLEDragDrop, OLEDragOver, OLEGiveFeedback, OLESetData, OLEStartDrag

Change()

Methods

Common Methods: Drag, Move, OLEDrag, Refresh, SetFocus, ShowWhatsThis, ZOrder

ReFill   *object*.ReFill

DBGrid

Properties

Common Properties: Appearance, BackColor, BorderStyle, Container, DataBindings, DataChanged, DragIcon, DragMode, Enabled, Font, ForeColor, Height, HelpContextID, hWnd, Index, Left,

Name, Object, Parent, TabIndex, TabStop, Tag, ToolTipText, Top, Visible, WhatsThisHelpID, Width

AddNewMode	*enum*AddNewModeConstants Enum
Align	Integer
AllowAddNew	Boolean
AllowArrows	Boolean
AllowDelete	Boolean
AllowRowSizing	Boolean
AllowUpdate	Boolean
ApproxCount	Long
Bookmark	Variant
Caption	String
Col	Integer
ColumnHeaders	Boolean
*Columns	Object Array
CurrentCellModified	Boolean
CurrentCellVisible	Boolean
DataMode	enumDataModeConstants Enum
DataSource	ICursor Object
DefColWidth	Single
EditActive	Boolean
ErrorText	String
FirstRow	Variant
HeadFont	IFontDisp Object
HeadLines	Single
hWndEditor	OLE_HANDLE Object
LeftCol	Integer
MarqueeStyle	enumMarqueeStyleConstants Enum
MarqueeUnique	Boolean
RecordSelectors	Boolean
Row	Integer
RowDividerStyle	enumDividerStyleConstants Enum

RowHeight	Single
ScrollBars	enumScrollBarConstants Enum
*SelBookmarks	Variant Array
SelEndCol	Integer
SelLength	Long
SelStart	Long
SelStartCol	Integer
SelText	String
Split	Integer
Splits	Object Array
TabAcrossSplits	Boolean
TabAction	enumTabActionConstants Enum
Text	String
VisibleCols	Integer
VisibleRows	Integer
WrapCellPointer	Boolean

Events

Common Events: Click, DblClick, DragDrop, DragOver, GotFocus, KeyDown, KeyPress, KeyUp, LostFocus, MouseDown, MouseMove, MouseUp

AfterColEdit([*index* As Integer,] ByVal *colindex* As Integer)

AfterColUpdate([*index* As Integer,] *colindex* As Integer)

AfterDelete([*index* As Integer,] *colindex* As Integer)

AfterInsert(*index* As Integer)

AfterUpdate(*index* As Integer)

BeforeColEdit([*index* As Integer,] ByVal *colindex* As Integer,
        ByVal *keyascii* As Integer, *cancel* As Integer)

BeforeColUpdate([*index* As Integer,] *colindex* As Integer,
        oldvalue As Variant, *cancel* As Integer)

BeforeDelete([*index* As Integer,] *cancel* As Integer)

BeforeInsert([*index* As Integer,] *cancel* As Integer)

```
BeforeUpdate([index As Integer,] cancel As Integer)

ButtonClick([index As Integer,] ByVal colindex As Integer)

Change([index As Integer])

ColEdit([index As Integer,] ByVal colindex As Integer)

ColResize([index As Integer,] colindex As Integer,
        cancel As Integer)

Error([index As Integer,] ByVal dataerror As Integer,
        response As Integer)

HeadClick([index As Integer,] colindex As Integer)

OnAddNew([index As Integer])

RowColChange([index As Integer, lastrow As String,
        lastcol As Integer])

RowResize([index As Integer,] cancel As Integer)

Scroll([cancel As Integer])

SelChange([index As Integer,] cancel As Integer)

SplitChange([index As Integer])

UnboundAddData(rowbuf As RowBuffer, newrowbookmark As
Variant)

UnboundDeleteRow(bookmark As Variant)

UnboundGetRelativeBookmark([index As Integer,]
        startlocation As Variant, ByVal offset As Long,
        newlocation As Variant, approximateposition As
Long)

UnboundReadData(rowbuf As RowBuffer, startlocation As
Variant,
        readpriorrows As Boolean)

UnboundWriteData(rowbuf As RowBuffer, writelocation As
Variant)
```

Methods

Common Methods: Drag, Move, Refresh, ZOrder

```
AboutBox              object.AboutBox

CaptureImage          object.CaptureImage
```

ClearFields	*object*.ClearFields
ClearSelCols	*object*.ClearSelCols
ColContaining	*object*.ColContaining (*coordinate*)
GetBookmark	*object*.GetBookmark (*value*)
HoldFields	*object*.HoldFields
ReBind	*object*.Rebind
RowBookmark	*object*.RowBookmark (*value*)
RowContaining	*object*.RowContaining (*coordinate*)
RowTop	*object*.RowTop (*value*)
Scroll	*object*.Scroll (*colvalue*, *rowvalue*)

DBList

Properties

Common Properties: Appearance, BackColor, Container, DataBindings, DataChanged, DataField, DragIcon, DragMode, Enabled, Font, ForeColor, Height, HelpContextID, hWnd, Index, Left, MouseIcon, MousePointer, Name, Object, OLEDragMode, OLEDropMode, Parent, RightToLeft, TabIndex, TabStop, Tag, ToolTipText, Top, Visible, WhatsThisHelpID, Width

BoundColumn	String
BoundText	String
IntegralHeight	Boolean
ListField	String
Locked	Boolean
*MatchedWithList	Boolean
RowSource	IRowCursor Object
*SelectedItems	Variant
Text	String
*VisibleCount	Integer
*VisibleItems	Variant Array

Events

Common Events: Click, DblClick, DragDrop, DragOver, GotFocus, KeyDown, KeyPress, KeyUp, LostFocus, MouseDown, MouseMove, MouseUp, OLECompleteDrag, OLEDragDrop, OLEDragOver, OLEGiveFeedback, OLESetData, OLEStartDrag

Methods

Common Methods: Drag, Move, OLEDrag, Refresh, SetFocus, ShowWhatsThis, ZOrder

ReFill   *object*.ReFill

DirListBox

Properties

Common Properties: Appearance, BackColor, Container, DragIcon, DragMode, Enabled, Font, FontBold, FontItalic, FontName, FontSize, FontStrikethru, FontUnderline, ForeColor, Height, HelpContextID, hWnd, Index, Left, MouseIcon, MousePointer, Name, OLEDragMode, OLEDropMode, Parent, TabIndex, TabStop, Tag, ToolTipText, Top, Visible, WhatsThisHelpID, Width

*List	String Array
*ListCount	Integer
ListIndex	Integer
Path	String
TopIndex	Integer

Events

Common Events: Click, DragDrop, DragOver, GotFocus, KeyDown, KeyPress, KeyUp, LostFocus, MouseDown, MouseMove, MouseUp, OLECompleteDrag, OLEDragDrop, OLEDragOver, OLEGiveFeedback, OLESetData, OLEStartDrag

Change([*index* As Integer])

Scroll()

Methods

Common Methods: Drag, Move, OLEDrag, Refresh, SetFocus, ShowWhatsThis, ZOrder

DriveListBox

Properties

Common Properties: Appearance, BackColor, Container, DragIcon, DragMode, Enabled, Font, FontBold, FontItalic, FontName, FontSize, FontStrikethru, FontUnderline, ForeColor, Height, HelpContextID, hWnd, Index, Left, MouseIcon, MousePointer, Name, OLEDropMode, Parent, TabIndex, TabStop, Tag, ToolTipText, Top, Visible, WhatsThisHelpID, Width

Drive	String
*List	String Array
*ListCount	Integer
ListIndex	Integer
TopIndex	Integer

Events

Common Events: DragDrop, DragOver, GotFocus, KeyDown, KeyPress, KeyUp, LostFocus, OLECompleteDrag, OLEDragDrop, OLEDragOver, OLEGiveFeedback, OLESetData, OLEStartDrag

Change([*index* As Integer)

Scroll()

Methods

Common Methods: Drag, Move, OLEDrag, Refresh, SetFocus, ShowWhatsThis, ZOrder

FileListBox

Properties

Common Properties: Appearance, BackColor, Container, DragIcon, DragMode, Enabled, Font, FontBold, FontItalic, FontName, FontSize, FontStrikethru, FontUnderline, ForeColor, Height, HelpContextID, hWnd, Index, Left, MouseIcon, MousePointer, Name, OLEDragMode, OLEDropMode, Parent, TabIndex, TabStop, Tag, ToolTipText, Top, Visible, WhatsThisHelpID, Width

Archive	Boolean
FileName	String
Hidden	Boolean
*List	String Array
*ListCount	Integer
ListIndex	Integer
*MultiSelect	Integer
Normal	Boolean
Path	String
Pattern	String
ReadOnly	Boolean
Selected	Boolean Array
System	Boolean
TopIndex	Integer

Events

Common Events: Click, DblClick, DragOver, GotFocus, KeyDown, KeyPress, KeyUp, LostFocus, MouseDown, MouseMove, MouseUp, OLECompleteDrag, OLEDragOver, OLEGiveFeedback, OLESetData, OLEStartDrag

PathChange([*index* As Integer])

PatternChange([*index* As Integer])

Scroll()

Methods

Common Methods: Drag, Move, OLEDrag, Refresh, SetFocus, ShowWhatsThis, ZOrder

Form

Properties

Common Properties: Appearance, BackColor, Enabled, Font, FontBold, FontItalic, FontName, FontSize, FontStrikethru, FontTransparent, FontUnderline, ForeColor, hDC, Height, HelpContextID, hWnd, Left, LinkMode, LinkTopic, MouseIcon, MousePointer, Name, OLEDropMode, RightToLeft, ScaleHeight, ScaleLeft, ScaleMode, ScaleTop, ScaleWidth, Tag, Top, Visible, Width

*ActiveControl	Control Object
AutoRedraw	Boolean
*BorderStyle	Integer
Caption	String
*ClipControls	Boolean
*ControlBox	Boolean
*Controls	Object
*Count	Integer
CurrentX	Single
CurrentY	Single
DrawMode	Integer
DrawStyle	Integer
DrawWidth	Integer
FillColor	Long
FillStyle	Integer
Icon	IPictureDisp Object
*Image	IPictureDisp Object
KeyPreview	Boolean

*MaxButton	Boolean
*MDIChild	Boolean
*MinButton	Boolean
*Moveable	Boolean
Palette	IPictureDisp Object
PaletteMode	Integer
Picture	IPictureDisp Object
*ShowInTaskbar	Boolean
*StartUpPosition	Integer
*WhatsThisButton	Boolean
*WhatsThisHelp	Boolean
WindowState	Integer

Events

Common Events: Click, DblClick, DragDrop, DragOver, GotFocus, KeyDown, KeyPress, KeyUp, LinkClose, LinkError, LinkExecute, LinkOpen, LostFocus, MouseDown, MouseMove, MouseUp, OLECompleteDrag, OLEDragDrop, OLEDragOver, OLEGiveFeedback, OLESetData, OLEStartDrag

Activate()

Deactivate()

Initialize()

Load()

Paint()

QueryUnload(*cancel* As Integer, *unloadmode* As Integer)

Resize()

Terminate()

Unload(*cancel* As Integer)

Methods

Common Methods: Move, OLEDrag, Refresh, Scale, ScaleX, ScaleY, SetFocus, ZOrder

Circle	*object*.Circle [Step] (*x*, *y*), [*color*, *start*, *end*, *aspect*]
Cls	*object*.Cls
Hide	*object*.Hide
Line	*object*.Line [Step] (*x1*, *y1*) [Step] (*x2*, *y2*), [*color*], [B][F]
PaintPicture	*object*.PaintPicture(*picture*, *x1*, *y1*, *width1*, *height1*, *x2*, *y2*, *width2*, *height2*, *opcode*)
Point	*object*.Point(*x*, *y*)
PopupMenu	*object*.PopupMenu(*menuname*, *flags*, *x*, *y*, *boldcommand*)
PrintForm	*object*.PrintForm
PSet	*object*.PSet [Step] (*x*, *y*), [*color*]
Show	*object*.Show(*style*, *ownerform*)
TextHeight	*object*.TextHeight(*string*)
TextWidth	*object*.TextWidth(*string*)
WhatsThisMode	*object*.WhatsThisMode

Frame

Properties

Common Properties: Appearance, BackColor, BorderStyle, Container, DragIcon, DragMode, Enabled, Font, FontBold, FontItalic, FontName, FontSize, FontStrikethru, FontUnderline, ForeColor, Height, HelpContextID, hWnd, Index, Left, MouseIcon, MousePointer, Name, OLEDropMode, Parent, RightToLeft, TabIndex, Tag, ToolTipText, Top, Visible, WhatsThisHelpID, Width

Caption	String
*ClipControls	Boolean

Events

Common Events: Click, DblClick, DragOver, MouseDown, MouseUp, OLECompleteDrag, OLEDragDrop, OLEDragOver, OLEGiveFeedback, OLESetData, OLEStartDrag

Methods

Common Methods: Drag, Move, OLEDrag, Refresh, ShowWhatsThis, ZOrder

HScrollBar

Properties

Common Properties: Container, DragIcon, DragMode, Enabled, Height, HelpContextID, hWnd, Index, Left, MouseIcon, MousePointer, Name, Parent, RightToLeft, TabIndex, TabStop, Tag, Top, Visible, WhatsThisHelpID, Width

LargeChange	Integer
Max	Integer
Min	Integer
SmallChange	Integer
Value	Integer

Events

Common Events: DragDrop, DragOver, GotFocus, KeyDown, KeyPress, KeyUp, LostFocus

Change([*index* As Integer])

Scroll()

Methods

Common Methods: Drag, Move, Refresh, SetFocus, ShowWhatsThis, ZOrder

Image

Properties

Common Properties: Appearance, BorderStyle, Container, DragIcon, DragMode, Enabled, Height, Index, Left, MouseIcon, MousePointer, Name, OLEDragMode, OLEDropMode, Parent, Tag, ToolTipText, Top, Visible, WhatsThisHelpID, Width

DataChanged	Boolean
DataField	String
Picture	IPictureDisp Object
Stretch	Boolean

Events

Common Events: Click, DblClick, DragDrop, DragOver, MouseDown, MouseMove, MouseUp, OLECompleteDrag, OLEDragDrop, OLEDragOver, OLEGiveFeedback, OLESetData, OLEStartDrag

Methods

Common Methods: Drag, Move, OLEDrag, Refresh, ShowWhatsThis, ZOrder

ImageList

Properties

Common Properties: BackColor, Index, Name, Object, Parent, Tag

hImageList	OLE_HANDLE Object
ImageHeight	Integer
ImageWidth	Integer
ListImages	ListImages Collection
MaskColor	OLE_COLOR Object
UseMaskColor	Boolean

Events

No events

Methods

Overlay   *object*.Overlay(*key1*, *key2*) As IPictureDisp

Internet Transfer (Inet)

Properties

Common Properties: Index, Name, Object, Parent, Tag

AccessType	AccessConstants Enum
Document	String
*hInternet	Long
Password	String
Protocol	ProtocolConstants Enum
Proxy	String
RemoteHost	String
RemotePort	Integer
RequestTimeout	Long
*ResponseCode	Long
*ResponseInfo	String
*StillExecuting	Boolean
URL	String
UserName	String

Events

StateChanged(ByVal *state* As Integer)

Methods

Cancel	*object*.**Cancel**
Execute	*object*.Execute(*url*, *operation*, *data*, *requestheaders*)
GetChunk	*object*.GetChunk(*size* [, *datatype*])
GetHeader	*object*.GetHeader(*hrdname*)
OpenURL	*object*.OpenURL(*url* [, *datatype*])

Label

Properties

Common Properties: Appearance, BackColor, BorderStyle, Container, DataChanged, DataField, DragIcon, DragMode, Enabled, Font, FontBold, FontItalics, FontName, FontSize, FontStrikethru, FontUnderline, ForeColor, Height, Index, Left, LinkItem, LinkMode, LinkTimeout, LinkTopic, MouseIcon, MousePointer, Name, OLEDropMode, Parent, RightToLeft, TabIndex, Tag, ToolTipText, Top, Visible, WhatsThisHelpID, Width

Alignment	Integer
AutoSize	Boolean
BackStyle	Integer
Caption	String
UseMnemonic	Boolean
WordWrap	Boolean

Events

Common Events: Click, DblClick, DragDrop, DragOver, LinkClose, LinkError, LinkNotify, LinkOpen, MouseDown, MouseMove, MouseUp, OLECompleteDrag, OLEDragDrop, OLEDragOver, OLEGiveFeedback, OLESetData, OLEStartDrag

Change()

Methods

Common Methods: Drag, LinkExecute, LinkPoke, LinkRequest, LinkSend, Move, OLEDrag, Refresh, ShowWhatsThis, ZOrder

Line

Properties

Common Properties: BorderStyle, Container, Index, Name, Parent, Tag, Visible

BorderColor	Long
BorderWidth	Integer
DrawMode	Integer
X1	Single
X2	Single
Y1	Single
Y2	Single

Events

No events

Methods

Common Methods: Refresh, ZOrder

ListBox

Properties

Common Properties: Appearance, BackColor, Container, DataChanged, DataField, DragIcon, DragMode, Enabled, Font, FontBold, FontItalic, FontName, FontSize, FontStrikethru, FontUnderline, ForeColor, Height, HelpContextID, hWnd, Index,

Left, MouseIcon, MousePointer, Name, OLEDragMode, Parent,
RightToLeft, TabIndex, TabStop, Tag, ToolTipText, Top, Visible,
WhatsThisHelpID, Width

Columns	Integer
*IntegralHeight	Boolean
ItemData	Long Array
List	String Array
*ListCount	Integer
ListIndex	Integer
*MultiSelect	Integer
*NewIndex	Integer
*SelCount	Integer
Selected	Boolean Array
*Sorted	Boolean
*Style	Integer
Text	String
TopIndex	Integer

Events

Common Events: Click, DblClick, DragDrop, DragOver, GotFocus,
KeyDown, KeyPress, KeyUp, LostFocus, MouseDown, MouseMove,
MouseUp, OLECompleteDrag, OLEDragDrop, OLEDragOver,
OLEGiveFeedback, OLESetData, OLEStartDrag

ItemCheck(*item* As Integer)
Scroll()

Methods

Common Methods: Drag, Move, OLEDrag, Refresh, SetFocus,
ShowWhatsThis, ZOrder

AddItem	*object*.AddItem(*item* [, *index*])
Clear	*object*.Clear
RemoveItem	*object*.RemoveItem(*index*)

ListView

Properties

Common Properties: Appearance, BackColor, BorderStyle, Container, DragIcon, DragMode, Enabled, Font, ForeColor, Height, HelpContextID, hWnd, Index, Left, MouseIcon, MousePointer, Name, Object, OLEDragMode, OLEDropMode, Parent, TabIndex, TabStop, Tag, ToolTipText, Top, Visible, WhatsThisHelpID, Width

Arrange	ListArrangeConstants
ColumnHeaders	ColumnHeaders Collection
DropHighlight	ListItem Object
HideColumnHeader	Boolean
HideSelection	Boolean
Icons	Object
LabelEdit	ListLabelEditConstants
LabelWrap	Boolean
ListItems	ListItems Collection
MultiSelect	Boolean
SelectedItem	ListItem Object
SmallIcons	Object
Sorted	Boolean
SortKey	Integer
SortOrder	ListSortOrderConstants
View	ListViewConstants

Events

Common Events: Click, DblClick, DragDrop, DragOver, GotFocus, KeyDown, KeyPress, KeyUp, LostFocus, MouseDown, MouseMove, MouseUp, OLECompleteDrag, OLEDragDrop, OLEDragOver, OLEGiveFeedback, OLESetData, OLEStartDrag

AfterLabelEdit(*cancel* As Integer, *newstring* As String)

BeforeLabelEdit(*cancel* As Integer)

ColumnClick(*colheader* As ColumnHeader)

ItemClick(*item* As ListItem)

Methods

Common Methods: Drag, Move, OLEDrag, Refresh, SetFocus, ShowWhatsThis, ZOrder

FindItem	*object*.FindItem (*string*, [*value*], [*index*], [*match*]) As ListItem
GetFirstVisible	*object*.GetFirstVisible() As ListItem
HitTest	*object*.HitTest (*x*, *y*) As ListItem
StartLabelEdit	*object*.StartLabelEdit

MAPIMessages

Properties

Common Properties: Index, Name, Object, Parent, Tag

Action	Integer
AddressCaption	String
AddressEditFieldCount	Integer
AddressLabel	String
AddressModifiable	Boolean
AddressResolveUI	Boolean
AttachmentCount	Long
AttachmentIndex	Long
AttachmentName	String
AttachmentPathName	String
AttachmentPosition	Long
AttachmentType	Integer
FetchMsgType	String
FetchSorted	Boolean
FetchUnreadOnly	Boolean
MsgConversationID	String
MsgCount	Long

MsgDateReceived	String
MsgID	String
MsgIndex	Long
MsgNoteText	String
MsgOrigAddress	String
MsgOrigDisplayName	String
MsgRead	Boolean
MsgReceiptRequested	Boolean
MsgSent	Boolean
MsgSubject	String
MsgType	String
RecipAddress	String
RecipCount	Long
RecipDisplayName	String
RecipIndex	Long
RecipType	Integer
SessionID	Long

Events

No events

Methods

Compose	*object*.Compose
Copy	*object*.Copy
Delete	*object*.Delete ([*value*])
Fetch	*object*.Fetch
Forward	*object*.Forward
Reply	*object*.Reply
ReplyAll	*object*.ReplyAll
ResolveName	*object*.ResolveName
Save	*object*.Save
Send	*object*.Send ([*value*])
Show	*object*.Show ([*value*])

MAPISession

Properties

Common Properties: Index, Name, Object, Parent, Tag

Action	Integer
DownloadMail	Boolean
LogonUI	Boolean
NewSession	Boolean
Password	String
SessionID	Long
UserName	String

Events

No events

Methods

SignOff	*object*.SignOff
SignOn	*object*.SignOn

Masked Edit (MaskEdBox)

Properties

Common Properties: Appearance, BackColor, BorderStyle, Container, DataBindings, DataChanged, DataField, DragIcon, DragMode, Enabled, Font, ForeColor, Height, HelpContextID, hWnd, Index, Left, MouseIcon, MousePointer, Name, Object, OLEDragMode, OLEDropMode, Parent, TabIndex, TabStop, Tag, ToolTipText, Top, Visible, WhatsThisHelpID, Width

AllowPrompt	Boolean
AutoTab	Boolean
ClipMode	ClipModeConstants
ClipText	String

Format	String
FormattedText	String
Mask	String
MaxLength	Integer
PromptChar	String
PromptInclude	Boolean
SelLength	Long
SelStart	Long
SelText	Long
Text	String

Events

Common Events: DragDrop, GotFocus, KeyDown, KeyPress, KeyUp, LostFocus, OLECompleteDrag, OLEDragDrop, OLEDragOver, OLEGiveFeedback, OLESetData, OLEStartDrag

Change()

ValidationError(*invalidtext* As String, *startpos* As Integer)

Methods

Common Methods: Drag, Move, OLEDrag, Refresh, SetFocus, ShowWhatsThis, ZOrder

MDIForm

Properties

Common Properties: Appearance, BackColor, Enabled, Height, HelpContextID, hWnd, Left, LinkMode, LinkTopic, MouseIcon, MousePointer, Name, OLEDropMode, RightToLeft, ScaleHeight, ScaleWidth, Tag, Top, Visible, Width

*ActiveControl	Control Object
*ActiveForm	Object
AutoShowChildren	Boolean

Caption	String
*Controls	Object Collection
*Count	Integer
Icon	IPictureDisp Object
*Moveable	Boolean
Picture	IPictureDisp Object
*ScrollBars	Boolean
StartUpPosition	Integer
*WhatsThisHelp	Boolean
WindowState	Integer

Events

Common Events: Click, DblClick, DragDrop, DragOver, LinkClose, LinkError, LinkExecute, LinkOpen, MouseDown, MouseMove, MouseUp, OLECompleteDrag, OLEDragDrop, OLEDragOver, OLEGiveFeedback, OLESetData, OLEStartDrag

Activate()

Deactivate()

Initialize()

Load()

QueryUnload(*cancel* As Integer, *unloadmode* As Integer)

Resize()

Terminate()

Unload(*cancel* As Integer)

Methods

Common Methods: Move, OLEDrag, SetFocus, ZOrder

Arrange	*object*.Arrange(*arrangement*)
Hide	*object*.Hide
PopupMenu	*object*.PopupMenu(*menu*, [*flags*], [*x*], [*y*], [*defaultmenu*])
Show	*object*.Show([*modal*], [*ownerform*])
WhatsThisMode	*object*.WhatsThisMode

Microsoft Tabbed Dialog (SSTab)

Properties

Common Properties: BackColor, Container, DataBindings, DragIcon, DragMode, Enabled, Font, ForeColor, Height, HelpContextID, hWnd, Index, Left, MouseIcon, MousePointer, Name, Object, OLEDropMode, Parent, TabIndex, TabStop, Tag, ToolTipText, Top, Visible, WhatsThisHelpID, Width

Caption	String
Rows	Integer
ShowFocusRect	Boolean
Style	StyleConstants
Tab	Integer
TabCaption	String Array
TabEnabled	Boolean Array
TabHeight	Single
TabMaxWidth	Single
TabOrientation	TabOrientationConstants
TabPicture	IPictureDisp Array
Tabs	Integer
TabsPerRow	Integer
TabVisible	Boolean Array
WordWrap	Boolean

Events

Common Events: Click, DblClick, DragDrop, DragOver, GotFocus, KeyDown, KeyPress, KeyUp, LostFocus, MouseDown, MouseMove, MouseUp, OLECompleteDrag, OLEDragDrop, OLEDragOver, OLEGiveFeedback, OLESetData, OLEStartDrag

Methods

Common Methods: Drag, Move, OLEDrag, SetFocus, ShowWhatsThis, ZOrder

MSChart

Properties

Common Properties: BorderStyle, Container, DataBindings, DragIcon, DragMode, Enabled, Height, HelpContextID, hWnd, Index, Left, Name, MousePointer, Object, Parent, TabIndex, TabStop, Tag, ToolTipText, Top, Visible, WhatsThisHelpID, Width

*ActiveSeriesCount	Integer
AllowDithering	Boolean
AllowDynamicRotation	Boolean
AllowSelections	Boolean
AllowSeriesSelection	Boolean
AutoIncrement	Boolean
*BackDrop	Backdrop Object
BorderStyle	VtBorderStyle Enum
*Chart3d	Boolean
ChartData	Variant
ChartType	VtChChartType Enum
Column	Integer
ColumnCount	Integer
ColumnLabel	String
ColumnLabelCount	Integer
ColumnLabelIndex	Integer
Data	String
*DataGrid	DataGrid Object
DoSetCursor	Boolean
DrawMode	VtChDrawMode Enum
*Footnote	Footnote Object
FootnoteText	String
*Legend	Legend Object
*Plot	Plot Object
RandomFill	Boolean

Repaint	Boolean
Row	Integer
RowCount	Integer
RowLabel	String
RowLabelCount	Integer
RowLabelIndex	Integer
SeriesColumn	Integer
SeriesType	VtChSeriesType Enum
ShowLegend	Boolean
Stacking	Boolean
TextLengthType	VtTextLengthType Enum
*Title	Title Object
TitleText	String

Events

Common Events: Click, DblClick, DragDrop, DragOver, GotFocus, KeyDown, KeyPress, KeyUp, LostFocus, MouseDown, MouseMove, MouseUp

AxisActivated(*axisid* As Integer, *axisindex* As Integer, *mouseflag* As Integer, *cancel* As Integer)

AxisLabelActivated(*axisid* As Integer, *axisindex* As Integer, *labelsetindex* As Integer, *labelindex* As Integer, *mouseflag* As Integer, *cancel* As Integer)

AxisLabelSelected(*axisid* As Integer, *axisindex* As Integer, *labelsetindex* As Integer, *labelindex* As Integer, *mouseflag* As Integer, *cancel* As Integer)

AxisLabelUpdated(*axisid* As Integer, *axisindex* As Integer, *labelsetindex* As Integer, *labelindex* As Integer, *updateflags* As Integer)

AxisSelected(*axisid* As Integer, *axisindex* As Integer, *mouseflag* As Integer, *cancel* As Integer)

AxisTitleActivated(*axisid* As Integer, *axisindex* As Integer, *mouseflag* As Integer, *cancel* As Integer)

AxisTitleSelected(*axisid* As Integer, *axisindex* As Integer, *mouseflag* As Integer, *cancel* As Integer)

AxisTitleUpdated(*axisid* As Integer, *axisindex* As Integer, *updateflags* As Integer)

AxisUpdated(*axisid* As Integer, *axisindex* As Integer, *updateflags* As Integer)

ChartActivated(*mouseflag* As Integer, *cancel* As Integer)

ChartSelected(*mouseflag* As Integer, *cancel* As Integer)

ChartUpdated(*updateflags* As Integer)

DataUpdated(*row* As Integer, *column* As Integer, *labelrow* As Integer, *labelcolumn* As Integer, *labelsetindex* As Integer, *updateflags* As Integer)

DonePainting()

FootnoteActivated(*mouseflag* As Integer, *cancel* As Integer)

FootnoteSelected(*mouseflag* As Integer, *cancel* As Integer)

FootnoteUpdated(*updateflags* As Integer)

LegendActivated(*mouseflag* As Integer, *cancel* As Integer)

LegendSelected(*mouseflag* As Integer, *cancel* As Integer)

LegendUpdated(*updateflags* As Integer)

PlotActivated(*mouseflag* As Integer, *cancel* As Integer)

PlotSelected(*mouseflag* As Integer, *cancel* As Integer)

PlotUpdated(*updateflags* As Integer)

PointActivated(*series* As Integer, *datapoint* As Integer, *mouseflag* As Integer, *cancel* As Integer)

PointLabelActivated(*series* As Integer, *datapoint* As Integer, *mouseflag* As Integer, *cancel* As Integer)

PointLabelSelected(*series* As Integer, *datapoint* As Integer, *mouseflag* As Integer, *cancel* As Integer)

PointLabelUpdated(*series* As Integer, *datapoint* As Integer, *updateflags* As Integer)

PointSelected(*series* As Integer, *datapoint* As Integer, *mouseflag* As Integer, *cancel* As Integer)

PointUpdated(*series* As Integer, *datapoint* As Integer, *updateflags* As Integer)

SeriesActivated(*series* As Integer, *mouseflag* As Integer, *cancel* As Integer)

SeriesSelected(*series* As Integer, *mouseflag* As Integer, *cancel* As Integer)

SeriesUpdated(*series* As Integer, *updateflags* As Integer)

TitleActivated(*mouseflag* As Integer, *cancel* As Integer)

TitleSelected(*mouseflag* As Integer, *cancel* As Integer)

TitleUpdated(*updateflags* As Integer)

Methods

Common Methods: Drag, Move, Refresh, SetFocus, ShowWhatsThis, ZOrder

AboutBox	*object*.AboutBox
EditCopy	*object*.EditCopy
EditPaste	*object*.EditPaste
GetSelectedPart	*object*.GetSelectedPart (*part*, *index1*, *index2*, *index3*, *index4*)
Layout	*object*.Layout
SelectPart	*object*.SelectPart (*part*, *index1*, *index2*, *index3*, *index4*)
ToDefaults	*object*.ToDefaults
TwipsToChartPart	*object*.TwipsToChartPart (*xval*, *yval*, *part*, *index1*, *index2*, *index3*, *index4*)

MSComm

Properties

Common Properties: Index, Name, Object, Parent, Tag

Break	Boolean
CDHolding	Boolean
CommEvent	Integer
CommID	Long
CommPort	Integer
CTSHolding	Boolean

DSRHolding	Boolean
DTREnable	Boolean
EOFEnable	Boolean
Handshaking	HandshakeConstants Enum
InBufferCount	Integer
InBufferSize	Integer
Input	Variant
InputLen	Integer
InputMode	InputModeConstants Enum
NullDiscard	Boolean
OutBufferCount	Integer
OutBufferSize	Integer
Output	Variant
ParityReplace	String
PortOpen	Boolean
RThreshold	Integer
RTSEnable	Boolean
Settings	String
SThreshold	Integer

Events

OnComm()

Methods

No methods

MSFlexGrid

Properties

Common Properties: Appearance, BackColor, BorderStyle,
Container, DataBindings, DragIcon, DragMode, Enabled, Font,
ForeColor, Height, HelpContextID, hWnd, Index, Left, MouseIcon,

MousePointer, Name, Object, OLEDropMode, Parent, RightToLeft,
TabIndex, TabStop, Tag, ToolTipText, Top, Visible,
WhatsThisHelpID, Width

AllowBigSelection	Boolean
AllowUserResizing	AllowUserResizingSettings Enum
BackColorBkg	OLE_COLOR Object
BackColorFixed	OLE_COLOR Object
BackColorSel	OLE_COLOR Object
CellAlignment	Integer
CellBackColor	OLE_COLOR Object
CellFontBold	Boolean
CellFontItalic	Boolean
CellFontName	String
CellFontSize	Single
CellFontStrikeThrough	Boolean
CellFontUnderline	Boolean
CellFontWidth	Single
CellForeColor	OLE_COLOR Object
*CellHeight	Long
*CellLeft	Long
CellPicture	IPictureDisp Object
CellPictureAlignment	Integer
CellTextStyle	TextStyleSettings Enum
*CellTop	Long
*CellWidth	Long
Clip	String
Col	Long
ColAlignment	Integer Array
ColData	Long Array
ColIsVisible	Boolean Array
ColPos	Long Array
ColPosition	Long Array

Cols	Long
ColSel	Long
ColWidth	Long Array
DataSource	IRowCursor Object
FillStyle	FillStyleSettings Enum
FixedAlignment	Integer Array
FixedCols	Long
FixedRows	Long
FocusRect	FocusRectSettings Enum
FontWidth	Single
ForeColorFixed	OLE_COLOR Object
ForeColorSel	OLE_COLOR Object
FormatString	String
GridColor	OLE_COLOR Object
GridColorFixed	OLE_COLOR Object
GridLines	GridLineSettings Enum
GridLinesFixed	GridLineSettings Enum
GridLineWidth	Integer
HighLight	HighLightSettings Enum
LeftCol	Long
MergeCells	MergeCellsSettings Enum
MergeCol	Boolean Array
MergeRow	Boolean Array
*MouseCol	Long
*MouseRow	Long
*Picture	IPictureDisp Object
PictureType	PictureTypeSettings Enum
Redraw	Boolean
Row	Long
RowData	Long Array
RowHeight	Long Array
RowHeightMin	Long

*RowIsVisible	Boolean Array
*RowPos	Long Array
RowPosition	Long Array
Rows	Long
RowSel	Long
ScrollBars	ScrollBarsSettings Enum
ScrollTrack	Boolean
SelectionMode	SelectionModeSettings Enum
Sort	Integer
Text	String
TextArray	String Array
TextMatrix	String Array
TextStyle	TextStyleSettings Enum
TextStyleFixed	TextStyleSettings Enum
TopRow	Long
*Version	Integer
WordWrap	Boolean

Events

Common Events: Click, DblClick, DragDrop, DragOver, GotFocus, KeyDown, KeyPress, KeyUp, LostFocus, MouseDown, MouseMove, MouseUp, OLECompleteDrag, OLEDragDrop, OLEDragOver, OLEGiveFeedback, OLESetData, OLEStartDrag

Compare(*row1* As Integer, *row2* As Integer, *cmp* As Integer)

EnterCell()

LeaveCell()

RowColChange()

Scroll()

SelChange()

Methods

Common Methods: Drag, Move, OLEDrag, Refresh, SetFocus, ShowWhatsThis, ZOrder

AddItem	*object*.AddItem (*item*, [*index*])
Clear	*object*.Clear
RemoveItem	*object*.RemoveItem (*index*)

MSRDC (Remote Data Control)

Properties

Common Properties: Appearance, BackColor, Container, DragIcon, DragMode, Enabled, Font, ForeColor, Height, Index, Left, Name, Parent, Tag, ToolTipText, Top, Visible, WhatsThisHelpID, Width

Align	Integer
*BatchCollisionCount	Long
*BatchCollisionRows	Variant
BatchSize	Long
BOFAction	BOFActionConstants Enum
Caption	String
Connect	String
Connection	rdoConnection Object
CursorDriver	CursorDriverConstants Enum
DataSourceName	String
EditMode	Integer
Environment	rdoEnvironment Object
EOFAction	EOFActionConstants Enum
ErrorThreshold	Long
KeysetSize	Long
LockType	LockTypeConstants Enum
LoginTimeout	Long

LogMessages	String
MaxRows	Long
*Object	Object
Options	Integer
Password	String
Prompt	PromptConstants Enum
QueryTimeout	Long
ReadOnly	Boolean
Resultset	rdoResultSet Object
ResultsetType	ResultsetTypeConstants Enum
RowsetSize	Long
SQL	String
UpdateCriteria	Integer
UpdateOperation	Integer
UserName	String
*Version	String

Events

Common Events: DragDrop, DragOver, MouseDown, MouseMove, MouseUp

Error(*number* As Long, *description* As String, *scode* As Long, *source* As String, *helpfile* As String, *helpcontext* As Long, *canceldisplay* As Boolean)

QueryCompleted()

Reposition()

Validate(*action* As Integer, *reserved* As Integer)

Methods

Common Methods: Drag, Move, Refresh, ShowWhatsThis, ZOrder

BeginTrans	*object*.BeginTrans
Cancel	*object*.Cancel
CommitTrans	*object*.CommitTrans

RollbackTrans	*object*.RollbackTrans
UpdateControls	*object*.UpdateControls
UpdateRow	*object*.UpdateRow

Multimedia MCI

Properties

Common Properties: BorderStyle, Container, DataBindings, DragIcon, DragMode, Enabled, Height, HelpContextID, hWnd, Index, Left, MouseIcon, MousePointer, Name, Object, OLEDropMode, Parent, TabIndex, TabStop, Tag, ToolTipText, Top, Visible, WhatsThisHelpID, Width

AutoEnable	Boolean
BackEnabled	Boolean
BackVisible	Boolean
CanEject	Boolean
CanPlay	Boolean
CanRecord	Boolean
CanStep	Boolean
Command	String
DeviceID	Integer
DeviceType	String
EjectEnabled	Boolean
EjectVisible	Boolean
Error	Integer
ErrorMessage	String
FileName	String
Frames	Long
From	Long
hWndDisplay	Long
Length	Long

Mode	Long
NextEnabled	Boolean
NextVisible	Boolean
Notify	Boolean
NotifyMessage	String
NotifyValue	Integer
Orientation	OrientationConstants Enum
PauseEnabled	Boolean
PauseVisible	Boolean
PlayEnabled	Boolean
PlayVisible	Boolean
Position	Long
PrevEnabled	Boolean
PrevVisible	Boolean
RecordEnabled	Boolean
RecordMode	RecordModeConstants Enum
RecordVisible	Boolean
Shareable	Boolean
Silent	Boolean
Start	Long
StepEnabled	Boolean
StepVisible	Boolean
StopEnabled	Boolean
StopVisible	Boolean
TimeFormat	Long
To	Long
Track	Long
TrackLength	Long
TrackPosition	Long
Tracks	Long
UpdateInterval	Integer
UsesWindows	Boolean
Wait	Boolean

Events

Common Events: DragDrop, DragOver, GotFocus, LostFocus, OLECompleteDrag, OLEDragOver, OLEGiveFeedback, OLESetData, OLEStartDrag

BackClick(*cancel* As Integer)

BackCompleted(*errcode* As Long)

BackGotFocus()

BackLostFocus()

Done(*notifycode* As Integer)

EjectClick(*cancel* As Integer)

EjectCompleted(*errcode* As Long)

EjectGotFocus()

EjectLostFocus()

NextClick(*cancel* As Integer)

NextCompleted(*errcode* As Long)

NextGotFocus()

NextLostFocus()

PauseClick(*cancel* As Integer)

PauseCompleted(*errcode* As Long)

PauseGotFocus()

PauseLostFocus()

PlayClick(*cancel* As Integer)

PlayCompleted(*errcode* As Long)

PlayGotFocus()

PlayLostFocus()

PrevClick(*cancel* As Integer)

PrevCompleted(*errcode* As Long)

PrevGotFocus()

PrevLostFocus()

RecordClick(*cancel* As Integer)

RecordCompleted(*errcode* As Long)

RecordGotFocus()

```
RecordLostFocus()

StatusUpdate()

StepClick(cancel As Integer)

StepCompleted(errcode As Long)

StepGotFocus()

StepLostFocus()

StopClick(cancel As Integer)

StopCompleted(errcode As Long)

StopGotFocus()

StopLostFocus()
```

Methods

Common Methods: Drag, Move, OLEDrag, Refresh, SetFocus, ShowWhatsThis, ZOrder

OLE

Properties

Common Properties: Appearance, BackColor, BorderStyle, Container, DragIcon, DragMode, Enabled, Height, HelpContextID, hWnd, Index, Left, MouseIcon, MousePointer, Name, Object, TabIndex, TabStop, Tag, Top, Visible, WhatsThisHelpID, Width

Action	Integer
AppIsRunning	Boolean
AutoActivate	Integer
AutoVerbMenu	Boolean
BackStyle	Integer
Class	String
Data	Long
DataChanged	Boolean
DataField	String

DataText	String
DisplayType	Integer
FileNumber	Integer
Format	String
HostName	String
*LpOleObject	Long
MiscFlags	Integer
*ObjectAcceptFormats	String Array
*ObjectAcceptFormatsCount	Integer
*ObjectGetFormats	String Array
*ObjectGetFormatsCount	Integer
*ObjectVerbFlags	Long Array
*ObjectVerbs	String Array
*ObjectVerbsCount	Integer
OLEDropAllowed	Boolean
*OLEType	Integer
OLETypeAllowed	Integer
*PasteOK	Boolean
*Picture	IPictureDisp Object
SizeMode	Integer
SourceDoc	String
SourceItem	String
UpdateOptions	Integer
Verb	Integer

Events

Common Events: Click, DblClick, DragDrop, DragOver, GotFocus, KeyDown, KeyPress, KeyUp, LostFocus, MouseDown, MouseMove, MouseUp

ObjectMove(*left* As Single, *top* As Single, *width* As Single, *height* As Single)

Resize(*newheight* As Single, *newwidth* As Single)

Updated(*code* As Integer)

Methods

Common Methods: Drag, Move, Refresh, SetFocus, ShowWhatsThis, ZOrder

Close	*object*.Close()
Copy	*object*.Copy()
CreateEmbed	*object*.CreateEmbed(*sourcedoc*, [*class*])
CreateLink	*object*.CreateLink(*sourcedoc*, [*sourceitem*])
Delete	*object*.Delete()
DoVerb	*object*.DoVerb([*verb*])
FetchVerbs	*object*.FetchVerbs()
InsertObjDlg	*object*.InsertObjDlg()
Paste	*object*.Paste()
PasteSpecialDlg	*object*.PasteSpecialDlg()
ReadFromFile	*object*.ReadFromFile(*filenum*)
SaveToFile	*object*.SaveToFile(*filenum*)
SaveToOle1File	*object*.SaveToOle1File(*filenum*)
Update	*object*.Update()

OptionButton

Properties

Common Properties: Appearance, BackColor, Container, DragIcon, DragMode, Enabled, Font, FontBold, FontItalic, FontName, FontSize, FontStrikethru, FontUnderline, ForeColor, Height, HelpContextID, hWnd, Index, Left, MouseIcon, MousePointer, Name, Parent, RightToLeft, TabIndex, TabStop, Tag, ToolTipText, Top, Visible, WhatsThisHelpID, Width

*Alignment	Integer
Caption	String
DisabledPicture	IPictureDisp Object
DownPicture	IPictureDisp Object

MaskColor	Long
Picture	IPictureDisp Object
*Style	Integer
UseMaskColor	Boolean
Value	Boolean

Events

Common Events: Click, DblClick, DragDrop, DragOver, GotFocus, KeyDown, KeyPress, KeyUp, LostFocus, MouseDown, MouseMove, MouseUp, OLECompleteDrag, OLEDragDrop, OLEDragOver, OLEGiveFeedback, OLESetData, OLEStartDrag

Methods

Common Methods: Drag, Move, OLEDrag, Refresh, SetFocus, ShowWhatsThis, ZOrder

PictureBox

Properties

Common Properties: Appearance, BackColor, BorderStyle, Container, DataChanged, DataField, DragIcon, DragMode, Enabled, Font, FontBold, FontItalic, FontName, FontSize, FontStrikethru, FontTransparent, FontUnderline, ForeColor, hDC, Height, HelpContextID, hWnd, Index, Left, LinkItem, LinkMode, LinkTimeout, LinkTopic, MouseIcon, MousePointer, Name, OLEDragMode, OLEDropMode, Parent, RightToLeft, ScaleHeight, ScaleLeft, ScaleMode, ScaleTop, ScaleWidth, TabIndex, TabStop, Tag, ToolTipText, Top, Visible, WhatsThisHelpID, Width

Align	Integer
AutoRedraw	Boolean
AutoSize	Boolean
*ClipControls	Boolean
CurrentX	Single

CurrentY	Single
DrawMode	Integer
DrawStyle	Integer
DrawWidth	Integer
FillColor	Long
FillStyle	Integer
*Image	IPictureDisp Object
Picture	IPictureDisp Object

Events

Common Events: Click, DblClick, DragDrop, DragOver, GotFocus, KeyDown, KeyPress, KeyUp, LinkClose, LinkError, LinkNotify, LinkOpen, LostFocus, MouseDown, MouseMove, MouseUp, OLECompleteDrag, OLEDragDrop, OLEDragOver, OLEGiveFeedback, OLESetData, OLEStartDrag

Change()

Paint()

Resize()

Methods

Common Methods: Drag, LinkExecute, LinkPoke, LinkRequest, LinkSend, Move, OLEDrag, Refresh, Scale, ScaleX, ScaleY, SetFocus, ShowWhatsThis, ZOrder

Circle	*object*.Circle(*step, x, y, radius, color, start, end, aspect*)
Cls	*object*.Cls
Line	*object*.Line(*flags, x1, y1, x2, y2, color*)
PaintPicture	*object*.PaintPicture(*picture, x1, y1, [width1], [height1], [x2], [y2], [width2], [height2], [opcode]*)

Point	*object*.Point(*x*, *y*) As Long
PSet	*object*.PSet(*step*, *x*, *y*, *color*)
TextHeight	*object*.TextHeight(*str*) As Single
TextWidth	*object*.TextWidth(*str*) As Single

PictureClip

Properties

Common Properties: Height, hWnd, Index, Name, Object, Parent, Tag, Width

CellHeight	Integer
CellWidth	Integer
Clip	IPictureDisp Object
ClipHeight	Integer
ClipWidth	Integer
ClipX	Integer
ClipY	Integer
Cols	Integer
GraphicCell	IPictureDisp Object Array
Picture	IPictureDisp Object
Rows	Integer
StretchX	Integer
StretchY	Integer

Events

No events

Methods

No methods

Printer

Properties

Common Properties: Font, FontBold, FontItalic, FontName, FontSize, FontStrikethru, FontTransparent, FontUnderline, ForeColor, hDC, Height, RightToLeft, ScaleHeight, ScaleLeft, ScaleMode, ScaleTop, ScaleWidth, Width

ColorMode	Integer
Copies	Integer
CurrentX	Single
CurrentY	Single
*DeviceName	String
DrawMode	Integer
DrawStyle	Integer
DrawWidth	Integer
*DriverName	String
Duplex	Integer
FillColor	Long
FillStyle	Integer
*FontCount	Integer
*Fonts	String Array
Orientation	Integer
*Page	Integer
PaperBin	Integer
PaperSize	Integer
*Port	String
PrintQuality	Integer
TrackDefault	Boolean
*TwipsPerPixelX	Single
*TwipsPerPixelY	Single
Zoom	Long

Events

No events

Methods

Common Methods: Scale, ScaleX, ScaleY

Circle	*object*.Circle(*step*, *x*, *y*, *radius*, *color*, *start*, *end*, *aspect*)
EndDoc	*object*.EndDoc
KillDoc	*object*.KillDoc
Line	*object*.Line(*flags*, *x1*, *y1*, *x2*, *y2*, *color*)
NewPage	*object*.NewPage
PaintPicture	*object*.PaintPicture(*picture*, *x1*, *y1*, [*width1*], [*height1*], [*x2*], [*y2*], [*width2*], [*height2*], [*opcode*])
PSet	*object*.PSet(*step*, *x*, *y*, *color*)
TextHeight	*object*.TextHeight(*str*) As Single
TextWidth	*object*.TextWidth(*str*) As Single

ProgressBar

Properties

Common Properties: Appearance, BorderStyle, Container, DragIcon, DragMode, Enabled, Height, hWnd, Index, Left, MouseIcon, MousePointer, Name, Object, OLEDropMode, Parent, TabIndex, Tag, ToolTipText, Top, Visible, WhatsThisHelpID, Width

Align	Integer
Max	Single
Min	Single
Value	Single

Events

Common Events: Click, DragDrop, DragOver, MouseDown, MouseMove, MouseUp, OLECompleteDrag, OLEDragDrop, OLEDragOver, OLEGiveFeedback, OLESetData, OLEStartDrag

Methods

Common Methods: Drag, Move, OLEDrag, ShowWhatsThis, ZOrder

Property Page

Properties

Common Properties: Appearance, BackColor, Font, FontBold, FontItalic, FontName, FontSize, FontStrikethru, FontTransparent, FontUnderline, ForeColor, hDC, Height, HelpContextID, hWnd, MouseIcon, MousePointer, Name, OLEDropMode, RightToLeft, ScaleHeight, ScaleLeft, ScaleMode, ScaleTop, ScaleWidth, Tag, Width

*ActiveControl	Control Object
AutoRedraw	Boolean
Caption	String
Changed	Boolean
*ClipControls	Boolean
*Controls	Object Collection
*Count	Integer
CurrentX	Single
CurrentY	Single
DrawMode	Integer
DrawStyle	Integer
DrawWidth	Integer
FillColor	Long
FillStyle	Integer
*Image	IPictureDisp Object
KeyPreview	Boolean

Palette	IPictureDisp Object
PaletteMode	Integer
Picture	IPictureDisp Object
*SelectedControls	SelectedControls Collection

Events

Common Events: Click, DblClick, DragDrop, DragOver, GotFocus, KeyDown, KeyPress, KeyUp, LostFocus, MouseDown, MouseMove, MouseUp, OLECompleteDrag, OLEDragDrop, OLEDragOver, OLEGiveFeedback, OLESetData, OLEStartDrag

ApplyChanges()

EditProperty(*propertyname* As String)

Initialize()

Paint()

SelectionChanged()

Terminate()

Methods

Common Methods: OLEDrag, Refresh, Scale, ScaleX, ScaleY, SetFocus

Circle	*object*.Circle(*step*, *x*, *y*, *radius*, *color*, *start*, *end*, *aspect*)
Cls	*object*.Cls
Line	*object*.Line(*flags*, *x1*, *y1*, *x2*, *y2*, *color*)
PaintPicture	*object*.PaintPicture(*picture*, *x1*, *y1*, [*width1*], [*height1*], [*x2*], [*y2*], [*width2*], [*height2*], [*opcode*])
Point	*object*.Point(*x*, *y*) As Long
PopupMenu	*object*.PopupMenu(*menu*, [*flags*], [*x*], [*y*], [*defaultmenu*])
PSet	*object*.PSet(*step*, *x*, *y*, *color*)
TextHeight	*object*.TextHeight(*str*) As Single
TextWidth	*object*.TextWidth(*str*) As Single

RichTextBox

Properties

Common Properties: Appearance, BackColor, BorderStyle, Container, DataBindings, DataChanged, DataField, DragIcon, DragMode, Enabled, Font, Height, HelpContextID, hWnd, Index, Left, MouseIcon, MousePointer, Name, Object, OLEDragMode, OLEDropMode, Parent, TabIndex, TabStop, Tag, ToolTipText, Top, Visible, WhatsThisHelpID, Width

AutoVerbMenu	Boolean
BulletIndent	Single
DisableNoScroll	Boolean
FileName	String
HideSelection	Boolean
Locked	Boolean
MaxLength	Long
MultiLine	Boolean
*OLEObjects	OLEObjects Collection
RightMargin	Single
ScrollBars	ScrollBarsConstants Enum
SelAlignment	Variant
SelBold	Variant
SelBullet	Variant
SelCharOffset	Variant
SelColor	Variant
SelFontName	Variant
SelFontSize	Variant
SelHangingIndent	Variant
SelIndent	Variant
SelItalic	Variant
SelLength	Long
SelProtected	Variant

SelRightIndent	Variant
SelRTF	String
SelStart	Long
SelStrikethru	Variant
SelTabCount	Variant
SelTabs	Variant Array
SelText	String
SelUnderline	Variant
Text	String
TextRTF	String

Events

Common Events: Click, DblClick, DragDrop, DragOver, GotFocus, KeyDown, KeyPress, KeyUp, LostFocus, MouseDown, MouseMove, MouseUp, OLECompleteDrag, OLEDragDrop, OLEDragOver, OLEGiveFeedback, OLESetData, OLEStartDrag

Change()

SelChange()

Methods

Common Methods: Drag, Move, OLEDrag, Refresh, SetFocus, ShowWhatsThis, ZOrder

Find	*object*.Find(*string*, [*start*], [*end*], [*options*])
GetLineFromChar	*object*.GetLineFromChar(*charpos*)
LoadFile	*object*.LoadFile(*pathname*, [*flags*])
SaveFile	*object*.SaveFile(*pathname*, [*flags*])
SelPrint	*object*.SelPrint(*hdc*)
Span	*object*.Span(*characterset*, [*forward*], [*negate*])
UpTo	*object*.UpTo(*characterset*, [*forward*], [*negate*])

Screen

Properties

Common Properties: Height, MouseIcon, MousePointer, Width

*ActiveControl	Control Object
*ActiveForm	Form Object
*FontCount	Integer
*Fonts	String Array
*TwipsPerPixelX	Single
*TwipsPerPixelY	Single

Events

No events

Methods

No methods

Shape

Properties

Common Properties: BackColor, BorderStyle, Container, Height, Index, Left, Name, Parent, Tag, Top, Visible, Width

BackStyle	Integer
BorderColor	Long
BorderWidth	Integer
DrawMode	Integer
FillColor	Long
FillStyle	Integer
Shape	Integer

Events

No events

Methods

Common Methods: Move, Refresh, ZOrder

Slider

Properties

Common Properties: BorderStyle, Container, DataBindings, DragIcon, DragMode, Enabled, Height, HelpContextID, hWnd, Index, Left, MouseIcon, MousePointer, Name, Object, OLEDropMode, Parent, TabIndex, TabStop, Tag, ToolTipText, Top, Visible, WhatsThisHelpID, Width

*GetNumTicks	Long
LargeChange	Long
Max	Long
Min	Long
Orientation	OrientationConstants Enum
SelectRange	Boolean
SelLength	Long
SelStart	Long
SmallChange	Long
TickFrequency	Long
TickStyle	TickStyleConstants Enum
Value	Long

Events

Common Events: Click, DragDrop, DragOver, GotFocus, KeyDown, KeyPress, KeyUp, LostFocus, MouseDown, MouseMove, MouseUp, OLECompleteDrag, OLEDragDrop, OLEDragOver, OLEGiveFeedback, OLESetData, OLEStartDrag

Change()

Scroll()

Methods

Common Methods: Drag, Move, OLEDrag, Refresh, SetFocus, ShowWhatsThis, ZOrder

ClearSel   *object*.ClearSel

StatusBar

Properties

Common Properties: Container, DragIcon, DragMode, Enabled, Font, Height, hWnd, Index, Left, MouseIcon, MousePointer, Name, Object, OLEDropMode, Parent, TabIndex, Tag, ToolTipText, Top, Visible, WhatsThisHelpID, Width

Align	Integer
Panels	Panels Collection
ShowTips	Boolean
SimpleText	String
Style	SbarStyleConstants Enum

Events

Common Events: Click, DblClick, DragDrop, DragOver, MouseDown, MouseMove, MouseUp, OLECompleteDrag, OLEDragDrop, OLEDragOver, OLEGiveFeedback, OLESetData, OLEStartDrag

PanelClick(*panel* As Panel)

PanelDblClick(*panel* As Panel)

Methods

Common Methods: Drag, Move, OLEDrag, Refresh, ShowWhatsThis, ZOrder

Sysinfo

Properties

Common Properties: Index, Name, Object, Parent, Tag

*ACStatus	Integer
*BatteryFullTime	Long
*BatteryLifePercent	Integer
*BatteryLifeTime	Long
*BatteryStatus	Integer
*OSBuild	Integer
*OSPlatform	Integer
*OSVersion	Single
*ScrollBarSize	Single
*WorkAreaHeight	Single
*WorkAreaLeft	Single
*WorkAreaTop	Single
*WorkAreaWidth	Single

Events

Common Events: None.

ConfigChangeCancelled()

ConfigChanged(*oldconfignum* As Long, *newconfignum* As Long)

DeviceArrival(*devicetype* As Long, *deviceid* As Long, *devicename* As String, *devicedata* As Long)

DeviceOtherEvent(*devicetype* As Long, *eventname* As String, *datapointer* As Long)

DeviceQueryRemove(*devicetype* As Long, *deviceid* As Long,

devicename **As String,** *devicedata* **As Long,** *cancel* **As** Boolean)

DeviceQueryRemoveFailed(*devicetype* As Long, *deviceid* As Long, *devicename* As String, *devicedata* As Long)

DeviceRemoveComplete(*devicetype* As Long, *deviceid* As Long, *devicename* As String, *devicedata* As Long)

DeviceRemovePending(*devicetype* As Long, *deviceid* As Long, *devicename* As String, *devicedata* As Long)

DevModeChanged()

DisplayChanged()

PowerQuerySuspend(*cancel* As Boolean)

PowerResume()

PowerStatusChanged()

PowerSuspend()

QueryChangeConfig(*cancel* As Boolean)

SettingChanged(*item* As Integer)

SysColorsChanged()

TimeChanged()

Methods

No methods

TabStrip

Properties

Common Properties: Container, DataBindings, DragIcon, DragMode, Enabled, Font, Height, HelpContextID, hWnd, Index, Left, MouseIcon, MousePointer, Name, Object, OLEDropMode, Parent, TabIndex, TabStop, Tag, ToolTipText, Top, Visible, WhatsThisHelpID, Width

ClientHeight	Single
ClientLeft	Single
ClientTop	Single

ClientWidth	Single
ImageList	Object
MultiRow	Boolean
SelectedItem	Tab Object
ShowTips	Boolean
Style	TabStyleConstants Enum
TabFixedHeight	Integer
TabFixedWidth	Integer
Tabs	Tabs Collection
TabWidthStyle	TabWidthStyleConstants Enum

Events

Common Events: Click, DragDrop, DragOver, GotFocus, KeyDown, KeyPress, KeyUp, LostFocus, MouseDown, MouseMove, MouseUp, OLECompleteDrag, OLEDragDrop, OLEDragOver, OLEGiveFeedback, OLESetData, OLEStartDrag

BeforeClick(*cancel* As Integer)

Methods

Common Methods: Drag, Move, OLEDrag, Refresh, SetFocus, ShowWhatsThis, ZOrder

TextBox

Properties

Common Properties: Appearance, BackColor, BorderStyle, Container, DataChanged, DataField, DragIcon, DragMode, Enabled, Font, FontBold, FontItalic, FontName, FontSize, FontStrikethru, FontUnderline, ForeColor, Height, HelpContextID, hWnd, Index, Left, LinkItem, LinkMode, LinkTimeout, LinkTopic, MouseIcon, MousePointer, Name, OLEDragMode, OLEDropMode, Parent, RightToLeft, TabStop, Tag, ToolTipText, Top, Visible, WhatsThisHelpID, Width

Alignment	Integer
*HideSelection	Boolean
Locked	Boolean
MaxLength	Long
*MultiLine	Boolean
PasswordChar	String
*ScrollBars	Integer
SelLength	Long
SelStart	Long
SelText	String
Text	String

Events

Common Events: Click, DblClick, DragDrop, DragOver, GotFocus, KeyDown, KeyPress, KeyUp, LinkClose, LinkError, LinkNotify, LinkOpen, LostFocus, MouseDown, MouseMove, MouseUp, OLECompleteDrag, OLEDragDrop, OLEDragOver, OLEGiveFeedback, OLESetData, OLEStartDrag

Change()

Methods

Common Methods: Drag, LinkExecute, LinkPoke, LinkRequest, LinkSend, Move, OLEDrag, Refresh, SetFocus, ShowWhatsThis, ZOrder

Timer

Properties

Common Properties: Enabled, Index, Name, Parent, Tag

Interval	Long

Events

Common Events: None

```
Timer()
```

Methods

No methods

Toolbar

Properties

Common Properties: Appearance, BorderStyle, Container, DataBindings, DragIcon, DragMode, Enabled, Height, HelpContextID, hWnd, Index, Left, MouseIcon, MousePointer, Name, Object, OLEDropMode, Parent, TabIndex, Tag, ToolTipText, Top, Visible, WhatsThisHelpID, Width

Align	Integer
AllowCustomize	Boolean
ButtonHeight	Single
Buttons	Buttons Collection
ButtonWidth	Single
*Controls	Controls Collection
HelpFile	String
ImageList	Object
ShowTips	Boolean
Wrappable	Boolean

Events

Common Events: Click, DblClick, DragDrop, DragOver, MouseDown, MouseMove, MouseUp, OLECompleteDrag, OLEDragDrop, OLEDragOver, OLEGiveFeedback, OLESetData, OLEStartDrag

```
ButtonClick(button As Button)
```

```
Change()
```

Methods

Common Methods: Drag, Move, OLEDrag, Refresh, ShowWhatsThis, ZOrder

Customize	*object*.Customize
RestoreToolbar	*object*.RestoreToolbar(*key*, *subkey*, *value*)
SaveToolbar	*object*.SaveToolbar(*key*, *subkey*, *value*)

TreeView

Properties

Common Properties: Appearance, BorderStyle, Container, DragIcon, DragMode, Enabled, Font, Height, HelpContextID, hWnd, Index, Left, MouseIcon, MousePointer, Name, Object, OLEDragMode, OLEDropMode, Parent, TabIndex, TabStop, Tag, ToolTipText, Top, Visible, WhatsThisHelpID, Width

DropHighlight	Node Object
HideSelection	Boolean
ImageList	Object
Indentation	Single
LabelEdit	*LabelEditConstants* Enum
LineStyle	TreeLineStyleConstants Enum
Nodes	Nodes Collection
PathSeparator	String
SelectedItem	Node Object
Sorted	Boolean
Style	TreeStyleConstants Enum

Events

Common Events: Click, DragDrop, DragOver, GotFocus, KeyDown, KeyPress, KeyUp, LostFocus, MouseDown, MouseMove, MouseUp, OLECompleteDrag, OLEDragDrop, OLEDragOver, OLEGiveFeedback, OLESetData, OLEStartDrag

```
AfterLabelEdit(cancel As Integer, newstring As String)

BeforeLabelEdit(cancel As Integer)

Expand(node As Node)

NodeClick(node As Node)
```

Methods

Common Methods: Drag, Move, OLEDrag, Refresh, SetFocus, ShowWhatsThis, ZOrder

GetVisibleCount	object.GetVisibleCount() As Long
HitTest	object.HitTest(x, y) As Node
StartLabelEdit	object.StartLabelEdit

UpDown

Properties

Common Properties: Container, DragIcon, DragMode, Enabled, Height, HelpContextID, hWnd, Index, Left, Name, Object, Parent, TabIndex, TabStop, Tag, ToolTipText, Top, Visible, WhatsThisHelpID, Width

Alignment	AlignmentConstants Enum
AutoBuddy	Boolean
BuddyControl	Variant
BuddyProperty	Variant
Increment	Long
Max	Long
Min	Long
OLEDropMode	OLEDropConstants Enum
Orientation	OrientationConstants Enum
SyncBuddy	Boolean
Value	Long
Wrap	Boolean

Events

Common Events: DragDrop, DragOver, GotFocus, LostFocus, MouseDown, MouseMove, MouseUp, OLECompleteDrag, OLEDragDrop, OLEDragOver, OLEGiveFeedback, OLESetData, OLEStartDrag

Change()

DownClick()

UpClick()

Methods

Common Methods: Drag, Move, OLEDrag, SetFocus, ShowWhatsThis, ZOrder

UserControl

Properties

Common Properties: Appearance, BackColor, BorderStyle, Enabled, Font, FontBold, FontItalic, FontName, FontSize, FontStrikethru, FontTransparent, FontUnderline, ForeColor, hDC, Height, hWnd, MouseIcon, MousePointer, Name, OLEDropMode, Parent, RightToLeft, ScaleHeight, ScaleLeft, ScaleMode, ScaleTop, ScaleWidth, Tag, Width

AccessKeys	String
*ActiveControl	Control Object
*Ambient	AmbientProperties Object
AutoRedraw	Boolean
BackStyle	Long
*ClipControls	Boolean
*ContainedControls	ContainedControls Collection
*Controls	Object Collection
*Count	Integer
CurrentX	Single

CurrentY	Single
DrawMode	Integer
DrawStyle	Integer
DrawWidth	Integer
*EventsFrozen	Boolean
*Extender	Object
FillColor	Long
FillStyle	Integer
*Hyperlink	Hyperlink Object
*Image	IPictureDisp Object
KeyPreview	Boolean
MaskColor	Long
MaskPicture	IPictureDisp Object
Palette	IPictureDisp Object
PaletteMode	Integer
ParentControls	ParentControls Collection
Picture	IPictureDisp Object
PropertyPages	String Array

Events

Common Events: Click, DblClick, DragDrop, DragOver, GotFocus, KeyDown, KeyPress, KeyUp, LostFocus, MouseDown, MouseMove, MouseUp, OLECompleteDrag, OLEDragDrop, OLEDragOver, OLEGiveFeedback, OLESetData, OLEStartDrag

AccessKeyPress(*keyascii* As Integer)

AmbientChanged(*propertyname* As String)

AsyncReadComplete(*asyncprop* As AsyncProperty)

EnterFocus()

ExitFocus()

Hide()

Initialize()

InitProperties()

```
Paint()
ReadProperties(propbag As PropertyBag)
Resize()
Show()
Terminate()
WriteProperties(propbag As PropertyBag)
```

Methods

Common Methods: OLEDrag, Refresh, Scale, ScaleX, ScaleY, SetFocus

AsyncRead	object.AsyncRead(target, asynctype, [propertyname])
CancelAsyncRead	object.CancelAsyncRead([property])
CanPropertyChange	object.CanPropertyChange(propname) As Boolean
Circle	object.Circle(step, x, y, radius, color, start, end, aspect)
Cls	object.Cls
Line	object.Line(flags, x1, y1, x2, y2, color)
PaintPicture	object.PaintPicture(picture, x1, y1, [width1], [height1], [x2], [y2], [width2], [height2], [opcode])
Point	object.Point(x, y) As Long
PopupMenu	object.PopupMenu(menu, [flags], [x], [y], [defaultmenu])
PropertyChanged	object.PropertyChanged([propname])
PSet	object.PSet(step, x, y, color)
Size	object.Size(width, height)
TextHeight	object.TextHeight(str) As Single
TextWidth	object.TextWidth(str) As Single

UserDocument

Properties

Common Properties: Appearance, BackColor, Font, FontBold, FontItalic, FontName, FontSize, FontStrikethru, FontTransparent, FontUnderline, ForeColor, hDC, Height, hWnd, MouseIcon, MousePointer, Name, OLEDropMode, Parent, RightToLeft, ScaleHeight, ScaleLeft, ScaleMode, ScaleTop, ScaleWidth, Tag, Width

*ActiveControl	Control Array
AutoRedraw	Boolean
*ClipControls	Boolean
ContinuousScroll	Boolean
*Controls	Object Collection
*Count	Integer
CurrentX	Single
CurrentY	Single
DrawMode	Integer
DrawStyle	Integer
DrawWidth	Integer
FillColor	Long
FillStyle	Integer
HScrollSmallChange	Single
*Hyperlink	Hyperlink Object
*Image	IPictureDisp Object
KeyPreview	Boolean
MinHeight	Single
MinWidth	Single
Palette	IPictureDisp Object
PaletteMode	Integer
Picture	*IPictureDisp* Object
ScrollBars	Integer

*ViewportHeight	Single
ViewportLeft	Single
ViewportTop	Single
*ViewportWidth	Single
VScrollSmallChange	Single

Events

Common Events: Click, DblClick, DragDrop, DragOver, GotFocus, KeyDown, KeyPress, KeyUp, LostFocus, MouseDown, MouseMove, MouseUp, OLECompleteDrag, OLEDragDrop, OLEDragOver, OLEGiveFeedback, OLESetData, OLEStartDrag

AsyncReadComplete(*asyncprop* As AsyncProperty)

EnterFocus()

ExitFocus()

Hide()

Initialize()

InitProperties()

Paint()

ReadProperties(*propbag* As PropertyBag)

Resize()

Scroll()

Show()

Terminate()

WriteProperties(*propbag* As PropertyBag)

Methods

Common Methods: OLEDrag, Refresh, Scale, ScaleX, ScaleY, SetFocus

AsyncRead	*object*.AsyncRead(*target, asynctype,* [*propertyname*])
CancelAsyncRead	*object*.CancelAsyncRead([*property*])
Circle	*object*.Circle(*step, x, y, radius, color, start, end, aspect*)

Cls	*object*.Cls
Line	*object*.Line(*flags*, *x1*, *y1*, *x2*, *y2*, *color*)
PaintPicture	*object*.PaintPicture(*picture*, *x1*, *y1*, [*width1*], [*height1*], [*x2*], [*y2*], [*width2*], [*height2*], [*opcode*])
Point	*object*.Point(*x*, *y*) As Long
PopupMenu	*object*.PopupMenu(*menu*, [*flags*], [*x*], [*y*], [*defaultmenu*])
PrintForm	*object*.PrintForm
PropertyChanged	*object*.PropertyChanged([*propname*])
PSet	*object*.PSet(*step*, *x*, *y*, *color*)
SetViewport	*object*.SetViewport(*left*, *top*)
TextHeight	*object*.TextHeight(*str*) As Single
TextWidth	*object*.TextWidth(*str*) As Single

VScrollBar

Properties

Common Properties: Container, DragIcon, DragMode, Enabled, Height, HelpContextID, hWnd, Index, Left, MouseIcon, MousePointer, Name, Parent, RightToLeft, TabIndex, TabStop, Tag, Top, Visible, WhatsThisHelpID, Width

LargeChange	Integer
Max	Integer
Min	Integer
SmallChange	*Integer*
Value	Integer

Events

Common Events: DragDrop, DragOver, GotFocus, KeyDown, KeyPress, KeyUp, LostFocus

Change()

Scroll()

Methods

Common Methods: Drag, Move, Refresh, SetFocus, ShowWhatsThis, ZOrder

Winsock

Properties

Common Properties: Index, Name, Object, Parent, Tag

*BytesReceived	Long
*LocalHostName	String
*LocalIP	String
LocalPort	Long
Protocol	ProtocolConstants Enum
RemoteHost	String
*RemoteHostIP	String
RemotePort	Long
*SocketHandle	Long
*State	Integer

Events

Common Events: None

Close()

Connect()

ConnectionRequest(*requestid* As Long)

DataArrival(*totalbytes* As Long)

Error(*number* As Integer, *description* As String, *scode* As Long, *source* As String, *helpfile* As String, *helpcontext* As Long, *canceldisplay* As Boolean)

SendComplete()

SendProgress(*bytessent* As Long, *bytesleft* As Long)

Methods

Common Methods: None

Accept	*object*.Accept(*requestid*)
Bind	*object*.Bind([*localport*], [*localid*])
Close	*object*.Close
Connect	*object*.Connect([*remotehost*], [*remoteport*])
GetData	*object*.GetData(*data*, [*type*], [*maxLen*])
Listen	*object*.Listen
PeekData	*object*.PeekData(*data*, [*type*], [*maxLen*])
SendData	*object*.SendData(*data*)

Summary

This appendix provided a quick-reference for many objects commonly used in Visual Basic, including all the standard and professional controls plus objects such as Screen and Printer. For each object, the chapter lists all its properties, methods, and events. Other information, such as the data type of properties, the syntax of methods, and the arguments of events, was also provided.

Glossary

Active Server Page (ASP) A Web-based application containing a combination of HTML, ActiveX components, and VBScript code. Active Server Pages can be used to dynamically provide different content for different users when viewed through each user's Web browser.

ActiveX A set of technologies based on Microsoft's Component Object Model (COM) for creating reusable binary objects.

ActiveX component (Formerly OLE automation server) A physical file that contains classes from which objects can be defined. ActiveX components generally have file extensions .exe, .dll, or .ocx.

ActiveX control An object that can be placed on a form so that users can interact with applications. ActiveX controls have events, properties, and methods and can be incorporated into other controls. ActiveX controls have an .ocx file extension.

ActiveX Data Objects (ADO) An object model—including data connection, data manipulation, and recordset objects—used for data access. ADO is an OLE DB consumer.

ActiveX DLL An ActiveX in-process component, an object that requires another application's process space. See also *ActiveX EXE.*

ActiveX document A Visual Basic application that can be viewed within a container application such as Microsoft Internet Explorer (version 3.0 or later) or Microsoft Office Binder. ActiveX documents don't require HTML code in order to be viewed or manipulated.

ActiveX EXE An ActiveX out-of-process component, an object that runs in its own address space. See also *ActiveX DLL.*

add-in A software component that extends Visual Basic's capability. Some add-ins, such as the Visual Basic Class Builder Utility add-in, are included with Visual Basic; many more are available from third-party sources. Within the IDE, you use the Add-In Manager to install and remove add-ins.

ambient property A property that a child object can assume during runtime. Ambient properties are controlled by a container object and are used so that objects within the container can take characteristics of the container.

ANSI The acronym for *American National Standards Institute*. ANSI provides a unique integer code for a character set that includes 256 characters. ANSI includes the 128-character ASCII character set and contains international letters, symbols, and fractions.

API The acronym for *Application Programming Interface*. An API is a set of functions that are exposed by a software module and provide access to the services the module provides. In Windows, the API is a set of core functions that allow direct access to many operating system–provided services, such as window management and printer services. The Windows API consists of three main files: user32.dll, gdi32.dll, and kernel32.dll.

application One or more software components that do some action or provide some service, a compiled Visual Basic project. Other examples of applications include Microsoft Visual Basic and Microsoft Word. Also known as a *program*.

argument Data sent to a procedure. An argument can be a constant, a variable, or some other expression.

array An indexed group of related data. Elements within an array must be of the same data type (such as all integers or all strings), and each element has a unique, sequential index number.

ASCII The acronym for *American Standard Code of Information Interchange*. ASCII provides a unique integer code for a character set that includes 128 numbers, letters, and symbols found on a standard U.S. keyboard. A subset of the ANSI character set. In Visual Basic, the ASC function returns the ASCII value of a character.

authentication The process by which the identity of an ActiveX control is proven to a Web browser. During authentication, the Web browser determines that the control meets a predetermined set of criteria, in essence, verifying that the control hasn't been tampered with and that it will behave in the way the control's developer originally intended.

automation server See *ActiveX component*.

bind To connect an object to a data source. See *bound control*.

bit The smallest amount of data storage available on a computer. A bit is either 0 or 1.

bookmark A marker for a specific location. A bookmark can be a specific record in a database, a line of code within a project, or a specific Web page.

Boolean A binary data type. Boolean values are 16-bit (2-byte) values that can hold the True or False constants or their equivalents (–1 and 0). The Boolean data type uses the prefix bln but doesn't have a type-declaration character.

bound control A data-aware control attached to a database through a Data control. At runtime, when users manipulate the Data control by changing from one row of the database to the next, the bound control changes to display the data found in the columns of the new row. If users change the data stored in a row, the new data is saved to the database when the users switch to a new row.

breakpoint A specific line within a block of code where program execution automatically stops (during runtime). Breakpoints are user selectable. You can toggled them on and off during design time by pressing F9.

browser An application used to browse content on the Web. Browsers, such as Microsoft Internet Explorer, can show HTML pages, Active Server Pages, and various other types of content.

buffer string A temporary holding location in memory for data that will be parsed or otherwise modified. For example, if an application were to take two string values from a user and then extract a specific section from their sum, each value would be placed in a buffer string. Then these would be concatenated (and placed into another buffer string) before the desired value is parsed from the input data.

Byte An 8-bit data type that can hold numbers in the range of 0–255. The `Byte` data type uses the prefix `byt` but doesn't have a type-declaration character. `Bytes` are the basis for all Visual Basic data types; for example, the `Single` data type is a 4-byte (32-bit) number.

CAB file Short for *cabinet file*. A group of files compressed into one larger file to conserve disk space. CAB files are often used to distribute applications. During installation, the Setup program extracts files from the CAB file and copies them to the appropriate location on the hard disk.

call To transfer control of an application to a different procedure. Procedures are sometimes called with the `Call` keyword.

child object An object contained within another object (its parent). See *object*.

class A template used to create user-defined objects. A class defines an object's properties and methods. All instances created from the class use the properties and methods defined by the class.

class module A module that defines a class. See *module*.

code block A selection of code. A code block usually consists of all lines necessary to complete a specific task within the application.

COM The acronym for *Component Object Model*. A standard by which applications can expose objects to the system for use by other applications and, conversely, by which applications can use objects that have been exposed by other applications.

compile To prepare code for execution. In Visual Basic, code can be compiled into either P-code (which results in faster compilation) or native code (which results in faster execution). The type of compilation can be selected from the Compile page of the Project Properties dialog box.

component object An object that supports automation through exposed properties and methods. Examples of component objects include ActiveX controls, ActiveX documents, and ActiveX code components.

compressed file A file that has been modified to take up less space when stored on the hard drive. Generally, compressed files can't be opened or manipulated until they're decompressed.

concatenate To join two or more strings in an expression.

conditional statement A logical statement involving a comparison, which yields a Boolean (True or False) value.

constant A variable or object whose value doesn't change.

constituent control A control that's encapsulated inside another ActiveX control to provide some of the constituent control's functionality when using the ActiveX control.

context-sensitive help Information about a specific concept or object within in an application that users can easily find. To access context-sensitive help, press Shift+F1 or click the What's This? help (question mark) button; then select the confusing item.

control An object that can be manipulated at design time or runtime to present or change data. Controls are manipulated by changing properties during design time and by calling methods or responding to events during runtime.

control array An indexed group of similar controls that are of the same type and have the same name. Individual elements within the control array are identified by a unique index number.

coolbar A type of toolbar characterized by flat buttons that raise when the mouse pointer moves over them and, when clicked, they depress. This is the type of toolbar found in the Visual Basic IDE. The Coolbar object is used to create user-modifiable coolbars.

Currency A numeric data type particularly suited to store money data. Currency values are 64-bit (8-byte) integers, scaled by 10,000 to provide four digits to the right of the decimal point. Currency values use the prefix cur and the type-declaration character @ (the *at* sign).

data consumer An object that's bound to a data provider. A data consumer lets programmers connect to a data source and manipulate information within it.

data member Private variable of a class. Data members are seen only by the class that defines them.

data provider A data source that exposes information for data access, such as Microsoft Jet, Microsoft SQL, or Oracle.

data type A set of rules describing a specific set of information, including the allowed range and operations and how information is stored. Data types in Visual Basic include Integer, String, Boolean, and Variant.

Date A numeric data type used to represent dates. Date values are 64-bit (8-byte) floating-point numbers that represent dates from January 1, 100, to December 31, 9999, and times from 0:00:00 to 23:59:59. The Date data type uses the prefix dat but doesn't have a type-declaration character.

DCOM The acronym for *Distributed Component Object Model*. An extension of COM by which applications can expose objects to computers across a network, and, conversely, by which computers can use objects that have been exposed from across a network.

Decimal A numeric data type, ranging from 0 to 28, used to specify the number of digits to the right of the decimal point. Decimal values are 96-bit (12-byte) unsigned integers, so with a scale of 28, the largest possible Decimal value is +/-7.9228162514264337593543950335; with a scale of 0, +/-79,228,162,514,264, 337,593,543,950,335. The Decimal data type must be used with a Variant, uses the prefix dec, and doesn't have a type-declaration character.

deployment The period during which an application is distributed for use by customers or by other applications.

design time The time spent creating forms and writing functions during the creation of an application. Forms and functions can be altered only during design time. See *runtime*.

designer An object or application that's used as a basis for creating more advanced objects or applications.

destination system The system on which an application will be installed and used.

device independence The concept that software components don't directly control hardware devices. Device-independent software controls hardware by manipulating objects that abstract and expose the functionality of a class of hardware devices.

DLL The acronym for *dynamic link library*. An executable file containing a set of functions that other applications can call during runtime. DLLs generally don't have a graphical user interface; instead, they're usually accessed by applications without user intervention.

Document Object Model (DOM) A method for storing information so that a document can display its content in a variety of in-place views.

domain name A unique name that identifies an Internet or network server, such as www.mcp.com or www.microsoft.com. Domain names are actually text representations of numeric IP addresses and must be registered with international authorities such as InterNIC.

Double A numerical data type. Double values are 64-bit (8-byte) floating-point number. Double values use the prefix dbl and the type-declaration character # (the pound sign).

dynamic A changing object or expression.

Dynamic HTML (DHTML) A series of extensions to the HTML language that enable an HTML page to be dynamically modified. A group of HTML pages that work together can be used to create a Web-based application. DHTML applications contain objects and events and are processed on the client within the Web browser.

dynaset A recordset that can include data from one or more tables from a database. A dynaset can be used to view or modify data contained in the underlying database.

early binding A technique that an application uses to access an object. In early binding, objects are defined from a specific class. Early binding is often faster than late binding because the application doesn't have to interrogate the object at runtime to determine the object's properties and methods. In Visual Basic, early binding enables the AutoComplete features to work correctly.

Easter egg A hidden signature within an application, included by programmers to demonstrate that they wrote it. Activating Easter eggs often requires a complex set of user actions.

element A single member of an array. Each element of an array is assigned a unique index value, which is used to locate and manipulate specific elements in an array.

encapsulation The act of placing code or data in a location, such as a module or control, that's isolated from the rest of an application. Encapsulation hides both the implementation details and the internal complexity of an object but still enables the application to use functions contained within it.

enterprise computing A computing model in which multiple users access applications and data stored on a server. In an enterprise computing environment, multiple servers and multiple networks can be linked together. This is an advanced form of general networking in which users can share information directly, without the use of a dedicated server.

entry point The starting point in the code of an application. In Visual Basic 6, entry points include a `Sub Main` procedure or a `Form_Load` event.

event A signal fired by the operating system in response to a user action. For example, when a user clicks (and holds down) a mouse button, a `MouseDown` event is sent by the operating system. The active application intercepts this signal and executes the code attached to the `MouseDown` event.

event-driven programming A method of programming in which blocks of code are run as users do things or as events occur while a program is running. This varies from procedural programming, in which code blocks are contained within a module and called from other procedures.

event procedure The place in a project where code is written to respond to an event. Event procedures are named by joining the object name with the event name, such as `cmdButton_Click()`.

extensibility The capability to extend an object's or application's functionality through the use of a programming language or an add-in.

field A discrete element of a record in a database, a column in a database—for example, a database of music CDs might have many fields, including the CD title, artist name, and CD label.

file A unit of storage on an external storage device such as a hard disk retrievable block of data. Usually stored on a hard drive, files can contain executable programs, word processor documents, or bitmap picture files. In Visual Basic, each form, module, and project are saved as a file.

file handle A structure that identifies and provides access to a file on disk.

File Transfer Protocol (FTP) A method used to transfer files between computers, across a network, or over the Internet by using the TCP/IP network protocol.

flag A `Boolean` (`True` or `False`) variable used to determine whether a condition has been met or an event has occurred. For example, the flag `blnPasswordSet` would be set to `True` when a password is set and to `False` when the password is cleared.

flat-file database A database file in which every record contains all the information required to describe it. Flat-file databases often contain redundant information. For example, every record in a flat-file database of music CDs would require multiple fields to describe the contact information for the artist's fan club. See also *relational database*.

focus The state in which an object can receive input from the mouse or keyboard. At any given time, only one object can have focus; this object is usually highlighted with a different color and contains the text cursor, where appropriate.

form The basis of an application's graphical user interface. Forms contain objects with which users manipulate data and otherwise control an application.

Form Designer A part of the Visual Basic 6 Integrated Development Environment. You use the Form Designer to create an application's graphical user interface by placing objects on forms during design time. At runtime, objects appear where they have been placed on the forms.

Form Layout window A part of the Visual Basic 6 Integrated Development Environment (MDI version only). The Form Layout window is used to position an application's forms during design time, visually rather than through code. At runtime, forms appear where they have been placed in the Form Layout window.

function A procedure, beginning with `Function functionname()` and ending with `End Function`, that returns a value to the calling procedure when it's complete.

Get A Visual Basic keyword, the part of a `Property` procedure that gets the value of a property.

global variable A variable that can be accessed from anywhere within a program and maintains its value while the program is being run. Global variables are defined within code modules with the `Public` keyword.

gotcha A detail that can cause problems when overlooked.

graphical user interface (GUI) A set of forms and objects that enable users to view and manipulate data and otherwise control an application. A graphical user interface is the part of the application that sits between users and an application's underlying procedures.

hard-coding The act of setting a value by directly coding it into the application without allowing for a way to easily change it. For example, the hard-coded statement `Set picPictureBox.Picture=LoadPicture("C:\windows\bubbles.bmp")` won't work if the file bubbles.bmp is moved from the Windows folder, and it doesn't allow users to change the image loaded into the PictureBox. To avoid this situation, it would be better to define a string variable that contains the image's path and filename and then

provide tools (such as an Open common dialog box) to help users search for it.

header A commented section of code at the beginning of a procedure, usually placed before the `Sub` or `Function` statement. The header describes the purpose of the procedure, specifies all variables declared within it, and can contain information identifying the developer(s) who wrote it.

help compiler An application used to combine information into a help file.

help context ID A number that defines a position within a help file. The Windows help system uses context IDs to move to new locations within help files as users navigate through the help system.

high-level language A computer language, such as Visual Basic, that can simplify coding by enabling programmers to write code with highly developed functions and keywords. See also *low-level language*.

hovering The act of holding the mouse pointer over an object. For example, a ToolTip can appear when the pointer hovers over a command button.

HTML The acronym for *Hypertext Markup Language*. HTML files are plain text files that include data and instructions for presenting it. When viewed with an Internet browser, an HTML file can contain text, multiple colors, and graphics. Using HTML files, which you can link via hyperlinks, is the primary way to display information on the Web.

HTML element A portion of an HTML page, such as a graphic, a CommandButton, or a table, that may or may not be created dynamically using Visual Basic.

HTTP The acronym for *Hypertext Transfer Protocol*. An Internet protocol used by Web browsers to exchange information and to receive and present data to the browser's user.

hyperlinks References between documents that, when selected by users, call and display other documents.

IDE The acronym for *Integrated Development Environment*. The IDE includes all the tools necessary to create applications with Visual Basic 6, such as the Form Layout window and the Object Browser.

index A unique number that identifies a single element in an array or a control array.

index (database) A cross-reference of fields across the tables of a database that enables faster retrieval to specific records in the database.

inheritance The act of passing property values from a class to objects created by the class.

initialization The act of setting the value of a variable or expression to a specific starting value.

input box A dialog, created with the `InputBox()` statement, that waits for users to enter text or click a button.

When users close an input box, a string containing the contents of the text box is returned to the calling procedure.

instance A single object created from a class. Also, a variable is an instance of a data type.

Integer A numerical data type. `Integer` values are 16-bit (2-byte) numbers within the range of −32,768 to 32,767. `Integer` values use the prefix `int` and the type-declaration character `%` (the percent sign).

Integrated Development Environment (IDE) See *IDE*.

Internet Information Server (IIS) Microsoft's network file and application server. IIS is primarily used to support transmission of HTML pages using the HTTP protocol.

Internet service provider (ISP) A company that provides access to the Internet via a dial-up or direct connection.

interpreted language A language, such as Visual Basic, which doesn't enable compilation to native code. When an application created with an interpreted language is run, the application's code is passed through an interpreter, which modifies the code into a form the computer can understand and execute.

intrinsic ActiveX control An ActiveX control included with Visual Basic, such as the CommonDialog or Winsock control.

intrinsic control Also known as *standard controls*. A control included with Visual Basic, such as the Label or CommandButton controls. Intrinsic controls can't be removed from the ToolBox.

intrinsic function A predetermined function included with Visual Basic. Examples of intrinsic functions include the type conversion functions, such as CStr(), which usually converts a numeric expression to a string value.

JScript The Microsoft implementation of the JavaScript scripting language.

key field The field in a database table that uniquely describes each record. For example, the key field in a database table of employees might be the employee number. Also known as the *primary key*.

keycode A constant value that represents a keystroke. Keycodes are sent to the application when a key on the keyboard is pressed; they are used to determine which key the user pressed.

keyword A word (function, constant, or command) recognized by Visual Basic. You can't use keywords to name user-defined structures such as variables or constants (see *name collision*).

language independent Any file, object, or other structure that can be used by any programming language. For example, the Windows API can be used by Visual Basic, C, or Visual C++.

late binding A method of using an object by an application. In late binding, objects are defined as Object. Late binding is slower than early binding because the application must interrogate the object to determine its properties and methods.

Let A Visual Basic keyword. The part of a Property procedure that assigns a value to a property. Also used to assign a value to a variable, such as Let x = 10.

literal statement Any expression consisting of ASCII characters, enclosed in quotation marks, and used literally in a procedure. For example, if the code MsgBox("This is a button") were contained within the Click event of a command button, a dialog box containing the text This is a button would appear onscreen when the user clicks the button. Also known as a *literal* or *string literal*. Literals are also numbers used directly within code.

local variable A variable defined and used only within a specific procedure in an application. Other procedures can't see local variables.

Long A numerical data type. Long (long integer) values are 32-bit (4-byte) numbers within the range of –2,147,483,648 to 2,147,483,647. Long values use the prefix lng and the type-declaration character & (the ampersand).

loose typing Defining and using variables without declaring or following a specific data type, such as when Variant values are used. This can lead to type-mismatch errors at compile time because expressions or values can encounter data types that they don't support. See also *strict typing*.

low-level language A computer language, such as machine language, that requires a programmer to write code with less developed instructions so that the computer can directly understand.

make To compile code into a standard application (EXE), dynamic link library (DLL), or ActiveX control (OCX).

member functions See *method*.

menu A list of user-selectable items within a program. Also, a control used to add menus to an application.

menu bar The part of the Visual Basic IDE, located directly below the title bar, that lets you select functions and commands included with the application. By using the Menu Editor, you can add menu bars to applications created with Visual Basic.

message box A dialog, created with the MsgBox() function, that displays a message for users. Message boxes include one or more command buttons that enable users to clear the dialog or respond with an answer to a query. A message box returns an Integer value describing which button was selected.

method A procedure, associated with a class, that manipulates an object. For example, one method of a command button is SetFocus, which moves the focus to the command button that invoked the method.

module A block of code saved as a file with the extension .bas. Modules contain declarations and may or may not contain procedures.

name collision An error that occurs when different structures are named identically. For example, if a variable were named string, a name collision would occur because the word String is a Visual Basic keyword. Name collisions also occur when identically named variables are defined within the same scope.

naming convention A specific style used to reference objects in code. See *variable prefix* and *variable suffix*.

native code Binary code that can be directly understood and executed by the computer's processor system. Visual Basic can be set to compile to native code by setting options on the **Compile** page of the Project Properties dialog.

nesting The act of including Loop or Select Case statements within similar statements. For example, a Do...Loop can be placed within one case of the Select Case statement. Then the repetitive action controlled by the Do...Loop executes only if the proper value is passed to the Select Case statement.

object A discrete combination of code and data, such as a ListBox or CommandButton, that can be manipulated. Objects contain properties and methods and are defined by a class.

Object Browser A part of the Visual Basic IDE, the Object Browser enables you to see all the objects (and all the properties, methods, and events of each object) available for use on the system. To access the Object Browser, press F2, choose **Object Browser** from the **View** menu, or click the Object Browser icon 🔡 on the toolbar.

object-oriented programming (OOP) A programming style and a type of programming language that involves the use of software modules called *objects* to encapsulate data and processing.

OLE automation server See *ActiveX component*.

OLE DB A Microsoft technology that allows access to data from various, multiple data sources.

Option Explicit A Visual Basic keyword, the use of which forces each variable or expression in an application to be defined with a specific data type through the use of the Dim, Private, Public, ReDim, or Static keywords. Using Option Explicit can help reduce the likelihood of typographical errors when typing the names of existing variables. If Option Explicit isn't used, undefined variables are automatically defined as Variants.

P-code Code that can't be directly understood and executed by the Windows operating system. In Visual Basic, code compiled to P-code is interpreted to native code at runtime. When you are creating an executable file, you can force Visual Basic to compile to P-code by setting the appropriate options in the **Compile** tab of the Project Properties dialog box.

parameter A numeric or string value that can be changed to modify an expression.

parse To use string manipulation functions to change user-inputted string information. For example, the string

"Microsoft+Visual&Basic&6.0" might be parsed into company ("Microsoft") and application ("Visual Basic 6.0") strings.

pattern wildcards Characters such as the asterisk (*) or question mark (?) that cause a query to broaden its result or that enable an expression to restrict inputted data. For example, a database query on all records containing *ain would return all records that end in ain, such as *Spain*, *train*, and so on. SQL databases typically use the percent sign (%) instead of an asterisk.

persistence The concept of keeping an object's data stored in memory or on disk.

pixel The smallest and most commonly used screen-dependent measure of screen distance. Objects on a form, however, generally aren't sized and located via pixels because the number of pixels on a screen varies for different resolutions and for different types of display systems. See *twip*.

prefix See *variable prefix*.

primary key The field in a database table that uniquely describes each record. For example, the primary key in a database table of employees might be the employee number. Also known as the *key field*.

private A Visual Basic keyword. Variables or procedures defined with the Private keyword are available only in the module in which the variable or procedure is defined.

procedural language A programming language, such as Visual Basic, in which data is manipulated by calling procedures rather than proceeding line by line through all code contained in the application.

procedure A block of code that can be called from within an application. A procedure might be used to position objects on a form or to calculate information from a set of user data. Various types of procedures include Functions and Subs.

program See *application*.

project A set of forms and modules that make up an application while it's being developed into an application.

Properties window A part of the Visual Basic IDE. This window enables you to view and modify all the properties of a given object during design time. It's not available during runtime.

property An attribute of an object as defined by a class. For example, one property of a command button is Caption, which is the text that appears on the button's face.

property bag An object that holds a set of property values and can restore those values to a new invocation of an object.

property procedures Procedures used to view and modify the properties of an object, such as the Let and Get statements. The Get statement returns the value of a private variable of an object, whereas the Let statement modifies the value if the new value is of the correct type.

protocol A formal set of rules that enable two computers to communicate (such as the HTTP or FTP protocols) or a set of rules used to define an action such as argument passing or creation of an object from a class. See *File Transfer Protocol (FTP)* and *Hypertext Transfer Protocol (HTTP)*.

prototype An application that simulates the behavior of another, more fully developed application. Visual Basic is often used as a prototyping tool, for example, to quickly develop a possible graphical user interface (GUI) for an application before the application is developed.

Public A Visual Basic keyword. Variables defined with the Public keyword can be seen by any procedure of any module contained in the application. If a public variable is defined within a class module, the object name must be specified to use the variable.

query A subset of a database that fits specific criteria. For example, a query might be placed on a music CD database for all jazz CDs. The query would return a recordset that contains only jazz CDs and no classical or rock CDs.

record All the data required to describe one retrievable item in a database and made up of one or more fields. A row in a database. For example, one record in a music CD database would contain all the data necessary to describe the CD, including artist, label, number of songs, and so on.

recordset A set of records from a single database table that meets specific criteria.

recursion The process of a procedure calling itself.

relational database A database file in which records can include pointers to other tables that contain some of the information required to describe the record. Relational databases can be a more efficient means of storing information. For example, a relational database of music CDs would require only one field to describe the contact information for the artist's fan club. This field would hold a pointer to another table containing the fan club information for every artist in the database. Contrast with *flat-file database*.

robust A term used to describe an application that can trap and react to errors occurring during execution. For example, a robust calculator application won't crash when users try to divide a number by zero. Instead, users see a dialog explaining that numbers can't be divided by zero.

round To change a value to a less precise value. When rounding a value, if the next most precise digit ends with 5 or higher, round up; otherwise, round down. For example, if rounding to the nearest tenth, the value 1.652 would be rounded to 1.7 because the next most precise (one hundredth) digit is 5. If rounding to the nearest one hundredth, 1.652 would be rounded to 1.65. See *truncate*.

runtime The time when the code is actually running during the creation of an application. Forms and functions can't be altered during runtime. See *design time*.

scope An attribute of a variable or procedure that determines which sections of which modules recognize it. There are three levels of scope: public, module, and procedure. Variables declared with the `Public` keyword can be accessed by any module, whereas variables declared within a specific module (with the `Private` keyword) can be used only within that module. Variables declared within a procedure can be used only in that procedure.

scroll buttons The buttons at the top and bottom of a scrollbar that enable users to move through the data within the object.

scrollbar A window element that enables users to view more available data when all available data can't be displayed within an object at one time.

server side In a Web-based application, the part of the application run by the server instead of the client's Web browser.

server-side components In a Web-based application, the portions of the application located on and run by the server.

Set A Visual Basic keyword. The part of a `Property` procedure that sets a reference to an object.

Single A numerical data type. `Single` values are 32-bit (4-byte) floating-point numbers, within the range of $-3.402823E38$ to $-1.4012989E\text{-}45$ for negative values and 1.401298E45 to 3.402823E38 for positive values. `Single` variables use the prefix `sng` and the type-declaration character ! (the exclamation point).

SQL The acronym for *Structured Query Language*. A set of rules that can control many types of relational databases, including Microsoft Access and SQL Server databases.

standard control See *intrinsic control*.

standard EXE A traditional executable application. A standard EXE is a self-contained application that doesn't expose objects to the system for use by other objects or applications.

statement A section of code that fully expresses a single declaration or action.

static variable A variable, defined with the `Static` keyword, that maintains its value between calls to different procedures.

step The act of moving through a section of code line by line. Stepping, used with a breakpoint, is useful in determining which line is causing a problem in code.

strict typing Always declaring and following a specific data type when defining and using variables. This can reduce the number of errors at compile time because expressions or values will encounter only data types that they support. Contrast with *loose typing*.

String An alphanumeric data type. `String` values are either variable length (up to 2 billion characters) or fixed length (approximately 64,000 characters);

longer strings require more memory. Strings can include numbers, letters, and ASCII symbols. `String` values use the prefix `str` and the type-declaration character $ (the dollar sign).

Sub A procedure, beginning with `Sub` *sub-name()* and ending with `End Sub`, that doesn't return a value to the calling procedure when it's complete.

subclassing The act of modifying the standard behavior of an object provided by Windows. Visual Basic doesn't directly support subclassing.

subscript The index value of an element in an array.

syntax The specific method by which functions or lines of code are written. Important elements of syntax might include spelling, spacing, and punctuation.

system modal A window or dialog that holds control of the entire system until the user responds to it.

table The basic mechanism of data storage in a database, made up of tables and rows. In a relational database, multiple tables might be used to store different categories of related information. For example, in a music CD database, one table might contain only artist information, whereas others might contain label information or fan club information.

toolbar A collection of buttons, contained in a strip or in a dedicated window, that enable users to control an application.

ToolBox A part of the Visual Basic 6 Integrated Development Environment (IDE). The ToolBox contains the objects and controls available for use in an application; objects are dragged from the ToolBox and added to forms during design time.

traverse To move through records in a database, elements in an array, or data contained within an object.

truncate To shorten or reduce a string value. For example, the value This is My String might be truncated to My String. Contrast with *round*.

twip A screen-independent measure of screen distance equal approximately to 1/1440 of an inch. Objects on a form should be sized and located by using twips instead of pixels so that they appear similarly on various types of display systems.

type The attribute of a variable that determines what kind of data it can contain. Various types of data include Integer, Long, Variant, and String.

typecasting Explicitly converting a variable or expression from one data type to another.

type-declaration character A character added to a variable's name that determines a variable's data type. A type-declaration character can be used as a shorthand way of automatically setting a data type when defining a variable and can be useful when defining a local variable. For example, the type-declaration

character of the Integer data type is the percent sign (%), so an Integer variable x could be automatically defined with the statement Dim x%.

type safety The concept of keeping the data type of a variable or expression correct and consistent. In Visual Basic, type safety can be forced through the use of the Option Explicit keyword.

user control A subobject of a control. User controls are properties or methods that can be added to an object.

user-defined data types A data type not intrinsic to Visual Basic and defined by using the Type keyword, a list of declared elements, and the End Type keyword. User-defined data types can contain one or more elements of any data type.

validation The act of ensuring that data is of an appropriate format before it's written to a database.

variable A named storage location that contains data and can be modified during runtime. Variables are generally defined to be a specific data type at design time.

variable prefix A combination of characters added to the beginning of a variable name, used to help describe the variable throughout your code. For example, a global variable used to accept user input might be called gInput; the prefix g indicates that the variable is global. See also *naming convention*.

variable suffix A combination of characters added to the end of a variable name, used to define and describe the data type the variable holds. For example, a global variable used to accept user input might be called `gInput$`; the suffix `$` indicates that the variable contains a string value. See also *naming convention* and *type-declaration character*.

Variant A data type that can be either numeric or alphanumeric. A `Variant` is automatically created when a variable is not defined to be a specific data type. `Variants` don't have a type-declaration character.

VBA The acronym for *Visual Basic for Applications*. Similar to but a subset of the Visual Basic language. VBA is the programming language included with programs such as Access and Excel. In these programs, VBA can be used to create macros.

VBScript A scripting language, similar to but a subset of the Visual Basic language, especially suited to be embedded into HTML files because it must be interpreted by a Web browser. VBScript enables objects to be added to Web pages to accomplish such tasks as password authentication or surveys for data collection.

Visual Basic runtime DLL One of a set of files required to run an application developed in Visual Basic. Automatically installed with Visual Basic, the runtime DLLs must be copied to any machine on which an application is deployed.

watch A variable whose value is tracked during runtime. When a watch is set, it appears in the Watch window (part of the IDE). Watches are updated whenever a breakpoint is reached; thus, changes to values can be seen by placing breakpoints at specific events.

whitespace When coding, the space within the code editor that doesn't contain text, such as blank lines or tab spaces. Whitespace makes it easier to follow the flow of code—especially more complex structures such as nested loops—within a procedure.

Wintel An abbreviation for Windows/Intel, the platform used by most computer users. Wintel refers to a computer running a version of Microsoft Windows running on an Intel processor.

wizard An application, or part of an application, that helps users complete a difficult task. For example, Visual Basic's Data Form Wizard consists of multiple steps, each asking for specific information required to create and bind a form to a database.

Index

Symbols

^ (caret), exponential operator, 140, 147

_ (underscore)
  constant naming conventions, 128
  continuation symbol, 215

! (exclamation point), data-type suffix, 132

" (quotation marks), strings, 134

(pound sign)
  data-type suffix, 133
  footnote character (RTF files), 463

$ (dollar sign)
  data-type suffix, 133
  footnote character (RTF files), 463

% (percent sign), data-type suffix, 120, 132

& (ampersand)
  access keys, 256
  concatenating strings, 218
  concatenation operator, 142-143
  data-type suffix, 120, 132
  menu captions, 253

' (apostrophe), 112

() (parentheses), 142, 152

* (asterisk)
  fixed-length string declarations, 135
  multiplication operator
    sample program, 136-139
    syntax, 136

+ (plus sign), addition operator, 134-135

- (hyphen), subtraction operator, 135

… (ellipsis), Windows menu conventions, 249

\ (backslash), integer division operator, 139

/ (forward slash), floating-point division operator, 139

:=, passing arguments, 355

= (equals operator), Select Case statement, 157

@ (at symbol), data-type suffix, 133

3D forms, Appearance property, 289

A

a prefix (variables), 114

About dialog, 276

Abs function, syntax, 647

abstraction, 292

accelerator keys. See shortcut keys

Access
  Data Form Wizard, 589
  VBA, 498-500, 504-508

access keys. See also shortcut keys
  adding with Menu Editor, 256-257
  Windows conventions, 249

ActiveDocument object (MS Word), 486

ActiveX Control Interface Wizard, 534

ActiveX controls, 527
  adding, 76
  adding functionality, 535-538
  building, 530
  Calendar program, 15, 18
    Timer control, 18-20
  compared to HTML elements, 551
  compiling, 538-539
  CoolBar control, 37
  deploying, 540-541
  Label control, displaying time, 21
  MS Word spell checker, 486
  Properties window, 62

registration, GetAutoServerSettings function, 674

Scripting RunTime, 40

server-side, 546

Slider, adding to DHTML, 574-576

Timer control, 20

UserControl object, 533
  adding to forms, 534

VB6 enhancements, 36

VBA Object Browser, 480-481

windowless, VB6 enhancements, 46

ActiveX DLLs, 43, 521-526
  registering, 525

Add File command (Project menu), 86

Add Form dialog box, About boxes, 276

Add method, controls at runtime, 42

Add Procedure command, 349

Add Procedure dialog box (IDE), 516

Add Project command (IDE File menu), 87

Add Watch dialog box (IDE), 406

Add-In Connect Designer (IDE), 593

Add-In Manager (IDE), 580
  Data Form Wizard, 588

add-in toolbar, 581
  Data Form Wizard, 588

Add-Ins (IDE)
  API Viewer, 440

  Application Wizard, 582-583, 586-587

  attaching to Add-Ins menu, 580

  attaching to Add-Ins toolbar, 581

  custom, 593-595
    IDE object model, 596, 599-601

  Data Form Wizard, 588

  VB6 enhancements, 47

Add-Ins menu, Data Form Wizard, 614

AddHeaderProc() function, 597

adding strings. See con-catenating strings

AddItem method, adding strings at runtime, 195

addition operator (+), 134-135

ADO (Active Data Objects)
  Data control, 632
    DataList control, 641
    linking DataGrid control, 636

  Data Form Wizard, 644

  DataCombo control, 643

  DataGrid control, 636
    form design, 639
    grid columns, 637-639
    properties, 640

DataList control, 641
  properties, 642

VB6 enhancements, 44

ADO Data control, 614, 635-636

AdvTedit.vbp, 367

aligning forms to screen, 102

always-on-top (windows), 448

Amazing Text Editor, 260
  Checked property, 262

Ambient property, 534

AmbientProperties object, 534

ampersand (&)
  access keys, 256

  concatenating strings, 218

  concatenation operator, 142-143

  data-type suffix, 120, 132

  menu captions, 253

AND operator, in place of If...Then, 454

ani prefix (variables), 114

API Viewer, 440. See also **Windows API**
  as an add-in, 581

  configuring, 441

  data definition, 442

  GetCursorPos function, 445

apostrophe ('), 112

App object
HelpFile property, 469
version information, 386

AppActivate statement, syntax, 648

Appearance property, 289

Application Setup Wizard. See **Package and Deployment Wizard**

Application Wizard, 582-587
menus, 249-252
settings, saving, 251

applications
adding help files, 468
tracking mouse pointer, 445
VBA, 482-486
MS Word search program, 491-497
MS Word spell checker, 486-491
version information, 386-389

arguments
data types, 354
HTML elements, 552
Index, 423
KeyPress event, 293
message boxes, 269
passing, Windows API, 448
passing to subs/ functions, 352
named, 355

arithmetic operators.
See **math operators**

Arrange method, 289

Array function, syntax, 648

arrays, 182
adding items to list/combo boxes, 193-195
arrays of strings, 226
combining with Join() function, 231
converting a string into an array, 227
sublists with Filter() function, 230
Baseball ScoreKeeper program, 201-202, 205, 208-209
changing number of elements, 185-187
control. See control arrays
declaring
like single variable, 184-185
with To keyword, 185
first element as 1, 184
GetAllSettings() function, 378
LBound function, 686
lists
clearing, 199
removing items, 198
selecting items, 196-198
multidimensional, 188-191
redimensioning, 186

reinitializing elements (Erase statement), 668
resizing with ReDim, 507
retrieving settings with GetAllSettings() function, 378
traversing with For...Next loops, 191-193

As keyword, 118, 130
redimensioning arrays, 186

Asc function, syntax, 648

ASCII
common characters, 294
control characters, 296

assigning
variable types
As keyword, 118, 130
data-type suffixes, 120, 132-133
variable values, 132

assignment statements, 132

asterisk (*)
fixed-length string declarations, 135
multiplication operator
sample program, 136-139
syntax, 136

at symbol (@), data-type suffix, 133

Atn function, syntax, 648

automatic error detection, disabling, 120

automation (ActiveX), 524

AutoShowChildren property, 289

AutoSize property, 336

B

b prefix (variables), 113

background pictures, 35

backslash (\), integer division operator, 139

Band objects, CoolBar control, 38

Baseball ScoreKeeper program, arrays, 201-202, 205, 208-209

Beep statement, syntax, 648

binding to Data control, 613

block statements
If...Then, 149
Select Case, relational operators, 157-158

Boolean data type, 117

Boolean functions, IsNumeric(), 242

BorderStyle property, 28
button properties, 322
ControlBox property settings, 323
settings, 90

bound controls, DataGrid, 641

bound forms, database, 614-615, 618-619

breaking infinite loops, 171

breakpoints
checking code segments, 404
Run to Cursor, 410
stepping, 408
variable values, 407
watches, 405

browsers
DHTML, 568
scripts, 557

buffer strings, 220

build numbers. See revision numbers

buttons
custom, 336-338
form properties, 323
Help, 469

byte data type, 117

ByVal keyword, 448

C

c prefix (variables), 113

CAB files, 393
deploying custom ActiveX controls, 540

Calculator program, If...Then statement, 147

Calendar program, 14-18
CommandButton control, 22, 25-26
improving, 26

Call keyword, 349

Call Stack dialog box (IDE), 412

Call statement, syntax, 648

calling
class properties, 519
subs, 349

capitalization, find operations, 214

Caption property, clearing text from ListBox control, 199

Caption text box (Menu Editor), separator lines, 261

captions, menu items, Checked property, 262

caret (^), exponential operator, 140, 146

carriage return character, 372

cascading errors, 418

Case statement, 154

CausesValidation property, 33

cbo prefix (variables), 114

CBool function, syntax, 649

CByte function, syntax, 649

CCur function, syntax, 649

CDate function, syntax, 649

CDbl function, syntax, 649

CDec function, syntax, 650

CGI (Common Gateway Interface), 552

Change event, TextBox control, 304

changing
control names, 72
project properties, 83

characters
ASCII, 294
delimiters, 228

ChDir statement, syntax, 650

ChDrive statement, syntax, 650

check boxes
INPUT tag (HTML), 555
Keep on Top, 451
Windows conventions, 249

CheckBox control, 70

Checked property, 262

CheckSpelling method (VBA), 486

child controls, defined, 75

child elements (HTML forms), 553

child forms (MDI), 285

chk prefix (variables), 114

Choose function, syntax, 650

Chr function, syntax, 650

CInt function, syntax, 651

CInt() function, type-casting, 241

class IDs, 573
compiling DHTML apps, 577

class modules, 513

classes
adding properties, 515-519
as ActiveX DLLs, 521-526
compared to user-defined types, 510
creating, 512
creating objects, 513
creating objects from, 520-521

Clear method, 199

Click event, 303, 306

click event handlers, control arrays, 424

Click() event procedure
custom buttons, 338
MoveIt program, 100
saving data to files, 370

client area, 453

client-side programs, 546

clients, 43, 544

Clipboard object, 263

CLng function, syntax, 651

Clock feature. See Timer control

Clock program
Format() function, 324-326
Timer control, 321-324

Close statement, 371
syntax, 651

closing files, 371

clp prefix (variables), 114

cmd prefix (variables), 114

cmdAddRun_Click() procedure, Baseball ScoreKeeper, 202

cmdEnlarge_Click() event procedure, 346

cnt files, 458

code headers, custom add-ins, 595

code listings. See listings

code reuse, procedure arguments, 353

Code window (IDE), 60
Add Procedure command, 349
catching syntax errors, 402
checking with break-points, 404
Run to Cursor, 410
stepping, 408
variable values, 407
watches, 405
class modules, 515
compiling, 389
continuation symbol (_), 215
debugging, find and replace, 413
event procedures, 22, 95
MsgBox statement/function syntax, 271

CodeModule object, custom add-ins, 597

CodePane object, custom add-ins, 597

collections
databases, 506
SpellingSuggestions, 490

color, RGB function, 708

Color dialog box, retrieving colors in CommonDialog control, 283

columns (database), displaying with DataGrid control, 637

com prefix (variables), 114

combining strings. See **concatenating strings**

combo boxes, FileType, 280

ComboBox control, 70
adding strings at design time, 194
adding strings at runtime, 195
array items, 193-195
Baseball ScoreKeeper program, 201-202, 205, 208-209
Clear method, 199
mouse events, 303
RemoveItem method, 198
SELECT tag (HTML), 556
styles, 199

ComboItem object, VB6 enhancements, 38

command codes (ASCII), 295

Command function, syntax, 651

command syntax. See **syntax**

CommandButton control, 22, 70
MoveIt program, 97

CommandButtons
control array, 422
message boxes, 269
MsgBox() function, return values, 272

commands (IDE)
File menu
Add Project, 87
New Project, 82
Open Project, 85
Save Project, 84
Project menu
Add File, 86
Components, 76
Remove, 87

comments, 98, 112
documenting procedures, 359
HTML, 559

CommonDialog control, 276
Color dialog box, 283
DBTransport program, 505
File dialog box, 278, 280-281
FileName property, 280
Filter property, 279

Flags property, 281
Font dialog box, 281
Print dialog box, 284
properties, 277

Compile On Demand option, 120

compiling, 389, 391
custom ActiveX controls, 538-539
DHTML apps, 577-578
native code, 390
P-code, 389

Complete Word, 52

components, 527-528
server-side, 546

Components command (Project menu), 76

Components dialog box (IDE), 277

Composer.vbp project, 470

concatenating strings, 142-143, 217
concatenation operator (&), 142-143
example, 143
syntax, 142
defined, 161
For...Next loops, 161-162

conditional compilation, 415-417

conditional loops. See **Do loops**

Connect Designer add-in, 596

Const statement, syntax, 651

constants, 138-139
  HWND_TOPMOST, 449
  KeyCode parameter (KeyUp/KeyDown events), 298
  message boxes, 268
  naming conventions, 128
  vbCrLf, 163

constituent controls, 533

containers
  controls, adding, 76
  defined, 75
  frames, 429
  mouse events, 313

content files, 458

context-sensitive help, 469-473

continuation symbol (_), 215

control arrays, 42, 422
  common event handlers, 426-428
  creating at design time, 422-424
  extending at runtime, 424-426
  For...Next loops, 432-436
  frame control groupings, 428-429
  scroll bar controls, 429-431
  Visible value, 425

control characters (ASCII), 296

control statements, 146. See also **decision statements**
  Do...Loop statement, syntax, 660, 667
  On...GoTo, 692, 699
  On...GoSub statement, syntax, 692, 699

ControlBox property, 323

controls. See also **ActiveX controls**
  ActiveX controls, adding, 76
  adding to forms, with ToolBox, 57
  ADO, 632
  child controls, defined, 75
  ComboBox, mouse events, 303
  common methods, 91
  common properties, 90
  CommonDialog, 276
    Color dialog box, 283
    File dialog box, 278-281
    Font dialog box, 281
    Print dialog box, 284
  constituent, 533
  containers, 76
    defined, 75
  Data, 609
    connecting to database, 611-614
  Data Report Designer, 623
  DataCombo, 643
  DataGrid, 636
    form design, 639
    grid columns, 637-639
    properties, 640
  DataList, 641
    properties, 642
  events, listed, 702
  FlatScrollBar, VB6 enhancements, 39
  Frame, child controls, 429
  graphics, VB6 enhancements, 34
  HelpContextID property, 469
  ImageCombo, VB6 enhancements, 38
  intrinsic controls, 57
    adding, 71
    CheckBox, 70
    ComboBox, 70
    CommandButton, 70
    Data, 70
    defined, 68
    DirListBox, 70
    distributing, 68
    DriveListBox, 70
    FileListBox, 70
    Frame, 70
    HscrollBar, 70
    Image, 70
    Label, 70
    Line, 70
    ListBox, 70
    moving, 75
    naming conventions, 72-74
    OLE Container, 70
    OptionButton, 70
    PictureBox, 70
    removing, 71
    Shape, 70

sizing, 74
TextBox, 70
Timer, 70
VscrollBar, 70
Label, 21
ListView, VB6 enhancements, 34
loading, nested loops, 179
menu properties, 256
methods, listed, 702
mouse events, VB limitations, 313
Name property, 24
PictureBox, 334
properties, listed, 702
RptLabel, 624
Slider, VB6 enhancements, 35
TabStrip, VB6 enhancements, 34
Timer, 318-320
static variables, 329-331
UserControl, 530
VB6 enhancements, 32
VB6 features, 42
VBA, adding to projects, 481
window handles (hWnd), 448
windowless, 20

Controls collection, Add method, 42

conversion functions, 241

CoolBar control, VB6 enhancements, 37

Copies property, 284

copying text, Clipboard object, 263

Cos function, syntax, 652

counter loops. See **For...Next loops**

counter variables (For loops)
changing values, 163
decrementing, 161
defining, 160
incrementing, 161
types, 163

counters, static variables, 329

CounterVar. See **counter variables**

CreateObject function, syntax, 652

CreateTextFile() method, 381

CSng function, syntax, 652

CStr function
syntax, 652
typecasting, 241

ctr prefix (variables), 114

CurDir function, syntax, 653

currency data type, 116

custom add-ins, 593-595
IDE object model, 596, 599-601

custom buttons, 336-338

custom icons, embedding, 341

cutting text, Clipboard object, 263

CVar function, syntax, 653

CVErr function, syntax, 653

D

d prefix (variables), 113

DAO (Data Access Objects), DBTransporter program, 498

dat prefix (variables), 114

data
persistence, 366
retrieving, 371
storing, 366

Data control, 44, 70, 609
ADO, 632
connecting to database, 611-614

data elements, 512

Data Environment Designer, 45, 624

Data Form Wizard, 588, 614-619
ADO controls, 645

Data Report Designer, 622
building reports, 623, 626-629
controls, 623
VB6 enhancements, 45

data sources, ADO Data control, 633

data structures, arrays, 182
changing number of elements, 185-187
declaring, 184
list/combo boxes, 193-195
multidimensional, 188, 191
traversing with For...Next loops, 191-193

data types, 115-116
assigning
As keyword, 118, 130
data-type suffixes, 120, 132-133
Boolean, 117
byte, 117
currency, 116
date, 117, 318
default values, 133
double, 116
integers, 116
Jet database engine, 608
long, 116
object, 117
passing arguments, 354
single, 116
string, 117
type mismatch errors, 129
typecasting, 240-241
user-defined, 510-512
variant, 117-118
VBScript, 547
Windows-defined, 439

data-bound forms, Data Form Wizard, 593

DatabaseName property (Data control), 611

databases, 606-609
ADO, 632
Data control, 632
DataCombo control, 643-644
DataGrid control, 636-640
DataList control, 641-642
ADO Data control, 635-636
bound forms with Data Form Wizard, 614-619
Data control, 609
connecting, 611-614
Data Form Wizard, 588
elements, 607
Jet engine, 608

DataCombo control, 643

DataGrid control, 636
form design, 639
grid columns, 637-639
properties, 640
VB6 enhancements, 45

DataList control, 641
properties, 642

DataSource property, reports, 627

date data type, 117, 318

Date function, 320
syntax, 653

Date statement, syntax, 653

DateAdd function, syntax, 654

DateDiff() function, 326-327

source code, 328
syntax, 654

DatePart function, syntax, 654

dates
calculating differences, 326
controls, VB6 enhancements, 37
Format() function, 325

DateSerial function, syntax, 654

DateTimePicker control, VB6 enhancements, 37

DateValue function, syntax, 655

Day function, syntax, 655

db prefix (variables), 113-114

DblClick event procedure, 306

DBTransporter program, 498

DDB function, syntax, 655

DebDbl statement, syntax, 657

Debug toolbar (IDE), 52, 410

Debug.Print statement, 415-416

debugging
application design, 415
breakpoints, 404
Run to Cursor, 410

stepping, 408
variable values,
405-407
catching undeclared
variables, 402-404
conditional compilation,
415
find and replace, 413
Immediate window, 411
Locals window, 410
tools, 410-412

decision statements
If, nested, 153
If...Then, 146
multiple line, 149
single line, 146-147
If...Then...Else, 150
If...Then...ElseIf, 151
Select Case, 153-155
relational operators in
blocks, 157-158

Declare statement, 438
syntax, 655

declaring
arrays
like single variable,
184-185
with To keyword, 185
objects, 521
variables, 25
Dim keyword,
111-112
error detection, 120,
132
explicit declarations,
117-119, 131-132
implicit declarations,
119, 131
local variables, 137

public variables,
136-137
static variables,
137-138

decrementing counter
variables (For loops),
161

default buttons, message
boxes, 273

default variable values,
133

DefBool statement, syn-
tax, 656

DefByte statement, syn-
tax, 656

DefCur statement, syn-
tax, 656

DefDate statement, syn-
tax, 657

DefDec statement, syn-
tax, 657

DefInt statement, syn-
tax, 657

DefLng statement, syn-
tax, 658

DefObj statement, syn-
tax, 658

DefSng statement, syn-
tax, 658

DefStr statement, syn-
tax, 659

DefVar statement, syn-
tax, 659

DeleteSetting statement,
378
syntax, 659

deleting
controls, 71
files
from project list, 86-87
Kill statement, 686

delimiters, 228

deploying
compiling projects, 389
custom ActiveX con-
trols, 540-541
Package and
Deployment Wizard,
391
version information,
386

depreciation, DDB func-
tion, 655

design
for debugging, 415
menus, 248

design time
adding strings to box
controls, 194
control arrays, 422-424
MinButton/MaxButton
properties, 323

Designer, 43

designers, 565, 593

device input, 292
KeyPress event,
293-297
KeyPreview property,
302
KeyUp/KeyDown
event, 297-300
mouse, 303
Click event, 303, 306
VB limitations, 313

MouseDown/MouseUp events, 306-311
MouseMove event, 311-312

device-independent operating system, 292

DHTML, 43, 564-569
class ID, 573
compiling apps, 577-578
RAD, 570, 573-574
sample program, 568-570
Slider ActiveX control, 574-576
VB Designer, 43

dialog boxes
Add Procedure (IDE), 516
Add Project (IDE), 87
Add Watch (IDE), 406
Call Stack (IDE), 412
Font, 27
Help Topics, 463
InputBox function, 677, 683
Load Picture, 335
Map, 471
MsgBox function, syntax, 690, 697
New Project (IDE), 82
Open Project (IDE), 85
Project Properties (IDE), 83
Quick Watch (IDE), 412
Save File As (IDE), 84

Dim keyword, 25, 111
declaring arrays, 184
VBScript, 557

Dim statement, syntax, 659

Dir function, syntax, 660

dir prefix (variables), 114

DirListBox control, 70

disabling automatic error detection, 120

distributing, intrinsic controls, 68

division
floating-point division, 139
integer division, 139
remainder division, 140

division-by-zero error, 419

DLLs, 438
ActiveX, 521-526
commonly used, 438
Declare statement, 655
DHTML, 567
native code, 390

dlq prefix (variables), 114

Do...Loop statements, 166
Do...Until, 170
example, 170-171
syntax, 170
Do...While, 166-169
example, 167-168
retrieving files from disk, 372
syntax, 166-167
syntax, 660

Document Object Model (DOM), 553

documentation. See

online help

documenting procedures, 359

documents, adding to Word session, 485

DoEvents function, syntax, 660

dollar sign ($), data-type suffix, 133

domain names, 545

double data type, 116

dragging objects, windows (SendMessage API function), 452-454

dragging the mouse, 314

Drive Not Ready error, 419

DriveListBox control, 70

drv prefix (variables), 114

ds prefix (variables), 113

dsr extension, 576

dt prefix (variables), 113

DTPicker. See DateTimePicker

dynamic Web page, 564

dynasets (database), 609

E

Easter eggs, displaying, 307

Edit toolbar(VB IDE), 52

editing
control names, 72
project properties, 83

elements collection (HTML), 558-563

ellipsis (...), Windows menu conventions, 249

Else statement, 150

ElseIf statements, 151

encapsulation, 348, 518
file system objects, 379
MS Word (VBA), 486

End If statement, 149

End Select statement, 154

End statement, syntax, 661

end user, 14

end-of-line sequence, 372

ending. See terminating

entry points (procedures), 361

Enum statement, syntax, 661

Environ function, syntax, 661

EOF() function, 372
syntax, 662

Erase statement, syntax, 662

Error function, syntax, 662

error handling, 417-420
automatic error detection, disabling, 120
cascading errors, 418

On Error statement, 679
Replace() function, 217
reporting with message boxes, 269
Resume statement, syntax, 688
type mismatch errors, 129
variable declarations, 120, 132

error reporting, message boxes, 473

Error statement, syntax, 662

estimation utility (listing), 137-139

event handling
common for control arrays, 426-428
VBScript, 564

event notification, 96

event procedures, 22
control arrays, 426
DblClick, 306
Form_KeyPress(), 302
itmAdd_Click(), 288
MouseDown, MoveIt program, 102
MouseUp, MoveIt program, 102

Event statement, syntax, 662

event-driven programming, 94

events, 90
Click, 303-306
event notification, 102
GotFocus, 92

KeyPress, 293-297
KeyUp/KeyDown, 297-300
LostFocus, 92
MouseDown/MouseUp, 306-311
MouseMove, 311-312
procedures, 94
relation to properties/methods, 93
stepping through code, 408
Timer, 318
user-initiated, 92
VB limitations on mouse input, 313

Excel
objects, 506
VBA, 498-500, 504-508

exclamation point (!), data-type suffix, 132

executables
compiling, 391
compiling to, 389
embedding icons, 341

Execute method, Range object, 496

Exit keyword, 355

Exit statement, syntax, 663

ExitEarly() function, 356

exiting procedures, 355

Exp function, syntax, 663

explicit declarations, 117-119, 130-132

error detection, 120, 132

example, 118, 131

exponential operator (^), 140, 145

Extensibility Model. See **IDE, object model**

extensions
.cnt, 458
.hlp, 458
.hpj, 459
.rtf, 459
.vbg, 61, 534
dsr, 576

F

F1 key
Help key, 299
online help, 458

fields (database), 606

fil prefix (variables), 114

File dialog box, retrieving files in CommonDialog control, 278-281

file extensions
.cnt, 458
.dsr, 576
.hlp, 458
.hpj, 459
.rtf, 459
.vbg, 534

file handles, 366

File menu commands
Add Project, 87
New Project, 82
Open Project, 85
Save Project, 84

file modes, 369

File objects, 382

file system objects, 379-383
comp to FileSystemObject, 379
VB6 features, 39-40

file types, Filter property (CommonDialog control), 279

file-open mode, 278

file-save mode, 278

FileAttr function, syntax, 663

FileCopy statement, syntax, 663

FileDateTime function, syntax, 664

FileLen function, syntax, 664

FileListBox control, 70
loading graphics, 343
WordSearch program, 496

FileName property, 280

files
adding to projects, 85-86
deleting, Kill statement, 673
Input function, 670
project files, 80
removing from projects, 86-87
storing data, 366
types, 80

FileSystemObject object
comp to file system objects, 379
VB6 language enhancements, 40

FileType combo box, 280

Filter property, 279

Filter() function, 230

find and replace, debugging, 413

Find object (MS Word), 491

finding strings, Replace() function, 214

Fix function, syntax, 664

fixed-length strings, 135. See also **strings**

Flags property, CommonDialog control, 281

flat style, 35

flat-file databases, 606

FlatScrollBar control, VB6 enhancements, 39

FlatScrollBars property, 35

floating-point division operator (/), 139

focus
KeyDown event, 297
message box CommandButtons, 273
performing other commands, 302

Font dialog box, 27
retrieving fonts in
CommonDialog con-
trol, 281

fonts
Calendar program, 27
Checked property
(menus), 262

**footnote character ($),
463**

footnote characters
#, 463
k, 463

**footnotes (RTF files),
462**

**For Each...Next state-
ment, syntax, 664**

For...Next loops, 160
control arrays, 432-436
counter variables
changing values, 163
decrementing, 161
defining, 160
incrementing, 161
types, 163
early termination,
164-165
nesting, 172-173, 179
stepping through, 161
strings, concatenating,
161-162
syntax, 160, 671
traversing arrays,
191-193
Baseball ScoreKeeper
program, 202

**For...Next statement,
syntax, 664**

**Form Designer window,
60**

**Form Editor toolbar (VB
IDE), 55**

Form Layout window
IDE, 50
setting form position,
63

FORM tag, 552-553

**Format function, syntax,
665**

**Format menu com-
mands, Form Editor
toolbar, 55**

**Format() function,
324-326**
Clock program, 323

forms, 14. See also **controls; windows**
3D, Appearance proper-
ty, 289
adding controls, with
ToolBox, 57
adding graphics,
334-335
adding UserControl
object, 534
aligning to screen, 102
binding to databases,
614
chaining Form_Load()
event procedure, 361
client area, 453
compared to HTML
FORM element, 553
data-bound, Data Form
Wizard, 593
DataGrid control, 639
defined, 68

icons, 340
IDE, 50
KeyPreview property,
302
message boxes, 268
naming, 97
predefined, 275
properties, 323
resizing, sizing handles,
75
restricting sizing, 28
setting position at run-
time, 63
VB limits on mouse
input, 313

**Form_Load() event pro-
cedure**
Baseball ScoreKeeper
program, 202
Clock program, 322
MoreGrfx.vbp, 343
MoveIt program, 97-99

fra prefix (variables), 114

Frame control, 70

frame control
grouping objects,
428-429
removing child con-
trols, 429

FreeFile function, 366
syntax, 665

**frm prefix (variables),
114**

FromPage property, 284

**FTP (File Transfer
Protocol), 544**

**Function statement, syn-
tax, 665**

functions. See also **statements**

Abs, syntax, 647
AddHeaderProc(), 597
Array, syntax, 648
Asc, syntax, 648
Atn, syntax, 648
CBool, syntax, 649
CByte, syntax, 649
CCur, syntax, 649
CDate, syntax, 649
CDbl, syntax, 649
CDec, syntax, 650
Choose, syntax, 650
Chr, syntax, 650
CInt
  syntax, 651
  typecasting, 241
CLng, syntax, 651
Command, syntax, 651
conversion, typecasting, 241
Cos, syntax, 652
CreateObject, syntax, 652
CSng, syntax, 652
CStr
  syntax, 652
  typecasting, 241
CurDir, syntax, 653
CVar, syntax, 653
CVErr, syntax, 653
Date, 320
  syntax, 653
DateAdd, syntax, 654
DateDiff, 326-327
  syntax, 654
DatePart, syntax, 654
DateSerial, syntax, 654
DateValue, syntax, 655
Day, syntax, 655

DDB, syntax, 655
defined, 128
Dir, syntax, 660
documenting, 359
DoEvents, syntax, 660
entry point, 361-363
Environ, syntax, 661
EOF, 372
  syntax, 662
Error, syntax, 662
ExitEarly(), 356
exiting, 355
Exp, syntax, 663
FileAttr, syntax, 663
FileDateTime, syntax, 664
FileLen, syntax, 664
Filter(), 230
Fix, syntax, 664
Format, 324-326
  Clock program, 323
  syntax, 665
FreeFile, 366
  syntax, 665
FV, syntax, 666
Get, 518-519
GetAllSettings, syntax, 667
GetAttr, syntax, 667
GetAutoServerSettings, syntax, 667
GetCursorPos (WinAPI), 439, 445-447
GetFirstName(), 235
GetLastName(), 235
GetObject, syntax, 667
GetSetting, syntax, 668
Hex, syntax, 668
Hour, syntax, 668
IIf, syntax, 669

IMEStatus, syntax, 669
Input, syntax, 670
InputBox, syntax, 670
InStr, 224
  syntax, 670
Int, syntax, 671
IPmt, syntax, 671
IRR, syntax, 671
IsArray, syntax, 671
IsDate, syntax, 327, 671
IsEmpty, syntax, 672
IsError, syntax, 672
IsMissing, syntax, 672
IsNull, syntax, 672
IsNumeric, 139, 205, 242
  syntax, 672
IsObject, syntax, 672
IsValid(), 238
Join(), 231
LBound, 497
  syntax, 673
LCase, 233, 500
  syntax, 673
Left, 220
  syntax, 673
Len, 219
  syntax, 673
Let, 518-519
LoadPicture, 339-340, 373
  syntax, 674
LoadResData, syntax, 674
LoadResPicture, syntax, 674
LoadResString, syntax, 675
Loc, syntax, 675
LOF, syntax, 675
Log, syntax, 676

LTrim, syntax, 676
Mid, 222-224
    syntax, 676
Minute, syntax, 677
MIRR, syntax, 677
Month, syntax, 677
MsgBox, 268-269
    icons, 270
    returning values,
    271-273
    syntax, 677
Now, 320
    syntax, 678
NPer, syntax, 678
NPV, syntax, 678
Oct, syntax, 679
Partition, syntax, 681
passing arguments, 352
    named, 355
Pmt, syntax, 681
PPmt, syntax, 681
PV, syntax, 686
QBColor, syntax, 686
RaiseEvent, syntax, 686
Rate, syntax, 687
Registry, saving/retriev-
    ing data, 375
Replace(), 214-217
RGB, syntax, 688
Right(), 220
    syntax, 688
Rnd, syntax, 688
RTrim, syntax, 689
Second, syntax, 689
Seek, syntax, 689
SendMessage (Windows
    API)
    dragging windows,
    452-454
    enhancing list boxes,
    454

SetWindowPos
    (Windows API),
    447-452
Sgn, syntax, 691
Shell, syntax, 691
Sin, syntax, 691
SLN, syntax, 691
Space, syntax, 692
Spc, syntax, 692
Split(), 227
Sqr, syntax, 692
Str, syntax, 692
StrComp, syntax, 693
string parsing, 235,
    238-240
StrReverse(), 212-214
Switch, syntax, 694
SYD, syntax, 694
syntax, 351-352
Tab, syntax, 694
Tan, syntax, 694
Time, 320, 695
Timer, syntax, 695
TimeSerial, syntax, 695
TimeValue, syntax, 695
Trim, syntax, 696
TypeName, syntax, 696
type conversion, 242
UBound, 497
    syntax, 696
UCase(), 233, 500
    syntax, 697
Val, syntax, 697
VarType, syntax, 698
Weekday, syntax, 698
While...Wend, syntax,
    698
Windows API, 438
wrapper, 446
Year, syntax, 699
FV function, syntax, 666

G

garbage collection,
    object variables, **490**
gau prefix (variables),
    114
General Declarations
    section, Declare state-
    ment, 438
Get function, 518-519
Get statement, syntax,
    666
GetAllSettings function,
    378
    syntax, 667
GetAttr function, 667
GetAutoServerSettings
    function, syntax, 667
GetCursorPos API func-
    tion, ActiveX controls,
    536
GetCursorPos function
    (Windows API), 439,
    445-447
GetFirstName() func-
    tion, 235
GetLastName() func-
    tion, 235
GetObject function, syn-
    tax, 667
GetSetting function, 376
    syntax, 668
GetSpellingSuggestions
    method (VBA), 486
gf_ prefix, 327
Global Property Bag, 44

GoSub...Return statement, syntax, 668

GotFocus event procedure, 92
  MoveIt program, 102

GoTo statement, syntax, 668

gpb prefix (variables), 115

graphics
  adding to forms, 334-335
  adding with LoadPicture() function, 339-340
  changing at runtime, 336
  ComboItem object, VB6 enhancements, 38
  custom buttons, 336-338
  form icons, 340
  ImageCombo control, VB6 enhancements, 38
  loading with file list box, 342-344
  saving/retrieving, 373
  special effects, 345
  VB6 enhancements, 34

grd prefix (variables), 115

grid columns (DataGrid control), 637-639

groupings, frame control, 428-429

groups (project), 87-88
  defined, 87

H

h prefix (variables), 114

handling errors. See error handlers

hardware, device input, 292

Hardware Abstraction Layer (HAL), 292

HasDC property, 46

HEAD tag, 549

headers (documentation), 359

Height property, form alignment, 102

Hello World program, VBScript, 548

help
  context-sensitive, 469-473
    InputBox function, 670
  online, 458, 461
    adding files to apps, 468
    creating help files, 462-465, 468
    Help Workshop 4.0, 458-459
    RoboHelp, 461

Help button, 469

Help key, 299

Help menu, Windows standard, 248

Help Topics dialog box, 463

Help Workshop 4.0, 458

HelpContextID property, 469

HelpFile property, 469

Hex function, syntax, 668

hlp files, 458

HotTracking property, 35

Hour function, syntax, 668

hpj files, 459

hsb prefix (variables), 115

Hscrollbar control, 70

HScrollBar control, control arrays, 429

HTML (Hypertext Markup Language)
  ActiveX control equivalents, 551
  comments, 559
  elements of, 551-552
  FORM tag, 552-553
  HEAD tag, 549
  incorporating VBScript, 558-559, 563-564
  INPUT tag, 553-555
  sample code with VBScript, 550
  SCRIPT tag, 549, 557
  SELECT tag, 556
  TEXTAREA tag, 556

HTML Help, 467

HTTP (Hypertext Transfer Protocol), 544

hWnd (window handle), 448

HWND_TOPMOST constant, 449

hypertext (online help), 463

hyphen (-), subtraction operator, 135

I

i prefix (variables), 114

Icon property, 341

icons, message boxes, 270

id property, DHTML, 568

IDE (Integrated Development Environment), 50
  ActiveX DLL projects, 522
  Add-In Manager, 580
  Add-Ins, API Viewer, 440
  add-ins
    Application Wizard, 582-583, 586-587
    attaching to Add-Ins menu, 580
    attaching to Add-Ins toolbar, 581
    custom, 593
    Data Form Wizard, 588
  adding ActiveX DLLs, 524
  adding Scripting Runtime, 379
  Call Stack dialog box, 412

Code window, 60
  Add Procedure command, 349
  catching syntax errors, 402
  checking with breakpoints, 404
  class modules, 515
  compiling, 389
  continuation symbol (_), 215
  debugging, find and replace, 413
  event procedures, 22, 95
  MsgBox statement/function syntax, 271
Complete Word, 52
Data Form Wizard, 615
Debug toolbar, 52, 410
debugging
  breakpoints, 404-407
  find and replace, 413
  Option Explicit statement, 402-404
  Run to Cursor, 410
  stepping, 408
  tools, 410
designers, 565
Edit toolbar, 52
Form Designer window, 60
Form Editor toolbar, 55
forms, 14
Form_Load() event procedure, 99
Immediate window, 411
loading Calendar program, 15
Locals window, 410

MDIs, 290
options, Auto Syntax Check, 402
Project Explorer, 61
project groups, 535
Properties window, 62
Quick Watch dialog box, 412
Report Layout window, 622
shortcut keys, duplicate entries, 258
Standard toolbar, 55
syntax errors, catching, 402
toolbars, adding/removing, 51
Toolbox
  adding CommonDialog control, 277
  adding controls to forms, 57
ToolTips, 51
UserControls, 530
VB6 enhancements, 43
VBA, 477
  MS Word search program, 491-497
  MS Word spell checker, 486-491
  Object Browser, 480-482
  Record Macro tool, 478-479
  simple app, 482-486
  viewing (MDI/SDI), 64
Watch window, 407

IE (Internet Explorer), VBScript, 548-551
  HTML elements, 551-556

If statements, nested, 153

If...Then statement, 146
AND operator in place of, 454
multiple line, 149
single line, 146-147

If...Then...Else statement, 150
syntax, 669

If...Then...ElseIf statement, 151
rewriting as Select Case, 155

IIf function, syntax, 669

IIS, 545
file system objects, 40

Image control, 70
custom buttons, 338
SavePicture statement, 374
special effects, 345

Image Editor, 341

ImageCombo control, VB6 enhancements, 38

images
INPUT tag (HTML), 555
loading, LoadPicture function, 674

IMEStatus function, syntax, 669

Immediate window (IDE), 411
error handlers, 418

Implements statement, syntax, 669

implicit declarations, 119, 131

imq prefix (variables), 115

incrementing, counter variables (For loops), 161

Index (online help), 463

Index argument, control array event procedures, 426

Index property, control arrays, 423

indexes (database), 607

infinite loops
example, 171, 179
preventing, 172, 179
terminating, 171

initialization, 99

initializing variables, 132

input, device, 292

Input # statement, syntax, 670

Input function, syntax, 670

Input mode, 371

INPUT tag, 553-555

InputBox function, syntax, 670

inserting controls
ActiveX controls, 76
intrinsic controls, 71

inserting lines (MS Word), TypeParagraph method (VBA), 479

InsertLines() method, 600

installing
CAV files, 393

Help Workshop, 458
Package and Deployment Wizard, 391

InStr function, syntax, 670

InStr() function, 224

Int function, syntax, 671

intCompare argument, 214

integer data type, 116

integer division operator (\), 139

interactivity, Internet documuments, 544

Interface Wizard, 534

Internet, 544-546
CGI, 552
deploying custom ActiveX controls, 540
DHTML, 565-567
compiling apps, 577-578
RAD, 570, 573-574
sample program, 568-570
Slider ActiveX control, 574-576
VB6 enhancements, 43
VBScript, 546-548
event handling, 564
HTML elements, 551-556
IE, 548-551
incorporating with HTML, 558-559, 563-564

interpreted code, 390

Interval property, Timer control, 20, 319

intrinsic controls, 18, 57. See also **containers**
  adding, 71
  CheckBox, 70
  ComboBox, 70
  CommandButton, 70
  Data, 70, 609
    connecting to database, 611-614
  defined, 68
  DirListBox, 70
  distributing, 68
  DriveListBox, 70
  FileListBox, 70
  Frame, 70
  HscrollBar, 70
  Image, 70
  Label, 70
  Line, 70
  ListBox, 70
  moving, 75
  names
    changing, 72
    naming conventions, 73-74
  OLE Container, 70
  OptionButton, 70
  PictureBox, 70
  removing, 71
  Shape, 70
  sizing, 74
  TextBox, 70
  Timer, 70
  UserControls, 530
  VscollBar, 70

IP addresses, 545

IPmt function, syntax, 671

IRR function, syntax, 671

Is keyword, Select Case statements, 157

IsArray function, syntax, 671

IsDate function, 327
  syntax, 671

IsEmpty function, syntax, 672

IsError function, syntax, 672

IsMissing function, syntax, 672

IsNull function, syntax, 672

IsNumeric function, 139
  syntax, 672

IsNumeric() function, 205, 242

IsObject function, syntax, 672

ISPs (Internet Service Providers), 545
  compiling DHTML applications, 577

IsValid() function, 238

itmAdd_Click() event procedure, 288

J - K

Jet database engine, data types, 608

Join() function, 231

Julian time, 318

k (footnote character, RTF files), 463

Keep on Top check box, 451

key prefix (variables), 115

KeyAscii argument, 293

keyboard events
  KeyPress, 293-297
  KeyPreview property, 302
  KeyUp/KeyDown, 297-300

keyboard input, Help key, 299

KeyCode parameter (KeyUp/KeyDown events), constants, 298

KeyDown event, 297-300

KeyPress event, 293-297

KeyPreview property, 302

KeyUp event, 297-300

keywords
  As, 118, 130
    redimensioning arrays, 186
  ByVal, 448
  Call, 349, 649
  defined, 111
  Dim, 25, 111
    declaring, 184
  Exit, 355
  Is, Select Case statements, 157
  New, 521
  Nothing, 490
  Option Explicit, 119, 131

Optional, arguments, 355
Preserve, 186
Private, declaring arrays, 184
Public, declaring arrays, 184
ReDim, 186, 507
Set, 490
Static, 126, 138
counter variables, 330
Step, For...Next loops, 161
To
declaring arrays, 185
multidimensional, 191
Type, 511
UserControl, 534
Kill statement, syntax, 673

L

l prefix (variables), 114
Label control, 70
displaying time, 21
LANGUAGE attribute (SCRIPT tag), 557
lbl prefix (variables), 115
LBound() function, 497
syntax, 673
LCase() function, 233, 500
syntax, 673
Left property, form alignment, 102
Left() function, 220
syntax, 673

Len() function, 219
reversing strings, 213
syntax, 673
length property (HTML), 563
Let function, 518-519
Let statement, syntax, 673
Libraries drop-down list (VBA), 481
licensing agreements, 540
lin prefix (variables), 115
Line control, 70
line feed character, 372
Line Input # statement, syntax, 674
Line Input statement, 366, 371
list boxes, enhancing with SendMessage API function, 454
List property, 193
ListBox control, 70
adding strings at design time, 194
adding strings at run-time, 195
array items, 193, 195
Baseball ScoreKeeper program, 201-202, 205, 208-209
Clear method, 199
RemoveItem method, 198
styles, 199
WordSearch program, 491

ListIndex property, 197
DBTransporter program, 506
listings
AddHeaderProc function (add-ins), 597
API declaration, 439
App object, reading properties, 387
arrays
adding items to ListBox control, 196
assigning values, 185
redimensionable, 187
traversing with For...Next loops, 192
ASCII code, converting to string, 295
Baseball ScoreKeeper program
cmdAddRuns_Click event, 206
Form_Load() event procedure, 203
lstTeamOne_Click procedure, 208
Checked property, 263
classes, adding properties, 517
Click() event procedures for CommandButtons, MoveIt program, 100
clipboard, retrieving text, 264
cmdAdd event procedure, 111-112
ComboItems, creating, 38
control arrays
Click event handler, 424

listings

*Click() event proce-
dure, 426*
*removing elements
with For..Next loop,
434*
*runtime
CommandButtons,
425*
*traversing with
For...Next loop, 433*
controls collection, Add
method, 42
Custom Button Image
control, 337
DateDiff() function
source code, 328
debugging, typing
errors, 404
decision statements,
OptionButton values,
147
DHTML
class IDs, 573
*VBScript with HTML,
571*
Do...Until loop,
170-171
Do...While loop,
167-168
documenting functions,
359
ElseIf statements, 152
enlarging pictures, 346
estimation utility,
137-139
event procedures, Time,
Date, Now functions,
321
events
counting clicks, 305

*KeyPress event proce-
dure, 303*
*MouseDown event pro-
cedure, 308*
*MouseMove event pro-
cedure, 312*
*MouseMove with loops,
312*
Shift parameter, 308
file object properties,
382
For...Next loop
*early termination,
164-165*
*string concatenation,
162*
Form_Load() event
procedure, Clock pro-
gram, 322
functions, 352
arguments, 353
exiting, 355
*within event procedure,
354*
GetCursorPos API
function, ActiveX con-
trols, 537
help files, context sensitive, 472
If...Then statement,
commands in, 149
key events, checking for
function keys, 300
Line Input statement
(reading text file), 372
ListBoxes, removing
strings, 198
MDI apps, itmAdd
Click() event proce-
dure, 287

MoreGrfx program
*Click() event proce-
dure, 344*
*FileListBox Pattern
property, 343*
mouse event proce-
dures, MoveIt pro-
gram, 103
MSFlexGrid control,
parameters, 179
MsgBox() function,
return values, 274
nested loops
long integer array, 179
*multiple For loops,
172-174, 179*
SavePicture statement,
374
saving files, 370
scope, 358
Select Case statement
extending, 156
*rewriting
If...Then...ElseIf as,
155*
testing equality, 155
*testing for a range,
155*
*with relational opera-
tors, 158*
strings
array of strings, 226
case changing, 234
concantenating, 218
Filter() function, 231
InStr() function, 225
*joining arrays of
strings, 232*
Len() function, 219
*Mid() function,
223-224*

parsing, 236
reversing with Len()
function, 213
reversing with
StrReverse() function,
213
splitting into arrays,
229
testing for space chars,
238
truncating, 221
validating user input,
243
subs, calling from event
procedure, 349
Sub_Main(), 362-363
TextBox secret message,
24
TextStream object
Write method, 381
reading, 380
Timer events
global variable, 330
static variables, 330
Timer1_Timer() event
procedure, 322
user-defined types,
511-512
variable naming, 510
VBA
adding text to Word
document, 484
finding field names
with DAO, 501
finding table names
with DAO, 499
moving data from
Access to Excel, 501
Word search program,
493
Word spell checking,
488

Word.Document Open
method, 495
VBScript, 549
with HTML elements,
558
Windows API
dragging windows
(SendMessage func-
tion), 453
GetCursorPos function,
446
keeping a window on
top, 451
SetWinPos() wrapper
function, 449
lists, 193
arrays of strings, 226
Filter() function, 230
clearing, 199
removing items, 198
selecting items, 196,
198
**ListView control, VB6
enhancements, 34**
**Load Picture dialog box,
335**
Load statement
runtime control arrays,
424
syntax, 674
**loading, controls, nested
loops, 179**
**LoadPicture function,
339-340, 373**
syntax, 674
**LoadResData function,
syntax, 674**
**LoadResPicture func-
tion, syntax, 674**

**LoadResString function,
syntax, 675**
**Loc function, syntax,
675**
local variables, 137. See
also **variables**
**Locals window (IDE),
410**
**Lock statement, syntax,
675**
**LOF function, syntax,
675**
**Log function, syntax,
676**
**logical operators, AND,
in place of If...Then,
454**
**login page, DHTML,
570**
long data type, 116
Loop blocks, 403
loops, 160
Do, 166
Do...Until, 170
example, 170-171
syntax, 170
Do...While, 166-169
example, 167-168
syntax, 166-167
For...Next, 160
counter variables,
160-163
early termination,
164-165
stepping through, 161
string concatenation,
161-162
syntax, 160

infinite loops
  example, 171, 179
  preventing, 172, 179
  terminating, 171
nested loops
  advantages, 179
  *data loading applica-
    tion, 179*
  defined, 172, 179
  *For loops, 172-174,
    179*
  *long integer arrays,
    179*

LostFocus event, 92

**LSet statement, syntax,
676**

lst prefix (variables), 115

**LTrim function, syntax,
676**

M

m prefix (variables), 114

**Macro Recorder (VBA
macros), 478**

Map dialog box, 471

**markup language (online
help), 464-467**

math operations, 134
  addition (+), 134-135
  exponential (^), 140
  floating-point division
    (/), 139
  If statement, 147
  integer division (\), 139
  modulus, 140
  multiplication (*)
    *sample program,
      136-139*
    syntax, 136

order of precedence
  *defaults, 141, 148,
    152*
  specifying, 142, 152
subtraction (-), 135

**MaxButton property,
323**

**MDI (Multiple
Document Interface)
applications, 285-289**
  Appearance property,
    289
  AutoShowChildren
    property, 289
  creating with
    Application Wizard,
    583
  viewing IDE, 64

**mdi prefix (variables),
115**

MDIForm object, 285

member functions, 518

member variables, 518

**memory, passing argu-
ments with Windows
API, 448**

menu bars. See menus

Menu Editor, 253
  access keys, 256-257
  pop-up menus, 259
  setting properties, 255
  shortcut keys, 258

**Menu object, properties,
255**

**menus. See also Menu
Editor; toolbars**
  Amazing Text Editor
    program, 260

Application Wizard,
  249-252
captions, ampersands
  (&), 253
Checked property, 262
Clipboard object, 263
MDI child forms, 285
pop-up, 259
selecting text, 265
separator bars, 583
separator lines, 261
standard Windows,
  248-249

message boxes, 268-269
  displaying context-sen-
    sitive help, 472
  icons, 270
  MsgBox() function,
    returning values,
    271-273

**messaging, SendMessage
API function, dragging
windows, 452**

methods, 90
  AddItem, adding strings
    at runtime, 195
  Arrange, 289
  CheckSpelling (VBA),
    486
  Clear, 199
  Clipboard object, 263
  CreateTextFile(), 381
  Execute, Range object,
    496
  GetSpellingSuggestions
    (VBA), 486
  InsertLines(), 600
  PopupMenu, 259
  Print, saving data to
    file, 370

ProcStartLine(), 600
relation to
    properties/events, 93
RemoveItem, 198
SaveAs,
    ActiveDocument
    object, 486
SetText, 264
Show, 362
ShowColor, 283
ShowFont, 282
ShowOpen, 278
ShowPrinter, 284
ShowSave, 279
TypeParagraph (VBA),
    479
using values with, 196

**Microsoft Developers
Network CD-ROM,
440**

Mid function, 222-224
    syntax, 676

**Mid statement, syntax,
676**

**MinButton property,
323**

**Minute function, syntax,
677**

**MIRR function, syntax,
677**

**mismatch errors (data
types), 129**

**MkDir statement, syn-
tax, 677**

**mnu prefix (variables),
115**

**modality, keeping a win-
dow on top
(SetWindowPos API
function), 447-452**

modes, file, 369

**modules, Sub_Main()
procedure, 361**

modulus operator, 140

**Month function, syntax,
677**

MonthView control, 17
    VB6 enhancements, 37

mouse events, 303
    Click, 303, 306
    DblClick event, 306
    MouseDown/MouseUp,
        306-311
    MouseMove, 311-312
    VB limitations, 313

**mouse movement,
GetCursorPos function
(Windows API), 447**

mouse pointer
    GetCursorPos function
        (Windows API), 445
    locating with
        GetCursorPos API
        function, ActiveX con-
        trols, 536
    position reporting, 310

**MouseDown event,
306-311**
    event procedure,
        MoveIt program, 102

**MouseMove event,
311-312**

**MouseUp event,
306-311**

MouseUp event proce-
dure, 102

MoveIt program, 96
    Click() event, 100
    event notification, 102
    Form_Load() event
        procedure, 97-99

moving controls, 75

MS Office VBA, 476-477
    Access/Excel, 498-500,
        504-508
    MS Word search pro-
        gram, 491-497
    MS Word spell checker,
        486-491
    Object Browser,
        480-482
    Record Macro tool,
        478-479
    simple app, 482-486

**MSFlexGrid control,
setup commands, 179**

**MsgBox function,
268-269**
    icons, 270
    returning values, 271
    default button, 273
    syntax, 677

MsgBox statement, 268

**multidimensional arrays,
188, 191**

**multiplication operator
(*), sample program,
136-139**
    syntax, 136

**MultiSelect property,
492**

N

Name property, 24
Data control, 611
SpellingSuggestion
object, 487
Timer control, 318

**Name statement, syntax,
678**

named arguments, 355

naming conventions
constants, 128
controls, 72-74
forms, 97
projects, 84
variables, 112
name collisions, 137
prefixes, 113-115
restrictions, 112-113
suffixes, 120, 132-133

**native code, versus
P-code, 390**

**natural logarithms, Log
function, 676**

nested loops
advantages, 179
data loading applica-
tion, setup commands,
179
defined, 172, 179
For loops, 172-173, 179
long integer arrays, 179

**nesting, If statements,
153**

New keyword, 521
Word.Application
object, 485

New operator, 288

**New Project command
(IDE File menu), 82**

**New Project dialog box,
82**

**Northwind Traders
database, reports, 623**

Nothing keyword, 490

Now function, 320
syntax, 678

**NPer function, syntax,
678**

**NPV function, syntax,
678**

O

**Object Browser, ActiveX
components, 525**

**Object Browser (VBA),
480-482**

object data type, 117

**object models, IDE, 596,
599-601**

**object variables, custom
add-ins, 599**

objects
AmbientProperties, 534
App, version informa-
tion, 386
Clipboard, 263
CodeModule, custom
add-ins, 597
CodePane, custom add-
ins, 597
ComboItem, VB6
enhancements, 38
creating from classes,
520-521

Excel, 506
file system objects, 379
FileSystemObject, VB6
language enhance-
ments, 40
Find (Word), 491
IDE object model, 596
MDIForm, 285
MS Office, 480
Printer, fonts, 283
Range (Word), 491
Screen, 100
Selection (VBA), 479
setting variables to
nothing, 490
TextStream, 380
UserControl, 533
VBA, 476
Word Application, 485

**Oct function, syntax,
679**

**OCX files, compiling
ActiveX controls to,
538**

**OLE Container control,
70**

**ole prefix (variables),
115**

**On Error Resume Next
statement, 417**

**On Error statement,
syntax, 679**

on-the-fly, 42

**On...GoSub statement,
syntax, 679**

**On...GoTo statement,
syntax, 679**

**one-dimensional arrays,
188**

online help, 458, 461
creating help files, 462-468
help files, adding to apps, 468
Help Workshop 4.0, 458-459
HTML Help, 467
hypertext, 463
markup language, 464-467
RoboHelp, 461
strikethrough text, 463-465

OOP (Object Oriented Programming)
abstraction, 292
classes, 512
components, 527-528
creating objects, 513
data elements, 512
encapsulation, 518
Get/Let functions, 518-519
Public/Private schema, 518
VB6 enhancements, 46

Open Project command (File menu), 85

Open Project dialog box, 85

Open statement, 367
syntax, 680

opening projects, 85

operating system, storing data, 366

operators, 134
=, Select Case statement, 157
addition (+), 134-135

concatenation (&), 142-143
syntax, 142
exponential (^), 140
floating-point division (/), 139
integer division (\), 139
modulus, 140
multiplication (*)
sample program, 136-139
syntax, 136
New, 288
order of precedence
defaults, 141, 149, 152
specifying, 142, 152
subtraction (-), 135

opt prefix (variables), 115

Option Base statement, syntax, 680

Option Compare statement, syntax, 680

Option Explicit statement, 119, 131, 402-404
syntax, 680

Option Private statement, syntax, 681

Optional keyword, arguments, 355

OptionButton control, 70
Calculator program, 147
control arrays, 428
ZOrder property, 55

order of precedence (operators)
defaults, 141, 151-152
specifying, 142, 152

P

P-code, versus native code, 390

Package and Deployment Wizard, 391-394, 397
custom ActiveX controls, 540

Page Designer (DHTML), 565

page footers (reports), 628

parameters. See arguments

parent elements (HTML forms), 553

parentheses (), 142, 152

Partition function, syntax, 681

passwords, INPUT tag (HTML), 554

pasting text, Clipboard object, 263

percent sign (%), data-type suffix, 120, 132

persistence, 366
Registry, 375

Picture property, 336

PictureBox control, 70, 334
Picture property, 336
VB limits on mouse events, 313

plus sign (+), addition operator, 134-135

Pmt function, syntax, 681

pnl prefix (variables), 115

pop-up menus, Menu Editor, 259

populating, TextBoxes
Do...While loops, 167-168
For...Next loops, 161-163

PopupMenu method, 259

positioning. See moving

pound sign (#), data-type suffix, 133

PPmt function, syntax, 681

precedence (operators)
defaults, 141, 150-152
specifying, 142, 152

predefined forms, 275

prefixes
control names, 73-74
variable naming conventions, 113-115

Preserve keyword, 186
with ReDim statement, 187

primary key, 606

Print # statement, syntax, 682

Print dialog box, setting printer options in CommonDialog control, 284

Print method, saving data to file, 370

Printer object, fonts, 283

printers, setting options in CommonDialog control, 284

Private data, 518

Private keyword, declaring arrays, 184

Private statement, syntax, 682

prjFileSystem.vbp, 40

prjFSObj.vbp, 383

procedures, 94, 348
documenting, 359
entry point, 361-363
exiting, 355
functions, 351-352
passing arguments, 352, 355
named, 355
subs, 348
adding with Add Procedure, 349
variable scope, 358
VBA macros, 478

ProcHeader (custom add-in), 593

ProcStartLine() method, 600

profiles, Application Wizard settings, 251

program listings. See listings

programs. See projects

Project Explorer, 61, 80-82
IDE, 50

project groups, 61, 87-88, 534
defined, 87

Project menu commands
Add File, 86
Components, 76
Remove, 87

Project Properties dialog box, 83
App object properties, 387

projects
ActiveX controls, 530
ActiveX DLL, 522
adding class modules, 513
Application Wizard, 587
compiling, 389-391
Composer.vbp, 470
creating, 82
defined, 80
DHTML, compiling, 577
file types, 80
files
adding, 85-86
file types, 80
project files, 80
removing, 86-87
integrating online help, 468
MDI, 286
naming, 84
opening, 85
Project Explorer, 80-82
project groups, 87-88
defined, 87

properties, editing, 83
reports, 624
saving, 25, 84
VBA, adding controls,
481

properties, 90
adding to classes,
515-519
Ambient, 534
App object, 386
Appearance, 289
AutoShowChildren, 289
AutoSize, 336
BorderStyle, 28
settings, 90
CausesValidation, 33
Checked, 262
ControlBox, 323
Copies, 284
Data control, 611
DatabaseName (Data
control), 611
DataGrid control, 640
DataSource, reports,
627
fil File object, 382
FileName, 280
Filter, 279
FlatScrollBars, 35
form alignment, 102
FromPage, 284
HelpContextID, 469
HelpFile, 469
HotTracking, 35
Icon, 341
id, DHTML, 568
Interval, Timer control,
319
KeyPreview, 302
length (HTML), 563

List, 193
ListIndex, 197
*DBTransporter pro-
gram, 506*
Menu object, 255
menus (Menu Editor),
255
MoveIt program, 97
MultiSelect, 492
Name, Timer control,
318
Name (Data control),
611
Picture, 336
PictureBox control,
334-335
project properties, edit-
ing, 83
RecordSource, 611
relation to
methods/events, 93
scroll bar controls, 429
ScrollBars, 27
SelText, 265
SpellingSuggestion
object, 487
Stretch, 345
Style, 200
TextPosition, VB6
enhancements, 36
Timer control, 319
ToPage, 284
Visible, 497
WindowState, 324
ZOrder, 55
Properties window, 62
CommonDialog con-
trol, 277
**Property Bag, VB6
enhancements, 46**

**Property Get statement,
syntax, 683**
**Property Let, syntax,
684**
**Property Pages,
CommonDialog con-
trol, 277**
**Property Pages dialog
box, ADO Data con-
trol, 633**
**Property Set statement,
syntax, 684**
protocols, 544
Public data, 518
**Public statement,
declaring arrays, 184**
syntax, 685
**public variables,
136-137. See also vari-
ables**
**Put statement, syntax,
686**
PV function, syntax, 686

Q - R

q prefix (variables), 114
**QBColor function, syn-
tax, 686**
queries (database), 608
**Quick Info window,
user-defined functions,
357**
**Quick Watch dialog box
(IDE), 412**
**QuickBasic, QBColor
function, 686**

quotation marks ("),
strings, 134

RAD (Rapid Application
Development),
DHTML, 570, 573-574

radio buttons, INPUT
tag (HTML), 555

RaiseEvent function,
syntax, 686

Randomize statement,
syntax, 686

Range object (MS
Word), 491

Rate function, syntax,
687

record data type. See
user-defined types

Record Macro tool
(VBA), 478-479

records, navigating with
Data control, 609

recordsets (database),
608

RecordSource property,
611

ReDim keyword, 186,
507

ReDim statement, syn-
tax, 687

redimensioning arrays,
186

Registry
class IDs, DHTML,
573
DeleteSetting state-
ment, 378, 659
deploying custom
ActiveX controls, 540

GetAllSettings function,
378, 667
GetSetting() function,
376
SaveSetting statement,
377, 689

relational databases, 606

relational operators, 157
Select Case blocks,
157-158

ReleaseCapture() API
call, 453

Rem statement, syntax,
687

remainder division, 140

Remove command
(Project menu), 87

RemoveItem method,
198

removing. See **deleting**

Replace() function,
214-217

Report Layout window,
622

reports, 622
adding data, 627
building, 623, 626-629
column-based, 628
Data Report Designer,
VB6 enhancements, 45
page footers, 628
page numbers, 628
report viewer, 629

Require Variable
Declaration feature
(Editor options), 119

reserved words. See **key-**
words; statements

Reset statement, syntax,
687

resizing
controls, 74
forms, sizing handles,
75

resource files
Application Wizard,
586
loading data from,
674-675

Resume statement, syn-
tax, 688

retrieving data, 371
Registry functions, 375
GetAllSettings(), 378
GetSetting(), 376

return values
MsgBox() function, 271
default button, 273
Replace() function, 216

revisions, 386

RGB function, syntax,
688

Rich Text Format, sec-
tions of, 462

Right function, 220
syntax, 688

RmDir statement, syn-
tax, 688

Rnd function, syntax,
688

RoboHelp, 461

rows, editing in a grid,
641

rows. See **records**

RptLabel control, page
footers, 628

RptLabel controls, 624

RSet statement, syntax, 689

rtf files, 459

RTrim function, syntax, 689

Run to Cursor command (IDE), 410

runtime, 42
  adding strings to List property, 195
  changing graphics, 336
  control arrays, 424-426
  setting form position, 63

runtime errors, handling, 417

S

s prefix (variables), 114

Save As dialog, File dialog box, 278

Save File As dialog box, 84

Save Project command (File menu), 84

SaveAs method, ActiveDocument object, 486

SaveGrfx.vbp, 374

SavePicture statement, 374
  syntax, 689

SaveSetting statement, 377
  syntax, 689

saving
  Application Wizard settings, 251
  compiled projects, 392
  projects, 25, 84

saving data, Registry functions, 375
  SaveSetting statement, 377

saving to files, Open statement, 367

scope, 358
  class modules, 517
  user-defined types, 512
  variable scope
    defaults, 136
    defined, 135
    local variables, 137
    public variables, 136-137
  variables, 123

Screen object, 100
  aligning forms to screen, 102

SCRIPT tag, 549, 557

scripting
  VBA, 476
  VBScript, 546
  vs programming, 547

Scripting RunTime, 40

scroll bar controls, control arrays, 429-431

ScrollBars property, 27

SDI (Single Document Interface), viewing IDE, 64

search and replace. See find and replace

search program (MS Word VBA), 491-497

searching for strings, Replace() functions, 214

Second function, syntax, 689

Seek function, syntax, 689

Seek statement, syntax, 690

Select Case statement, 153-155
  control array Click() event procedure, 426
  relational operators in blocks, 157-158
  syntax, 690

SELECT tag, 556

selecting text, 265

Selection object (VBA), 479

SelText property, 265

SendKeys statement, syntax, 690

SendMessage function (Windows API)
  dragging windows, 452-454
  enhancing list boxes, 454

separator bars, 583

separator lines (menus), 261

serial time, 318

server-side applications, IIS, 40

server-side components, 546

server-side programs, 546

servers, 544

Set statement, syntax, 690

Set keyword, 490

SetAttr statement, syntax, 691

SetText method, 264

Setup Wizard, VB6 enhancements, 44

SetWindow function (Windows API), 447-452

Sgn function, syntax, 691

Shape control, 70

Shell function, syntax, 691

Shift parameter
KeyDown event, 297
MouseDown event, 307

shortcut keys
adding with Menu Editor, 258
Amazing Text Editor program, 261
Windows conventions, 249

Show method, 362

ShowColor method, 283

ShowFont method, 282

ShowOpen method, 278

ShowPrinter method, 284

ShowSave method, 279

shp prefix (variables), 115

SimpleCD.VBP, 276

Sin function, syntax, 691

single data type, 116

single-line If statement, 146

sizing
controls, 74
forms, sizing handles, 75
variables, 116

slash (/), floating-point division operator, 139

Slider ActiveX control, adding to DHTML app, 574-576

Slider control, VB6 enhancements, 35

source code listings. See listings

Space function, syntax, 692

spaces, strings, 223

Spc function, syntax, 692

spelling checker app, 486-491

Split() function, 227

spn prefix (variables), 115

SQL (Structured Query Language), reports, 627

SQL Builder, reports, 627

Sqr function, syntax, 692

Standard toolbar (VB IDE), 55

startup object, 362

statements, 658, 665. **See also functions**
AppActivate, syntax, 648
assignment, 132
Beep, syntax, 648
Call, syntax, 648
ChDir, syntax, 650
ChDrive, syntax, 650
Close, 371
syntax, 651
Const, syntax, 651
Date, syntax, 653
Debug.Print, 415
Declare, 438
syntax, 655
DefBool, syntax, 656
DefCur, syntax, 656
DefDbl, syntax, 657
DefDec, syntax, 657
DefInt, syntax, 657
DefLng, syntax, 658
DefObj, syntax, 658
DefSng, syntax, 658
DefStr, syntax, 659
DefVar, syntax, 659
DeleteSetting, 378
syntax, 659
Dim, syntax, 659
Do...Loop, syntax, 660
End, syntax, 661
End Select, 154
Enum, syntax, 661
Erase, syntax, 662
Error, syntax, 662
Event, syntax, 662
Exit, syntax, 663

FileCopy, syntax, 663
For Each...Next, syntax, 664
For...Next, syntax, 664
Function, syntax, 665
Get, syntax, 666
GoSub...Return, syntax, 668
GoTo, syntax, 668
If...Then...Else, syntax, 669
Implements, syntax, 669
Input #, syntax, 670
Kill, syntax, 673
Let, syntax, 673
Line Input, 371
Line Input #, syntax, 674
Load, syntax, 674
Lock, syntax, 675
loops. See loops
LSet, syntax, 676
Mid, syntax, 676
MkDir, syntax, 677
MsgBox, 268
Name, syntax, 678
On Error, syntax, 679
On Error Resume Next, 417
On...GoSub, syntax, 679
Open, 368
  syntax, 680
Option Compare, syntax, 680
Option Explicit, 402-404
  syntax, 680
Option Private, syntax, 681
Print #, syntax, 682

Private, syntax, 682
Property Get, syntax, 683
Property Let, syntax, 684
Property Set, syntax, 684
Public, syntax, 685
Put, syntax, 686
Randomize, syntax, 686
ReDim, syntax, 687
Rem, syntax, 687
Reset, syntax, 687
Resume, syntax, 688
RmDir, syntax, 688
RSet, syntax, 689
SavePicture, 374
  syntax, 689
SaveSetting, 377
  syntax, 689
Seek, syntax, 690
Select Case, syntax, 690
SendKeys, syntax, 690
Set, syntax, 690
SetAttr, syntax, 691
Static, syntax, 692
Stop, syntax, 692
Sub, syntax, 693
Time, syntax, 695
Type, syntax, 696
Unload, syntax, 697
Unloc, syntax, 697
Width #, syntax, 698
With, syntax, 698
Write #, syntax, 699
Static keyword, 126, 138
  counter variables, 330
Static statement, syntax, 692

static variables, 137-138.
  See also **variables**
  Timer control, 329-331
static Web pages, 564
Step keyword, For...Next loops, 161
stepping through code, 408
stepping through loops, For...Next loops, 161
Stop statement, syntax, 692
storing data, 366
Str function, syntax, 692
StrComp function, syntax, 693
StrConv function, syntax, 693
str prefix (variables), 114
Stretch property, 345
strikethrough text (online help), 463-465
String function, syntax, 693
string functions
  Filter(), 230
  InStr(), 224
  Join(), 231
  LCase(), 233
  Left(), 220
  Len(), 219
  Mid(), 222-224
  parsing, 235, 238-240
  Replace(), 214-217
  Right(), 220
  Split(), 227
  StrReverse(), 212-214
  UCase(), 233
  VB6 features, 41

strings, 117
  array of strings, 226
    combining with Join()
    function, 231
    converting a string into
    an array, 227
    sublists with Filter()
    function, 230
  buffer, 220
  case, 233
  concatenating, 142-143,
    217
    defined, 161
    For...Next loops,
    161-162
  converting to lowercase,
    673
  defined, 133
  delimiters, 228
  determining length
    (Len() function), 219
  fixed-length strings, 135
  Format() function, 324
  highlighting in textbox,
    328
  List property, selecting
    items in, 196
  lists, 193
  parsing, 235, 238-240
  quotation mark (")
    notation, 134
  replacing (Replace()
    function), 214-217
  returning chars inside,
    222-224
  reversing order
    (StrReverse() func-
    tion), 212-214
  truncating
    (Left()/Right() func-
    tion), 220

typecasting variables,
  240
validating (IsNumeric()
  function), 242
values, 134
variable-length strings,
  134

**StrReverse() function,
212-214**

Style property, 200
  DataCombo control,
    644

sub procedures. See also
functions
  adding with Add
    Procedure, 349
  code changes, 348
  documenting, 359
  entry point, 361, 363
  exiting, 355
  On...GoSub statement,
    679
  passing arguments, 352,
    355
    named, 355
  syntax, 348

**subclassing, mouse
events, 315**

**Submit button (INPUT
tag), 554**

subroutines. See sub
procedures

**subtraction operator (-),
135**

**Sub_Main() procedure,
361-363**

**Sub statement, syntax,
693**

**suffixes, variable data-
type suffixes, 120,
132-133**

**Switch function, syntax,
694**

**SYD function, syntax,
694**

syntax
  Abs function, 647
  AppActivate statement,
    648
  Array function, 648
  Asc function, 648
  Atn function, 648
  Beep statement, 648
  Call statement, 648
  CBool function, 649
  CByte function, 649
  CCur function, 649
  CDate function, 649
  CDbl function, 649
  CDec function, 650
  ChDir statement, 650
  ChDrive statement, 650
  Choose function, 650
  Chr function, 650
  CInt function, 651
  CLng function, 651
  Close statement, 651
  Command function,
    651
  Const statement, 651
  Cos function, 652
  CreateObject function,
    652
  CSng function, 652
  CStr function, 652
  CurDir function, 653
  CVar function, 653
  CVErr function, 653

Date function, 653
Date statement, 653
DateAdd function, 654
DateDiff function, 654
DatePart function, 654
DateSerial function, 654
DateValue function, 655
Day function, 655
DDB function, 655
Declare statement, 655
DefBool statement, 656
DefByte statement, 656
DefCur statement, 656
DefDate statement, 657
DefDbl statement, 657
DefDec statement, 657
DefInt statement, 657
DefLng statement, 658
DefObj statement, 658
DefSng statement, 658
DefStr statement, 659
DefVar statement, 659
DeleteSetting statement, 659
Dim statement, 659
Dir function, 660
Do...Loop statement, 660
DoEvents function, 660
End statement, 661
Enum statement, 661
Environ function, 661
EOF function, 662
Erase statement, 662
Error function, 662
Error statement, 662
Event statement, 662
Exit statement, 663
Exp function, 663
FileAttr function, 663

FileCopy statement, 663
FileDateTime function, 664
FileLen function, 664
Fix function, 664
For Each...Next statement, 664
For...Next statement, 664
Format function, 665
FreeFile function, 665
Function statement, 665
FV function, 666
Get statement, 666
GetAllSettings function, 667
GetAttr function, 667
GetAutoServerSettings function, 667
GetObject function, 667
GetSetting function, 668
GoSub...Return statement, 668
GoTo statement, 668
Hex function, 668
Hour function, 668
If...Then...Else statement, 669
IIf function, 669
IMEStatus function, 669
Implements statement, 669
Input # statement, 670
Input function, 670
InputBox function, 670
InStr function, 670
Int function, 671

IPmt function, 671
IRR function, 671
IsArray function, 671
IsDate function, 671
IsEmpty function, 672
IsError function, 672
IsMissing function, 672
IsNull function, 672
IsNumeric function, 672
IsObject function, 672
Kill statement, 673
LBound function, 673
LCase function, 673
Left function, 673
Len function, 673
Let statement, 673
Line Input # statement, 674
Load statement, 674
LoadPicture function, 674
LoadResData function, 674
LoadResPicture function, 674
LoadResString function, 675
Loc function, 675
Lock statement, 675
LOF function, 675
Log function, 676
LSet statement, 676
LTrim function, 676
Mid function, 676
Mid statement, 676
Minute function, 677
MIRR function, 677
MkDir statement, 677
Month function, 677
MsgBox function, 677

Name statement, 678
Now function, 678
NPer function, 678
NPV function, 678
Oct function, 679
On Error statement, 679
On...GoSub statement, 679
On...GoTo statement, 679
Open statement, 680
Option Base statement, 680
Option Compare statement, 680
Option Explicit statement, 680
Option Private statement, 681
Partition function, 681
Pmt function, 681
PPmt function, 681
Print # statement, 682
Private statement, 682
Property Get statement, 683
Property Let statement, 684
Property Set statement, 684
Public statement, 685
Put statement, 686
PV function, 686
QBColor function, 686
RaiseEvent function, 686
Randomize statement, 686
Rate function, 687

ReDim statement, 687
Rem statement, 687
Reset statement, 687
Resume statement, 688
RGB function, 688
Right function, 688
RmDir statement, 688
Rnd function, 688
RSet statement, 689
RTrim function, 689
SavePicture statement, 689
SaveSetting statements, 689
Second function, 689
Seek function, 698
Seek statement, 690
Select Case statement, 690
SendKeys statement, 690
Set statement, 690
SetAttr statement, 691
Sgn function, 691
Shell function, 691
Sin function, 691
SLN function, 691
Space function, 692
Spc function, 692
Sqr function, 692
Static statement, 692
Stop statement, 692
Str function, 692
StrComp function, 693
StrConv function, 693
String function, 693
Sub statement, 693
Switch function, 694
SYD function, 694
Tab function, 694

Tan function, 695
Time function, 695
Time statement, 695
Timer function, 695
TimeSerial function, 695
Trim function, 696
Type statement, 696
TypeName function, 696
UBound function, 696
UCase function, 697
Unload statement, 697
Unlock statement, 697
Val function, 697
VarType function, 698
Weekday function, 698
While...Wend function, 698
Width # statement, 698
With statement, 699
Write # statement, 699
Year function, 699

system clock, accessing, Time function, 320

T

Tab function, syntax, 694

table of contents, online help, 459

tables (database), 606

TabStrip control, VB6 enhancements, 34

tagged languages, 551

Tan function, syntax, 695

td prefix (variables), 114

telephone touch pad program, control arrays, 426

terminating loops
For...Next loops, 164-165
infinite loops, 171

text, selecting, 265

text editor program, 260

text files
reading, custom add-ins, 600
reading with TextStream object, 380
retrieving from disk, 371

TEXTAREA tag, 556

TextBox control, 70
Change event, 304
highlighting strings, 328
KeyPress event, 295
mouse Click event, 303
populating
Do...While loops, 167-168
For...Next loops, 161-163
StrReverse() function, 212

TextPosition property, VB6 enhancements, 36

TextStream object, 380

third-party tools, add-ins, 582

three-dimensional arrays, 190

time
Format() function, 325
serial, 318

Time function, 320
syntax, 695

Time statement, syntax, 695

Timer control, 70, 318-320
Calendar program, 18-20
Clock program, 321-324
configuring, 20
Format() function, 324-326
Interval property, 20
Now function, 328
properties, 319
static variables, 329-331

Timer event, 318

Timer function, syntax, 695

Timer() event procedure, ReportMousePos() API function, 447

Timer1_Timer() event procedure, 322

TimeSerial function, syntax, 695

TimeValue function, syntax, 695

title bar, dragging windows, 452

tmr prefix (variables), 115

To keyword
declaring arrays, 185
multidimensional arrays, 191

ToolBar control, VB6 enhancements, 36

toolbars
Add-In, 581
CoolBar control, 37
Debug (IDE), 410
Edit (IDE), 52
Form Editor (VB IDE), 55
IDE
adding/removing, 51
Debug, 52
Standard, 55
Record Macro (VBA), 479

Toolbox (IDE), 50
adding ADO Data control, 632
adding CommonDialog control, 277
adding controls to forms, 57
adding DataGrid control, 636
CommandButton control, 22
Data Report Designer, 623
Label control, 21
Timer control, 18

tools
Application Wizard, 582
menus, 249
Data Environment Designer, 624

Data Form Wizard, 588
debugging, 410-412
  find and replace, 413
designers, 593
Help Workshop 4.0,
  458
Record Macro (VBA),
  478-479

ToolTips
enhanced list boxes, 454
IDE, 51

**Top property, form
alignment, 102**

ToPage property, 284

Topic ID
context-sensitive help,
  HelpContextID prop-
  erty, 469
online help, 464

traversing arrays, 191

**Trim function, syntax,
696**

truncating strings, 220

**twips, mouse pointer
position, 310**

**two-dimensional arrays,
188**

txt prefix (variables), 115

Type keyword, 511

**type mismatch errors,
129**

**Type statement, syntax,
696**

**typecasting, VBScript,
557**

**typecasting variables,
240-241**

**TypeName function,
syntax, 696**

**TypeParagraph method
(VBA), 479**

types. See data types

typing errors, 404

U

UBound() function, 497
syntax, 696

**UCase() function, 233,
500**
syntax, 697

**underscore (_), constant
naming conventions,
128**

Unload statement
control arrays, 434
syntax, 697

**Unlock statement, syn-
tax, 697**

user interaction
ASCII control charac-
  ters, 296
CommonDialog con-
  trol, 276
  Color dialog box, 283
  *File dialog box,
  278-281*
  Font dialog box, 281
  Print dialog box, 284
control arrays, 426
keeping a window on
  top, 451
KeyPress event, 293
message boxes, 268
  return values, 271

mouse events
  Click, 303, 306
  *MouseDown/MouseUp,
  306-311*
  MouseMove, 311-312
  VB limitations, 313
showing MDI child
  forms, 289
validating
  *IsNumeric() function,
  242*
  Validate event, 33

user interfaces
MoveIt program, 96
Windows standard
  menus, 248

user-defined functions
GetGreaterNum() code
  listing, 353
Quick Info window, 357

user-defined subs, 348

**user-defined types,
510-512**

user-initiated events, 92

UserControl object, 533
adding to forms, 534

UserControls, 530

V

Val function, syntax, 697

Validate event, 33

**validating data,
IsNumeric() function,
242**

**validation functions,
parsing strings, 238**

**variable-length strings.
See strings**

variables, 25, 110. See
also **constants**
  arguments, 352
  arrays, 182
  catching undeclared,
    402-404
  checking values with
    watches, 405-407
  counter variables (For
    loops)
      changing values, 163
      decrementing, 161
      defining, 160
      incrementing, 161
      types, 163
  data types, 115-116
      assigning, 118-120,
        130-133
      Boolean, 117
      byte, 117
      currency, 116
      date, 117
      double, 116
      integers, 116
      long, 116
      object, 117
      single, 116
      string, 117
      type mismatch errors,
        129
      variant, 117-118
  debugging with watch-
    es, 406
  declaring
      Dim keyword,
        111-112
      Dim statement, 659
      error detection, 120,
        132
      explicit declarations,
        117-119, 131-132

      implicit declarations,
        119, 131
  Immediate window
    (IDE), 411
  Locals window, 410
  naming conventions,
    112
      prefixes, 113-115
      restrictions, 112-113
      suffixes, 120, 132-133
  scope, 123, 358
      defaults, 136
      defined, 135
      local variables, 137
      public variables,
        136-137
  sizing, 116
  static variables, 137-138
  string functions, 212
  testing with Select
    Case, 154
  typecasting, 240-241
  user-defined types, 510
  values
      assigning, 132
      default values, 133
  VBScript, 557

**variant data type,
117-118**

**VarType function, syn-
tax, 698**

VB6
  enhancements
      ADO, 44
      CausesValidation prop-
        erty, 33
      CoolBar control, 37
      Data Environment
        Designer, 45
      FlatScrollBar control,

        39
      Global Property Bag,
        44
      HotTracking, 35
      ImageCombo control,
        38
      ListView/TabStrip con-
        trols, 34
      MonthView/DateTime
        Picker controls, 37
      OOP, 46
      Slider control, 35
      TabStrip control, 35
      ToolBar control, 36
      Validate event, 33
  new features, 32
  new language features
      dynamic control cre-
        ation, 42
      file system objects,
        39-40
      string functions, 41

**VBA (Visual Basic for
Applications), 476**
  IDE, 477
  MS Access, 498-500,
    504-508
  MS Excel, 498-500,
    504-508
  MS Word search pro-
    gram, 491-497
  MS Word spell checker,
    486-491
  Object Browser,
    480-482
  Record Macro tool,
    478-479
  simple app, 482-486

vbCrLf constant, 163

vbg files, 534

VBScript, 43, 546-548
Dim keyword, 557
event handling, 564
HTML elements,
551-556
incorporating with
HTML, 558-559,
563-564
Internet Explorer,
548-551
server-side ActiveX
components, 546
typecasting, 557
variables, 557

versions, 386-389

Visible property, 497

**Visible value, control
arrays, 425**

**Visual Basic Editor. See
VBA**

**Visual InterDev,
VBScript, 547**

**vsb prefix (variables),
115**

VscrollBar control, 70

**VScrollBar control, con-
trol arrays, 429**

W - Z

Watch window, 407

watches, 406

Web pages, 544
custom ActiveX con-
trols, 540
DHTML, 570
dynamic, 564
registering with search
engines, 578

static, 564

**Width property, form
alignment, 102**

window handles, 448

windowless controls, 20

windows. See also forms
client area, 453
dragging (SendMessage
API function),
452-454
keeping on top
(SetWindowPos API
function), 447-452

Windows 95
common dialog boxes,
277
device independence,
292
printing, 284
standard menus,
248-249

Windows API, 438-440
API Viewer, 440-444
GetCursorPos, 445
GetCursorPos function,
447
passing arguments, 448
ReleaseCapture() API
call, 453
SendMessage function
*dragging windows,
452-454*
*enhancing list boxes,
454*
SetWindowPos func-
tion, 447-452

Windows NT, HAL, 292

**Windows Registry. See
Registry**

**WindowState property,
324**

WinHelp.exe, 464

WithEvents keyword
Private statement, 703
Public statement, 706

wizards
ActiveX Control
Interface, 534
Application, 249-252,
582
Data Form, 614-615,
618-619
Package and
Deployment, 391-394,
397

Word (Microsoft)
adding new documents,
485
adding text to docu-
ment, 482
running unseen, 497
sample app, 482
search program,
491-497
spell checker app,
486-491

**Word Application object,
485**

**Word object model
(VBA), 479**

**word processing,
Replace() function, 214**

**wrapper functions,
ReportMousePos(),
446**

**Write method,
FileSystemObject, 381**

ZOrder property, 55

Special Edition Using Visual Basic 6

—Brian Siler and Jeff Spotts

Special Edition Using Visual Basic 6 is organized to serve as an easy-to-use reference. Individual topics and material are organized so they are easy to locate and read. Special Edition Using Visual Basic 6 also teaches Visual Basic in a straightforward manner. It is assumed that the reader is new to Visual Basic. This book teaches programming with Visual Basic in a steady, consistent pace. After instructing the reader about the Visual Basic programming language, the book progresses into more advanced topics. Such hot topics include creating ActiveX controls, using Visual Basic with Active Server Pages, VB database programming, and more. Because of its straightforward approach, *Special Edition Using Visual Basic 6* covers more topics in more detail than equivalently sized books. This new edition incorporates many changes to Visual Basic 6. Additionally, the authors have added more hands-on examples throughout the book, making it even easier to learn the topics within Visual Basic. *Special Edition Using Visual Basic 6* builds on the success of the best-selling previous edition of this book. This book also goes beyond most Visual Basic books by providing expanded coverage of hot topics such as creating ActiveX controls, database programming, creating distributed applications, and much more. With version 6, Visual Basic becomes an integrated tool that developers can use with other development tools.

$39.99 US/$36.84 CDN   *Intermediate - Advanced*

0-7897-1542-2   *900 pages   Que*

Sams Teach Yourself Database Programming with Visual Basic 6 in 21 Days

—Curtis Smith

Sams Teach Yourself Database Programming with Visual Basic 6 in 21 Days is a tutorial that allows the reader to learn about working with databases in a set amount of time. The book presents the reader with a step-by-step approach to learning what can be a critical topic for developing applications. Each week focuses on a different aspect of database programming with Visual Basic. Week 1—data controls and Microsoft Access databases. Learn about issues related to building simple database applications using the extensive collection of data controls available with VB. Week 2—programming with the Microsoft Jet Engine. Concentrate on techniques for creating database applications using Visual Basic code. Week 3—programming with ODBC and SQL. Study advanced topics such as SQL data definition and manipulation language, and issues for multiuser applications such as locking schemes, database integrity, and application-level security.

$45.00 US/$64.95 CDN   *Intermediate*

0-672-31308-1   *900 pages   Sams*

Doing Objects in Visual Basic 6

—Deborah Kurata

Doing Objects in Visual Basic 6 is an intermediate-level tutorial that begins with the fundamentals of OOP. It advances to the technical aspects of using the VB IDE to create objects and interface with databases, Web sites, and Internet applications. This revised edition features more technical information than the last edition, which was the #1 OOP title for Visual Basic programmers and developers. It specifically highlights the features of the new release of Visual Basic. Text focuses on the technical aspects of developing objects and covers the Internet and database programming aspects of version 6 of Visual Basic.

$49.99 US/$46.18 CDN *Intermediate - Expert*

1-56276-577-9 *560 pages   Que*

Dan Appleman's Developing COM/ActiveX Components with Visual Basic 6

—Dan Appleman

Dan Appleman's Developing COM/ActiveX Components with Visual Basic 6 is a focused tutorial for learning component development. It teaches the reader the programming concepts and the technical steps needed to create ActiveX components. Dan Appleman is the author whom Visual Basic programmer's recommend to their friends and colleagues. Appleman is one of the foremost developers in the Visual Basic community and the author of *Visual Basic 5.0 Programmer's Guide to the Win32 API.* He consistently delivers on his promise to break through the confusion and hype surrounding Visual Basic and ActiveX. Appleman goes beyond the basics to show readers common pitfalls and practical solutions for key problems. This edition is complete with a new CD and all new material.

$49.99 US/$71.95 CDN *Programming Intermediate*

1-56276-576-0 *850 pages   Que*

The Waite Group's Visual Basic 6 How-To

—Eric Brierley, Anthony Prince, and David Rinaldi

The Waite Group's Visual Basic 6 How-To is a programmer-oriented, problem-solving guide that teaches readers how to enhance their Visual Basic skills. Chapters are organized by topic and divided into How-Tos. Each how-to describes a problem; develops a technique for solving the problem; presents a step-by-step solution; furnishes relevant tips, comments, and warnings; and presents alternative solutions where applicable. This book offers illustrated solutions and complete working code. Whenever possible, the code is modularized and fully encapsulated for easy transplant into other applications. *The Waite Group's Visual Basic 6 How-To* demonstrates how to take advantage of new interface options and Windows APIs, contains expanded coverage of Visual Basic 6, and contains all-new How-Tos on building multitier Web-based applications, Advanced Data Objects (ADO), and much more. The previous edition of this book has sold over 50,000 copies to date and won the *Visual Basic Programmer's Journal* Reader's Choice Award in 1995.

$39.99 US/$57.95 CDN *Intermediate*

1-57169-153-7 *800 pages   Sams*

Sams Teach Yourself More Visual Basic 6 in 21 Days

—Lowell Mauer

This book provides comprehensive, self-taught coverage of the most sought-after topics in Visual Basic programming. This book uses the step-by-step approach of the best-selling *Sams Teach Yourself* series to continue more detailed coverage of the latest version of Visual Basic. Not only does this book cover a wide array of topics, but it also goes into each topic to a level that the reader will be able to apply to his or her own programs. In addition, *Sams Teach Yourself More Visual Basic 6 in 21 Days* includes various tips and tricks of Visual Basic programming that will help the more inexperienced programmer. Topics include enhanced controls, collections, and loops; procedures, functions, and logic; MDI and SDI window types; database processing and designing a database application; data-bound controls, the Data Form Wizard, and OLE drag and drop; Internet programming, ActiveX documents, building on-line help, and using Crystal Reports. This book includes complete coverage of database applications and uses real-world applications to demonstrate specialized programming.

$35.00 US/$50.95 CDN   *Beginner - Intermediate*

0-672-31307-3   *700 pages   Sams*

Using Visual C++ 6

—Jonathan Bates and Timothy Tompkins

Based on market research by Market Decisions Corp., Visual C++ is being used by 73% of the professional developers using C++. *Using Visual C++ 6* provides a reference to help teach programmers Visual C++—Microsoft's leading development tool for developing the fastest and most efficient components and applications. *Using Visual C++ 6* takes a straightforward, no-nonsense approach to teaching C++. The book is broken into a number of sections. The first part creates a foundation for the reader. The use of Developer Studio as well as wizards, editors, and debuggers is covered. The book progresses into the Microsoft Foundation Classes (MFC)—the libraries of pre-built classes that Microsoft provides to make Visual C++ programming much easier. By understanding how to use the classes within MFC, the reader will be able to create nearly any type of program. Unlike many books, *Using Visual C++ 6* does not try to be a compendium of all the questions a user may ever have; rather, the book focuses on teaching the reader to use Visual C++ and on providing quick and easy access to answers and information on Visual C++ basics. *Using Visual C++ 6* provides its readers with a reference that will help them learn Visual C++ quickly, plus it is designed to allow readers to re-use it as a reference to find the answers to questions they have later.

$29.99 US/$42.95 CDN   *Beginner - Intermediate*

0-7897-1635-6   *848 pages   Que*

Using Visual J++ 6

—Scott Mulloy

Using Visual J++ 6 is a task-based reference that uses clear organization, step-by-step tasks, abundant code samples, and new cross-indexing techniques to teach Visual J++. This book covers all aspects of using Visual J++ to build a wide range of Java applets and applications, ActiveX objects, COM/DCOM objects, and more. The book also covers some of the more advanced features of the Java 1.2 language. *Using Visual J++ 6* accomplishes these goals by anticipating the needs of the user, providing strong navigation and accessibility to the content. This book provides a powerful price/content value proposition versus other books in the marketplace. This thorough and easy-to-use reference helps inexperienced readers quickly learn Visual J++. Hands-on practical approach and well-documented code examples ensure that readers understand and learn Java programming techniques. Strong content and organization, a leading author, new packaging, and 700 pages of material for $29.99 makes *Using Visual J++ 6* an excellent value.

$29.99 US/$42.95 CDN   *Beginner - Intermediate*

0-7897-1400-0   *800 pages   Que*

Add to Your Sams Library Today with the Best Books for Programming, Operating Systems, and New Technologies

To order, visit our Web site at www.mcp.com or fax us at

1-800-835-3202

ISBN	Quantity	Description of Item	Unit Cost	Total Cost
0-7897-1542-2		Special Edition Using Visual Basic 6	$39.99	
0-672-31308-1		Sams Teach Yourself Database Programming with Visual Basic 6 in 21 Days	$45.00	
1-5627-6577-9		Doing Objects in Visual Basic 6	$49.99	
1-5627-6576-0		Dan Appleman's Developing COM/ActiveX Components with Visual Basic 6	$49.99	
1-57169-153-7		The Waite Group's Visual Basic 6 How-To	$39.99	
0-672-31307-3		Sams Teach Yourself More Visual Basic 6 in 21 Days	$35.00	
0-7897-1635-6		Using Visual C++ 6	$29.99	
0-7897-1400-0		Using Visual J++ 6	$29.99	
		Shipping and Handling: See information below.		
		TOTAL		

Shipping and Handling

Standard	$5.00
2nd Day	$10.00
Next Day	$17.50
International	$40.00

201 W. 103rd Street, Indianapolis, Indiana 46290   1-800-835-3202 — Fax

Book ISBN 1-7897-1633-x

You can't define it. Can't quantify it. But you know when it's missing. Working with Cap Gemini America, you can feel the difference our spirit makes every day. The essence of it is the way we use ideas, people, and technology to help you achieve your business goals. It's the way we team with you to make your projects successful.

That's the spirit that has helped us earn one of the highest satisfaction ratings in the systems integration business, and made Cap Gemini one of the world's top consulting and IT services companies. And it's one powerful reason why you should contact us about your next information technology challenge.

People

CAP GEMINI

Ideas People Technology

1-414-273-3321 • www.usa.capgemini.com